1971

COMPENSATORY EDUCATION
A National Debate

Volume 3

DISADVANTAGED CHILD

COMPENSATORY EDUCATION
A National Debate

Jerome Hellmuth, Editor

BRUNNER/MAZEL Publishers

Published by
BRUNNER/MAZEL, INC.
80 East 11th Street
New York, N. Y. 10003

Library of Congress Catalog Card No. 67-7639
SBN 87630-033-6

MANUFACTURED IN THE UNITED STATES OF AMERICA

INTRODUCTION
PERIOD OF CONSOLIDATION

In assigning a label to the seventh decade of the twentieth century, historians will have a wide range of descriptive terms from which to choose. Within the field of education, however, the choice could hardly be a difficult one, for it has most assuredly been the decade of the disadvantaged child, especially the young disadvantaged child. Although programs were not formulated and fielded to any extent before the middle of the decade, the theorizing, the research, and the assimilation of available information that were the necessary precursors of programmatic efforts were engaged in with great fervor from approximately 1960 until and beyond the time that programs became operational.

Determinants of our interest in the young disadvantaged child have not been restricted to the scientific domain. In 1960 we elected a young and vigorous new president, one who spoke about a new frontier and asked people to forget about what might be done for them and to think instead about what they could do for others. During that time "invisible men" (to use Ralph Ellison's term) became visible, the "other" American (to use Michael Harrington's phrase) suddenly was there to be observed and could not be overlooked. The increasing visibility of minority groups brought into clearer focus the impedimenta which handicapped their development and their attainment of educational and vocational competence. Change along a variety of dimensions seemed the only solution, and, even though fundamental change in human institutions never comes easily or quickly, the multiple adjustments necessary to accommodate relevant changes began.

Obviously there was no one single point of entry that could accomplish everything that was needed. Simultaneous changes in many dimensions would be necessary. And yet something was needed to serve as the primary point of entry that had a reasonable likelihood of success in a fairly short period of time. Educational intervention during early childhood plus supplementation of existing services (such as health) was selected as the showcase operation. There is no question in this author's mind but that this was the proper choice, as it was firmly grounded in developmental theory and as we had available a repertoire of skills (though not enough people) to put a program into operation.

Although there were several experimental programs in operation between the period of 1960 to 1964, and although early education for middle-class children had been available for many years, the movement did not gain any real momentum until that fateful spring of 1965 when Project Head Start was launched. This launching gave instant status to a field that had long been a step-child of both education and psychology. Instant status is a heady thing, and it often leads to some of the excesses and ineptitudes of the parvenu.

One such excess is sure to be boasting and the making of exaggerated claims. That such boasts were made—and possibly even believed—is now a matter of history. They characterized the mood of the period— one of *enthusiasm* and *optimism*. So excited were many of us by the possibilities of the program that we did not go on record to protest that a six-week summer program could not hope to develop a positive self concept, produce new levels of language competence, discover and correct an accumulation of five years worth of medical and nutritional problems, and convince parents that education was the solution to all their problems. Plus many other miracles. It was as though there existed an unverbalized fear that if one dared suggest that too much was being expected it would remove the opportunity to make even a small beginning. So we all surfed on the excitement and hoped we would not drown in our own foamy rhetoric. But many of us were uneasy. In an address given in the fall of 1965, by which time the enthusiasm had not diminished to any significant extent, by which time no formal evaluation had appeared and the informal essays were all still favorable and optimistic, this author warned that the inevitable sequel to over-sell was over-kill. Others began to express similar notes of caution. Then by the spring of 1966 the first trickles of data began to appear—an initial rise followed by a plateau or a decline, initial superiority over control groups followed rather quickly by a catch-up phenomenon. At this time we entered what I would call the period of *skepticism.*

Skepticism is always healthy, and so it was with respect to early education of the disadvantaged child. It helped reorient our thinking from *whether* effects were produced to the more reasonable questions of how, what kinds, and with which children. With the skepticism also came closer atention to the educational fare being offered under the rubric of compensatory early education. No longer was it assumed that *any* early education would produce effects; rather, a healthy, if often partisan, debate began to appear regarding the nature of the educational experience that would be associated with the most desirable effects.

With the release in 1969 of what has come to be called the Westinghouse Report, it is probably accurate to state that on many fronts the skepticism changed to *disillusionment*. Was the human organism really less modifiable during this early period than had been hoped? Were all our gains to prove evanescent and inconsequential? Was enrichment without continuity an exercise in futility? Or were there errors in the design and execution of the study that made conclusions unstable and unreliable? Were the programs evaluated in areas that did not have relevance? These questions are discussed at length in the chapters by White, Wilkerson, Gordon and others later in this book. The disillusionment may have taken its toll in the number of professionals working in the field and possibly in funds available for new programs (although other forces would be equally if not more responsible for any reduction in available monies), but it has not seriously weakened the thrust of the movement.

At the beginning of the seventies, education for the disadvantaged child might be described as being in a period of *consolidation*. The easy days are over, and with their departure went some of the confusion and frenzy that characterized our endeavors for several years. What is left is more than enough to work with and grow with—namely, a sound theoretical base for interest in the effects of early experience, an awareness of the need to search for new concepts in terms of which to structure operating programs, and a recognition of the need to search for ways to organize the learning environment so as to sustain as well as stimulate growth. Actually, most of the serious workers in the field are relieved at having the onus of unrealistic expectations removed. Things are now in better perspective.

This book brings together a set of paper written by many of the people who have helped make this short history. Various chapters chronicle in greater detail the attitudinal eras referred to in this introduction. Others offer important notes of caution lest some of our earlier indiscretions be repeated. Finally the book presents a brief overview of existing programs geared to meet the needs of the disadvantaged child—programs that have either been in operation long enough to have demonstrated their usefulness, or else new programs that are building upon what has been learned in this exciting decade of research and education. They all have in common the ultimate objective of helping to remove the prefix from the word "dis"advantaged in so far as it refers to experience-sensitive personal characteristics which are inimical to optimal development.

BETTYE M. CALDWELL, PH.D.
Director, Center for Early Development
and Education
University of Arkansas
College of Education

TABLE OF CONTENTS

Table of Contents

SECTION III. PROGRAMS AND PRACTICES:
DEFINING SUCCESS
(page 247)

Section I

HISTORY
AND
ISSUES

1

IN THE DARK ... REFLECTIONS ON COMPENSATORY EDUCATION 1960-1970

James F. Winschel, Ed.D.

Associate Professor of Special Education
School of Education, Division of Special Education
and Rehabilitation, Syracuse University

I

> Seamen have a custom, when they meet a whale, to fling him out
> an empty tub by way of amusement, to divert him from laying
> violent hands upon the ship.
>
> JONATHAN SWIFT
> *Tale of a Tub* (1704), Preface

Compensatory education may be a fraud perpetrated upon a poor and unsuspecting citizenry which has traditionally looked to education to lead it out of bondage. Compensatory education may be a hoax by which the politicians and educators of middle class America salve their consciences and maintain the status quo. Or compensatory education may be simply the best efforts of a politico-educational complex blinded in one eye by prejudice and in the other by do-goodness—both equally detrimental to the welfare of children and society. Because compensatory education has resulted in a rising tide of expectations among the poor, the Black, and the disadvantaged, its failure to achieve a noble end presents a danger to the very fabric of American education that cannot long be ignored. It is for this reason that the "National Debate on Compensatory Education" has been set in motion.

The 60's was a decade of paradox: hunger in the midst of plenty, strife in the struggle for peace, riots in the citadels of learning, and poverty the plague of prosperity. Youth in search of freedom imprisoned themselves with drugs, soldiers trained to kill refused to fight, and the recipients of public welfare refused to be everlastingly grateful.

It was an age of madness, too. A popular president was assassinated, the disciple of non-violence was murdered, and a promising politician—

3

some would say a rare species—was cut down in a crime more absurd than monumental. "With all deliberate speed" meant endless delay, and the "war on poverty" seemed uncertain of victory as its goal. The invasion of privacy became a national concern, but with unremitting zeal educators demanded that teachers get into the homes of the poor to "see" how *they* lived.

The decade 1960-69 was an era in which the old truths were challenged as never before. The never-ending God was dead; patriotism lost its sheen; the dirty book was surpassed by the dirty movie—and both were accepted as mature art. The casually accepted prejudice inherent in the black list, black ball, black market, black sheep and black beard were exposed by a new concept, "Black is Beautiful." The Negro community would never again accept an inherent inferiority in social roles, education or intelligence. Statistics be damned; if education cannot deliver the promise of full equality under whatever name, then, as Larry Cuban (1967) has suggested, "the structure of education must be rethought and, ultimately, revised . . . (p. 220)." And while Cuban limited his observations to the education of inner city youth, it is likely that substantial changes in the education of the disadvantaged would be but a prelude to sweeping changes throughout public and private education. That these changes may be born on the edge of social chaos or in the shadow of political revolution, if not a foregone conclusion, is at least a sober and frightening possibility.

Christmas in Purgatory, The Manufacture of Madness, Biological Timebomb, God is Dead, and compensatory education. In the tide of our times one questions whether the latter was a sufficiently bold concept; the challenge seemed somehow to call for a greater imagination, a more splendid effort. As Jennings has stated,

> The continuing challenge, then, is to provide an education as various as the diversity of the country, which will allow the least advantaged, the most gifted, and the ordinary to grow together, to learn to communicate (and to have significant experiences and feelings and opinions to communicate), to be able to work and live in communities which are not merely tolerant of but genuinely hospitable to uniqueness and even to heresy. At the same time these communities must be capable of cherishing the ordinary and the commonplace. Unless this is achieved, we will be diminished as a nation. (1967, pp. 351-353)

To the extent that compensatory education was thought capable of achieving the above goals, it has failed; to the extent that it has been utilized to modify the dissidents and cool the scene, it has had the opposite effect. Contrary to widespread opinion, compensatory education was an unpretentious idea capable of modest success. Unfortunately, it has been puffed up beyond its potential and is now about to burst. In illustration of what has happened, Evline Omwake (1968) tells of attending an early conference in which the possibility of a head-start-like program was explored. The authorities agreed that such a program might help children to begin school with greater confidence and pleasure, but that school success in academic terms would not necessarily be promoted.

> In short, children themselves might indeed benefit but the elementary school would still face the problem of large numbers of poor learners. Now, three years later, it seems that new experiences, greater self-confidence, and a positive feeling about school are not considered sufficient reason for so expensive and elaborate a program; children must have made up for their deficiencies in academic skills and knowledge, as well. . . . This seems to be the result of adults being carried away by fantasies of their own magical powers . . . (1968, p. 539).

The problem, then, is that we have promised too much and in the promising have floundered upon the rising expectations of our clients. An examination of most compensatory education programs with their emphasis on guidance, reading and language development, parental and community involvement, modified curriculums and more adequately trained teachers suggests that we have nothing so very new to offer the disadvantaged learner. Certainly all of the preceding should be a part of any good educational program. Perhaps the problem lies in our having failed with many to do the ordinary with any extraordinary skill—and we have sought to hide our omissions behind labels: *the disadvantaged child* and *compensatory education.*

II

> Nothing is better calculated to drive men to desperation than when, in attempting to carry out beneficial reform, they find the whole world aligned against them. The more especially so if amongst those so aligned they discover men who had preached the same ideal, but now dreaded its concrete realization.
>
> HEWLETT JOHNSON
> *The Soviet Power: The Socialist*
> *Sixth of the World* (1940)

Black is beautiful. What an improbable statement! Red is beautiful, or blue or green. One might even accept magenta or chartreuse. And while white is not exactly beautiful, it is at least pure and clean as they say "like the driven snow." *Don't give up the ship, Remember Pearl Harbor, Ask not what your country . . . , Yankee, go home!* One can sense in these the call to patriotism and pride, self-respect and duty. But "Black is Beautiful"? What can it possibly mean?

In one sense it stands as a powerful rejection of the 'melting pot' ideal. We had dreamed that groups of diverse background would relinquish most of their identifying characteristics in exchange for the American character. And while for many the image became reality, it was for the Negro only a mirage—a dream from which he was, with rare exception, systematically excluded. Having gloried in their success with a great flow of immigrants, our schools must now bear the responsibility for failure with twenty million black Americans. Black is beautiful because America allowed itself to be blinded by color, and in losing its vision must now adapt to new realities.

But Black is also beautiful because there is no alternative in cities which John Gardner described as "fragmented worlds of ignorance, fear and hostility, not communities, but encampments of strangers (Holmes, 1969, p. 200) ." And it is beautiful because the seemingly inexhaustible patience of the Negro has worn thin, and a people long committed to non-violence grow restless amidst the patronage of their oppressors, tired of loving, determined not to emulate. It is because lynchings, murder, discrimination, poverty, ignorance and hate are ugly that Black is beautiful. In a larger sense it is because America is rather unpretty. "Our universities are in deep trouble," writes Peter Rossi "our cities sink further into a morass of decay and anarchy, and our school systems fail both the society and the pupils they are supposed to serve (1969, p. 332) ."

In reply to the new reality of color and pride in an oftentime sick society, the educational community shuddered briefly, labored timidly, and brought forth compensatory education. They said it was for the disadvantaged, the deprived, and the poor, but the target was unmistakably Black. Compensation in the educational process was to be an affluent society's payoff for two and a half centuries of exploitation and humiliation, the reward for a history of servitude and neglect. Compensatory education was to be carried out with a certain flair and rhetoric so as to disguise its basic quality, that of offering more of what hadn't worked in the past. A black author addressed himself to the problem:

> A number of panaceas, for instance, involve the assumption that quantitative inputs will effect qualitative outputs. Thus, one finds sincere attempts to fight cancer with corn plasters. The proponents of this view hold that we must sensitize the teachers, inject Negro history, reduce class size, and add some new services (but only when substantial outside pressure to do so is exerted) . Where these initial attempts to patch up the system fail, schools can always fall back upon the processes of labeling and stigmatizing inner-city children as deviants either culturally, socially or emotionally, and thus placing them in "special" or "compensatory" programs. Then

the children can be blamed, rather than the racism which permeates our educational institutions (Johnson, 1969, p. 244).

The problem, of course, is that compensatory education has attempted to solve the problems of racial and social class isolation in schools which are themselves isolated by race and class, staffed by teachers who have been systematically steeped in the passive acceptance of discrimination and underachievement, and led by an intellectual elite more committed to the rhetoric of democracy than to its practice. Label the child; parrot the cliche; accept the subtle prejudice; send your daughter to a private school, and advise the President on the "benign neglect" of things racial. It is this mixture that continues to nourish a growing separatism within the black community and may yet result in the tragedy of parallel social and political structures, color coded and competitively hostile.

The lesson America must learn is not that black is beautiful, but rather that "black is." The lesson is not without precedent, for white and black alike recognize that "white is." "White" is people, stupid and smart, good and bad, ugly and beautiful, some glorying in the history of their ancestors, but many unconcerned. Black is much the same, I think, and we should not be goaded into accepting slogans which are usually the first and most dramatic step in the cessation of thought and feeling. Schools have a dramatic task before them: to close the gap between races so that in education and in all other aspects of life *white is* and *black is* are replaced by *people are*. It is not a task for "compensatory education" with its division of learners and its inherent suggestion of inferiority, but rather for education, straightforward and not always exciting, unadulterated by qualifying terms no matter how glamorous.

A peaceful revolution within education may yet stave off the portents of human conflict which surround us. Action is called for which will rescue black children from schools which produce failure and white children from a world which gives acquiescence to the intolerable. Starkly before us—if we fail—is the prospect that "Black is Beautiful" may yet turn ugly.

III

The office of government is not to confer happiness, but to give men opportunity to work out happiness for themselves.

WILLIAM ELLERY CHANNING
*The Life and Character of
Napoleon Bonaparte*

War is too potent in the affairs of man to be left to the miiltary; education too subject to control—with too great a portent for the manipulation of human beings—to be left in the hands of government. "What is needed," writes Joseph Durham, "is a massive reordering of social and political power so that education again becomes a national passion (1969, p. 22)." It is not a passion—personal, intimate, all-pervasive—because compulsory education has been imposed from without, and the individual, his family and community have increasingly lost any sense of its control or direction. Nowhere has this fact been more evident than among the poor.

The literature is replete with characteristics of the disadvantaged. Poverty, alienation, delinquency and low achievement are but a few. While accurate in varying degrees, these characteristics miss the essence of disadvantagement, which is a severe restriction on freedom of choice and freedom of response. Indeed educational disadvantagement might best be gauged by the extent, both in distance and degree, to which what is "good" for children has had its germination and received its direction from beyond the individual, his family and community. As the disadvantaged are those for whom others decide what is good, the educationally disadvantaged are those for whom others decide what is good education. It is apparent that, in whatever form, disadvantagement is the product of forces outside the individual, and that only change in the advantaged can alter the plight of the disadvantaged. The danger in compensatory education lies in focusing our efforts on the few when change is demanded of the many. To some extent it was recognition of this fact that led Durham to conclude, "The challenge is to relegate compensatory education to the museum of educational antiquities along with corporal punishment and the Lancastrian system (1969, p. 22)."

Public education today constitutes the nation's largest monopoly. Like all monopolies, it is in turn arrogant, rigid, paternalistic, and coercive. Like all monopolies, it is as much interested in perpetuating itself as in the welfare of its clients. More than that, self preservation is a tenet of its faith. Frightened by lawlessness, shamed by overt prejudice and discrimination, and chagrined at its low achieving products, public education spawned compensatory education. Then, in a subtle distortion of purpose, it offered the disadvantaged not merely equality of opportunity but equality of achievement as well. It is upon this shoal that compensation as an educational doctrine has run aground. Public education has not (probably cannot) deliver on its promise as the work of Coleman (1966), Durham (1969), Freeman (1969), Jensen (1969), and others have amply suggested.

We do not castigate compensatory education for its failure to improve in any dramatic way the education of the disadvantaged. Rather we question its implied promise to eliminate those differences in ability and achievement which are a part of the richness of a people no less than is the equality of opportunity, once attained, a part of the wealth of a nation. Of the differences in educational achievement among people Glazer wrote:

> History and social research convince me there are deep and enduring differences between various ethnic groups, in their educational achievement and in the broader cultural characteristics in which these differences are, I believe, rooted; that these differences cannot be simply associated with the immediate conditions under which these groups live, whether we define these conditions as being those of levels of poverty and exploitation, or prejudice and discrimination; and that if we are to have a decent society, men must learn to live with some measure of group difference in educational achievement, to tolerate them, and to accept in some degree the disproportion in the distribution of rewards that may flow from differences in educational achievement (1969, p. 187).

I believe we have to accept differences in ability and attainment if we are to live in harmony, one with another, or if we are to stave off the relentless pressures which accelerate us on the path to a faceless society.

In support of man's uniqueness Jennings writes:

> He can be dealt with as a statistic, but he will not behave like one. He can be usefully described by a stereotype, but in his recalcitrant uniqueness, he will not always perform in a fixed or general pattern (1967, p. 352).

In spite of this optimism, breakthroughs in biology have accelerated the prospects of genetic engineering and modern techniques of communication and persuasion leave one unaware of the erosion of free choice. Operant conditioning is hailed as a sometime savior, and the vision of a salivating dog is but a distant memory. Technology is placing in the impersonal hands of monolithic government and its increasingly beholden servant, public education, such potential for the destruction of individuality that new forms of education and new protections for the rights of man must be developed without delay.

A step in this direction might pattern itself upon the successful educational aspects of the popular G.I. Bill of Rights. Parents would be obligated or at least encouraged to purchase the educational process which best met their needs. Limited profits would be permitted and the purveyors of a shoddy process or a faulty product would at least now be more subject to judicial restraint and the loss of clientele. Sounder, more imaginative plans than the foregoing are even now being developed by individuals who are concerned with the disadvantaged and are disillusioned by the failures of compensatory education (see Jencks, 1968). As innovations begun with the least advantaged have invariably been incorporated into the broad spectrum of educational practice, so too can we expect these new forms to alter the face of education for all and thereby frustrate indefinitely the nightmares of Huxley and Orwell.

The quality of education offered minority group children has seldom met with widespread approbation. Second class schools, worn out teachers, and ineffective programs have been the lot of the disadvantaged child. These conditions exist in the face of herculean efforts to alter the pattern, largely because minority group parents have been denied their share of responsibility for making decisions pertinent to the education of children. There is among the poor an abiding faith in education which, if acknowledged, respected, and utilized can be a mainspring to the improvement of education for all.

As we move forward in this venture let us not speak of community control; such terms easily become the focal point of strife and dissensions. Let us think instead of involving people, black and white, rich and poor, ignorant and educated alike in a new passion for education. If we are successful, the need for compensatory education will indeed have been relegated to the "museum of educational antiquities." The goal, after all, is not one of equivalent people achieving equally, but rather of equal people achieving through equivalent opportunities. In the pursuit of this goal we will find safety from the oppression of government and honor in the quest for individuality.

IV

There is nothing on earth intended for innocent people so horrible as a school. To begin with, it is a prison. But it is in some respects more cruel than a prison. In a prison, for instance, you are not forced to read books by the wardens and the governor. . . . In prison they may torture your body, but they do not torture your brains.

BERNARD SHAW
Parents and Children

It is difficult to find anyone to mourn the passing of the sixties. Perhaps the issues which divided society had been too finely honed, the conflicts brought too sharply into focus. Alienation was the prevailing mood of the country, and nowhere was this more apparent than in the disenchantment with the educational establishment evidenced by millions of miseducated Americans. Symbolic of this disillusionment, and occurring in disproportionately large numbers among the disadvantaged, was the school dropout.

While dropout may be descriptive of the final act, it fails miserably to convey the nature of the problem or the direction of its solution. Why did youth cut short their school experiences? At times dropouts were the end product of low expectations for achievement endemic to the teaching profession and directed extensively toward poor and minority group children. At other times students left because out-of-school experiences had promoted a degree of independence incompatible with continued educational servitude. In still other cases, dropping out was the student's ultimate refutation of an educational stratagem which presumed that all could achieve equally if only sufficient pressure or expertise was brought to bear upon the learner. This strategy resulted from a misreading of both compensatory education and civil rights. The attempt to equalize achievement, while sometimes instrumental in motivating teachers, inevitably ended in disappointment. Achievement could not be equalized.

The contribution of the school to the dropout problem stems from the long term inability of education to adjust curriculum and methodology to the 15% of youth that Havighurst and Stiles (1961) termed "the alienated group" and for whom schooling is an uncertain path to adulthood. As Strom succinctly stated,

> Every year a significant number of basically sound young Americans discover that they are not really wanted and that neither their teachers nor their curricular experiences seem to pay any attention to who they are, what they have and what they have not, and what they can do and what they cannot do. Instead, imposed upon them is a nonsensical experience which goes under the name of education (1966, p. 60).

It is an education in which children of the poor have been passive recipients and for which dropping out is often an escape from an oppression of body, mind and spirit. Rapid changes in society make tradition-bound schools irrelevant and foster among students a rejection of the school, its processes and control. It may be that we should speak of the school as dropout rather than the student. In its unresponsiveness to the demands of the poor, particularly the Blacks, for a greater say in decisions affecting their education, the school drops out of the child long before the student drops out of the school. One may at least postulate that the needed revisions of theory and practice which will preclude this happening cannot be accommodated within the present framework of compensatory education and must await more basic changes in the democratic structure—changes not only in education but in people as well.

In retrospect the ten years spanning 1960-69 was a decade of dropouts. Spiraling divorce rates gave testimony to the marriage dropout, and decreased attendance figures sent paroxysms of holy reform through church leaders. College professors urged students to drop out and "turn on," and with the help of drugs they did so in alarming numbers; years of education had apparently given them little skill in "turning on" on their own. One nationally circulated publication captioned an idyllic picture of a dropout family as follows: "Refugees from affluence fled from the rat race into older, steadier rhythms (Life, Dec. 25, 1969, p. 25)." Surely millions of readers, fed up with the pressures of living and disillusioned in the quest for a good life, must have lingered upon that portrait with more than a tinge of envy. And of course, as school administrators across the country could testify, teachers also dropped out. One teacher in an urban Junior High School put it this way:

> I know the teachers in my school. Several of them are young and inexperienced, but they are also devoted and energetic. A large number are Negroes who have a special interest in these young-sters. And yet in the end, well-nigh every teacher, no matter who he is or why he is teaching, gives up and leaves the school or the profession altogether (Ornstein, 1965, p. 105).

Obviously, the scope of our problem is not confined to children who fail to complete school. The student dropout is only a manifestation of a larger social malady affecting the moral standards, mental health, and social welfare of a nation. To suggest remediation through compensation, whether within education or without, is a little like throwing a cork to a drowning man. It may be indicative of our good will, but the victim is going to go under.

Interestingly, the rate of dropouts among secondary school students has declined impressively in the last fifty years. Schrieber (1967) estimated that in 1964 two out of every three children who had entered 5th grade eight years earlier had graduated and that the trend is toward ever larger percentages. Open to conjecture, however, is whether these students remain in school because of more meaningful programs, or in the broadest sense benefit from the experience. Wasserman and Reimann (1969) have suggested that the "law" of competitive accreditation may be partially responsible for the school's holding power. This "law," in effect, denies entrance to the ladder of independent adulthood for those who have not been accredited at a high school level, regardless of the individual's potential for success or the idiocy of the program from which he withdrew. A kind of coercive retention takes place in which schools glory in their new found holding power at the same time they become overburdened with the psychological dropout, the student whose withdrawal is complete in all but body. It seems probable that students so retained will acquire a growing disrespect for the conventions of society and in so doing will develop a susceptability to discontent, mayhem, and revolution. Indeed, forced feeding is the antithesis of education, and *argumentum baculinum*—the argument of the cudgel—

even when subtlely stated is little likely to solve the problems of disenchanted learners.

"The ultimate prevention of the school dropout and consequent conservation of human resources is quality education which takes into account the unique needs and characteristics of the individual student." So wrote then Commissioner of Education, James E. Allen, Jr. (1969, p. 8), aware, no doubt, that knowledge poorly taught and poorly learned is both the progenitor and sustainer of the dropout problem; aware, no doubt, that the multitude of causes which appear so voluminously in the professional literature are more excuse than cause; aware, no doubt, of education's attempt to attribute cause to factors outside itself and then to demonstrate its good will with a flurry of activity designed to smother the problem and obfuscate its origin. Lack of motivation and poor achievement attitudes may be a challenge to teaching, but they do not cause dropouts; poor education does that. Meaningful school retention, then, will not be the product of the numerous and sometimes imaginative plans sponsored by government and industry except as these are catalysts for an educational experience which preserves individuality, recognizes the right of self-determination, and promotes self-respect.

In January, 1968, approval of the Title VIII amendments to the Elementary and Secondary Education Act placed the federal government in the battle to improve education so as to reduce the number of children failing to complete their elementary and secondary schooling. In recognition of the complexity of the problem and the paucity of reliable information in this area, the Office of Education refrained from developing a model for funded programs. The uncertainties surrounding ameliorative efforts and the resistance of the problem to solutions have since been described by Kruger.

> Numerous studies and experimental programs have made it clear that no simple cause-and-effect relationship explains why some students leave school. No socioeconomic level, intelligence strata, physical classification, or ethnic group is immune from the problem. No panaceas have been discovered, and few situations are responsive to short term or inexpensive remedies (Kruger, 1969, p. 7).

Model projects under Title VIII have not been lacking in imagination. Sensitivity training for teachers (students are presumably already too sensitive), storefront schools (education purchased through involvement and hard work), curriculum innovations (students in one project learn academic skills by studying welfare programs), students paid to learn (presumably penalties for not learning are inappropriate as long as teachers who fail to teach go scot free) and home visitations by teachers (a subtle invasion of privacy often foisted upon the poor by halo wearing, spy prone educators) are only a few of the techniques sponsored by the Model Projects of Title VIII in what supporters and critics alike must recognize as a random search for solutions to the dropout problem. But then, even when questioning, one must recognize that problems are as often solved through the random as through the systematic, and that the problem of school dropouts is even now decreasing in size, if not intensity.

We are inclined to agree with Roy Wilkins who suggested that the ultimate objective of healthy schools in a wholesome society is to create love, "the kind of affection that endears us to our brothers, of whatever color they are and whatever language they speak (*The Urban Review,* 1969, p. 22) ." Dropouts haven't been in love with schools, and schools haven't much loved them. It is a deficiency for which compensation is inadequate; the challenge is greater than that.

V

The chief wonder of education is that it does not ruin everybody concerned in it, teachers and taught.
HENRY ADAMS
The Education of Henry Adams

New approaches to teacher training have been a crucial aspect of the compensatory education movement. Nevertheless the literature on training teachers of the disadvantaged continues to be misleading and subtly (unintentionally, no doubt) dishonest. Few authors actually extoll the virtues of teaching in a slum school, but unmistakably they give the impression that merit and satisfaction in abundance await the "specially" trained neophyte. Teaching children the rest of us have mostly failed to teach is invariably presented as a challenge; between the lines, however, is the clearly written promise of success, recognition, and reward. For the majority of new teachers the challenge is real, the promise mere phantasy.

Most of the efforts to modify teacher training programs are variations and expansions of a five point program suggested by Riessman (1967) and generally include: 1) changed attitudes toward the disadvantaged on the part of teachers through formal and informal study experiences, 2) extensive pre-teaching experiences (prepared exposure), 3) an understanding of rapport, management, and motivational techniques specific to poor and minority group children, 4) the utilization of appropriate educational technology, including innovations in curriculum, methods, and materials, and 5) a concern with the art of teaching so as to utilize "the idiosyncratic potential of each teacher (p. 326) ." At a na-

tional level the Higher Education Act of 1965 provided funds for a
National Teacher Corps as a means of promoting more and better
trained teachers for low income areas; numerous NDEA institutes have
also promoted interest and provided expertise for this cause. Support
for colleges and universities has resulted in a rash of programs; representative of these are the Urban Teacher Preparation Program at Syracuse University, the Capitol Campus plan of Pennsylvania State University (Sinclair, 1968), Operation Fair Chance of the California State
College at Hayward (Olsen, 1967), and Project Mission (Epstein, Fink
& Hauserman, 1967), a cooperative program sponsored by Baltimore
and three of the Maryland State Colleges. All of these special training
programs have been marked by great enthusiasm, energy, and conviction.
Since unsuccessful programs seldom continue to receive funded support, one surmises that the above programs have met with some degree
of modest success. They are what Epstein, Fink, and Hauserman (1967)
called "little breakthroughs in our search for educational change (p.
16)."

Better trained teachers, however, will have little impact on children
if, as Ornstein (1965) has stated, "education is not the primary concern
of the school in the depressed areas of our large cities (p. 107)." While
not extremely typical, Ornstein's teacher's-eye-view of the school's purpose is typical of the extreme:

> For the children, it is a broadway for free meals, gang warfare, and
> delinquency. For the parents, it is a place where they can deposit
> their children so that they can work or have a short-lived respite
> from their onerous lives. For the neighborhood, it is a center which
> temporarily clears some of the young malfactors off the streets
> (1965, p. 107).

Little wonder that Ornstein describes the experience as "frightening."
Goldberg (1966) presents a description of the depressed area school
which is the more awesome for its inclusion in a reasoned and tem-
perate discussion. She lists inadequate and hostile supervision, harassed
principals, uncovered classes, discipline problems, school involvement
with the police, and the absence of teaching activities as but some of
the "challenges" awaiting the new teacher. In recognition of the chaos
that has gripped many of our urban schools, teacher training programs
have offered special programs of instruction. The problem, of course, is
that the specially trained teacher may become more adept at understanding the disadvantaged than in the teaching of children. If she manages a
class, handles problems, or fosters social relationships to the exclusion of
effective instruction in the content areas, a teacher may quash dissent but
she will not have improved the education of disadvantaged children.

The current gush of rhetoric on contemporary education and the unbridled (sometimes shallow) enthusiasm for teaching the disadvantaged child that has so recently taken hold of our teacher training programs has obscured the almost prosaic need for cognitively sound instruction. I have watched this enthusiasm for teaching minority group children with some dread that in their affective-social involvement our teachers-in-training will have lost sight of the need for instruction which is not only culturally appropriate but sequentially sound. As Ausubel (1963) noted:

> An effective and appropriate teaching strategy for the culturally deprived child must therefore emphasize these three considerations: (a) the selection of initial learning material geared to the learner's existing state of readiness; (b) mastery and consolidation of all ongoing learning tasks before new tasks are introduced, so as to provide the necessary foundation for successful sequential learning and to prevent unreadiness for future learning tasks; and (c) the use of structured learning materials optimally organized to facilitate efficient sequential learning. Attention to these three factors can go a long way toward insuring effective learning for the first time, and toward restoring the child's educational morale and confidence in his ability to learn (1963, p. 455).

In the past, teacher training programs willfully neglected the education of disadvantaged children. They have not now developed a special wisdom and should not now be accorded a pedagogical monopoly on instruction. Reports too numerous to mention cite the superior teaching of involved individuals from diverse backgrounds of experience and learning. Indeed, there is reason to think that public education in its present form should relinguish its grip on teacher certification and its influence on teacher training. Local communities must be free to purchase the services of personnel they deem best qualified to cope with the educational problems of their youth, and whole communities must be free to make outlandish errors as the price to society of this freedom. "Providing more services to the poor may only add to the humiliation," writes Pearl. "The solution might rest in getting more service from the poor (1970, p. 56)." The extent to which this could be done is restricted only by one's imagination and his faith in people. The effect of compensatory education on teacher training programs, while laudatory as it represents the good will of concerned educators, is on another level a subtle evasion of our responsibility to get "more service from the poor." At worst it is but another ploy in the game of keeping all of education firmly in the grip of favored middle America.

VI

". . . we should recognize that a smug paternalism has characterized the attitudes of many white Americans toward school questions."

Presidential Message
on Desegregation, 1970

Dear Anne: Little girls grow up so quickly fathers are quite unprepared for the sudden bursts of independence that bespeak the onrush of maturity. I sometimes wish your curiosity in films was of another hue than (Yellow), and I confess to doubts about the purpose of your march upon the White House. And I wonder, too, what motivates you to spend your Saturday mornings tutoring black children. There are dangers, you know. Pornography masquerades as freedom of expression, anarchy poses as the right to protest, and the exploitation of human beings is sometimes characterized by high sounding names like Upward Bound and Operation Bootstrap. What you must come to understand is that freedom is corrupted by license, and the desire to help is often thwarted by the need to dominate.

There is much to be proud of in what our schools have done for you. Scholarship, hard work, and good manners are but a few aspects of the Protestant ideal which has formed your character and given you a certain allegiance to the values of middle class America. Unfortunately —often deliberately—we have not done nearly so well with millions of poor and minority group Americans. And in the process of failing others, education has cheated you—and me. That is, to the extent that the richness of opportunity has been denied to any, we are all the poorer, not so much in the materials of life but rather in the quality of living.

The Upward Bound program of which you are a part has been praised and damned in equal measure—as have most of our compensatory education programs—and I will leave to you and those you teach to judge the merits of your efforts. What I am concerned with is that you may engage in educational and other social welfare causes as a sanctioned path to the subtle manipulation of people. After all, few of us are of sufficient modesty not to want to emulate the deity, that is, not to want to create man in our own likeness and image. It is imperative that you sense the difference between working for people and working with them. When you do things for people, you tend to perpetuate a state of dependency, a violation of the purpose of your aid and a source of eventual resentment and hostility. Doing things with people, on the other hand, by not providing the ready-made solution, permits them to develop their own concepts for dealing with problems and thereby promotes the exercise of independence compatible with the personal and cultural uniqueness of the individual. The tactic calls for restraint, for the goal, simply stated, is to help people be what they *are,* not what they *ought* to be; to help children be what they *could be,* not what they *should be.*

Perhaps that's a little too preachy for a teenage daughter. The questions you need to ask yourself are really quite simple: can I aid without dominating?; am I privileged to give (of myself) rather than they privileged to receive?; am I willing to accept direction from those I seek to help? In summary, is loving my neighbor as myself still relevant? In commenting on the compensatory education programs of the sixties, President Nixon's message on desegregation in education noted that "most of them are not yet measurably improving the success of poor children in school (*Newsweek,* March 16, 1970, p. 113)." The President called for more research; don't scoff, but I rather wish he had called for more love.

Anne, I say love because I'm a little disenchanted with research and technology. I say love because manpower and funding alone have succeeded so little in ministering to the ills of education. Love, because without it special programs are often dedicated to the self-interest of their promoters; love, because it is the only antidote I know for the domination of mind and spirit which has so often characterized our helping relationships. Fortunately, a new spirit stirs within education in which selflessness and love in teaching may yet become a reality. It is of this spirit that you are a part and it is this spirit which has now almost inevitably led you to the ghetto and Upward Bound.

But I said there was a danger in your work with slum children. The danger lies in the unconscious ways in which teachers, convinced of their own superiority and unaware of their own prejudices, heap small but telling indignities upon the very children they purport to help. Gerald DeWitt said it like this:

> There are limitless subtle and sometimes unconscious ways we can damage children, strip them of their dignity, shatter their feelings of self worth. And such practices have no economic or racial boundaries. They can happen in any school that has failed to develop a humane climate and humane attitudes toward children (1970, p. 41).

DeWitt suggests that we need to respect children at least to the same extent we have demanded respect. It's not a new idea; it just seems a trifle foreign because we have never taken it too seriously.

Whitney Young, Jr. tells the story of South African diamond miners trapped below ground, dying of thirst and starvation amidst untold riches. He draws an analogy between this situation and a society which has surrounded itself with the fruits of research and science but is spiritually dead to the Sermon on the Mount and the Golden Rule.

"Somehow in our scheme of things," he writes, "there must be developed some appreciation for those broad human values that transcend things, or else we shall find ourselves entombed to our death in our own diamond mine of materialism (1970, p. 24)." The Elementary and Secondary Education Act of 1965 provided the material sustenance by which education for the poor and poorly educated could be improved. What you and I do with this opportunity will always say more about us than about those we seek to aid. We can enjoin the educational dilemma in a spirit of love and freedom for all, or we can make of it but another sophisticated example of the exploitation of people. What I fear is that we may be as much motivated by the inconvenience of the poor as by the opportunity to serve our fellow man.

I have proceeded from the need for restraint to the need for love of children unrestrained. In passing I referred briefly to only one of the thousands of special programs for disadvantaged children. I have done this because we *know* too much about the disadvantaged and too little about ourselves. Perhaps progress in compensatory education will have to await a righting of the balance. Anne, work *with* children; know them; know yourself. Love,

VII

The folly of mistaking a paradox for a discovery, a metaphor for a proof, a torrent of verbiage for a spring of capital truths, and oneself for an oracle, is inborn in us.

> PAUL VALERY
> *Introduction to the Method of*
> *Leonardo Da Vinci* (1855)

There is too much written about the disadvantaged child and his school-related corollary, compensatory education. It is fired by the gluttonous appetite of mediocre journals, and feeds on the insatiable demands of school and university promotion committees. The bulk of this literature is replete with unwitting lies, prejudices, misconceptions, stupidities, double talk, and worse. In example:

1964—*The dropout*

> Low or failing marks are not used as a motivational device. Their efficacy for this purpose, if we accept the findings of numerous studies, has long been seriously questioned. However, low or failing marks are sometimes used, though they are confined to accurate reporting of insufficient progress in terms of reasonable expectations based on the child's functional ability.

Translation?—Don't bank on getting *these* kids to work for marks. The best you can do is make some guess about what they ought to be able to do, and then zap them if they don't do it.

Comment: Millions of words are written and thousands of programs are funded, but almost nothing changes. The packaging is different but the prize is still a ring that turns your finger green. The ploy in this case is to suggest change by implying that the very practice in which you now engage (assigning low or failing marks) was somehow different when engaged in by your predecessor.

The imperviousness of institutions to change is illustrated by Henry Kaiser's unsuccessful attempt to alter the automobile industry. He commented in effect that it was the fastest way he knew to drop a fortune without making a splash. Kaiser, it is assumed, was not acquainted with compensatory education.

1965—*Beginning reading*

> Culturally disadvantaged children frequently end the reading habit before it is begun.

Translation?—Culturally disadvantaged children frequently end the reading habit before it is begun.

Comment: Huh? What?!?

1966—*Impoverished homes*

> . . . the life experiences of a child from an impoverished home are often so limited . . .

> Such a child may never have walked in a park or ridden in an automobile or played with other children. A little girl may never have had a doll to call her own. A little boy may never have seen himself in a mirror; indeed, he may not even know his own name. When children like these go to school, they can't understand the simplest story the teacher might read because the words mean nothing to them.

Translation?—Those niggers live like animals. You couldn't imagine how they neglect their children. Why, do you know that some of their kids don't even know their own names? And dumb; you wouldn't believe it! They can't understand the simplest story that even a baby could follow.

Comment: Prejudice travels in many guises. One of the most apparent is the bleeding heart. Should reputable journals print these banalities? Doesn't this mawkish bleating do as much to promote prejudice as to eradicate it? Perhaps it's just another case of bathos for pathos and only children are the worse for our subrogation.

1969—*the slow learner*

> . . . many children raised in the central city possess certain characteristics. They learn at a slow rate. They forget quickly. They lack the quality of being responsible for their own learning. They see little purpose in learning today for a far off tomorrow. They deal fairly well with rote material, but have difficulty dealing with abstractions, analysis, or critical thinking. They see little relevance in their own lives for what is being taught in school.

Translation?—Inner city kids are different—they're stupid.

Comment: The criticisms cited in the above selection have their embarrassing origin in the literature on mental retardation. Our pedagogical adherence to these clichés has restricted the intellectual and academic growth of retarded children—and can nicely do the same for the youth of our inner cities. What proportion of children actually possess these negative learning characteristics? *Many* is not an answer. Under what circumstances are the characteristics manifested? *In school* is an evasion, not a reply. The indictment is too serious to speak in generalities; there is an obligation to be precise. To be otherwise is neither ethical nor helpful.

1970—*the warped personality*

> Ways must be discovered for helping disadvantaged youth to deal with difficult trying situations. The inhospitable environment in which these youths live has caused the development of submerged, warped, and distorted personalities. This causes the child to be unable to cope with the normal flow of events and he may withdraw completely or "act out" in defiant and delinquent behavior.

Translation?—Disadvantaged children are unable to deal with life's problems because they are sick, the symptoms of which they manifest by acting crazy or becoming delinquent.
Comment: This kind of explanation as applied to Black children was protested by Johnson when he wrote, "The rule of thumb for Black children is: IQ under 75 = learning problem or stupidity; and IQ above 75 = behavior problem or crazy (1969, p. 244)." Let's be done with this nonsense!

1970—*the rioter*

> Finally, a complex, industrial and democratic society can't afford to have ignorance motivating the behavior of many of its citizens.

Behavior that is motivated by ignorance, with accompanying frustration, is a threat to the security, and perhaps the survival, of a democratic society. The riots that have taken place in the disadvantaged areas of our large cities suggest this.

Translation?—Riots are motivated by the ignorance of the rioters who, if they were not an ignorant lot, would not be frustrated, i.e. would not riot.

Comment: What ever happened to the collective frustrations of poverty, substandard housing, exorbitant rents, rotten meat, and discriminatory law enforcement? Ignorance? The rioters have only been undereducated; it is the rest of us who have been ignorant.

Only the most naive would doubt that education in the United States is in a state of crisis or that the turmoil continues largely as a result of our inability or unwillingness to provide minority group children with a first class education. But just possibly we have reached a point of negative return in the flood of words about disadvantaged children. It becomes increasingly difficult to tell truth from half-truth, half-truth from fiction, and fiction from falsehood.

Some years ago I asked a wise old woman—a noted professional in her field—how she dealt with the unremitting flood of literature. Her reply is worthy of our consideration. "What I try to do," she said, "is to read a little, and think a lot." Perhaps we might emulate that philosophy as we look forward to education in the seventies. After all, the failures of compensatory education stem not so much from a misunderstanding of the disadvantaged as from a failure to understand ourselves. *That* is the problem about which we must "think a lot."

REFERENCES

AUSUBEL, D. P. A teaching strategy for culturally deprived pupils: cognitive and motivational considerations. *School Review,* 1963, 71, 454-463.

BLACK, M. H. Characteristics of the culturally disadvantaged child. *Reading Teacher,* 1965, 18, 465-470.

CLIFT, V. A. Further considerations in the education of the disadvantaged. *The Educational Forum,* 1970, 34, 223-228.

COLEMAN, J. S. et al *Equality of educational opportunity.* Washington, D.C.: Government Printing Office, 1966.

Commissioner Allen stresses importance of guidance in dropout programs. *American Education,* 1969, 5 ,8.

CUBAN, L. Cardozo project in urban teaching. *Education,* 1967, 88, 216-220.

DeWITT, G. Humanizing the elementary school: a deterrent to student unrest. *The National Elementary Principal,* 1970, 49, 40-42.

DiPASQUALE, V. C. Dropouts and the graded school. *Phi Delta Kappan,* 1964, 46, 129-133.

DURHAM, J. T. Who needs it? Compensatory education. *Clearing House,* 1969, 44, 18-22.

EPSTEIN, J., FINK, C. H., & HAUSERMAN, B. D. Teachers for the disadvantaged: project mission. *The National Elementary Principal,* 1967, 46, 13-16.

FREEMAN, R. A. The alchemists in our public schools. In J. M. Ashbrook, *Congressional Record—extension of remarks*, April 24, 1969, E3374-E3381.

GLAZER, N. Ethnic groups and education: towards the tolerance of difference. *The Journal of Negro Education*, 1969, 38, 187-195.

GOLDBERG, M. Adapting teacher style to pupil differences. In J. L. Frost & G. R. Hawkes (Eds.), *The disadvantaged child*. Boston: Houghton-Mifflin, 1966. Pp. 345-362.

HAVIGHURST, R. J. & STILES, L. J. National policy for alienated youth. *Phi Delta Kappan*, 1961, 42, 283-291.

HOLMES, E. C. A philosophical approach to the study of minority problems. *The Journal of Negro Education*, 1969, 38, 196-203.

JENCKS, C. Private schools for black children. *New York Times Magazine*, Vol. 118, Pp. 30, 132-140 (November 3, 1968).

JENNINGS, F. G. Educational opportunities geared to diversity. In *The sixty-sixth Yearbook of the National Society for the Study of Education, Part I*. Chicago: The University of Chicago Press, 1967. Pp. 351-353.

JENSEN, A. How much can we boost I.Q. and scholastic achievement? *Harvard Educational Review*, 1969, 39, 1-123.

JOHNSON, J. L. Special education and the inner city: a challenge for the future or another means for cooling the mark out? *The Journal of Special Education*, 1969, 3, 241-251.

JOHNSON, K. R. The culturally disadvantaged—slow learners or different learners? *Journal of Secondary Education*, 1970, 45, 43-47.

KRUGER, W. S. They don't have to drop out. *American Education*, 1969, 5, 7-8.

LEWIS, P. A. Materials for inner city schools. *The National Elementary Principal*, 1967, 46, 21-24.

Life. The sweep of the '60s. 1969, 67, (26), 12-31 (December 24, 1969).

NEA Journal. Project get set. 1966, 55, 16-18.

Newsweek. Education-Delayed Impact. 1970, 75, (11), 113-114 (March 16, 1970).

Nixon on Desegregation: "It is time to strip away hypocrisy and prejudice." *U.S. News & World Report*. 1970, 48, 80-87. (April 6, 1970).

OLSEN, E. G. Teacher education for the deprived: a new pattern. *School & Society*, 1967, 95, 232-234.

OMWAKE, E. Head start—measurable and immeasurable. In J. Hellmuth (Ed.), *Disadvantaged Child, Vol. II, Head Start and Early Intervention*. New York: Brunner/Mazel, Inc., 1968, Pp. 531-544.

ORNSTEIN, A. C. Effective schools for "disadvantaged" children. *Journal of Secondary Education*, 1965, 40, 105-109.

PEARL, A. Education, employment, and civil rights for Negro youth. In W. C. Kvaraceus, J. S. Gibson & T. J. Curtin (Eds.), *Poverty, education and race relations: studies and proposals*. Boston: Allyn and Bacon, 1970. Pp. 49-60.

RIESSMAN, F. Teachers of the poor: a five point plan. *The Journal of Teacher Education*, 1967, 18, 326-336.

ROSSI, P. H. The education of failures or the failure of education? *The Journal of Negro Education*, 1969, 38, 324-333.

SCHREIBER, D. The school dropout. In *The sixty-sixth Yearbook of the National Society for the Study of Education, Part I*. Chicago: The University of Chicago Press, 1967. Pp. 211-236.

SINCLAIR, W. Teacher preparation for urban schools. *School & Society*, 1968, 96, 339-340.

STROM, R. D. The school dropout and the family. In J. L. Frost & G. R. Hawkes (Eds.), *The disadvantaged child*. Boston: Moughton-Mifflin, 1966. Pp. 58-61.

Urban Review, The. Interview with Roy Wilkins. 1969, 3, (6), 16-23.

WASSERMAN, M. & REIMANN, J. Student rebels vs. school defenders: a partisan account. *The Urban Review*, 1969, 4, 9-17

YOUNG, W. M. JR. Order or chaos in our schools. *The National Elementary Principal*, 1970, 49, 24-33.

2

COMPENSATORY EDUCATION: DEFINING THE ISSUES

Doxey A. Wilkerson, Ph.D.

*Professor of Education and Chairman of the
Department of Curriculum and Instruction
Ferkauf Graduate School of Humanities and Social Sciences
Yeshiva University, New York City*

The compensatory education movement that emerged in the early 'sixties has produced a large number of varied programs and a vast literature. There is little hard evidence, however, that it has substantially improved the academic performance of disadvantaged children; and it certainly has not developed a consensus among theorists and practitioners in the field. Indeed, there seems to be less agreement at the end of the decade than at the beginning on the theory and practice of compensatory education; unresolved issues abound.

An objective definition of these issues would be very difficult even for an "outside" observer with no involvement in the field; his theoretical orientation and social values would necessarily influence his conception and formulation of the issues. Such a definition is quite impossible for one whose whole professional career has centered around the education of children of the poor, especially black children, and who is strongly partisan in most controversies over compensatory education. Thus, there is no claim of objectivity for this introductory essay. An effort is made, however, to interpret fairly what an admittedly biased observer understands to be the main points of dispute in the field, and to do so with a minimum of polemics.

The debate over compensatory education involves scores of specific issues, of both theory and practice; but they tend to cluster around a few, somewhat overlapping, major themes. Paramount among them are questions concerning the causes of the academic retardation that prevails among children of the poor; whether the school can reasonably be expected to improve substantially the academic performance of such children; and, if so, through what types of curricular experiences. There are also clusters of questions about approaches to the evaluation of compensatory programs; the role of the local community in both the development and appraisal of such programs; and, perhaps most fundamental, whether the effective education of disadvantaged children is, indeed, an important value of our society.

Compensatory education emerged to prominence nearly a decade after the United States Supreme Court decision in "The Segregation Cases," at a time when the civil rights movement was burgeoning, and when public school officials were under massive pressure to improve the education of impoverished Negro children through desegregating the schools. By then, the interactionist theory of the development of intellectual function was in the ascendancy; and the long-renowned doctrine that disadvantaged racial and social-class groups of people are "poorly endowed by nature" had seemingly been put to rest. It was no longer respectable in professional circles to attribute substandard performance among large population groups, in school or elsewhere, to presumed inadequacies in their genetic equipment. Rather, explanations were sought in the quantity and quality of these groups' encounters with their environment.

Consistent with this social, political and ideological setting, the rationale of early approaches to compensatory education was based on the hypothesis of "cultural deprivation." The academic failure and progressive retardation so common among children of the poor was mainly a function of their early socialization under conditions of poverty and discrimination. Deprived of preschool experiences essential for normative cognitive and affective development, these children entered school poorly equipped for academic work; and the function of special programs of compensatory education was to "make up" for their socially-induced handicaps. The origins of impoverished pupils' academic problems were mainly sociological, not biological. On this, there was at the beginning —and there continues to be—a broad consensus among professional advocates of compensatory education.

This cultural-deprivation premise was challenged at the outset by a small number of prominent educators who attributed widespread academic failures among disadvantaged children to grossly inept practices in the schools. Early socialization under conditions of poverty and discrimination, although hardly conducive to optimum development, by no means precluded effective learning in school. Impoverished children were fully capable of such learning, and demonstrated this potential when guided in appropriate learning experiences. The fact that most such children did not perform well in school was mainly a function of negative attitudes and low expectations among professional staff, and especially of instructional methods and materials ill-suited to their de-velopmental needs. The observed academic deficiencies of such children called not for special programs of compensatory education, but simply for good teaching; and this necessarily implied the adaptation of school methods and materials and affective climates to the differing needs of learners from impoverished backgrounds.

This point of view is strongly opposed by most school teachers and administrators—defensively, it would seem—but it has grown in accept-ance among students of public education. Increasing numbers of them now tend to discount the hypothesis of "cultural deprivation," and to explain the widespread and cumulative academic retardation among disadvantaged children on the basis of seriously dysfunctional charac-teristics of the school.

Although the early rationale of compensatory education eschewed doc-trines of inherent racial and social-class differences in ability to learn, such ideas—propagated under respectable auspices for centuries—lay deep in our culture; and they frequently emerged, even though fur-tively, among practitioners in the field. During most of the decade, however, there was no substantial support for such doctrines in the scientific community; the very few diehards espousing them had long been discredited among their peers. But this situation changed at the end of the decade, when an outstanding behavioral scientist—writing in a prestigious educational journal—impressively developed the argument that genetic influences were paramount in the poor school performance of disadvantaged children, especially Negroes. Compensatory education sought unattainable goals, because of hereditary limitations on the po-tential of the lower classes for intellectual development.

This modern-day reaffirmation of the doctrine of racial and social-class differences in "native endowment" was promptly repudiated by eminent scientists in the several behavioral fields, including genetics; but its impact abides. A long-dormant issue has been resuscitated. The educability of the population to which compensatory education is ad-dressed has emerged, once again, to the level of respectabiliity in scien-tific inquiry and debate.

Still another etiological issue has recently been raised by educators who question the relevance of etiology to educational practice. Un-moved by hereditary, environmental, or even interactionist analyses of the causes of academic retardation among children of the poor, they ask: "So what?" Given the wide variability among human beings, even valid etiological generalizations based on large populations provide no guidance whatever to diagnosing the needs and directing the learning experiences of the individual pupils in a teacher's classroom. Moreover, in the management of behavior—which formal education undertakes to do—the antecedents of observed patterns of behavior are of little consequence; how to effect change is the crucial question. Proponents of this point of view grant the general theoretical importance of etiological inquiry into the academic performance of disadvantaged children, but they deny its relevance to the development of specific educational programs.

Why, then, do disadvantaged children tend to perform poorly in school? Is it encounters with the negative environment of poverty and discrimination? Is it inept and dysfunctional school practice? Is it genetic inferiority? Is it important? All of these etiological issues remain unresolved at the end of the first decade of compensatory education.

REVERSIBILITY

Contending points of view concerning the etiology of the sub-standard academic performance that tends to prevail among disadvantaged children correspond in large measure to disputes concening reversibility—that is, the extent to which such children's negative developmental patterns can be redirected toward growth in academic competence. Several issues of importance to compensatory education bear directly on this general question.

Confidence in reversibility is implied in the very concept "compensatory education." The basic premise of special compensatory programs is that children of the poor—whatever their academic deficiencies—are teachable, that appropriate intervention can overcome the educational retardation that prevails among them. Even so, the case for "cultural deprivation" has been pressed so strongly in the literature—with massive documentation of the cognitive and affective "deficits" born of widespread pathology in the ghetto—that its apparently compensatory aim has often been turned into its opposite. Oversold on the seriousness and magnitude of these alleged deficits, many practitioners in the field—and seemingly some of the theorists—tended toward a kind of sociological determinism that all but precluded reversibility. The children of the poor were so scarred by encounters with poverty and discrimination that their potential for cognitive growth—whatever it may have been at birth—was severely limited by the time they entered school. Thus, even within the presumably optimistic camp of compensatory education, there were—and there still are—many professionals with serious doubts about the capacity of disadvantaged children for normative academic development.

Such doubts about the reversibility of poverty-induced educational handicaps were strengthened several years ago by one finding of the national study of *Equality of Educational Opportunity.* Using the method of regression analysis to assess the relative impact of different variables upon academic performance, it was found that socio-economic influences appeared to explain most of the variability in pupils' achievement, and that school influences appeared to explain but little. Subsequent analyses of data from this study have raised serious technical questions about the finding noted, the most basic being the appropriateness of the statistical techniques involved. A number of researchers have pointed out that when indices for two such closely correlated "independent" variables as socio-economic status and school service are subjected to regression analysis, the one entered first into the regression equation seems to show the greater explanatory power, since it tends to exhaust the major portion of the total variance carried by the two sets of indices together. The "Coleman Study" entered socio-economic-status variables into the equation first, with the results reported. Had the school-service variables been entered first, the results would have shown the school to be the major influence on pupil performance. Thus, constrary to widespread beliefs, the "Coleman Study" has not established that schooling makes but little difference in the academic development of children. It affords no confirmation of the thesis that the educational handicaps of disadvantaged children are irreversible.

Confidence in the reversibility of such handicaps is most pronounced, of course, among those scholars who view inept school practice as the main source of academic retardation among children of the poor. The children can learn if effectively taught. The pressing need is substantially—or perhaps radically—to modify professional attitudes, methods and materials. The most immediate target of change is the school.

The findings of research evaluations of compensatory education have tended both to support and to undermine confidence in the reversibility premise. Many systematic studies have revealed substantial cognitive growth by disadvantaged children, in this country and also in Israel— where problems in the education of disadvantaged children are strikingly similar and where notable compensatory programs are being developed. Programs demonstrated to be successful are addressed mainly to preschool youngsters, but not exclusively; more than a few show impressive gains among adolescents on the secondary and collegiate levels. Substandard patterns of academic behavior characteristic of children in these programs are clearly shown to be reversible.

The findings are different, however, with those large-scale compensatory programs in big-city school systems that have been evaluated by careful research techniques. The common conclusion is these programs made "no significant difference" in the academic achievement of the disadvantaged children involved; and this, of course, has tended to buttress doubts about the reversibility of the educational handicaps generally characteristic of children of the poor. The acting superintendent of one large school system was moved by such findings to declare recently that it is a "mystery" why these children do not learn, a sentiment ominously echoed shortly afterward from the White House. It has appropriately been asked, however, whether such negative findings tell us more about the inadequacies of large-scale compensatory programs than about the educability of disadvantaged children.

Among the biological determinists, of course, there is no mystery about the negative findings from research evaluations of large compensatory programs. The children involved are by nature incapable of normative intellectual development; demonstrably, the premise of reversibility is unsound.

Thus, as in the case of questions about the etiology of educational retardation among children of the poor, there persist sharply-drawn issues over whether their sub-standard academic performance is reversible.

CURRICULUM

"Curriculum" is here used to designate the experiences pupils have under the guidance of the school—which, of course, determine what they learn. Most issues in this area are predicated upon the assumption that appropriate school experiences can, indeed, make a significant difference in the academic performance of disadvantaged children.

Probably the most persistent of such issues concerns the validity for compensatory education of the kinds of learning experiences generally suggested in the regular curriculum bulletins. Such experiences tend to predominate in compensatory programs, supplemented by more or less intensive efforts at remediation; and they are defended as appropriate by most professional personnel. All that is needed to make them functional is smaller classes, or more supplies and equipment, or greater support by pupils' parents. Many critics contend, however, that prevailing types of school learning experiences—variously characterized as excessively verbal and abstract, alien to the "real world," unduly formal, "lock step," etc.—are far less than optimum even for the middle-class children for whom they were designed, and are wholly inadequate to serve the educational needs of children nurtured in poverty and discrimination. Clearly indicated is curriculum reform more thorough-going than is generally found in compensatory education. Among the reforms often proposed are learning experiences in all curriculum areas that relate directly to the out-of-school lives of the learners; creative and discovery and problem-solving activities; a wide range of printed and other instructional materials, especially including resources available in the community; informal patterns of instructional organization; nongraded classes and other approaches to individualized instruction—and many more. Although prescriptions vary widely among advocates of change, the issue of curriculum reform in compensatory education is sharply drawn.

An increasingly prominent aspect of that issue concerns the incorporation of "The Black Experience" and similar content from other minority-group sub-cultures in the curriculum on all educational levels. Should such content be taught as a separate "subject" or integrated into the general curriculum of compensatory programs? Does the use of such content enhance the ego-strength and academic achievement of disadvantaged children? There is a fair amount of empirical evidence on the latter question, but the findings of systematic studies tend to be inconclusive or contradictory.

The affective climates of school and classroom powerfully influence the quality of pupils' learning experiences, and there are important issues for compensatory education in this curricular dimension. Is it true, as critics contend and professional staff deny: That negative racial and social-class attitudes among many teachers and school administrators aggravate the learning problems of disadvantaged children? That many teachers' low expectations of their pupils lead toward the acceptance of unduly low standards of academic performance? That such low expectations, subtly or explicitly communicated to pupils, tend to erode their incentive to achieve? The debate around such questions as these is widespread and intense in both the profession and the communities it serves.

Whether children attend schools that are segregated along racial and social-class lines also conditions the nature and quality of their learning experiences; hence, disputes in this realm are in a very real sense "curricular." Moreover, such questions are especially relevant to compensatory education, because almost all of the programs are conducted in segregated schools. Indeed, some observers interpret the rapid growth of compensatory education in the early 'sixties as an off-target response to the then powerful demands for school integration. In any case, there are at least two issues in this area with important implications for the development of compensatory programs.

First, is school desegregation desirable as general social policy? Several years ago, the Negro community was united around the demand for school integration; and its struggles toward that goal were strongly supported by white allies in the civil rights movement and by the Federal Government. This is no longer true. An aggressive and highly articulate minority of the Negro people, especially in large northern cities, now deny the importance, the possibility, and the desirability of school integration in the education of black children; and support for integration in the white community and the Federal Government has definitely waned. In the country as a whole, however—especially among black people—the demand for desegregating the schools continues strong.

Second, are curricular experiences that foster desirable affective and cognitive development more likely to be provided for disadvantaged children—especially black youngsters—in segregated or desegregated schools? This question, of course, is subject to scientific inquiry; and a number of systematic studies have sought the answer. The findings of most of these studies suggest that desegregated schools tend to afford more productive learning experiences for impoverished minority-group children than segregated schools. Desegregated school settings with compensatory services to children who need them would seem, therefore, to be indicated; but considerations beyond the data of research investigations keep this issue very much alive.

There are many other specific issues relevant to curriculum development in compensatory education; but the most important current disputes seem to cluster around the questions here noted—general curriculum reform, black and ethnic studies, attitudes of professional staff, and school desegregation.

EVALUATION

As in the case of American education generally, systematic and rigorous evaluation is not a common characteristic of the special compensatory programs; impressionistic appraisals based on the subjective judgments of participants tend to prevail. Although there is general recognition that more careful evaluation is needed, there is considerable dispute over the appropriateness of different criteria and emphases.

The most fundamental of these issues is whether the appraisal of compensatory programs—indeed, all educational programs—should be based mainly on inputs or on outputs. Prevailing practice, generally favored by practitioners, is to focus on the organization and conduct of the programs—stated objectives, instructional methods and materials, qualifications of professional staff, community participation, administrative efficiency, etc.—all indices of inputs. Many critics insist, however, that evaluation in education is properly conceived as assessment of the growth of children toward educational goals. They would focus on increments of learning associated with compensatory programs, on outputs.

The common rationale for evaluations that are based on inputs rather than outputs is that it is practically impossible to differentiate clearly between school and non-school influences on pupils' learning; which, of course, is true. It is noted, further, that available techniques for measuring educational outcomes are crude; which is also generally true. There remains, however, the question of whether there can be any serious evaluation of compensatory or any other educational programs without major effort to assess their contributions to pupil learning.

A kindred issue concerns the relative emphasis to be given to different domains of behavior in evaluations that do focus on the outcomes of compensatory programs. Many researchers tend to emphasize cognitive development as measured by standardized tests of intelligence and of academic achievement—in reading, mathematics, science, and the like. Many practitioners tend to emphasize social and emotional development as assessed through the systematic or informal observation of social behavior, attendance rates, attitudes toward self and others, educational and vocational aspirations, and the like. It would seem that adequate appraisal of compensatory programs calls for the assessment of behavioral changes in both of these broad domains. The issue is posed by tendencies among many evaluators to concentrate on one and to discount the importance of the other.

There are also issues concerning the validity of standardized tests of intelligence and achievement in the appraisal of compensatory programs. In the first place, are tests of "intelligence" at all appropriate? Such tests are widely used in research evaluations of compensatory programs, but their relevance is questioned by some observers. Compensatory education, they argue, undertakes (among other things) to enhance the academic achievement of disadvantaged pupils, not their "potential" for learning, which it is assumed intelligence tests seek to gauge. Second, are even standardized achievement tests appropriate for measuring the academic performance of disadvantaged children? On the one hand, it is argued that the content and norms of such tests are based on the culture and performance of white, middle-class children, and are of doubtful validity when used with black and other minority-group children from impoverished backgrounds. Moreover, the special developmental handicaps experienced by children of the poor make it unreasonable to assess their academic performance by the same standards used with middle-class children. On the other hand, it is contended that the academic performance of disadvantaged children should be evaluated by the same instruments and norms that are used with other children. Otherwise, compensatory programs will tend toward development of an inferior, special "lower-class" type of education, thus further aggravating the coping problems of disadvantaged youth in the real world beyond the school.

Questions concerning the relative emphasis to be placed on different evaluative criteria and the appropriateness of standard instruments and norms are important in the appraisal of compensatory programs. The more basic question, however, is whether these programs are to be evaluated mainly in terms of what professionals do or what children learn.

COMMUNITY

The principle that community support is essential for effective school programs is almost universally accepted in the profession; there is no issue here, at least in theory. What this principle implies for school practice, however, is the subject of considerable debate; and this is especially true in the urban ghettoes, which most programs of compensatory education are designed to serve.

The characteristic alienation of school and community in poverty areas undoubtedly minimizes parental support of compensatory programs and negatively influences the academic behaviors of pupils. Where lies the main responsibility for correcting this state of affairs? Professional staffs tend to disavow such responsibility, blaming parental lack of interest and non-support for their problems in managing and teaching the children. Community leaders should educate and organize their people to support the school. Parents and community leaders tend to blame the school, alleging indifference—and even hostility—to the local population. Teachers and administrators should work to develop rapport with the community, and especially to involve parents substantively in the program of the school. The central question here, it would seem, is whether community support of the school is a value professional staff has the right to expect or the obligation to win.

A far more explosive issue of school-community relations in ghetto areas is posed by the recent movement for "community control." Frustrated by early efforts to desegregate the schools, and outraged by the continued failure of schools to educate their children—even in compensatory programs—Negro organizations in many large cities are demanding that the school be made accountable to the people it serves; and their demand is increasingly echoed by communities of Puerto Ricans, Mexican-Americans and American Indians. Authority over school policy, program, personnel and budget should be transferred in large measure from the central educational bureaucracy to elected representatives of the local community. Perceiving this demand as a threat to their autonomy and job security, teachers and school administrators overwhelmingly resist what they consider community encroachment upon their domain. Professionals, not laymen, must exercise decisive control over the school. This particular issue is expressive of current tendencies to challenge institutional authority on many fronts. Its resolution will not come through academic debate, but through confrontation in the arena of political struggle.

These issues concerning the relations of school and community have relevance beyond the limited realm of compensatory education. They are most sharply drawn, however, in those disadvantaged areas where compensatory programs are concentrated.

SOCIAL VALUES

Affirmations of the principle of equality of educational opportunity abound in the rhetoric of American democracy. Yet, throughout the history of our country, there never has been even the approximation of such equality for the masses of children of the poor. The question arises: Is equality of educational opportunity, indeed, an important value of our society?

The promise of compensatory education was substantially to redress prevailing inequality between the education of the affluent and the poor, but its failure thus far to do so is evident from the experience of the past decade. Why? Because our nation could not or would not fulfill this commitment?

The effective education of disadvantaged children is a goal genuinely cherished by a large proportion of the American people, but it is patent that many of our citizens are indifferent or opposed to its realization. Indeed, there are those who explicitly advocate a European-type of limited "class education" for the children of the poor; and, as is apparent from one essay in this volume, their views are welcomed in high councils of the Federal Government. Could it be, despite professions to the contrary, that this negation of the goal of educational equality reflects values that really are commanding in our country?

The institution of education is an interacting and highly dependent unit of the whole society, decisively influenced by the values that there prevail. Considering the unparalleled resources that our nation can and does marshal in pursuit of what are clearly priority goals—as in space, in Vietnam, in the production of munitions—our persistent failure to develop good school programs for most children of the poor necessarily raises questions about the position of this goal in our national scale of values.

Compensatory education, after a decade of development, is beset by many important issues of educational theory and practice. Most fundamental to its further development, however, is whether the effective education of disadvantaged children is—or can be made—an imperative value of American society.

REFERENCES

1. BLOOM, BENJAMIN S. *Stability and Change in Human Characteristics*. New York: Wiley, 1964.
2. COHEN, S. ALAN. *Teach Them All to Read*. New York: Random House, 1969.
3. COLEMAN, JAMES S. AND OTHERS. *Equality of Educational Opportunity*. Washington: Government Printing Office, 1966.
4. CORDASCO, FRANCESCO, HILLSON, MAURIE and BULLOCK, HENRY A. (Eds.). *The School in the Social Order*. Scranton, Pa.: International Textbook Company, 1970.
5. DAVIDSON, HELEN H. and GREENBERG, JUDITH W. *Traits of School Achievers from a Deprived Background*. New York: The City College and the City University of New York, 1967.
6. DEUTSCH, MARTIN. *The Disadvantaged Child*. New York: Basic Books, 1967.
7. Educating the Children of the Welfare Poor: A *Record* Symposium. *The Record*, Vol. 68, No. 4, pp. 301-319, January, 1968.

8. Education, Ethnicity, Genetics and Intelligence. *IRCD Bulletin,* Vol. V, No. 4, Fall, 1969. (ERIC Information Retrieval Center on the Disadvantaged, Teachers College, Columbia University, New York, N. Y.).

9. FANTINI, MARIO D. and WEINSTEIN, GERALD. *The Disadvantaged: Challenge to Education.* New York: Harper and Row, 1968.

10. FUCHS, ESTELLE. *Teachers Talk.* Garden City, N.Y.: Doubleday and Company, Anchor Books, 1969.

11. GROSS, RONALD and BEATRICE (Eds.). *Radical School Reform.* New York: Simon and Schuster, 1969.

12. GUTHRIE, JAMES W. and others. *A Survey of School Effectiveness Studies.* Paper presented at the Conference on How Do Teachers Make a Difference? U.S. Office of Education, Bureau of Educational Personnel Development, Washington, D.C., February 4, 1970.

13. HAMILTON, CHARLES C. Race and Education: A Search for Legitimacy. *Harvard Educational Review,* 38: 669-684, Fall, 1968.

14. "How Much Can We Boost IQ and Scholastic Achievement?": A Discussion. *Harvard Educational Review,* 39: 273-356, Spring, 1969.

15. HUNT, J. Mc V. *Intelligence and Experience.* New York: Ronald Press, 1961.

16. JENSEN, ARTHUR R. Reducing the Heredity-Environment Uncertainty: A Reply. *Harvard Educational Review*: 39: 449-483, Summer, 1969.

18. KLINEBERG, OTTO. *Race Differences.* New York: Harper and Brothers, 1935.

19. LEACOCK, ELEANOR BURKE. *Teaching and Learning in City Schools.* New York: Basic Books, 1969.

20. LIGHT, RICHARD J. and SMITH, PAUL V. Choosing a Future: Strategies for Designing and Evaluating New Programs. *Harvard Educational Review,* 40: 1-28, February, 1970.

21. MAYESKE, GEORGE W. and others. *A Study of Our Nation's Schools: A Working Paper.* U.S. Department of Health, Education and Welfare, Office of Education, N.D. (circa 1969).

22. PETTIGREW, THOMAS A. *A Profile of the Negro American.* Princeton, N.J.: Van Nostrand, 1964.

23. ROSENTHAL, ROBERT and JACOBSON, LENORE. *Pygmalion in the Classroom.* New York: Holt, Rinehart and Winston, 1968.

24. RUBINSTEIN, ANNETTE T. (Ed.). *Schools Against Children: The Case for Community Control.* New York: Monthly Review Press, 1970.

25. SCHWEBEL, MILTON. *Who Can Be Educated?* New York: Grove Press, 1968.

26. SHUEY, AUDREY M. *The Testing of Negro Intelligence.* New York: Social Science Press, 1966.

27. SKEELS, HAROLD M. *Adult Status of Children with Contrasting Early Life Experiences: A Follow-Up Study.* Society for Research in Child Development, University of Chicago Press, 1966.

28. SMILANSKY, MOSHE. Fighting Deprivation in the Promised Land. *Saturday Review,* 49: 82+, October 15, 1966.

29. United States Commission on Civil Rights. *Racial Isolation in the Public Schools.* Washington: Government Printing Office, 1967.

3

AN EDUCATIONAL IMPERATIVE
AND ITS FALLOUT IMPLICATIONS

James O. Miller, Ph.D.

Director, National Laboratory on Early Childhood Education

INTRODUCTION

If the educational decade of the sixties is remembered for its student revolts on university and college campuses, it must also be remembered for the unprecedented awakening of interest and commitment to early childhood education. That these seemingly two disparate movements should occur simultaneously is not fortuitous. They must be considered a part of a dynamic social revolution in the United States, of whose scope we are only recently becoming fully aware. The student revolts are a direct response to the intransigence of the educational system to social reality. Society has embraced Early Childhood Education as a constructive alternative to a mass sit-in on the Educational system.

Following World War II, the social revolution which had its roots in the depression years gained new impetus with an exuberant economic growth throughout the country. This growth was in part the result of rapid technological development during the war which was then put to peaceful production. With high production came economic affluence for the majority of the population.

But technological development and affluence etched a much sharper picture in the contrast between skilled and unskilled, both socially and economically. Highly developed abstracting and symbolic abilities necessary to compete in a technological society were lacking in a significant segment of the work force. Agricultural automation decreased opportunities for the unskilled and semiskilled in the labor market. Technological displacement increased and continues to increase at an alarming rate. An increasing gap between the affluent majority of the citizens in the country reaping the material benefits and those who were denied the fruits of the expanding economy became apparent. The accumulated educational deficit of a significant number of the population came sharply into focus. Economically deprived ctizens found themselves to be deprived of equal educational opportunity. A crisis in civil rights was inevitable. In the early fifties, the American education system became the battleground for equal educational opportunity in a confrontation of power. As the battle for equal opportunity was being fought and skirmishes won, society faced yet another crisis, that of human rights. Equality of educational opportunity, a civil right, was a hollow victory indeed for the individual, if doors were closed to him because environmental circumstances had failed to provide the necessary support to insure educational success.

Society's confrontation with conscience continues as it looks for means to insure that young children have adequate environmental support for building the skills, abilities, and motivations necessary for success. Nowhere is the need greater or the inequality more sharply defined than among those socially powerless in the large metropolitan inner-cities and the southeastern region of the United States whose emigrants feed the ghetto. Markedly higher juvenile crime rates, premature school dropout and truancy, alienation of the citizens from the school are the bitter fruits of the inner-city schools' inability to establish and retain relevancy with their constituents. Schools organized and staffed in mirror image of the white middle class culture fail, but the children they serve bear the burden of failure.

In part, a response to the schools' failure to be effective with the disadvantaged child, the movement to early education has been supported by substantial evidence accumulating in the behavioral sciences over the past decade and a half as to the crucial importance of the early years in the development of personal competence. Long held beliefs in the relatively set pattern and pace of development have had to yield, in the face of increasing evidence that environmental circumstances play a major role in the shaping of both the developmental course and rate of the abilities required for environmental mastery. The accumulating evidence has had a dramatic effect upon developmental theory, which in turn has begun to affect practice. While earlier conceptions saw growth and development occurring according to a fixed genetic pattern and pace in a closed system, the evidence now seems to point to growth and development being an interacting process between the individual's genetic endowment and his environmental circumstances *in an open system*. This new conception will have a profound effect upon child rearing and educational practices in the development of a competent and productive citizenry.

Our emphasis has been on shaping the child to fit the school. Too little has been done to shape the system to fit the child. We must develop the capacity for the system to be continuously relevant. I believe that an essential condition for systemic development is the capacity to accommodate change rather than resist it if the system is to be effective in its mission. Further, it must not only be able to accommodate change (essentially a respondent position), it must be able to utilize the effects of change to manage and optimize the development of the total system. Here a total system is defined as broadly as the educational system or as narrowly as an individual staff member. Tragically, our educational institutions seem to be caught in an inability to accommodate and utilize change which puts them constantly into a failure posture.

Clearly, American society during the sixties has invested its educational system with more than the responsibility of acting as a repository for the cultural heritage and passing on its accumulated wisdom to the next generation (a job up to now it has done on a very selective basis, indeed, on both counts!). It has stated, in deed as well as word, that the educational system must become relevant to all sectors of the population and prepare children to cope effectively with rapidly changing societal conditions. This is more than a challenge, it is an educational imperative.

Early childhood education programs have been conceived as agents of change aimed directly at the problems of the impoverished and the inner-city, and only thinly disguised as agents of change in the educational system that serves disadvantaged populations (witness the Follow-Through Program). The choice, if deliberate, has been well made since early childhood education is not strapped with the bureaucratic paraphernalia which inhibits innovation. The problems and crises which beset early childhood education provide an arena for research and experimentation not readily available in other areas of education. One of the most crucial problems facing the field is the critical shortage of trained personnel to mount quality programs targeted for disadvantaged groups.

THE PROBLEMS

"I have yet to see any problem, however complicated, which when you looked at it the right way did not become still more complicated."

Poul Anderson

In order to fully appreciate the staffing crisis being experienced in early childhood education, one must go back to 1964 and look at the field as it then existed. Up to that time most programs in early childhood education were privately sponsored, principally as nursery and kindergarten schools for the more affluent middle class. Those day care facilities available for children of working parents were primarily custodial in nature with little concern for an educational program per se. A few programs existed on college and university campuses where they served as laboratories for professionals interested in child growth and development. Some training occurred in these laboratory preprimary units. But, few training programs of magnitude existed, nor have they been developed.

Trained personnel were in short demand. What demand there was at the publicly-supported kindergarten level could be staffed by teachers trained in an elementary school program. Privately sponsored programs paid such low salaries that formal educational preparation was not worth the investment. The practicing professional field was kept alive primarily by holdovers from the Lanham Act and WPA child care centers. No reliable statistics are available as to the number of trained and qualified teachers available in the professional pool prior to 1964.

Further, it is difficult to assess with any accuracy the extent of pre-primary education prior to that time. No standard lexicon was in use and over the past five years only a minimum amount of headway has been made in developing standard terminology. As we look at the period from 1965, the marker date for the rapid expansion of the field, the term early childhood education will be restricted to the age range of birth to six years of age. Preprimary education covers the age range of three to six, primarily because formal educational programs are few in number for children from birth to three years of age even in away-from-home day care settings. The problem of trying to assess where we are in the field is further confounded by the diversity of settings, the proliferation of responsible regulatory agencies, public versus private, non-profit versus private-for-profit sponsorship, and even the length of time the child spends in the facility. With that caveat, a look at the field during its period of maximum growth is in order.

In 1964 it was estimated that 25.5 per cent of the three to five year old population was enrolled in prekindergarten and kindergarten educational programs (Table 1). By contrast, in 1967 enrollment reached 31.6 per cent of the age group. Since the number of children in the three to five year age group has remained relatively stable over this period of time, somewhat in excess of 12 million, this represents an increase of approximately 700,000 children enrolled in preprimary educational programs. Head Start and programs for the disadvantaged under the Elementary and Secondary Education Act have been estimated to account for 400,000 of the increase. The rest is due to non-targeted federally sponsored programs and other public and privately supported increases. Table 1 clearly indicates where the impact of these programs has been. While an increase in enrollment can be seen across all income groups, by far the greatest increase has occurred at the two lower income levels, a little over 6 per cent in each category. Clearly, this is a function of Head Start and targeted preprimary ESEA programs. However, the affluent enroll a far greater proportion of their children in preprimary programs than do any of the other three categories. The range is from

a minimum of 10 per cent to a maximum of 20 per cent greater enrollment. Obviously, we are not yet reaching a significant proportion of
those most in need of preprimary educational programs. In fact, to bring
the enrollment of the least served to the level of the most affluent would
add in excess of 800,000 children to preprimary educational programs.
Such an increase would match the growth over the three years represented, but certainly is a poor rationale for determination of need. It
simply would bring the level of use to that of the most affluent economic
groups, those whose family income is in excess of $7,500 per year. It
would also create the need for 114,000 additional classroom personnel.

Of the 25 million preschool children (0-6) in the United States, a
little over 12 million are in the preprimary age bracket (3, 4 and 5 year
olds). Thirty-one point six per cent are estimated to be enrolled, with the
greatest percentage appearing in kindergarten programs which benefit
from state aid in 29 of the states. At the present time, approximately

TABLE 1

PERCENTAGE DISTRIBUTION OF OCTOBER ENROLLMENT OF 3-5
YEAR OLD CHILDREN BY FAMILY INCOME GROUP FOR THE
UNITED STATES: 1964, 1965, 1966, AND 1967

Income Group and Year	Percentage
Under $3,000:	
1967	21.2
1966	19.3
1965	14.4
1964	15.1
$3,000 to $4,999:	
1967	26.0
1966	21.3
1965	21.0
1964	19.8
$5,000 to $7,999:	
1967	29.0
1966	29.0
1965	26.3
1964	25.8
$7,500 and over:	
1967	38.5
1966	37.8
1965	37.4
1964	37.2

Adapted from "Preprimary Enrollment of Children Under Six," October, 1967 published by
Office of Education, U.S. Department of Health, Education, and Welfare. OE-20113.

225,000 children are served in licensed day care facilities. Approximately 70 per cent of the preprimary educational programs are publicly supported. Sixty-six per cent are kindergarten with publicly supported programs serving but 5 per cent of those enrolled three years of age and under. Public support of day care is presently on a small scale with only California providing comprehensive state aid.

The highest impact area for the federally sponsored programs has been in the larger metropolitan areas (Table 2). The rural areas have been served much less than have the more densely populated urban and suburban areas. Non-white enrollment is greater than that of the white group in general and must be accounted for by federally sponsored programs at the four-year-old level since at both the three-year-old level and the five-year-old level white enrollment exceeds that of the non-white. This is certainly an indictment of the public school kindergarten in the inner-cities.

Table 3 summarizes enrollment by income, occupation, residence, and region. The level of public support for kindergarten is higher than for prekindergarten programs which serve mainly three and four year olds. Enrollment of children in white collar families greatly exceeds that of children in manual or service workers' families. This undoubtedly reflects both a higher motivation for educational services and the wherewithal to pay for them. The level of enrollment of children of the unemployed is similar to that of the manual or service workers' children. Referrals by welfare agencies are probably instrumental in bringing this about. Enrollment in rural areas and in the southern region of the United States is much less. The South lags behind by approximately 10 per cent. If migration from the rural South to the inner-cities continues, the need for preprimary education will undoubtedly increase.

In the aggregate, the foregoing demonstrates vividly the accelerated growth in the field of the early childhood education since 1965. If one accepts a ratio of seven children to one adult in the classroom, as called for by most guidelines, there was a minimum increase of 100,000 positions over this three year span. One must calculate the impact of such an explosion in megatons when one considers the lack of training capabilities in existence.

In the main, the staffing problem has been met at the professional level with short term training drawing on a pool of people with training and experience in other educational fields. Classroom assistants have been recruited from the areas served and usually have had no professional training whatsoever. In fact, some have viewed the Head Start Program as more a job opportunity project for the poor than an educational program for disadvantaged children.

Head Start has provided data on the characteristics of classroom personnel. It seems reasonable to accept this picture as typical of the field

TABLE 2

NUMBER OF 3-, 4-, AND 5-YEAR-OLD CHILDREN IN THE POPULATION AND NUMBER AND PERCENT ENROLLED IN PREPRIMARY PROGRAMS, BY RESIDENCE, AGE, AND COLOR: UNITED STATES, OCTOBER 1967

[Numbers in thousands]

Age and color of children	SMSA* central cities			SMSA* outside central cities			Non-SMSA*		
	Population	Enrolled in preprimary programs Number	Percent	Population	Enrolled in preprimary programs Number	Percent	Population	Enrolled in preprimary programs Number	Percent
Total, 3-5 years old....	3,348	1,227	36.6	4,342	1,542	35.5	4,548	1,098	24.1
White.............	2,343	855	36.5	4,029	1,422	35.3	3,910	990	25.3
Nonwhite	1,005	372	37.0	313	120	38.3	638	108	16.9
Total, 3 years old	1,069	96	9.0	1,427	110	7.7	1,497	68	4.5
White.............	749	68	9.1	1,317	95	7.2	1,279	54	4.2
Nonwhite	320	28	8.8	110	15	13.6	218	14	6.4
Total, 4 years old	1,131	303	26.8	1,459	383	26.3	1,496	185	12.4
White.............	789	195	24.7	1,356	340	25.1	1,288	153	11.9
Nonwhite	342	108	31.6	103	43	41.7	208	32	15.4
Total, 5 years old	1,148	828	72.1	1,456	1,049	72.0	1,555	843	54.2
White.............	806	593	73.6	1,356	987	72.8	1,342	781	58.2
Nonwhite	342	235	68.7	100	62	62.0	213	62	29.1

Note.—Excluded from the enrollment data in this table are 444,000 5-year-olds in programs above the kindergarten level. Also excluded are the population and the preprimary enrollment (157,000) of 6-year-olds.

* SMSA = Standard Metropolitan Statistical Area.

TABLE 3

SUMMARY OF CHARACTERISTICS OF 3-, 4-, AND 5-YEAR-OLD CHILDREN ENROLLED IN PREKINDERGARTEN AND KINDERGARTEN PROGRAMS: UNITED STATES, OCTOBER 1967

[Numbers in thousands]

Characteristics	Total population	Total enrolled in preprimary programs		Enrolled in prekindergarten programs		Enrolled in kindergarten programs	
		Number	Percent	Number	Percent	Number	Percent
Total	12,242	3,869	31.6	712	5.8	3,157	25.8
White	10,283	3,267	31.8	563	5.5	2,704	26.3
Nonwhite	1,959	601	30.7	149	7.6	452	23.1
Family income[1]							
Under $3,000	1,333	282	21.2	46	3.5	236	17.7
$3,000 to $4,999	1,973	513	26.0	99	5.0	414	21.0
$5,000 to $7,499	3,439	997	29.0	140	4.1	857	24.9
$7,500 to $9,999	2,358	780	33.1	127	5.4	653	27.7
$10,000 and over	2,269	1,002	44.2	243	10.7	759	33.5
Occupation of family head[2]							
White-collar	4,178	1,652	39.5	395	9.5	1,257	30.1
Manual or service	6,085	1,687	27.7	236	3.9	1,451	23.8
Farm	540	101	18.7	12	2.2	89	16.5
Unemployed or not in labor force	1,097	304	27.7	47	4.3	257	23.4
Residence							
SMSA—Central cities	3,348	1,227	36.6	274	8.2	953	28.5
SMSA—Outside central cities	4,342	1,542	35.5	289	6.7	1,253	28.9
Outside SMSA's	4,548	1,098	24.1	149	3.3	949	20.9
Region							
Northeast	(3)	(3)	34.6	(3)	6.2	(3)	28.4
North Central	(3)	(3)	34.0	(3)	5.1	(3)	28.8
South	(3)	(3)	23.3	(3)	5.0	(3)	18.3
West	(3)	(3)	38.4	(3)	7.8	(3)	30.6

Note.—Excluded from the enrollment data in this table are 444,000 5-year-olds in programs above the kindergarten level. Also excluded are the population and the primary enrollment (157,000) of 6-year-olds.

[1] Excludes children with family income not reported.
[2] Excludes children with occupation of household head not reported.
[3] No figures shown, since regional data are not controlled by independent population estimates.

in general. Inspection of Table 4 indicates clearly that the preprimary programs have been staffed by people with relatively little formal academic training, even less experience with primary age children from disadvantaged environments. (The Westinghouse report on Head Start evaluation should come as no great shock.) In light of the dearth of investment in applied research and development on instructional content, one is left wondering as to the meaning of preprimary "educational" programs. Almost a third of the professional staff have had less than two full years of college work. Nearly 80 per cent have practically no experience with preprimary education and a whopping 80 per cent have had little experience, if any, with children from impoverished environments. The effects of cultural shock must have an impact upon the problem of educational relevancy in the ghetto. These data clearly suggest that the classroom staff has insufficient knowledge and experience concerning the children and the communities to be served. While there is no question of the concern and dedication of the people who have assumed classroom responsibilties, there is a definite question as to their ability to design and implement an instructional curriculum. Without such ability, programs are forced to be custodial depending upon the "natural unfolding" of the child to develop competence. I see little reason to promote the myth of unfolding abilities. Nurturance is an active endeavor requiring skill and knowledge of the significant adults in contact with the child.

Unfortunately, the investment in training has been pitifully small in light of demonstrated need. Short term training institutes sponsored by OEO have never been counted as substitutes for career development training. They might best be characterized as "how to get started" sessions with the hope that the regional training officer could lend the helping support on the job required for program maintenance.

Under the Educational Professional Development Act, only 494 fellowship support slots are presently available for general early childhood education. An additional 170 fellowships are targeted for preprimary education of the handicapped. Only one of the funded programs, with support for 20 participants, is located in an area with direct access to an inner-city. The training plans of the other programs were not available to ascertain whether provision is being made for direct contact with the inner-city environment and its problems. Not only is the support available for career training impossibly minute, but it is being distributed far from the source of need. It is questionable if the real training expertise is located upon college and university campuses where investment in early childhood education training has been scarce historically.

I would like to be optimistic that institutions of higher learning are moving away from simply stacking courses in the development of training programs. This would be such a radical shift, however, that it is

TABLE 4

SELECTED CHARACTERISTICS OF HEAD START STAFF FOR
FULL YEAR PROGRAM, 1967[1]

Staff Characteristics	Per Cent Professional Staff*	Per Cent Program Assistants**
Ethnicity		
Caucasian	53.4	30.6
Negro	31.6	45.1
American Indian	3.9	8.0
Puerto Rican	5.2	5.1
Mexican-American	2.3	6.7
Other	4.3	4.5
School Years Completed		
Less than high school	5.5	30.2
High school	10.5	50.8
1 to 2 years college	13.7	11.6
3 to 4 years college	45.5	5.9
5 or more years college	23.8	1.3
Not reported	1.4	.7
Paid experience with preschool children before Head Start		
None to less than 6 months	55.9	75.8
6 months to 3 years	22.4	12.3
4 to 5 years	4.7	1.9
Over 5 years	13.6	4.0
Not reported	3.7	6.3
Paid experience with poor children before Head Start		
None to less than 6 months	53.7	76.2
6 months to 3 years	23.7	11.6
4 to 5 years	4.7	1.4
Over 5 years	12.9	2.3
Not reported	5.2	8.7

* Teachers constitute 72.1 per cent of the total professional staff surveyed.
** Teacher aides constitute 79.2 per cent of the total program assistant staff surveyed.
[1] Project Head Start 1965-1967: A Descriptive Report of Programs and Participants.

doubtful that such is the case. Brady (1968) has expressed the problem well when she states

> "Higher education respondeth not. . . . Many faculty and adminis-
> trators in teacher education do not think of developing a program
> in an area until it is mandated by the existence of a credential.
> They do not generate programs based on evidence of need or as the
> result of research. At times the circle appears unbreakable. There
> is resistance to establishing a credential at a quality level because
> few people could meet the standard. The number of qualified people
> will not markedly increase until there are programs of preparation,
> and these will not be established until the credential makes them
> imperative. To further complicate matters, faculty members who
> can prepare early childhood teachers are rare; the doctorate is in-
> creasingly required, but few universities offer doctoral programs
> through which individuals can qualify themselves as college faculty."

In summary, the field of early childhood education has experienced a phenomenal growth which is continuing. The proliferation of programs has created a crisis in staffing. The problem has been met by using inadequately trained classroom personnel. Training capabilities have lagged far behind demonstrated need. Those training programs which are being developed probably reflect little understanding or conversance with the inner-city and its people. The meager resources available for development of training programs appear to be distributed on the basis of inappropriate criteria.

THE FUTURE

Children's Bureau estimates that approximately 38,000 children are left totally uncared for while their mothers work and double that number are looked after by other children under the age of 16. It is esti-mated that 1,050,000 disadvantaged children from zero to six years of age need full day care. Presently there are only 110,000 places in day care programs for these children. Of the 12 million children in the three through five year age bracket, approximately 4 million come from disadvantaged environments. As earlier reported, only about 400,000 or 10 per cent of the children are being served who should be enrolled in preprimary education.

These facts are influencing pending legislation and policy. At the federal level, enabling legislation is before Congress to allow collective bargaining to include provision of day care for the children of employ-ees. The administration has committed itself to doubling the Parent and Child Center experimental program. Recently passed amendments to the Social Security Act make provisions for day care of children receiving aid under AFDC.

The federal panel on early childhood recently issued its *Federal Inter-agency Day Care Requirements*. These program standards and regulations are applicable to all programs supported wholly or in part by federal funds. Of particular significance are the mandatory provisions requiring educational opportunities to be provided for every child in federally sponsored programs. The educational activities must be under the supervision of a person trained in child growth and development. The program must contain activities designed to influence "a positive concept of self and motivation and to enhance his social, cognitive and communication skills." Materials and equipment to implement the program are also mandatory.

There are kindergartens for five year olds in slightly more than half of the states now. Several states which do not yet allow or provide public support for kindergarten are passing legislation enabling it or making it mandatory. Beginning with the fall term of 1969, all handicapped children who might benefit from an educational program from the age of two must be provided such services by the local school district in the state of Connecticut. Similar legislation is pending in the state of New York.

In addition, other organizations are advocating increased investment in early childhood education. The Educational Policies Commission of the National Education Association (1960) maintains that "All children should have the opportunity to go to school at public expense beginning at the age of four."

The Research and Policy Committee of the Committee for Economic Development (July, 1968), stated

> "We believe that early schooling is probably desirable for all children and that it is a necessity for the children of culturally disadvantaged areas. We, therefore, recommend extensive experimental activity in preschooling, not only in the substance and process of instruction but also in organization, administration, and finance. We urge the establishment of both public and private nursery schools, especially in the neighborhoods of the disadvantaged."

A straight line projection over the next five years would predict the development of 200,000 direct classroom contact positions. A more realistic estimate, given attrition and a more accelerated growth curve, would place the number close to 300,000. The need for ancillary services and the staff involved is not considered here.

It is apparent that the decisions we make this year will cast a long shadow into the next decade. The mandate is clear that society should deliver education to children before first grade.

SOME MODEST PROPOSALS

The most immediate pressing need is the development of in-service training programs. Several promising models have been developed. Katz and Weir (1969) have summarized the cogent characteristics of these models and they conclude that the success of an in-service helping approach is based upon the following requirements.

    a. It must occur largely in the teacher's classroom. To be helpful, the trainer or helper must see the real-life physical and interpersonal conditions in which the teacher is working.

    b. It must emphasize the practical "how to" needs of new and inexperienced teachers. Theory, knowledge, history, philosophy, etc., must follow upon the expressed interests of the trainees.

    c. It must be based on a relationship characterized by mutual trust between teacher and trainer. The customary "supervisor" or "inspector" roles developed in many public school districts do not seem to give teachers the support and encouragement they seek.

    d. It must encourage the trainee to see herself as experimenter, innovator, learner and problem-solver and to see these qualities as inherent in the role of the teacher of young children.

    e. It should lead to professionalism, using the term "professional" to denote commitment to high standards of performance and continuous efforts to grow in competence, to develop new skills and to acquire deeper and broader knowledge of the nature of development and learning.

To create an instrumentality which could put such concepts into practice, I would propose the creation of a minimum of six regional teacher-demonstration centers which would be the main diffusion instrumentality of the focused national research and development effort in early childhood education. These centers would demonstrate a variety of proven instructional programs emanating from the research and development effort and would serve as the headquarters for in-service helping teams. Appropriate affiliations with the community colleges and other institutions of higher learning would be established to facilitate career development programs. Sites for these centers would be chosen on the basis of direct access to the environment containing the on-line programs being served. Charged with the responsibility of outreach on an in-service training basis, the trainer and the content of training would emphasize appropriate community contact and involvement by the trainee to develop greater skills and sensitivity for maintaining social-educational relevancy.

To develop greater pre-service training capabilities, I would advocate a much heavier investment in the community college. Pre-service field involvement would be more readily accomplished in that setting. It could be terminal for teaching assistants and preliminary to a final two years of professional training at a four year institution leading to regular beginning teacher qualification.

I believe it is time to do a very careful analysis of the purposes served by certification. Much is to be lost by too rapid a movement toward prescription of requirements. Pre-service preparation is only the beginning to the task of establishing and creating teacher competence. Many factors enter into the equation. The match between the teacher's experience and the children she must teach, personality adjustments to supervisors and colleagues play important roles in developing competence. Simply establishing that an individual is prepared to teach is only one step in certifying teacher competence. Edelfelt (1968) points out that in-service teachers need more motivation and reward to stay in teaching than merely the status of being certified or on the basis of college credits received. They need desirable working conditions, career patterns and differentiated levels of compensation.

In early childhood education, we have the opportunity to experiment with a number of career development patterns which could demonstrate advancement in competency without promoting the teacher out of the classroom. Certification should reflect identification of levels of competence so that compensation can be made in terms of differentiated teaching roles and responsibilities rather than simply length of service. With flexible and differentiated certification, steps should be taken to implement the standards at a national level. Perhaps the chief responsibility for certification should be in the hands of the professional organizations who would act for the legal regulatory agencies at the local and state levels.

Finally, but most importantly, I would propose the establishment of a National Institute on Early Childhood. Clearly, we have the need to bring order and a concentrated effort to this field which has such high social priority. An educational field as new as this to public support offers a golden opportunity to establish fresh patterns of attacking educational problems. We must develop institutions which are anticipatory and future oriented rather than merely respondent. Such an institute would be the focal point of the national commitment to early childhood. Autonomous in organization, its major function would be to develop the national perspective through its integrative activities.

I see such an institute as having five functional capacities; four of which would be at the level of direct action. They are: (1) A research capacity which would be concerned with the production of knowledge and applied experimentation. (2) A development capacity which would translate knowledge and results of experimentation into effective products for application. (3) A diffusion and installation capacity which would provide the capability to rapidly move the newest and best from the research and development effort into field practice. The major means would be the regional teacher demonstration centers previously mentioned. (4) A resources production capacity which would include the operational and support capability necessary for the previous three functions. It would include such capabilities as information retrieval and dissemination, storage systems such as data banks and media production.

The fifth functional capacity is the key to a focused national effort in early childhood. It is an integrative capacity. All of the action elements of the institute, whether they be university based, field based or in the private sector, can go on in isolation as has been the case thus far. What we desperately need is the power to integrate all of these efforts on some rational and data oriented basis. Program integration would include the capability to analyze the needs of the field and to conceptualize these needs into alternative strategies for solution of the problems. It would also have the ability to integrate existing knowledge and synthesize this knowledge for potential development and application. Long term planning and evaluation capabilities would be essential in order to appropriately allocate resources as they were made available. The institute would have the ability to manage and coordinate the total program, thus avoiding the fragmentation which now exists.

Other programs of national commitment have demonstrated the importance of an integrated effort. This month a dream may be fulfilled which only ten years ago seemed beyond imagination. If man can walk the lands of the moon in 1969, all children, no matter what their environmental circumstances may be, should in the short span of time that it takes to reach adulthood be able to walk the lands of the earth with competence and self-assurance.

Section II

TESTING
AND
EVALUATION

4

ANOTHER LOOK AT CULTURE-FAIR TESTING

Arthur R. Jensen, Ph.D.

Professor, School of Education
University of California, Berkeley

It is galling, but not wholly unrewarding, to be misquoted in a popular magazine. I had the experience when *Life* (March 31, 1967) ran a feature article on "early learning" and incorrectly stated that I had invented a culture-free test of intelligence. The results of this misunderstanding were instructive to me and provided much of the stimulus for writing the present paper.

In the several weeks following the appearance of the *Life* article, I had to send out more than two hundred copies of a form letter in answer to inquiries about the culture-free test erroneously attributed to me. I had not invented any culture-free test, I explained, and all I had were some not at all unusual experimental techniques for studying the learning abilities of children, including children called "culturally disadvantaged."

This spate of mail (and several long-distance phone calls) gave me some interesting insights into the passionate aspects of intelligence testing. Only a few of the letters were from persons writing as parents, and still fewer were from psychologists. Most were from public school people—teachers, counselors, principals, heads of school research bureaus, and administrators of special education, compensatory education, and the like. Some wanted further information, but mostly they wanted copies of the "test"—a few ordered hundreds of "copies" and sent billing numbers without even asking the price. Others were skeptical, saying they had tried everything on the market without finding a test that wiped out status or race differences but would be delighted to find any test that could really do so. One schoolman said he was in "hot water" because the tests being used in his school district discriminated among groups as well as among individuals, and there were public spirited persons in the community who were quite upset by this. Somewhat more

Presented at the Educational Testing Service's 1968 Western Regional Conference on Testing Problems. Reprinted by permission.

ominous to me was that the sincere expression of what might very well prove to be a false hope was accompanied in some letters by derogatory, hostile censure of conventional standardized tests—a brand of outrage which almost makes one wonder if the writers believe there are some mean, hateful persons somewhere who can be blamed for deliberately making up culturally unfair, biased tests to discriminate against children of the poor. It gave me mixed feelings to be praised for helping to combat this evil conspiracy!

Let me say right off that I fully agree with my correspondents that many of the problems of public education which give rise to their worries about testing are real indeed, and much must be done to solve them. But I doubt that a culture-free test—even if we had one—could do any more than highlight the problem. Of course, this in itself might be of value. As far as I can tell, problems are never resolved by tests; but tests can help to define and evaluate the problems—and I mean the crucial problems that now confront public education in its struggle to be of tangible benefit to all children in all segments of the population.

In so far as the role of culture-free tests may be involved in this endeavor, this article is my *present* answer to many of these misguided but nonetheless informative letters from readers of *Life*. I emphasize "present," because this is my answer as of May, 1968—not guaranteed to be perfectly correlated with my views on the subject six months or a year from now, although I would surely expect a substantial positive correlation, for we are not totally without bearings in this field. The current pace of relevant research, however, is such that anyone who hopes to view these issues constructively and creatively must assiduously eschew a doctrinaire stance.

AN OLD ISSUE

The issue of cultural bias or status bias in intelligence tests is as old as intelligence testing itself. Alfred Binet in 1905 made a clear distinction between the kinds of judgment, adaptability, and general problem solving ability he called intelligence and attempted to measure by means of his mental age scales, on the one hand, and, on the other, the kinds of information acquired in schools or in a cultured home. Despite his efforts to come as close as possible to assessing the child's innate endowment of general intelligence by means of his scales, he consistently found systematic differences between various social status groups. The first formal study of this social aspect of intellectual assessment was published by Binet just five years after the appearance of the first edition of his now famous intelligence test, which became the prototype of nearly all subsequent individual tests of intelligence (3). Binet reported evidence from France and Belgium that children of professional workers did better on his new intelligence tests, on the average, than did children in working-class neighborhoods. Since then, the question of social-class bias in tests versus real social-class differences in intelligence has been an issue of dispute among psychologists, sociologists, and educators. Innumerable investigations have been made in the United States, in Europe, and in Asia, of the relationship of social status to performance on intelligence tests. These investigations have used a wide variety of intelligence tests and many different methods of measuring social status. Without a single exception, the studies show a positive correlation between intelligence test scores and social status; half of the studies yield correlations between .25 and .50, with a central tendency in the region of .35 to .40. When children selected from the total population are grouped into social status categories, the mean IQs of the groups differ by as much as one to two standard deviations (15 or 30 IQ points), depending on the method of status classification. The fact of social class differences in measured intelligence is thus about as solid a fact as any that we have in psychology, and apparently it has long since ceased being a point of dispute. Most of this evidence has been reviewed by Kenneth Eells and others (14).

There is an even greater number of studies of racial differences in measured intelligence, most of them involving comparisons of Negroes and Caucasians. The results of the more than 380 studies of Negro intelligence up to 1965, comprehensively reviewed by Audrey Shuey (44), are highly consistent in showing mean Negro-Caucasian IQ differences of between 10 to 20 points and an average median overlap (i.e., the percentage of Negroes exceeding the Caucasian median) of 12 per cent. In most, if not all, of these estimates racial classification is confounded with socioeconomic status (SES); when the racial groups are roughly "matched" on the usual SES factors, the mean IQ difference is diminished to about 10 points. The logic and validity of such "matching" is, of course, highly questionable, since it involves comparing quite different proportions of the two populations, and, furthermore, SES is not strictly a *causal* variable in relation to IQ. But more on this point later—here I am just sketching the raw empirical findings without trying to explain them. They are the generally agreed upon results of testing with the kinds of instruments we call intelligence tests. Whether the results are "fair" or not is the point at issue.

STATUS-FAIR VERSUS CULTURE-FAIR TESTS

What we shall be talking about here are social status differences within the same national culture. In this context the terms "culture-free," "culture-fair," or "culture-controlled" as applied to most such tests of intelligence are really misnomers. We should be using the preferable terms "status-free" or "status-fair" instead. I wish to avoid extending the discussion in the present paper to the slippery problem of the cross-cultural assessment of mental abilities in primitive cultures or other essentially anthropological uses of tests for which the designation "culture-fair" may constitute a legitimate use of this term. Cross-cultural testing is a complex problem in its own right, and part of what I have to say may be relevant to it, but it should be clear now that our chief concern is with test results as related to social status and ethnic background factors within a single national culture. The much more difficult subject of true cross-cultural testing will probably remain hopelessly problematical so long as the nature of the environmental differences between widely disparate cultural groups cannot be conceptualized in a generally agreed upon fashion with reference to common dimensions on which differences range. In the absence of such schemata there is the risk of perceiving and describing environments post hoc in terms of performance on particular tests, which is putting the cart before the horse. Thus we shall stick to the more mundane task of looking at status-fair tests, and shall bypass the usual polemics in the area of cross-cultural testing, like debating how Einstein would rate on an aborigine's "IQ" test consisting of throwing boomerangs and tracking wallabies.

WHY INTELLIGENCE TESTS ARE LIKE THEY ARE

It should not be forgotten that intelligence tests as we now know them evolved in close conjunction with the educational curricula and instructional methods of Europe and North America. Schooling was not simply invented in a single stroke. It has a long evolutionary history and still heavily bears the imprint of its origins in predominantly aristocratic and upper-class European society. Not only did the content of education help to shape this society, but, even more, the nature of the society shaped the content of education and the methods of instruction for imparting it. If the educational needs and goals of this upper segment of society had been different, and if their modal pattern of abilities —both innate abilities and those acquired in these peculiar environmental circumstances—were different, it seems a safe conjecture that the evolution of educational content and practices and consequently the character of public education in modern times would be quite different from what it is. And our intelligence tests—assuming we had them under these different conditions—would most likely also have taken on a different character.

The particular direction taken by education at its origins in Western European cultures emphasized a host of conditions which will largely characterize moden education: beginning formal instruction at the same age for all children—universally between five and six years of age; instruction in groups; keeping the same age groups together in a lockstep fashion at least throughout the first several years of schooling; learning under instructional conditions of relative teacher activity and pupil passivity—a showing-seeing and telling-listening relationship between teacher and pupil. This approach capitalized on the attentiveness and obedience of children in a telling-listening relationship with an adult. These habits were thoroughly inculcated in the children by their parents long before the children entered school. Of even more fundamental importance is that the success of this method of schooling depended heavily upon the child's possession of certain abilities, both innate and acquired: an attention span long enough to encompass the teacher's utterances and demonstrations; verbal comprehension—extracting meaning from verbal forms; ability to grasp the relationship between things or events and their symbolic representations; and, largely because of the overtly passive nature of the pupil's role, the demand for *covert* activity on the pupil's part—to repeat things to himself, to voluntarily focus his attention where it is called for; when confronted with new tasks to be learned or problems to be solved, to talk to himself in relevant ways for self-direction, for self-provided cues, for active scanning of memory stores for pertinent bits of information—in short, the capacity overtly to inhibit large-muscle activity and covertly to respond to the instructional inputs. Physical activity had to give way to mental activity—an active processing of the instructional input, not just a passive reception. To succeed, pupils had to learn not only the manifest educational content and skills explicitly imparted by the teacher, but they also had to acquire the skills of self-instruction without which group instruction by the teacher leads to little actual learning.

The interesting and important fact is that the system worked. It worked satisfactorily for the majority of children who were exposed to it, not because it was a gift of God or an inspired invention of man; but for the simple reason that the class of children whom it served had largely shaped it to their capabilities. Thus, school methods were not *designed*. They were not *imposed*. They *evolved*. This evolution was shaped by the predominantly bookish educational content valued by the well-to-do classes of Europe and by the particular learning capabilities of their children. If the system had not worked to the satisfaction of the majority whom it served, or proved unduly frustrating to the teachers and pupils, it seems safe to say it would have evolved in a different direction.

The extension of public education over the years to an increasingly broader segment of the population, toward the goal of universal education through the twelfth grade or even beyond, has caused pressures to be exerted to change the rather highly crystalized (some would say fossilized) structure of the educational system. The system now, in fact, does appear to impose itself—often with consequent frustration and defeat—on many in our population whose cultural and racial forebears played no part in the evolution of the system.

Returning now to the subject of intelligence tests, my contention is that our definitions of intelligence and our methods of measuring it have been significantly shaped by the schools and the historical and geographical factors involved in their development. Intelligence tests, as we all know, were originally made to be able to rank-order children in terms of their probable success in profiting from the traditional curriculum under the traditional methods of school instruction. They were not intended to measure the typical *outcomes* of such instruction, but to assess, by means relatively independent of scholastic performance, the probable scholastic attainments of children given more or less the same standard instruction in school.

Tests were made to perform this function very well indeed, and despite many auxiliary advances in test theory and test construction, the high predictive power of intelligence tests for scholastic performance has remained essentially unchanged for decades.

Psychologists became interested in intelligence as more than just scholastic ability and devised tests which could rank persons along a supposedly broader "bright-dull" continuum, differences which are intuitively, though roughly, recognized by nearly all persons who thoughtfully observe other persons—at play, at school, and at work. Various terms designating roughly agreed upon differences along such a continuum have been used throughout recorded history and probably longer. Without specifying precisely what the behaviors consist of, this "brightness" continuum along which persons range is recognized by all teachers, employers, and parents (especially if they have more than one child). Intelligence tests were intended by their makers as a means for objectifying, quantifying, and sharpening these subjective judgments.

From the very beginning, differences in what came to be called intelligence were regarded as largely inborn, and it was the inborn aspect of intelligence that psychologists were mainly attempting to assess by means of their new tests.

Whether tests were made to correspond to subjective judgments of relative brightness or to predict scholastic performance, they looked much alike and were, in fact, much alike in whatever it was they measured, as shown by their high intercorrelations. Tests that failed to correlate highly also failed to meet the external criteria of intelligence.

Spearman's concept of a *general factor* of intelligence, accounting for the substantial correlations among all tests and criteria that were independently agreed upon in general as representing samples of intelligent behavior, was practically inevitable. It is difficult and rare to find ability tests of any degree of complexity that do not show substantial positive intercorrelations when administered to a cross-section of the population.

When the intercorrelations among a dozen or more different tests of mental ability (like the vocabulary, general information, memory span, block designs, figure copying, mazes, and other subtests of the Wechsler and Binet scales) are subjected to a factor analysis or principal components analysis, typically 50 per cent, and often more, of the individual differences variance in subtest scores is attributable to a general factor common to all the subtests. Henceforth, when we speak of intelligence, we will have in mind mainly this general factor, *g*. Thus we need not tie the concept of intelligence to any particular test or method of measurement, but shall use the term to refer to the general factor (*g*) common to practically all tests of complex mental abilities.

FLUID AND CRYSTALIZED INTELLIGENCE

Raymond B. Cattell (9) has made an important conceptually and empirically justified distinction between what he calls *fluid* general intelligence (g_f) and crystalized general intelligence (g_c). Fluid intelligence is a basic, general "brightness" that can be marshalled for new learning and novel problem-solving and adaptibility; it is relatively independent of education and experience but it can be invested in the particular opportunities for learning afforded by the individual's life circumstances, motivations and interests. Tests of fluid intelligence are essentially like those intended to minimize the importance of cultural and educational attainments. Examples are Cattell's *Culture Fair Tests* and Raven's *Progressive Matrices Test*. Crystalized intelligence (g_c), on the other hand, consists of acquired knowledge and intellectual skills. Since the original acquisition of such knowledge and skills depends upon fluid intelligence, there will usually be a substantial correlation between measures of g_f and g_c, and thus within a common culture there will be a super general factor common to both g_f and g_c. John L. Horn has characterized crystalized intelligence as "a precipitate out of experience. It results when fluid intelligence is 'mixed' with what can be called 'the intelligence of the culture.' Crystallized intelligence increases with a person's experiences and with the education that provides new methods and perspectives for dealing with that experience (23)." This distinction between fluid and crystallized intelligence parallels closely one of the major distinctions between "culture-free" and "culture-loaded" tests, although not all attempts to minimize cultural loading in tests are based on this distinction.

INTELLIGENCE A, B, AND C

An important set of distinctions that seems essential to any discussion of culture-free or status-fair testing is Donald O. Hebb's well-known distinction between intelligence A and B and the further refinement, added by Philip Vernon, of intelligence C.

Intelligence A refers to the individual's *genotype* as regards mental ability; it is the genetic code or "blueprint," established at the moment of conception by the uniting complements of genes received from each parent, which genetically conditions the internal biological factors involved in the individual's mental development. Intelligence A is, of course, not directly observable or measurable. It is only inferable on a probabilistic basis from evidence on the heritability of intelligence.

Intelligence B refers to the individual's *phenotype* for mental ability, that is, the actual manifest mental ability resulting from the interaction of genetic and environmental influences. It should be emphasized that the term "environment" really means *non-genetic* and includes much more than just those influences arising from cultural, social, and interpersonal factors. It includes also a host of prenatal, perinatal, and postnatal factors related to the nutrition and physical health of the mother and the child. Intelligence B is in part directly assessable by means of various psychological tests, observation of the individual's actual achievements, and so forth. It is the sum total of the individual's mental abilities, which are not measurable by any one test and in their totality probably not by any combination of presently existing tests.

This brings us to *intelligence C,* that aspect of mental ability which is actually measured by a particular intelligence test, since no single test draws upon the entire domain of mental abilities. When we speak of a person's score on a typical test of intelligence, such as the Stanford-Binet or the Wechsler, both of which are highly loaded with the g factor, we are referring to intelligence C. Each test measures a somewhat different constellation of abilities, as shown by the less than perfect intercorrelations among tests even after correction for unreliability of measurement.

PURPOSES OF TESTING

Another preliminary consideration in our discussion of status-free tests is one's purpose in assessing abilities.

Prediction of Scholastic Performance. If one is interested only in predicting the individual's scholastic performance under certain relatively unchanging conditions of instruction, the question of the status-fairness of the test is of no real concern. All one attempts to do in this situation is to maximize the validity of the test for predicting the criterion, say, students' grade point averages. If the test's validity can be increased by including culturally and educationally loaded items, it is probably because these kinds of knowledge play a part in performance on the criterion. If the regression equation for predicting the criterion can be made more powerful by including items of background information of the subjects (e.g., previous school grades, sex, socioeconomic status of parents, race, scores on interest and personality inventories), so much the better. That is, if all we want is to maximize prediction of success or failure in a given academic setting. Whether this is a worthy goal is another issue entirely. It is not a technical matter but one of educational and social policy.

However, if a test is used for selection and it predicts well for group A and has low predictive validity for group B, the test can be said to be unfair to group B. It may be unfair because of its cultural bias, but this is not the main point. It is really unfair because it selects or predicts with less precision in group B than in group A. If removing culture-loaded items from the test improves validity for group B without lowering it for group A, this is well and good. If overall prediction is improved by giving each group entirely different tests, while both groups are measured on the same criterion, this is well and good. The necessary safeguard to fairness in any selection program is continually to examine the validity coefficients of the selection tests within every significant identifiable subgroup in the population which competes in the selection process.

In terms of the foregoing criteria, there has been little, if any, indication that the standard scholastic aptitude tests used in selection for higher education—the major sphere in which tests play a role in selection—are unfair in terms of differential validity across social-class and racial lines within the United States. (This generalization does not extend to the selection of foreign students, for certain groups of whom the standard tests do not have the same predictive properties as they have for American students.) The Educational Testing Service, for example, studied the *Preliminary Scholastic Aptitude Test* (PSAT) and the *Scholastic Aptitude Test* (SAT), (among the most widely used tests for college selection), to determine whether they were biased in such a way as to deny Negro students equal opportunity in the selection for admission to three integrated colleges (2). Two criteria of test bias were examined: (*a*) individual item biases, and (*b*) the total score's predictive validity for grade point average (GPA). If the rank order of item difficulty were different for Negroes and white, or, in terms of analysis of variance, if there were an "item $\times$ race" interaction or an "item $\times$ social-class within race" interaction, this would constitute evidence of item bias for race or socioeconomic status (SES). No significant race or SES bias was found. The "item $\times$ race" and "item $\times$ SES within race" interactions made the smallest contributions to the total variance. As for the predictive validity of total scores for GPA, it was found that in two of the three colleges studied, the validity coefficients were essentially the same for Negro and white students; it made little difference whether predictor scores for Negroes or whites were plugged into the common regression equation or the equation for any subgroup. In short, the same test scores predicted GPA equally accurately in all groups. In one of the three colleges the Negro students' GPA was slightly overpredicted by the use of the common regression line, a bias which increased Negro applicants' chances of being accepted in that college.

Studies of test bias in selection in Negro colleges in the South, by Professor Julian C. Stanley of the Johns Hopkins University, have revealed that a kind of pseudo-bias exists when the SAT test is used in these colleges (43). The predictive validity of the SAT is markedly lower in the Negro colleges than in white or integrated colleges because the test is too difficult, causing the distribution of scores to be markedly skewed, with a piling up of scores at the lower end of the scale and consequently a severe restriction of variance. When an easier test—the *Secondary School Admissions Test* (SSAT)—was used, so that the distribution of scores was approximately normal, the predictive validities were just as high as those achieved by the SAT in white colleges. In other words, for the purpose of predicting academic performance, the evidence indicates that our tests work as well for Negroes as for whites, provided the difficulty level of the test is such as to avoid ceiling or floor effects which seriously skew the distribution of scores or restrict the variance.

Employment Selection. It is probably in this realm more than in any other that test practices can be improved to reduce SES and race bias. In every situation where psychological tests are used for personnel selection or promotion, care must be taken to insure that the tests are truly valid for the actual job to be performed. If there is a negligible correlation between the test and actual work performance criteria, the test, no matter how good it may be on other grounds, is worse than a random lottery to the extent that it may deny equal opportunity for employment in terms of socio-cultural factors with which the test is correlated but which are irrelevant to performance on the job. The problem is underlined by the fact that most intelligence and aptitude tests correlate as highly with social-class factors as with job performance. If a test is shown to select differentially among social-class or racial groups of applicants for a particular occupation, the test may be considered unfairly discriminatory if the correlation between the test and the criterion is not significantly lowered when the variables of social-class or race are partialed out of the correlation. In other words, when race or social classes are correlated with the test but are not independently correlated with the criterion, the test may be regarded as biased. Note that this criterion of bias does not necessarily imply that various groups should obtain the same scores on an unbiased test, nor does it say that social background factors should not be correlated with the criterion. It simply says that if the social background factors are irrelevant to the criterion performance, they should not surreptitiously creep into selection via tests that are correlated with both the criterion and the social status factors.

The risk of such bias is emphasized by the known surprisingly low correlations between a wide variety of intelligence tests and actual proficiency on the job. Such correlations average about .20 to .25, and thus predict only four or five per cent of the variance in work proficiency (17). Intelligence correlates more highly with occupational status, however, since intelligence is highly correlated with educational attainment, which in turn is a major determiner of eligibility for various occupations. Speed and ease of training show correlations with mental tests of around .50, which is four or five times the predictive power that the same tests have in relation to job proficiency *after* training. From the standpoint of sheer economy of job training, tests can therefore make a substantial contribution. The same criteria for ruling out test bias as described above should, of course, be applied also to the use of tests in selection for training. Furthermore, the economy of job training should be viewed in the broad perspective of the long-term economy of increasing productive employment in previously undereducated or underskilled persons. In this endeavor the speed or ease with which persons can be trained for a specific job may be a far less important criterion in the long run than the final level of their performance on the job. Here previous scholastic performance or scores on tests which are predictive of school achievement may be quite irrelevant. And where some selection for job training is necessitated by a great disparity between the number of job opportunities and the number of applicants, tests quite different from those now generally in use may prove just as predictive without introducing socially biasing factors that are irrelevant to success in training or job performance. One type of such test, called "direct learning tests," are described later on. The *Porteus Maze Tests* are also promising in this respect (11).

Diagnosis of School Learning Problems. An intelligence test is just one among a number of techniques used by school psychologists for assessing the learning and adjustment problems of children whose progress in their school work is markedly deviant from that of their age mates. Intellectual assessment of such children should be based upon more than a single instrument in order to take into consideration a greater variety of cognitive functions than are exposed by any one test. A diversity of tests is needed to discover the child's cognitive strengths as well as his deficiencies. This is important for all children who perform scholastically below the normal range (more than one standard deviation below grade level) and it is especially important for children from an educationally disadvantaged background, since there is evidence of less uniformity among these children in their individual profiles of abilities. Any single test of ability is therefore apt to be less generally

representative of low SES children's capabilities for profiting from education than is the case for middle-class children. It is also likely that
there is a greater diversity and unevenness among the various cognitive
capabilities of children viewed as "slow learners" in school than of "average" or "fast" learners. A relatively uniform but merely slowed and
watered down version of the regular instructional program is not what
so-called "slow learners" need. They need a greater diversity of course
content and instructional approaches than are necessary for the average
run of children. But this goal becomes feasible only if there is some
rational and empirically valid basis for assessing individual differences
in patterns of abilities and for relating these to differential educational
treatments. We know that children who are grouped together on the
basis of scores on any one test are still extremely heterogeneous in a
variety of other abilities, and this is especially true of those children in
the bottom half of the distribution. When grouping based on a single
test or a narrow criterion of scholastic achevement cuts across the full
socioeconomic spectrum in the population as well, the heterogeneity of
capability within groups is made even greater. I have become reasonably
convinced by our own research at Berkeley that the pattern of abilities
of the majority of lower-class children who become identified as "slow
learners" in school is quite different from that of the majority of middle-
class children with the same designation. This difference appears to be
more fundamental than the kinds of differences that would be wiped out
if we had perfectly culture-free or culture-fair intelligence tests. Consequently, I suspect that the instructional requirements of the two groups
referred to would be quite different if the school hopes to provide optimal educational advantages for both. The socioeconomic factor, it
should be emphasized, is not the primary basis of this distinction. It
is the ability patterns that matter; the fact that these may be correlated
with SES is incidental, and it should not be construed to mean that
children would be given different educational treatment *because* of their
SES background. One major aspect of this difference in ability patterns
is described in a later section.

Discovering Abilities. One of the important functions of tests is the
discovery of abilities in children that may ordinarily escape notice by
teachers. The discovery and development of abilities in socioeconomically
heterogeneous schools and in educationally disadvantaged groups calls
not only for status-fair tests of general intelligence but for a broad coverage of other abilities which may not be highly correlated with g but
which may nevertheless be developed to the educational and social advantage of the child. Tests of g which are free of obvious cultural content,
like Raven's *Progressive Matrices* (41), Cattell's *Culture-Fair Tests* (8),
and the *Domino* test (19), should be used much more widely in schools
that serve the educationally disadvantaged in order to spot those chil-

dren with potentially strong academic aptitude. One important criterion of a school's excellence is the level of scholastic performance attained by its pupils from disadvantaged backgrounds who score above the general average on culture-fair tests of *g* such as those just mentioned. Poor scholastic performance despite high scores on these tests, in the absence of other severely disabling conditions, is a strong indication that the child's abilities are going to waste where formal education is concerned. Every urban school should assess its population by means of such tests and lavish special attention on the scholastic progress of those children from relatively poor backgrounds who score above the general average. They will have the basic intellectual equipment to compete successfully with children from any other strata of society, but they may need to be given extra encouragement and more individual help, especially in the first years of school, if they are to make the most of their ability. For many of these children, the school or some allied community agency will have to provide the motivational and tutorial supports to scholastic achievement that are normally provided for most middle-class children by their educationally oriented parents.

What about those who get low scores on these relatively culture-fair tests of *g*? Are they doomed to failure in school? No. But to profit maximally from school they may need a different instructional program from that which is suitable for those who are relatively high on *g*. There are other educationally important abilities that are not highly correlated with *g* and are not assessed by means of the tests mentioned so far, but which, with appropriate instructional techniques, may be utilized to achieve mastery of the traditional school subject matter. It is probably only when *all* children are indiscriminately taught by methods which depend heavily upon *g*—a heritage from the days when education was intended for only a select few—that a substantial proportion of children called disadvantaged fail ever to master even the subject matter of the elementary grades.

One of the worst examples I ever saw of needlessly infusing verbal-academic criteria of success in an essentially non-academic course was in my wood shop course in junior high school. A week before the end of the term the teacher announced that the course grade would be based entirely on a written test of our knowledge of the full names of each of the more than 150 wood-working tools in the shop! I would be surprised if there were better than zero correlation between the grades in the course and the actual wood-working skills and interests displayed by the students. How often do such essentially irrelevant criteria work against the less academically inclined children in our schools?

Comparisons of Schools and School Systems. Statewide or nationwide testing programs supposedly permit a comparative assessment of different regions of the country or state and of different neighborhoods and schools within a single school system. Because these group tests are usually administered by the teachers in each classroom under quite variable conditions, the test scores have an unknown but probably large degree of error variance. Although the errors may tend to cancel out in large samples to give reasonably stable means, the usefulness of the data for correlational analysis is greatly impaired. Small random samples of the school population tested under highly controlled, uniform conditions by expert testers with no vested interest in the performance of a particular school would actually yield much more satisfactory data from a statistical and psychometric standpoint. Test score means and standard deviations per se are the least revealing aspect of the differences among schools and school systems, for the means and standard deviations are largely a function of the particular segments of the population served by the school. More important in comparing schools or educational practices is the regression of scholastic achievement on intelligence test scores. And for this purpose status-fair tests of intelligence are the most desirable, since they are less loaded on scholastic content and should remain relatively stable across a variety of educational treatments. In a statewide testing program, the mean achievement scores of various schools and districts by themselves tell us practically nothing. The regression of achievement scores on culture-free or status-free intelligence measures, on the other hand, tell us how successful different schools are in translating their raw material—the pupils' intelligence—into scholastic achievement. Other community and pupil status variables may also be entered into the regression equation for predicting test scores. Schools that depart markedly in either direction from the common regression line could profitably be subjected to a thorough study.

MEANS OF ACHIEVING STATUS-FAIR TESTS

Nearly all attempts to devise culture-free or status-free tests have resorted to the principle of reducing test content to the lowest common denominator of experiences encountered in the various cultures or social strata across which the test is intended to give a "fair" assessment of individuals' intelligence. In practice, the attempts to make tests that sample the common elements from a wide range of cultural, social, and educational backgrounds have taken a number of forms. Each has its advantages and disadvantages.

Common Information. The least satisfactory method of attempting status-fairness of tests is by seeking items of information that are common across various status groups. Information tests consisting of questions like "Who was the first President of the United States"?, "Whose picture is on a penny?", and so on, make poor test items mainly for two reasons: (*a*) they do not get at complex mental processes, and (*b*) they cannot be steeply graded in difficulty level without introducing items of information to which there is a relatively low probability of exposure, in which case social status and educational differences become practically impossible to avoid. The same thing holds true for vocabulary tests, including picture vocabulary. Consider these three items from the information subtest of the old *Wechsler-Bellevue Intelligence Scale.* They vary markedly in "difficulty" level (indicated by the percentage of the population giving the right answer): "Who is the President of the United States?", "Who wrote Hamlet?" "Who wrote Faust?". Knowledge of the answers to all three questions involves the same kind and degree of mental ability. The difficulty levels differ only because of frequency of exposure. Such items based on information and vocabulary are rightly regarded as more culturally loaded than items which vary in difficulty because of the complexity of the mental processes involved. One can think of this in terms of the kinds of computer programs that would be required to handle the test items. One and the same simple program could handle "Who wrote Faust?" and "Who is President of the United States?", but the same would not be true for the easy and the difficult items of Raven's *Progressive Matrices Test,* which would call for programs differing markedly in complexity.

Thus, in examining classes of test items for their potential value in constructing status-fair tests, one should distinguish between *intrinsic* and *incidental* correlates of intelligence. Scores on information and vocabulary tests do, in fact, correlate substantially with g in a culturally more or less homogeneous segment of the population, since amount of information acquired under fairly equal exposure reflects learning capacity. But such items are here regarded as *incidental* correlates of mental ability, since the mental processes of acquisition are themselves not involved in response to the test question. One can go a step further, as Harrison Gough (18) has done, and devise a thoroughly incidental test of intelligence which contains not a single item calling for the use of any mental ability (other than the ability to read the questions and mark the true-false answers). All 52 items in Gough's test are "personality" questions, such as "I have often been frightened in the middle of the night" (keyed *False*) and "I gossip a little at times" (keyed *True*). Yet this "test" correlates about .50 with conventional IQ measures in a high school population. This non-intellectual intelligence test is so obviously culturally loaded that it may serve a useful function in evaluating the culture-fairness of other tests. If the Gough test reflects the culture-laden values, attitudes, and interests associated with measured intelligence, it would be interesting to compare different social status and racial groups on conventional IQ tests, controlling with scores on the Gough test. In other words, what is the correlation between SES and IQ after their correlation with Gough scores is partialed out? It would also be interesting to know how the Gough variance is distributed in a factor analysis of a variety of tests of mental ability, and to compare the factor scores of different sub-populations on factors with high and low loadings on the Gough test. One would expect the factor with low loadings on the Gough to be more status-fair.

The distinction between intrinsic mental test items and incidental-correlate items parallels E. L. Thorndike's distinction between *altitude* and *breadth* of intelligence. General information and vocabulary tests mainly get at intellectual breadth; tests involving problem solving get at altitude. Since the breadth factor depends so much on amount and range of exposure, as well as the person's interests and values, status-fair tests have generally tried to minimize the breadth factor. In the general population, breadth and altitude measures are both highly correlated with g, but test content reflecting breadth is more influenced by environment and training. It is on breadth tests, like the *Peabody Picture Vocabulary Test*, for example, that it is easiest to show IQ gains in programs such as Head Start. Although measures of breadth and altitude are usually highly correlated, there is a real psychological distinction between the two. Any moderately endowed person may, for example, learn to play chess, checkers, dominoes, bridge, and many other games moderately well and the person who can play ten games at this level is not necessarily more able than the person who can play only one or two; they probably differ mainly in the amount of time they have devoted to learning the games. But only a few persons can ever become chess masters even by concentrating all their effort on chess alone. Similarly, given sufficient time, almost anyone can learn to play a dozen different musical instruments, but most persons cannot achieve a virtuoso level even on a single instrument, given any amount of time, training, and drive. The altitude factor thus seem much more dependent on innate endowment than the breadth factor. In the strictly intellectual realm this distinction parallels Cattell's distinction between fluid (altitude) and crystalized (breadth) intelligence (9).

In his first attempts to increase the culture fairness of tests, Cattell made use of items testing word knowledge, but he used all quite familiar (high frequency) words to which we could expect that almost everyone had been more or less equally exposed. He manipulated the difficulty of the items by requiring subjects to make increasingly difficult choice or discriminations between the meanings of highly familiar words. This, of course, introduces the altitude component, but it would now be argued by most students of social-class differences that subtleties of word meanings and fine shades of distinction in the use of language are more highly valued and given more attention and emphasis in high status homes. Cattell wisely gave up this method in his later versions of culture-fair tests.

A classic example of attempting to make a test that used presumably status-common content to measure the altitude of the problem solving aspect of intelligence was the *Davis-Eells Games,* now defunct because it proved to have less satisfactory reliability and validity for its stated purposes than conventional tests of intelligence. The *Davis-Eells Games* consisted of cartoon pictures of persons engaged in activities familiar and recognizable to everyone in our society. The examiner asked questions about the pictures in simple language. One item, for example, shows a series of pictures of a boy trying to climb over a high fence by several different methods, only one of which appears very practicable. The subject has to pick out the picture he thinks shows the best method of scaling the fence.

Today an informational test based on television programs would probably have greater universality than any other source of content. A recent study of low SES inner-city Negro boys in Washington, D.C. failed to identify content areas of interest to this disadvantaged group that would set them off from middle-class groups (40). The source of this common core of interest areas seems mostly attributable to television, which now apparently is equally spread throughout the entire SES range.

Eliminating Status-Biasing Factors. In addition to avoiding content of a scholastic or specific cultural nature, construction of status fair tests have tried eliminating or minimizing the role of factors such as reading, language, and speed. Dependence on reading skill is a strongly biasing factor in group tests when they are used in educationally heterogenous populations. To avoid this bias Orr and Graham (40) have devised a *Listening Comprehension Test* to identify educational potential among disadvantaged junior high school students who had failed to develop reading and writing skills commensurate with their grade level. It was thought that these students would also show better comprehension on auditory measures than on visual measures. The test devised by Orr and Graham drew on a common core of interests in sports, TV, and comic books. The authors note that interest in these subjects is shared across economic strata among 8th grade boys. They also comment that on the basis of interviews intended to sample interest content areas in the disadvantaged population, "It did not appear possible to construct a test that would be entirely specific to disadvantaged subjects of Negro ethnic background." The common core of content served as the basis of orally administered (on a tape recorder) test items that required students to draw conclusions, to make inferences, to learn, remember, and follow directions. To increase understanding, the audio tape was narrated by a native of the disadvantaged neighborhood who spoke with a Washington Negro accent. They found a correlation of .60 between the Listening Test and total score on a conventional scholastic aptitude test (SCAT). The Listening Test had negligible correlations with an economic index within the disadvantaged population. The test statistics, however, were not compared with a middle-class group or other ethnic groups. In such group comparisons, this test, with its emphasis on sports and entertainment and narrated in a Negro accent, if it has any bias at all, would seem to favor low SES Negroes. If such a test were to be used for making status and ethnic comparisons, it should be factor analyzed within each group along with a number of other tests of *g* to determine whether it has the same *g* saturation in both groups. The test may still be useful even if it were not a test of *g* in certain subpopulations, but the interpretation of the scores would depend on knowledge of their factorial composition. The test's satisfactory reliability (.85 to .89), the existence of equivalent forms, and the correlation with scholastic performance (.45) surely recommend it for further investigation. What needs most to be determined is whether the *uniqueness* of the test (that part of its total variance which is not shared by other ability tests) consists of any educationally relevant variance.

Spatial-Quantitative Relations. If one eliminates reading, language, scholastic content and pictorial representation of real objects, what is left from which to make up intelligence test items? About all that is left, and forms the basis for what are probably the most satisfactory culture-free and status-free tests, are spatial and quantitative concepts. Spatial tests make use of elementary topological properties and relationships which are common features of all environments. The basic forms of spatial percepts are common to all cultures and are largely uninfluenced by material aspects of the culture. Thus the basis for test items can be found in such universal topological concepts as "inside-outside," "up-down," "above-below," "left-right," "behind-in front," "in-out," "full-empty" and such space-form percepts as "straight-curved," "smooth-jagged," and so forth. Add to these such elementary quantitative concepts as "many-few," "increase-decrease," "large-small," etc., and one has virtually all the basic elements with which to make a Raven's *Progressive Matrices,* Cattell's *Culture-Fair Tests,* and the *Domino Test* (19). These three tests generally show higher loadings of *g*, when factor analyzed with other measures of intelligence, than any other tests. This shows that it is possible to measure general intelligence with a high degree of reliability simply by means of the elemental topological-quantitative properties mentioned above. They are one of the few forms of test content which can cross many language and cultural differences which are often barriers to the use of conventional tests. Kidd and Rivoire (30) have analyzed the items in tests such as the Cattell and Raven from the standpoint of their topological properties and point out that most of the concepts employed appear in the pottery, baskets, carvings, face paintings, body paintings, blankets, and clothing of a majority of primitive societies.

Gough and McGurk (20) have made up what they call a group *Test of Perceptual Acuity,* consisting largely of visual illusions and discriminations. Although the test reliably measures individual differences in perceptual functions which show an age-gradient, nothing has been reported concerning the relationship of these measures to other cognitive abilities.

Another test in the same vein but which has been shown to correlate satisfactorily with conventional intelligence tests is the *Johns Hopkins Perceptual Test* devised by Leon Rosenberg (42). It is still in a developmental stage and its factorial content has not been explored.

CONTROL OF EXTRINSIC FACTORS IN TAKING TESTS

Test performance can be influenced by extrinsic factors that may be associated with social status but are not central to the psychological functions the test attempts to measure. Personality factors, motivation, "test anxiety," "test sophistication" and other test-taking attitudes, "personal empo," "clerical" skills, and susceptibility to distraction all come under this category of extrinsic contributors to individual and group differences in intelligence, aptitude, and achievement tests. The contribution to variance of many of these factors can be reduced by improving testing procedures, wording instructions to make them perfectly clear to all subjects, using simplified forms of the test for preliminary practice, and the like. Answer sheets and other "clerical" aspects of test taking can be minimized by eliminating complexities in the mechanics of test taking and by giving subjects training and practice on the mechanics.

In our research we have found that low SES children are relatively more distracted in a classroom testing situation than when they are tested individually and there is thus a greater discrepancy between group and individual test scores for low SES than for middle-class children. Testing procedures can probably be devised which will minimize this gap.

But improvements in testing procedures alone will not eliminate all variance due to extrinsic factors. Further steps are necessary. Personality scores and other relevant measures may be entered into prediction equations along with the intelligence test scores. We have found, for example, that college students who obtain high scores on extraversion in the *Eysenck Personality Inventory* rush through untimed tests faster than more introverted subjects and thereby obtain slightly lower scores. In one study, extraversion scores correlated—.45 with time spent on Raven's *Progressive Matrices* when college subjects were allowed more time than needed and could quit when they thought they had done their best on this test. Extraversion correlated—.13 with total number correct (26).

Timed tests introduce a speed factor, part of which may be irrelevant to what the test intends to measure. There is evidence of at least two kinds of speed factors (37). One is an intellectual factor involving speed and efficiency of mental operations in problem solving. This is an important component of intelligence and enters into complex problem solving. The other speed factor is essentially non-cognitive. Although its effects are spread throughout all difficulty levels of a test, it shows up in relatively pure form in the easiest items. As an extreme example, suppose a 100-item test is made up of 50 very easy problems followed by 50 very difficult problems. Subjects will differ in the time they need to get through the easy items and to begin working on the difficult items, and consequently they will have unequal amounts of time for the difficult items. The chief source of variance on the easy items is not intellectual ability but is essentially a non-cognitive speed factor. I call it a "speed and persistence" factor, since it involves the ability not only to work fast but also to avoid taking rest pauses. Subjects who are low in this trait are at a disadvantage in timed tests. A group of mathematics graduate students given a timed test consisting of several hundred simple addition problems, for example, will show reliable individual differences in their total time scores, but the scores will reflect nothing of their mathematical ability. It will represent a pure speed and persistence factor. The same factor enters into timed tests at all levels from kindergarten through graduate school.

We are attempting to assess the importance of this factor in group testing in elementary schools across a wide range of socioeconomic levels by measuring speed and persistence independently of intelligence and using the speed scores as a control variable in making group comparisons. It should be possible to determine how much of the variance in social status differences on intelligence tests is due to the noncognitive speed and persistence factor. It is measured by having subjects mark Xs in 150 boxes, given 1.5 minutes. The procedure is given twice, first under instructions that make no mention of speed and second with instructions to work as fast as possible in order to do much better than the first time.

Listening attention is another factor that plays an important role in group administered tests at the elementary level. We have devised a "Listening-Attention" test which helps to separate the variance due to this factor from the more strictly cognitve factors we wish to measure with intelligence tests. To separate listening attention from memory span for digits, for example, children are given a test which shows whether they can listen to digits on a tape recorder and simultaneously check those digits that they hear on a special answer sheet. The task makes no memory demands but shows whether the subject can hear, understand, and pay attention to digits read on a tape recorder. If the child cannot do this, his score on a test of auditory digit span cannot be regarded as a valid test of his auditory memory span.

By thus sorting out the sources of variance in social class differences in intelligence test scores we can arrive at more status-fair conclusions and uses of the tests, and we can better determine the kinds of instructional procedures most likely to improve the performance of the educationally disadvantaged.

IMPROVING SUBTESTS WITH STATUS-FAIR POTENTIAL

Various subtests of omnibus intelligence tests such as the Stanford-Binet and Wechsler show different degrees of discrimination between status groups, yet they may have approximately equal correlations with total IQ. This is presumptive but not conclusive evidence that the subtests differ in status-fairness. Digit span correlates almost as highly with total IQ as vocabulary in the normative population, when both are corrected for attenuation. We have found, however, that digid span has a much lower correlation with total IQ in Negroes of low socio-economic status (29). A possible interpretation of this finding is that digit span is one of the more status fair subtests in the Stanford-Binet and Wechsler. The usefulness of the digit span test, however, is impaired by its relatively low reliability due to the brevity of the test as it is usually presented in omnibus batteries. We have lengthened the digit span test, added procedural variations (e.g., immediate vs. delayed recall and single vs. multiple repetitions of the same digit series), and standardized administration by presenting the digits by tape recorder at a metronomic one-second rate. Reliabilities are over .90. Social status differences are much smaller than for other tests. Whether the test still measures the intellective *g* factor of mental ability in low status groups, however, is now seriously open to question (29). It appears that digit span gets at an important component of mental ability, but it is different from *g*. Its substantial loading on *g* in factor analyses of the Stanford-Binet and Wechsler in the white and predominantly middle-class normative groups may be explained by the hypothesis that memory span is a component of mental ability which is necessary but not sufficient for the development of *g*. The *g* factor is indexed mainly by tests involving complex reasoning.

Another subtest with apparently little status bias but a very substantial *g* loading is *Block Design*. Its reliability is in the .80s for various age groups and could be made still higher if the test were lengthened and more difficult items were added. The Kohs block design test improves on the Wechsler in these respects. The high *g* saturation of the test, despite its nonverbal and nonscholastic character, suggests its great potential as a status-fair measure of intelligence. The test involves a speed factor and could be improved by providing a means of assessing noncognitive speed. Performance time on a series of very easy block designs could be used for this purpose. Time scores on more difficult designs could be "regressed" on time scores for the easy designs in order to get an estimate of intelligence relatively uncontaminated by the non-cognitive speed factor.

The *Porteus Maze* test is another example of a more elaborate form of one of the Wechsler subscales in the children's form. The *Porteus Maze* test has been shown to discriminate between behaviorally retarded and non-retarded Negro adolescents all of whom had Wechsler and Stanford-Binet IQs in the retarded range (11). The maze test distinguished those regarding whom the following eight questions could be answered in the affirmative:

Is he socially alert? Is he socially effective? Is his general activity level high? Is he mentioned more often? Is his vocational ability high? Does he have sports ability? Is his physical appearance good? Is his social judgment accurate?

This study indicates that the Porteus test measures a socially important dimension of behavior which is relatively undetected by conventional tests of intelligence in an educationally disadvantaged population.

A BIAS IN AGE-GRADED SCALES

The vocabulary and digit span subtests are not given at every age level in the Stanford-Binet. The same thing is true for other subtests as well; they are staggered over the age scale. This raises a question of whether the particular selection of subtests in one age grouping are equated with those of another age grouping in their status-fair properties.

If the age groupings differ in the status fairness of their subtests, the biasing effect could be exaggerated well beyond the bias in the individual items, because of the way age scales are administered. That is, the testing is discontinued when the child fails all the subtests in one age category. A preponderance of status-biased items concentrated at one age level could therefore prevent many subjects from even having a chance at the less biased items at the next age level. In this respect the Wechsler tests, which are not construed in accord with the age-scale notion, are superior to the Stanford-Binet. In the Wechsler the subject has an equal chance at every type of item, so that the single effects of status-biased items are not magnified in their effect on the total score. We do not know how large a status bias this factor causes in Stanford-

Binet scores, but it should be investigated and, if it is found to be significant, some change in the Stanford-Binet testing procedures would be called for. An index of status discrimination could be obtained for every item in the test and the age groupings of the items could be rearranged, if necessary, to yield the same average discrimination index at each age level.

PHYSIOLOGICAL INDEXES OF INTELLIGENCE

Is there a possibility of bypassing cultural factors in tests altogether by measuring the brain or its neurological efficiency directly? So far no one has found any single brain measurement or combination of measurements that correlates sufficiently with behavioral criteria of mental ability to be of practical use. Even if high correlations between electrophysiological brain measurements and intelligence test scores were found, however, we would still have to establish by means of factor analysis that the physiological measure was loaded on the g factor in all the various social class or racial groups for whom the test is intended to be "fair."

From the laboratory of Dr. John P. Ertl, director of the center for cybernetic studies at the University of Ottawa, there is now good evidence of a common factor in IQ and the rapidity of evoked potentials in brain wave patterns as recorded by the electroencephalograph (EEG) (46). While the subject's brain waves are being recorded in a darkened room, a bright light is flashed in the subject's eyes for a fraction of a second. The stimulus is registered as an "evoked potential"—a spike—in the subject's brain waves. The brief period of time between the flash of light and the peak of the evoked potential which follows it has been found to correlate with IQ. But so far the only reliable discriminations that have been reported are between children differing as widely in IQ as retarded and gifted children. Technical improvements, however, may lead to substantial correlations with psychometric measures of g and we would have a culture-free method for studying individual and group differences in the brain processes that underlie intelligent behavior. If status differences are associated with nutritional or other biological factors that affect the brain's development early in life, these factors would be reflected also in electrophysiological measurements. No one claims a test that can "read through" environmental factors that have direct biological influences on mental growth. As pointed out previously, we cannot directly measure Intelligence A (the individual's genotype). But physiological techniques may ultimately permit measurement of Intelligence B free of all environmental factors but those of a strictly biological nature.

The literature on culture-free and culture-fair testing reveals an almost total confusion and misconception concerning the definition of "fairness" and the criteria by which it is to be recognized. One author of a culture-fair test stated as the criterion of fairness: ". . . a test is culture-fair if the obtained scores are demonstrated to be free of the influence of socioeconomic differences between subjects." In other words, the degree of culture-fairness is judged in terms of the degree of reduction in SES variance in obtained scores. When tests designed to be culture-fair, such as the *Davis-Eells Games*, the *Davis-Hess Individual Test of Intelligence*, and the *Cattell Culture-Fair Tests*, are shown still to differentiate between social status groups, as they do, this is claimed as evidence that the tests are not "fair" and that the authors have failed in their purpose. It is a fact that no tests of intelligence have yet been derived which consistently wipe out social class and racial differences.

Does this mean that the tests are culturally biased? To claim the absence or reduction of group differences as the criterion of fairness is to beg the question completely. It is a wholly inappropriate criterion. A culture-fair or status-fair test should, in principle, be capable of showing status differences where such differences are not due solely to cultural factors but to genetic factors as well. The notion that culture-fair tests should wipe out SES differences is based on the implicit assumption that high and low SES groups do not differ in their genetic potential for the development of intelligence. Such an assumption is not only unwarranted by the evidence but is in fact contradicted by the preponderance of the relevant evidence. This evidence cannot be reviewed in detail here. It consists of highly consistent findings from diverse studies of the inheritance of intelligence: identical twins separated in the first year of life and reared in widely differing social classes still show greater resemblance in IQ than unrelated children reared together or even than siblings or fraternal twins (who have half their genes in common) reared together (7); the IQs of children adopted in infancy show a much lower correlation with the socioeconomic and educational level of the adopting parents than do the IQs of children reared by their own parents (36); the IQs of children reared in an orphange from infancy and who have never known their true parents show approximately the same correlation with their true father's occupational status as is found for children reared by their own parents (35); the correlations between the IQs of children adopted in infancy and the educational level of their true mothers is close to that of children reared by their own mothers ($r = .44$), while the correlation between children and their adopting parents is close to zero (22); children of low and high SES show, on the average, an amount of regression from the parental IQ toward the mean of the general population that is predicated by a polygenetic model (6); when full siblings (who, on the average, have half their genes in common) differ significantly in intelligence, those who are above the family average tend to move up the SES scale and those who are below the family average tend to move down (49). In view of these lines of evidence, it would be surprising to find a test that claimed to wipe out SES differences in measured intelligence; one would question whether the test was actually measuring intelligence—an issue that could be checked by factor analyzing the test along with other standard tests and noting its *g* loading.

Anastasi (1) has stated that a test is not culture-fair "when it fails to control relevant cultural parameters." This is an extremely slippery criterion. It is always applied in a *post hoc* manner. If what is thought to be a relevant cultural parameter is controlled and the test still discriminates between status groups, a new relevant cultural parameter is then invoked as an explanation for the difference. Anastasi, for example, points to findings which challenge the belief that nonverbal tests are more culture-fair than verbal tests. When American Negroes perform less well than other groups on a highly verbal test like the Stanford-Binet, the explanation is that their language background is different or impoverished in the kinds of words or syntax common to white middle-class society. Then, according to Anastasi, it was found that Negroes generally perform more poorly on tests involving concrete objects, numerical problems, and spatial relations than on most verbal tests. "One explanation proposed for these differences," Anastasi continues, "centers around problem-solving attitudes. Insofar as the social environment of the American Negro has traditionally encouraged attitudes of passive compliance rather than active exploration, it would be more conducive to rote verbal learning than to perceptual manipulation of stimuli and problem solving." This may or may not be true. The point is that since an unlimited number of "cultural parameters" can be hypothesized that would have to be controlled to make a test "fair" by Anastasi's criterion, and since presumably the only criterion that all relevant factors have been controlled is the absence of group differences (the presence of any difference would always be seen as the result of another cultural parameter that was not controlled), I regard Anastasi's definition of culture-fairness as quite meaningless and useless from an objective, operational standpoint. Obviously, some other criterion of culture-fairness or status-fairness is needed.

What are some other possible criteria by which we might judge the status fairness of a test?

We have already mentioned the criterion of predictive validity. If a test has different predictive validities for different groups in the population and these differences cannot be attributed to differences in variance on the test or the criterion, it is likely that the test is biased in favor of some groups and not others.

Another indicator of a test's loading on environmental influences is its correlation with environmental ratings or other indices of relevant environmental factors. Other things being equal, the test with lower environmental correlations is probably more status fair than tests with higher environmental correlations. It is an especially strong indication of culture-fairness if the mean test scores of a number of widely different cultural groups are not monotonically related to mean environmental ratings for the groups, when the environments are rated on a scale of experiential and educational similarity to that of the population on which the test was standardized. Probably the most powerful test of environmental influence on test scores can be achieved by determining the multiple correlation between the scores and indices of a large number of environmental factors.

The effects of training and practice on test scores may also reflect the test's susceptibility to environmental influence. Performance on all tests shows practice effects, but some tests show more than others. Although high suspectibility to improvement with practice does not rule out the test's lack of bias, high resistance to practice gains strongly suggests that the test is getting more at internally regulated developmental processes than at environmental attainments. Tests on which gains in score resulting from practice rapidly reach asymptote, and which show little transfer across equivalent forms, and which leave little or no residue in measurements obtained with the same tests or equivalent forms a few months later, can probably be regarded as more status fair than tests which do not show these properties to as high a degree. Seventy-eight practice sessions on a variety of memory span tasks spread over a period of four and a half months, for example, showed a significant gain in young children in relation to an unpracticed matched group, but after another four and a half months without additional practice both groups performed the same. Then both groups were given 22 days of intensive training on memory span tasks; at the end both groups were approximately equal. There was no evidence of any permanent effect of the seventy-eight days of practice (16). Thus it seems highly unlikely that memory span tests manifest any appreciable status bias. Raven's *Progressive Matrices* appears to have a similar resistance to training, as shown by recent, as yet unpublished, research by Paul Jacobs of the Educational Testing Service. Transfer of training on the matrices is surprisingly small, even when there is high similarity between the training items and the test items.

Copying geometric figures of varying difficulty also seems to get at developmental rather than experiential aspects of mental ability (25). There is an age scale for ability to copy such figures, going from a circle to a cube drawn in perspective. My experience in testing children on these figures and in trying to teach children how to copy figures that are beyond their developmental level makes me believe that this type of ability is highly resistant to specific training. It is interesting to observe a five-year-old who can copy a circle, a cross, a square, and a triangle as perfectly as any adult, and then cannot begin to copy a diamond. Instead, the child will usually draw an ellipse with little arrow points on the top, bottom, and sides. Training and practice, using imitation, verbal instructions, tracing, and the like, do not improve the child's performance. Wait a year or so, and the child will copy the diamond without any difficulty. Piaget's conservation problems evince this same resistance to specific training. Piaget tasks have been found to have very substantial loadings on the g factor when analyzed with conventional psychometric tests (47).

Probably the major pitfall for most attempts to devise status-fair tests results from uncritical acceptance of the following common criteria of fairness: (*a*) the test score means and variances should be the same in high and low status groups, and (*b*) the test should correlate highly with conventional tests of intelligence in the high status group. We have found a number of tests that meet these criteria, the best example being digit span (30). But these two criteria are insufficient. They do not tell us whether the test measures the same intelligence in the low status group as in the high status group. My own research has shown that digit span and various types of associative learning do not measure much of the variance in intelligence in low status groups. Even though scores on conventional tests may be depressed by a poor environment, subjects should remain in about the same rank order of ability on both status-fair and conventional tests. When there is almost no correlation between the two kinds of tests, it is highly doubtful that they are measuring the same psychological processes. A principal components analysis or factor analysis of a status-fair test can help to answer this question. Since there is no necessary connection between the means of various tests in a population and their intercorrelations, a requirement of a status-fair test should be that it show essentially the same factorial composition in a low status as in a high status group. The test's g saturation, especially, should be by far its largest component, if the test is claimed to measure intelligence, and it should be of about the same magnitude in both lower and upper status groups. As stated before, it is not at all necessary that the test yield the same means across low and high status groups. So far no culture-fair intelligence test yet devised that meets the criterion of measuring *g* in both high and low status groups fails to show significant social class and racial differences (e.g. (39)). As already pointed out, the "fairness" of these tests is not disproved by the findings of status group differences. How then can their fairness be judged? Are there any objective criteria we can apply?

CRITERIA DERIVED FROM QUANTITATIVE GENETICS

I propose the following definition of status fairness of a test: a test is status fair to the degree that its correlation with "Intelligence A" in the population in which the test is used approaches unity. In other words, the higher the correlation between phenotype and genotype, the higher is the "fairness" of the test. If the genotype-phenotype correlation is perfect, after correction for attenuation, the test can be said to measure innate ability. The phenotype-genotype correlation for individual tests like the Stanford-Binet is approximately 0.9 in the normative Caucasian population. This figure is actually the square root of the heritability of intelligence test scores. The heritability of intelligence as measured by conventional tests has been estimated by the methods of quantitative genetics in a large number of studies in Europe and North America. The average value of these heritability estimates is about .80 (27), which means that about 80 per cent of the true-score variance on intelligence tests is attributable to genetic factors and about 20 per cent is attributable to nongenetic factors. "Nongenetic" includes all environmental influences—physical, biological, and social—acting on the individual from the moment of conception.

The Concept of Heritability. The equation for the total population variance of the phenotypes (i.e., actual measurements) for a given characteristic can be specified as follows:

$$V_P = \underbrace{(V_G + V_{AM}) + V_D + V_i}_{\substack{V_H \\ \text{Heredity}}} + \underbrace{V_E + 2\,\text{Cov}_{HE} + V_I}_{\substack{V_E \\ \text{Environment}}} + \underbrace{V_e}_{\text{Error}} \quad (1)$$

where: V_P = phenotypic variance.
V_G = genic (or additive) variance.
V_{AM} = variance due to assortative mating.
$\quad\quad V_{AM} = 0$ under random mating (panmixia).
V_D = dominance deviation variance.
V_i = epistatis (interaction among genes at 2 or more loci).

V_E = environmental variance.

Cov_{HE} = covariance of heredity and environment.

V_r = true statistical interaction of genetic and environmental factors.

V_e = error of measurement (unreliability).

Each of these variance components can be further partitioned into a Between Families component and a Within Families component. The Between Families component in the case of the genetic variance is that proportion of the variance which relatives have in common by virtue of common ancestry; the Within Families component is that proportion of the variance which they do not share in common, since relatives receive a random selection of genes from their ancestral pool. In the case of environmental variance, the Between Families component in the variance is shared in common by virtue of the individuals' being *reared* in the same family setting; the Within Families component is the variance not shared in common by individuals reared in the same family, since environmental variations occur within the family setting.

The estimation of heritability by any one of several known methods is an attempt to estimate the proportion of phenotypic variance attributable to genetic factors. Not every heritability formula takes into account all the components shown in Equation 1. What geneticists refer to as heritability in the "narrow" sense (or "strict" sense) is:

$$H_N = \frac{V_G + V_{AM}}{V_P - V_e}. \tag{2}$$

Heritability in the "broad" sense is:

$$H_B = \frac{V_G + V_{AM} + V_D + V_i}{V_P - V_e}. \tag{3}$$

Other kinds of H are, of course, possible, with values ranging between H_N and H_B, depending on the components included in the numerator. The variance due to the correlation between heredity and environment and to the statistical interaction of genetic and environmental factors do not get included in these fundamental definitions of heritability. The interaction of heredity and environment could be included with the genetic components with as much justification as there is for including it with the environmental components. The technical definitions of heritability, however, put the genetic-environmental interaction on the side of environment and in this sense may be regarded as "conservative."

In practice, some formulas intended to estimate H tend to give an underestimate because of the heredity-environment interaction. Loehlin (38) has shown that the generalized heritability formula (Equation 4 below) proposed by Jensen (27) is unaffected by the genetic-environmental interaction. However, the correlation between geno-type and environmental influences causes some degree of under-estimation of H by the Jensen formula, as it does with every other formula designed for extracting heritability estimates from twin data. Fortunately, empirical estimates in the case of intelligence test scores have shown that the

TABLE 1

ANALYSIS OF VARIANCE FOR INTELLIGENCE TEST SCORES (BURT, 1958)

Source of Variance	Per cent
Genetic:	
Genic (additive)	40.5
Dominance & Epistasis	16.7
Assortative mating	19.9
Environmental:	
Covariance of H & E	10.6
Random (including V_I)	5.9
Unreliability (test error)	6.4
Total	100.0

covariance of genotype and environment and the genetic-environmental interaction constitute a very minor proportion of the total variance. One of the best estimates of these components shown in Equation 1 was made by Sir Cyril Burt (4) from many different kinship correlations in large samples of the London schools population. The results are shown in Table 1.

The variance components that account for the correlation between different degrees of kinship, reared apart or reared together, are shown in Table 2. The intraclass correlation between members of any particular relationship is:

$$r_i = \frac{\text{sum of components in common}}{\text{total variance}}.$$

The total variance, of course, consists of the sum of all the variance components (in common and not in common) shown in Table 2. If we wished to include the interaction and covariance terms of Equation

1 in Table 2, they would go on the side of "components not in common" in every case. Thus, they would always lower the intraclass correlation between relatives.

Table 2 should highlight the fact that heritability estimates based on comparison of identical or monozygotic (MZ) twins with fraternal or dizygotic (DZ) twins gives values of H that are actually somewhat inflated in proportion to the degree that dominance and epistasis are important sources of trait variance. MZ twins have *all* of the genetic components in common; DZ twins have something less than half in common overall. The method for estimating the dominance variance is also apparent in Table 2: compare DZ twins or sibs, who have $\frac{1}{4}$ of their dominance variance in common, with half-sibs or parent-child relationships, which have none of the dominance in common. Examination of the entries in Table 2 will reveal which comparisons will yield estimates of other variance components. The same components can often be estimated by comparing different sets of relationships, which provides evidence of the consistency of estimates in the population under consideration.

One of the most valuable relationships from the standpoint of heritability analysis is half-siblings. (I have not been able to find studies of half-siblings reported anywhere in the literature of human genetics.) For one thing, a comparison of half-siblings (of the same mother) and full siblings probably yields the best single estimate we can get of the dominance variance. More important, however, is the fact that half-siblings can give us some information about the effects of individual differences among mothers in the quality of the prenatal environment they provide. A comparison of the correlations between half-sibs having the same mother with those having different mothers should give an indication of the amount of environmental variance attributable to maternal differences in prenatal environment. It is hard to see why the necessary data should be hard to obtain in a society with as high a rate of divorce and remarriage as ours. There must be many half-siblings in the population. Double first cousins could also be used in such comparisons, since they are genetically as much alike as half-sibs but, of course, always have different mothers. Unfortunately, double first cousins are rare in human populations.

ESTIMATION OF NARROW HERITABILITY (H_N)

The proportion of variance due to additive genic effects is important to know if one is interested in the rate of change from one generation to the next under selective breeding. It is only the additive component that "breeds true." Sir Ronald Fisher referred to this component as "the

TABLE 2

VARIANCE COMPONENTS IN VARIOUS KINSHIPS

Relationship	Reared	Components* in Common				Components Not in Common					
		A	D	E_p	E_{BF}	A	D	E_p	E_{BF}	E_{WF}	e
MZ Twins	Together	1	1	1	1	0	0	0	0	1	1
MZ Twins	Apart	1	1	1	0	0	0	0	1	1	1
DZ Twins (Sibs)	Together	1/2	1/4	<1/4	1	1/2	3/4	>3/4	0	1	1
DZ Twins (Sibs)	Apart	1/2	1/4	<1/4	0	1/2	3/4	>3/4	1	1	1
1/2 Sibs	Together	1/4	0	<1/16	1	3/4	1	>15/16	0	1	1
1/2 Sibs	Apart	1/4	0	<1/16	0	3/4	1	>15/16	1	1	1
Parent-Child	"Together"	1/2	0	<1/4	?>0	1/2	1	>3/4	?<1	1	1
Parent-Foster Child	"Together"	0	0	0	?>0	1	1	1	?<1	1	1
Unrelated Children	Together	0	0	0	1	1	1	1	0	1	1
Unrelated Children	Apart	0	0	0	0	1	1	1	0	1	1

*
A = Additive
D = Dominance
E_p = Epistasis

E_{BF} = Between-Families Environment
E_{WF} = Within-Families Environment
e = Error

essential genotype." It is estimated by H_N—heritability in the narrow sense. The value of H_N cannot be determined by the twin method, however. Comparison of parent-child with half-sibs would seem to be the easiest method of estimating H_N. (This estimate would include something less than $\frac{1}{4}$ of the epistatic variance, which can be considered as negligible.) The appropriate correlations are simply entered into Jensen's generalized formula (Equation 4). Another estimate of H_N is given directly by the mid-parent—mid-child correlation. H_N, in fact, can be defined theoretically as the correlation between the mid-parent (i.e., mean of the parents) and the mean of an infinite number of their offspring. This offspring mean rapidly asymptotes, so a correlation based on a large sample of average-size families gives a fair estimate. The one attempt I have found to estimate H_N for Stanford-Binet IQ in this fashion is by Jones (32). The mid-parent—mid-child raw correlation was .693. Corrected for attenuation (i.e., test unreliability) this gives a value of $H_N = .72$.

A final reason for cross-checking heritability estimates by various methods is the large sampling error of estimate obtained by any one set of data, especially when the sample size is not large, as is typically the case in twin studies. There may also be systematic biasing factors in one set of kinship correlations that do not exist in correlations for some other degree of kinship. This is why I am impressed by the Erlenmeyer-Kimling and Jarvik (15) survey of 52 studies of the correlation of relatives for tested intellectual abilities, using a wide variety of intelligence tests and involving some 30,000 correlational pairings obtained from 8 countries in 4 continents. The median values of these correlations probably constitute the best estimates we have of kinship correlations for intelligence. They are shown in Table 3, which also includes the expected values if only genetic factors were involved and no assumptions were introduced about assortive mating, selective placement of foster children, and so forth. The expected values are those given by the simplest possible polygenic model. We can obtain three independent estimates of heritability from Table 3. (Because the correlations have not been corrected for attenuation, the values of H in every case are slightly underestimated by about five per cent.) The correlation between identical twins reared apart gives one estimate of $H = .75$. The comparison of correlations for MZ and DZ twins (reared together), using Jensen's formula (Equation 4) gives a value of $H = .75$. Still another estimate consists of 1 minus the difference between correlation of unrelated children reared together, and from this we obtain $H = .77$. These independent estimates are highly consistent and if the correlations were corrected for attenuation the H values would average very close to .80.

A Generalized Heritability Formula. In 1967 I proposed a generalized heritability formula which can be used to derive heritability estimates from any two sets of kinship correlations where one degree of kinship is closer than the other, e.g., identical (MZ) vs. fraternal (DZ) twins, sibs vs. half-sibs, sibs. vs. cousins, and sibs. vs. unrelated children (27). In all cases the two groups should consist of pairs either reared together or reared apart; that is to say, both groups must either share or not share the Between Families environmental component (Table 2). When pos-

TABLE 3

CORRELATIONS FOR INTELLECTUAL ABILITY OBTAINED AND EXPECTED
AMONG RELATIVES ON THE BASIS OF MENDELIAN INHERITANCE

Correlations between	Number of Studies	Median Correlation, r	
		Obtained*	Expected
Unrelated persons, reared apart	4	—.01	. 0
Unrelated persons, reared together	5	+.23	. 0
Foster parent—child	3	+.20	. 0
Parent—Child	12	+.50	+ .50
Siblings, reared apart	2	+.42	+ .50
Siblings, reared together	35	+.49	+ .50
Fraternal twins, opposite sex	9	+.53	+ .50
Fraternal twins, same sex	11	+.53	+ .50
Identical twins, reared apart	4	+.75	+1.00
Identical twins, reared together	14	+.87	+1.00

* Erlenmeyer-Kimling & Jarvik, 1963

sible, all correlations should be corrected for attenuation, or H will be underestimated. The proposed generalized formula is:

$$H = \frac{r_{AB} - r_{CD}}{\rho_{AB} - \rho_{CD}} \qquad (4)$$

where: r_{AB} is the obtained correlation (corrected for test unreliability) between pairs of individuals of a particular degree of kinship.

      r_{CD} is the correlation between pairs of individuals whose degree of kinship is less than that of group AB.

      ρ_{AB} is the theoretical genetic correlation (i.e., proportion of genes in common) between pairs A and B.

      ρ_{CD} is the theoretical genetic correlation between pairs C and D.

With random mating, the theoretical genetic correlations, ρ, between relatives is 1 for identical twins; .50 for fraternal twins, siblings, and parent-child; .25 for half-siblings, grandparent-grandchild, and double first cousins; .125 for first cousins; and 0 for unrelated persons. The values of ρ under a known degree of assortative mating (i.e., parental correlation on the trait in question) can be determined from formulas given elsewhere (see (12, 27)).

When applied to twin data (MZ and DZ reared together), this formulation can be used to obtain estimates of the proportions of Between-Families and Within-Families environmental variance. The proportion of Between-Families variance is:

$$E_B = \frac{r_{DZ} - \rho_s r_{MZ}}{1 - \rho_s} \tag{5}$$

where ρ_s is the genetic correlation between siblings (it is .50 under random mating and .55 when the parental genetic correlation is .25, a conservative estimate). The proportion of Within-Families environmental variance is:

$$E_W = 1 - H - E = 1 - r_{MZ} \tag{6}$$

Formulation of Correlation Between Persons. An interesting derivation from Equation 4 yields a conceptualization of the correlation between any set of paired individuals, where A is the first in the pair and B is the second:

$$r_{AB} = \rho_G H + \rho_E E_B. \tag{7}$$

ρ_G is the theoretical genetic correlation between members of the pair and ρ_E is a parameter for the correlation between their environments. ρ_E is generally assumed to be 1 when the individuals are reared together and 0 when they are reared apart. If there are direct, independent estimates of the degree of environmental similarity, there would, of course, be a basis for substituting other values of ρ_E that lie somewhere between 0 and 1.

Estimating the Mean of a Population from Theoretical Genetic Parameters. If the mean of a population on a given trait can be closely estimated, without being directly estimated from a random sample of the population, by making use of genetic parameters, this would constitute evidence for the genetic determination of the trait. Continuously distributed physical traits that are highly determined by polygenic inheritance, such as stature, head circumference, and fingerprint ridges show a highly precise degree of "regression to the mean" of the population—for offspring, siblings, and other degrees of kinship, the amount of regression being directly proportional to the remoteness of kinship. The genetically expected value (EX) of a characteristic for a relative (R) of a "target" person (T) can be expressed as:

$$EX_R = \rho_G (X_T - M_P) + M_P. \tag{8}$$

where: EX_R = the expected value of the relative of the target person.

X_T = value of target person.

M_P = mean value for the population from which T and R are drawn.

ρ_G = the theoretical genetic correlation between T and R. (Under the assumptions of random mating, no dominance, epistasis, or genetic-environment interaction, these values are 1 for MZ twins, .50 for parent-child, DZ twins and full siblings, .25 for half-siblings and double first cousins, and 0 for unrelated persons.)

From this equation it should be possible to estimate M_P by measuring a target group (T) and measuring their relatives, even if the target group is a highly select sample, such as children in gifted classes or classes for the educable mentally retarded. It should little matter how the target group is selected, so long as they are not pathological. The expected value of the population mean (EM_P) is obtained by transposing Equation 8:

$$EM_P = \frac{\Sigma[\,(X_R - \rho_G X_T)\,/\,(1 - \rho_G)\,]}{N} \tag{9}$$

where: EM_P = expected mean of population.

X_T = value of target person, T.

X_R = value of relative, R, of target person.

N = number of T-R pairs.

If T and R are siblings, ρ_G = .50 under the simplest assumptions, and Equation 9 can be simplified:

$$EM_P = \frac{\Sigma\,(2X_S - X_T)}{N} \tag{10}$$

where: X_S = the value of the sibling of T.

The discrepancy between EM_P as obtained by Equations 9 or 10 and M_P as obtained from a random sample of the population provides an indication of the degree to which the population distribution of scores can be accounted for by assuming a simple polygenic model. We can work this procedure in reverse, and estimate ρ_G simply by selecting subjects at random from a defined population and computing the correlation between relatives and seeing how discrepant the obtained values of r are from the theoretical ρ_G for any given degree of kinship. The data summarized by Erlenmeyer-Kimling and Jarvik (15), shown in Table 3, are the median values of such correlations from a large number of studies. The discrepancies between obtained and expected values are, of course, assumed to be due to the influence of nongenetic factors. (The discrepancies, however, are slightly reduced if the expected values are derived from a more complex genetic model (7).) The considerable consistency of the degree to which environmental factors (excluding prenatal effects) cause discrepancies between correlations among relatives is shown by plotting the median values of all the correlations reported in the literature for various kinships reared together and reared apart, as shown in Figure 1.

FIGURE 1

MEDIAN VALUES OF ALL CORRELATIONS REPORTED IN THE LITERATURE FOR THE INDICATED KINSHIPS[15]

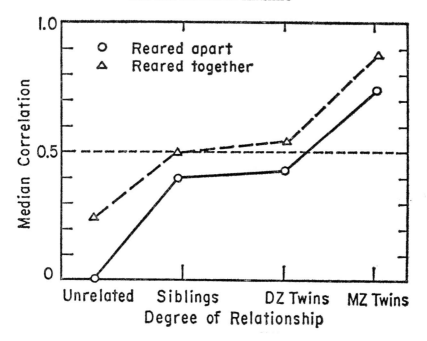

Checks on the Obtained Correlations for Different Kinships. At times there may be some doubt about the reported kinship of relatives in the population under study. This is probably extremely rare in the case of twins, but may constitute a serious source of error for siblings and half-siblings, especially in populations with high rates of illegitimacy and multiple paternities within the same nominal family unit. Correlations can be checked and corrected, however, in terms of "baseline" correlations based on physical characteristics of known high heritability. Perhaps the most ideal measurement for this purpose is fingerprint ridge count, which Sir Ronald Fisher originally suggested could be used as a "sheet anchor" for assessing other kinship correlations. Fingerprint ridges may be measured with a high degree of reliability and the quantitative values when used in kinship correlations correspond perfectly to a simple additive genetic model without assortative mating. The correlations between relatives come as close to the theoretical values as reliability of measurement and sampling error permit (21). For large samples (N 100), the obtained correlations (corrected for attenuation) show a virtually perfect fit to the theoretical values. This only means, of course, that the heritability of fingerprints is 100%. Since fingerprints may not always be available or obtainable, correlations for other highly heritable physical traits may serve the purpose nearly as well. Head circumference and standing height, standardized for chronological age, have heritabilities only slightly lower than fingerprints (24). Correlations (corrected for attenuation) between relatives on the trait under study can be further "corrected" simply by dividing them by the correlations (corrected for attenuation) on a highly heritable physical trait in the same sample. Given the precision of fingerprint correlations and a fairly large sample size, it should be possible quite accurately to estimate the proportion of half-sibs in a group of all nominal siblings which actually contain some proportion of half-sibs. If one wanted to go even further in "purifying" the sample, a number of independent genetic polymorphisms could be used in a discriminant function analysis to exclude, with a specified probability of error, individual pairs of subjects from the sample as not belonging to the particular kinship classification in question. This is essentially the same method as used for determining the zygosity of twins.

Sibling Correlations Alone. Can sibling correlations alone provide us with any information at all concerning the heritability of test scores? I believe they can, but only in a one-sided fashion. If the correlation is close to the genetically expected value, we can say it is consistent with a genetic model and the heritability of the test in question may be high. But this is not proved by a sibling correlation alone, because a correlation of .50 could arise also from strictly environmental factors without any genetic determination whatsoever. If, on the other hand, the correlation significantly departs in *either* direction from the theoretical genetic value, we can be quite sure that the trait variance has a significant environmental component. This information can be used for roughly classifying measurements of various psychological characteristics for their degree of environmental determination in the population on which they are obtained. For example, psychological tests range along a continuum of the absolute deviation of the sibling correlation from the theoretical genetic value. This use of sibling correlations is proposed only as a less than optimal substitute for heritability estimates which require correlations in at least two kinship groups.

Heritability and Psychometrics. Characteristics of psychological and educational tests such as the mean, standard deviation, reliability, validity, and factorial composition are unquestionably important parameters of psychological tests and have a long tradition of being the main questions asked about any test. The heritability of the test in the normative population (or various subpopulations) should be added to this list. We should know more about the degree to which score variance on particular tests is attributable to genetic and environmental sources within the population in which the test is used. The heritability of a test is, of course, not a constant value; it can vary from one age group to another, from one subpopulation to another, and from one generation to another in the same population. It is an interesting index in the case of ability and achievement tests in that it tells us a good deal about equality of environmental conditions for mental development in the population. With increasing improvement and equalization of the environmental conditions needed for children's optimal mental development, including greater equality of educational opportunity, there should be an increase in the heritability of intelligence and scholastic achievement scores. Greater increases in H should be expected in subpopulations whose environmental conditions are upgraded and equalized most. Because of much potentially valuable information about population changes that can be gotten from heritability estimates, I would urge that large-scale assessment programs make a point of obtaining various kinship correlations, especially for twins and siblings, that can be used in heritability formulas. For this reason I urged the National Assessment Program, which proposes to test a representative sample of over 150,000 of the U.S. population on a kind of general intelligence and educational achievement test, to obtain test results on MZ and DZ twins, a large number of which should turn up in a sample of 150,000 persons. The heritability of the test in different socioeconomic and racial subgroups of the population could be determined from these data and would provide a basis for assessing future changes in an important population parameter, in addition to the changes in means and variances. My suggestion along these lines to the Director and Advisory Board of the National Assessment Program unfortunately was rejected. At present the only large-scale testing programs I know of that have systematically collected twin data in this country are the National Merit Scholarship Corporation and the American Institute of Research in the Project Talent study. The Scandinavian countries are far ahead of us in this sphere; they have established national twin registries, in which are kept records on every pair of twins in the entire population. Such a data bank is of great potential value to researchers in the fields of medicine, psychology, sociology, and criminology, to name a few. We would do well to follow suit. We are especially lacking such data in our minority populations.

Heritability as a Criterion of the Status-Fairness of Ability Tests. The inventors and developers of intelligence tests—men such as Galton, Binet, Spearman, Burt, Thorndike, and Terman—clearly intended that their tests assess as clearly as possible the individual's innate brightness or mental capacity. If this is what a test attempts to do, then clearly the appropriate criterion for judging the test's "fairness" is the *heritability* of the test scores in the population in which the test is used. The quite high values of H for tests such as the Stanford-Binet attests to the success of the test-maker's aim to measure innate ability. The square root of the heritability, $(\sqrt{H})$, represents the correlation between phenotype and genotype, and, as pointed out before, this is of the order of .9 for our best standard intelligence tests. However, I would be hesitant to generalize this statement beyond the Caucasian population of the United States and Great Britain, since nearly all the major heritability studies have been performed in these populations. At present there are no really adequate data on the heritability of intelligence tests in the American Negro population. In my own work so far I have not gone beyond obtaining IQ correlations between a large number of Negro sibling pairs. The intraclass correlation for siblings ($N = 380$) was .46 (.50 when corrected for attenuation) for a group-administered intelligence test. The fact that this value does not differ significantly from the sibling correlation for Caucasians would lead me to predict that heritability estimates obtained in the Negro population probably will not differ markedly from the values of H typically found in the Caucasian population. But this is far from certain, as I have indicated elsewhere (28), and the facts should be determined directly by means of full-fledged heritability studies. Values of H may well differ for Negroes and Caucasians from one test to another. The "fairness" of various tests in each population is indexed by the test's H value in that population. It is quite conceivable that tests having the same *predictive* validity in two populations may have quite different H values in those populations. Though two tests may give the same degree of prediction of success in college, in the Armed Services, or in industry, if the tests differ in H, their results may lead to differences in just who gets screened out in the selection procedure. This is why I believe H should be determined especially on tests used in selection procedures wherever there is concern about eliminating unfair discrimination and an effort is made to insure equality of opportunity. I believe we should estimate the H of current widely used tests and develop methodologies for maximizing or minimizing H values, so that tests with very high and very low H values can be made for use wherever tests of high or low heritability seem most appropriate. We know almost nothing of the predictive validities of tests intended for various purposes such as academic and personnel selection, as a function of their H values.

Heritability and Group Comparisons. Can heritability estimates tell us anything about whether group differences are attributable to genetic or environmental factors or to some specifiable proportion for each source of between-groups variance? My conclusion is that heritability by itself cannot answer this question, but that heritability estimates combined with other data and certain assumptions, which may or may not be tenable, may provide some reduction in uncertainty concerning the nature-nurture controversy with respect to social class and race differences in abilities.

If the heritability of a trait is 100% in both groups A and B, and if A and B are reared in environments that "overlap" each other on factors relevant to the development of the trait, then it would probably be safe to say that a mean difference between groups A and B is due to a difference in genotypes. When heritability is considerably less than 100%, as in the case of measures of intelligence and other important psychological characteristics, the answer to the questions of group differences becomes considerably more speculative. If H is less than 100% but is the same in groups A and B, and if groups A and B are reared under conditions which on the average are indistinguishable, then, too, it would probably be safe to say that a mean difference between groups A and B is due to genetic factors.

What can we say, however, when the environment is *not* the same for A and B? Assume that we can rate or measure environments on some scale that is relevant to the development of the trait in question, say, intelligence as measured by our typical tests. If groups A and B show no overlap in their distributions of environmental ratings, then I believe nothing can be said about their genotypes if the group with the lower mean intelligence also has the poorer environment. If the group with the lower mean intelligence has the better environment, however, one could then claim this as evidence that the groups differ genetically.

In most cases, however, the group with the lower mean also has poorer environmental conditions. Can heritability estimates throw any light on group comparisons in this situation? I believe it can if there is substantial overlap between the relevant environmental conditions of the groups being compared; the environments need not be equal in the two populations, but they must overlap. Then we can take the following tack, which I put forth at this point only for discussion and criticism. If it is inadequate it may at least help to suggest a better method. If $M_A <$ M_B and $H_A = H_B$, and if we hypothesize that groups A and B do *not* differ genetically on the trait in question, we must conclude that there is a constant environmental decrement for each member of group A. Thus, if individuals from groups A and B are matched by pairs on the test scores (i.e., $M_A = M_B$), then the genetic value of group A would have to be higher than the genetic value of B. If we then compare these matched groups on a different measure of the same trait, but one which has higher heritability in both groups, group A should exceed group B, $(M_B < M_A)$. On the other hand, if we used still another test of the same trait which had lower heritability in both groups, we should expect the reverse, that is, $M_B > M_A$. (Of course, in each case correction would be made for regression due to measurement error.)

This, then, illustrates the rationale of one method by which heritability estimates may serve to reduce the heredity-environment uncertainty. The method can, of course, be made more general in practice. As a beginning, for example, one could estimate the heritabilities of a variety of mental abilities tests in the population subgroups one wishes to compare. We would expect a considerable range of values of H for the various tests, and there could be different values of H for any one test in the two population groups, A and B. The next step would be graphically to plot separately for each group the median overlap (i.e., the percentage of subjects in group A who exceed the median of group B) between groups A and B on the various tests as a function of the test's heritability. (Median overlap is on the ordinate; heritability is on the abscissa.) If the median overlap between A and B increases with an increase in H, it would favor the hypothesis that the difference between groups A and B is mainly the result of differences in environmental factors. If median overlap decreased with increases in H, on the other hand, it presumably would be indicative of a genetic difference between the groups. I will leave it to the statisticians to work out the optimal test of the statistical significance of the slopes of these plots relating median overlap to the H values of different tests. I imagine the statistical problems are not insurmountable, since confidence limits can be established both for H and for median overlap. It seems fairly certain that a large sample size would be needed to make this type of analysis statistically worthwhile.

I think we might learn important things if analyses of this type were made. To go far out in search of any data that even begins to resemble the requirements for such an analysis, I note some of the data in the well-known Coleman Report (10). Other studies have shown that intelligence tests, especially nonverbal tests, have generally higher heritabilities than scholastic achievement tests and highly verbal tests of intelligence (27), at least in British and American populations. The Coleman study did not attempt to determine the heritability of its psychological and educational tests. But it came up with some interesting findings which could be better understood if we did have heritability estimates on the tests in the various population categories used in the Coleman study. For example, it was found that Southern Negro children scored higher on verbal and scholastic achievement tests, relative to the nonverbal intelligence test, while Negroes in the North and West scored lower on the verbal and scholastic tests relative to the nonverbal test. Negroes in the rural South showed the largest discrepancy between the nonverbal and achievement tests, with higher scores on the scholastic achievement tests. What is the meaning of these findings? I submit we would be closer to knowing the answer if we knew the heritabilities of these various tests in the different subpopulations.

The Achievement of More Refined Genetic Models. So long as we depend only upon omnibus-type psychological tests on which the individual's score represents a conglomerate of mental processes, skills, response tendencies, and their interactions with procedural factors in psychological testing—all with unknown weightings in the composite score—we will not be able to advance our understanding of the inheritance of mental abilities beyond the crudest and simplest models of polygenic inheritance. In order to advance further our knowledge of human behavioral genetics, especially as regards individual differences in mental abilities, I believe we will have to make more highly analytical studies of the psychological components of particular abilities. I have suggested one approach to this problem elsewhere (26). Memory span (digit span), for example, is a subtest in many omnibus tests of intelligence such as the Stanford-Binet and the Wechsler. Corrected for attenuation, it correlates .75 with both Stanford-Binet and Wechsler total scores (minus digit span). It has a loading of .80 on the g factor in these tests. It can therefore be regarded as an important test of mental ability. In my laboratory we are taking digit span apart through a combination of experimental analysis and factor analysis. First of all, it is gratifying to find that individual differences in digit span are highly reliable and stable in young adults. It is possible to obtain measurements of individual differences that are as reliable as measures of physical characteristics such as height and weight. Furthermore, it is apparent that digit span is not a unitary ability. It has a number of subcomponents on which there are reliable individual differences. I plan to go on fractionating digit span ability until just about all conceivable reliable sources of individual differences have been exhausted. How many dimensions of "ability" will ultimately be found to constitute what we call "memory span" is still anyone's guess. I put "ability" in quotes, because the components of digit span ability may not even resemble *abilities* as we ordinarily use this term. When digit span (to use only one example) is thus fractionated into reliably measurable factors or components, will these components better lend themselves to quantitative genetic analysis than the more conglomerate score or than conventional intelligence test scores? May not the components—the "atoms" of ability, so to speak—be controlled by fewer genes and by more specific environmental factors? If so, it would seem that such experimental analysis of abilities, hand in hand with quantitative genetic analysis, should make possible greater progress in understanding the nature and nurture of mental abilities than we have known heretofore.

EXTENDING THE SPECTRUM OF MEASURED ABILITIES

What if it turns out that tests of g which do in fact meet acceptable criteria of status-fairness still show mean differences between various social class and racial groups? And what if such tests have the same predictive power for all groups in the present educational system? How could such a state of affairs be reconciled with our ideals and hopes for equality of educational and occupational opportunity for all persons in all segments of the population?

The answer will come, I believe, by putting g in its proper place. It now carries much more weight in school than it ever has in life outside of school. And much of its importance in the world of occupations is derived from their often unwarranted dependence upon formal educational attainments as selection criteria.

The educational system operates in such a way as to maximize the importance of g as a source of variance in scholastic attainment. Yet g is only one aspect, perhaps not even a major aspect, of mental ability. Throughout the preceding discussion I have used the terms "intelligence" and "mental ability." I have not used them interchangeably. By "intelligence" I have referred to that aspect of ability that is tapped by tests heavily loaded on g—the capacity for abstract reasoning, or "the education of relations and correlates," to use Spearman's original definition. By "mental ability" I refer to the full spectrum of abilities, of which g is only a part. If tests are "unfair," it is more likely to be because of their limited sampling of the total spectrum of abilities than because of culturally biased content. Even if our intelligence tests meet all the usual criteria of fairness, they could still be unfair in the sense that they fail to tap other abilities that could be just as important as g for educational and occupational achievement.

It is possible to design instruction in school subjects (or almost anything else) in such a way as to maximize the importance of g and minimize the importance of all other abilities. We know it is possible because it is what we are doing all the time in school. In such a situation intelligence tests heavily loaded on g will inevitably have high predictive validity. But does this mean that g is the most essential ability for learning under any and all conditions of instruction? I seriously doubt it.

It seems to me that the *sine qua non* of educability under any conditions is not g, but learning ability—the ability to acquire information and skills by one means or another. What I call basic learning ability is, in the final analysis, the most fundamental source of individual differences. It is not the same as g. While it is rare to find children high on measures of g who do not also perform well on measures of basic learning ability, we find many children, especially among groups called disadvantaged, who score low on tests of g but whose performance on direct learning tests is average or above in relation to middle-class norms.

It is a common observation of many teachers of children called disadvantaged that those in the IQ range from 60 to 80 seem much brighter than their IQs would suggest on the basis of experience with middle-class children of the same IQ. Usually the brightness shows up, however, only in nonscholastic activities. We have found in our research that although this brightness is not tapped by any standard IQ tests, it can be tapped by direct learning tests. Most of these children are capable of learning with an ease and speed far beyond what one would predict on the basis of their conventional IQs. The two main reasons that they do not perform better scholastically than would be expected from their IQs are (*a*) the instruction is geared to their weakest abilities and not their strongest, and (*b*) after the first year or two in the classroom they become "turned off" for scholastic activities because of lack of the reinforcement that comes from success in learning.

At least part of the answer will consist of discovering abilities other than g that can be brought into play by appropriate instructional techniques to achieve useful and realistic educational goals, which includes the 3 Rs and other traditional forms of scholastic attainment in addition to more specific occupational knowledge and skills. Thus, the true meaning of culture-fair or status-fair testing, it seems to me, is to assess as broad a spectrum of abilities as possible and to design instruction so as to capitalize on existing strengths. For many children in our school population we should strive to *lower* the correlation between conventional IQs and scholastic attainment and boost the correlation between direct learning measures and scholastic attainment.

Our research on learning abilities in disadvantaged children shows that their strength exists in their fundamental ability to learn, whether they are high g or low g. If they are high g, they can learn in the traditional classroom. If they are low g, they fail in the traditional classroom.

But most of those in the latter group have shown that they can learn just as well as any other children when given learning tasks in our laboratory.

On learning tasks involving memory span, serial learning, paired-associate learning, trial-and-error selective learning, and free recall of certain kinds of informational input, we find highly reliable individual differences in performance but no significant differences in the distribution of scores as a function of social class or racial background. Some of this research has been described elsewhere (28, 29, 30, 31). To summarize briefly, we have found that children of low SES whose IQs are in the range below 90 on standard intelligence tests are quite different from middle-class children of the same IQs in associative learning ability. Low SES children of relatively low measured IQ are generally markedly superior to their middle-class counterparts in IQ tests involving free recall, serial learning, paired-associate learning, and digit span. Low SES children of average IQ or above, on the other hand, do not differ from their middle-class counterparts in these associative learning abilities. This interaction among IQ, associative learning ability, and socioeconomic status has been found in children sampled from Caucasian, Mexican-American, and Negro populations.

My current attempts to conceptualize these findings in a theoretical model that will suggest further hypotheses and empirical investigations is based on the notion of a hierarchy of mental abilities going from associative learning to conceptual thinking, in which the development of lower levels in the hierarchy is necessary but not sufficient for the development of the more complex levels involving symbolic or abtract thinking, conceptual learning, semantic generalization, and the use of language as a "tool of thought" in learning and problem solving. A crucial question concerns the extent to which the development of these complex abilities are determined by the nature of environmental inputs. The fact that the best tests of these abilities, such as the *Progressive Matrices,* have quite high heritability suggests that the development of these complex mental abilities depends upon the development of innate neural structures, so that appropriate environmental influences may be necessary but not sufficient for their manifestation in performance. As for associative learning ability, which may be a necessary but not sufficient substrata in the development of conceptual abilities, there is no reason to believe that it is not at least as heritable as psychometric intelligence, although there is little direct evidence on the heritability of associative learning ability in humans. It is likely that both types of ability, associative and conceptual, are highly determined by genetic factors. The important point is that individual differences in associative learning ability per se apparently are not differentially distributed according to socioeconomic background.

But such exploration of learning ability has only begun, and it is possible that instructional techniques can be developed that will mobilize various learning capacities in the classroom to achieve much the same educational goals that have traditionally depended in such large measure on a limited pattern of cognitive processes, generally characterized by *g*. Perhaps more thought and effort should go into discovering ways of radically making over our educational methods to accord with the full variety and range of children's innate patterns of mental abilities. The long-term rewards from such efforts, I believe, will be greater than any derived from massive efforts to shape all children to the requirements of an instructional system which inordinately emphasizes one type of ability at the expense of all others. The ideal of equality of educational opportunity should mean the opportunity for every child to put his *best* foot forward on the path to achieving his educational and occupational goals.

REFERENCES

1. ANASTASI, ANN. Culture-fair testing. *Educational Horizons*, Fall, 1964, Pp. 26-30.
2. Are aptitude tests unfair to Negroes? ETS investigates two kinds of "bias." *ETS Developments*, 1966, 14, 1.
3. BINET, A., & SIMON, T. *The development of intelligence in children.* (Trans. by Elizabeth S. Kite). Baltimore: Williams and Wilkins, 1916.
4. BURT C. The inheritance of mental ability. *Amer. Psychol.*, 1958, 13, 1-15.
5. BURT, C. Class differences in general intelligence: III *Brit. J. Stat. Psychol.*, 1959, 12, 15-33.
6. BURT, C. Intelligence and social mobility. *Brit. J. Stat. Psychol.*, 1961, 14, 3-24.
7. BURT, C. The genetic determination of differences in intelligence: A study of monozygotic twins reared together and apart. *Brit. J. Psychol.*, 1966, 57, 137-153.
8. CATTELL, R. B. *Handbook for the Culture Fair Intelligence Test: A measure of "g."* Champaign, Ill.: Institute for Personality and Ability Testing, 1959.
9. CATTELL, R. B. Theory of fluid and crystalized intelligence: A critical experiment. *J. educ. Psychol.*, 1963, 54, 1-22.
10. COLEMAN, J. S., et al. *Equality of educational opportunity.* U.S. Dept. of Health, Education, and Welfare, 1966.
11. COOPER, G. D., YORK, M. W., DASTON, P. G., & ADAMS, H. B. The Porteus Test and various measures of intelligence with Southern Negro adolescents. *Amer. J. ment. Defic.* 1967, 71, 787-792.
12. CROW, J. F., & FELSENSTEIN, J. The effect of assortative mating on the genetic composition of a population. *Eugenics Quart.*, 1968 (June).
13. ECKLAND, B. K. Genetics and sociology: A reconsideration. *Amer. Soc. Rev.*, 1967, 32, 173-194.
14. EELLS, K., et al. *Intelligence and cultural differences.* Chicago: Univ. Chicago Press, 1951.
15. ERLENMEYER-KIMLING, L., & JARVIK, L. F. Genetics and intelligence: a review. *Science*, 1963, 142, 1477-1479.
16. GATES, A. I., & TAYLOR, G. A. An experimental study of the nature of improvement resulting from practice in mental function. *J. educ. Psychol.*, 1925, 16, 583-593.
17. GHISELLI, E. E. *The measurement of occupational aptitude.* University of California Publications in Psychology, Vol. 8, No. 2. Berkeley, Calif.: Univ. of Calif. Press, 1955.

18. Gough, H. G. A nonintellectual intelligence test. *J. consult. Psychol.,* 1953, 17, 242-246.

19. Gough, H. G., & Domino, G. The D 48 Test as a measure of general ability among grade school children. *J. consult. Psychol.,* 1963, 27, 344-349.

20. Gough, H. G., & McGurk, Ethel. A group test of perceptual acuity. *Percept. motor skills,* 1967, 24, 1107-1115.

21. Holt, S. B. Inheritance of dermal ridge patterns. In Penrose, L. S. (Ed.) *Recent advances in human genetics.* London: Churchill, 1961.

22. Honzik, M. P. Developmental studies of parent-child resemblance in intelligence. *Child Developm.,* 1957, 28, 215-228.

23. Horn, J. L. Intelligence—why it grows, why it declines. *Trans-action,* Nov., 1967, pages 23-31.

24. Huntley, R. M. C. Heritability of intelligence. In Meade, J. E., and Parkes, A. S. (Eds.), *Genetic and environmental factors in human ability.* New York: Plenum Press, 1966.

25. Ilg, F. L., & Ames, L. B. *School readiness.* New York: Harper and Row, 1964.

26. Jensen, A. R. *Individual differences in learning: Interference factor.* Cooperative Research Project No. 1867, U.S. Office of Education, 1965.

27. Jensen, A. R. Estimation of the limits of heritability of traits by comparison of monozygotic and dizygotic twins. *Proceedings of the National Academy of Sciences,* 1967, 58, 149-157.

28. Jensen, A. R. Social class, race, and genetics: Implications for education. *Amer. Educ. Res. J.,* 1968, 5, 1-42.

29. Jensen, A. R. Patterns of mental ability and socioeconomic status. *Proceedings of the National Academy of Sciences,* 1968, 60, Pp. 1330-1337.

30. Jensen, A. R. Intelligence, learning ability, and socioeconomic status. *Journal of Special Education.* August, 1968.

31. Jensen, A. R., & Rohwer, W. D., Jr. Mental retardation, mental age, and learning rate. *J. educ. Psychol.,* 1968, in press.

32. Jones, H. E. The environment and mental development. In Carmichael, L. (ed.) *Manual of child psychology.* (2nd ed.) New York: Wiley, 1954. Pp. 631-696.

33. Kennedy, W. A., Van De Riet, V., and White, J. C., Jr. A normative sample of intelligence and achievement of Negro elementary school children in the Southeastern United States. *Monogr. Soc. Res. Child Developm.,* 1963, 28, No. 6.

34. Kidd, Aline H., and Rivoire, Jeanne L. The culture-fair aspects of the development of spatial perception. *J. genet. Psychol.,* 1965, 106, 101-111.

35. Lawrence, E. M. An investigation into the relation between intelligence and inheritance. *Brit. J. Psychol. Monogr. Supplmt.,* 1931, 16, No. 5.

36. Leahy, Alice M. Nature-nurture and intelligence. *Genet. Psychol. Monogr.,* 1935, 17, 241-305.

37. Line, W., and Kaplan, E. The existence, measurement and significance of a speed factor in the abilities of public school children. *J. exper. Educ.,* 1932, 1, 1-8.

38. Loehlin, J. C. Psychological genetics, from the study of human behavior. In Cattell, R. B. (Ed.) *Handbook of modern personality theory.* New York: Aldine, in press.

39. Ludlow, H. G. Some recent research on the Davis-Eells Games. *School and Society,* 1956, 84, 146-148.

40. Orr, D. B., and Graham, W. R. Development of a listening comprehension test to identify educational potential among disadvantaged junior high school students. *Amer. educ. Res. J.,* 1968, 5, 167-180.

41. Raven, J. C. *Guide to using Progressive Matrices.* London: Lewis, 1952.

42. Rosenberg, L. A., Rosenberg, Anna M., and Stroud, M. The Johns Hopkins Perceptual Test: The development of a rapid intelligence test for the preschool child. Paper presented at the *Eastern Psychological Association* annual meeting, April, 1966, New York, N. Y.

43. Stanley, J. C., and Porter, A. C. Correlation of Scholastic Aptitude Test score with college grades for Negroes versus Whites. *J. educ. Meas.,* 1967, 4, 199-218.

44. Shuey, Audrey M. *The testing of Negro intelligence.* (2nd ed.) New York: Social Science Press, 1966.

45. Tyler, Leona E. *The psychology of human differences.* (3rd ed.) New York: Appleton-Century-Crofts, 1965.

46. Using speed of brain waves to test I.Q. *Medical World News,* 1968, 9, 26.

47. Vernon, P. E. Environmental handicaps and intellectual development: Part I and Part II. *Brit. J. educ. Psychol.,* 1965, 35, 1-22.

48. Wright, S. Systems of mating. III. Assortative mating based on somatic resemblance. *Genetics,* 1921, 6, 144-161.

49. Young, M., and Gibson, J. B. Social mobility and fertility. In *Biological aspects of social problems,* J. E. Meade and A. S. Parkes (Eds.), Edinburgh: Oliver and Boyd, 1965.

5

THE JENSEN REPORT
REVIEW OF THE PAST, FOCUS FOR THE FUTURE

Frederick G. Brown, Ph.D.

Professor of Psychology, Iowa State University

The Winter 1969 issue of the *Harvard Educational Review* featured a 123-page article by Arthur Jensen (University of California, Berkeley) titled, "How Much Can We Boost IQ and Scholastic Achievement?" The article began with the now oft-quoted statement, "Compensatory education has been tried and it apparently has failed" (p. 2), then discussed the reasons for the apparent failure, particularly emphasizing the question stated in the title.

I cannot remember many articles that have stimulated such intense reaction, both in the psychological and educational literature and in the news media. The next issue of the *Review* (Spring 1969) contained solicited reactions from seven geneticists and behavioral scientists; the subsequent (Summer) issue was devoted almost entirely to reactions to Jensen's article, including another article by Jensen replying to his critics. In addition, articles and comments have appeared in various magazines—e.g., *Time, the New York Times Magazine, Psychology Today,* the *Saturday Review*—and the controversy has received wide coverage by the news media.

Reaction has ranged from complimentary to hostile, from reasoned commentaries to diatribes, from broadscale rebuttals to disagreement with the finer points of Jensen's arguments, from comments on the adequacy of his data and methodology to *ad hominem* attacks. To attempt to summarize these reactions would be impossible; suffice it to say that most have centered on (a) Jensen's statement that compensatory education has been tried and apparently failed; (b) his stress on the genetic determiners of mental ability, and the consequent deemphasis

Reprinted from MEASUREMENT AND EVALUATION IN GUIDANCE: Vol. 3 No. 1 Spring 1970. Copyright 1970, American Personnel and Guidance Association.

of environmental influences; and (c) the implications of his data and conclusions for current social issues, particularly the race problem.

The focus of this article will be limited. Rather than attempting a broad evaluation of Jensen's article and the surrounding controversy, I will consider only its implications for those of us who are concerned with the development, evaluation, and use of tests and other measures of psychological characteristics.

WHAT DID JENSEN SAY?

Because such widely divergent conclusions have been drawn from Jensen's article, it would be well to preface my reactions with a précis of what I think Jensen was saying.

Jensen is concerned with the reasons for the apparent failure of compensatory education programs. He feels that these programs are based on several questionable, though seldom questioned, assumptions. One is the "average child" concept, which is the belief that all children, except those with severe neurological disorders, are basically similar in their capacities and mental development. Consequently, observed differences between children are assumed to reflect primarily differences in their upbringing and early environments. More particularly, children of ethnic minority groups and from lower socioeconomic classes perform at lower levels because they have been deprived of certain crucial early experiences. These assumptions are strongly environmentalistic, emphasizing the malleability of the individual in the wake of his experiences. Jensen questions the validity of these assumptions.

Surveying the extant compensatory education programs he finds little persuasive evidence that other than small and ephemeral changes in IQ are produced by these programs. Gains in achievement and developed skills (e.g., reading ability) seem to be larger and more permanent. Jensen stresses the need to study changes in specific behaviors and skills, rather than relying on global evaluations, and to identify the effective causal agents—those aspects of the program that actually produce the changes. He also questions whether raising IQ is either an obtainable or a desirable goal.

The failure to find significant increases in IQ leads to an extensive discussion of the determiners of mental ability. After surveying various lines of evidence (no single one of which he considers definitive) Jensen is persuaded that the preponderance of the evidence is less consistent with a strictly environmental hypothesis than with a genetic hypothesis. Similar conclusions are reached for both interindividual and intergroup differences in mental ability. In other words, Jensen concludes that differences in mental abilities are primarily a reflection of genetic differences. Thus attempts to raise mental ability or to decrease differences between individuals will be limited by genetic constraints. This conclusion is, of course, antagonistic to the environmentalist views currently held by most behavioral scientists.

A third point that Jensen makes—which has received less attention than his comments on the failure of compensatory education programs and the genetic determinants of ability—is that there are several types of mental abilities. Although he accepts the construct of general intelligence (g) as an empirical fact, he also emphasizes his research, which differentiates associative learning and abstract problem-solving, and Cattell's distinction between fluid and crystallized intelligence. That there are several types of mental abilities implies: (a) that different persons or groups may exhibit different patterns of abilities; (b) that different ability patterns may come into play in various educational and occupational situations; and (c) that different educational methods may be used for students of differing ability.

There is also a hidden agenda in Jensen's article. He refuses to accept some of the common, though perhaps gratuitous, generalizations that are currently fashionable. He is against side-stepping an issue because of its social or political implications. While recognizing that the data pertaining to the issues he discusses are neither complete nor definitive, he is in favor of looking at the available data as objectively as possible and planning future courses of action in light of these data, while continuing to collect more, and hopefully better, data.

Finally, it should be noted that, in spite of the attention he devotes to group differences, Jensen strongly advocates treating each person as an individual. "The variables of social class, race, and national origin are correlated so imperfectly with any of the valid criteria on which [educational or employment] decisions should depend, or, for that matter, with any behavioral characteristic, that these background factors are irrelevant as a basis for dealing with individuals—as students, as employees, as neighbors" (p. 78).

WHAT, THEN, ARE THE IMPLICATIONS?

Let us now turn to the implications of Jensen's article for test development, evaluation, and use. It seems to me that Jensen has not pointed out any problems or issues that thoughtful psychologists and educators have not already been aware of; he has discussed them, however, in both a manner and a context that serve to reemphasize their importance. To discuss these issues one more time may seek like a waste of journal pages, and even like a short course in tests and measurements; yet they are some of the persistent problems of testing, but ones that we too often ignore.

To me, the following implications are worthy of special note.

Test scores are multiply determined

This statement is obviously trite; thus, we often neglect its implications when interpreting test scores. Any test score will be a function of three classes of variables: the individual's genetic makeup, his prior experiences, and the testing conditions. To the extent that test development and standardization minimize variability in testing conditions, scores will reflect the first two classes of variables. The relative influence of the genetic and experiential factors, in turn, will depend on the characteristic tested and the heterogeneity with respect to the other variables. Therefore, for example, when persons having similar backgrounds are tested, genetic factors will play a larger role in producing individual differences than when groups with greater heterogeneity of experience are tested. One interpretation of the high heritability of intelligence in our culture ($h=.80$) is that individuals have been subjected to environments that are more similar than one might suppose. With greater diversity of environments, experiential factors would have a stronger influence on individual differences in mental ability.

As a corollary, a single test score indicates only current status. It indicates the level of performance on the test, not how or why the individual attained this status. Although we often have a body of empirical data that allows us to predict future behavior or performance from test scores, and sometimes even to infer why the score was obtained, these are generally only statements of empirical relations, not cause-and-effect statements.

Test scores must be interpreted with respect to a particular population

All tests are developed and most appropriately utilized within a designated population. For example, the Stanford-Binet was developed and is most appropriately used with English-speaking children in the United States, aged 2-18; the CEEB Scholastic Aptitude Test was developed and is most appropriately used with American high school juniors and seniors who are preparing to enter college. Consequently, the interpretation of scores on any test (within the limits of the available validity and normative data) is limited to members of the designated population. Attributing meaning to scores of other persons is inferential.

This does not mean that a test developed for one population cannot be used with another. It does mean that when the test is used with other populations, it is incumbent on the test user to establish the transferability (Cattell, 1964) of the test scores. Such evidence has sometimes been collected; for example, several studies indicate that although college admissions tests have been developed using primarily middle class white students, scores on these tests also predict the academic performance of black college students. However, the burden of proof of the test's applicability to the new population rests on the test user.

Tests have several functions

A distinction can be made between two broad functions of tests: (a) as measures of psychological traits and characteristics; and (b) as aids in decision-making. In the latter case, we are interested in the information the test provides that can be used to make a decision regarding some practical problem; we are concerned with criterion-related validity, with the test as a predictor. In the former case, we are concerned with the trait the test measures and the variables that determine the test score. Here the appropriate measure of validity is construct validity.

Jensen is more concerned with tests as measures of basic mental abilities, particularly intelligence. The difficulty arises, not when he defines intelligence operationally as a cluster of inter-correlated behaviors (as he clearly does when discussing *g*), but from the fact that people attribute a "reality" to the construct of intelligence over and above its summarizing function as an intervening variable. That is, while the term "intelligence" may be neutral to the tester it is value-laden for most persons. Thus they react to statements about an individual's intelligence as implying something about the individual's worth as a person, rather than as a description of his developed skills in the domain of mental ability.

One must also remember that in any situation or behavioral domain many possible behaviors might be measured. The test developer selects those skills, behaviors, or characteristics which appear most relevant and important in light of his purposes, and then builds a test to measure these dimensions. (For example, intelligence tests were originally developed to measure those characteristics which identified children who would have trouble learning in the classroom situation.) Nothing in the procedure implies that these are the only important characteristics that an individual might possess. Neither, however, should the fact that a test measures only a limited range of characteristics denigrate the value of the test.

Mental abilities are plural

Although "general mental ability" is a useful concept (see McNemar, 1964), the evidence clearly shows that there are numeous mental abilities. Jensen discusses two categorizations: his distinction between associative learning and abstract problem-solving and Cattell's (1963) distinction between fluid and crystallized intelligence. He mentions that even finer categorizations can be made, an obvious fact to anyone familiar with factor-analytic studies of abilities (e.g., Guilford, 1967).

One implication of the diversity of abilities is that the psychologist's armamentarium of tests must be large if he is to measure any variety of human abilities. Although new types of tests appear on the market— multiple-aptitude batteries, Guilford's tests for his structure-of-intellect model, measures of creativity, tests of cognitive styles—there are still many gaps in the testing arsenal. Although, as Buros has repeatedly stated, in many areas we need fewer but better tests, there are other areas where no acceptable tests are currently available.

Of more importance, however, is the fact that individuals possessing different patterns of ability may learn better under different conditions or perform better in different jobs. Testers and educators have too long accepted what Gough has aptly called the idea of "one true path to grace." That is, while paying lip-service to the idea of individualized instruction, we have continued to subject every child in a class to the same educational process. Not surprisingly, some learn and others do not. While computers provide the technology to adapt instruction to individuals (Glaser, 1968), we need more research to provide a firmer foundation for the assignment of individuals to instructional treatments (Cronbach, 1967; Wittrock, 1969).

Are our models adequate?

Another important issue implicit in Jensen's article is the adequacy of our present models for conceptualizing test scores. One example is Jensen's "threshold" approach to the role of environmental experiences. The prevailing view assumes that if a given amount of stimulation produces a certain change in behavior or test scores, then a greater amount of the same stimulus will produce a larger change. Jensen questions this view, suggesting that the crucial factor may be whether or not the person has been exposed to the threshold level of stimulation. Thus, while enriched environments may raise the IQ's or achievement levels of severely deprived children (those who have not experienced even the minimal necessary level of stimulation), enriching the environment will not have a significant effect on the performance of persons who have been exposed to the threshold level, even if their experiences have been somewhat limited.

A second question was touched on by Jensen but emphasized by many of his critics. This is whether certain experiences or educational procedures will (or should) have the effect of increasing differences between individuals or of raising everyone to a desired level of performance or proficiency, thereby reducing individual differences. The testing analog is norm-referenced and criterion-referenced scores (Glaser, 1963), norm-referenced scores being those which compare an individual to other persons, criterion-referenced scores being those which compare the individual to an external standard. The relevance for test developers and curriculum evaluators is that tests designed to measure criterion-referenced standards must meet different technical requirements than those developed to measure individual differences (Popham & Husek, 1969). For example, our usual measures of reliability and item discrimination become meaningless when every person obtains the same score on a test.

Jensen also points out the distinction between scores of groups and those of individuals. Of necessity, all item statistics, reliability and validity data, and normative information are based on the performance of groups. When studying differences between designated groups, or when evaluating the validity of a test as a selection or classification instrument, such statistics suffice. When we interpret the scores of an individual, however, we must jump from group data to the individual case, a procedure that has no logical rules to follow. To know that a college admissions test is 95 percent accurate in identifying which students will succeed at Midwest College may be valuable information for the admissions office; it is not so comforting to the 5 percent of the students who are misclassified.

THE CONSEQUENCES OF TESTING

The previous section focused on some of the implications of Jensen's article for the development, evaluation, and interpretation of test scores. While these points are open to disagreement and debate, for the most part they are issues that can be solved by the accumulation of empirical evidence and rational discussion of alternative methods and models.

But much of the controversy surrounding Jensen's article concerns not the data per se, but the potential social and political consequences of his data and conclusions. To report that there are differences in the mental abilities of various groups, or that genetic constraints may limit our attempts to improve the skills of some individuals, is to make not mere statements of empirical facts but statements having social and political consequences.

The implications for testing are obvious. No longer can we use tests without carefully considering their effects on the individuals and institutions concerned. This, of course, is not a simple task, particularly in a pluralistic society such as ours. That college admissions tests predict the academic success of black students as well as white students may imply to some persons that blacks who score low do not have the potential to do acceptable college work and thus should be denied admission. To other persons the same data may indicate that colleges are not doing an effective job of teaching students but are only selecting winners (Astin, 1969). Furthermore, neither alternative necessarily implies that any college should admit any student. It does imply that colleges should spend more effort in clarifying their goals and priorities.

Testers should also be constantly reviewing their goals and priorities and the possible effects of their tests on the persons concerned. In the past decade a number of studies have been concerned with the social implications of testing (Ebel, 1964; Fishman, et al., 1964; Goslin, 1963; Rosenthal & Jacobson, 1968; Schwebel, 1968). In fact, looking at the history of testing, the present period is probably best characterized as one of concern over the social implications of testing. That further study is needed of the uses and misuses of tests and their values and limitations should go without saying. Hopefully, too, these studies will be balanced and objective and made by persons both knowledgeable about testing and aware of the social context in which tests are used.

Finally, I cannot agree with those critics of Jensen who seem to imply that because his article may be misinterpreted, or used in support of certain causes, it should not have been published. To me, publication of the article, and the open airing of the surrounding controversy, will be beneficial to both those concerned with testing and those interested in compensatory education. My hope for those of us interested in testing is that we will rearrange our priorities so that we spend less time and effort on topics such as esoteric refinements of reliability theory and more time considering the impact of testing on our society and its individual members.

REFERENCES

Astin, A. W. Folklore of selectivity. *Saturday Review,* December 20, 1969. P. 57.

Cattell, R. B. Theory of fluid and crystallized intelligence: a critical experiment. *Journal of Educational Psychology,* 1963, 54, 1-22.

Cattell, R. B. Validity and reliability: a proposed more basic set of concepts. *Journal of Educational Psychology,* 1964, 55, 1-22.

Cronbach, L. J. How can instruction be adapted to individual differences? In R. M. Gagné (Ed.), *Learning and individual differences.* Columbus, Ohio: Charles E. Merrill, 1967. Pp. 23-39.

Ebel, R. L. The social consequences of educational testing. Proceedings of the 1963 Invitational Conference on Testing Problems. Princeton, N. J.: Educational Testing Service, 1964. Pp. 130-143.

Fishman, J. A., Deutsch, M., Kogan, L., North, R., & Whiteman, M. Guidelines for testing minority group children. *Journal of Social Issues,* 1964, 20, 127-145.

Glaser, R. Instructional technology and the measurement of learning outcomes: some questions. *American Psychologist,* 1963, 18, 519-521.

Glaser, R. Adapting the elementary school curriculum to individual performance. Proceedings of the 1967 Invitational Conference on Testing Problems. Princeton, N. J.: Educational Testing Service, 1968.

Goslin, D. A. *The search for ability: standardized testing in social perspective.* New York: Russell Sage Foundation, 1963.

Guilford, J. P. *The nature of human intelligence.* New York: McGraw-Hill, 1967.

Jensen, A. R. How much can we boost IQ and scholastic achievement? *Harvard Educational Review,* 1969, 39, 1-123.

McNemar, Q. Lost: our intelligence. Why? *American Psychologist,* 1964, 19, 871-882.

POPHAM, W. J., & HUSEK, T. R. Implications of criterion-referenced measurement. *Journal of Educational Measurement,* 1969, 6, 1-9.

ROSENTHAL, R., & JACOBSON, L. *Pygmalion in the classroom.* New York: Holt, Rinehart & Winston, 1968.

SCHWEBEL, M. *Who can be educated?* New York: Grove Press, 1968.

WITTROCK, M. C. *The evaluation of instruction: cause and effect relations in naturalistic data.* Los Angeles: Center for the Study of Evaluation, University of California. 1969.

6

PROBLEMS AND PROSPECTS OF GENETIC ANALYSIS OF INTELLIGENCE AT THE INTRA- AND INTERRACIAL LEVEL

Luigi L. Cavalli-Sforza, M.D.

Visiting Professor, Genetics Department
School of Medicine, Stanford University,
on leave from Instituto di Genetica
Universita di Pavia, Italy

Genetic analysis has proved extremely constructive in many ways, but only or mostly when situations investigated involved only one or two gene differences, and the environmental effects in creating variation between individuals were well under control. Neither condition applies, as far as we know today, to the study of intelligence. A polygenic character, namely one which is affected by many genes, especially if it is subject to environmental influence, is difficult to study genetically at the intra-racial level. It is even worse at the interracial level.

RACIAL DIFFERENCES IN MAN

It may be worth summarising very briefly what we know about racial differences in general, concerning the human species. We know that the paleontological record does not offer any clear evidence of racial differentiation (see e.g. Le Gros Clark). Races may differ in the flesh, but they do not differ enough in the bones, which are the objects of paleontological study. On the other hand, there are differences between humans who live in different parts of the world, which have prompted the distinction into "races." Groupings in races are largely arbitrary; there is no unequivocal biological category, the "race." There is no unambiguous and simple criteria that can help us to establish which groups should be considered as forming, or not forming different races. One can, however, measure differences between groups. This will permit us to establish hierarchies of differences, in the sense that some groups will

111

be more different than others. Which minimum level of difference should be considered as "racial" is largely arbitrary.

An important problem is that of the sources of the differences that we observe between races. It would be difficult to discuss this problem here, except for saying that differentiation is likely to be in part random, and therefore essentially non-adaptive, and in part due to adaptation to different environments. At least relative isolation is usually a prerequisite for the development of the differences. It should be kept in mind that genetic adaptation, the consequence of natural selection, takes a very long time to evolve. It should not be confused with the short term adaptation, or generally with the environmental effects which have only short term duration, and would be reversible over a very short time, usually one generation.

Thus, for genetic study of race formation, it is essential to confine attention to characters which are known to be reasonably free from short range environmental effects. An analysis of racial differentiation in man has been recently carried out, using characters most suitable to this aim. The best characters are those for which evidence is available that they are due to single gene differences. The requirement is to be able to tell, from the *phenotypes*—that is what we see and measure on the individual—the *genotypes*, or their inherited constitution. These characters, the inheritance of which is well-known, are commonly called *genetic markers* (blood groups, plasma and red cells proteins and enzymes, etc.). There are several for which there is today sufficient information in man to be able to measure racial differences on their basis. An analysis of these differences has led to a construction of the probable history of racial divergence in man (Edwards and Cavalli-Sforza, Cavalli-Sforza and Edwards). The major groups that can be thus differentiated are Africans, Indo-Europeans or Caucasoids (indicating by this name all Caucasoids whether living in Europe or not) and a heterogenous group called Easterners, comprising all aboriginal population which live in the Pacific area and including Mongolians, American Indians, Australians and Melanesians. Without going into the details of the analysis, the main result can be indicated by a triangle (see opposite page) in which Indo-Europeans are roughly intermediate between the other two. The scale in which the difference between racial group is indicated in the figure is a scale of gene substitution. If the divergence has proceeded to completion, this quantity would be one. The averages of thirteen genes with a total of thirty-eight alleles on which the figures are based indicate that the differences accumulated are relatively small.

This may be surprising at first, because the racial differences which we are used to consider may seem larger. Some are, in fact, larger. For instance we know, for skin color, that there are probably at least four gene differences determining the divergence between the extremes of

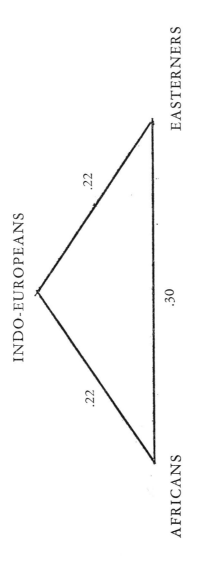

skin pigmentation (Harrison et al.). This character, like any other character the genetics of which is not precisely known, has not been included in the analysis. I believe this is not likely to produce a serious bias. One should keep in mind that we are used to considering racial differences on the basis of what we see. We usually base our everyday criteria for classifying the race of a person on characters such as the pigmentation of skin, hair and eye, hair texture and distribution, facial traits, and body build. Often we also use, subconsciously, other criteria such as clothes, hair dressing, etc. which are hardly genetic. Practically all traditional classifications of races are based on superficial characters, and it is not entirely surprising that these more conspicuous differences are also the larger ones. All of these characters are subject to fairly intense selection, some of which is adaptive, and some of which is not (as, for instance, sexual selection). For instance, it is not surprising that the skin is the tissue which shows perhaps the greatest variation among races and was thus made a basis for racial classification. In an almost hairless organism, living in extremely different conditions, such as man, skin color is likely to be subject to strong selection differentials in various environments. It may, therefore, show a relatively fast adaptation, still requiring, however, a time which might be guessed to be of the order of five or ten thousand years at least to develop some of the extreme differences. Even skin color, however, like any other trait which is consciously or subconsciously detected through our senses, may be affected also by sexual selection. This type of selection is likely to be as erratic and unpredictable as fashions are, and probably largely non-adaptive. It will thus contribute, in a way, to the "random" component of differentiation.

The characters which we have used in the analysis of racial differences are probably less subject, on the average, to such extreme selection differentials, and therefore, show a smaller variation. They were not selected on this basis, however, but merely upon that of a clear-cut Mendelian behavior. This choice makes them more useful for deepening the kinetic analysis of the process, a point on which, again, it would be impossible to give any detail here.

It is, however, of interest to consider the possible time of separation between the various branches of humanity. Using as a yardstick the separation between American Indians and other Easterners, which can be dated at about 15,000 years, it would seem that the earliest split, which is probably that between Africans on on side, Easterners and Indoeuropeans on the other, may have occurred some 50,000 years ago. On making this estimate we use the assumption that, averaging over all genes, the rate of evolution is constant in the various branches. We also use some other assumptions concerning the evolutionary model. Various hypotheses would alter this estimate which must be considered as highly preliminary; a probable range of 25,000 to 100,000 years is indicated (L. Cavalli-Sforza, 1969).

This is a fairly small fraction of the total time available for evolution of our genus, Homo. Some people like to give it a start with our nearer ancestors and therefore at half a million years ago. Some people prefer to extend our genus to the toolmaking hunters of Olduvai gorge which are dated to 1.75 million years ago. Just to give some further ideas of evolutionary rates, the time of separation between us and the nearest primates, the anthropoid apes is of the order of over 10 million years ago.

Naturally, even during such a relatively small separation as that between the main racial groups, even large differences could have been produced for at least some traits (as must have happened for skin color) if there is a very strong difference in selection pressures in various parts of the area inhabited by the species. But there is no reason that we know to assume such a difference in selection pressure in the different branches of humanity regarding other traits, such as in particular intelligence.

INHERITANCE OF INTELLIGENCE

We can measure, today, the mean phenotype of intelligence in ways that seem, to some, entirely satisfactory, and to others more superficial and vague. One may thus find differences between races. How this measurement depends on the cultural background is a difficult problem, but there is evidence to show that tests are sensitive even to the skin color of the interviewer (see Pettigrew). As a geneticist, I am certain that even if tests could be considered as fair, they still could not be independent of the environment of growth, as long as there are cultural, social, biological differences. My persuasion, as every experimental geneticist could confirm, depends on the number of examples in experimental organisms that show how the environment can affect *any* phenotype. It is a very exacting task in the laboratory to obtain perfectly controlld environments that can be used to obtain reproducible phenotypes, especially for polygenic characters.

Heritability measurements have been introduced, which try to overcome this difficulty by measuring the relative importance of variation in genetic, and in environmental differences between individuals. A classification of the possible ways in which the environment can act will help to understand the limits of this approach.

Differences due to the environment can be found at many different levels:

1. At the level of the family.—Different children of the same parents are inevitably subject to different environmental conditions. Parental age, birth order, different teachers, friends, etc., and

simply the fact that different children are different individuals create these conditions.

2. Different families, even if they belong to the same socio-economic layer, offer inevitably different environments for development.

3. Differences between socio-economic strata are certainly very important in creating differences of educational opportunities, motivation and number of other factors which can deeply affect intelligence.

4. Differences in culture, when one considers the variety of human cultures in existence, must be the most important factor of them all.

Usual heritability measurements based on twins are sensitive only to environmental variation of type 1, and even that in a biased way. Moreover, they will relate to the environmental differences that exist today, for the particular population examined, and might change considerably in the future or in other places. Thus, they form a very incomplete measurement of environmental effects. When twins reared apart can be examined, there is some chance of measuring some of the effects of levels 2 or 3. But this category of twins is very rare and thus only large effects can be found to be statistically significant in this material. Standard errors of the observed correlation coefficients are high. Also, the cases considered are not likely to be unbiased. To make the effects of separation fully meaningful, this should occur at birth, for random twins and with random allocation. The actual observations are probably very far from the conditions which would be desirable for making the data entirely unbiased.

Correlations on relatives other than twins might help to understand more on levels 2 and 3. This analysis is difficult even in experimental organisms and more so in an organism like man. The existence of large genotype-environment interactions contributes to obscure the picture. Another consideration is that heritability measurements are somewhat arbitrary and can be given in a number of different ways. They were originally introduced to help breeders to predict expected gains in artificial selection. To this aim, what is usually called "genetic variance" is broken down into various parts, e.g.: that due to additive effect of single genes; that due to non-additive effects of genes (epistacy); that due to dominance; that due to non-random mating. It is only when these are cumulated together, that the impressive figure of almost 90% genetic variance for intelligence is obtained (Burt, 1956). But the fraction that could be fixed in a selection experiment or in evolutionary divergence could be much smaller, and is given by the additive variance, plus perhaps an unknown fraction of epistacy. The fraction of genetic variance for intelligence, computed in this way, is less striking and might be less than 50% from the same data. These estimates take into account, without analyzing it and probably in part confounded with other sources of variation, only the environmental variance of levels 1 to 3, but there is no study which includes level 4. Finally, all conclusions are essentially limited to Caucasoids.

Ways of considering the other levels might also use studies of foster children. These are rare. They show effects, but they are usually far from being unbiased, because of the social factors involved in the selection and assignment of foster children to their foster parents.

EFFECTS OF ENVIRONMENT ON INTELLIGENCE

The best one can say is that we know very little of the effects of environment in the development of intelligence, and that it is likely to be important, certainly more important than is detectable by studies of inheritance in twins alone. There are also many factors other than intelligence as measured by intelligence tests which affect social performance and are not perhaps revealed directly in this way, and are likely to be even more largely determined by the environment.

In the poverty of direct evidence it may be useful to extrapolate, in order to consider what might be the effects of environment on human intelligence.

It is worth citing a classical example of an experimental study of a performance which is usually referred to intelligence, namely maze behavior in rats. It was possible, by a long selection experiment, to develop lines that were very fast and made few mistakes ("bright"), and lines that were slow and made more mistakes ("dull"). Still, growing these two lines in different living conditions, in particular in what could be described as a "poor" living environment, the phenotypic difference between them disappeared (Cooper and Zubek).

The extrapolation from rat to man may seem unsatisfactory. There is another extrapolation which can be effected in man, using a polygenic trait which has approximately the same heritability as intelligence: stature. This character has shown, in the last 70 to 100 years, a very remarkable increase, for reasons that are still very poorly understood. The increasre observed in this period is of the order of one standard deviation. Very little of this can be hereditary.

It is worth noting that there is here a common fallacy: some workers (Tanner, Hulse) have accepted the fact that the progeny of consanguineous marriage is smaller (as shown incidentally by only some populations) as evidence of heterosis, a known genetic effect which is the equivalent of hybrid vigor. A criticism of this conclusion is given e.g. by Morton. When noted, the consanguinity effect is so large that it must have (as is well ascertained in some instances), a socio-economic origin. It is probable that similar criticisms apply to the relationship of parental consanguinity and intelligence.

Effects of socio-economic differentials are well known for stature and they are large. In addition, it is known that there is a strong negative correlation between family size and stature. If taller people tend to have fewer children, stature, being so highly heritable, should decrease. Instead, it increases at a very fast rate. This paradox cannot easily be resolved unless we accept the fact that the character is strongly affected by the environment, in spite of its apparently high heritability. The fact is that heritability measurements do not take into account secular changes in the environment or some special types of environment differentials which may be of the greatest importance.

Extrapolations of this kind do not supply direct information, but certainly warn us to be very cautious in this field. There is moreover some direct evidence that the environment can be of importance in determining intelligence. Leaving aside recent findings on nutrition and intrauterine decompression, which may require confirmation, it is worth commenting on one clearcut environmental effect: the difference between twins and non-twins. Twins have, on the average, a lower IQ than non-twins, irrespective of whether they are identical or fraternal (Zazzo). The difference is marked, and above one-third of a standard deviation. The origin of the difference can hardly be genetic; the twinning process is itself believed to be largely nongenetic. The effect is probably due to a poorer nutrition or other biological effects of the intrauterine development of twins. It might also be due to the decreased care which children can get from their parents when there are two of them instead of one of the same age. This would be in agreement with the observation that the mean IQ decreases so markedly with increasing sibship size.

If we are asked the question: *are the differences in intelligence which can be observed in races inherited, or due to short-term environment effects?,* the answer is, in my opinion, we do not and cannot easily know. If we have to express a guess, we would think that if they are inherited, they must be so only to a limited extent. The basis of this persuasion is that biological evolution is very slow, while cultural evolution, which can produce important but also rapidly reversible effects, is fast. Many of the behavioral differences that we note between races could well be and perhaps are entirely due to differences in the cultural background and socio-conomic position. The experiment that would be necessary to test it, namely to grow children of different races in closely similar environments, is practically impossible, especially now that there is such a deep emotional involvement with problems of skin color. In our environment, the factors which might affect the results would be difficult to eliminate entirely from any experiment of this kind, at least with our present social setup. Th ethical sides of such an experiment are also open to question.

SOCIAL CONSEQUENCES OF THE SCIENTIFIC CONCLUSIONS

It seems very difficult to give a fair answer to all questions regarding behavioral traits of different races. Naturally, one should carefully distinguish the scientific problems and the social ones. Inevitably, the social planners may be influenced by the scientific conclusions. At the moment, scientific data on the genetic basis of behavioral differences between "races" are non-existent, and very difficult to get, in my opinion.

Is this conclusion fully useless for the social planner and the educator? I do not think so. Recent reports, presumably unbiased, find a phenotypic difference in intelligence between white and non-white, especially black, American children of school age which is of the order of one standard deviation. If this difference is not or is only to a small part heritable, this means that in order to close the existing gap, a greater effort and larger amount of money should be proportionately spent for the education of the handicapped fraction. But the results cannot be satisfactory if a major effort will not be put into all the aspects of social and cultural life which can deeply affect motivation. Also if the difference is fully or highly heritable, more money should be spent, anyhow, to decrease the gap. The main difference in the social consequences of the two hypotheses is that in the first case, this money will be spent only once; over a finite and not too long period of time, say of the order of one or two generations, the gap may be permanently closed or modified. In the second case, the higher expense would have to continue also in the later generations in order to keep the gap closed or small.

The people of the United States are of many different origins, and various groups showed widely different lags before they participated fully in the American way of life. Immigrants from poorer areas inevitably showed a longer lag, which seems to have lasted in many cases, on the average, for more than one generation. Among all of them, black Americans had by far the worst start. Freedom from slavery, which took place only some three generations ago, could not, and certainly was not, followed by immediate socioeconomic upgrading. Instead, the first period after slavery was marked, among other things, by a complete disruption of the family pattern, (Franzier) which has perhaps not even now been completely repaired. It is possible, and even likely, that the first years of life, when school has not started and only or mostly the family environment counts, are of great importance in establishing the pattern of reaction of children when they will later be exposed to schooling. If this is true, it is probable that, because of their present social structure, black children are still put at a great handicap by the insufficient instruction and stimulation which they receive in their preschool years. This will add up to difficulties due to interaction with the rest of society. Such a situation may considerably increase the time necessary to close the gap, unless measures are taken to favor the process of effective equalization of opportunities.

The problem raised by the recognition of a difference in IQ between layers of different ethnic origins is of enormous social importance. It will require a considerable investment in research, and in education and social relief of the handicapped faction. There seems to be no other way of solving a problem, which might undermine the basis of the present society.

By contrast, the scientific problem itself seems of dubious validity, if one considers how great are the difficulties of dissecting environmental and genetic causes of the difference, at least on the basis of present knowledge and techniques.

FUTURE PROSPECTS IN THE INVESTIGATION OF INTELLIGENCE

Are future prospects of investigation in this general area of the genetics of intelligence as dim as they seem at present? I can see some ways of improvement.

Genetics can give an important contribution to the understanding of intelligence if its possibilities of analysis are fully exploited. To this aim one important avenue of research is that of isolating individual genes affecting the character. This is possible today, but the experimentation required is heavy. The method is that of using linkage with known genetic differences such as blood groups and any of the inherited biochemical differences known in man (the usual genetic markers). If two genes, one of which is a marker and the other is one of the many that can affect intelligence, are on the same chromosome, they will be more often than not transmitted together to the progeny. This is genetic *linkage,* and it offers a possibility of dissecting the total genetic variation into its individual components. Moreover, traits that are of uncertain inheritance could thus be tested for heritability in a foolproof way. Should clearcut genetic differences in intelligence or other behavioral traits be isolated by the way of linkage with standard markers, they could be further studied at the physiological and biochemical level, with confidence that some interesting correlation could be found. The approach has been tested very successfully in experimental animals (Thoday). The statistical machinery necessary for the study in man has been created (Jayakar). The difficulty is that the successful detection of linkage would require large scale observations. At least several thousand children would have to be examined. The program should be the following: pairs of sibs should be examined for intelligence (and/or any other quantitative character, behavioral physiological trait, etc.) and their blood tested in the laboratory for as many useful markers as possible. Their parents need not be examined for the same behavioral trait, but it would greatly increase the efficiency if their blood could be examined also for the same markers. The analysis would then be based on the resemblance for the traits between the sibs who received from their parents certain markers. To increase efficiency, it would be convenient to choose large families, and in particular those in which parents have certain combinations of markers.

This would be a very ambitious project, and not an easy one to carry out. It could be very usefully applied, also, in interracial marriages.

Another type of investigation which might throw light on the potentials of education and therefore, indirectly, on environmental influences on intelligence, which would be of great interest for education, is that of using identical twins for testing educational procedures. We are still largely unaware of possible sensitive periods in education; of the relative efficacy of different teaching methods; of individual differences in educability and in response to different methods. Identical twins can offer an ideal material, in that they are easy to find, they are not too rare, and they are really identical in genotype. Any differences observed between members of an identical pair can be ascribed to the environment and, therefore, could be taken as indicators of the experimental difference. Naturally, there may be variations in the genotypes in various twin pairs, creating variation in the differential response of each pair. Observations carried out on a single twin pair would already be valuable, but they cannot be generalized if they are not repeated on a sufficient number of pairs. Whenever there are new teaching methods to be tested against the old, I would suggest that a new method be tested on one member of an identical pair and the old traditional method be administered to the other. This kind of experimentation should well be acceptable on an ethical basis, as long as it is not imposed but suggested, and voluntarily accepted by the twins and their parents. If it demands separation of the twins for a period, it could be encouraged by scholarships. The surveillance of a psychologist would help in preventing possible trauma due to the separation and differential treatment.

Experimentation like this can considerably improve the value of information obtained from twins. Nature has provided us with a splendid chance for genetic study by producing identical twins. But the value of the experiment is greatly reduced by the possible formation of a more similar environment around identical twins. This is a consequence of their overall similarity and perhaps their desire to resemble each other. Identical twins are happier at being twins than unidentical ones (Conterio and Chiarelli), and this may affect their tendency to be like each other. Even parents aid identical twins to resemble each other more closely. This has prompted a well-known geneticist, L. S. Penrose, to warn against the possible dangers of conclusions based on uncritical use of twin comparisons. He noted, in fact, that if resemblance between identical twins were taken too literally, one might conclude that clothes are an inherited character, because parents of identical children clothe them more often alike than those of non-identical ones.

Even so, the method of twins remains one of the best tools we have to test the power of inheritance. But its limitations should be appreciated and its potential expanded.

SUMMARY

Interracial differences in intellectual performance have been found in American school children and have prompted the question whether differences are genetic or environmental in nature. A review of present knowledge on interracial divergence in man makes it unlikely that a difference as large as the observed one is genetic. The difficulties in the analysis of a polygenic character like I.Q. or related measurements, subject to mostly unknown environmental influences that may affect intellectual development—among which are early biological and psychological, as well as motivational factors—make conclusions on the basis of present knowledge unwarranted. In any case, such conclusions could hardly affect the obvious necessity of trying all known means to close the gap, and of looking for more efficient procedures to reach this aim.

Some possibilities of sharpening methods of genetic analysis, by linkage of polygenic traits with standard markers, and by experiments in education on identical twins, are mentioned and briefly discussed.

REFERENCES

BURT C. The Inheritance of Mental Ability, *American Psychologist* 1958, 13: 1-15.

CAVALLI-SFORZA L. L. and EDWARDS, A. W. F. Analysis of Human Evolution, Genetics Today Proc. of The XI Inter. Congress of Genetics, The Hague, 1963, 3: 923-933.

CAVALLI-SFORZA, L. L. Human Diversity, XII Intern. Congress of Genetics, Tokyo, 1968 (in press).

COLEMAN, J. S. et al. Equality of Educational Opportunity, National Center for Educational Statistics, U.S. Dept. of Health, Education and Welfare (Washington) 1966, 737 p.

CONTERIO, F. and CHIARELLI B. Study on the Inheritance of Some Daily Life Habits, *Heredity*, 1962, 17: 347-359.

COOPER, R. M. and ZUBEK, J. M. Effects of Enriched and Constricted Early Environments on the Learning Ability of Bright and Dull Rats, *Cand. J. Psychol.*, 1958, 12: 159-164.

EDWARDS, A. W. F. and CAVALLI-SFORZA, L. L. Reconstruction of Evolutionary Trees, *Systematic Association Publication* 1964, 6, Phenetic and Phylogenetic Class., 67-76.

HARRISON, AINSWORTH G. and OWEN, J. J. T. Studies on the Inheritance of Human Skin Color, *Ann. Hum. Genet.* 1964, 28: 27-37.

HULSE, F. S. The Breakdown of Isolates and Hybrid Vigor Among the Italian Swiss, Proceed. of the XII Inter. Congress of Genetics, Tokyo, 1968 (in press).

JAYAKAR, S. D. On the Detection and Estimation of Linkage Between a Locus Influencing a Quantitative Character and a Marker Locus (in press).

LEGROS, CLARK W. E. The Fossil Evidence for Human Evolution, The Univ. of Chicago Press (Ed. 2), 1964.

MORTON, N. E., YASUDA, N., MIKI, C., and YEE, S. Population Structure of the ABO Blood Groups in Switzerland, *Am. J. of Human Genetics* 1968, 20, 5: 420-429.

PETTIGREW, T. F. Race, Mental Illness, and Intelligence: A Social Psychological View, *Eugenics Quart.*, 1964, 11, 1: 189-215.

TANNER, J. M. Earlier Maturation in Man, *Scientific American* 1968, 218: 21.

THODAY, J. M. New Insights into Continuous Variation, Proceed. of the 111 Inter. Congress of Human Genetics 1966, 339-350.

ZAZZO, R. Les Jumeaux, le Couple et la Personne. 2 Vols. Paris: Presses Universitaires de France, 1960.

7

CAN WE AND SHOULD WE STUDY RACE DIFFERENCES?

Arthur R. Jensen, Ph.D.

Professor, School of Education
University of California, Berkeley

Most persons experience some difficulty in discussing the topic of race differences in intelligence—a difficulty over and above that which is ordinarily inherent in the scientific study of any complex phenomenon. There is an understandable reluctance to come to grips with the problem, to come to grips with it, that is to say, in the same straightforward way that we would try to approach the investigation of any other problems in the behavioral sciences. This reluctance is manifested in a variety of "symptoms" found in most writings and discussions of the psychology of race differences, particularly differences in mental ability: a tendency to remain on the remotest fringes of the subject, to sidestep central questions; to blur the issues and tolerate a degree of vagueness in definitions, concepts, and inferences that would be unseemly in any other realm of scientific discourse; to express an unwarranted degree of skepticism about reasonably well established quantitative methods and measurements; to deny or belittle already generally accepted facts— accepted, that is, when brought to bear on inferences outside the realm of race differences; to demand practically impossible criteria of certainty before even seriously proposing or investigating genetic hypotheses, as contrasted with extremely uncritical attitudes toward purely environmental hypotheses; a failure to distinguish clearly between scientifically answerable aspects of the question and the moral, political, and social policy issues; a tendency to beat dead horses and to set up straw men on what is represented as the genetic side of the argument; appeals to the notion that the topic is either really too unimportant to be worthy of scientific curiosity or too complex, or too difficult, or even forever impossible for any kind of research to be feasible, or that answers to key questions are fundamentally "unknowable" in any scientifically acceptable sense; and, finally, the complete denial of intelligence and race as realities, or as quantifiable attributes, or as variables capable of being related to one another, thereby dismissing the subject altogether.

These tendencies will be increasingly overcome the more widely and openly the subject is discussed among scientists and scholars. As some of the taboos against the public discussion of the topic fall away, the issues will become clarified on a rational basis, we will come to know better just what we do and do not yet know about the subject, and we will be in a better position to deal with it objectively and constructively.

IS INTELLIGENCE AN ATTRIBUTE?

Intelligence is an attribute of persons. Probably for as long as man has been on earth it has been a common observation that persons differ in brightness, in speed of learning, in ability to solve problems, and so on. Parents, teachers, and employers are able roughly to rank children and adults in terms of a subjective impression of brightness or capability, and there is a fairly high agreement among different observers in the rank order they assign in the same groups of children. It is helpful to think of the subjective perception of intelligence as analogous to the subjective perception of temperatures, which is also an attribute. Before the invention of the thermometer, temperature was a matter of subjective judgment. The invention of the thermometer made it possible to objectify the attribute of temperature, to quantify it, and to measure it with a high degree of reliability. With some important qualifications, the situation is similar in the case of intelligence tests. The most essential difference is that intelligence, unlike temperature, is multidimensional rather than unidimensional. That is to say, there are different varieties of intelligence, so that persons do not maintain the same rank order of ability in every situation or test that we may regard as indicative of intelligence. It so happens that from among the total spectrum of human behaviors that can be regarded as indicative of some kind of "mental ability" in the broadest sense, we have focused on one part of this spectrum in our psychological concept of intelligence. We have emphasized the abilities characterized as conceptual learning, abstract or symbolic reasoning, and abstract or verbal problem solving. These abilities were most emphasized in the composition of intelligence tests because these were the abilities most relevant to the traditional school curriculum and the first practical intelligence tests were devised to predict scholastic performance. They naturally had a good deal in common with the tests devised for scholastic prediction, since the educational system is intimately related to the occupational demands of a given society. Much the same abilities and skills that are important in schooling, therefore, are important also occupationally. Thus, we find that in industrialized countries practically all intelligence tests, scholastic aptitude tests, military classification tests, vocational aptitude tests, and the like, are quite similar in composition and that the scores obtained on them are all quite substantially intercorrelated. In short, there is a large general factor, or *g*, which the tests share in common and which principally accounts for the variance among individuals. When tests are devised to measure this *g* factor as purely as possible (i.e. in a factor analysis including a host of other tests it will have nearly all of its variance loaded on the general factor common to all the other tests and have little or no variance loaded on factors found only in certain tests [group factors]), examination of their item content leads to the characterization of it as requiring an ability for abstract reasoning and problem solving. Raven's Progressive Matrices Test is an example of such a test. Tests having quite diverse forms can have equally high loadings on the *g* factor—for example, the verbal similarities and block design tests of the Wechsler Intelligence Scales are both highly loaded on *g*. Tests of *g* can be relatively high or relatively low in degree of "culture fairness." (The question "In what way are a wheel and a penny alike?" is probably more culture fair than the question "In what way are an oboe and a bassoon alike?") In short, it is possible to assess essentially the same intelligence by a great variety of means.

Standard IQ tests measure the kinds of behavior in abstract and verbal problem situations that we call abstract reasoning ability. These tests measure more of *g*—the factor common to various forms of intelligence tests—than of any of the other more special ability factors, such as verbal fluency, spatial-perceptual ability, sensory abilities, or mechanical, musical, or artistic abilities, or what might be called social judgment or sensitivity. But a test that measured everything at once would not be very useful. IQ tests do reliably measure one important, though limited, aspect of human performance. The IQ qualifies as an appropriate datum for scientific study. If we are to study intelligence, we are ahead if we can measure it. Our measure is the IQ, obtained on tests which meet certain standards, one of which is a high *g* loading when factor analyzed among other tests. To object to this procedure by arguing that the IQ cannot be regarded as being interchangeable with intelligence, or that intelligence cannot really be measured, or that IQ is not the same as intelligence, is to get bogged down in a semantic morass. It is equivalent to arguing that a column of mercury in a glass tube cannot be regarded as synonymous with temperature, or that temperature cannot really be measured with a thermometer. If the measurements are reliable and reproducible, and the operations by which they are obtained can be objectively agreed upon, this is all that need be required for them to qualify as proper scientific data. We know that individually administered IQ tests have quite high reliability; the reliability coefficients are around

.95, which means that only about 5 percent of the total individual differences variance is attributable to measurement error. And standard group administered tests have reliabilities close to .90.

The standard error of measurement (which is about $\pm$ 5 for the Stanford-Binet and similar tests) must always be taken into consideration when considering any individual's score on a test. But it is actually quite unimportant in comparison of the means of large groups of subjects, since errors of measurement are more or less normally distributed about zero and they cancel out when N is large. The reliability (i.e., consistency or freedom from errors of measurement) per se of the IQ is really not seriously at issue in making comparisons between racial groups. If the samples are large, the mean difference between groups will not include the test's errors of measurement.

The validity or importance of the measures derives entirely from their relationship to other variables and the importance we attach to them.

The IQ correlates with many external criteria, and at the most general level it may be regarded as a measure of the ability to compete in our society in ways that have economic and social consequences for the individual. In the first place, the IQ accords with parents' and teachers' subjective assessments of children's brightness, as well as with the evaluations of children's own peers. In terms of assessments of scholastic performance, whether measured in terms of school grades, teachers' ratings, or objective tests of scholastic achievement, the IQ accounts for more of the individual differences variance than any other single measurable attribute of the child. IQ accounts for about 50 percent of the variance in scholastic achievement at any single grade level, and over the course of several years or more of schooling it accounts for over 70 percent of the variance in overall scholastic performance.

Since considerably less than 100 percent of the variance is accounted for, it means the IQ is not an infallible predictor of the performance of any one individual. When used for individual diagnosis it must be evaluated in terms of many other factors in the child's makeup and background and condition at the time of testing, and even then not too much stock should be placed in the IQ in predicting *for the individual case,* since the predictive validity of the IQ is not sufficiently high to override the effects of possibly unassessed traits or unpredictable unusual future circumstances which may radically alter the course of the individual's development or performance in a statistically small proportion of cases. Thus, I am emphasizing the importance of evaluating the IQ somewhat differently when used for individual diagnosis and prediction than when used in making statistical predictions on large groups of individuals. It is somewhat analogous to actuarial predictions of insurance risks. Predictions for large groups classified by various criteria can be made with high degrees of certainty, while predictions for individual cases are highly uncertain.

Recently I received a letter from a high school senior who described himself as coming from a disadvantaged background. He had a strong desire to go on to college in hopes of becoming a lawyer, and he was wondering about his IQ and how much stock he should put in it in deciding his further course. I doubt if there is much more sense in worrying about one's own IQ than in worrying about the age at which one will die, as predicted by the insurance company's actuarial tables. Among other things, I wrote the following to my student inquirer: "My own attitude toward tests, when I was a student, was not to give much thought to them but simply to set my sights on what seemed to me a realistic goal and then do my best to achieve it. You find out from those who have already made it what you have to know, what you have to be able to do, what skills you need to develop, and you set about doing these things just as you'd go about doing any kind of job that you know has to be done. If you set your goals too low, it's too easy and you won't develop your potential. If you set goals that are unrealistically high, you become discouraged. I recommend one step at a time, each step being something you really think you can achieve if you really work for it. When you have made the first step successfully, then you will have a better idea of how to take the next step. That way, if you have whatever it takes, you'll make it; if you haven't got whatever it takes, you'll find this out. But you'll never really know without trying your best. I wouldn't let any kind of test score determine what I try for. The reality of your own performance in meeting the competition in striving toward your goals is the only real test. I believe this approach gives one the best chances of finally doing what he is best suited for, and this is one of the conditions for a satisfying life."

In statistical terms, however, the correlation is quite substantial between IQ and occupations, when the latter are merely ranked in the order of persons' average judgment of the occupation's prestige. Various studies have shown correlations in the range of .50 to .70. This is sufficiently high that the mean differences between groups of persons in occupations arranged according to a prestige hierarchy (which is highly related to income) show highly significant differences in IQ or other mental test scores. In general, any two groups which differ in possessing what are perceived as "the good things in life" according to the criteria and values of our society, will be found on the average to differ significantly in IQ. Upward social mobility is related to IQ: the brighter children in a family tend to move up in socioeconomic level and the least bright tend to move down. There are exceptions to the general rule. Those who are born to wealth tend to be less able than those who made it themselves—a quite predictable finding in terms of "regression to the mean." Usually the regression of ability is much greater than the regression of cumulated wealth. The most conspicuous exceptions, however, involve various disadvantaged minorities, whose social and economic positions are different from what one would predict in terms of IQ. For example, Negroes earn less income than whites of comparable IQ, education, family background, and work experience (Duncan et al., 1968). And American Indians, though considerably more impoverished than Negroes in the United States, score higher than Negroes on tests of intelligence and scholastic achievement (Kuttner, 1968). Oriental children, who generally score at least as high on IQ as white children, also score considerably higher than would be predicted from their socioeconomic status (SES). This appears especially true of low SES Oriental children, who perform on a par with middle-class white children on nonverbal tests (Lesser, Fifer, & Clark, 1965). In predicting scholastic performance in school and in college, however, the evidence indicates that IQ tests and scholastic aptitude tests work with about equal accuracy for all persons from whatever background. In this one respect, at least, the educational system seems to be one of the least discriminatory institutions in our society. For example, there is no evidence that IQ tests predict scholastic performance of Negro children less well than for white children, or that college entrance exams predict college grades less well for Negro than for white students (Jensen, 1968c; Stanley & Porter, 1967). The predictive validity of such tests could be lowered or changed, of course, by altering the curriculum such that the predictors would no longer be as relevant and other predictors might then become more valid.

When groups are selected from the lower or upper extremes of the IQ distribution, the contrasts are enormous. A classic example is Terman's study of gifted children, selected in elementary school for IQs over 140, which constitutes the upper one percent of the population. These 1,528 children have been systematically followed up to middle age (Terman & Oden, 1959). The group as a whole greatly exceeds a random sample of the population on practically every criterion of a successful life, and not just intellectual criteria. On the average the Terman group have markedly greater educational attainments, have higher incomes, engage in more desirable and prestigious occupations, have many more entries in *Who's Who,* have brighter spouses, enjoy better physical and mental health, have a lower suicide rate, a lower mortality rate, a lower divorce rate, and have brighter children (their average IQ is 133). These results should leave no doubt that IQ is related to socially valued criteria.

The evidence on this point is very clear. There is no doubt of a large genetic component in individual differences in IQ. The methodology of determining the heritability of intelligence (or other traits) and the results of the applications of these methods to the study of intelligence have been reviewed in detail elsewhere (Burt, 1958; Jensen, 1967, 1969a,b). Heritability (H) refers to the proportion of individual differences variance in a measurable trait, like intelligence, that can be attributed to genetic factors. $1 - H$, therefore, is the proportion of variance attributable to non-genetic factors. These non-genetic factors are both biological and psychological. Some substantial proportion of the non-genetic IQ variance is unidentifiable, that is, it is due to random environmental effects and to random stochastic biological processes in embryonic development.

The heritability of IQ as estimated from the average of all published studies of the subject is .80, which means that on the average the studies show that 80% of the population variance in IQ is attributable to genetic variation, and 20% to nongenetic factors. The value of .80 is merely an average of many studies which yield H values that range from about .60 to about .90. There is no single true value of the heritability of a trait. Heritability is not a constant, but a population statistic, and it can vary according to the test used and the particular population sample tested. H will be affected by the range of genetic and environmental variation that exists in the population. It should be noted that all the studies of the heritability of intelligence have been based on European and North American Caucasian populations. The results cannot strictly be generalized to other populations such as American Negroes. We would need to conduct heritability studies within the Negro population if we are to have any certainty that our IQ tests are measuring a genetic component to the same degree in the Negro as in the white population. (Determining H in both populations still would not answer the question whether the group mean IQ difference between Negroes and whites has a genetic component.)

Non-genetic or environmental sources of variance can be analyzed into two major components: variance attributable to differences *between* families in the population and variance attributable to differences *within* families. The sum of the *between* families and the *within* families variances constitutes the total of the nongenetic or environmental variance. Expressed as a proportion, it is $1 - H = E$, and, as already pointed out, the average value of H reported in the literature is .80, making the average value of $E = .20$. The conceptually simplest method for estimating E is to obtain the correlation between identical (monozygotic) twins reared apart (r_{MZA}) in uncorrelated environments (families). E

$= 1 - r_{MZA}$. The correlation between identical twins reared together (r_{MZT}) in the same family is used to estimate the *within* families environmental variance $E_W = 1 - r_{MZT}$. The *between* families variance is then $E_B = E - E_W$ or $r_{MZT} - r_{MZA}$. When these formulations are applied to all the relevant twin data reported in the literature, the average values they yield are $E = .20$, $E_B = .12$ and $E_W = .08$ (Jensen, 1967). Little, if any, of the E_W is controllable. Some of it is due to prenatal effects related to mother's age, health, accidental perinatal factors, ordinal position among other siblings, etc. In terms of our present knowledge, no prescription could be written for reducing E_W. Some of it, in fact, is almost certainly due to random, stochastic developmental processes in the first weeks after conception, which means that even if we had perfect control over all the identifiable factors usually classified as environmental, genetically identical individuals would still show some differences. The *between* families component, E_B, is probably much more attributable to what we commonly think of as environmental differences in terms of cultural-educational advantages, quality of nutrition, general health care, and the like.

SPECIFIC COMMENTS ON GENETICS AND IQ

To say that an IQ test like the Stanford-Binet "measures present ability, not inborn capacity" is misleading. Surely it measures present ability or performance. But the fact that the heritability (H) of the Stanford-Binet IQ is about .80 in English and North American Caucasian populations also means that the test measures "innate capacity," if by this term we mean the individual's genotype for intellectual development. Since H is the proportion of variance in IQs (which are phenotypes) attributable to variance in genotypes, the square root of H represents the correlation between phenotype and genotype, and this correlation is about .90, a very high correlation indeed. (This is the correlation that exists *after* correction for attenuation, that is, test unreliability.) What the evidence on heritability tells us is that we *can*, in fact, estimate a person's genetic standing on intelligence from his score on an IQ test. If the correlation between phenotype and genotype were perfect (i.e., 1.00), a person's test score would, of course, be an exact index of his genetic potential. But since the correlation is only about .90, such statements can only be made on a probabalistic basis.

If education and culturally-derived motivation strongly affect intelligence test performance, then these factors should show up as part of the E variance, mostly E_B, i.e., *between* families environmental variance. Heritability studies, as pointed out, show the E variance to be only about 20% of the total and E_B only about 12% of the total. If *group* differences in IQ are to be explained in terms of educational and motivational factors, and if the heritability of IQ were the same in both groups, it would have to be assumed that all the members of one group differed from the mean of the other group by a *constant amount* in these motivational or other environmental variables. More will be said on this point in the later section on proposed genetic research.

The twin method may actually *underestimate,* rather than overestimate, the heritability of IQ. The reason is that there is considerable evidence that twins are more subject to prenatal stresses and nutritional disadvantages than singletons. This is reflected in the much lower birthweights of twins, the higher infant mortality of twins, and the fact that twins average 6 to 7 points lower in IQ than single-born children. One member of the twin pair is usually prenatally favored over the other, and this is especially true for monozygotic twins, as reflected in their differing birthweights. Birthweight of twins is positively correlated with later IQ (Willerman & Churchill, 1967). These prenatal differences, reflected in later IQ differences between the members of twin pairs, are very probably greater for twins than for singletons and therefore suggest a larger component of (prenatal) environmental variance in twins than in singletons. Thus the argument that the twin method of estimating heritability leads to an overestimate and thereby underestimates the environmental component is very weak. A stronger case can be made for just the opposite conclusion. The fact that the estimates of *H* from the twin methods are in close agreement with estimates based on other kinships indicates that the twin estimates are not very deviant in *either* direction. Indeed, it is the consistency of *H* estimates arrived at by different methods that makes them so impressive and reinforces their validity and scientific credibility (see Crow, 1969).

Cultural and educational differences are probably the most important *non-biological* sources of individual differences in intelligence, but they are not necessarily the most important *non-genetic* source of differences. It is likely that prenatal and nutritional factors are at least as important sources of variance as social-psychological factors. The sociological emphasis on the non-biological aspects of the environment has resulted in a relative neglect of probably important nutritional factors and maternal factors (age, health, diet, number of births, spacing of births, etc.) which can affect the prenatal and early childhood development of the individual.

In reply to suggestions that our national IQ may be declining due to the possibility that the least able segment of the population is reproducing at a faster rate than the most able segment, some writers draw the familiar analogy between intelligence and physical stature. Both IQ and height are polygenetic traits and the same quantitative genetic model can be applied to both and can predict the various kinship correlations for IQ and height about equally well. It is also known that height, like intelligence, shows a positive correlation with socioeconomic status. Thus, if poor people have larger families than the well-to-do, we should expect the average height of the population to decrease over a number of generations. Exactly the same line of reasoning applies also in the case of intelligence. To counter this pessimistic prediction, it has been noted that despite what we should predict from simple genetic principles, the mean height of the population not only has not decreased in the past 200 years or so, but has in fact *increased* by a very significant amount. The increase, it is assumed, is due to environmental factors such as improved nutrition. And the implication is, of course, that intelligence, too, will increase over generations because of improvements in the environmental factors relevant to intellectual development. I believe this line of argument is weak and can lead to an unwarranted complacency about a possibly serious social trend.

First of all, Carter (1962) and Tanner (1965, 1968) have pointed out that much if not all of the increase in adult height in the past 200 years can be attributed to genetic factors, namely, the outbreeding effect. Increase in height is closely associated with the increase in the population's mobility. The offspring of parents from different Swiss villages, for example, are taller than the offspring of parents born in the same village. This outbreeding effect, or hybrid vigor, tends to saturate or level off in the population in a few generations, as has already occurred with respect to height in the United States. Nutritional factors have their greatest effect on *rate* of growth rather than on final adult height. In World War I men reached their full adult height at age 26; today they attain their full height at 18 or 19.

Although it is true that height is positively correlated with socioeconomic status (SES) and that low SES families are larger than high SES families, these facts alone are not sufficient to warrant the prediction that the mean height of the population should decline. It would have to be shown that the same *numbers* of low SES persons as high SES persons have offspring. When this point was investigated for intelligence, it was found that persons of below average IQ have larger families than persons of above average IQ, but that fewer of the below average ever marry or have any children at all (Higgins, & Reed, 1962; Bajema, 1963, 1966). The net result is a balance between the low and high IQ groups in the number of offspring they produce. This finding holds only for the white population of the U. S. of a generation ago. No studies of this type have been conducted in the U. S. Negro population. Since the bases for marriage and mate selection may be quite different in various subcultures, the results of investigation of this problem in one group cannot be generalized to other population groups with any confidence. The analogy with height is not convincing, since we have established only a negative correlation between height and family size, but have not taken into account the relative proportion of short and tall persons who never marry or produce offspring. Since we know there is selective mating for height in our population (that is, taller persons are viewed as more desirable) it is likely that fewer short persons marry or reproduce and that therefore a similar equilibrium between reproductive rates of short and tall persons exists as in the case of low and high intelligence. As I have noted elsewhere (Jensen, 1968a, 1969a), certain statistics raise the question of whether Negro intelligence is declining relative to white intelligence as a result of more extreme differential birthrates in lower and upper social classes among Negroes than among whites. Negro middle- and upper-class families have fewer children than their white counterparts, while Negro lower-class families have more. In 1960, Negro women married to professional or technical workers had only 1.9 children as compared with 2.4 for white women in the same circumstances. Negro women of ages 35 to 44 who were married to unskilled workers had 4.7 children compared with 3.8 for non-Negro women in the same situation, and Negro women with incomes below $2000 per year averaged 5.3 children (Moynihan, 1966). This could mean that the least able segment of the Negro population is reproducing most rapidly, a condition that could alone produce and increase a genetic difference between the Negro and white populations in a few generations. The possible genetic and social implications of these trends have not yet come under investigation and there are no data at present which would warrant complacency about this important question.

Can genetic changes in a population take place only very slowly, so that selective pressures acting over several generations would be of negligible consequence? The answer, of course, depends largely on the degree of selective pressure. We already know enough to permit fairly accurate estimates of genetic trends given certain criteria of selection. If selection were extremely rigorous, an enormous shift in the population mean would be possible, as can be inferred from the average IQ of the offspring of the Terman gifted group. The Terman subjects were selected for Stanford-Binet IQs of 140 and above; they had a mean of 152. There was no selection of their spouses, except by the normal assortative mating that occurs for intelligence in our society (i.e., a correlation of .5 to .6 between spouses' IQs). The offspring of the Terman gifted had an average IQ of 133 (Terman & Oden, 1959). This is more than two standard deviations above the mean IQ of children born to a random sample of the population. There is a regression from the selected parent generation toward the general population mean, but the regression happens only once, and the offspring of the selected parents will in turn have offspring without further regression, provided, of course, they do not mate outside the group of offspring from the selected parents.

Rats have been bred for maze learning ability and it has generally required from six to nine generations of selection to produce two strains of rats whose distributions of maze learning scores are completely non-overlapping.

One of the easiest ways of avoiding the issue of race differences in intelligence is to make the claim that there is no such thing as race and therefore it is not a variable that can be related to any other variables. Thus, proponents of this view would claim that the concept of race is merely a myth, not a phenomenon that can be subjected to scientific study. This is, of course, utter nonsense. But it will pay to clarify the concept of race as it figures in comparative studies of intelligence.

There are two general definitions of race: the social and the biological (or genetic). Both are arbitrary, but this need not mean they are unreliable or lacking in precision. Although most of the studies of racial differences in intelligence are based on social definitions of race, it should be noted that there is usually a high correlation between the social and the biological definitions, and it is most unlikely that the results of the research would be very different if the investigators had used biological rather than social criteria of race in selecting groups for comparisons.

The social criteria of race are simple: they are the ethnic labels people use to describe themselves and the more obvious physical characteristics such as skin color, hair texture, facial features, and so on, by which persons roughly determine one another's "race." Admitted, the social definition is crude. It does not take account of "borderline" or ambiguous cases that are hard to categorize and which make for some unreliability in classification, and it does not take account of the fact that there are no pure racial types—and especially in the case of American Negroes there is considerable racial admixture. Almost no American Negroes are of pure African descent; most have from 5% to 90% Caucasian genes, the average degree of admixture now being between 20% and 30%. Thus there is great genetic diversity *within* socially defined racial groups.

Does this make the social definition of race useless as a variable? No. In the first place, there is undoubtedly a high correlation between social and biological classification. That is to say, if one were to sort school children, for example, into three socially defined racial groups, Negro, Oriental, and Caucasian, one would find a very high concordance of classification if he used strict biological criteria based on the frequencies of blood groups, anthropometric measures, and other genetic polymorphisms. What one would not have obtained from the crude social classification is degrees of racial admixture. In other words, the major racial categories would be much the same whether constituted by social judgments or strict biological criteria. But if we wanted to go beyond this crude system of classification to make more refined differentiations, we would have to resort to biological criteria. Social judgments of degrees of racial admixture are quite unreliable. The broad categories, however, *are* reliable. They also qualify as variables in the sense that they show significant correlations with other variables such as IQ and scholastic performance. This is not to say that such correlations by themselves tell us anything about a biological or genetic basis for the correlation, which might be due to other environmental, social-class and cultural variables related to the socially defined racial classification. If the crucial variables in IQ differences are not racial classification per se, but other correlated environmental factors, then, at least in theory, one should be able to reduce the racial correlation with IQ to zero by partialling out the truly causal factors that are only incidentally correlated with both race and IQ. So far no one has succeded in doing this as regards Negro-white comparisons. Every combination of environmental variables that anyone has partialled out has always left behind some significant correlation between race (socially defined) and IQ (Shuey, 1965). One can always claim that all the relevant environmental variables were not taken into account. This is a real weakness of such studies and they can be legitimately criticized on this score. It is largely for this reason that our understanding of racial differences will not be greatly advanced until more refined criteria of race based on biological criteria are employed. Specific proposals are made in a later section.

It is strange that those who claim that there are no genetic racial differences in ability are often the most critical of studies that have employed the social criterion of race rather than more rigorous genetic criteria. If the observed IQ differences are due only to social factors, then the social definition of race should be quite adequate, and, in fact, should be the only appropriate definition. If it is then argued that the two socially defined racial groups being compared are not "pure" and that each group contains some genetic admixture of the other, it can only mean that the biological racial aspects of the observed IQ differences has been *under*estimated by comparing socially defined racial groups.

The biological definition of race is based on gene frequencies. Races are breeding groups which differ in the frequencies of one or more genes. A breeding group is one in which there is a higher proportion of matings among members of the group than of matings in which one member of the pair is from outside the group. Breeding groups result from relative degrees of geographical, racial, and cultural isolation of different population groups. The definition of race by these criteria is arbitrary only in the sense that differences in gene frequencies are a continuous variable, and where one wishes to draw the lines as criteria for classification purposes is not dictated by nature but by the taxonomic considerations of the investigator. Rather than thinking in terms of races, we should think in terms of groups with different gene frequencies. The question we would ask is whether various groups differing in gene frequencies also differ in IQ, other things being, in effect, equal. The major races are simply breeding populations that have a relatively high degree of inbreeding and differ from one another in the relative frequencies of many genes. They differ in so many known gene frequencies, in fact, that it seems highly improbable that they would not also differ in the frequencies of genes related to behavioral traits such as intelligence.

A major block to clear thinking about race is to think of it as a kind of Platonic essence, independent of any particular population group. General statements about the mental abilities of the "white race," the "black race," "the yellow race," and so on, make no sense in terms of any studies that have yet been done or that seem at all feasible for the future. Strictly speaking, to ask if there are race differences in any characteristic is scientifically meaningless if what we mean by race is not clearly specified. All we can do is study samples selected from certain specified populations. These samples cannot be regarded as representative of some Platonic racial groups. They are merely representative (if properly selected) of the clearly specified population group from which they are selected.

We could ask, for example, whether a population subgroup that differs from the general population in its average response to the educational and occupational requirements of our society differs in its gene pool from other population subgroups which are more successful, and if so, are some of the genetic differences related to ability factors with high heritability?

Population subgroups which have immigrated are not necessarily representative of their native parent populations. Studies of racial or national groups in the United States, therefore, cannot be generalized abroad, and the reverse is also true. This does not mean, however, that meaningful comparative studies of various population subgroups within the United States are not feasible.

The notion that there are no genetic mental ability differences among population subgroups that differ in many other gene frequencies is, in principle, hard to defend. Populations that have been widely separated geographically or socially for many centuries and which have been exposed to climatic and cultural conditions that exert different selective pressures are almost certain to differ genetically in many ways. And, in fact, they do. Nearly every anatomical and physiological system studied has shown race differences. It is not at all necessary to invoke the factor of differential selective pressures to validate or explain some of these genetic differences, many of which confer no discernible advantage or disadvantage to survival or adaptation in any particular environment. A chemical substance, phenylthiocarbamide (PTC), is one illustration. To some persons PTC is completely tasteless; to others it has a very unpleasant bitter taste. Whether a person is a taster is determined by a single gene. This gene has markedly different frequencies in different racial groups. No one knows why this should be. Similarly, blood types have markedly different distributions in various racial groups, although it is not at all clear that one blood type is more advantageous than another in any given environment. In short, genetic diversity is the rule; genetic uniformity is the rare exception. By definition the gene pools of racial groups differ, and it is not at all an unreasonable hypothesis that genetic factors that condition behavioral development also differ.

Biological evolution generally is a slow process, but genetic changes with respect to particular traits can occur relatively fast in response to selective pressures in the environment. In any case, biological evolution, whatever its rate, has resulted in marked genetic differentiation of human populations. Concerning the one standard deviation average IQ difference between Negro and white American populations, one writer stated, "A review of present knowledge on interracial divergence in man makes it unlikely that a difference as large as the observed one is genetic." This hardly seems tenable in view of the fact that other traits show even greater racial differences than are found for intelligence. Height, like intelligence, is a polygenically inherited characteristic and is probably less subject to selective pressures than intelligence, and yet we find racial (and even national or regional) differences of more than one standard deviation. In fact, two racial subgroups on the African continent, the Pygmies and the Watusi, differ in height by five to six standard deviations. Obviously biological evolution has, in fact, been sufficient to create marked differences in genetic characteristics.

It is hard to imagine that there have not been different selection pressures for different abilities in various cultures and that these pressures would not be as great for intelligence as for many physical characteristics which are known to differ genetically among racial groups. Individual differences in the abilities most relevant to a particular culture are highly visible characteristics and if they have consequences for the individual's status in the social hierarchy or the culture's system of rewards they will be traits subject to the genetic effects of sexual selection and assortative mating. If a trait is not very relevant to the demands of a particular culture it will not become highly visible, it will not be a basis for selective mating, and its genetic basis will not be systematically affected by pressures in the social environment.

Selective mating refers to the fact that certain characteristics are viewed as desirable in mate selection by virtually all members of the breeding population. The usual consequence is that those standing higher on the desired trait will have greater opportunities for mating and reproduction while those at the lowest end of the distribution on the trait in question will be least likely to find a mate and to leave progeny. The net effect is to boost the mean value of the trait in the population. Assortative mating refers to the fact that like tends to marry (or mate with) like. It is sometimes an inevitable consequence of selective mating with respect to generally desirable traits, but also holds for traits which are merely subject to various individual preferences. It is noteworthy that of all measurable human characteristics the one with the highest coefficient of assortative mating (i.e., the correlation between mates) is intelligence. The correlation between spouses' IQs, for example, is around .5 to .6 in various studies, as contrasted with a correlation of .3 for height and of zero for fingerprints. The high degree of assortative mating for intelligence means that it is highly subject to genetic change through social influences. For example, the variance of the IQ distribution in the population would be reduced by approximately 20% if there were no assortative mating for just one generation. Assortative mating increases the variance of the characteristic in the population, and if there is selective mating (as well as assortative) for the characteristic, the individuals at the lower (least desirable) end of the distribution will be least likely to reproduce. The net effect is to raise the average of the population on the trait in question. Such trends have probably taken place with respect to different traits in different societies for many centuries. While sexual selection may be capricious and nonadaptive with respect to many physical characteristics (e.g., various societies have different criteria of beauty), selection is not likely to be capricious with respect to those abilities which are salient in the competition in a given society. There has probably been quite strong and consistent selection for different patterns of ability in different cultures. A high degree of genetic adaptation to the demands of one environment might not constitute optimal adaptive capabilities to the demands of another, quite different, environment. As stated by Spuhler and Lindzey (1967, p. 413) in their chapter on the behavior-genetics of race difference:

> . . . it seems to us surprising that one would accept present findings in regard to the existence of genetic, anatomical, physiological, and epidemiological differences between races and still expect to find *no* meaningful differences in behavior between races.

They continue to point out that there are

> enormous discrepancies between races in the efficiency with which culture is transmitted (for example, the difference between literate

and nonliterate societies). Some of these differences are closely associated with race differences, have existed for many thousands of
years, and presumably have been accompanied by very different
selection pressures in regard to character potentially relevant to
culture transmission, such as 'intelligence.'

Thus, it seems highly improbable that there have been no markedly
differing selective pressures on different subpopulations even within the
United States. The selective pressures on Negroes must have been very
different from those in European immigrant populations. The history
of slavery suggests quite extreme selective factors, involving even the
deliberate breeding of slaves for certain characteristics which were irrelevant or perhaps even negatively correlated with intellectual prowess. It
would be surprising indeed if more than 300 years of slavery did not
have some genetic consequences. But since the possible nature of these
consequences are highly speculative and cannot be accurately inferred
from historical accounts, this retrospective approach to the study of
racial differences is too unreliable to be of much real scientific value.
Direct genetical studies of present population groups can provide the
only really satisfactory basis for the scientific study of genetic differences
in abilities.

ARE THERE RACIAL DIFFERENCES IN IQ?

In the United States persons classed as Negro by the common social
criteria obtain scores on the average about one standard deviation (i.e.,
15 IQ points on most standard intelligence tests) below the average for
the white population. One standard deviation is an *average* difference,
and it is known that the magnitude of Negro-white differences varies
according to the ages of the groups compared, their socioeconomic status,
and especially their geographical location in the United States. Various
tests differ, on the average, relatively little. In general, Negroes do
slightly better on verbal tests than on non-verbal tests. They do most
poorly on tests of spatial ability, abstract reasoning and problem solving
(Shuey, 1966; Tyler, 1965). Tests of scholastic achievement also show
about one standard deviation difference, and this difference appears to
be fairly constant from first grade through twelfth grade, judging from
the massive data of the Coleman study (1966). The IQ difference of
1 SD, also, is fairly stable over the age range from about 5 years to
adulthood, although some studies have shown a tendency for a slight
increase in the difference between 5 and 18 years of age. Another point
that has been suggested, but which requires much more systematic investigation before any firm conclusions can be reached, is that there is
a larger sex difference in IQs for Negroes than for whites (Bronfenbrenner, 1967). The presumed difference favors the females. The point

is especially worthy of research because, if true, it would have considerable social and educational consequences, which would be especially evident in the upper tail of the IQ distribution. For example, if girls are a few IQ points higher than boys, on the average, one should expect a greatly disproportionate number of Negro girls to qualify, as compared with boys, in any selection based on cut-off scores well above the mean, such as selection for college. Assuming a general mean of 85, an SD of 15, and a normal distribution, a 5 point IQ difference between Negro boys and girls and a college selection cut-off score of 115, for example, we would expect the number of qualified girls to boys to be approximately in the ratio of 2 to 1.

A statistic which has been much less studied than the mean difference is the standard deviation (SD), that is, the measure of dispersion of scores within the distribution.

Most studies agree in finding a smaller SD in Negro than in white IQs. The single largest normative study of Stanford-Binet IQs in a Negro population, for example, found an SD of 12.4 as compared with 16.4 in the white normative sample (Kennedy, Van de Riet, and White, 1963). This study is based on a large sample of school children in five Southeastern states and therefore may not be representative of the Negro population in other regions of the U.S. In general, however, most studies of Negro intelligence have found a smaller standard deviation than the SD of 15 or 16 generally found in white samples. The point is of some consequence in considering the relative merits of the opposing hypothesis relating to the *causes* of the observed average IQ difference between Negroes and whites, namely, the hypothesis of genetic equality versus the hypothesis of genetic differences. If the distribution of IQs in the Negro population does, in fact, have a smaller SD than in the white population, and if we hypothesize no genetic differences between the two populations, we must conclude that there is less variance due to environmental differences within the Negro group than within the white group. Since the genetic variance is hypothesized to be exactly the same in both groups, the difference in the variances (i.e., the square of the SD) of the groups must be all environmental variance. Thus, if the total variance of Negro IQs is less than of white IQs, the genetic equality hypothesis is forced to predict a higher heritability of IQ in the Negro population than in the white; that is to say, more of the variance in Negro IQs would have to be due to genetic factors. If a study of the heritability of IQ in the Negro population yielded a heritability coefficient equal to or less than that found in the white population, this finding would contradict the genetic equality hypothesis, at least as regards the equality of genetic variance in the two populations.

Let us take another look at the Kennedy et al. (1963) data in this connection, to see how the hypothesis of genetic equality of variances comes out for this one set of data comparing the distribution of Negro IQs with the distribution of the white population sample on which are based the norms for the Stanford-Binet Intelligence Test. It will be recalled that the SDs for Negroes and whites were 12.4 and 16.4, respectively. The variances are thus $(12.4)^2 = 153.76$ and $(16.4)^2 = 268.96$. Now, the best estimate of the heritability of Stanford-Binet IQs in white population samples similar to that on which the Stanford-Binet was standardized is .80 (Jensen, 1969a). This means that 80% of the variance of the white IQ distribution is *genetic* variance: thus, $.80 \times 268.96 = 215.17$ is the white genetic IQ variance. But this is still greater than the *total* Negro IQ variance. The heritability of IQ in the white group would have to be assumed to be .57 for the white *genetic* variance to equal the *total* IQ variance of the Negro group, and surely some of this total variance is non-genetic. Furthermore, no reported study of the heritability of Stanford-Binet IQs is as low as .57. Thus, a hypothesis of genetic equality with respect to variances leads to highly untenable conclusions when applied to the data of Kennedy et al. (1963). By any canon of statistical and logical reasoning one is forced to reject the hypothesis that the distributions of genotypes for intelligence are equivalent in these two samples. By assuming genetic equivalence, one simply cannot make any sense out of the available data. This is not to say that one cannot question the data with respect to every parameter that is involved in this line of reasoning.* But if one accepts the validity of the heritability estimates in the white population and the SDs given by Kennedy et al., it logically follows that a genetic equivalence hypothesis is untenable. It is, of course, statistically unwarranted to generalize this conclusion beyond the populations sampled in the study by Kennedy et al. The causes of the lesser variance of IQ in the Negro group are not known. One can only speculate and suggest hypotheses. From the evi-

---

* For example, one need not accept the IQ scale as the most appropriate. If it could be argued and demonstrated that some transformation of the IQ scale produced more orderly and lawful data in studies of heritability, in the degree of normality of the distribution of scores, and in more closely approximating a genetic model, then such a transformation would be justified. It could very well affect the variances of the distributions in different population subgroups. Berkeley geneticist Dr. Jack King, for example, has suggested that if we assume that the factors (genetic and environmental) that affect intelligence do not behave additively but interact multiplicatively (i.e., a factor adds or subtracts a given *percentage* to the total measure rather than a fixed *amount*) a logarithmic transformation of the IQ scale is theoretically justified. In the multiplicative model, the logarithm of the observed measure is normally distributed. The logarithmic transformation in fact makes the IQ distribution more normal (Gaussian) in a number of studies, and it tends to equalize the variances of the Negro and white distributions, although it also has the effect of pulling their means slightly further apart. The proper transformation is 100 (1 + ln IQ/100), which leaves the general population mean at IQ 100. (ln is the natural logarithm.) Past studies of the heritability of intelligence should be re-analyzed using this logarithmic transformation of the IQ scale to see if it gives a closer and more parsimonious fit to a polygenic model.

dence on the white population, for example, we know that some 15 to 20 percent of the total variance is attributable to assortative mating for intelligence; if the correlation between mates' IQs was markedly reduced, the white IQ variance would be substantially reduced. (Variance due to assortative mating is all *genetic* variance.) Also, the covariance of heredity and environment (i.e., there is some correlation between children's genotypes for intellectual development and the quality of the environment in which they are reared) constitutes some 5 to 10 percent of the total IQ variance in the white population. If environments were more similar, there would be less covariance and this source of variance would be diminished in the total. We could find out if these factors or others, or some combination of factors, are responsible for the lesser variance in the Negro population only by carrying out complex heritability studies in the Negro population.

A point that should be stressed is the fact that neither the white nor the Negro population, by common social classification, is genetically homogeneous. It has already been noted that the American Negro is not of pure African ancestry but has, on the average, an admixture of 20% to 30% Caucasian genes, varying from less than 5% in some regions of the country to 40% or 50% in others (Reed, 1969). The white population contains many different subgroups which most probably differ genetically in potential for intellectual development. To point to one particular subgroup of one socially defined racial population as being higher or lower in IQ than some subgroup in another racial population proves nothing other than the fact that there exists an overlap between the racial groups. The fact that relatively large mean IQ differences are found between certain subgroups within the same race does not mean that these differences must be entirely of environmental origin and that therefore racial differences of similar magnitude must also be entirely attributable to environment.

Finally, it should be noted that IQ tests are taken by individuals. There is no such thing as measuring the IQ of a group as a group. Individuals' IQs are obtained as individuals. The basis on which individuals may be grouped is a separate issue, depending upon the purposes of the investigator. When test scores are grouped according to some criteria of racial classification, we find mean differences between the groups. If we group test scores by some criteria of socioeconomic status, we find mean differences between the groups. Conversely, if we group persons by levels of IQ, we find the groups differ in their proportions of persons of different races and social classes.

ARE RACE DIFFERENCES IMPORTANT?

There is, of course, nothing *inherently* important about anything. Race differences in intelligence are important only if people think these differences, or their consequences, are important. It so happens that in our society great importance is given to these differences and their importance is acknowledged in many official public policies. Racial inequality in educational and occupational performance, and in the social and economic rewards correlated therewith, is today clearly one of the uppermost concerns of our nation.

Most persons are not concerned with those racial characteristics that are patently irrelevant to performance. The real concern results from the observed correlation between racial classification and educational and occupational performance. Persons who feel concerned about these observed differences demand an explanation for the differences. It is apparently a strongly ingrained human characteristic to need to understand what one perceives as a problem, and to ask for answers. People inevitably demand explanations about things that concern them. There is no getting around that. We have no choice in the matter. Explanations there will be.

But we do have a choice of essentially two paths in seeking explanations of intelligence differences among racial groups. On the one hand, we can simply *decree* an explanation based on prejudice, or popular beliefs, or moral convictions, or one or another social or political ideology, or on what we might think it is best for society to believe. This is the path of propaganda. Or, on the other hand, we can follow the path of science and investigate the problem in the same way that any other phenomena would be subjected to scientific study. There is nothing to compel us to one path or the other. This is a matter of personal preference and values. And since persons differ markedly in their preferences and values, we will inevitably see both of these paths being followed for quite some time. My own preference is for a scientific approach to the study of these phenomena. It is certainly the more interesting and challenging intellectually. And our experience tells us that the scientific approach, by and large, leads to more reliable knowledge of natural phenomena than any other method that man has yet devised. If solutions to educational problems depend upon recognizing certain psychological realities in the same sense that, say, building a workable spaceship depends upon recognizing certain physical realities, then surely we will stand a better chance of improving education for all children by choosing the path of scientific investigation. In facing the issue of race differences in abilities we should heed the statement of John Stuart Mill:

> If there are some subjects on which the results obtained have finally received the unanimous assent of all who have attended to the proof, and others on which mankind have not yet been equally successful; on which the most sagacious minds have occupied themselves from the earliest date, and have never succeeded in establishing any considerable body of truths, so as to be beyond denial or

doubt; it is by generalizing the methods successfully followed in the former enquiries, and adapting them to the latter, that we may hope to remove this blot on the face of science.

Once we subscribe to a scientific approach, we are obligated to act accordingly. This means, for one thing, that we entertain alternative hypotheses. To entertain a hypothesis means not just to pay lip service to it or to acknowledge its possible merit and let it go at that. It means to put it into a testable form, to perform the test, and report the results with information as to the degree of statistical confidence with which the hypothesis in question can be accepted or rejected. If we can practice what is called "strong inference," so much the better. Strong inference consists of formulating opposing hypotheses and pitting them against one another by actually testing the contradictory predictions that follow from them. This is the way of science. How much of our educational research, we may ask, has taken this form? How much of the research that we see catalogued in the already gargantuan ERIC bibliography on the causes of the educational handicaps of children called culturally disadvantaged has followed this path? The only sensible conclusion one can draw from a perusal of this evidence is that the key question in everyone's mind about racial differences in ability—are they genetic?— has, in effect, been ruled out as a serious alternative hypothesis in the search for the causal factors involved in inequalities of educational per- formance. Sundry environmental hypotheses are considered, but rarely, if ever, are alternative genetic hypotheses suggested. If a genetic hypoth- esis is mentioned, it is usually for the sake of dismissing it out of hand or to point out why it would be impossible to test the hypothesis in any case. Often, more intellectual ingenuity is expended in trying to find reasons why a particular genetic hypothesis could not be tested than in trying to discover a way of formulating the hypothesis so that it could be put to a test. The emotional need to believe that genetic factors are unimportant in individual or group differences in ability can be seen in many statements by dedicated workers in those fields of psychology and education most allied to the problems of children called disadvan- taged. For example, Dr. Bettye Caldwell, a prominent worker in com- pensatory and early childhood education, has noted:

> Most of us in enrichment . . . efforts—no matter how much lip service we pay to the genetic potential of the child—are passionate believers in the plasticity of the human organism. We need desper- ately to believe that we are all born equalizable. With any failure to demonstrate the effectiveness of compensatory experiences offered to children of any given age, one is entitled to conclude parsimo- niously that perhaps the enrichment was not offered at the proper time. (Caldwell, 1968, p. 81)

But genetic factors in rate of development are never considered as a possible part of the explanation.

It is important not to evaluate persons in terms of group membership if we are to insure equality of opportunity and social justice. All persons should be treated as individuals in terms of their own merits, if our aim is to maximize opportunities for every person to develop his abilities to their fullest capacity in accord with his own interests and drives. But the result of *individual* selection (for higher education, better jobs, etc.) makes it inevitable that there will be unequal representation of the parent populations in any subgroup that might be selected whenever there are average differences between parent populations.

Many questions about the means of guaranteeing equality of educational opportunity are still moral and political issues at present. When there is no compelling body of scientific evidence on which policy decisions can be based, such decisions must be avowedly made in terms of one's personal social philosophy and concepts of morality. Many goals of public policy must be decided in terms of values. The results of research are of greatest use to the technology of achieving the value-directed goals of society. The decision to put a man on the moon was not a scientific decision, but once the decision was made the application of scientific knowledge was necessary to achieve this goal. A similar analogy holds for the attainment of educational goals.

CAN RACE DIFFERENCES BE RESEARCHED?

It is sometimes argued that even though it is not unreasonable to hypothesize genetic racial differences in mental ability, we cannot know the direction or magnitude of such genetic differences and the problem is much too difficult and complex to yield to scientific investigation. Therefore, the argument often continues, we should go on pretending as though there is no question of genetic differences, as was officially stated by the U. S. Office of Education in 1966: "It is a demonstrable fact that the talent pool in any one ethnic group is substantially the same as that in any other ethnic group."

First, we will never know to what extent research can yield answers on a subject unless we at least try our best to do the research. It is doubtful that any major scientific advances could have been made in any field if it were decided beforehand that the problems could not be researched. I cannot agree that a scientific approach should be restricted to only the easy problems. If all the necessary methodology for studying the genetics of race differences in psychological characteristics is not yet sufficiently developed, this should not be surprising, since so little effort has been made thus far. The methodology of a field of inquiry does not grow in a vacuum. Scientists do not *first* develop a complete methodology for the investigation of a complex area and then apply it all at once to get the final answers. An appropriate methodology evolves as a result of grappling with difficult problems in the spirit of scientific research. Darwin's theory of evolution did not begin with a fully developed methodology adequate to prove the theory, nor did the theory of the inheritance of acquired characteristics—a theory which was later disproved after the development of an adequate methodology, a methodology which would not have developed in the absence of attempts to research this theory. No one would have been inclined to invent the necessary research methods in the absence of the problems these methods were needed to solve. One critic states "The scientific problem [of genetic race differences in ability] itself seems of dubious validity, if one considers how great are the difficulties . . . , at least on the basis of present techniques." The same statement could have been made about research on the theory of evolution, the atomic theory, the gene theory, and so on. We do not expect any single study or experiment to reduce all the uncertainty about a complex subject to absolute zero in one bold stroke! But as in dealing scientifically with most other complex phenomena, we should not regard ourselves as so intellectually impotent as to be unable to gradually chip away at the heredity-environment uncertainty with whatever tools that scientists can muster or devise with their present knowledge and ingenuity.

What are some of the thinking blocks in this area? One is the frequent failure to distinguish between raw facts, on the one hand, and inference from the facts in terms of some hypothesis, on the other. The Society for the Psychological Study of Social Issues (SPSSI), for example, in a press release (May 2, 1969) criticizing my article in the *Harvard Educational Review* (Jensen, 1969a), stated, "There is no *direct* [italics mine] evidence that supports the view that there is an innate difference between members of different racial groups." Of course there is not *direct* evidence, nor can there be direct evidence if by "direct" we mean evidence that is immediately palpable to our physical senses. The gradual disappearance of ships over the horizon is not *direct* evidence of anything, but it can be interpreted in terms of the hypothesis that the earth is round. It would be harder to explain if we hypothesized that the earth is flat. So even as relatively simple an hypothesis as that the world is round cannot be proved by direct evidence, but depends upon logical inference from diverse lines of evidence. If all that was needed was direct evidence, even a monkey would know that the world is round, in the same sense that it knows that a lemon is sour. The substantiation of an hypothesis in science depends upon *objective* evidence but does not necessarily depend upon direct evidence alone.

Another inhibition to thought on this topic is the notion that before research can yield any answers, the environment must be absolutely equal for all groups involved in comparisons. The SPSSI statement went so far as to say that ". . . a more accurate understanding of the contribution of heredity to intelligence will be possible only when social conditions for all races are equal and when this situation has existed for several generations." Since no operationally testable meaning is given to "equal" social conditions, such a statement, if taken seriously, would completely preclude the possibility of researching this important question, not just for several generations, but indefinitely. Actually, large environmental differences between racial groups can be revealing when the environmental ratings are positively correlated with IQ or scholastic performance *within* the groups but show a negative correlation *between* the groups. If group A on the average has a poor environment in terms of variables claimed to be important to intellectual development and group B has a good environment, and if group A performs better than group B on intelligence tests which are appropriate to the experience of both groups, this is evidence that some factors other than the measured environmental variables are involved in the relatively higher intellectual performance of group A as compared with group B. If environmental factors cannot be found that will account for the difference, it is presumptive evidence in favor of the genetic hypothesis. Genetical tests of the hypothesis are preferable, of course. (These are discussed in a later section). But what one also looks for are consistencies among various lines of evidence, especially lines of evidence that lead to opposite predictions from different hypotheses.

Many investigators now would question the view that the lack of early stimulation in the preschool years can be counted among the chief causes of the poorer IQ performance of Negro children, since when children are grouped in several categories according to their parents' socioeconomic status, the Negro children in the highest SES category still score two to three IQ points below white children in the lowest SES level (Shuey, 1966). Thus, what we generally think of as a reasonably good environment is apparently not sufficient to equalize the performance of Negro and white groups.

Such findings lead to hypothesizing increasingly subtle and hard to measure environmental effects. But it should be recognized that at present most of the environmentally "damaging" effects that are assumed to be accountable for performance differences are hypothetical and not factual. Poor self-concept and alienation are among the currently prevailing explanations, but what has not yet been satisfactorily explained is why such general motivational dispositions should affect some cognitive abilities so much more than others. Performance is not uniformly low on all tasks, by any means. There are distinct high and low points in the profile of various abilities in different ethnic groups (Stodolsky

& Lesser, 1967), and no one has yet attempted to explain how such profile differences, which are invariant across social classes, could come about as a result of differences in generalized attitudes and motivation in the test situation.

Finally, unnecessary difficulties arise when we allow the scientific question to become mixed up with its possible educational, social, and political implications. The scientific question and its solution should *not* be allowed to get mixed up with the social-political aspects of the problem, for when it does we are less able to think clearly about either set of questions. The question of whether there are or are not genetic racial differences in intelligence is independent of any questions of its implications, whatever they may be. But I would say that the scientific question should have priority and the answer should be sought through scientific means. For although the answer might have educational and social implications, and there are indeed grave educational and social problems that need to be solved, we must first understand the causes of problems if we are to do anything effectively toward solving them. Gaining this knowledge is a scientific task. As it is accomplished, we are then in a better position to consider alternative courses of action and evaluate their feasibility and desirability in terms of society's values and goals. This moves the problem into the realm of public policy, where all the answers cannot be scientifically derived. But policy cannot be wisely or effectively formulated unless it is informed by the facts. No matter how well-intentioned it may seem to be, it can only be less effective and less beneficial if it is based on false premises or in contradiction of reality.

GENETIC RESEARCH TO REDUCE THE HEREDITY-ENVIRONMENT UNCERTAINTY

Today there is virtually no uncertainty among those who have attended to the evidence that individual variation in intelligence is predominantly conditioned by genetic factors and that environmental factors account for a lesser proportion of the phenotypic variance. One can point to variations among studies that have estimated the heritability of intelligence. Such variations in estimates of the proportion of variance attributable to genetic factors are to be expected in view of the great variety of populations sampled and the differences among the variety of tests of mental ability that have been used. Despite these expected variations in heritability estimates, it is important to note that no major study contradicts the conclusion that heredity contributes something more than twice as much to the variance in IQ as environment in *white* European and American populations. (We do not have good heritability data on other populations.)

The term "heredity-environment uncertainty" refers mainly to the question of race differences in intelligence. The answer to this question is still in the realm of uncertainty in terms of the normal scientific meaning of this word. *Absolute* certainty is never attained in an empirical science. Absolute certainty can be had only in pure mathematics, the certainty of which rests upon the fact that pure mathematics is, as Bertrand Russell pointed out, just one vast tautology. Empirical science deals in probability statements, and "certainty" refers to a high degree of probability that a proposition is "true," meaning that certain objective consequences can be predicted from the proposition with a stated probability. A decisive increase in this probability with respect to any given scientific proposition rarely results from a single experiment or discovery. I take exception to the impression that might be given by some writers that unless a scientific study can be perfect and 100% certain, we cannot know anything. This is not how scientific knowledge advances. We do not devise perfect methods or obtain complete answers on the first try. Certainty, in the sense of probability, is generally increased very incrementally in science. Research aims to add reliable increments to statements of probability.

This we must continue to do with respect to the question of genetic race differences in intelligence. It is still an open question by all reasonable scientific standards. The existing evidence is in all cases sufficiently ambiguous, due largely to the confounding of racial and environmental factors, as not to permit statements with a sufficiently high probability such that all reasonable and qualified persons attending the evidence will agree that it is conclusive. The issue of genetic race differences may be likened to theories of the moon's craters—whether they were caused by volcanic eruptions or by the impact of meteors. All the evidence obtainable by astronomers could support either interpretation, and different scientists could argue for one theory or the other. A substantial increment could be subtracted from this uncertainty only by obtaining new evidence not obtainable through telescopic study, namely, directly obtaining and analyzing material from the surface of the moon.

I believe that, similarly, the heredity-environment uncertainty about race differences in IQ will be substantially reduced only by obtaining new evidence—new *kinds* of evidence. Exclusive reliance on anthropological, sociological, and psychological evidence would probably not substantially advance our knowledge. I believe that application of the methods of biometrical genetics (also called population genetics or quantitative genetics) to the question of race differences will substantially reduce our uncertainty.

Someone suggested that the only way one could prove race differences in intelligence would be to dye one member of a pair of white identical twins black and adopt it out to a Negro family while the co-twin is reared by a white family. How much difference would it make in their IQs? Better yet is the suggestion of Professor Arthur Stincombe (1969):

find pairs of identical twins in which one member of each pair is Negro and one is white, separate them at birth and rear them in Negro and white families and see how their IQ differences compare with those found for twins where both are of the same race! These suggestions sound ridiculous; one is unfeasible and the other is impossible. Yet as conceptual experiments they are good, because they suggest the necessary ingredients of the information we must obtain to reduce the heredity-environment uncertainty. Both examples rightly recognize skin color (and, by implication, other visible racial features) as a part of the individual's environment. They are based on comparing genetically equivalent persons reared in different environments. Another possibility consists of rearing genetically and racially different persons in essentially similar environments—including the factor of skin color, etc. Is such a study possible? Yes.

Geneticists already know the frequencies of a large number of genetically independent blood groups in European and African populations. On the basis of such data, it is entirely possible to determine the proportion of Caucasian genes in a population sample of Negroes, socially defined. Furthermore, it should be possible by the same means to classify individuals on a probabilistic basis in terms of their relative proportions of African and Caucasian genes. Since the *average* admixture of Caucasian genes for American Negroes is between 20 and 30 percent, there should be enough variance to make it possible to assign large numbers of individuals to at least several categories according to their amount of admixture, and the probable error in classification could be quite definitely specified. A sufficient number of blood groups or other genetic polymorphisms with known frequency distributions in African and Caucasian populations would have to be employed to ensure a high degree of statistical certainty that the categories represented different degrees of genetic racial admixture. A wide range of admixtures probably exists among Negroes living in highly similar environments, so that it should be quite possible in such a study to obtain samples which do not differ across the admixture categories in a number of socioeconomic or other environmental indices. What about skin color? It is polygenetic and is very imperfectly correlated with the amount of Caucasian admixture. Individuals, for example, whose genes are derived in equal (50-50) proportions from African and Caucasian ancestors evince the full range of skin colors from white to black, including all the shades between. This makes it possible statistically to control the effect of skin color; that is, one can compare a number of persons all of whom have the same skin color but different degrees of African/Caucasian admixture, or conversely, the same degree of admixture but different skin colors. (Skin color can be quantified precisely and objectively by means of a photoelectric device which measures reflectance.) The question, then, would be: do the mean IQs (or any other mental ability tests) of the several categories of racial admixture differ significantly and systematically? The genetic equality hypothesis would predict no difference; the genetic inequality hypothesis would predict a difference between the groups.

A further refinement, in order to ensure greater equality of environmental conditions across the admixture categories, *including* prenatal environment, would be to include in the study a large number of half-siblings all related through the mother and reared together. Some half-siblings will inevitably fall into different admixture categories. Do they differ significantly on mental tests when skin color is controlled? Birth order, maternal age, and other factors would have to be noted, but in large samples these factors would probably tend to be random with respect to racial admixture. One would also want a white control group with no African admixture in order to rule out the remote possibility that the blood groups themselves are causally related to IQ, since they are intended in this study only as genetic markers or indices of racial admixture. Such a study would go further toward answering the question of Negro-white genetic differences in intelligences than the sum total of all the other studies that we now have.

The possibility has been suggested of using genetic linkages for studying the inheritance of intelligence and race differences, but evaluation of its potential merits will have to be decided by geneticists. If the genes for some clearly identifiable physical trait are located on the same chromosome as the genes for some measurable mental ability, we should expect to find a marked correlation in the population between the appearance of the physical characteristic and the mental attribute whose genes share the same chromosome. The physical characteristic would thus serve as an objective genetic marker for the mental trait.

The major difficulty with this approach may be that what we call intelligence is so polygenetic that the relevant genes are carried on most or all of the chromosomes, so that specific linkages could never be established. If intelligence consists of a large number of subabilities, each of which is conditioned independently by a very limited number of genes which are carried on a single chromosome, then it may be possible to study linkages, provided we can reliably measure the subabilities. I have described elsewhere how psychologists might make their measurements of abilities of greater interest and value to researchers in genetics (Jensen, 1968c). Briefly, it would consist of the fractionation of mental abilities to the most extreme limits that reliability of measurement will permit, and then seeing if these subabilities show any signs of relatively simple genetic inheritance (such as showing Mendelian ratios) or genetic linkages.

Are there any known linkages between physical and mental characteristics in the normal distribution of intelligence? I do not know of any established examples. We should begin looking for such possible mental linkages with blood groups, biochemical variations, and other physical traits. One set of interesting findings concerns the association between uric acid level in the blood and intellectual achievement. Whether this is an instance of genetic linkage or whether there is a causal connection between uric acid and brain functions is not yet established. Stetten and Hearon (1958) reported a correlation between serum uric acid concentration and scores on the Army intelligence test of 817 inductees. A study of serum urate levels of 51 University of Michigan professors found a positive correlation with drive, achievement, and leadership (Brooks and Mueller, 1966), and high school students have been found to show a similar relationship (Kasl, Brooks, & Cobb, 1966). It would be interesting to know if these correlations are found within other racial groups and also if there are differences between groups in serum uric acid levels. Every bit of such various kinds of information, if it points consistently in the same direction, reduces to some extent the heredity-environment uncertainty.

There are other promising approaches to this problem through biometrical genetics, but explication of the technical aspects of these methods is clearly beyond the possible scope of the present discussion.

IMPLICATIONS FOR EDUCATION

Since educators have at least officially assumed that race and social class differences in scholastic performance are not associated with any genetic differences in growth rates or patterns of mental abilities but are due entirely to discrimination, prejudice, inequality of educational opportunity, and factors in the child's home environment and peer culture, we have collectively given little if any serious thought to whether we would do anything differently if we knew in fact that all educational differences were not due solely to these environmental factors.

There have been and still are obvious environmental inequities and injustices which have disfavored certain minorities, particularly Negroes, Mexican-Americans, and American Indians. Progress has been made and is continuing to be made to improve these conditions. But there is no doubt still a long way to go, and the drive toward further progress in this direction should be given top priority in our national effort. Education is one of the chief instruments for approaching this goal. Every child should receive the best education that our current knowledge and technology can provide. This should not imply that we advocate the same methods or the same expectations for all children. There are large individual differences in rates of mental development, in patterns of ability, in drives and interests. These differences exist even among children of the same family. The good parent does his best to make the most of each child's strong points and to help him on his weak points but not make these the crux of success or failure. The school must regard each child, and the differences among children, in much the same way as a good parent should do.

I believe we need to find out the extent to which individual differences, social class differences, and race difference in rates of cognitive development and differential patterns of relative strength and weakness in various types of ability are attributable to genetically conditioned biological growth factors. The answer to this question might imply differences in our approach to improving the education of all children, particularly those we call the disadvantaged, for many of whom school is now a frustrating and unrewarding experience.

Individuals should be treated in terms of their individual characteristics and not in terms of their group membership. This is the way of a democratic society, and educationally it is the only procedure that makes any sense. Individual variations within any large socially defined group are always much greater than the average differences between groups. There is overlap between groups in the distributions of all psychological characteristics that we know anything about. But dealing with children as individuals is not the greatest problem. It is in our concern about the fact that when we do so, we have a differentiated educational program, and children of different socially identifiable groups may not be proportionately represented in different programs. This is the "hang-up" of many persons today and this is where our conceptions of equal opportunity are most likely to go awry and become misconceptions.

Group racial and social class differences are first of all individual differences, but the causes of the *group* differences may not be the same as those of the *individual* differences. This is what we must find out, because the prescription of remedies for our educational ills could depend on the answer.

Let me give one quite hypothetical example. We know that among middle-class white children, learning to read by ordinary classroom instruction is related to certain psychological developmental characteristics. Educators call it "readiness." These characteristics of readiness appear at different ages for different kinds of learning, and at any given age there are considerable individual differences among children, even among siblings reared within the same family. These developmental differences, in middle-class white children, are largely conditioned by genetic factors. If we try to begin a child too early in reading instruction, he will experience much greater difficulty than if we waited until we saw more signs of "readiness." Lacking readiness, he may even become so frustrated as to "turn off" on reading, so that he will then have an emotional block toward reading later on when he should have the optimal readiness. The readiness can then not be fully tapped. The child would have been better off had we postponed reading instruction for six months or a year and occupied him during this time with other interesting activities for which he was ready. Chances are he would be a better reader at, say, 10 or 11 years of age for having started a year later, when he could catch on to reading with relative ease and avoid the unnecessary frustration. It is very doubtful in this case that some added "enrichment" to his preschool environment would have made him learn to read much more easily a year earlier. If this is largely a matter of biological maturation, then the time at which a child is taught in terms of his own schedule of development becomes important. If, on the other hand, it is largely a matter of preschool environmental enrichment, then the thing to do is to go to work on the preschool environment so as to make all children equally ready for reading in the first grade. If a child's difficulty is the result of both factors, then a combination of both enrichment and optimal developmental sequencing should be recommended.

There is a danger that some educators' fear of being accused of racial discrimination could become so misguided as to work to the disadvantage of many minority children. Should we deny differential educational treatments to children when such treatment will maximize the benefits they receive from schooling, just because differential treatment might result in disproportionate representation of different racial groups in various programs? I have seen instances where Negro children were denied special educational facilities commonly given to white children with learning difficulties, simply because school authorities were reluctant to single out *any* Negro children, despite their obvious individual needs, to be treated any differently from the majority of youngsters in the school. There was no hesitation about singling out white children who needed special attention. Many Negro children of normal and superior scholastic potential are consigned to classes in which one-fourth to one-third of their classmates have IQs below 75, which is the usual borderline of educational mental retardation. The majority of these educationally retarded children benefit little or not at all from instruction in the normal classroom, but require special attention in smaller classes that permit a high degree of individualized and small group instruction. Their presence in regular classes creates unusual difficulties for the conscientious teacher and detracts from the optimal educational environment for children of normal ability. Yet there is reluctance to provide special classes for these educationally retarded children if they are Negro or Mexican-American. The classrooms of predominantly minority schools often have 20 to 30 percent of such children, which handicaps the teacher's efforts on behalf of her other pupils in the normal range of IQ. The more able minority children are thereby disadvantaged in the classroom in ways that are rarely imposed on white children for whom there are more diverse facilities. Differences in rates of mental development and in potentials for various types of learning will not disappear by being ignored. It is up to biologists and psychologists to discover their causes, and it is up to educators to create a diversity of instructional arrangements best suited to the full range of educational differences that we find in our population. Many environmentally caused differences can be minimized or eliminated, given the resources and the will of society. The differences that remain are a challenge for public education. The challenge will be met by making available more ways and means for children to benefit from schooling. This, I am convinced, can come about only through a greater recognition and understanding of the nature of human differences.

REFERENCES

BAJEMA, C. Estimation of the direction and intensity of natural selection in relation to human intelligence by means of the intrinsic rate of natural increase. *Eugen. Quart.*, 1963, 10, 175-187.

BAJEMA, C. J. Relation of fertility to educational attainment in a Kalamazoo public school population: A follow-up study. *Eugen. Quart.*, 1966, 13, 306-315.

BRONFENBRENNER, U. The psychological costs of quality and equality in education. *Child Developm.*, 1967, 38, 909-925.

BROOKS, G. W., & MUELLER, E. Serum urate concentrations among university professors. *J. Amer. Med. Ass.*, 1966, 195, 415-418.

BURT, C. The inheritance of mental ability. *Amer. Psychol.*, 1958, 13, 1-15.

CALDWELL, B. The fourth dimension in early childhood education. In R. Hess and R. Bear (Eds.) *Early Education: Current Theory, Research and Action.* Chicago: Aldine Publishing Co., 1968.

CARTER, C. O. *Human heredity.* Baltimore, Md.: Penguin Books, 1962.

COLEMAN, J. S., et al. *Equality of educational opportunity.* U. S. Dept. of Health, Education, and Welfare, 1966.

CROW, J. F. Genetic theories and influences: Comments on the value of diversity. *Harvard Educational Review*, 1969, 39, 301-309.

DUNCAN, O. D., FEATHERMAN, D. L., & DUNCAN, BEVERLY. Socioeconomic background and occupational achievement: Extensions of a basic model. Final Report, Project No. 5-0074 (EO-191) U. S. Dept. of Health, Education, and Welfare, Office of Education, Bureau of Research, May, 1968.

HIGGINS, J., REED, S.. & REED, E. Intelligence and family size: A paradox resolved. *Eugen. Quart.*, 1962, 9, 84-90.

JENSEN, A. R. Estimation of the limits of heritability of traits by comparison of monozygotic and dizygotic twins. *Proc. Nat. Acad. Sci.*, 1967, 58, 149-157.

JENSEN, A. R. Social class, race, and genetics: Implications for education. *Amer. Educ. Res. J.*, 1968, 5, 1-42. (a)

JENSEN, A. R. Another look at culture-fair testing. In *Western Regional Conference on testing Problems, Proceedings for 1968,* "Measurement for Educational Planning." Berkeley, Calif.: Educational Testing Service, Western Office, 1968. Pp. 50-104. (c)

JENSEN, A. R. How much can we boost IQ and scholastic achievement? *Harvard Educ. Rev.*, 1969, 39, 1-123. (a)

JENSEN, A. R. Reducing the heredity-environment uncertainty. In *Environment, Heredity, and Intelligence. Harvard Educ. Rev.* Reprint Series No. 2. 1969, pp. 209-243. (b)

KASL, S. V., BROOKS, G. W., & COBB, S. Serum urate concentrations in male high school students. *J. Amer. Med. Ass.*, 1966, 198, 713-716.

KENNEDY, W. A., VAN DE RIET, V., & WHITE, J. C. A normative sample of intelligence and achievement of Negro elementary school children in the Southeastern United States. *Monogr. Soc. Res. Child Developm.*, 1963, 28, No. 6.

KUTTNER, R. E. Letters to and from the editor. *Perspect. Biol. Med.*, 1968, 11, 707-709.

LESSER, G. S., FIFER, G., & CLARK, D. H. Mental abilities of children from different social-class and cultural groups. *Monogr. Soc. for Res. in Child Developm.*, 1965, 30, (4).

MOYNIHAN, D. P. Employment, income, and the ordeal of the Negro family. In T. Parsons, & K. B. Clark (Eds.) *The Negro American.* Cambridge: Houghton-Mifflin, 1966. Pp. 134-159.

REED, T. E. Caucasian genes in American Negroes. Unpublished manuscript. March, 1969.

SHUEY, AUDREY M. *The testing of Negro intelligence.* (2nd ed.) New York: Social Science Press, 1966.

SPUHLER, J. N. & LINDZEY, G. Racial differences in behavior. In J. Hirsch (Ed.), *Behavior-genetic analysis.* New York: McGraw-Hill, 1967.

STANLEY, J. C., & PORTER, A. C. Correlation of Scholastic Aptitude Test score with college grades for Negroes versus whites. *J. educ. Meas.*, 1967, 4, 199-218.

STETTEN, D., JR., & HEARON, J. Z. Intellectual level measured by Army classification battery and serum acid concentration. *Science*, 1969, 129, 1737.

STINCHCOMBE, A. L. A critique of Arthur R. Jensen's "How much can we boost IQ and scholastic achievement?" *Harvard Educ. Rev.*, 1969, 39, no. 3.

STODOLSKY, S. S., & LESSER, G. Learning patterns in the disadvantaged. *Harvard Educ. Rev.*, 1967, 37, 546-593.

TANNER, J. M. The trend towards earlier physical maturation. In J. E. Meade & A. S. Parkes (Eds.), *Biological aspects of social problems.* New York: Plenum Press, 1965. Pp. 40-66.

TANNER, J. M. Earlier maturation in man. *Sci. Amer.*, 1968, 218, 21-28.

TERMAN, L. M. & ODEN, M. *The gifted group at mid-life.* Stanford: Stanford University Press, 1959.

TYLER, LEONA E. *The psychology of human differences.* (3rd ed.) New York: Appleton-Century-Crofts, 1965.

WILLERMAN, L., & CHURCHILL, J. A. Intelligence and birth weight in identical twins. *Child Developm.*, 1967, 38, 623-629.

8

IQ: GOD-GIVEN OR MAN-MADE?
A DISCUSSION OF "JENSENISM"

Gilbert Voyat, Ph.D.

Associate Professor of Psychology
Ferkauf Graduate School of Humanities and Social Sciences
Yeshiva University

Who would believe that in the declining decades of the twentieth century the antique psychological argument between environment and heredity would grab headlines and ignite academic tempers?

Last winter, in the *Harvard Educational Review*, Arthur R. Jensen, professor of educational psychology at the University of California at Berkeley, suggested that intelligence is a trait not unlike eye color and hardly more susceptible to change. The study presents an interesting renewal of the genetic argument. Many of the ideas defended are neither new, self-evident, nor irrefutable. The fact that Dr. Jensen's findings are corroborated by statistical evidence does not make them true. It makes them misleading.

His central thesis is simple: Intelligence is a natural trait, inscribed in the genetic pool, unequally distributed among individuals. Theoretically, genius can be found anywhere, regardless of race or social milieu. In practice, however, Jensen insists that in terms of the average IQ, whites are more intelligent than blacks. The average IQ for blacks is, according to his calculations, approximately 15 points below the average for whites. Furthermore, only 15 percent of the Negro population exceeds the white average.

Jensen makes the further assertion that Indians, who are even more disadvantaged than Negroes, are nevertheless more intelligent. Jensen is cautious about this differential intelligence. Negro infants, he claims are more precocious in sensory-motor development in their first year or two than Caucasian infants. The same holds for motor skills. But, he believes, what is critically missing among Negroes is what constitutes

---

genuine formal intelligence: conceptual learning and problem-solving ability.

Jensen describes the roles of genetic and environmental factors as he defines intelligence. His strategy in demonstrating the roles is to use exclusively statistical evidence. It is a typical case of validation by quantification. It is impressive, precise, and wrongheaded.

Jensen's notion of "heritability" is a statistical mean, allowing him to state the extent to which individual differences in intelligence can be accounted for by genetic factors. He concludes that this heritability is quite high in the human species, meaning that genetic factors are much more important than environmental factors in producing IQ differences. And this relationship is displayed in achievement on IQ tests which Jensen sees as related to genetic differences.

These analyses lead Jensen to the conclusion that genetic factors are strongly implicated in achievement in the average Negro-white intelligence differences. Given these conclusions, Jensen ascribes the failure of compensatory education and other enrichment programs to genetic differences, because any attempt to raise intelligence probably lies more in the province of the biological sciences than in that of psychology and education.

Jensen's recommendations are based on distinguishing between two genotypically distinct processes underlying a continuum ranging from "simple" associative learning, which he calls Level I, to complex conceptual learning, which he calls Level II. Object memory, serial rote learning, and selective trial and error learning are good examples of Level I. Concept learning and problem solving in a range of experiences are good examples of Level II. The ideal educational world of Jensen would provide two types of education: one directed toward the acquisition of basic skills and simple associative learning which is training, not education.

The thesis that given such training children with Level I skills will "perfectly" adapt to any society is based mainly on validity of IQ tests. The crucial question concerns the value of IQ tests themselves. The very basis of Jensen's findings must be questioned in the light of what experimental psychology tells us today about the nature of cognitive development and operations.

For example, 50 years ago biology texts opened by giving a definition of "life." Today this is not possible. A definition of life is never adequate because the dynamic aspects of the concept are incompatible with a static and fixed definition. In like manner, IQ tests essentially quantify static definitions. As biology can no longer define life statically, so, too, in psychology a static definition of intelligence is impossible.

PIAGET'S POINT OF VIEW

To understand the limitations of Jensen's basic assumption, it is helpful to consider the point of view of the Swiss psychologist, Jean Piaget. During more than 40 years of experimentation, Piaget has arrived at a formal description of cognitive development and has divided it into four stages. The strong contrasts of Piaget's approach with Jensen's point of view can be demonstrated without a minute detailing of the structure of Piaget's four-stage formal description of cognitive development.

Piagetian "tests" clearly differ from IQ tests. Typical IQ tests are essentially an additive progression of acquired skills. They give a state, a global or overall result for a specific population; their quantitative aspect allows one to place a child among children of his age and development. In contrast, Piagetian tests are hierarchical: they describe a progressive organization and individual potentialities. They provide a detailed analysis of the functioning of thinking. They qualify thinking; they do not quantify it. They always respect the intelligence of a specific child.

Given Piaget's theory we can describe intelligence functionally; we can formalize its structural development. It avoids assigning to intelligence a specific, static definition, in terms of properties, for this directly contradicts the idea of development. Any static definition reduces intelligence either to exclusively environmental factors or to exclusively genetic factors without implying the necessary *equilibrated* interaction between them.

The two levels proposed by Jensen are inadequate to provide a clear idea of the *development* of intelligence. Piaget never gives a static definition of intelligence, he gives a functional one. The two functions of intelligence are to understand the external world and to build or discover new structures within it. Piaget's experiments are involved with a description of a progressive organization directed by logic and not greatly influenced by culture. A whole set of Piagetian experiments have been carried out in Africa, Algeria, Iran, and elsewhere.

The main result is that sequential development, in comparable terms, is observed irrespective of the culture or the race. In other words, the stages of developing intelligence are respected in their succession and do not permit, even in a theoretical continuum, division into the type of level differences that Jensen describes, and they most strongly suggest the irrelevance of these genotypically distinct basic processes.

In contrast, IQ tests, designed by whites for Western culture, have value limited to the culture within which they were designed. In any testing of intelligence, relativity, not absolutism, should be the criterion.

Even the correction of IQ tests for other populations is not valid. Furthermore, IQ tests are simply not adequate to measure processes of thinking. They provide results, they do not lead to an understanding of how intelligence functions. Piaget's approach not only allows an understanding of how intelligence functions but describes it. Since the interests of Piaget's tests lie in describing the mechanism of thinking, they permit an individual, personalized appraisal of further potentialities independent of the culture. This is neglected in IQ tests where the global population is assessed rather than individual potentialities estimated.

Jensen's methodology may have its merits. The problem is that the point of departure is wrong. To decide compensatory and other programs are failures is an important, responsible act. To base judgment on IQ measurements is questionable.

One must have a way to judge such programs. But to decide IQ gains are small and do not justify the money poured into such educational enterprises can give the impression that psychologists and educators know what they are talking about concerning processes of learning. But one problem of education is that very little is known about the underlying processes of learning. Furthermore, pedagogy provides generalized techniques for what must be individualized teaching. Not much is known about how the child grasps notions such as conservation, seriation, number, mass, motion, time, and logical categories. Psychologists who place their confidence in IQ tests forget the real issue—how the child learns.

Our tragic situation of lacking knowledge about the learning process should make us modest. We should accept that the nature of cognitive learning is an open question for experimental and developmental psychology.

Jensen's position is a dangerous one strictly on cognitive grounds. It prescribes a limitation on experience for the four- or five-year-old who already has an egocentric view of his world. If learning is to take place in the often confusing circumstances of childhood, the precise purpose of teaching is to exploit such circumstances, not to limit them.

Dr. C. Kamii of Ypsilanti (Mich.) Public Schools makes the point relative to her experience following Piaget's model: If we really want children to learn, the *process* of interacting with the environment must be emphasized rather than a specific response already selected by the teacher. This idea of process is never considered in Jensen's approach, either in his theoretical position or in his pedagogical evaluation. In Piaget's conception of process, emphasizing logical conflicts is naturally involved.

A primary role of the teacher is to follow the process and to provide creative conflict at appropriate moments. In the long run, the imposition of rules is a less efficient way to teach than influencing development of underlying cognitive processes that will eventually enable the child to construct his own rules, which will square with physical reality.

The creative aspect of learning and teaching is lost in Jensen's point of view. The child is reduced to a ratio. Teaching becomes a mechanical adjustment of narrowly identified capacities to severely limited learning goals. Education must be more generous than this.

9

THE NATIONAL IMPACT STUDY
OF HEAD START

Sheldon H. White, Ph.D.

Roy E. Larsen Professor of Educational Psychology
Graduate School of Education, Harvard University
Laboratory of Human Development (Cambridge)

In April, 1969, preliminary results of a national study of the effectiveness of Head Start were released, showing marginal positive results of the program. The study was promptly controversial. Consultants to the study were divided, one publicly withdrawing his name from it and disclaiming it, others coming to its defense. Several prominent individuals not involved in the study issued public criticism of the work and of its conclusions. I was a consultant involved with the effort and, while I believe there are flaws in it, I also believe that the flaws are not critical and that the study's general conclusions are sound. None of the arguments I have yet seen has changed my mind about this.

The public discussion back and forth does not seem fully meaningful. As one testimony after another is given, all the phrases of claim or disclaim seem to fall into the simplest sort of adversarial pattern. One gathers that there are Fors and there are Againsts and that all have their reasonable-sounding reasons. It seems worthwhile to go over the study, to put the claims into a context and try to show how far apart the Fors and Againsts really are. The controversy about the Head Start evaluation is not a black-or-white affair. It arises out of a complicated collaboration, one whose limits and merit are still not fully understood, the collaborative decision-making between social scientists and government officials first in the construction of social programs and later in their evaluation.

Head Start was one of a series of extraordinarily swift moves by which, in 1964-1965, the government went to war on poverty. Head Start's authorization came under Title II, the educational provision of the Economic Opportunity Act of 1964, though at the time of the passage of that act Head Start had not yet been invented. Title II simply provided that there would be special programs for the education of the poor located outside the usual framework of public education. The crystalization of this mandate into Head Start preschools began with the establishment of a Planning Committee in November, 1964. The public announcement was made in January, 1965. Head Start was operational, nationwide, by the Summer of 1965.

In the light of what was known then, the Head Start program must be seen as a bold gamble, which drove over theoretical and practical hesitancies and which sought to bury them under the weight of a *fait accompli*. We do not yet know whether the gamble has succeeded or failed. Why Head Start? Why so quickly?

—There was a problem. It had become clear, in 1964, that legal re-assertions of the civil rights of minorities had only opened doors to rooms that the Black could not enter. The Black was burdened by an educational handicap visible on the day he entered school and defini-tive on the day he left it. He was, generally, one-half year behind na-tional norms in kindergarten, one year behind in the third grade, three years behind in the twelfth grade.

—There was a new cadre of professional reformers that could pick out that problem and make its solution an immediate national need. Daniel P. Moynihan's recent book, *Maximum Feasible Misunderstanding*, de-scribes the history of one sector of the war on poverty, the Community Action Programs, and in so doing it describes the forces that created Head Start. Here, too, there was social action dictated not by grass roots demands but by the social diagnostician; there was the urge to establish a solution outside The System, which had "failed"; there was scientific backing offered by the expert-turned-advocate.

—There was scientific backing, supportive research evidence, but of a mixed quality. The traditional wisdom tended to be negative and/or confused; it had leaned towards the view that human intelligence was largely inherited and constant throughout life; it had tried preschool education to raise the IQ a few times and had decided that it didn't work; it knew little about the processes by which preschool children learn. All this from the somewhat somnolent domains of child psychol-ogy and preschool education.* But there were also some bright new

---

* On February 7-9, 1966, not long after the initiation of Head Start, the Social Science Research Council held a Conference on Pre-School Education. As a discussant at that meeting, I discussed the traditional wisdom in the words given here:

"Five or ten years ago, a developmental psychologist asked the important ques-tions which are on the table today would have given generally predictable answers:

"—If he were asked whether the IQ can be augmented by pre-school experience, he would have answered that there have been some claims to that effect but that the weight of evidence seemed to discount those claims, the generally accepted, conservative interpretation being that the IQ is fairly constant.

"—If he were asked what kinds of pre-school experiences could be used to further intellectual development, he might or might not have made allusion to the somewhat forgotten works of Maria Montessori. He might have argued

challenges to that traditional wisdom. In 1961, J. McVicker Hunt's book, *Intelligence and Experience,* had attacked the notion of predestined intelligence and had argued that intelligence could be changed. In 1964, Benjamin Bloom's book, *Stability and Change in Human Characteristics,* presented analyses suggesting that intelligence was most likely to be plastic in the preschool years, that it reaches stability at age 6 or 7. Neither book's arguments were ironclad, but they drew attention to the importance of learning in the early years and their point was augmented. There had been some attempts to teach in the preschool years—Martin Deutsch's compensatory preschool in New York City, Susan Gray's preschool in Nashville, O. K. Moore's autotelic teaching of reading to preschoolers—and the early reports from these efforts sounded promising. So, from Academia, with a little picking and choosing, one could find some positive backing.

Thus, in 1964, one could argue a need for Head Start preschools and find research work to suggest their promise. The political support was duly forthcoming. It was sure that the country did not have the resources, in experienced personnel or in established facilities, for a national network of compensatory preschools, but one could expect that the program would build its resources as it grew. Early planning had envisaged a beginning with 50,000 to 100,000 children in an eight-week summer program, but the idea of Head Start was a natural. It had a kind of magic for everyone. Sixty-five percent of the counties in the

---

that such a question was beside the point, that the many pre-schools in every large city existed principally on social justifications, to teach children how to play with other children or to serve as pleasant custodial places for the convenience or the necessity of parents.

"—If he were asked to describe what a child learns during the pre-school years, he might have answered by reference to normative studies which compile age-changes in indices of language, motor skills, social attitudes, etc. The aggregate of these normative studies, to be sure, would have amounted to a rather adventitious sampling of the easily measured indices of intellectual growth, not a comprehensive view of the intellectual growth of the child.

"—If he were asked how a child learns during the pre-school years, his answer would have been a largely hypothetical account in one or more of the terminologies with which we discuss children's adaptation—the terminology of environmental contingency and habit, the terminology of differentiation and integration, of social and emotional adjustment, of imitation and identification, of self-actualization. Whichever way he chose to answer the question, his answer would have been hypothecated on the basis of studies with animals and adults, very little on the basis of actual observations and experiments done with children of differing ages.

"Such questions would have been approached rather casually by most developmental psychologists; it did not seem so urgent to form exact judgments about these questions then. The vagueness of our information about the fundamental questions has not been alleviated noticeably, but there has been a breakthrough in our need for understanding. Society's needs press in upon us suddenly. Placed in the uncomfortable role of experts without expertise, we are all in the business of trying to supply educated guesses about the nature of children's cognitive development."

Quote taken from R. D. Hess and R. M. Bear (Eds.) *Early Education: Current theory, research, and practice.* Chicago: Aldine Publishing Co., 1968, pp. 203-204.

nation applied for Head Start programs and, ultimately, 40% were granted them.

During its first summer, in 1965, Head Start served 561,000 children in some 2400 communities in the United States and its possessions. Federal antipoverty funds provided 83 million dollars on a 90%-of-support basis. With local supplementation, the cost of Summer, 1965 came to 95 million dollars. Succeeding Summer operations have been of about the same magnitude. Beginning in Fall, 1965, Full-year Head Start programs were initiated, serving 20,000 children and then increasing tenfold by 1967, when 215,000 children were enrolled. Summer and Full-year components together have by now reached over 2 million children since the inception of Head Start. At present, Head Start operates on a budget of about $350 million a year.

The central focus of Head Start has been preschool education but the Child Development Centers sponsored by the program were given the responsibility for a more comprehensive intervention, actually a sixfold mission: (1) an educational program; (2) health services, to provide medical diagnosis and treatment; (3) social services, aid to the child's family; (4) psychological services; (5) nutrition; (6) a parent participation program. One had an expensive intervention, running to $220 per child in Summer programs and $1050 per child in the Full-year, but one had a program which was trying to reach out at all the possible roots of educational deficit.

But the gamble lurked beneath all of this implementation. Politicians could vote for Head Start; bureaucrats could carefully place the funds out; willing teachers, parents, nurses, doctors, etc. could then establish over 12,000 Head Start Centers around the country.* The preschools

---

* The following is a quote from a letter written on September 11, 1965 by Keith Osborn, an early consultant to Head Start:

"I wish I knew how to tell this part of the story—the many nonprofessionals (the secretaries at OEO and other personnel) who worked 12-15 hours every day between February and June—because they wanted these children to have a Head Start in school. The bus driver in West Virginia who took time off from his regular job and went to the Center to have juice and crackers with "his" children because they asked him to. The Head Start Center in Mississippi that met in a church which was burned to the ground by some whites—and they opened the next day in a tent. The farmer who lived near an Indian Reservation and who each morning saddled his horse, forded a river and picked up an Indian child—who would not have attended a Center otherwise. An ADC (Aid-to-Dependent-Children) mother who worked four hours daily in one center—without pay—she paid a baby-sitter to care for her other children—why? Because she wanted these children to get the schooling she never had. The Kentucky principal who worked at two jobs for four months so his county could have Head Start. The Negro principal in Georgia who will probably lose his position in the school system because of his stand in following the "spirit" that Head Start is for *all* children regardless of color. Numerous consultants who, on an hour's notice, dropped everything and flew all over the country to help communities plan for Head Start. I visited one cook (a volunteer) working in a "tenant farm" center—there were no fans and only one small window in the kitchen—the temperature was 97° outside—she was cooking fried chicken and baking rolls

offered an intensive encounter for the child, 1 teacher for every 15 children, 1 adult for every 5 children. All this did not erase the gamble. The heart of the gamble lay in that which the experts were not so certain about, what to do in a preschool program and how to evaluate it.

There was not then—and there is not now—any tested and generally accepted way to mount a curriculum for preschool children. Head Start has been, and is, the corporate name for a nationally implemented series of preschool programs, but Head Start has never specifically dictated the curriculum of these programs. In view of the current state of the art of preschool education such a prescription would be quite controversial.

Throughout all education one finds confusion about what should be taught to whom, but in the primary and secondary grades there are rough agreements about curriculum which keep the arguments within bounds: there will be reading, and writing and arithmetic in some form in the early grades and, in the higher grades, there will be such things as history and algebra and geometry and foreign languages. The range of opinions about what could or should happen in preschool education is, at the present time, almost unbounded. Most people do not know how deep the confusion is, simply because it takes time and repeated exposures to reveal the diversity of strongly-voiced opinions, and the ambiguity beneath them all. One recognizes, at first, a great polarity between less-structured, adjustment-centered goals versus more-structured, teaching-centered goals. But this is largely an organization of the rhetoric and as one penetrates beneath it one gets to a second layer of the problem. There are remarkably few preschool curricula spelled out in such a way as to be prescriptive for their users, capable of being disseminated from an originator to a follower. Such spelled-out training— Montessori, Bereiter, Moore—is either difficult to obtain, or ideologically repugnant, to a good majority of preschool educators. When one gets past the spelled-out programs and one listens again and again to people talking about their preschool programs, it is very hard to tell whether two people who talk alike or differently actually run their programs alike or differently.

Periodic unofficial descriptions of the Head Start curriculum have placed emphasis on teaching to overcome handicaps in learning,* but

---

for the children. Or even the school superintendent who received funds for 30 migrant children and then returned the funds because the families moved before the Center opened.
    "I don't know how you tell these stories in an article—it is really unfortunate— since they represent the true flavor of Head Start."

(From a letter quoted in J. L. Frost (Ed.) *Early Childhood Education Rediscovered.* New York: Holt, Rinehart, and Winston, 1968, pp. 285-286.)

* "These programs are shaped largely by assumptions about the characteristics of 'culturally deprived' children which underlie their inferior academic performance. These characteristics, which follow patterns of both cognitive and affective deficit—at

such descriptions do not seem to square with the emphases of a majority of Head Start directors as they themselves report them.

A national sample of Summer, 1966 Head Start was surveyed by Educational Testing Service, which concluded that:

> "Response patterns to statements related to curriculum orientation were rather consistent. They reveal a preference for a supportive, unstructured socialization program rather than a structured, informational program."

At the same time that survey did reveal that 36% of Center directors agreed with the statement, "It is through organized and systematic stimulation, through a structured and articulated learning program that a child is best prepared for the demands of school."* Data revealed by the Head Start Official's Interview Questionnaire in the 1969 Westinghouse/Ohio study give much the same distribution of approaches.

All of this is not to say that the Head Start Center directors are wrong or right in their emphases, only that there is no one description of what they are doing. About the curricula of the many local implementations of Head Start, one can say this. They are not well known. They are heterogeneous. They reflect the existing dispute between adjustment-centered versus teaching-centered goals. They have been significantly biased towards the adjustment emphasis. All this variation is reasonable and desirable, but it does pose a problem for the evaluation of Head Start as a national effort. With local variations in approach augmented by all the other local variations in circumstance—ethnicity of children, geographical area, size of program, background of teacher, health of children, rural vs. urban setting, etc.—the demonstrated success or failure of one Center is not immediately indicative of the success of the others.

---

least from the middle-class point of view—include poor language facility, constriction in dealing with symbolic and abstract ideas, narrowness of outlook because of the narrowness of the familiar environment, passivity and lack of curiosity, low self-esteem, and lack of motivation for achievement."

(Clay V. Brittain, "Some Early Findings of Research on Preschool Programs for Culturally Deprived Children." In J. L. Frost (Ed.) *Early Childhood Education Rediscovered*. New York: Holt, Rinehart, and Winston, 1968, p. 287.)

> "The educational program is designed to help the children develop vocabulary and verbal fluency, spontaneity in expression, familiarity with school routines, trust in and rapport with teachers, interest in books, a motivation to want to learn to read, and a broadened concept of the world around them. Cultural enrichment is stressed in the educational program and teachers are encouraged to utilize community resources for exposure to enrichment experiences."

(William F. Brazziel, "Two Years of Head Start." In J. L. Frost (Ed.) *Early Childhood Education Rediscovered*. New York: Holt, Rinehart, and Winston, 1968, p. 298.)

* From an Educational Testing Service Final Report, *Project Head Start Summer 1966*, Section Two, "Facilities and Resources of Head Start Centers," by Joseph L. Boyd.

Head Start, like other divisions of OEO, had at first been given responsibility for its own evaluation. The evaluation mission was hampered by the fact that Head Start has not had a continuous, full-time research director during its three-year history, but a number of studies of the effects of the program were commissioned and completed. The results of these evaluation efforts were inconclusive. Some studies were poorly done and their conclusions not fully trustworthy. The well-executed evaluation studies, of which there are a reasonable number, have either been short-term studies just following the children through the Head Start training period or else, if they have gone after longer-term effects, they have been localized to one Center or a few adjacent Centers.

The consistent pattern of the findings was this: some effect of the training, demonstrated benefit to Head Start pupils as compared with matched control children on a number of instruments, followed later by a "levelling off." The Head Start children maintained their gains but the control children in their first year of schooling showed increases which brought them level with the Head Start group. But this was a pattern inferred by reading across studies. Clearly, there had to be a larger study which examined long-range effects among a national sample of Head Start children.

Early in 1968, the Office of Economic Opportunity reviewed its program evaluation, not only in Head Start but in all its divisions, and it reorganized the effort. Three kinds of evaluation were distinguished. One, sometimes called *summative evaluation,* would assess the impact of a program as a whole, averaging over local variations in implementation. The second, *formative evaluation,* would be concerned with locating and analyzing strong programs, more effective approaches, to find ways to improve the overall effort. The third, *monitoring,* would be custodial, the periodic review of each local activity to see to it that minimum expectations about performance were being met.

The 1968 OEO reorganization gave the broadest evaluation, the summative, to its Office of Evaluation which would henceforth serve as a kind of scientific auditing arm of the agency. Formative evaluation and monitoring were left to the responsibility of separate programs. Because a comprehensive national assessment of the effects of Head Start seemed needed, one of the early moves of the Office of Evaluation was to design such a study and issue an "RFP" (a Request for Proposals) to organizations which might do such a study. Other comprehensive studies commissioned at about that time were concerned with various manpower programs, the Community Action Programs, Neighborhood Health Centers, Family Planning, and JOBS.

The successful bidder for the Head Start evaluation was the Westinghouse Learning Corporation, joined for the execution of the contract with Ohio State University, and its study was carried through in the period from June, 1968 to June, 1969.

The original RFP staked out a great many of the conditions under which Westinghouse/Ohio were expected to operate. The questions to which the study was to be directed were the following:

> Does the school readiness or early school performance of children who have been through Head Start differ on the average nationally from that of comparable children who have not been through Head Start?
>
> If so, about how much improvement, on the average, does Head Start bring about?
>
> What is the relative benefit of Summer Head Start versus Full-year Head Start?
>
> Is there a difference in net benefit attributable to Head Start depending on whether the children are in the first, second, or third year of school (possibly attributable to changes in Head Start over the years or to "levelling" effect)?

The most favorable approach to such questions would be a "before-after" design. Head Start and Control children would be tested before the school session to establish their similarity, then retested after the Head Start children had received their training to see if they were now dissimilar. Such a before-after design, particularly if it sought to trace Head Start effects through to the third grade, would take years to accomplish. The study needed to be done quickly and, therefore, an "after only" design was called for in the RFP. Children who had had Head Start training would be identified in the first, second, and third grades and then Control children would be sought who matched them according to certain background factors which would suggest that they had once been comparable.

The RFP specified the universe to be sampled (children in the first three years of school, in disadvantaged neighborhoods, in areas where Head Start programs existed), but it did not specify the size of the sample, nor the strategy by which it was to be located. The RFP outlined characteristics of the children to be tested, but did not specify which tests to use. After the award of the proposal, the sampling procedure and the evaluative instruments were arrived at by Westinghouse/Ohio in consultation with the OEO Evaluation Office and a specially recruited panel of consultants, who were regularly called upon for reactions and advice.

As the sampling was finally worked out, it went this way. From the list of 12,927 Head Start Centers existing in 1966-1967, a random sample of 104 was drawn. In that year, 70% of Head Start programs were Summer and 30% Full-year. The selected group of 104 centers preserved that proportionality: 75 had Summer programs and 29 Full-year. Once the 104 Head Start Centers had been located, each Center was construed as the nucleus of one of 104 "target areas." The target area was a geographical area including the Head Start Center, the several public schools into which Head Start graduates entered, and the residential area served by that set of schools. From the school's lists, Head Start graduates were sought in the first to third grades, eight graduates at each grade level. Such Head Start children having been identified, an equal number of Control children were sought in the same target area— children who had not attended Head Start, but who had lived in the area at the time of the inception of the local Head Start program and who would have met the local eligibility requirements.

Head Start and Control children were thus, by the constraints of this search process, matched for school grade, area of residence, length of residence, and qualification for Head Start. Certain further matches were made. Head Start and Control children were alike according to race, sex, and whether or not the children had attended kindergarten in addition to Head Start. All this matching did not include a deliberate attempt to determine the social class status of the Head Start and Control child and assure its equality. This would have been difficult to do properly during the sampling, and it was because of this difficulty that a covariance analysis was projected—a type of treatment of test scores which could change them to take out effects of differences in "SES" (socioeconomic status) among the children.

There were vicissitudes in the sampling process—shortages in projected subjects, problems in obtaining necessary cooperation, variations in local practices—which superimposed on the logic of the sampling plan a hundred little local judgments about the proper way to handle special situations. Some of these called for side investigations.

—Two hundred and twenty-five Head Start Centers had to be investigated in order to settle on 104 which could furnish the kind of cooperation and information the study needed. A subsidiary analysis then had to be done to establish that there was no significant bias involved in the selection of the centers actually used.

—The Head Start children seen in the study were necessarily those who had remained in the target area after their training, but this remainder might be a biased group whose performance would not fully reflect the benefits of Head Start. Suppose the program had some effect on the family that enabled it to move out of the residential area into a better location. This, in itself, would be a noteworthy effect of Head Start. Furthermore, the migration might remove from the area exactly those children whose performance might best reflect the educational benefits of Head Start. The possibility was a little more than imaginary; anecdotal reports from Susan Gray's work in a housing project in Nashville suggest that such reactive migration occurs at least occasionally.

Accordingly, a side study on out-migration of Head Start families from target areas had to be conducted. Ten representative target areas were selected for a subsidiary analysis of migration which showed that about 12% of Head Start graduates had moved away from the first three grades. This value was low, and the side study ended with this figure. Pressures of time and cost did not allow the subsidiary study to proceed ahead and fully nail down the migration issue; that is, to show that rates of migration are comparable for Head Start and non Head Start families in the target areas and, also, to show that there was no difference academically between Head Start children who moved and those who stayed.

Out of a possible total of 3,984 subjects, the study found 3,963. The sample was composed of 1,980 Head Start and 1,983 Control children (the numbers unequal because four Head Start children and one Control child did not complete their testing program, and no replacements for them were available). The sample included about half the number of cases in the third grade as were located in second and first. Grade 3 Head Start children were graduates of Summer, 1965 or Full-year 1965-1966. These were the beginning years of the Summer and Full-year programs and, since the first full year was on a relatively small scale, its graduates were in short supply in the third grade.

Another significant set of decisions had to be made about the tests used to evaluate the sample. Three kinds of instruments were put together, one set intended as indices of the cognitive status of the child, a second trying to determine his affective status, and a third set of background instruments to be given to significant adults in the child's environment.

The cognitive evaluation could proceed on the surest ground, using well-established instruments which have been widely used and whose characteristics are relatively well understood. The first graders were given the Metropolitan Readiness Test, a test used to diagnose children's readiness for first grade subject matter and highly correlated with success in the first grade. The second and third graders were given consecutive versions of the Stanford Achievement Test, a comprehensive battery of tests nationally accepted as a standard for the achievement to be expected in those grades. All children were given the Illinois Test of Psycholinguistic Abilities, one of the most sophisticated of existing instruments for use at this age level. The test analyses the child's ability to comprehend symbolic material as a number of subabilities. It diagnoses special problems, and at the same time gives a total score which is about equivalent to the usual test of verbal intelligence. The test, given individually, requires some skill to administer properly and Westinghouse/Ohio mounted a training program for its field examiners in order to prepare them for its use.

In contrast to the cognitive evaluation, the affective evaluation presented enormous difficulties. Most preschool educators, as has been said, believe that the most significant goal of preschool work should be to change the child's attitude towards himself and school, and improve his motivation to learn. There are only a few existing instruments which get at such attitudes, and their utility is either unimpressive or not known. Westinghouse/Ohio undertook to build three suitable instruments even though there was great time pressure. One instrument, the *Children's Self-Concept Index,* tried to detect how positively or negatively the child felt about himself. The child was presented with pairs of stick figures, one described by a positive statement and the other by a negative statement, and he was asked to choose which figure was most like himself. A second instrument, the *Classroom Behavior Inventory,* went after the child's motivation to achieve in school by asking his teacher to rate him. ("Does he try to figure things out for himself before asking for help?"—the question replied to on a five point scale ranging from "Always" to "Never"). The third instrument, the *Children's Attitudinal Range Indicator,* asked the child how positively he felt about peers, home, school, and society. Picture stories were used, three frames outlining a story (Bobby going to school, approaching the building, going inside) and the fourth frame asking the child to choose an emotional outcome (stylized faces looking happy, neutral, or sad).

The three affective measures look reasonable; they have "face validity." Working with preliminary samples of children, Westinghouse tried to establish a more rigorous validity. The results of this preliminary work, as given in the draft report, are all right as far as they go, but they do not go very far. Though the affective measures were ultimately used to come to conclusions in the main body of the draft report, I am inclined to feel that this is a little misleading. I believe that the contractor could have pleaded *nolo contendere* about the issue of attitude measurement. Possibly, subsequent work may establish the credibility of the instruments. Then, one might look back on the published Westinghouse comparisons as meaningful comparisons of attitude.

The third set of instruments, all given to adults in the child's environment, had a mixed purpose. They were to locate background factors which might influence the child's reaction to his Head Start experience and, at the same time, they might reveal indirect effects of Head Start on the child's family life. There was a *Head Start Official's Interview Questionnaire,* designed to get a picture of each of the nuclear Centers' organization, staff, population of children, parental involvement, program objectives, facilities, and relationship with the public schools. There was a *Parent Interview Questionnaire* designed to get at factors in the psychological atmosphere of the home which might help or hinder schooling, and also to get descriptive information about the family and its situation. Parents were also given a *Vocational Aspiration-Expectation*

Index, one form if the child was a boy and another if a girl, designed to reveal the parent's occupational hopes for his child. Finally, there was a *School Environment Measure,* a set of descriptive sentences about a classroom with which a teacher might agree or disagree, which were designed to establish dimensions of classroom atmosphere and management in the post-preschool classroom.

Looking at the whole battery of evaluation instruments, one might fairly characterize it as adequate for the task. The central issue in the evaluation of Head Start, the subsequent performance of the child in school, was to be approached with substantial instrumentation. While the attitudes of the child were approached with instruments which were, in my opinion, not proven, it must be understood that in this context of evaluation the value of those attitudes should have been registered in the school achievement measures. The weakness of the attitude instruments left a small loophole. If the cognitive measures failed to register a difference between Head Start and Control children, and if the attitude measures were defective, then one might still argue that Head Start produces a sleeper effect, a change in attitude which does not influence schooling in the early years but does affect it later. The third set of background instruments were reasonably comprehensive in their search through possibly-relevant factors in Head Start program, home, and school classroom. As it happened, however, partly because of the nature of the sampling and partly because of the pattern of the results, those factors could not be applied to sorting out the Head Start effects.

We turn now to the results of the study, which can be quickly characterized. Separate determinations of the effects of Head Start were made for Summer Head Start and Full-year Head Start. Each grade was looked at separately. The data for each of the cognitive and affective tests were examined separately, each test as a whole and subtest by subtest. Groupings of Head Start Centers were examined according to gross geographical area (Western, Northeast, Southeast), and according to population unit (Core cities, Small cities, Small cities near Core cities, Small cities far from Core cities, Villages and rural), and according to ethnic mix (90-100% Negro and 0-10% white; 10-90% Negro and 10-90% white; 0-10% Negro and 90-100% white; 90-100% Mexican-American and 0-10% white; other racial/ethnic combinations). The data were treated using the covariance analysis first planned for and then once again using another analytic technique which avoids some of the assumptions necessary for covariance analysis.

The study, generally, did not detect any positive effect of Summer Head Start programs, either across-the-board or in most of the compartments of the differentiated comparisons. This was true in each of the three grades. There was an indication that Summer Head Start had a slight positive effect for Black children. There did appear, in the cognitive instruments, the suspicion of a reverse trend; with some regularity, there were slight differences favoring the *Control* children registered on all three cognitive instruments and in all three grades. Such a trend could most simply be explained by an imperfection in the matching of Head Start and Control children, such that the Control children were drawn from a slightly more advantaged background. The draft report goes over this possibility and discounts it. But comparisons of the circumstances of Head Start and Control families, possible through detailed questionnaire data given in an appendix, show that the matching was not perfect. Control families seem to be slightly better off. This would account for the reverse findings.

The study's determinations of the effects of Full-year Head Start showed some positive effects of Head Start in the first and second grades, with the number of cases in the third grade too small to make a meaningful determination. In the first grade, the Head Start children were superior to the Control children on the Metropolitan Readiness Test. Otherwise, in first grade and second grade, there was a pattern of scattered positive effects. There was some suggestion that Head Start Full-year training might be selectively potent in the Southeast region of the country, and for Blacks. The affective instruments failed to detect consistent differences between Head Start and Control children in the Full-year programs but, for the reasons indicated earlier, my own inclination is to discount this.

So, on the whole, the results showed that only Full-year Head Start had produced detectable positive effects on the cognitive measures. A good many of these effects were large enough to be statistically significant (likely to be found again by a study of this scope), but they were not large enough to make one believe that the child's academic prospects were much improved. There is a rough convention in educational evaluation which holds that only an improvement on a test which amounts to half a standard deviation should be considered educationally significant. No positive effect of Full-year Head Start met this criterion of practical significance. Viewing the position of the Full-year Head Start children in more absolute terms, they were estimated at about eight months behind national norms on the Illinois Test of Psycholinguistic Ability, at the 44th percentile of the first grade Metropolitan Readiness Test, and at the 20th percentile on the second-grade Stanford Achievement Test.

We turn now to the controversy about the National Impact study, and its results. Controversy brewed up because of several factors: first, the fact that the process of working out the final report of the study was made awkward by some unforeseen circumstances; second, because of a general question raised by Head Start officials and others both before and after the study, the question whether one could do a definitive evaluation of Head Start at this time; and third, because of weaknesses, real or imagined, in the techniques of the study itself.

The original contract arrangements called for delivery of the final report in April, 1969, and in early March a first working draft of a final report was submitted to consultants for their reactions. Two of the consultants—Dr. William G. Madow, a mathematical statistician at Stanford who was ultimately to withdraw his name from the report, and myself—had been conducting a campaign for some basic changes in the analysis of the study as it had been originally planned. (There had originally been a plan to begin the attack on the data by a gross analysis which lumped effects of Summer and Full-year programs together. We felt that such an analysis would be meaningless and misleading. Originally, the data analysis was to be entirely through covariance analysis; the scores of each test were to be "corrected" in accordance with measured differences in socioeconomic status and, thus, effects of differences between Head Start and Control children in socioeconomic status would be "taken out" of the analysis. Covariance analyses are tricky. They depend upon assumptions which are hard to guarantee. In the case of this study, there was a conceivable possibility—if the gains from Head Start are positively correlated with the child's socioeconomic status— that the covariance adjustments might incidentally lift some legitimate Head Start gains out of the data.)

These two issues had been the subject of long letters and conference calls—a process which was time-consuming, occasionally exasperating, but basically well-meaning and on its way to being worked out. It was agreed that Summer and Full-year Head Start would be separately evaluated. It was agreed that an alternative analysis which avoided the covariance problems would be done and would be described in the report.

The first working draft in March was not satisfactory with respect to the existing issues, and it raised others. It did not present either the covariance analysis or its alternative completely and satisfactorily. In addition, by laying out the findings of the study for the first time, it brought up a series of new questions about subsidiary analysis to establish the soundest interpretation of the data. There were other minor shortages and obscurities in the report. A rather substantial editing and revision had to be envisaged and so a new final date for submission was obtained.

Along about March, however, political heat entered to increase the already substantial time pressure. In late February and early March, Congress was going over the authorization for the poverty program. There was conflict between Congressional forces who sought continuation of the poverty program in its entirety and the new Nixon administration which sought to make changes in it. A national evaluation of Head Start was an important factor in such a contest, particularly if it was negative. It was possible to believe that the extension of time to May 31 was an attempt to submerge the impact of the National Impact study. Congress was unhappy, and there was talk of an investigation. This made the Administration unhappy and so the working draft, with only a few emendations, was released as a Preliminary Draft report on April 14.

The acceleration required to produce a draft report in April probably did add fuel to the public controversy. It interfered with an already difficult process of discussion among contractor and consultants, and thus helped to cause a behind-the-scenes technical discussion to "go public."

But controversy would have come anyway. The second kind of questioning directed at the Westinghouse study is more basic; it asks whether evaluation techniques could make a fair judgment of Head Start in 1968-1969. Should the Westinghouse evaluation have been undertaken at all? The readiness of Head Start for definitive evaluation was at least debatable. By going to the third grade, the Westinghouse study tapped all three years of Head Start's existence. The first summer, 1965, was by all accounts a chaotic affair in which everyone concerned with Head Start had to scramble amidst impossible confusion simply to make some semblance of a preschool program concrete. Given the general unpreparedness of 1965, it is highly probable that the three years since then have been a learning experience in which all concerned—Head Start administrators and teachers, Washington administrators and evaluators —have been slowly learning how to do their job properly. By evaluating the program over the years when it has been consolidating itself, might one not risk a premature negative conclusion about a potentially profitable venture?

This is a reasonable argument, but I believe that Head Start had to stand for an evaluation at this time, ready or not. The gamble of Head Start lay in its instant nationwide implementation. It could have been launched in a much less expensive way, by support of a series of small scale programs to demonstrate feasibility, then by progressive and prudent administrative steps to the scale of a nationwide program. During the early phase, when costs were low, one might have expected to wait until the time was ripe for a definitive evaluation. By going into nationwide implementation, Head Start quickly went into annual costs of 350 million dollars, a considerable sum which might be used for other kinds of approaches and whose value calls for justification. The study might have produced such justification and, if it did, the gamble would have won. In the actual case, with the finding of scant positive results, a prudent bureaucracy might be expected to acknowledge the possible prematurity of the evaluation and keep some form of Head Start going. At the same time, with findings showing that Head Start does not have an effect when given in any old way, a prudent bureaucracy might be expected to become interested in pilot projects which would show a right way to perform Head Start and to diminish emphasis on nation-wide implementation until there were some indications of that right way.

Were there evaluation instruments adequate for the enterprise? This is a question for judgment and, above, I have already discussed the individual tests and offered some judgments of them. The cognitive tests were by far the most important since all other effects must sooner or later channel their influence into academic work. The cognitive tests were substantial instruments and it would be hard to believe that Head Start could produce some worthwhile benefit to academic success in the first three grades which slipped by them. The instruments were sensitive enough to make the kind of gross determination this study called for, to decide that something had happened without deciding what. Of course, no test could detect an effect if the design of the study could not bring before it properly representative groups of Head Start children and properly matched controls, which brings us to the third line of criticism, the attacks on the techniques of the study.

The study has flaws and soft spots. No study of this scope, done so quickly, could be pristine. It is not sufficient criticism of a field study to find design flaws, avoidable or unavoidable, without considering whether they are of a kind and magnitude sufficient to destroy the main purpose of the study. Anyone who deals with field studies must use a moderated criticism which balances methods against mission.

The mission of the National Impact study was out of the ordinary. We discussed, earlier, the OEO separation between summative evaluation, formative evaluation, and monitoring. The National Impact study was a pure case of summative, or undifferentiated, evaluation. It was to try to estimate the size of the Head Start effect nationwide—not whether Head Start could have an effect, or whether it was now having localized effects, or whether there were antagonistic forces which were suppressing its long range effect. The study chose to deal with the first issue and, in my judgment, gave a valid answer to it. The study did not choose to deal with the alternative issues and, in the judgment of all present, did not give valid answers to them.

Why be concerned with so gross and uninformative a question in the first place? There is a question which I once heard an OEO official ask:

> "We are paying 350 million dollars for this program and 20 million dollars for that program. Why are we paying 350 million dollars for this program and 20 million dollars for that program? Why aren't we paying 20 million dollars for this program and 350 million dollars for that program?".

This is the question of the policy maker. It is a new kind of question, deceptively like the traditional forms of the evaluation question but different and worthwhile in its own terms. Is national implementation of Head Start now working?—Does it produce effects substantial enough to justify its cost and its preemption of funds which might be allocated towards other possible approaches?

The answer to the question given by the National Impact study is that Head Start is now not producing a nationwide effect through its Summer programs, and that it is now producing marginal positive effects through its Full-year programs. Are any of the imperfections of the study sufficient to discredit those answers, sufficient to mask a substantial nationwide effect? I do not believe so. The major questions about the techniques of this study have to do with four facets: (1) the sampling of Head Start programs; (2) the matching of Head Start and Control cases, and the covariance analysis which is dependent upon it; (3) the choices and use of the evaluation instruments; and (4) the differentiation of the analysis.

Head Start sampling. The study's unbalanced sampling of Head Start, 70% Summer to 30% Full-year, was not the best tactic. Generally, one wants more cases where one wants to detect smaller effects or where one expects to break apart the sample to look at subgroup effects. These concerns were equal for Summer and Full-year programs. The study ran the risk of drawing too small a sample of Full-year Head Start, and in fact the third grade Full-year sample was too small to be trusted. However, for other groups, the study must have had sufficient discriminating power. It did not detect an effect of Summer programs where it had placed most of its weight and at the same time it did detect Full-year effects far smaller than those which are considered educationally significant.

Matching. We have already noted that the matching of Head Start and Control children was imperfect. The Control children came from slightly more favorable backgrounds. The direction of this difference is important, because it could bias the study against Head Start. However, the design of the study envisaged this possibility and guarded against it by the covariance analysis. If one argues that that analysis is problematical, one then meets a second complete analysis, largely without the problems, whose results reconfirm those given by the covariance analysis.

Test instruments. The affective instruments were not good, and three of the four background instruments are subject to some question. But the nuclear cognitive instruments were sound, and defects in the other instruments can only moderate their findings to the extent that one is willing to believe in sleeper effects, dormant in the first three grades and potent in the later grades—or, in another direction, by making it difficult to differentiate out those factors in the child's environment which enhance or suppress the effects of Head Start upon him. These are not central weaknesses for the principal mission of the study. The weakness of so many instruments, it must be said, reflects an admirable effort by the contractor to go into important new ground, and cannot be considered an index of the quality of the effort.

Differentiation of effects. All criticism of the National Impact Study expresses dissatisfaction with the grossness of the evaluation. Much of this criticism fails to acknowledge the summative mission of the study. To begin with, the draft report should have been at more pains to spell the mission out, because it was unusual and because it was misleading. Only a policy maker, at this time at least, can understand the mission of a study designed to get at the amount of implementation—the amount of budget allocation—he is going to give to a program. Most people do not naturally think in terms of amount of emphasis. They think in terms of whether a program is Good or Bad. They are wrong, administratively—because administration is a matter of placing bets—but they are right fundamentally. The fundamental question is whether the idea of Head Start is any good or not.

The National Impact study sought to finesse the fundamental question, but this was probably an innocent mistake. One could not exclude it. Nowadays, social science data and policy questions are freely mingled in public discussions, and any study of this sort is going to be a political gesture, whatever its intentions. The study's implications will be digested in the most general way. There will be Fors and Againsts. And most people will simply skim through all the discussion to test their basic decision that Head Start is Good or Bad. Because of this, enlightened planning of the study could either have tried to communicate its specialized mission, a very difficult thing to do, or it could have included more differentiated comparisons in the design . . . simply to keep the study from being an issue. There are further arguments for a differentiated analysis even from the strict definition of the study's mission. For the policy maker, right next to the question of whether his program is having impact is the question of where he might prune or give emphasis to increase its manifest impact.

In fact, the National Impact study did provide for some differentiation of effects, but not completely enough. Then, the pattern of results came in badly. The background instruments could have been used to break down Head Start's impact. One needs a larger number of cases to make the breakdown, and the study had most cases for Summer Head Start, where there was no effect to be differentiated, and too few for Full-year programs, where we now have positive effects whose source we cannot attempt to localize. We emerge from such subanalyses as were possible basically dissatisfied, with some suspicion that Head Start may work best among Negroes and in the Southeast.

On the whole, the fundamental idea of Head Start—that compensatory preschools may significantly help a disadvantaged child to cope with school—has not been satisfactorily tested yet, by this study or any other. There is now in existence an argument that compensatory schooling has failed, and must fail, because it directly or indirectly tries to change intelligence, which cannot much be changed. The source is a recent, widely-publicized article by Arthur Jensen, an educational psychologist at Berkeley. This paper, appearing at about the same time as the draft of the National Impact Study, abolished any faint hope that the study might be nonpolitical and neutral because, in many minds, it set the seal on the negative findings of the study.

Jensen's paper begins with the premise that compensatory education has failed:

> "Why has there been such uniform failure of compensatory programs wherever they have been tried? What has gone wrong? In other fields, when bridges do not stand, when aircraft do not fly, when machines do not work, when treatments do not cure, despite all conscientious efforts on the part of many persons to make them do so, one begins to question the basic assumptions, principles, theories, and hypotheses that guide one's efforts. Is it time to follow suit in education?"*

The paper then proceeds into an elaborate and scholarly analysis of a thesis about the premise of failure. The paper is prodigious in its search through all the relevant research, and all the *kinds* of relevant research, which might have a bearing on the thesis. It reasserts the traditional wisdom—that intelligence is fixed by heredity and cannot be changed much by training. In order to do this, the paper tries to make the case that we can definitively measure human intelligence. It explores the calculations by which one can try to establish how much influence heredity and environment can have on intelligence, and by which one can assign a great majority of the influence to heredity. (Since we cannot do selective breeding studies with humans, we must arrive at our estimates through computations based on the correlations between IQs of individuals of known relationship—parent and child, grandparent and grandchild, brothers and sister, etc.) It considers socioeconomic class differences in intelligence test scores, and argues that socioeconomic status may be as much a measure of the heredity as of the environment of the individual. It takes up racial differences in intelligence, and argues that public discussion of educational policy has been hampered by an unwillingness to consider the possibility that they may exist. It rehearses evidence which leads up to the assertion of a Black-White dif-

---

* The reference is to Jensen, A. R. "How Much Can We Boost IQ and Scholastic Achievement?" *Harvard Educational Review,* 1969, 39, 1-123. The quote is on p. 3. For a set of invited comments, see the following number of the journal.

ference in intelligence, without making the assertion. It considers the question of raising the IQ by training, and argues that this has only been done when hereditary potential has not been fully allowed expression. Finally, it offers research findings to justify an argument for a new direction in policy—not towards compensatory education, but towards diversified public education aimed towards different patterns and levels of mental abilities.

The paper stops a hair short of asserting flatly that Blacks are racially below Whites in intelligence, but this is a difference that does not make a difference as far as the public discussion has gone. The juxtaposition of the arguments say it, even if the prose avoids it. But a clean case cannot be made. First, Jensen's formulae concede some environmental influence on intelligence, enough to account for Negro-White differences in IQ scores. Second, his argument holds that an individual's socioeconomic status is a statement about his heredity as well as his environment, but this is not so true for a suppressed minority. For the Negro, relative to the White, low social class must be relatively more a statement of environment than it is of heredity. Social suppression crowds all individuals, regardless of hereditary ability, towards the lower class environment. We consequently do not know what the calculations for hereditary and environmental variance would be for a suppressed group. In fact, we have the figures only for White samples, which are not comparable. Certainly, unless one can somehow manage to deny that social suppression is real, there must be a good number of minority members to fit one kind of changeability of the IQ conceded by Jensen, the case where performance is depressed below potential.

Jensen cannot rigorously make the case that Negro intelligence is inferior to White intelligence. Yet there has been talk that the *Harvard Educational Review* should never have published the article, or that comments about the article by six other men should not have been delayed until the next issue but should have been put right after the Jensen article—presumably, to instantly neutralize it. The general idea seems to be that one should not allow this kind of case to be laid down in such scholarly detail, because it will give ammunition to Them. Who are They? "They" are presumably some Southern White Protestants who have been publicly vociferous about the issue of racial differences in intelligence . . . but "They" are, I think, also a rather unpleasant set of doubts lodged in the minds of every single non-Southern-White-Protestant among us, Black and White. I find it unpleasant to say this, but I do not think any discussion of Head Start or compensatory education can ever be quite sane unless and until our discussion can include the issue which Jensen has had the courage to bring forth. Not the reality of his case, but its possibility.

The National Impact Study of Head Start and the Jensen article, both issued at the same time, may have had a healthy shock value. They may work together to bring to an end an uneasy and not-quite-healthy era in which social science and public policy became intertwined and went slightly out of bounds. On the administrative side, one had an impulsive, explosive, confused implementation of a nationwide program, without any clear prototype to guarantee feasibility, without any staged planning to try to mount the resources adequate to the program. On the social science side, one had an unpleasant rhetoric by some in or near the public press, immoderately concerned to "protect" the program by refusing to admit that any problems could or did exist for it.

We may, perhaps, be ready to move into a better time, less exuberant, when a more careful test of Head Start will be made. Jensen's conclusion that compensatory education has failed is distinctly premature . . . most fields that need a bridge or an airplane or whatever do not quit after three years of trying. If the very first Head Start cadre has only just come into the third grade, then we clearly do not know what Head Start can do in the third grade. Some specific issues need to be explored first:

There are compensatory preschool programs that have repeatedly produced large and significant-looking gains during their training period. These gains are subject to "levelling off" during the early primary grades, but the public schools may not act to sustain the effects of the Head Start experience. There are as yet very few cases in which there has been parallel work in the early elementary grades, though a program has gotten under way—the Follow-Through program—to establish such work.

If there is to be preschool work, we need more leverage on the preschool years—perhaps earlier access to the child but more importantly, I think, work with the parents. There has been work with parents on a pilot scale which looks interesting. Head Start had defined work with parents as part of its nationwide mission, but it is dubious that the possibility of a program of this sort has been adequately tested. Work of this sort will need to be tried.

There is, in the original base of the Head Start effort, continual need to develop, test, and disseminate prototype preschool curricula, and to foster the training of personnel. The adjustment emphasis reported by most Head Start directors at the present time has the unfortunate property, I believe, of being in one sense the highest possible wisdom in preschool education and, in another sense, its lowest common denominator. Which sense now predominates in the programs? There must, in all reason, be room for improvement in a program in its fourth year of existence.

It will take up to a decade before the fundamental idea of Head Start can be given something like a reasonable test. One must expect, because it takes so long to try and try again on a question of education-and-outcome, that simultaneous parallel exploration will be given to other approaches to poverty. It is quite probable that from here on in most of these avenues being explored will be evaluated by something like the Westinghouse/Ohio effort, smaller or larger, more or less argumentative. The reader, whom I have been belaboring with complexities for these many pages, may blanch at the prospect. I do, too. Yet this is, I think, a reasonable and productive basis for collaboration between social science and policy making.

10

HOW REGRESSION ARTIFACTS IN QUASI-EXPERIMENTAL EVALUA-TIONS CAN MISTAKENLY MAKE COMPENSATORY EDUCATION LOOK HARMFUL

Donald T. Campbell and Albert Erlebacher

Northwestern University

Evaluations of compensatory educational efforts such as Head Start are commonly quasi-experimental or *ex post facto*. The compensatory program is made available to the most needy, and the "control" group then sought from among the untreated children of the same community. Often this untreated population is on the average more able than the "experimental" group. In such a situation the usual procedures of selection, adjustment, and analysis produce systematic biases in the direction of making the compensatory program look deleterious. Not only does matching produce regression artifacts in this direction, but so also do analysis of covariance and partial correlation. These biases of analysis occur both where pretest scores are available and in *ex post facto* studies.

It seems reasonably certain that this methodological error occurred in the Westinghouse/Ohio University study (Cicirelli, et al, 1969) and it probably has occurred in others purporting to show no effects or harmful effects from Head Start programs. The occurrence of such tragically misleading misanalyses must be attributed to the slow diffusion of the isolated warnings. These have been long available for the process of matching (e.g. McNemar, 1940; 1949; Thorndike, 1942; Hovland, Lumsdaine & Sheffield, 1949; Campbell & Clayton, 1961; Campbell & Stanley, 1963), and for *ex post facto* designs (Campbell & Stanley, 1963). But for analysis of covariance, the warning message is newer (Lord, 1960; Evans & Anastasio, 1968; Werts & Linn, 1969; see also Lord 1967; 1969)

Supported in part by National Science Foundation Grant GS 1309X.

185

and most references are wrong in their recommendations (e.g. Thorndike, 1942; Peters & Van Voorhis, 1940; Walker & Lev, 1953; Winer, 1962; Campbell & Stanley, 1963; McNemar, 1969).

The purpose of this essay is the didactic one of illustrating with a detailed example why these biases appear. The initial focus will be on the case of the superior control group. Subsequently, data assemblies which could misleadingly make compensatory education look effective will be discussed. Several of the sections which follow involve statistical technicalities which some readers will want to skip. It could be hoped that every reader will stick it out through the section on *Matching*. But however that may be, we would like to call attention of all readers to some general conclusions: 1. For the *ex post facto* situation to which the Westinghouse/Ohio University study was unavoidably limited, no satisfactory analysis is possible. 2. Analysis of covariance in its usual forms is inadequate not only in such *ex post facto* settings, but also in those quasi-experimental settings where pretests are available. 3. For quasi-experiments with pretests similar in composition to the posttests, common-factor covariance adjustments developed by Lord (1960) and Porter (1967) may be appropriate. We would also like to call attention to the two non-statistical sections at the end, especially the argument in favor of randomly assigned control groups.

For the purpose of illustration, we have generated computer simulated data for two overlapping groups with no true treatment effect. Figure 1 shows the frequency distributions of these two groups. In the bottom portion are the two distributions representing the test scores that were obtained after the ameliorative treatment ("posttest"). It can be seen that the Experimental Group has a lower mean than the Control. However, as can be seen in the top portion of the figure, the difference between the two groups was already present prior to the treatment. The "pretest" shows precisely the same difference, except for the vagaries of random sampling.

With the data as displayed in Figure 1, few if any would be tempted to conclude that the treatment had any effect, helpful or harmful. However, our example is especially clear because we have kept the same means and standard deviations for the pretest and the posttest (as far as population parameters are concerned). Nevertheless we will be able to show that even in the present clear cut instance of no treatment effects, the common quasi-experimental analysis techniques will result in serious biases.

Figures 2, 3, and 4 display the relationship between pretest (or covariate) and posttest scores within each group, separately and then combined. The relationships there displayed could have been reported more economically as correlation coefficients (the pretest-post correlations are .489 for the Experimental Group, .496 for the Control, where the theo-

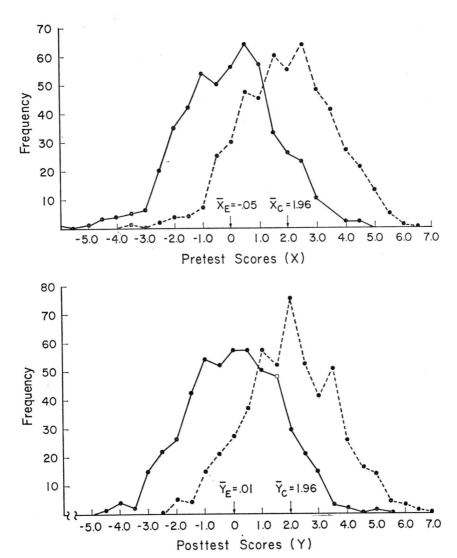

FIG. 1. Pretest and posttest distributions (simulated data) for an instance of a superior Control Group (dashed lines) and no treatment effect in the Experimental Group (solid lines).

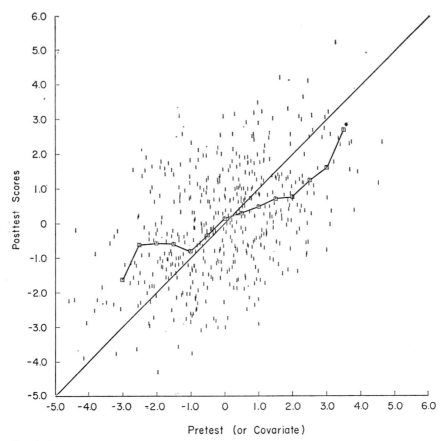

Fig. 2. Scatter plot of the correlation of pretest and posttest scores for the Experimental Group.

retical population values are each .500). But we feel that the display of relationships as scatter diagrams provides the easiest route to an intuitive understanding of regression artifacts.

The truisms we are going to demonstrate with these simulated data are not at all specific to our mode of generating them. The similarity of pretest and posttest means and variances makes the didactic exposition easier to follow, but is not essential. Any simulation would do in which the mean difference and overlap between experimental and control group exists to the same degree in both pretest and posttest (as shown for example by the *t* ratio for the mean difference between experimental and control). Thus posttest means and variances could be larger than for the pretest. Or still less restrictively, any simulation will do which distinguishes between pretest values and the common factor (or true

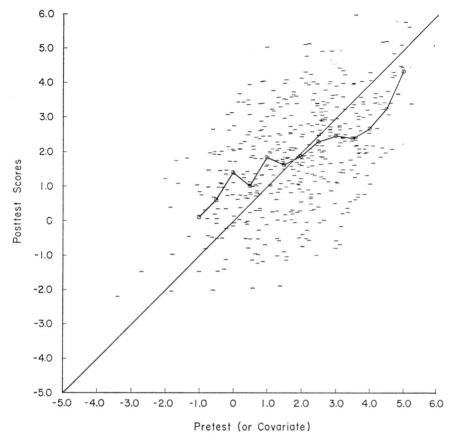

Fig. 3. Scatter plot of the correlation of pretest and posttest scores for the Control Group.

score component) shared by pretest and posttest, as by adding "error" or "unique variance" to the pretest as well as to the posttest. We believe that the reader may skip without loss the following paragraph on the details of our simulation.

The data were generated in the following way: A person's score was made up of three parts, added to each other. Thus for the pretest,

$$X_{ij} = G_{i.} + C_{ij} + E_{ij}, \text{ and}$$

for the posttest,

$$Y_{ij} = G_{i.} + C_{ij} + E'_{ij}, \text{ where}$$

X_{ij} is the pretest score of person j in Group i.
Y_{ij} is the posttest score of subject j in Group i.

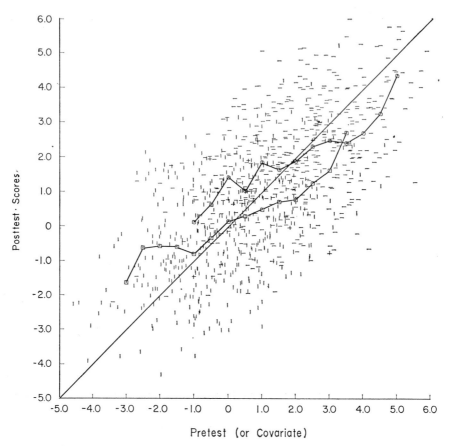

Fig. 4. Scatter plot of the correlation of pretest and posttest scores for Experimental and Control Group. (Vertical tally marks represent Experimental Group children, horizontal tallys Controls)

$G_{i.}$ is a group score common to all members of a group. It was taken as O for all members of the Experimental Group and 2 for all members of the Control Group. G is that portion of "true score" variance producing group differences.

C_{ij} is a common factor score for subject $i j$. It represents that component of "true score" variance accounting for persisting individual differences in ability within groups. C_{ij} was randomly chosen from a normal population with a mean of 0 and a standard deviation of 1. (In this simulation, neither pretest nor posttest contain "true score" components not shared with the other.)

E_{ij} and E'_{ij} are separate "error" scores for subject ij. They represent measurement errors. That is, if the same subject were tested again on the same test, because the test is not perfectly reliable, his E_{ij} would be different. E_{ij} and E'_{ij} were randomly chosen from a normal population with a mean of zero and a standard deviation of 1.

In Figures 2, 3 and 4 there is a tally mark for each of 500 individuals in each of the highly overlapping distributions. Each "Experimental" individual is diagramed with a vertical mark, each of the generally superior "Control" individuals with a horizontal mark. For each class interval of pretest scores (width = .500 points) the mean posttest score has been plotted (the boxed or circled points), separately for each group. A meandering line connects these means. To understand the diagrams, look at the plots of individuals and means in a given area: Each mean is based upon the tallys of its type above and below it in a narrow vertical column, the boundaries of which are not shown but which can be inferred. Where the number of cases in a column was fewer than 6 no mean was plotted on the grounds that its small N would lead to misleading variability. Checking visually some of the plotted details will insure comprehension. Begin at the left edge of Figure 2. The class interval —4.750 to —4.250 centered at 4.500 as read on the bottom line, has in the column it designates 3 cases, mean = 1.566, unplotted. The next column, centered around —4.000, with boundaries of —4.250 and —3.750, contains 4 cases, mean = —.2564, unplotted. The next interval, —3.750 to —3.250 has 5 cases, mean = —1.868, unplotted. In the next class interval, —3.250 to —2.750 there are 6 cases, mean = —1.643, providing our first plotted column mean, the boxed point above —3.000. From there rightward there is a plotted mean for the next 13 class intervals, plotted every .500 points, above points —2.500, —2.000, —1.500, —1.000 etc. Small numbers still create instability, leading to the high value for the Experimental category centered at pretest +3.500, where one very high point produces a column (posttest) mean of +2.711, leading it to cross over the corresponding Control Group value, as seen in Figure 4. (The complete set of values is presented in the statistical appendix.)

The straight line running diagonally through Figures 2, 3 and 4 can be designated the identity diagonal and represents the set of values which all tallys would have taken had pretest and posttest scores been identical. Note that the line of column means for each of the groups lies below this identity diagonal in the higher range of its scores, and lies above the identity diagonal for lower half of its scores. The meandering line ideally should cross the identity diagonal at that point representing the intersection of the pretest and the posttest means. A straight line fitted by least squares to the column means would be the regression line of posttest on pretest. If the correlation were perfect, there would be no scatter, and this line would coincide with the identity diagonal. If there were zero correlation, that is if pretest scores were totally useless in predicting posttest scores, then all column means would equal the posttest mean for the whole group (in universe values if not specific sample values) and the regression line would be perfectly horizontal. This case falls about halfway between. The correlation between pretest and posttest scores is .489 for the experimental Group, and .496 for the Control Group, where the universe values determined by the formula for generating the scores are both .500.

In a usual presentation of regression phenomena, there would also be a presentation of the regression of pretest on posttest. However, to avoid needless visual complexity, we have omitted presentation in Figures 2, 3 and 4 of row means, that is of the mean pretest scores for each class interval of posttest scores. These values would be tipped away from the identity diagonal in the direction of the vertical, would be to the left of the identity value above the means, and to the right of the identity value below the means. (These values are presented in the statistical appendix.)

The often referred to but less often understood "regression toward the mean" is portrayed in the departure of the column means from the identity diagonal. For each class of pretest scores, the corresponding mean posttest score lies closer to the overall population mean, posttest values being thereby lower in the case of high pretest values, and higher in the case of lower pretest values. (This verbal statement must be made more complex for situations in which pretest and posttest have different means and variances: For each pretest class interval, the corresponding mean score on the posttest is closer in standard-deviation units to the overall posttest mean than is the pretest class interval's distance from the pretest mean in pretest standard deviation units.) Note that *just as our Experimental and Control groups have different means on both pretest and posttest occasions, they thereby also have different regression lines.* This point will be expanded below.

Matching

With the details of the illustration before us, we can now look at several procedures commonly used in quasi-experimental situations to attempt to compensate for pretest inequality between experimental and control groups. Most widespread of these is *matching,* an ubiquitous error so supported by common sense that it is repeatedly reinvented as the way of "controlling for" initial inequalities of group means.

We have graphed in Figures 1 through 4, an absolutely null case, in which the supposed "treatment" applied solely to the "Experimental Group" had absolutely no effect. Suppose we attempt to examine the effect of the treatment on a matched sample. Let us start with sub-samples from each population matched on a specific pretest score, for example, 1.000 (class interval from .750 to 1.250). Looking at Figures 2 and 4, we see that for the "Experimental" sample, the posttest mean is .478, for the "Control" sample (Figures 3 and 4) the mean is 1.850, a difference in the direction of the Experimental Group becoming worse, the Control Group becoming better. If we expand this matched sample by taking equal numbers of experimentals in each of the overlapping class intervals, we add further replication of this same bias, easily getting a highly significant effect. The proper interpretation of this effect is that scores in each group are regressing toward different means—inevitable if the groups do in fact have different means. It is to be hoped that the why of this error is by now intuitively obvious from the form of display used in Figures 2, 3 and 4.

One reason why one is so often deceived by regression artifacts in the matching situation is that the matching score and the value of the dependent variable seem to be stated in the same metric, but actually are in different metric languages. In the example above, the two pretest values of 1.000 are in the language of scores selected just because they had that value. The posttest values of .478 and 1.850 are actually means of scores that have been free to vary, and all of the effects of error and independence in the relationship between pretest and posttest have been thrown into these posttest means.

We could generate the opposite picture by starting with selected, matched posttest scores of 1.000 and looking for the mean pretest score corresponding to each. While row means have not been graphed in Figures 2, 3 and 4 you can probably confirm by visual inspection that the row (pretest) mean for the Experimental subjects whose posttest score is in the .750 to 1.250 interval is about .505, while that for the Control Group is 1.152. (See the statistical appendix.) If one were a trapped director of a Head Start program who had to have experimental proof for the worth of a program which he knew on other grounds to be valuable, one could probably package this last result persuasively. "Of children scoring the same at time two, the Head Start children have gained .495 points while the Control children have lost .152." For a growth situation, the actual numerical values of our illustration are of course inappropriate in having pretest and posttest means the same. Normally both groups would have gained. Let us accommodate this by adding 1.000 to all posttest scores. This gets rid of the implausible loss on the part of the Control Group. Now our trapped director can say, "Of children scoring equally on the posttest, the Head Start children have gained 1.495 points, in comparison with a gain of only .848 on the part of the Control children." We recoil at such politically motivated sophistry, yet the analysis itself is no more fallacious than the complementary one we have fallen into inadvertently by matching on the pretest. The resulting implications for social policy might even be regarded as more benign, though neither bias is defensible.

Our simulated case has been based upon the psychometrician's traditional "true score" model. Along with this goes the derivation that a "fallible" ("obtained," "manifest") score is an unbiased estimate of the true score, given the normal definition of error as uncorrelated with true score. But this is correct only for *unselected* scores, that is, for total sets of scores that have been allowed to fall freely. Where scores have been selected *because* of their manifest values, they become biased estimates of true scores in the direction indicated by regression to the mean. Matching and any other classifying for analysis by obtained scores are just such biasing processes.

The magnitude of the pseudo-effect resulting from matching depends upon two parameters: First, the higher the pretest-posttest correlation, the less the regression. In a symmetrical situation such as this, or in a less symmetrical one when expressed in *z* scores, *r* directly shows the proportion of regression, or rather of non-regression. If the pretest-posttest correlation were .90, the scores would regress 1/10th of the distance toward the mean. In our simulation, the regression is $\frac{1}{2}$ the way to the mean. Second, the larger the difference between group means, the more regression. Verbally stated, the farther the group means are apart, the farther the matched cases will be from their respective means, hence, the more regression. Visually, it is obvious that the larger the mean difference of the two overlapping clouds of tallys in Figure 4, the larger the separation between the two parallel plots of column means. In our example, the differences in the means of the two groups is about 2.00, and the regression pseudo effect concomitant with a .50 correlation is half this, or about 1.00. If the mean difference were 4.00, the regression pseudo-effect would be half of that, or 2.00.

Matching on several variables simultaneously has the same logic and bias. The use of multiple matching variables may reduce the regression artifact, but will not remove it. It reduces it insofar as the multiple correlation of the several matching variables with the posttest is higher than the simple *r* of a single matching variable. Matching by means of qualitative dimensions or dichotomous variables has an equivalent bias. All such matching variables turn out to be imperfect indicators of the underlying variables we would like to match on. Parents' number of years of schooling have vastly different meanings from school to school, and within the same schools and classrooms. Living in the same neighborhood or block means widely different things as far as the educational quality of the home is concerned. Regression artifacts analogous to those of Figure 4 emerge. There is inevitably undermatching, in the sense that the population differences which one is trying to correct by matching are under corrected by the matching process. The initial matching in the Westinghouse-Ohio University study was of this qualitative nature. This undermatching showed up on the socio-economic status ratings subsequently made. Had they "corrected" their initial matching by further matching on the socio-economic ratings this composite would still have been an imperfect indicator of underlying achievement-ability, there would still have been undermatching, with resulting regression artifacts as in Figure 4, in the specific direction of making Head Start look damaging. Even had they had an achievement-ability pretest to match on, as some studies including Follow Through have, matching would produce this erroneous put down.

How can one tell which direction a matching bias will take? Only by having evidence on the nature of the population differences which matching attempted to overcome. Conceivably, in reporting a matching process, the researcher might neglect to say what kind of cases he found hard to get matches for, and what kind of cases existed in surplus in the control population. If so, we could not tell. In the Westinghouse-Ohio University study it *might* have been that matches were easily found for the most disadvantaged Head Start children, and hard to find for the more advantaged ones: It *might* have been, but it was not. If it had been, then regression artifacts would have artifactually made Head Start look effective. Instead, it seems clear that generally in the Westinghouse-Ohio University study, it was the most disadvantaged Head Starters that were hard to match and that the controls were selected from generally more able populations. The same direction of matching bias is probably prevalent in many of the small scale studies of compensatory education also. Whereas it would probably be the case in most fields as it is in pharmacology (Smith, Traganza, & Harrison, 1969) that the less rigorously designed studies show the most favorable effects, it seems to be the reverse in compensatory education studies. For example, McDill, McDill & Sprehe (1969) review eleven studies of compensatory education. Of five using randomly assigned control groups, all show significant gains on some cognitive measures. Of five with quasi-experimental controls, only one shows a significant effect. While an examination of control group selection in each of these cases has not been done, pending that, the most plausible explanation seems to us to be the bias of the superior control group in the quasi-experimental studies.

In situations such as this where control samples are chosen to have pretest scores equivalent to experimental samples, the question may be asked "Since the Head Start children are an extreme group, why don't they regress toward the overall population mean just as much as do the matched controls?" Comparable questions emerge when psychotherapy applicants are matched with a control sample chosen to have equally maladjusted test scores (e.g. Campbell & Stanley, 1963; 1966, pp. 11-12 and 49-50). Why are these controls expected to regress to the population mean while the therapy applicants are not? An initial answer is that person-to-person matching on individual scores involves the misleading exploitation of score instability phenomena to a much greater degree than do the complex of processes which produced the Head Start sample or the psychotherapy applicants. These groups turn out to be extreme when measured, but were not selected on the basis of their extreme scores. It is selection on the basis of extreme individual scores that creates most strongly the conditions under which obtained scores become biased estimates of true scores.

This is not to deny some small degree of regression toward a mean of all children on the part of the Head Start children. But since the Head Start children were not selected on individual characteristics, but rather as members of neighborhoods or school districts, the degree of such regression would be trivial in magnitude in comparison with the control children selected because of individual attributes. The mean test level of the hundred or so children in a neighborhood is a very stable value compared with the score of a single child. The test-retest correlation for neighborhood average, computed over all of the neighborhoods of a city, will be very high, perhaps as high as .98 or .99, even with tests for which the test-retest correlation for children within a single neighborhood is only .50. These considerations become very confusing in the abstract. But in the applied situation one can tell the direction of the bias by the specific nature of the difficulties one has in finding matches, and by the differences prior to matching in the groups from which the matched cases are sought.

ANALYSIS OF COVARIANCE

The posttest means in our simulation were .006 and 1.961 for the Experimental and Control groups, respectively. The difference, 1.955, when tested by analysis of variance gives F (1, 998) $= 374.31$ which is, of course, statistically significant. Analysis of covariance, a technique commonly prescribed and used in the Westinghouse/Ohio University study to statistically "equate" groups, yields adjusted means of .491 and 1.476 for the two groups. Although the difference between these has been reduced to .985, we obviously have a serious undercorrection which is further demonstrated by the analysis of covariance F (1, 997) $= 90.80$ which is also very large and also statistically significant. The mean difference is of the same general magnitude as that produced by matching, and again, makes the experimental treatment look damaging. Our simulation is like a pretest, rather than a qualitatively different co-variate, in that it is in the same metric as the posttest. The principle of undermatching due to error and unique factors in the covariate holds just as inexorably for the case of dissimilar covariates.

This underadjustment by the analysis of covariance has commonly been overlooked and the resulting bias makes the statistical criticisms of the Westinghouse/Ohio University study by Smith and Bissell (1970) seem trivial in comparison. While we do not have enough information to estimate the magnitude of the bias, we can confidently state its direction on the basis of the reported group differences on the socio-economic status rating used as a covariate. We can therefore confidently conclude that had the Head Start programs actually produced no effects whatsoever, the mode of analysis used in the Westinghouse/Ohio University study would have made them look worse than useless, actually harmful.

Porter (1969) has pointed out that in the Westinghouse/Ohio University tests of Summer Head Start programs, 44 out of 56 have outcomes in the direction of Head Start being worse than nothing, significantly different from a 50-50 split. For the summer programs, apparently, the true gains were not sufficient to overcome the inevitable regression artifacts coming from the fact that controls were selected from a superior population. For one year programs, on some measures at least, the regression artifacts were overcome, but with the inevitable result that the true effects were underestimated to an unknown degree.

GAIN SCORES

In our particular analysis, with its stationary pretest-posttest structure chosen for a simplicity of presentation, analysis in terms of gain scores would have avoided the regression artifacts which both matching and analysis of covariance generated. Applied as a *t* test of the difference between the mean gain scores of the total Experimental Group versus the mean gain score of the total Control Group, such an analysis would have shown no effect. As can be seen from Figure 1, these means would be equal, both being essentially zero. (A comparison of gain scores for only the overlapping parts of the distributions would of course be biased, as described under *matching*.) However, gain scores are in general such a treacherous quicksand, e.g. are so *non* comparable for high versus low scorers within any single sample, that one is reluctant to recommend them for any purpose. More important here is that for the setting of compensatory education the use of gain scores would involve an assumption that is certainly wrong. Again, the bias would be to make Head Start look damaging.

In a growth situation, unlike our simulation, the posttest mean would be higher than the pretest mean for both Experimental and Control groups, and this would be so whether or not the treatment had an effect. In this situation, the crucial assumption of gain score analysis is that the absolute amount gained would have been the same for both Experimental and Control pupils under the condition of no treatment

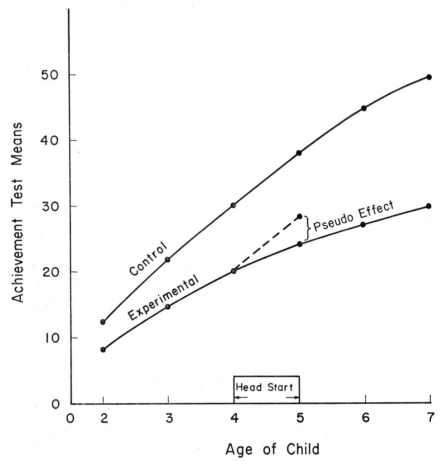

Fɪɢ. 5. Pseudo effect generated by assuming growth rate in the Experimental Group as in a superior Control Group.

effect. This assumption is inconsistent with the fact that the groups differ at the time of the pretest. That difference no doubt is there because of a previously more rapid rate of growth on the part of the Control Group, which would be expected to continue during the period of the experimental treatment. Figure 5 illustrates the situation.

In Figure 5 we have the growth curves for the two group under the condition of no treatment effect. Between the ages of 4 and 5 when a treatment was given, the Control Group increased 8 units in ability while the Experimental Group increased only 4 units. This would result in an interpretation of a decrement of 4 units due to the treatment received by the Experimental Group. If a true treatment effect were actually present, it would be underestimated to the same degree.

The bias in analysis of covariance comes from the presence of "error" and "uniqueness" in the covariate, i.e. variance not shared by the dependent variable. If the proportion of such variance can be correctly estimated, it can be corrected for. Lord (1960) has presented the basic algebraic derivation. Porter (1967) has extended the method and tested it on computer-simulated data. In the presentations of the method, the labels "fallible covariate," "true score," and "reliability" are used. These terms are apt to have misleading connotations to practitioners in quasi-experimental situations such as are under consideration here, inasmuch as true score components in the covariate which are *not* shared with the dependent variable have the same effect as error in biasing ordinary covariance analysis. For this reason we are using the label "common-factor covariance adjustment" for the method, rather than "true-score covariance" or "fallible-covariate analysis." Also for this reason we are using the term "common-factor coefficient" in place of "reliability coefficient." This coefficient should reflect only those components of the covariate shared with the dependent variable. Internal consistency, test-retest, alternate forms, or any reliability coefficient based solely on the covariate will usually be too high due to the presence of specific factors and changes in true scores over time, and thus lead to undercorrection.

Lest this suggestion seem incompatible with the usual assumptions of test score theory, we will be more explicit. Let us distinguish between two types of covariate, the "similar" and the "dissimilar." In the ordinary pretest-posttest design, the same test or parallel forms are used for pretest and posttest. Under these conditions, it is reasonable to assume for both a similar factorial composition. Such a pretest used as a covariate is a similar covariate, and has been illustrated in our basic simulation. A dissimilar covariate would be one with a factorial structure differing from the dependent variable, as by containing factors not found in the dependent variable. Such would be the situation, for instance, when socio-economic status is used as a covariate and a cognitive test score as a dependent variable.

Consider an extension of our simulation to include a dissimilar covariate, Z, containing a unique factor, U, not shared with Y. The covariate score for subject j in group i is:

$$Z_{ij} = G_{i.} + C_{ij} + U_{ij} + E''_{ij}$$

where G and T have the same values as in X and Y, where E'' is a new independent error term, again with unit variance, and where U is also a variate randomly chosen from a normal population with a mean of zero and a standard deviation of 1. To provide a reliability coefficient,

Z′ is also available, identical to Z except for an independent error, E‴, in place of E″:

If $r_{ZZ'}$ (for which the population value is .667) were to be used as the reliability coefficient for the Lord-Porter procedure, we would under-correct, since the variance due to U will have the same effect as another component of error insofar as its relationship with Y is concerned, since Y does not contain U as a component. A significant adjusted mean difference and F would result. On the other hand, if we used a "common-factor" coefficient, in which U is lumped with E as error, the coefficient (for which the population value = .333) would yield a trivial and insignificant adjusted mean difference.

In real situations, one would not have the benefit simulation provides of knowing the correct value for the common-factor coefficient. But it may be helpful to illustrate from the simulation a rule of thumb for checking on the adequacy of an estimate of the common-factor coefficient. This procedure involves computation of an estimate of an analogous coefficient for the posttest or dependent variable. The covariate-dependent variable correlation, r_{ZY}, (within groups) should become 1.00 when corrected for attenuation by the common-factor coefficients. In our simulation, the universe value for such a common-factor coefficient for Y is .500, (in this case also the ordinary reliability coefficient). The population value for r_{ZY} is .408, which becomes 1.000 when divided by $\sqrt{.333 \times .500}$.

In a pretest-posttest situation one may find it reasonable to make two assumptions that would generate appropriate common-factor coefficients. First, if one has only the pretest-posttest correlations, one may assume that the correlation in the experimental group was unaffected by the treatment. (We need a survey of experience in true experiments to check on this.) Second, one may assume that the common-factor coefficient is the same for both pretest and posttest. Under these assumptions, the pretest-posttest correlation coefficient itself becomes the relevant common-factor coefficient for the pretest or covariate, the "reliability" to be used in Lord's and Porter's formulas. More complexly, if one had internal consistency reliabilities computed for each group for each time period, and if these failed to bring the pretest-posttest correlation up to unity in correction for atenuation, one might proportionally decrease each until they did so, thus making use of the information on differential reliability.

Returning now to the worked-out simulation of X and Y, let us continue the example from where we left off in the section on *Analysis of Covariance*. For X and Y, the assumption of similarity is reasonable, and the within groups correlation of .492 becomes a reasonable estimate of the common-factor coefficient for X. Applying this in Porter's formula, the corrected means become .991 and .976 for the Experimental and

Control groups, respectively. The very small over-correction is a random sampling phenomenon and the difference between these means is not statistically significant. Porter's extension of Lord's true score analysis of covariance gives F (1, 997) $= .01$.

Because Porter's formulation is easier to work with than Lord's and because his study is not readily available, we wish to present the essence of his technique here. The only difference between ordinary analysis of covariance and his adjusted analysis of covariance is in the presence of the reliability coefficient in the formula for the adjusted total sum of squares (SS'_T). Thus,

$$SS'_T = SS_{T_Y} - \frac{(rSS_{W_{XY}} + SS_{B_{XY}})^2}{r^2 SS_{W_X} + SS_{B_X}} \quad , \text{ where}$$

SS_{T_Y} is the total sum of squares for the dependent variable

$SS_{W_{XY}}$ is the within groups sum of products

$SS_{B_{XY}}$ is the between groups sum of products

SS_{W_X} is the within groups sum of squares for the covariate

SS_{B_X} is the between groups sum of squares for the covariate

r is a reliability coefficient (our common factor coefficient)

It should be noted that if r were deleted in both numerator and denominator we would have the usual SS'_T. Since SS'_T is modified, so will be the adjusted between groups sum of squares (SS'_B) since

$$SS'_B = SS'_T - SS'_W, \text{ where}$$

SS'_W is the ordinarily used adjusted within groups sum of squares.

Does the fact of different growth rates rule out this analysis as it does gain scores? Not as clearly. If one assumes that the differential growth rate between Experimental and Control groups is accompanied by corresponding differential growth rates within, producing a correspondingly increased variance, then Lord's analysis would be appropriate. One would be assuming that had the treatment had no effect, the t test between experimental and control would have been the same for the posttest scores as for the pretest scores. One would be assuming a constant biserial correlation between the experimental-control distinction and the test scores. The reasonableness of these assumptions is an empirical matter, although assumed in normal use of I.Q. scores or Achievement Coefficients. Evidence of such proportional growth of means and variances on the standardization samples for the particular tests would be important. Still more relevant would be evidence, as in the Coleman report, that social class and black-white differences, when expressed as t ratios or biserial rs, were constant over age.

In using Lord's or Porter's adjustments, one is making the assumption that the "common factor coefficient" is the same for the experimental and control group, and also the assumption that the covariate-dependent variable correlation is the same. Test floor effects for the disadvantaged population often creates systematic departures from these assumed equalities. Porter (1969) calls attention to an analogous difference between the Experimental and Control samples of the Westinghouse/Ohio University study in regard to the socio-economic status ratings used as covariate.

In the light of the several considerations discussed above, it is clear that even in the case of repeated measurements on "the same" test, Lord's and Porter's corrected covariance analysis should only be undertaken with great tentativeness and caution. Can we find reasonable presumptions permitting its use in the Westinghouse/Ohio University study? While the answer must be no, it is nonetheless true that any such correction would make the report less biased, less misleading than it now is even after Smith & Bissell's well intentioned reanalysis. Thus to assume that the covariate-posttest correlations are appropriate common-factor coefficients (to assume, that is, that the social class ratings and the ability and achievement tests have identical factor loadings on the factors they have in common) would move an unjust analysis in the direction of greater justice. But the presumptions involved are so much less justified than in the similar test-retest situation that they become patently untenable.

If one by chance hit upon the right true score covariance correction here, would this also correct for the regression artifacts generated by the prior qualitative matching done in the Westinghouse/Ohio University study? Only under that unlikely case where all the true score factors shared by the qualitative matching variables and the posttest are identical to those shared between the social class rating and the posttest. Thus even if one could use Lord's and Porter's corrected covariance, artifacts from the prior matching process would probably remain operating, still in the direction of making Head Start look harmful.

BIASING PROCEDURES THAT COULD MAKE HEAD START LOOK GOOD

Selecting a control group from a generally more advantaged population has made Head Start look bad. Selecting a control from a generally less able population would make it look good. There are so many combinations of conditions that would produce this bias that we may be sure it has occurred in many studies. One could make Head Start voluntary, advertising its availability, then select as controls those non-Head Start children who eventually turn up at school from the same tenements and blocks as do the Head Start alumni. In this process, the control group would probably have mothers of lower contact with community information sources and of less concern for their child's school achievement. Or one could select as controls those who initially enrolled but who attended less than one fourth of the sessions. If we look to the probable biases in quasi-experimental evaluations of the "Sesame Street" preschooler's educational television program, they will no doubt be in this direction. In any given neighborhood, it will be the more competent homes that know of the program's existence, and make certain that their children get to see it.

SOCIAL SCIENCE'S UNREADINESS FOR APPLIED
QUASI-EXPERIMENTAL EVALUATION

It is tragic that the social experiment evaluation most cited by presidents, most influential in governmental decision making, should have contained such a misleading bias. The technical and political background of this error needs discussion, particularly since it involves so much that is correct and forward looking, and has produced extremely important social experiments such as the New Jersey negative income tax experiment.

In an important essay, Williams and Evans (1969) have described the political processes leading to the massive Head Start evaluation, and have provided valuable guidelines for the proper political postures to be taken when, as must often happen, accurate evaluations show specific ameliorative programs to be ineffective.

There were political pressures from Congress for hard-headed evaluation of specific programs. These pressures can only be commended, and may in the long run make possible an experimenting society (Haworth, 1960; Campbell, 1969) which will do reality testing with exploratory modifications of its own structure. These program evaluation pressures are probably the most valuable part of a movement which also includes demands for more generalized "social indicators" and "data banks."

Within O.E.O. the demand for evaluation led the Office of Planning, Research, and Evaluation to force evaluation of Head Start in spite of the reluctance of the Head Start administrators. Reluctance to expose operating programs to hard-headed evaluation is so common that in the general case a willingness to override such reluctance may be essential for social reality testing, even though in this instance the Head Start administrators were right, given the fact that the Head Start programs to be evaluated had been initiated without randomization or pretesting.

Commitment to reality testing on ameliorative programs should involve acceptance of the fact that some programs will turn out to be ineffective. When such outcomes are encountered, the political system should seek alternative approaches to solving the same problem, rather than abandon all remedial efforts. Williams and Evans do an outstanding job of clarification and advocacy on this point.

We academics are apt to assume that where things go wrong in collaborations between the political and scholarly communities, the failure comes from the political process, in the form of a failure to make use of our more than adequate wisdom. In this instance it was quite the reverse. As outlined in the preceding paragraphs, the political forces were positive, and if they survive or can be revived, are such as to make possible a reality-testing society. In this instance, the failure came from the inadequacies of the social science methodological community (including education, psychology, economics, and sociology) which as a population was not ready for this task. The one weakness in Williams and Evans' otherwise outstanding paper comes at this point. They state that *ex post facto* studies are a respected and widely used scientific procedure. While it would be hard to find any text since Chapin (1955) that has advocated them, most methodology texts are silent on the issue and condone comparable procedures. They cite "matching" as though it achieved its purpose. Warnings against matching as a substitute for randomization occur in a few texts, but probably 90% of social scientists teaching methodology at U.S. universities would approve the process. On using analysis of covariance to correct for pretreatment differences the texts that treat the issue are either wrong or noncommital (that is, fail to specify the direction of bias) and probably 99% of experts who know of the procedure would make the error of recommending it. Note again that the competitive reanalysis of the Westinghouse/Ohio University data by Smith and Bissell (1970) repeats the original error in this regard. The prestige of complex multivariate statistics and their associated computer programs will perpetuate such mistakes for years to come, under such terms as dummy variable analysis, multiple covariate analysis of covariance, step-wise multiple regression, and the like. The deep rooted seat of the bias is probably the unexplicit trust that although the assumptions of a given statistic are technically not met, the effects of these departures will be unsystematic. The reverse is in fact the case. The more one needs the "controls" and "adjustments" which these statistics seem to offer, the more biased are their outcomes.

THE CASE FOR TRUE EXPERIMENTS IN FUTURE EVALUATION OF COMPENSATORY EDUCATION

There are other possible quasi-experimental designs which avoid the biases here described although none are available for the data to which the Westinghouse/Ohio University study was limited. In a school system with good records of annual testings in the lower grades, a time series of such testings might be employed retrospectively (Campbell, 1970). Longitudinal studies which include some Head Start children offer another possibility (Campbell, 1969b). Looking to the future, by making explicit in quantified detail a policy of giving Head Start opportunity to the most needy, one could create Regression Discontinuity designs (Thistlethwaite & Campbell, 1960; Campbell, 1969) at the individual or school district level. Where highly similar pretests are available, where test-retest correlations are similar for experimentals and controls, and where the assumptions of homogeneous mean and variance growth are tenable, Lord's and Porter's common-factor covariance adjustments may be used with caution. But are there compelling reasons to limit ourselves to quasi-experimental designs when true experiments involving randomization would be so much more informative?

There are problems, of course, with randomization experiments. Randomization at the invitational level avoids the disappointment problem generated by randomly allocating eager applicants to the control condition. But it exaggerates the always present problem of experimental mortality inasmuch as not all those randomly invited accept the treatment. Using only those invited who accept as the experimental group produces a selection bias with favorable pseudo-effects. The unbiased solution of treating all those randomly assigned as though treated, dilutes experimental effects, but is at present the recommended solution (Campbell & Stanley, 1963; 1966, pp. 15-16). More sensitive and yet still unbiased procedures focusing on an upper edge of the experimental and control distributions rather than the whole are feasible (Campbell, 1965) and can be further developed. Randomization by neighborhoods or school districts rather than by individuals is an acceptable solution with superior external validity, but again *all* eligible children in the experimental areas must be compared with all eligible children in the control areas. While one can estimate what the magnitude of the effect would be if one could remove the dilution coming from including the untreated, the tests of significance must be made on the full samples created by randomization. These same strictures, however, apply to most quasi-experimental designs, and in particular to the very attractive Regression Discontinuity analysis.

Even though "true" experiments in the field setting are on these grounds more "quasi" than those in the laboratory, (and those in the laboratory more "quasi" than published reports and statistical treatments indicate), experiments with randomized assignment to treatments are greatly to be preferred where possible. We believe that any investigator fully attending to the presumptions he is making in using quasi-experimental designs will prefer the random assignment of children to treatments *where this is possible*.

Social ameliorative changes which are applied or made available to everyone do not readily permit the creation of control groups. These include across-the-board legal changes and television broadcasts. But those expensive remediations which are in short supply and which cannot be given everyone provide settings in which true experiments are readily possible. Once the decision makers in government and applied research are educated to their importance, they can become the standard evaluational procedure.

On the one hand, we must not create a political climate which demands that no ameliorative efforts be made unless they can be evaluated. There will be many things obviously worth doing which cannot be experimentally evaluated, and which should still be done. The shift to new math is an example. By making math achievement tests inappropriate it undermined the only convenient benchmark for its own evaluation. College education is another example, a boon for which we have almost no interpretable experimental or quasi-experimental evidence. (Since college education is given to those who need it least, the regression artifacts are biased to make it look effective.) We applied social methodologists should be alert to recognize such cases and not assume that every new program must be and can be evaluated. On the other hand, where we can experiment and where the social costs of such experimentation are outweighed by the social value of reality testing, we should hold out for the least biased, most informative procedures.

There exist in administrators, researchers, legislators, and the general public "ethical" reluctances to random assignment. These center around a feeling that the control group is being deprived of a precious medicine it badly needs. But if it be recognized that the supposed boon is in fact in short supply, then it can be seen that the experiment has not increased the number so deprived, but has instead reassigned some of that deprivation so that the ethical value of knowing may be realized. Is randomization as the mode of such reassignment ethically defensible? It might represent an ethical cost (one nonetheless probably worth paying) if all the children in the nation had been rank ordered on need, and those most needy given the compensatory education up to the budgetary and staff limits of the program. But instead, the contrast is with a very haphazard and partially arbitrary process which contains unjust inversions of order of need far more extensive than a randomization experiment involving a few thousand children would entail. These unjust deprivations are normally not forced to our attention, and so do not trouble our ethical sensitivities as does the deprivation of the control group. But there is no genuine ethical contrast here.

Within randomization, there are some designs and stances that may ease any residual ethical burden. For example, the randomization could be limited to the boundary zone, at the least needy edge of those to be treated, and the most needy edge of the untreated. For this narrow band of children, all considered as essentially tied at the cutting point on a coarse grained eligibility score, random assignment to treatment and non-treatment could be justified as a tie-breaking process. We would learn about the effects of the program only for a narrow band of talent. We would wonder about its effectiveness for the most disadvantaged. But this would be better than nothing, and better than quasi-experimental information.

The funds set aside for evaluation are funds taken away from treatment. This cost-benefit trade-off decision has already been made when quasi-experimental evaluation has been budgeted, or when funds are committed to any form of budgeting and accounting. Taking these evaluational funds, one could use nine-tenths of them for providing experimental expansions of compensatory instruction, one-tenth for measurement of effects on the small experimental and control samples thus created. Here the ethical focus could be on the lucky boon given to the experimentals. Since evaluation money would be used to expand treatment, the controls would not be deprived. In retrospect, we are sure that data from 400 children in such an experiment would be far more informative than 4,000 tested by the best of quasi-experiments, to say nothing of an *ex post facto* study.

REFERENCES

CAMPBELL, D. T. Invited therapy in an archival or institutional-records setting: with comments on the problem of turndowns. Duplicated Memorandum, Northwestern University, August, 1965, 13 pp.

CAMPBELL, D. T. Reforms as experiments. *American Psychologist,* 1969. 24, 409-429. (No. 4, April).

CAMPBELL, D. T. Treatment-effect correlations and temporal attenuation on relationships in longitudinal studies. Duplicated Memorandum, Northwestern University, December, 1969, 15 pp.

CAMPBELL, D. T. Time-series of annual same-grade testings in the evaluation of compensatory educational experiments. Duplicated Memorandum, Northwestern University, April, 1970, 4 pp.

CAMPBELL, D. T., & CLAYTON, K. N. Avoiding regression effects in panel studies of communication impact. *Studies in public communication,* Department of Sociology, University of Chicago, 1961, No. 3, 99-118. Bobbs-Merrill Reprint No. S-353.

CAMPBELL, D. T., & STANLEY, J. C. Experimental and quasi-experimental designs for research on teaching. In N. L. Gage (Ed.), *Handbook of research on teaching.* Chicago: Rand McNally, 1963, 171-246. Reprinted as *Experimental and quasi-experimental design for research.* Chicago: Rand McNally, 1966, paper.

CHAPIN, F. S. *Experimental designs in sociological research.* (Rev. ed.) New York: Harper, 1955.

CICIRELLI, V., et al. *The impact of Head Start: An evaluation of the effects of Head Start on children's cognitive and affective development.* A report presented to the Office of Economic Opportunity pursuant to Contract B89-4536, June, 1969. Westinghouse Learning Corporation, Ohio University. (Distributed by: Clearinghouse for Federal Scientific and Technical Information, U.S. Department of Commerce, National Bureau of Standards, Institute for Applied Technology. PB 184 328.)

EVANS, S. H. & ANASTASIO, E. J. Misuse of analysis of covariance when treatment effect and covariate are confounded. *Psychological Bulletin,* 1968, 69, 225-234.

HAYWORTH, L. The experimental society: Dewey and Jordan. *Ethics,* 1960, 71 (No. 1 October) 27-40.

HOVLAND, C. L., LUMSDAINE, A. A., & SHEFFIELD, F. D. *Experiments on mass communication.* Princeton, N. J.: Princeton University Press, 1949.

LORD, F. M. Large-scale covariance analysis when the control variable is fallible. *Journal of the American Statistical Association,* 1960, 55, 307-321.

LORD, F. M. A paradox in the interpretation of group comparisons. *Psychological Bulletin,* 1967, 68, 304-305.

LORD, F. M. Statistical adjustments when comparing preexisting groups. *Psychological Bulletin,* 1969, 72 (No. 5, November) 336-337.

McDILL, E. L., McDILL, M. S., & SPREHE, J. *Strategies for success in compensatory education: An appraisal of evaluation research.* Baltimore: Johns Hopkins Press, 1969.

McNEMAR, Q. A critical examination of the University of Iowa studies of environmental influences upon the I.Q. *Psychological Bulletin,* 1940, 37, 63-92.

McNEMAR, Q. *Psychological Statistics.* New York: Wiley, 1949; Fourth Edition, 1969.

PETERS, C. C., & VAN VOORHIS, W. R. *Statistical procedures and their mathematical bases.* New York: McGraw Hill, 1940.

PORTER, A. C. *The effects of using fallible variables in the analysis of covariance.* Ph.D. dissertation, University of Wisconsin, June, 1967. (University Microfilms, Ann Arbor, Michigan, 1968.)

PORTER, A. C. Comments on some current strategies to evaluate the effectiveness of compensatory education programs, and Comments on the Westinghouse-Ohio University study. Two memoranda prepared for Robert D. Hess for use at the Symposium on "The effectiveness of contemporary education programs in the early years: Reports from three national evaluations and longitudinal studies." Annual Meeting of the American Psychological Association, Washington D.C., August 31, 1969.

SMITH, A., TRAGANZA, E., & HARRISON, G. Studies on the effectiveness of antidepressant drugs. *Psychopharmacology Bulletin,* 1969, March, 1-53.

SMITH, M. S., & BISSELL, J. S. Report analysis: The impact of Head Start. *Harvard Educational Review,* 1970, 40, (No. 1, February) 51-104.

THISTLETHWAITE, D. L., & CAMPBELL, D. T. Regression-discontinuity analysis: An alternative to the ex post facto experiment. *Journal of Educational Psychology,* 1960, 51, 309-317.

THORNDIKE, R. L. Regression fallacies in the matched groups experiment. *Psychometrika,* 1942, 7, 85-102.

WALKER, H. M., & LEV., J. *Statistical inference.* New York: Holt, Rinehart & Winston, 1953.

WERTS, C. E., & LINN, R. L. Analysing school effects: ancova with a fallible covariate. Research Bulletin No. 69-59, Educational Testing Service, July, 1969. In press, *Educational and Psychological Measurement.*

WILLIAMS, W., & EVANS, J. W. The politics of evaluation: the case of head start. *The Annals,* 1969, 385, September, pp. 118-132.

WINER, B. J. *Statistical principles in experimental design.* New York: McGraw-Hill, 1962.

APPENDIX

STATISTICAL DETAILS OF THE SIMULATION

TABLE 1

MEANS OF SIMULATED DATA

	Group Experimental	Control
Pretest	—0.047	1.956
Posttest	0.006	1.961
Population Values	0.000	2.000

TABLE 2

STANDARD DEVIATIONS OF SIMULATED DATA

	Group Experimental	Control	Pooled Within Groups
Pretest	1.644	1.602	1.625
Posttest	1.595	1.597	1.597
Population Values	1.414	1.414	1.414

TABLE 3

CORRELATION COEFFICIENT BETWEEN PRETEST AND POSTTEST

Group	r
Experimental	.489
Control	.496
Within Groups	.492
Population Value	.500

TABLE 4

MEANS ON POSTTEST ACCORDING TO PRETEST SCORE

Pretest Score	Experimental Group n	Posttest Mean	Control Group n	Posttest Mean
5.75 — 6.25	0	—	1	5.098
5.25 — 5.75	0	—	5	3.558
4.75 — 5.25	0	—	13	4.375
4.25 — 4.75	2	1.774	21	3.271
3.75 — 4.25	2	.954	27	2.699
3.25 — 3.75	6	2.711	41	2.413
2.75 — 3.25	10	1.625	48	2.485
2.25 — 2.75	23	1.252	64	2.320
1.75 — 2.25	26	.773	55	1.892
1.25 — 1.75	33	.716	60	1.631
.75 — 1.25	57	.478	45	1.850
.25 — .75	64	.293	47	1.029
—.25 — .25	56	.138	30	1.412
—.75 — —.25	50	—.349	25	.611
—1.25 — —.75	54	—.813	7	.114
—1.75 — —1.25	42	—.609	4	1.058
—2.25 — —1.75	35	—.583	4	—.340
—2.75 — —2.25	20	—.631	2	—.076
—3.25 — —2.75	6	—1.643	0	—
—3.75 — —3.25	5	—1.868	1	—2.205
—4.25 — —3.75	4	—2.564	0	—
—4.75 — —4.25	3	—1.566	0	—

TABLE 5

MEANS ON PRETEST ACCORDING TO POSTTEST SCORE

Posttest Score	Experimental Group n	Pretest Mean	Control Group n	Pretest Mean
6.25 — 6.75	0	—	1	2.877
5.75 — 6.25	0	—	3	4.459
5.25 — 5.75	0	—	4	4.406
4.75 — 5.25	1	3.266	14	3.153
4.25 — 4.75	0	—	16	3.746
3.75 — 4.25	2	2.036	25	2.762
3.25 — 3.75	3	1.719	51	2.719
2.75 — 3.25	14	1.420	41	2.407
2.25 — 2.75	21	1.790	52	2.256
1.75 — 2.25	29	.164	75	1.916
1.25 — 1.75	48	.340	52	1.862
.75 — 1.25	50	.505	57	1.152
.25 — .75	57	.623	37	1.338
—.25 — .25	57	—.048	27	1.143
—.75 — —.25	52	—.101	21	1.209
—1.25 — —.75	54	—.719	15	.841
—1.75 — —1.25	42	—.506	4	—1.102
—2.25 — —1.75	26	—1.281	5	—.771
—2.75 — —2.25	22	—1.623	0	—
—3.25 — —2.75	15	—1.259	0	—
—3.75 — —3.25	2	—1.971	0	—
—4.25 — —3.75	4	—3.325	0	—
—4.75 — —4.25	1	—1.966	0	—

TABLE 6

SUMMARY OF ANALYSES OF VARIANCE ON SIMULATED DATA

	Pretest	Posttest
Between Groups F	379.93	374.31
Within Groups MS	2.640	2.552
Within Groups df	998	998
Point Biserial r	.525	.522

TABLE 7

SUMMARY OF ANALYSES OF COVARIANCE ON SIMULATED DATA

	Usual	Type of Analysis True Score
Adjusted Means		
Experimental Group	0.491	.991
Control Group	1.476	.976
Between Groups F	90.80	.01
Adjusted		
Within Groups MS	1.935	1.935
Within Groups df	997	997

10a

THE RELEVANCE OF THE REGRESSION ARTIFACT PROBLEM TO THE WESTINGHOUSE-OHIO EVALUATION OF HEAD START: A REPLY TO CAMPBELL AND ERLEBACHER

Victor G. Cicirelli, Ph.D.

Professor of Human Development
Purdue University

Campbell and Erlebacher have stated the general thesis that most evaluations of compensatory education programs to date have used quasi-experimental or ex post facto designs rather than true experiments. When such designs are used, there is a tendency to select a control group which is superior to the experimental group (or vice versa), and matching or covariance techniques are used to adjust or correct for the initial bias. However, under certain conditions, regression artifacts occur such that matching or covariance analysis does not remove (or only partially removes) the initial bias; but, the results are interpreted as if such a bias had been completely removed. Thus, compensatory education programs may be judged to be less successful than they are in reality. Campbell and Erlebacher use the Westinghouse/Ohio evaluation of Head Start as an example of the regression artifact phenomenon.

The Westinghouse/Ohio evaluation of Head Start was carried out after the children completed their Head Start experience. In this situation, the use of an *ex post facto* design was one of the few possible ways of carrying out such an evaluation. However, Campbell and Erlebacher have charged that the use of such a design has made Head Start look less effective than it actually is by attempting to adjust for initial bias in favor of the "control" or comparison groups through matching and

Victor Cicirelli was Research Director for the evaluation of Head Start carried out jointly by the Westinghouse Learning Corporation and Ohio University from June, 1968 to June, 1969.

covariance techniques which in fact failed to remove any bias which was present.

In the Westinghouse/Ohio study, the covariate used in the random replications covariance analyses was the Hollingshead Index of socio-economic status. During the sampling process, the Head Start and controls were matched on sex, racial-ethnic background and whether or not they attended kindergarten. (A further simple analysis of covariance used three covariates; income per capita, educational level of father, and occupational level of father.)

Basically, Campbell and Erlebacher's argument is as follows: In the Westinghouse/Ohio study, the control groups were drawn from a more able population than were the Head Start groups. (As indicated in the report itself, the controls were slightly superior on higher education, occupation and income per capita.) Use of matching and covariance techniques in the attempt to adjust for these initial differences between groups, while apparently equating groups on the above extraneous variables (the pre-test in Campbell and Erlebacher's example) does not in fact remove differences between the two groups on the dependent variable (the post-test in Campbell and Erlebacher's example, cognitive and affective measures in the Westinghouse study), since the scores of each of the groups regresses towards the corresponding population mean on the dependent variable.

The maximum size to which such a regression effect can occur depends primarily on the initial size of the difference between the two populations. The greater the difference, the greater the possible regression of dependent scores towards their population means. Also important is the degree of correlation between the extraneous and dependent variables, and finally, the measurement error in the instruments used to measure the variables. The less the correlation and the greater the unreliability of scores, the closer a sample mean score will be to the population mean on the dependent variable. (However, as Campbell and Erlebacher rightly contend, there is no way to accurately estimate the size of the regression artifact effect in the Westinghouse study, since such an estimation can be made only for the pretest-posttest situation.)

While we recognize the essential validity of Campbell and Erlebacher's argument, we would argue that such effects would be small in the Westinghouse study, too small to significantly alter its conclusions.

In the Westinghouse study, the population means for the various extraneous variables were not very different for the Head Start and controls. *Both* the Head Start and control populations were defined and selected from the larger population of children in the target area (the area served by a particular Head Start center) according to the same criteria of eligibility for Head Start. (These criteria were essentially socioeconomic, and were established according to OEO guidelines, although there was room for local variability in the interpretation of these guidelines.) Thus, both the Head Start and control groups were drawn from the *lower extreme of the population of all school children.* (The "least disadvantaged" Head Start children were not matched against the "most disadvantaged" controls, as Campbell and Erlebacher suggest, which of course would imply a greater difference between population means.)

If the populations means were similar, then we would expect to find little difference in measures of socioeconomic status between Head Start and controls, and no systematic difficulties in carrying out the matching on race, sex, and kindergarten attendance.

Once the two populations had been defined for each target area, the sample of Head Start children to be used in the study was drawn by a process of random sampling. From a list of control children drawn from the control subpopulation in random order, a control sample was matched to the previously drawn Head Start sample on sex, racial-ethnic group membership, and whether or not kindergarten was attended. Campbell and Erlebacher have suggested that systematic difficulties in matching may indicate the direction of bias. However, there was little difficulty in matching subjects on such variables as sex, race, and kindergarten in most target areas, and certainly no systematic difficulties.

The Head Start and control samples used in the study were then measured not only on socioeconomic variables but on other demographic variables and a number of attitudinal measures as well. Differences between the Head Start and control groups were very slight (even though statistically significant on some of the socioeconomic measures). Since the differences between the Head Start and control groups were small as expected, one would expect any effects of regression artifact to be correspondingly small.

As for the contribution of measurement error to the regression artifact phenomenon it would be minimal. In the main part of the study, the unit of analysis was the target area *mean score* and not individual scores. These should have a smaller measurement error than individual scores, and hence less regression effect. In the case of the matching variables (sex, race, kindergarten attendance or nonattendance), there is little score instability.

However, correlations between the socioeconomic status measures and the dependent measures were low (.2 to .3 in the Westinghouse study which was in part due to the limited range of the socioeconomic measures), and would allow for the existence of regression artifact. But if population differences and measurement error are small, the bias should not be great.

In summary, the conditions in the Westinghouse study do not imply a bias from regression effects which would be large enough to significantly alter the overwhelmingly negative outcomes of the Westinghouse study. It might also be mentioned that operation of the self-selection factor (inherent in the *ex post facto* design) —whereby some eligible parents send their children to Head Start and some do not—should lead to a bias in favor of the Head Start group on the dependent measures, as Campbell and Erlebacher point out. And such a self-selection effect would act to counter the regression effect.

Finally, regardless of how damaging the regression artifact might be, the performance of the Head Start sample alone on standardized achievement tests* (when compared with national norms) leads one to the inescapable conclusion that Head Start has not been effective in remediating the effects of poverty and social disadvantage.

Campbell and Erlebacher further propose that the most effective way to solve such problems as the regression artifact phenomenon is to refrain from using *ex post facto* and certain other quasi-experimental designs, and instead use true experiments involving random assignments of subjects to the experimental and control groups from the same initial population.

We agree with Campbell and Erlebacher that in the ideal case the use of true experiments would provide the most information in the evaluation of compensatory and other social action programs. However, we question the feasibility of implementing such experimentation in many situations. (Evans and Schiller discuss this point in detail in another article in this volume.) Essential to any true experiment is random assignment of subjects to treatment and control groups. (Essential also is the random selection of subjects from a relevant population, if generalization of the results to the population is to provide useful information. Many true experiments carried out with college freshmen or laboratory school subjects are not generalizable to a relevant population.)

The political and social conditions for true experimentation may not always exist, or if they do, time pressures may not permit long term experimentation. The *ex post facto* or quasi-experiment may indeed be useful under such circumstances, provided that one is willing to recognize and take the risk that results may be subject to certain biases. At the very least, such evaluation may signal that something is wrong with the status quo, and suggest intelligent hypotheses for changing the situation. Perhaps this degree of information is all we can hope for in certain areas of social action.

---

* According to the report, Head Start children are somewhat below the national norms on the MRT when tested at Grade 1, approximately one half year behind national norms at Grade 2 on the SAT, and a full year behind at Grade 3 on SAT.

REFERENCES

CAMPBELL, DONALD T. & ERLEBACHER, ALBERT. "How regression artifacts in quasi-experimental evaluations can mistakenly make compensatory education look harmful." (This volume.)

CICIRELLI, VICTOR G., EVANS, JOHN W., & SCHILLER, JEFFRY S. "The impact of Head Start: a reply to the report analysis." *Harvard Educational Review,* Vol. 40, No. 1 (February, 1970).

CICIRELLI, VICTOR G. "Project Head Start, a national evaluation: Summary of the study." *Britannica Review of American Education.* Vol. 1, Ed. by David G. Hays. Chicago: Encyclopedia Britannica, 1969.

EVANS, JOHN W. "The Westinghouse study: Comments on the criticisms." *Britannica Review of American Education.* Vol. 1, Ed. by David G. Hays. Chicago: Encyclopedia Britannica, 1969.

MADOW, WILLIAM G. "Project Head Start, a national evaluation: a methodological critique." *Britannica Review of American Education.* Vol. 1, Ed. by David G. Hays. Chicago: Encyclopedia Britannica, 1969.

SMITH, MARSHALL S. & BISSELL, JOAN S. "Report analysis: the impact of Head Start." *Harvard Educational Review.* Vol. 40, No. 1 (February, 1970).

Westinghouse Learning Corporation/Ohio University. *The Impact of Head Start: An Evaluation of the effects of Head Start on children's cognitive and affective development.* Volumes I and II, June 12, 1969. Copies may be obtained at $6 per volume from the Clearinghouse for Federal Scientific and Technical Information, Sales Department, U.S. Department of Commerce, Springfield, Virginia, Order No. PB 184329. A brief summary of the study is available from the Evaluation Division, Office of Planning, Research, and Evaluation, Office of Economic Opportunity, 1200 19th Street, N.W. Washington, D.C. 20506.

10b

HOW PREOCCUPATION WITH POSSIBLE REGRESSION ARTIFACTS CAN LEAD TO A FAULTY STRATEGY FOR THE EVALUATION OF SOCIAL ACTION PROGRAMS: A REPLY TO CAMPBELL AND ERLEBACHER

John W. Evans

U. S. Office of Education

Jeffry Schiller

Office of Economic Opportunity

Campbell and Erlebacher have written a technically elegant paper about the possible biasing effects of using matching procedures and covariance corrections in evaluations of social programs. We would like to begin this reply with the unusual statement that we agree entirely with their technical points, and we do not wish to challenge the virtuosity of their statistical arguments. We only wish it were possible in the evaluation of ongoing social action programs to follow the more classically correct approach they recommend. Unfortunately, it is not.

The main points we wish to make are two. First, the fact that regression artifacts can occur (especially in tailored, computer simulated data) does not necessarily mean that they must occur or that they did in fact occur to a damaging extent in the Westinghouse study. Regression artifacts resulting from "score instability phenomena" would seem to be at a minimum when the matching was carried out on such vari-

John W. Evans is presently Assistant Commissioner of Education for Planning and Evaluation. Previously he was Chief of OEO's Evaluation Division which prepared the general design for the Head Start Evaluation and contracted with the Westinghouse Learning Corporation and Ohio University to carry out the field work from June 1968 to June 1969. Jeffry Schiller was the OEO Project Director for the Westinghouse evaluation. The views expressed here are the authors' and not necessarily those of their respective institutions.

ables as sex, race, and kindergarten attendance. The differences between the Head Start and control groups on the socioeconomic status measures obtained later were very slight, and the required covariance corrections were minor. In any case, the magnitude of bias from any regression arti-facts would have to be very large indeed to significantly alter the over-whelmingly negative outcomes of the Westinghouse study.

The second and more important point we wish to make is that re-gression artifacts are only one of a number of biases, shortcomings, or imperfections which can occur in evaluation studies. The choice which the evaluators of social action programs face is not, as Campbell and Erlebacher imply, between a good design without regression artifacts and a bad one with them. It is rather a choice among a range of proce-dures, each of which has methodological deficiencies of one kind or another. The alternative approaches proposed by Campbell and Erle-bacher also have both practical and methodological defects—most of them, in our judgment, more severe and more biasing than the possible effects of regression artifacts.

Consider the difficulties with the three approaches they recommend as alternatives to *ex post facto* analyses. First is the *true experiment*. Camp-bell & Erlebacher assert that "experiments with randomized assignment to treatments are greatly to be preferred where possible." Certainly nobody can argue with that. But the real questions are: How often are such procedures possible? and What do we do when they aren't? Camp-bell and Erlebacher state that "once the decision makers in government and applied research are educated to their importance, [true experi-ments] can become the standard evaluational procedure." We think this view reflects remarkable naivete. Attempts to implement the re-quired condition of random assignment will continue to face the objec-tions of program clients on the grounds that such procedures involve an arbitrary deprivation of the program to those designated as controls. Among the dissatisfied, the vocal ones will complain to officials and congressmen. Program directors consequently will want to avoid this procedure and will be on the side of those opposing it.

Our experience leads us to conclude, though reluctantly, that in the actual time-pressured and politically loaded circumstances in which so-cial action programs inevitably arise, the instances when random assign-ment is practical are rare; and the nature of political and governmental processes makes it likely that this will continue to be the case. Unfor-tunately, the political process is not orderly, scheduled, or rational. Crests of public and congressional support for social action programs often swell quickly and with little anticipation. Once legislation is en-acted, the pressures on administrators for swift program implementation are intense. In these circumstances—which are the rule rather than the exception—pleas that the program should be implemented carefully, along the lines of a true experiment with random assignment of subjects so we can confidently evaluate the program's effectiveness, are bound to be ignored.

Even in those cases where the logistics and the politics of random assignment can be handled (and we would expect such cases to be in the minority), random assignment in the natural environment has its own array of serious methodological problems. First, people's awareness that they are among the "experimentals" or the "controls" can produce serious Hawthorne effects. Second, there is likely to be nonrandom mortality from both experimental and control groups: dissatisfied members of the control population may seek to get the program services or some equivalent treatment elsewhere; the higher (and lower) ends of the SES range are more likely to move out of the area and be difficult or impossible to locate; etc. Campbell and Erlebacher's "recommended solution" to the problem of experimental mortality is to regard "all those randomly assigned to the program as treated." This assumes, of course, that they can be located in order to be measured. More importantly, however, this substitute procedure for avoiding regression artifacts is an unusual "solution" indeed, since including numerous cases as treated when in fact they were not would seem to introduce biases enormously greater than any due to regression artifacts. Third, the attempt to use random assignment in a real world setting will encounter the problem of contamination of the controls by the experimentals. In education programs, the fact that the randomly assigned controls may be in the same classrooms, in the same schools, in the same play groups, in the same neighborhoods, and in some cases even in the same families will often vitiate the whole purpose of random assignment. One of the programmatic hopes of Head Start, for example, has been to generate spill-over effects among the untreated.

A second approach to *ex post facto* analyses which Campbell and Erlebacher recommend is *limiting randomization to the boundary zone between the needy and those just above*. They themselves note, however, that "we would learn about the effects of the program only for a narrow band of talent, [and] we would wonder about its effectiveness for the disadvantaged." This admitted shortcoming of this approach to evaluating a social action program specifically aimed at the disadvantaged is so fundamental that we do not see the need to comment on it further, except to say that randomization at the boundary zone in addition to producing results of extremely limited utility is also subject to all the difficulties with random assignment in general noted above.

Campbell and Erlebacher's third alternative to *ex post facto* evaluation is the *supplementing of regular programs by small experimental expansions* (e.g. on the order of 10%). They say they "are sure that data from 400 children from such an experiment would be far more informative than 4,000 tested by the best quasi-experiments to say nothing of an *ex post facto* study." We are equally sure it would not. In addition to all the standard logistical, political, and methodological difficulties with random assignment outlined above, there is the additional serious problem that such an evaluation approach would yield information only on how a program works under very special hot-house conditions, not on how effective it is under the real conditions of mass implementation.

The practical consequence of all the obstacles to implementing random assignment is that studies which start out as true experiments will not end up as such, and it will be just as necessary to adjust the final data from these studies (by matching and covariance procedures, for example,) as it is with *ex post facto* studies.

By ruling out all evaluation designs except those that meet the requirements of true experiments, Campbell and Erlebacher are proposing a position which is untenable practically. It would require, for acceptable evaluations, conditions which only rarely if ever can be met. It would also rule out the use of masses of census and survey data for assessing program effects and policy alternatives. Consider, for example, the problem of trying to arrive at a judgment about the relationship of cigarette smoking and lung cancer. Obviously, there are selective factors in determining whether people smoke or not, and we will most certainly never be able to randomly assign people to smoking and non-smoking groups for a thirty-year period. Attempts to match smokers and non-smokers and correct for any residual differences through covariance or similar procedures are subject to all the technically correct strictures raised by Campbell and Erlebacher. Yet we must arrive at some judgment using the best information we have at hand. This is what has been done and we have made national and medical policy on the basis of it.

Attempts to rationalize the public decision-making process cannot be placed in the procrustean bed of pure experimental procedure. Enlightened congressman, administration officials, and others will continue to demand that the process of policy analysis and program assessment be improved in the direction of making it more empirical. Such improvements, however, will never yield perfection.

What all this means as far as the larger question of the evaluation of real world social action programs is concerned is that we are always going to have to make decisions on the basis of imperfect research and imperfect knowledge. In light of the fact that true experiments are of such doubtful applicability where national, politically based social action programs are concerned, and in view of the fact that when implemented outside the laboratory they have as many, if not more, methodological deficiencies as well designed *ex post facto* studies, we think Campbell and Erlebacher's dismissal of *ex post facto* studies is without merit, and if followed would lead to a very limited approach to evaluating social action programs which would be unable to produce information that can influence the national policy process—and this, it should be remembered, is the real objective of such evaluations.

Apparently sensitive to the fact that true experimental procedures and random assignment just won't be possible in many instances, Campbell and Erlebacher seem to opt for having no evaluation at all if it cannot meet true experimental standards. They say we should "not assume that every new program must be and can be evaluated." This position fails to understand that every program *will* be evaluated. The problem is that in the absence of formal, objective studies, programs will be evaluated by the most arbitrary, anecdotal, partisan, and subjective means. Congressional committees will hold hearings and parade before them a stream of witnesses (duly recruited by the majority and minority members of the Committee) who will testify on the one hand how marvelous the program is and how many needy mothers and children are being helped by it, and on the other, how mismanaged and frivolous the program is and what a shameful waste it is of the taxpayers' money. It is on the basis of this kind of "evaluation" that Congress will finally decide either to approve a continuation or expansion of the program (often at a cost of several hundred million dollars a year) or cut it back drastically. Compared with the weaknesses of this method for making decisions, the problem of regression artifacts pales to a most minor flaw indeed. It is this antiquated process of partisan, subjective evaluation which it is the task of the evaluator of social programs to *improve*, and he is not likely to improve it much if he will only deign to carry out true experiments with random assignment of subjects.

In sum, we do not believe the Westinghouse Head Start evaluation in particular, or well designed *ex post facto* studies in general, are "tragically misleading misanalyses," the widespread use of which can be attributed to the "slow diffusion of isolated warnings." Quite the contrary, the Head Start evaluation is, in our opinion, a fundamentally sound study which greatly advanced the previous, sadly inadequate basis on which to make policy judgments about Head Start and which deservedly has been "cited by Presidents and those influential in Government decision-making." Probably the reason that "90% of social scientists teaching methodology at U.S. universities would approve the process [of using matching procedures and covariance corrections]" is not that these methodologists are unaware of regression artifacts, but rather that they appreciate the fact that they represent only one of a range of imperfect approaches among which a choice must be made.

10c

REPLY TO THE REPLIES

Donald T. Campbell and Albert Erlebacher

There remain major unresolved differences between us (Campbell and Erlebacher, this volume), Cicirelli (this volume), and Evans and Schiller (this volume). These differences are at both the technical level and the policy level, the latter being both the more serious and harder to resolve. Nonetheless the technical issues are complex and difficult, and our original exposition is awkward at many points. There has resulted enough evidence of misunderstanding in the replies that we are tempted to some point-by-point comments, even though these will have to be too brief to achieve agreement.

In his first paragraph, Cicirelli states that in the situation in which the control and experimental populations are unequal in ability, under "certain conditions" regression artifacts occur. This statement is misleading in that *under all such conditions* matching and analysis of covariance will only partially remove the group differences they are employed to adjust. Furthermore, such artifacts occur with lawful inevitability in both natural situations and computer simulations (see also the "possible biasing effects" of paragraph 1, and paragraph 2 of Evans and Schiller). Our simulation was designed merely to make clearer the fact of and reasons for under-adjustment. Both replies agree as to the direction of the bias in the Westinghouse/Ohio study (paragraphs 8 and 9 of Cicirelli, and paragraph 2 of Evans and Schiller) but argue that its magnitude was minimal. We emphasize that the degree is unascertainable for two reasons: first, the lack of information on the characteristics of the populations from which matches were chosen prior to matching; second, lack of information on the factorial composition of the covariates.

In Cicirelli's third and fourth paragraphs it is not clear that he understands or accepts that matching on qualitative variables involves regression artifacts just as much as does matching on quantitative variables. If one is matching to overcome group differences in ability, then matching on race, kindergarten attendance, and neighborhood will involve undermatching, understandably enough considering the difference in

Supported in part by National Science Foundation Grant GS 1309X.

educational value of homes within each race, of houses within neighborhoods, and of kindergarten experiences across kindergartens as well as within the same kindergarten. The last sentence in Cicirelli's eleventh paragraph and paragraph 2 of Evans and Schiller imply that the fact that matching variables such as race and sex have little or no score instability is somehow relevant. It is not. Such matching variables are quite fallible *when used as a means of matching on ability.* It is also not clear that Cicirelli recognizes that regression artifacts are fully as much due to unshared true-score components as to measurement error. In Cicirelli's paragraph 11, area mean scores are not less biased than individual scores if the individuals going into the mean have been selected by individual matching.

In their paragraphs 3, 6, and 7, Evans and Schiller point to difficulties, biases, and limitations which true experiments evaluating compensatory education would have even if they could be implemented. They seem to overlook that *point-for-point* these limitations also exist for quasi-experiments in general and for their own Head Start evaluations. (To be sure, quasi-experimental situations may be less apt to confront the researcher with the existence of these problems.) Thus quasi-experiments with pretests and *ex post facto* studies, were it to be known, will be biased by differential loss of cases from experimental and control groups, by controls that seek out equivalent treatment elsewhere, by differential availability for follow up, by presence of both experimentals and controls in the same grade school classrooms, by spill-over effects, etc.

In paragraph 14, Cicirelli argues that Head Start "has not been effective" because Head Start children end up below national norms. The sentence should read "has not been completely effective." More important is the policy strategy involved. Shall we discourage Head Start programs by pointing to the remaining gap, or shall we reward progress, where it has in fact occurred, by noting gains over no Head Start conditions. It is relevant that even if the environmental opportunity difference were entirely removed during the Head Start period, no learning theory would expect the learned achievement difference to be eliminated (Campbell and Frey, this volume).

The smoking-lung cancer illustration is raised by Evans and Schiller in paragraph 10. We agree in accepting it as a plausible non-experimental demonstration of cause but we must insist that this achievement does not at all vindicate the Westinghouse/Ohio mode of analysis. There exist some major differences between the two cases. The original observation in the lung cancer case is a simple correlation, not a complexly pseudo-adjusted one. Cause-effect interpretations of simple correlations gain credence when one is able to rule out the other available plausible rival hypotheses, and produce other corroborating evidence. The confidence in a smoking-to-lung cancer direction of causation is in part based on the great weakness of all the other explanations of the correlation so far brought forth. No plausible third variable has been proposed which causes both smoking and lung cancer and thereby the correlation between the two. Nor is the reverse causation plausible—namely that either lung cancer or cancer proneness causes smoking. The inferred causation is moreover supported by at least partially substantiated mediational theories (to say nothing of evidence from experiments on animals).

The correlation of Head Start experience with subsequent ability scores on the contrary is swamped with plausible third variable explanations, both general environmental and genetic. This is exactly the problem acknowledged when one—as was done in the Westinghouse/Ohio study—uses matching and analysis of covariance to "adjust" for possible alternate causes. These techniques, however, are demonstrably inadequate to the task, and have a systematic direction of bias.

To provide an equivalent methodological problem in the lung cancer area, let us consider an investigator with the psychosomatic hypothesis that lung cancer is caused by the guilt and anxiety about smoking, produced when one is advised by one's doctor to stop smoking and does not do so. Our investigator is too sophisticated to simply compare an experimental group that has been warned by doctors to stop smoking, but has not stopped, with a control group not receiving such advice. He recognizes the certainty that the warned group would contain more and heavier smokers as well as more patients with a history of childhood pulmonary illnesses. The investigator might at this point decide to adjust the difference in cancer rate between the two groups by using the amount of smoking and rate of childhood pulmonary illness as covariates in analysis of covariance. His hypothesis would receive pseudo confirmation due to the inevitable underadjustment. There should in such an instance be no pretense that this analysis had tested the hypothesis, however socially important that hypothesis might seem.

We wish now to address ourselves to questions of policy. Paragraphs 4 and 5 of Evans and Schiller present the obstacles to mounting true experiments, difficulties which we do not wish to deny, and have indeed described similarly elsewhere (Campbell, 1969). Yet we must persist in our "remarkable naivete" and insist that if the consensus of methodological authorities, including Cicirelli, Evans, and Schiller, were to affirm the great superiority of true experiments, they could become recognized as the "standard" and become the model and modal type of evaluation in the eyes of the important decision makers in government and applied research, a small and highly educable population. The methodological community has not yet communicated such a message to these decision makers. We hope it soon will.

For the purpose of communicating such a message or the alternative one proposed by Evans and Schiller, depending on the result of the deliberations, we propose the convening of a commission composed of experts who are not yet partisans in this controversy, but who are recognized by the present partisans on both sides as having the requisite competence and objectivity. Such a commission might be convened by the American Educational Research Association, the National Academy of Sciences, and the Social Science Research Council, in consultation with the Office of Economic Opportunity and the U.S. Office of Education. The commission should include scientists from government as well as from universities. However such a commission decided, the commission would be performing a very valuable and influential service. We, of course, advocate developing a consensus among methodologists that would 1.) rule out all *ex post facto* studies, i.e. studies lacking either a pretest similar in factorial structure to the posttest or random assignment to treatments. 2.) among quasi-experimental pretest-posttest control group designs, rule out those using matching or ordinary covariance analyses as means of adjusting for pretest differences. There remain the several acceptable quasi-experimental designs which we have cited, especially the following: Where there are pretests similar to posttests, and where the homogeneity and other assumptions are met, there are Lord's and Porter's adjusted covariance analyses. Without similar pretests, the regression discontinuity analysis is available if the grounds of eligibility to Head Start can be made explicit and quantified. There also remains random assignment to treatments, with or without pretests. We believe the issues are now becoming clear enough so that a commission of experts with sufficient study would achieve and recommend some such consensus.

As they cite us in paragraph 13, we do indeed recommend that no scientific evaluation be done at all in *ex post facto* situations and in other situations where none is possible. We recommend this not because we "fail to understand that every program will be evaluated," but rather because we judge it fundamentally misleading to lend the prestige of science to any report in a situation where no scientific evaluation is possible. Professional evaluators of social programs will fail to improve these social evaluations unless they make clear that after-the-fact and immediate evaluations are impossible, and that well planned prospective research designs, experimental or quasi-experimental, are essential to that hard-headed scientific social reality testing which Cicirelli, Evans and Schiller so ably advocate (see especially Evans, 1969, and Williams and Evans, 1969).

REFERENCES

CICIRELLI, V. G. The relevance of the regression artifact problem in the Westinghouse-Ohio evaluation of Head Start: A reply to Campbell and Erlebacher. (This volume.)

EVANS, J. W. & SCHILLER, J. How preoccupation with possible regression artifacts can lead to faulty strategy for the evaluation of social action programs. A reply to Campbell and Erlebacher. (This volume.)

CAMPBELL, D. T. & ERLEBACHER, A. How regression artifacts in quasi-experimental evaluations can make compensatory education look harmful. (This volume.)

CAMPBELL, D. T. & FREY, P. W. The implications of learning theory for the fade-out of gains from compensatory education. (This volume.)

CAMPBELL, D. T. Reforms as experiments. *American Psychologist,* 1969, 24, 409-429.

EVANS, J. W. Evaluating social action programs. *Social Science Quarterly,* 1969, 50, 568-581.

WILLIAMS, W. & EVANS, J. W. The politics of evaluation. The case of Head Start. *The Annals,* 1969, 385, 118-132.

11

FROM TEXTBOOKS TO REALITY:
Social Researchers Face the Facts of Life in the World of the Disadvantaged

Scarvia B. Anderson, Ph.D.
Educational Testing Service

Of Lowe's 40-year project to develop a palaeographical guide to all extant Latin literary manuscripts copied before the ninth century, John (1969) wrote:

> If Lowe's project [Codices Latini Antiquiores] had initially been proposed in words that would now accurately describe how it was actually carried out, there is no question that its chances of avoiding miscarriage would have seemed negligible at best. No prudent man, entrusted with a foundation's funds, could have bet them on C. L. A.

It is no small comfort to read of the history of some major researches in other disciplines (which, since they are not our own, always appear more distinguished) when one is embarking on a project that eminent advisers have said could not be done. Fortunately, for the dedicated investigators, two agencies (Head Start* and Educational Testing Service) were willing to place some bets on a "longitudinal study of disadvantaged children and their first school experiences." But it is certainly true that the words in the original proposal did not provide a very accurate description of what carrying out this study would be like. Furthermore, with less than two of a planned six years of data collection behind us, we are still a long way from solving many of the practical—not to mention theoretical—problems associated with this kind of research related to social action.

I am indebted to Samuel Barnett, Joseph Boyd, Virginia Shipman, Gray Sidwell, George Temp, Virginia Wilson, and Jane Wirsig for suggestions about this chapter.
* Originally Head Start/OEO, then Head Start/Office of Child Development/HEW.

Nevertheless, this paper will detail some of the personnel, community relations, and logistical challenges of the study and the means we have adopted to face them. The spirit is not so much that of an Apologia (see Schachter et al., 1961) or a revelation to graduate students of the prologues and "sediment" in educational research (Wittrock, 1969), as it is an interim progress report specific to one of the stated aims of the study: to learn how to do research of this kind in this kind of setting. At the same time, we shall be grateful if an occasional section enables a colleague to avoid a pitfall in his own social research or at least to feel some comfort of fellowship.

First, let us take a look at the study as a whole. It is a longitudinal study of children from the age of about $3\frac{1}{2}$ (before preschool) through grade 3. The present sample size is 1700, but some of these children will move and be unfindable, and the design allows us to add children who move into the preschool and school classes of children in the original sample. Thus, over the period of the study we expect we will be in touch with well over 2000 children but, of these, only about half will be veterans of a complete six years of measurement. Most of the children are from poor families; the majority of them are black. (Fortunately, the two are not completely confounded.) The children are from Lee County (including the city of Auburn), Alabama; Portland, Oregon; Trenton, New Jersey; and St. Louis, Missouri. Even brief visits to those four spots point up the lack of standardization of the term "disadvantaged."

The object of the investigation is to try to identify the components of early education that are associated with cognitive and personal-social development of children—and the family and community characteristics that may moderate these associations. In other words, it is evaluation of early education programs (especially Head Start), basic research on child development, social action, and a "practicum" in how to do research in the real world. It relies upon a naturalistic design: the sample includes all children in selected school districts who will be eligible to enter the first grade in the fall of 1971; some of them have enrolled in Head Start and others have not. We have managed to convince ourselves that this is the best design for the study purposes, just as we have managed to live with a number of other compromises with "elegance." For example, our first choice eastern city became ineligible at the last moment (their Head Start funds were cut off), and we had to change our whole rationale for the "purposive" sampling of cities. (For a more complete description of the study, see *Educational Testing Service,* 1968 and 1969, and Anderson & Doppelt, 1969.)

Local personnel

Very early in the study plans, we committed ourselves to using community people (mostly those described euphemistically as "indigenous") for local management and data collection. This commitment was less altruistic than practical and professional. We needed community acceptance to do the study at all, and we felt that local people had a better chance than outsiders of collecting valid data from children, their families, and community sources. At this point we are, unscientifically, unwilling to brook any debate on this commitment.

In each site we first employed a local coordinator. The qualifications listed for this job included familiarity with the power structure in the community and rapport with the diverse elements of it; ability to speak well and fluently; involvement with disadvantaged children, their families, and early education; administrative skills; good health; and ability to drive a car. It can be seen that at the earliest stages of operations we were most concerned about community relationships. Local coordinator problems fell into three main areas:

1. We had not defined "administrative ability" very well and indeed had not anticipated the tremendous demands we would make upon the coordinators. Each one wound up with a set of personnel, fiscal, and other administrative responsibilities comparable to those of the manager of a small factory. In addition, of course, they had the other full time job of keeping up with the children and creating a favorable image for the whole range of activities. With the bias in our selection process, it is not surprising that the local coordinators did far better at the second kind of work than at the first. We belatedly arranged for some specific management training sessions for the coordinators, sessions more typical of industry than of a research agency. In addition, we have put a great deal of effort into improving the forms and instructions we provide to aid them in dealing with payrolls, inventories of equipment and materials, purchasing, personnel problems, etc.

2. Not only did we err in underemphasizing management aspects of coordinators' jobs, but also we did not foresee adequately the conceptual problems they would face. Originally, we had thought that local coordinators could be present at all training sessions for testers and interviewers, that they would learn the tasks, and that they could then exercise general supervision over the collection of data in the field (with some monitoring from ETS of course). But the coordinators had more than enough to do without this; furthermore, effective monitoring of the technical aspects of data collection simply could not be done on the basis of brief training. Without a fund of basic knowledge about measurement and child development, they could not be expected to make adjustments or adaptations that would maintain the integrity of the study. Therefore, last year we kept ETS Princeton and regional office professional staff in the field constantly. This year we are trying something new: a technical director in each community, who is a member of a local university faculty in education or psychology and was able to arrange a limited teaching schedule. Technical directors came to

Princeton for intensive training specific to the data collection of the study and are now supervising local training and data collection activities, relieving the local coordinators in principle as well as in fact of concerns here.

3. The third and greatest problem, more evident in some situations than in others, arose from conflict in the coordinator's loyalties. He* had been hired primarily because he related well to his community. It should not have been surprising then that he would sometimes put project concerns below community concerns and pressures; for example, the purpose of the project was perceived more as providing jobs than as collecting data. We were very self-conscious about this problem at the beginning and spent more time talking around it than in confronting it directly. As one consequence, a serious rift developed in the project staff back home, and, most unfortunately, different interpretations and instructions about a situation were sometimes communicated to the local coordinators. The situation is substantially better today, partly because the staff worked conscientiously to "heal itself" and some social-professional compromises were effected, partly because the study has become fairly well accepted in the communities, and partly because the coordinators have become more knowledgeable about the purposes of the study and less distrustful of its management.

In each site, the local coordinators recruited local people to serve as testers. These women, mostly black, were trained to administer Hess-Shipman mother-child interaction tasks and one of the three test batteries. Training generally took six to eight weeks, much longer than we had hoped it would require. But the problems of and with the testers, as continuing association with them revealed, were related only tangentially to their abilities to learn new tasks and cope with a type of work that almost anyone would find unusual. Problems stemmed from a deeper source, a life style characterized by economic chaos, lack of personal support and back-up resources, short-term plans and expectancies, violence, and deep distrust of outsiders. Unfortunately, at the beginning of the association some of the actions that the home office took, or delayed, did not do much to dissipate this distrust.

Consider, for example, the matter of pay. ETS Princeton and regional office personnel are paid twice a month. Because of the unusual arrangements surrounding employment of personnel in the field, the first paychecks of testers were delayed even beyond the first two weeks of employment as trainees. Many of these women simply had no alternative means of sustaining themselves during this period. How were they going to buy groceries at the cash-and-carry market? How were they going to

---

* "He" is used generically. Actually, two of the four coordinators are female. (Three are black and one is white.)

pay their babysitters who demanded a few dollars each evening? It was shocking and understandable that the second time pay was delayed in one site (this time because the local coordinator did not get the payroll in) the testers went on strike. It took all the persuasive abilities of our coordinator of community activities to get them back to testing children again. Only a few of us who remembered the Depression were not surprised when the testers in St. Louis asked that "graduation" (a diploma-awarding ceremony marking the completion of training) be delayed a month so that they could buy or make new dresses. As one member of the staff put it, some of the needs of the testers were those of the daily maid: transportation, lunch (for some centers in Lee County there might not be a restaurant for miles), and pay by the day. We were able to furnish the first in most cases and make provision for the second. However, our accounting system could never be adjusted to allow for pay more frequently than twice a month. Gradually, and with several pay periods behind them, most of the women began to adjust to this fact of organizational life.

In the larger cities, the majority of the testers are divorced, widowed, or separated from their husbands; they frequently have several children to support. A number are involved in some kind of court litigation. There is a general atmosphere of violence around them. (One of our interviewers discovered a murder; shots were fired at one of our rented vehicles.) Some of the women have been victims of burglaries or husbands (ex- or otherwise) on a rampage. These angry men have in several cases appeared right at a testing center; and, at least once, we reassigned a tester to another center where her husband would not be likely to find her. Usually, however, the project staff's help is not sought in such domestic matters, nor do the testers get involved in husband-wife quarrels of their friends. Calling a cop is far beyond the pale of acceptable behavior in this society.

Frequent tester absences and some turnover are associated with home problems. If a school age child gets sick, there may be no one for the mother to leave him with. The excessive absences on Mondays, far more than we would expect from regular staff, are probably attributable to another kind of home or neighborhood event. Princeton office standards of good working habits were simply not met by many of the women in the early days of the study. And some of those who met them best left to accept long-term employment elsewhere. At least the project may have helped them see that they could make it in the business or educational world. We are keeping a tabulation of what happens to our ex-testers; so far, jobs as aides in Head Start or other preschool programs seem to have held the greatest attraction. Some of our turnover losses may represent community and personal gains! Moreover, as the project continues, many field employees have continued in a number of different roles and we have been greatly encouraged by the improvements in working habits.

In our original definition of the tester job, we naturally stressed the testing per se. Then, when we asked testers to do telephoning, answer sheet inspection, or other fill-in jobs, they sometimes refused stubbornly and sullenly. Yet unless they are occupied constantly, a whole new set of problems based upon gossip and rumor emerges. The most successful testing centers, in more ways than one, have been the busiest centers. As we have recruited new testers or started new phases of testing, we have made every attempt to communicate a broader definition of the tester job and to back up this broader definition with ample "seat work."

At least one more tester problem should be mentioned, but this one is not particular to the group of data collectors we used. It is certainly familiar to other researchers using any relatively untrained child testers. One of the hardest parts of the training was to make the testers assume roles different from those they might play with their own children; good testers, unlike good mothers, are neither teachers nor disciplinarians.

In spite of all the problems, however, most of the women have been very proud of their jobs and their "diplomas." (Many of them had never received a diploma for anything before.) And, by and large, they have produced useful data on children and their mothers.

There are at least three other categories of local personnel: Observers who go into classrooms (usually they are drawn from the ranks of those who test at other times), playroom supervisors, and drivers.

Playroom supervisors are generally tester trainees who "flunked." In their new tasks, most of them seem to forget their earlier lack of success. They are usually motherly types with considerable skill in comforting a frightened child, making a skinned knee well, or engaging a child's interest in a toy until it is time for him to go to a testing room. They also make quantities of peanut butter and jelly sandwiches and take charge of brothers and sisters of study subjects whom the mothers bring along.

Drivers should be as carefully screened as testers. In the early days of the project, we were not as aware of this as we should have been. Fortunately, we have had a number of good drivers who defined for us what the job should be. Drivers have to be able to answer questions about the study, they have to feel responsible for their charges, they have to be prompt. There are, for example, the drivers who take children home to find no one there; they may babysit for a while or take the children back to the testing center playroom, but they do not leave them unattended on their doorsteps. Some drivers help get Johnny or Susie dressed if they get to the house and find Mother behind schedule.

Since the same driver picks up the same children on succeeding days, he gets to know them in a way that few other study personnel do.

Community relations

A major consideration in the selection of study sites was the expressed willingness of school people, Head Start people, and other community people to be involved in, or at least accept the presence of, the research. To secure these expressions of willingness, members of the central project staff and ETS regional offices made "presentations," distributed brochures, went on local radio and television programs, and had informal discussions in offices, barbershops, and cafés. Project plans call for a continuation of publicity efforts throughout the six years; and to the conventional media we have added some others that seem to be especially effective in getting our messages across: notices in church bulletins, announcements from pulpits, flyers stuck under doors, and placards in laundromats.

However, we believe that our continuation in the communities is far more dependent on local involvement in the project than on our publicity about it. We staff from the community, buy from local merchants, and maintain a highly visible office there. We have now had local offices for over a year, and we think that this fact alone has helped establish that we are not a fly-by-night organization. We are listed in the local telephone directory; local companies deliver goods to us and send us bills; increasing numbers of the citizenry call upon us with requests of one kind or another.

Generally our testing centers are set up in churches or in church-related buildings. The original reasons for this choice were convenience, low rent, and the fact that many churches have a number of small Sunday school rooms ideal for individual testing. However, we feel that the use of churches had the supplementary advantage of adding an aura of respectability and responsibility important to our initial contacts with the families of study children.

Another activity, undertaken for measurement reasons, is also important in community relations. We appointed a Communities Advisory Panel consisting of two representatives from each site, one involved in some official capacity in education (e.g., school principal) and the other a member of the concerned but not professional community (e.g., Head Start mother). In an intensive meeting with the project measurement staff, this panel reviewed all of the tests in terms of the appropriateness of the items to the socio-economic level and local conditions of the young subjects. Their comments were varied and helpful (e.g., objects might be familiar to the children of rural Lee County but not familiar to the children from St. Louis housing developments, and vice versa), and we took account of as many as we could in revising the instruments. This panel will be asked to review instruments planned for later years of the study as well.

To deny that a project such as this would have some racial overtones would be exceedingly naive. In the early days of training testers, the Trenton group was brought to the ETS Princeton office, because the Trenton office was not large enough for the total group sessions. A chance rudeness in the cafeteria line by someone not connected with the project at all led to immediate shouts of "racism." That same cry was used several times in communities too when a local employee wanted to put down an ETS professional trainer and could not seem to think of a better way to do it. During the pay strike mentioned earlier, a black staff member had to contend with charges of "Uncle Tom-ism." But the shouts seem to be dying down, and fortunately they have been directed at Princeton employees, the "establishment," rather than at co-workers in the field.

In fact, there have been practically no problems of a racial nature within the testing centers. Black and white testers have worked together amicably in Lee County and St. Louis alike; black testers comfort white children and greet their mothers; white testers work equally effectively with black and white children. At one point, when it was suggested that we might have to segregate testing centers in order to reach the children of some rural white Alabama families, the testers expressed willingness to organize themselves in this way for the sake of the study, but they were obviously unhappy about the possibility. Fortunately, ETS policy against segregated testing centers and the feelings of the Alabama testers were congruent. Color blindness was also a matter of pride to interviewers. Although the relevant research evidence is not definitive, it was proposed that we send black interviewers to interview black mothers and white interviewers to interview white mothers. The Portland crew rebelled loudly: "What are we supposed to do," the black interviewers asked, "if a white mother answers the door? Say uh-oh, wrong color, I'll have to go get my friend?" We bowed to their demands to relax the requirement of matching interviewer and interviewee, but because of the neighborhood assignments of interviewers most of the interviews were color matched. At least that could be blamed on a larger problem of society and not on a provincial project policy. One race-related adjustment had to be made to a fact of the real world: if the driver was a black man, we sent a white tester along with him to pick up children in some predominantly white areas.

Some of the public relations problems were so subtle that it took us a very long time to find out that we had them. Even the name of the study came into question. Head Start had funded a study of "disadvantaged children and their first school experiences" but one does not walk up to a mother and say, "We want your child in our study of disadvantaged children." On all local communications we try to remember to drop the word "disadvantaged." We even have to be careful in referring to the "project." Some mothers in Trenton put our project in the same category as "housing projects" and "poverty projects" that they did not want to be associated with. We have a token payment for mothers, but we have to be careful not to appear condescending as we present it. We also have to be careful about who our local friends are or, more specifically, we have to try to be friends with everyone and not get identified with one particular group no matter how helpful they are. In one city, we got caught right in the middle of internecine warfare between two settlement houses.

Logistics

Getting an operation going requires trained personnel, facilities, materials/equipment, transportation/communication, and specified operating procedures. There were times in the early days of the project when many of us wished we had had more courses in business administration if fewer in the social sciences.

Before personnel training got underway, we rented and equipped offices. Finding a suitable site in a short time was especially difficult in the impacted areas of Trenton and St. Louis. In our target areas in St. Louis, if an office has been vacant for any length of time it is likely to have been so vandalized that it will require a major restoration effort. We have "made do" there with very inadequate space and are only now moving into suitable quarters. Beyond locating space, we had to equip our new rented offices with everything: window shades, used furniture, typewriters, $29.95 copying machines, wastebaskets, rubber bands, paper clips, stationery, etc., etc. In keeping with our general policy, most of these items were purchased locally, and serendipitously we usually saved money by doing it that way. (The project is operating under a grant that is relatively very large for educational research. However, we are trying to do so many things that—not unlike our testers—we seem always to be teetering on the brink of fiscal disaster.)

Our testing operations were to be in churches, and generally the churches provided basic furnishings. However, several did not have child-sized furniture and in a few cases we had to build or improvise partitions to obtain enough private testing space. The testing materials were, of course, the major equipment for the centers and, with manuals, answer documents, and the other components (pictures, food, toys, etc.) of 28 different measures for 3½-year-old children, the task of supply was formidable. Toy departments did not yield all of the materials the psychologists had put into their tasks or, in some cases, if they had an item, it was the wrong color. At one point in the project, while tester trainees were on call, they painted a large number of toys and pictures to conform to task specifications. Unfortunately, halfway in the testing all of the paint began to rub off, but we have improved upon the procedure this year. During the course of testing, the manufacturer of Etch-a-Sketch games (used in one mother-child interaction task) seemed to be producing increasingly poorly constructed ones or else our subjects were becoming increasingly aggressive; in any case, this equipment was subject to constant replacement. The projection equipment for the fixation task was so often out of commission that we had to involve the president of the large manufacturing company in the maintenance problems. Add to the list of equipment that seemed to be needed in testing centers in never ending supply: Tootsie Rolls and paper bags (for the delay of gratification and risk taking tasks), Polaroid film (pictures were essential to the self-concept task and also made nice souvenirs for the mothers), something more than juice and cookies for obviously unbreakfasted children (dry cereal and peanut butter were favorite menu items), coffee for waiting mothers, strong wrapping materials to return answer documents to ETS, and size 4 underpants (even the best trained children sometimes needed extras in the excitement of the new situation).

Safeguarding equipment in both offices and testing centers is a matter of serious concern to local coordinators. They need money but they are actually fearful of having it around, and locked metal boxes provide a relatively poor solution. Travelers checks are a somewhat better one. After two air conditioners were stolen from our office in Trenton we started renting a dog for nights and weekends. A continuing series of "losses" of small, readily negotiable equipment in one site was a clue to a drug problem.

We expected to provide transportation for mothers and children to the testing centers, but at first we offered parents the option of "own" transportation versus ours. However, at least two of our coordinators noted that the "no shows" were significantly greater for the "own" transportation group, and we started insisting that we would handle transportation arrangements. Last year, transportation was provided in rented station wagons. This year, we are the proud owners of eight small vans. The reasons: ownership is more economical in the long run, and the vans provide the flexibility of an extra testing room if needed.

Establishing policies and procedures for field operations was and is not easy. The two most troublesome areas, not unexpectedly, have been personnel and finances. Some of the problems have been related to attempts to integrate field and central office procedures.

The problem of semi-monthly pay periods has already been mentioned. This arrangement is satisfactory for ETS Princeton and regional office employees; it is far less satisfactory in the field. However, a dual system would require a major and very expensive change in ETS accounting procedures. Part of the reason for the initial delay in pay checks to testers in the field was that legal authorities were puzzling over whether testers should be considered "temporary employees" or "consultants." Initially, we explained their jobs to them in terms of the latter (this meant to them that we did not take out social security and federal income tax). However, we had to go back later and explain that all procedures had been changed: they would be considered temporary employees. (That status, incidentally, is a factor, along with personal characteristics, in the turnover problem mentioned earlier. Despite the fact that we are thinking of a six-year study, our budgets are handled on an annual basis. Furthermore, we cannot guarantee full-time work within the year. More permanent jobs are bound to be attractive.)

Then there were the problems of setting up cash resources for local coordinators to enable them to cope with "start up" expenses. Charge accounts are fine for dealing with large, conventional purchases. The corner dime store does not charge that suddenly needed extension cord; cash was required to take advantage of the surplus store's reasonable offering of child-sized chairs and tables; no one had quite anticipated the costs of paper cups, cookies, and juice at testing centers. But, at the time the study began, ETS policy allowed operations a maximum of $50 in petty cash, and receipts had to be processed before replacement funds could be provided. This policy was changed for the longitudinal study, but the change could not be effected before professional trainers in the field had used up their living allowances for equipment and the local coordinators had incurred personal debts.

Personnel recruitment, hiring, and especially firing are very different propositions in Portland or St. Louis, compared to ETS Princeton. In the Princeton office with over 1300 regular employees, relatives can easily be separated departmentally; if an employee is not doing well on one job there is the opportunity to try him on another; the job market is such that one week's notice is not necessarily a catastrophe; and, most important, jobs can be classified as "regular" rather than "temporary." We are slowly evolving personnel policies that are more realistic for our new colleagues.

*   *   *

We are obviously not far enough along to draw any firm conclusions about what our research thrust into the world of the disadvantaged has accomplished either for them or for us, but there are some signs in *us* that seem rather significant:

1. We write or say "them" and "us" much less easily, and the re-

searchers are as likely to talk about what they have learned from the field as about what they have taught.

2. We complain more than we used to about our graduate training in psychology and education and how ill equipped it left us to work on real problems.

3. We recognize that there are deadlines more important than APA papers, and we are not as afraid as we used to be of losing our personal professional identification in the kind of projects that require a team effort.

4. After being in the position of the "establishment" for a couple of years, we have new sympathy for some of the revolts against it.

5. We have developed considerable realism about time and money: everything seems to take twice as long and cost twice as much as we expect.

6. We can even hold up our heads in the face of nonrandom assignment of subjects to treatments.

REFERENCES

ANDERSON, S. B., & DOPPELT, J. (Chm.) Untangling the tangled web of education. Symposium sponsored by the National Council on Measurement in Education, New York, November 1968. Princeton, N. J. Educational Testing Service, RM-69-6, 1969.

Educational Testing Service. Disadvantaged children and their first school experiences: Theoretical considerations and measurement strategies. Report in 2 volumes, December 1968, Contract OEO 4206 and Grant OEO CG-8256, Office of Economic Opportunity.

JOHN, J. J. E. A. Lowe and *Codices Latini Antiquiores.* American Council of Learned Societies *Newsletter,* 1969, 20 (5), 1-17.

SCHACHTER, S., FESTINGER, L., WILLERMAN, B., & HYMAN, R. Emotional disruption and industrial productivity. *Journal of Applied Psychology,* 1961, 45, 201-213.

WITTROCK, M. C. Dirty data points: The case of the missing research equipment. Paper presented at the meeting of the American Educational Research Association, 1969, and published in *Educational Researcher,* 1969, 20 (9), 5-7.

12

HAS EVALUATION FAILED COMPENSATORY EDUCATION?

Herbert Zimiles, Ph.D.

Chairman, Resarch Division
Bank Street College of Education, New York

The long overdue search for an effective method of educating young deprived children has been diverted by seemingly authoritative claims and counterclaims of competing theoretical positions, and, more recently, by somber pronouncements that new efforts along these lines have failed. The basis for these judgments, both of success and failure, has been the outcome of evaluation studies involving pre-post comparisons of scores on various intellectual aptitude tests. How valid are the methods of evaluation which form the basis for these contentions? If tests are exclusively used to assess cognitive growth, what kind of information do they provide and how relevant is this information to how children are influenced intellectually by their early school experience? The purpose of this paper is to identify some issues which challenge the validity of current methods for evaluating the effectiveness of compensatory educational programs for young children.

The Narrow Band of Measurement and Its Marginal Relevance

It is a commonplace that no brief test can provide comprehensive measurement of a given trait or area of subject matter. Tests have traditionally been viewed as providing behavior samples which are representative of domains to be assessed. However, as the study of cognitive development in children advances, it becomes apparent that most tests sample only a small fraction of the cognitive domain. The tests used in evaluation studies are best suited to the measurement of stored information, perceptual and visual-motor skills and the ability to follow simple instructions. Tests help to measure products, i.e., they identify outcomes of previous formal or informal learning. They offer an index of the visible skills and levels of knowledge which have been achieved at the time of testing. However, they provide only scant and very indirect information regarding the cognitive processes which mediate the child's current intellectual functioning and are even less illuminating with regard to those personality-related attributes which support the development of effective intellectual functioning.

The area of conceptual functioning—how children order events and govern their inferential thinking, how they utilize thought to recreate and understand reality—which has only begun to receive systematic study since the recent rebirth of interest in Piaget's work, is minimally represented in most assessment studies. Yet, many observers tend to regard this sphere of functioning as lying at the core of the intellectual disability observed in disadvantaged children. Similarly, such personality-related attributes as curiosity, flexibility, initiative, perseverance, orderliness and imaginativeness, which have a decisive effect on the character of intellectual development, are only peripherally assessed by current testing procedures.

To the educator of young children who is primarily concerned with activating the processes which mediate and support intellectual growth, the task of evaluation seems premature and difficult to achieve. He usually adopts a long-term perspective with regard to the cultivation of inquiry, the expectation of order and the search for relationships, the development of initiative and perseverance. The interim products of such a course of development are not always specifiable, and when they are, they are often difficult to measure. It is clear that these educators need to be encouraged to devote more time to searching for signs of development, to establish benchmarks of progress, so that their efforts can begin to be validly assessed at intermediate points in the educational enterprise. Unfortunately, some essential technical knowledge is not yet available. The mapping of the domain of conceptual functioning has barely begun. Not a single aspect of this vast domain has undergone such detailed analysis of its development that it is possible to assess and record growth over relatively short periods of time. Yet many evaluation studies are concerned with gauging change in pre-post test performance over intervals considerably shorter than a year. Moreover, assessment of conceptual functioning is extremely time consuming. Demonstrating a single problem, with all of its intricacy, and communicating to the young child the nature of the response that is called for, followed by a series of problems large enough to ensure reliable measurement, require much more time than the simple cataloguing of knowledge of words, for example. It is not surprising, then, that the process-oriented educator sees evaluation as only marginally relevant to the operation of his program.

While it may be meaningful to distinguish between process and product-oriented educators and evaluators, it should be noted that virtually none of the tests currently employed in evaluation studies was explicitly designed to measure the outcome of a specific product-oriented educational program. Because their content so often consists mainly of intellectual products, it has been possible for the eclectic, product-oriented educator to design his program and define his objectives in terms which are compatible with, if not actually patterned after, the content of existing tests. The product-dominated quality of most tests is not the result of the deliberate effort to exclude the assessment of more dynamic elements of intellectual functioning. Technical and theoretical problems in defining and measuring the mediating processes have given rise to the product-process imbalance which exists. In defense of standard test content, it has been argued that the acquisition of language and information is not independent of the child's level of relationship thinking and his inquisitiveness and perseverance as well. While granting this point, it remains clear that omnibus tests of discrete bits of knowledge and specific skills provide only a haphazard and extraordinarily crude index of these more complex cognitive processes. Further, while a given instrument may seem comprehensive because of the sheer number of its items, the recording of change is limited to shifts in performance from pretest to posttest, to those items which were failed during the pretest and then passed during posttest. Since it frequently happens that many of the items which were failed at the outset were manifestly unrelated to the nature of the educational intervention, the results of the intervention can only be demonstrated on a comparative handful of items. Often, then, the image of intensive (if not comprehensive) measurement of change created by multi-itemed tests is illusory.

These considerations have emphasized how narrow and unordered is the band of cognition which is being measured in current evaluations of cognitive change. Currently used evaluation instruments, by virtue of their content, are more suited for use with product-oriented as opposed to process-oriented educational programs.

CONTEXTUAL FACTORS IN COGNITIVE FUNCTIONING

The current emphasis in child development research on the exploration of conceptual functioning has generally formulated its task to be that of identifying the major dimensions of conceptual functioning and establishing methods for their valid measurement. Conservation phenomena, for example, one of the first to be considered both conceptually meaningful and amenable to direct and reliable measurement, have undergone extensive investigation, first to determine the developmental level at which they emerge and to identify their correlates among other cognitive measures, and secondly to determine how non-conservers can be trained to more rapidly acquire the ability to conserve.

Most of the work in this area has had as its point of departure the assumption that conservation is either present or absent in a child, and that the task of research is to determine the nature of its cognitive content and its pattern of development. However, it has been suggested that conservation behavior does not simply entail the presence or absence of a specific concept, but rather is dependent on a complex of interrelated factors, each one of which may decisively affect performance on the conservative task (Zimiles, 1966).

Of greater significance to the present discussion is the observation that conservation performance, as well as the factors which appear to underlie it, do not seem to function with perfect reliability. They seem present and available for use on some occasions and unavailable or not called upon on others. These observations point to the important role of context in cognitive performance. It suggests that concepts are not simply present or absent, but rather that they are sometimes available and sometimes unavailable, and that the situation in which they are called forth determines in some lawful manner whether or not they will be utilized or found applicable. This stance changes the task of studying conceptual functioning (and other aspects of cognition as well) from an emphasis on determining the presence-absence of a particular concept to an analysis of the conditions under which it is available for use. In terms of its implications for evaluation, this orientation to the problem of conceptual functioning calls for a much more elaborate method of assessment, thereby further complicating the task of evaluation.

Consideration of the role of contextual factors in cognition tends to emphasize, too, the unsuitability of the testing situation as the only occasion for assessing a child's cognitive functioning. If the context of conceptual functioning is an important issue, children should be studied in a variety of situations as well as with a variety of tasks. The pervasive practice of exclusively assessing cognition in a test situation is especially inappropriate for the study of disadvantaged children. Labov (1969) has eloquently expressed the observation of other workers in the field in his analysis of how the asymmetrical social-psychological relationship between the disadvantaged child and the tester decisively curtails his responsiveness in the test situation. Because of the fear and suspicion aroused by the tester, knowledge and skills which may be available to the disadvantaged child under more relaxed, personally meaningful circumstances, may simply not be manifested during the test situation.

The way in which interpersonal-communicational dynamics may affect test performance has been shown in a recent study by Zigler and Butterfield (1968), who demonstrated that substantial differences in test performance can be induced by manipulating the relationship between child and tester. There are other indications that the process of accommodation to the world of adults, their style of communication and demands, can by itself produce significant gains in test performance. In a recent study of the effects of different preschool programs (Zimiles, Wallace and Judson, 1970) , an analysis of pre-post changes in individual item performance on a modified version of the Preschool Inventory revealed that one of the largest changes in the performance of a group of bright middle-class four year olds attending nursery school was their ability to give their first name upon request. Did these children have to attend nursery school to learn their names, or were they simply more ready or competent to respond to the examiner the next time (posttest) around? The example just cited is flagrant. The discrepancy between a child's spontaneously emitted classification behavior and performance evoked by a test of classification is more difficult to detect. The testing of young children is replete with instances in which the examiner is convinced that the child possesses the capability of responding correctly despite his failure to do so. This is not to deny that the availability of knowledge on demand, the ability to solve a problem presented in a test situation, does not reveal something significant about the character of cognitive organization and flexibility of functioning of the child, but it is not the definitive indicator of his current level of knowledge or ability, or even of the general availability of this knowledge, but rather of the availability of this knowledge under the very special conditions of testing.

THE MEANING OF CHANGE SCORES

While the disadvantages of testing as a method for assessing young children are well known, this method continues to command a surprisingly persistent level of credibility and loyalty, partly because of the absence of viable alternatives, and partly because investigators periodically report such large gains from a pre-post test analysis that the results are interpreted as upholding the validity of the test method. These occasional large gains encourage evaluators to believe that if a form of educational intervention is really effective, its excellence will be revealed by test scores. While some of these rare spurts in test scores are simply occasioned by chance or error, in those instances in which a particular program of intervention consistently produces large gains in test performance, clearly something systematic is happening. In such cases, it is most likely that the content or form of the training program is closely matched by the index of cognitive growth employed to evaluate the method. In some instances the material to be learned in a training program has so closely paralleled the actual item content of the evaluation instrument that there is no wonder that positive results were obtained. More often, however, positive results stem from the program's emphasis on the need to attend to detail and the familiarity it provides with a didactic communication process strikingly similar to the interrogation process used in testing. It requires the child to "tune in" and participate at a level which facilitates test performance. The training received by some educational intervention programs hones the child's ability to take a test in the same way that a newcomer to crossword puzzles, upon repeated exposures to the puzzles and without learning any new words, sharply increases his capacity to cope with the puzzle. He develops a capability of responding effectively by familiarizing himself with the framework of the interrogation and by learning to summon his already existing knowledge to the demands of the problem. If there is any generality to the effect of this type of learning, then it is quite valuable, but if its effect is specific to the particular structure and demands of the evaluation instrument, then one may justifiably question the usefulness of this form of cognitive growth and the concern with measuring it.

The usual defense of continued use of omnibus tests to evaluate educational programs begins by conceding that they provide only a crude estimate rather than an actual representation of the learning which transpires in a program, but then maintains that by virtue of a kind of filtering down process, the test becomes sensitive to the net effect of the program and offers a reliable index of the relative amount of growth produced by the program. This interpretation of the meaning of change scores seems less tenable than one which attributes test gains to the more direct (or indirect) training in effective test-taking performance provided by the programs being evaluated. These are, of course, not mutually exclusive interpretations of change scores.

Perhaps a more realistic view of the validity of current methods of evaluation would be achieved if evaluators were expected to provide a rationale for their choice of methods, that is, were required to explain the ways in which their pre-post testing was seen as relevant to the behavioral changes likely to be produced by the educational intervention program they are evaluating. And correspondingly, upon completion of the evaluation, it would be instructive if the evaluator were required to account for the changes found in test behavior on an item-by-item basis, if he were called upon to relate changes in item performance to the nature of the influence of the program. At the very least, the establishment of this mode of procedure might contribute to a more critical view of the relevance of existing evaluation methodology.

One of the most telling arguments in favor of the continued use of aptitude tests to evaluate educational programs has been the fact that they reveal how effectively the child will function in school at a later date. The substantial correlations found between Stanford-Binet performance and school grades are unquestionably attributable, in part, to the fact that both the traditional classroom and the test require attentiveness to detail, docility and mobilization to respond to adult demands. Whatever the basis for the covariance, however, it should be pointed out that the test scores which contribute to these empirical relationships with school performance served as an index of some internalized or stabilized set of attributes. Increments in test scores resulting from compensatory education training programs were not involved. It has yet to be established how such incremental IQ points, which may be much more transitory in nature, relate to school performance. It may well be that the sources of variance in change scores differ from those factors which contribute to pretest performance. Until this relationship can be established empirically, it may be wrong to assume that IQ increments are predictive of a child's functioning in school.

Whether or not it is true that the relationship between test scores and school performance can be largely attributed to the pervasive alienation of disadvantaged children and the consequent inaccessibility of their knowledge and abilities, a state of affairs which has adversely affected their test performance just as it has undermined their ability to function well in school, it must be borne in mind that tests merely serve as signs of future school performance. Because they provide the basis for useful predictions, they have often been mistaken for the dynamic forces which actually affect the development of intellectual competence. The task of the educator is not to remove the symptom of the condition, i.e., low test scores, but to intervene in a way which interrupts the disadvantaged child's lack of relatedness to school. The problem is not one of mechanically raising point scores on tests but of creating a school situation which establishes a meaningful framework for the child's full participation in school life. Once the child becomes invested in the school world and his talents are free to be expressed, the pattern of his abilities and disabilities will become more visible, and more productive educational planning will become possible. The educator must turn away from a preoccupation with the outward appearances of the disadvantaged child as a student to a concern with engaging him emotionally and intellectually in a school program which fosters an organic type of psychological growth.

The purpose of this discussion has been to identify some significant shortcomings of current methods for evaluating cognitive growth attributable to preschool compensatory educational programs. It has been shown that our incomplete understanding of how cognition develops during the preschool years prevents comprehensive assessment of intellectual functioning and fosters a regrettable reliance on measures of accomplishment rather than mediating cognitive processes. Further, it has been suggested that a refined analysis of cognitive functioning must take into account the context in which it is being studied, that the issue of the conditions of availability of knowledge and skill rather than its presence or absence needs to guide future assessment. Related to this issue is the fact that deprived children are probably systematically being assessed under conditions which put them at a disadvantage.

Finally, it has been maintained that many of the change scores which current, inadequate measures produce are more a reflection of studied efforts to improve test scores than to generate cognitive growth. It has yet to be shown that these change scores are predictive of school success. In light of these rather serious flaws in ongoing evaluation procedures, it does not seem appropriate or useful for their results to be used as definitive indications of the state of compensatory education, or to serve as a valid basis for comparing alternative educational approaches.

Although unrealistic in some of its expectations and premature in its timing, the present emphasis on evaluation has stimulated investigators to identify major gaps in existing theory of child development, especially as it relates to the psychological influence of school experience. It has also helped to pinpoint methodological needs which grow out of the theoretical network regarding the nature of school influence. Since this network of theory is at least as important to the educator as it is to the evaluator, the educator must be pressed to contribute much more than he has until now to a theoretical analysis of the basis for his program and its presumed interim and long-term effects. The evaluator, too, must begin to see the need for formulating the potential influence of a program in terms of the most sophisticated and comprehensive theoretical framework possible rather than in terms of accidentally available measuring instruments. This calls for a relaxation of the inflexible empiricism which dominates most of the evaluation work of today; it asks that measures be viewed as fallible instruments in the service of a complicated, basically theoretical enterprise (see Minuchin, Biber, Shapiro and Zimiles, 1969).

In the meantime, evaluation studies serve as a goad to advancing knowledge and theory. But when the shortcomings of the evaluations themselves are glossed over and they are mistakenly presented as offering definitive statements regarding the nature of school influence, and the imperfect indices they use to achieve crude assessment themselves become the basis for school planning, then it is time to recognize that they have overstepped their bounds and begun to interfere with the very processes they were intended to support.

REFERENCES

LABOV, W. "The Logic of Non-Standard English." In *Georgetown Monograph Series on Language and Linguistics,* Monograph No. 22, 1969.

MINUCHIN, PATRICIA, BIBER, BARBARA, SHAPIRO, EDNA, & ZIMILES, H. *The Psychological Impact of School Experience.* New York: Basic Books, 1969.

ZIGLER, E. & BUTTERFIELD, E. "Motivational Aspects of Changes in I.Q. Test Performance of Culturally Deprived Nursery School Children." *Child Development,* 1968, 39, 1-14.

ZIMILES, H. "The Development of Conservation and Differentiation of Number." *Child Development Monograph,* Serial No. 108, 1966, 31, No. 6.

ZIMILES, H., WALLACE, DORIS, & JUDSON, MARCIA. A Comparative Study of the Impact of Two Contrasting Educational Approaches in Head Start. Report of Office of Evaluation and Research of Project Head Start, OEO, 1970.

Section III
PROGRAMS AND PRACTICES: DEFINING SUCCESS

13

PROBLEMS IN THE DETERMINATION OF EDUCABILITY IN POPULATIONS WITH DIFFERENTIAL CHARACTERISTICS

Edmund W. Gordon, Ed.D.
Teachers College, Columbia University

INTRODUCTION

The determination of educability in children from populations which show wide differentials in intellective and social functioning is simple but also complex. When the question is posed as a political problem, the answer is simply to declare that all children are educable and assign the responsibility to the schools for educating all children. Some of our activities on behalf of economically and socially disadvantaged children and youth have taken that form. We have agreed that these children should be educated. We have acknowledged or assumed that they are educable. We have greatly increased money and human resources directed at improving their education. We have developed varieties of compensatory education. Yet we have not been highly successful in educating poor and minority group children. We are now told (or reminded) by Jensen (1969) that the problem may be that these children, particularly the black ones, are genetically different and inferior. The allegation of genetic inferiority is a value judgment based largely on speculation and inference from a quite disparate body of empirical data. The fact of genetic difference is obvious with respect to certain physical traits but not so clear with respect to intellective and social behavioral characteristics. It is clear, however, that children who come from certain ethnic, cultural, and economic groups show some characteristics in high incidence. The hypothesis that some of these characteristics are hereditable is of course tenable. The fact that differences exist, however, is not debatable and may have relevance for the determination of educability. It is when the determination of educability is posed as a pedagogical rather than political problem that the question becomes complex.

249

The complexity of this issue derives in part from the fact that educational treatments vary greatly with respect to content, focus, and goals, but are relatively non-variant with respect to method, while on the other hand patterns of intellective and social human functions vary with respect to affective qualities, cognitive styles motivational forces, task involvement, temperaments, etc. The variance in these patterns of human functions may require complementary variations in educational *method* as well as in content, focus, and goals. In the absence of such a match, individuals and groups with atypical patterns of intellective and social functions may be uneducable under that inappropriate set of conditions. These same individuals or groups may prove to be educable under a more appropriate set of pedagogical conditions. Thus, in the present crisis over education for black, Puerto Rican, Mexican American, American Indian, poor white, or other disadvantaged groups, the questions of educability may prove to be recalcitrant of solution until we move beyond political declarations to find pedagogical solutions and commit the necessary financial and human resources to the application of these solutions.

DIFFERENTIAL CHARACTERISTICS IN DISADVANTAGED POPULATIONS

Available research data permit the identification of several categories of behavior which are encountered with great frequency among socially disadvantaged youth. First there are several studies which suggest that children from disadvantaged backgrounds in comparison with middle class children are less able to make use of conventional verbal symbols in representing and interpreting their feelings, their experiences, and the objects in their environments. It is important to note that the apparent deficiency is in the use of such conventional verbal symbols—there is no definitive evidence that such children suffer from an underlying deficiency in symbolic representation.

Available evidence suggests that depressed language function can be the result of a variety of circumstances which make for disadvantaged status. Kellmer, Pringle, and Tanner (1958) found in a group of youth of comparable economic level, age, sex, and I.Q. differences on all quantitative measures of language function, differences which consistently favored children raised in their own homes as opposed to children raised in institutions. The authors suggested that youth raised in the institutions studied were disadvantaged by an insufficient language stimulation resulting in restricted capacity for language development. Other investigators have been concerned with language development in different economic groups. Davis (1937) found a considerably higher percentage of youth with good articulation among upper occupational groups than among lower. Beckey (1942) reported finding significantly more children with retarded speech among lower socioeconomic groups. Templin (1953) found a significant difference between children of upper and lower economic groups on tests of articulation, the difference being in favor of the higher economic group. Her data indicate that children of the lower socioeconomic groups take about a year longer to reach essentially mature articulation than do those of the upper group. Irwin (1948) reported that children after the age of one-and-one-half showed significant differences in their mastery of speech sounds according to their father's occupational status—with the advantage in the direction of the higher occupational groups.

Anastasi (1952) compared Negro and Caucasian children and found among the Caucasians a greater frequency of mature sentence types, more complex construction and better elaborated concepts. Hilliard (1957), approaching the questions inferentially, found that children with rich information backgrounds were better equipped for reading than were pupils whose previous experience had been meager. In studies by Thomas (1962) and Templin (1957) in which the variable studied was a number of words used per remark, Thomas' subjects drawn from a low socioeconomic group showed a mean of 5.6 words used, while Templin's subjects drawn from a middle class population showed a mean of 6.9 words per remark.

In what is probably the most careful, though limited, study of linguistic behavior in lower and middle class subjects, Bernstein (1961) reported that the language of lower class youths tends to be "restricted" in form. He characterized this language as serving to communicate signals and direction and to confine thinking to a relatively low level of repetitiveness. On the other hand, he described the language of the middle and upper classes as "elaborated" and serving to communicate ideas, relationships, feelings, and subjective states. These works suggest that symbolic representation is present in both classes, but also that important qualitative differences exist in the form and utilization of the symbol or language systems. These differences may have important implications for learning. However, since these studies have not included analysis of learning facility or lack of it in terms of language forms and vernacular peculiar to the population, the data do not enable us to determine accurately the specific nature of the learning disabilities involved.

But the inferential conclusions drawn from these studies, relating school failure to differences in language development in disadvantaged children, gain some support from studies of concept development in this population. Riessman (1962) has described concept formation among the disadvantaged as content centered rather than form centered, their reasoning as inductive rather than deductive. Such a conceptual style has been viewed as limiting the child's ability to make accurate generalizations and to transfer knowledge utilizing previously learned concepts, (Gordon, 1963).

Deutsch (1963) and Hilliard (1957) have noted that increasing age amplifies the difference in the quality of language usage between classes; and Deutsch has suggested that if the acquisition of language is a prerequisite of concept formation and problem solving, then these evidences of relative increasing language deficiency would indicate a tremendous lower class deficit in conceptual formation. Deutsch (1963) found that his subjects, drawn from a disadvantaged population, were relatively proficient on motor tasks, on tasks which required a short time span, and on tasks which could be most easily related to concrete objects and services; but, as he later reported (1964) he found lower class children generally inferior in abstract conceptualization and in the categorizing of visual stimuli. Ausubel (1963) concluded that when there was a delay in the acquisition of certain formal language forms, there was a resultant difficulty in making the transition from concrete to abstract modes of thought.

In a cross cultural inventory of the arithmetic concepts of kindergarteners, Montague (1964) found significant differences between social classes in favor of the higher SES group; but Deutsch (1960) found that arithmetic scores were higher than reading scores among a population of lower class children, even though both were depressed below national norms. In interpreting this finding, the investigator suggested that the difference might be accounted for by a hypothesis that reading involves motivations arising from specific value systems not shared by the disadvantaged society, while arithmetic may involve concrete acts, such as marketing, which are common to the society. In the work of the author (Gordon, 1965) in Prince Edward County, Virginia, arithmetic scores were similarly found to be less depressed than reading scores in the 7 to 10 year age groups. These children who had been deprived of formal education for four years are thought to have developed simple arithmetic skills in their everday chore experiences. These experiences did not, however, provide a basis for the casual or incidental acquisition of reading skills.

If these assumptions about the experience-based distinctions between acquisition of reading and arithmetic skills are correct, then the Montague, Deutsch, and Gordon data would seem to support the observation that disadvantaged children tend to depend more on concrete than symbolic experience in dealing with concepts. In a study by Siller (1957), however, this view is subjected to closer examination. Studying 181 white sixth graders, he found that higher status children (a) scored higher than lower status children on all tests of conceptual ability; (b) showed a significantly greater tendency toward abstraction in making choices between types of definitions than lower status children; and (c) when matched with lower status subjects on non-verbal tests, scored higher than their counterparts on tests of verbal concepts. When, however, the groups were matched on the basis of I.Q. scores, none of the above differences remained. The investigator suggests that this is due to an elimination of the lower extreme of the low status group which in turn suggests that differences with respect to conceptual style may be a result of generally lower levels of intellectual function (as measured on intelligence tests) among lower status children. Thus, while there is a considerable body of evidence to support the statement that lower status children tend to show preference for concrete as opposed to abstract frames of reference in concept formation, the origin and nature of this style dominance and its relationship to intelligence and the teaching-learning process are yet to be established.

Among other disadvantageous characteristics, disadvantaged children have been noted by several investigators and observers to demonstrate perceptual styles and perceptual habits which are either inadequate or irrelevant to the demands of academic efficiency. Although high levels of perceptual sensitization and discrimination are often present, these skills appear to be better developed in physical than in visual behavior and in visual than in aural behavior (Riessman, 1962). Probably the most significant characteristic in this area is the extent to which these children fail to develop a high degree of dependence on the verbal and written language forms of academicians for learning cues. Many of the children simply have not adopted the modes of reception and expression which are traditional to and necessary for success in school.

The extent to which styles of perception and expression differ among children of different backgrounds is well documented. In his study of retarded, average, and gifted children, Jensen (1963) concluded that many children viewed as retarded have merely failed to learn the verbal mediators which facilitate school learning. Earlier, Carson (1960) found white children superior to Negroes and northern Negroes superior to southern Negroes when it came to understanding the meanings of words used in communication. In a study of children's use of time in their own stories, LeShan (1952) found that time orientation varies with social class and that middle and upper class children told stories involving a more prolonged period of time than those of lower class children. Riessman (1962) includes slowness as a feature of the cognitive functioning of disadvantaged youngsters, a conclusion arrived at by Davidson some ten years earlier (1950) on finding differences in speed of response to be primarily responsible for racial differences in I.Q. estimated by timed performance tests. C. Deutsch (1964) found lower class children relatively poorer in auditory discrimination, in recognizing perceptual similarities, and in the syntactical manipulation of language. Earlier (1960),

M. Deutsch had found them inferior to a control group on tasks requiring concentration and persistence.

In fact, many of the children with whom we are concerned show a marked lack of involvement with, attention to, and concentration on the content of their academic experiences. There are few academic tasks which commit them to deep involvement. Their work habits are frequently insufficiently developed. Because of the high interest demands of non-academic experiences and the relatively low-interest demands of academic experiences, they are limited in their ability to inhibit responses to those stimuli which are extraneous to academic learning and to disinhibit responses which are pertinent to academic learning. Deutsch (1960) reported that lower class children tend to ignore difficult problems with a "so what" attitude and that as a result, over a period of time, their learning is decreased proportionately. Ausubel (1963) found that lower class children depend more on external as opposed to internal control than do children from the middle class.

Moreover, socially disadvantaged children have been determined by several investigators to be less highly motivated and to have lower aspiration for academic and vocational achievement than do their middle and upper class school peers. The degree of motivation and the direction which it takes among many of these children are often inconsistent with both the demands and the goals of formal education. But although the quality of aspiration is often depressed, it is usually consistent with the child's perceptions of the opportunities and rewards available to him. Symbolic rewards and postponements of gratification appear to have little value as positive motivators of achievement. For these children goals tend to be self-centered, immediate, and utilitarian, as are the goals of the dominant culture. However, children growing up under more privileged circumstances have available many sources of immediate satisfaction and immediate feedback as well as many more evidences of the utilitarian value of academic effort. The differences between the privileged and the disadvantaged in this area are not so much differences in values as differences in the circumstances under which the values are called into play. Although the values from which motivation is derived in the disadvantaged child seem to reflect the dominant-culture concern with status, material possessions, in-group morality, Judeo-Christian ethics, competition, etc., there is usually lacking a concern with the aesthetics of knowledge, symbolization as an art form, introspection, and competition with one's self. In other words, dominant societal goals and values are operative, but their direction and context may not be complementary to academic achievement.

Rosen (1956) observing a relationship between high motivation and high grades postulated that middle class children are more likely to be taught the motives and values which make achievement possible. Similarly, in Gould's study, (1941) only sons who internalized their parent's values of aspiration were sufficiently motivated to overcome obstacles which faced them in school. Bernstein (1960) found achievement strivings arising from parental demands for success to be a more central motivational factor among middle class than among lower class children.

Closely related to these motivational factors are attitudinal factors, and these too are often a source of problems in educational planning for disadvantaged children. Hieronymus (1951) found that higher socioeconomic status was correlated with a high level of aspiration and positive attitudes toward school while negative attitudes toward school and lower levels of aspiration were more frequently encountered in lower socioeconomic status groups. Sewell's (1957) finding that educational aspirations tend to be greatly influenced by class values in a manner favoring the middle and upper classes is consistent with the earlier work. Among other characteristics which have been referred to in this population are utilitarian attitudes toward knowledge and negative attitudes toward the pure pursuit of knowledge. Many of these children and their parents view education primarily in terms of its job market value and their orientation is toward achieving the minimum level of education commensurate with employability. Carrol (1945) sees the lower class ideal self as characterized by personal beauty and fame, not the moral and intellectual qualities which characterize the ideal self of middle class children.

As important as these attitudes toward school and learning may be, it is in the area of attitude toward self and others that the crucial determinants of achievement and upward mobility may lie, and it is in these areas that our data are least clear. It has been observed by some that disadvantaged children show affinity for ingroup members and demonstrate a sense of distance from or even hostility toward representatives of outgroups, whether in peer or nonpeer relationships. Contrastingly, other observers have noted the high degree of respect and awe in which these children hold selected outgroup status persons or idealized models. Tendencies toward self-depreciation and depressed self-concepts have been noted by several observers (Dreger, 1960; Keller, 1963; and Silverman, 1963). Goff (1954) found that lower class children have more feelings of inadequacy in school than do children from the middle class. On the other hand, some recent findings (Gordon, 1965) suggest that depressed self-concept is not so prevalent a condition, and that even where present it may have little negative bearing on achievement. In fact, it is entirely possible that positive or negative feelings of self-worth may operate respectively to depress or accelerate achievement. Furthermore, it is in this area that the rapidly changing national and world situations involving underdeveloped peoples are likely to be most influential, and it is difficult to predict the ultimate effect of these altered situations on self-perception and behavioral change. Our knowledge and even our researchable hunches are as yet limited. But it is around these changing situations that the school may yet find a fulcrum on which to lever up motivation, aspiration, and involvement. There is growing empirical evidence to support the view that young people actively associated with the current civil rights struggle draw from their involvement in that effort a new source of motivation and an enhanced view of themselves (Coles, 1963). The impression is gained that such experiences are reflected in greater application of effort to and greater achievement in academic endeavors. The evidence for such improvement is less clear, yet there can be little doubt that attitudes toward self and toward the environment in relation to self are crucial variables in academic as well as in social and emotional learning situations. One of the clearest findings coming from the Coleman Report (1966) indicates the crucial role of a sense of environmental control in academic achievement. The importance of an individual's sense of personal ability to influence his future through his own efforts is exceeded only by family background characteristics as a contributor to school achievement. With the notable exception of Riessman (1962) attempts at identification of positives or strengths in this population are hard to find. However, even in Riessman's treatment there is a tendency to romanticize these characteristics, which may be a more serious error than to ignore them. Among the several positives which may be identified are those behaviors and conditions which can be utilized and built upon for the purposes of educational improvement. It is extremely important to recognize that *selective* motivation, creativity, and proficiency are present in this population; and, as Riessman has consistently stressed, if we look for these characteristics in their traditional form and along traditionally academic dimensions, we shall merely insure that they not be found. These children, like others, *are* motivated by *some* factors in the field. They show creativity in *some* situations. They are proficient at *some* tasks and under *some* conditions.

Reference has earlier been made to problems in language development and use. In contrast to the colloquially accepted concept that language is inadequate in this population is the proposition that there exist in disadvantaged populations quite complex languages. The form in which the language is expressed may not be verbal nor may the specific symbols be consistent with those normative to the dominant culture. But the presence of a language system or a system of symbolic representation adequate to the needs of the culture in which it has developed should not be ignored. The important question then becomes not whether language exists, but to what extent a given language system may be utilized in understanding and managing advanced conceptual problems. If the facts and integrative relationships of science or the conceptual explorations of philosophy cannot be expressed in symbols capable of incorporation into the language system in question, then that language, though it may be adequate for the culture in which it exists, is inadequate to the demands of contemporary educational processes. To date, investigations into the utilitarian dimensions of divergent language patterns have not been conducted. Our research has established the fact of language differences (Deutsch, 1963, 1964; Jensen, 1963; John, 1964), and in addition we know something of the nature of these differences. The Bernstein work (1960, 1961) referred to earlier characterized lower class language as restricted and middle class language as elaborated. Strodbeck (1964) has described a mechanism by which such language systems may develop and be perpetuated. He identifies this mechanism in the context of intrafamilial decision theory where the elaborative characteristic of middle class language is a product of parity (and thus conflict) in the decision making process in the middle class home. Restricted language on the other hand develops as a product of unilateral decision making in the lower class home. In a situation involving equality and conflict of ideas the learner (child) early develops sensitivity to language as a vehicle for the elaboration of ideas. Where the opposite situation exists, the child early develops sensitivity to language as a vehicle for the communication of signals or directions. Some findings of C. Deutsch (1964) indicate that there are significant class differences in the time spent in parent-child communication—the length of such communication is considerably shorter for lower class than for middle class subjects. This difference has been viewed as a handicap, but it may be that given a different instructional method this proclivity for brief verbal communicative contact could be an advantage to the learner.

Much of our knowledge concerning children from socially disadvantaged backgrounds has been drawn by inference from the wide literature on juvenile delinquency. Sensitive analysis of this literature leads to an awareness of several other characteristics of this population. One cannot study the literature on boys' gangs or juvenile offenders without coming to the conclusion that these youngsters show ingeniousness and resourcefulness in pursuing self-selected goals and in coping with very difficult and complex conditions of life. Such coping behavior reflects accuracy of perception and generalization around a variety of social, psychological, and physical phenomena. It is at once obvious that these children are capable of meaningful and loyal personal relationships and operate with an ingroup morality that surpasses that of some more privileged segments of society. In many situations where the problems flow from the experiences and are important for the self-selected goal, such operations as memory, recall, computation, and representation have been demonstrated to be functionally adequate.

The second area to which research attention has been directed is the environment. Studies referrable to environmental concern have consisted largely of a cataloguing of the factors in homes and communities from which disadvantaged children come which may interfere with normal school achievement. Such studies have often been conducted with the ultimate aim of incorporating knowledge obtained from them in the training of school personnel so that they may "understand" the culture and the values of their pupils. The concurrence between certain conditions of life, certain population characteristics and poor school adjustment has been interpreted as indicating a causal relationship, though the evidence supports only the conclusion that these phenomena are correlated. Such studies, while they may have social-anthropological value, are of questionable use in planning educational programs for these children. It is probably true that adverse conditions of life do not facilitate academic achievement in most children, but we have no firm evidence that such conditions preclude academic success. In fact, there are sufficient cases of success despite adverse conditions to make untenable the conclusion that difficult life circumstances prevent success in school. Insufficient attention has been given to the fact that many "normal" and well-functioning individuals have such adverse circumstances in their lives. There are many good reasons for improving the living conditions of the disadvantaged, and there is certainly no good excuse for an affluent society to fail to do so, but a concern on the part of the school for changing poor conditions of life should not substitute for a primary concern with the improvement of the teaching-learning process.

THE PROTEAN NATURE OF EDUCABILITY

One of the traditional roles of education in the U.S.A. has been to broaden opportunities for productive, influential, and rewarding participation in the affairs of the society by developing those skills and entry credentials necessary for economic survival and social satisfaction. The idea of education for all grew gradually. In this country we extended this opportunity to more and more of our people by a steady increase in the quantity of educational experiences available and the quality of the educational product. While the quantity of available educational experiences has grown, there also has been a marked increase in the quality of the skills and competencies demanded of those who would achieve much. Similarly, the individual's goals are higher. He wants to be productive in the sense that the society sees his effort as resulting in a valued product; influential in the sense that his participation is viewed as having some influence on outcomes; and rewarded for his effort both materially *and* psychologically.

Increased perception of this role of education makes us want to equalize access to basic education of high quality. Spurred on by the civil rights movement of the 1950's and '60's, equal opportunity in education has become an issue of crucial national concern. By many, it is regarded as the base for all the rights, privileges, and responsibilities of membership in this modern democratic society.

Our country's desire to equalize educational opportunities is in part a product of advances in the organization and development of human societies during the past six centuries. In earlier periods when neither the need nor the resources for wide access to education existed, the ideal of universal equalization of educational opportunities also did not exist, certainly not in the public policy sphere. The concept itself and the concern for its implementation could not have emerged as an important issue, even now, if we had not earlier developed an awareness of the universality of educability. Human societies have always considered educable those categories of persons thought to be needed in the maintenance of the social order. Consequently as the human resource requirements of social orders have changed, concepts of educability have changed. Educability in human subjects has been defined less by the actual potentials of persons and more by the level of society's demand for people capable of certain levels of function. In more simplistic and exclusive social systems, most people were considered uneducable and effort was not "wasted" on their formal training. As long ago as the early Christian period and as recently as the early nineteenth century, it was only the religious and political nobility who were thought to be capable and worthy of academic learning. The social order was maintained by the machinations of those elite groups and the simple and routine gaming, farming, and crafting skills of the illiterate masses. Under the triple pressures of the reformation in religion, mechanization in industry, and institutionalization in commerce, categories of persons thought to be capable of academic learning were greatly expanded. Opportunities for active participation in religious activities and rituals made reading and writing more widely usable and salable skills. Similarly, the emergence of collective machine production in shops and the expansion of commerce and trade through institutions made necessary the broader distribution of these skills. The combined impact was a greatly increased societal need for computational and communicative skills in larger numbers of people. As a corollary, previously illiterate people were drawn into the small body of literates and the mass of "uneducables" was reduced.

In the United States, where religious freedom and diversity became widespread, where democracy in government became the ideal, and where industrialization and economic expansion advanced most rapidly, more and more literate persons were required. In mid-nineteenth century U.S.A., society's view of who could be educated quickly expanded to include all people in this country except slaves. With the end of slavery and the incorporation of exslaves into the industrial labor force, exslaves gradually came to be regarded as educable. Through the exercise of briefly held political power, together with uneducated poor whites, they literally forced increased access to public education as a vehicle for their education. These indigenous poor were later joined by waves of immigrants who also saw the public school as their major route to economic and social salvation. In the metropolitan areas of the period, the school also became the major vocational training resource that prepared semiskilled and commercial workers for rapidly expanding industries. Although the school did not succeed in educating all of these new candidates, the once narrowly defined concept of educability was now nearly universal in its inclusiveness.

Our conception of education has also changed over the years. In Thomas Jefferson's view the school was expected to provide the technical skills and basic knowledge necessary for work and economic survival. It was from newspapers, journals, and books, and from participation in politics that people were to be really educated. In reviewing Jefferson's position on education, Cremin (1965) has concluded that it never occurred to Jefferson that schooling would become the chief educational influence on the young. However, changes in the number and variety of persons served by the school, changes in the functioning of the society and changes in the nature of the skills and competencies required by the social order have also changed the nature of education.

By the middle of the nineteenth century in this country, public schools serving the upper classes had developed curriculums basic to a liberal education. In this period, the secondary school was quite selective and was designed to prepare a relatively few young people for entrance into college where most of them would pursue studies leading to one of the professions. While this trend continued through the latter half of that century, the first half of the twentieth century was marked by a high degree of proliferation in the development of technical and vocational training programs. Preparation in the liberal arts was considered a luxury and was thought by some to be relatively useless. It was the Jeffersonian concept of utilitarian education which prevailed. And it was this utilitarian education which came to be the mode in the growing acceptance of universal educability. "Everyone can and should be taught to do useful work and to hold a job" was the prevalent view.

The wide acceptance of this view contributed to the salvaging of education for Negroes following the betrayal of the Reconstruction Period and its leadership. In the great debate symbolized by verbal conflict between Booker T. Washington and William E. B. DuBois, the real struggle was between those who stood for the narrow but practical training of the hands of Negro and poor children so that they could work and those represented by DuBois who believed in the broad and somewhat less immediately practical education of the mind through the liberal arts and sciences. Those favoring the training of the hands won that debate. Educational facilities for Negroes and other poor people slowly expanded under the banner of technical and vocational training. This may have been a victory for expanded access to education, but the neglected concern for the "liberating" study of the arts and sciences made this a victory from which true equality in education has yet to recover. We will return to this point later in this paper. At the moment our concern is with the protean nature of educability and education.

In this country the battle for equality of educational opportunity was first waged to establish public responsibility for the education of children in states where public education did not exist. This was followed by the struggle for adequate educational facilities and diverse educational programs. The twentieth century was one-third spent before the struggle for equal though separate schools was engaged. By mid-century it was legally determined that in our society separate schools are intrinsically unequal. However, even before the 1954 Supreme Court school desegregation decision was promulgated, it was becoming clear that racially mixed school systems do not automatically insure education of high quality. This observation was supported by data on minority group children from schools in the North where varying degrees and patterns of ethnic mix were extant. Although the performance of minority group children in some of those schools was superior to that of such children in segregated systems in the South, differences in achievement and in the characteristics of their schools were notable.

The early nineteen sixties brought campaigns for education of high quality provided in ethnically integrated school settings. Some school systems responded with plans for the redistribution of school populations in efforts to achieve a higher degree of ethnic balance. Some of those, along with other schools, introduced special enrichment and remedial programs intended to compensate for or correct deficiencies in the preparation of the children or the quality of the schools. Neither these efforts at achieving integrated education nor efforts at developing compensatory education resulted in success. Ethnic balance and educational programs of high quality proved impossible to achieve instantaneously. Confronted with the failure to obtain ethnic integration and high quality in education, and given the recalcitrant presence of segregation in schools north, south, and west, the goals for many minority group parents shifted. In the late nineteen sixties the demand is made for education of high quality, where possible, on an ethnically integrated basis. However, where segregation exists (and it does exist for the great majority of ethnic minorities in this country) the demand increases for control of those schools serving such children, by groups indigenous to the cultures and communities in which they live. Hence the demand for "black schools run by black people."

Alongside this growing acceptance and promotion of ethnic separation, there continues to be concern for ethnic integration in education and compensatory education as complementary strategies in the equalization of educational opportunity. The introduction of the concept "compensatory education" grew out of the recognition that learners who did not begin from the same point may not have comparable opportunities for achievement when provided with equal and similar educational experiences. To make the opportunity equal, it is argued, it may be necessary to make education something more than equal. It may be necessary to compensate for the handicaps if we are to provide education of equal quality. It may be necessary to change the educational method and create new models in order to meet the learning need and style of the youngster who comes to school out of a different background of experiences.

EDUCABILITY AND THE PROCESSES OF EDUCATION

To give meaning to the concept of educability in populations where there is deprivation of developmental and educational opportunity, several educational preconditions are indicated. These include (1) provision for a more appropriate distribution of emphasis between the affective, cognitive, and conative aspects of learning; (2) a shift in emphasis in educational appraisal from quantitative measures and static prediction to qualitative measures and dynamic prescription; (3) increased attention to individually prescribed learning experiences; and (4) greater concern for insuring that the learning experience is relevant to the general experience of the learner.

Affective, Cognitive, and Conative Aspects of Learning

Zigler (1966) has suggested that the relative lack of success in many of our programs of compensatory education may be due in part to the fact that so much of this effort has been directed at attempting to modify the cognitive function of inefficient and retarded learners. He reminds us, however, that cognitive function may be the least malleable of human adaptive systems. The affective and conative systems may be more susceptible to change. In his research he has been able to demonstrate significant shifts in intellective function (reflected in intelligence test scores) as attributable to changes in motivation and task involvement without perceptible change in the quality of basic cognitive function. It may be that our efforts at improving the general functioning of these children would be more productive if the emphasis were placed instead on tapping the sources of motivation known to be intrinsic to these learners and on the design of learning experiences directed at basic skills mastery. Productive function in these areas may lead to improved cognitive functions as a byproduct. Experimentation in these areas is not very extensive, save for the work of the behavioral analysis-contingency management plan.

Qualitative vs. Quantitative Approaches to Measurement

The heavy emphasis on reduced demand in curriculum modification for disadvantaged and retarded learners is partially a byproduct of our heavy dependence on quantitative approaches to measurement. When psycho-educational appraisal data are reported in terms of a score or a level of normalcy or retardation, educational planners have little basis for the design of learning experiences. On the other hand, qualitative appraisal data which are descriptive of intellective and social function lend themselves to the prescription of learning experiences which accommodate or complement cognitive style, temperamental traits, achievement patterns, and motivational states. Under such conditions, the predictive validity of measures of status may break down since the basis of predictions is our knowledge of how others of similar status have performed in fairly well standardized educational or treatment situations. Where the characteristics of the target population vary greatly and traditional approaches to education prove ineffective, a shift in educational appraisal may be necessary from quantitative measurement and static prediction to qualitative measurement and dynamic prescription.

Individually Prescribed Learning

In prescriptive design in education, the concern is with matching learning experiences to the characteristics and needs of children who vary in a number of ways. The major efforts so far have been directed at prescribing learning units which match the achievement level, learning rate, or special interests of individual children. Each child is encouraged to move at his own rate and in areas which are of greatest interest to him. Most of these programs use existing curriculum materials with varying degrees of modification. None of the programs have seriously engaged the problems of diagnosing affective and cognitive style and developing materials and techniques which match stylistic variations in learning behavior. As sophistication in qualitative appraisal advances, increased specification in the prescription of learning experiences becomes more possible. However, the ultimate value of individuation in education is dependent upon our ability to translate educational prescriptions into appropriate units of learning experience.

Learning Experiences Which Have Relevance for the Learner

In order to be maximally meaningful to a child, education must be relevant in three areas: 1) it must relate to him as an affective being through its materials, experiences, and people with which he can identify; his motivation to learn will be more easily tapped when the learning task leads to goals which he perceives himself as valuing; (2) the content and form of the learning experience must be suited to his cognitive style and temperamental characteristics, and must complement his stage of cognitive development; this implies a sensitive determination of the curriculum to be presented as well as the manner in which it is offered to the child; and (3) it must have social or utilitarian relevance; i.e. it must offer those skills and competencies which will expand the realm of functional choice available to the child. In this concern with expanding choices, it may be necessary to include some educational areas with which he does not immediately identify, since it will be based not only on what he would need for adaptation to society at present, but on the projections of what he might need in the future.

In general, the emphasis in attempts to provide relevant education has tended to shift back and forth between a stress on cognitive achievement or development and an emphasis on socialization or "development of the whole child," with few attempts to focus on both simultaneously in an integrated manner. In the recent flurry of activity to improve education for disadvantaged learners, considerable effort has been directed at somehow changing cognitive functioning. Unfortunately, to date there has been relatively little success in developing effective tools to shape this area of functioning. At the same time, emerging research is beginning to make more respectable a renewed emphasis on affective (attitudinal and motivational) processes in learning.

This renewed concern with affect, however, must be distinguished from much of the traditional approach which has concentrated on means of motivating, rather than on ways of using existing motivation. Little attention has been given to providing role models with which the child can identify or to modifying the school so that it and its values have meaning for the child.

Educability may be defined as the condition of being capable of academic learning mastery. The educability of mentally subnormal children, be they mentally defective or socially and educationally deprived, continues to elude definitive determination. Undoubtedly, some of these children are irreversibly retarded. Just how many is an unanswered question. Possibilities for the determination of educability through more appropriate and diligently applied educational processes are asserted to exist. It has been suggested that the failure of compensatory education for disadvantaged children may be the result of insufficient and inappropriate resources and methodology. Given the high incidence of characteristics in this population which are non-supportive of academic achievement and the relative non-variant nature of traditional approaches to education, there may be greater promise in effort directed at the development of a match between the individual's behavioral style and background of experience on the one hand, and the nature and content of the learning experience on the other. The fact that they are atypical requires that we give greater attention to what we know about and is implied by our concept of individual differences.

REFERENCES

ANASTASIA, ANNE & D'ANGELO, RITA Y., "A Comparison of Negro and White Preschool Children in Language Development and Goodenough Draw-A-Man IQ." *Pedagogical Seminary and Journal of Genetic Psychology (Journal of Genetic Psychology)*, Vol. 81, December 1952, pp. 147-165.

AUSUBEL, DAVID P. & AUSUBEL, PEARL, "Ego Development Among Segregated Negro Children," pp. 109-141 in Passow, A. Harry, ed., *Education in Depressed Areas*. New York: Bureau of Publications, Teachers College, Columbia University. 1963. 359 pp.

BECKEY, RUTH ELIZABETH, "A Study of Certain Factors Related to Retardation of Speech." *Journal of Speech Disorders*, September 1942, Vol. 7, pp. 223-249.

BERNSTEIN, BASIL, "Language and Social Class." *British Journal of Sociology*, Vol. II, September 1960, pp. 271-276.

BEBNSTEIN, BASIL, "Social Class and Linguistic Development: A Theory of Social Learning," Chap. 24, pp. 288-314 in Halsey, A. H.; Floud, J.; and Anderson, C. A., eds., *Education, Economy, and Society*. New York: Free Press of Glencoe, Inc. 1961. 640 pp.

CARROLL, REBECCA EVANS, "Relation of Social Environment to the Moral Ideology and the Personal Aspirations of Negro Boys and Girls." *School Review*, Vol. 53, January 1945, pp. 30-38.

CARSON, ARNOLD S. & RABIN, A. I., "Verbal Comprehension and Communication in Negro and White Children." *Journal of Education Psychology*, Vol. 51, April 1960, pp. 47-51.

COLEMAN, JAMES S., and others. *Equality of Educational Opportunity*. Washington, D.C.: U.S. Government Printing Office, 1966. 737 pp.

COLES, ROBERT. *The Desegregation of Southern Schools: A Psychiatric Study*. New York: Anti-Defamation League, July 1963. 25 pp.

CREMIN, LAWRENCE A. *The Genius of American Education*, University of Pittsburgh Press, Pittsburgh, Pa., 1965.

DAVIDSON, KENNETH S., and others. "A Preliminary Study of Negro and White Differences on Form I of the Wechsler Bellevue Scale." *Journal of Consulting Psychology*, Vol. 14, October 1950, pp. 489-492.

DAVIS, EDITH A. *The Development of Linguistic Skill in Twins, Singletons with Siblings, and Only Children from Age Five to Ten Years*. Institute of Child Welfare Monograph Series No. 14. Minneapolis, Minnesota: University of Minnesota Press, 1937. 165 pp.

DEUTSCH, CYNTHIA. "Auditory Discrimination and Learning: Social Factors." *Merrill-Palmer Quarterly*, Vol. 10, July 1964. pp. 277-296.

DEUTSCH, MARTIN. *Minority Group and Class Status as Related to Social and Personality Factors in Scholastic Achievement*. Society for Applied Anthropology Monograph No. 2, Ithaca, New York: Cornell University. 1960. 32 pp.

DEUTSCH, MARTIN. "The Disadvantaged Child and the Learning Process," pp. 163-179 in Passow, A. Harry, ed., *Education in Depressed Areas*. New York: Bureau of Publications, Teachers College, Columbia University, 1963. 359 pp.

266   *Compensatory Education: A National Debate*

DEUTSCH, MARTIN, & BROWN, BERT. "Social Influences in Negro-White Intelligence Differences." *Journal of Social Issues,* Vol. 20, April 1964. pp. 24-35.

DREGER, RALPH MASON, & MILLER, KENT S. "Comparative Psychological Studies of Negroes and Whites in the United States." *Psychological Bulletin,* Vol. 57, September 1960, pp. 361-402.

GOFF, REGINA M. "Some Educational Implications of the Influence of Rejection on Aspiration Levels of Minority Group Children." *Journal of Experimental Education,* Vol. 23, December 1954, pp. 179-183.

GORDON, EDMUND W. "The Relevance of Behavior Theory for Directed Learning in Disadvantaged Children." *Unpublished paper, presented at Annual Meeting of the American Association of Orthopsychiatry,* March 1963.

GORDON, EDMUND W. *Educational Achievement in the Prince Edward County Free School,* 1963-64. New York: Ferkauf Graduate School of Education, Yeshiva University. 63 pp. Mimeographed. 1965.

GORDON, EDMUND W. "Help for the Disadvantaged?" *American Journal of Orthopsychiatry,* Vol. 35, April 1965, pp. 445-448.

GOULD, ROSALIND. "Some Sociological Determinants of Goal Strivings." *Journal of Social Psychology,* Vol. 13, May 1941, pp. 461-473.

HIERONYMUS, A. N. "Study of Social Class Motivation: Relationships Between Anxiety for Education and Certain Socio-Economic and Intellectual Variables." *Journal of Educational Psychology,* Vol. 42, April 1951, pp. 193-205.

HILLIARD, GEORGE H., & TROXWELL, ELEANOR. "Informational Background as a Factor in Reading Readiness and Reading Progress." *Elementary School Journal,* Vol. 38, December 1957, pp. 255-263.

IRWIN, ORVIS C. "Infant Speech: The Effect of Family Occupational Status and of Age on Use of Sound Types." *Journal of Speech and Hearing Disorders,* Vol. 13, September 1948, pp. 224-226.

JENSEN, ARTHUR R. "Learning Ability in Retarded, Average, and Gifted Children." *Merrill-Palmer Quarterly,* Vol. 9, April 1963, pp. 123-140.

JENSEN, ARTHUR R. "How Much Can We Boost IQ and Scholastic Achievement?" *Harvard Educational Review,* Vol. 39 No. 1, Winter 1969, pp. 1-123.

JOHN, VERA P., & GOLDSTEIN, LEO S. "The Social Context of Language Acquisition." *Merrill-Palmer Quarterly,* Vol. 10, July 1964, pp. 265-276.

KELLER, SUZANNE. "The Social World of the Urban Slum Child: Some Early Findings." *American Journal of Orthopsychiatry,* Vol. 33, October, 1963, pp. 823-831.

LESHAN, LAWRENCE L. "Time Orientation and Social Class." *Journal of Abnormal and Social Psychology,* Vol. 47, July 1952, pp. 589-592.

MONTAGUE, DAVID O., "Arithmetic Concepts of Kindergarten Children in Contrasting Socioeconomic Areas." *Elementary School Journal,* Vol. 64, April 1964, pp. 393-397.

PRINGLE, M. L. KELLMER, & TANNER, MARGARET. "The Effects of Early Deprivation on Speech Development: A Comparative Study of Four Year Olds in a Nursery School and in Residential Nurseries." *Language and Speech,* Vol. I, October-December 1958, pp. 269-287.

RIESSMAN, FRANK. *The Culturally Deprived Child.* New York: Harper & Row, 1962. 140 pp.

ROSEN, BERNARD C. "The Achievement Syndrome: A Psychocultural Dimension of Social Stratification." *American Sociological Review,* Vol. 21, April 1956. pp. 203-211.

SEWELL, WILLIAM H., HALLER, ARCHIE O., & STRAUS, MURRAY A. "Social Status and Educational and Occupational Aspiration." *American Sociological Review,* Vol. 22, February 1957, pp. 67-73.

SILLER, JEROME. "Socioeconomic Status and Conceptual Thinking." *Journal of Abnormal and Social Psychology,* Vol. 55, November 1957, pp. 365-371.

SILVERMAN, SUSAN B. *Self-Images of Upper-Middle Class and Working Class Young Adolescents.* Unpublished master's thesis, University of Chicago.

STRODTBECK, FRED L. "The Hidden Curriculum of the Middle Class Home," pp. 15-31, in Hunnicutt, C. W., ed., *Urban Education and Cultural Deprivation.* Syracuse, N. Y.: Syracuse University Press, 1964, 126 pp.

TEMPLIN, MILDRED C. "Norms on Screening Test of Articulation for Ages Three Through Eight." *Journal of Speech and Hearing Disorders,* Vol. 18, December 1953, pp. 323-331.

TEMPLIN, MILDRED C. *Certain Language Skills in Children; Their Development and Interrelationship.* Institute of Child Welfare Monograph Series No. 26. Minneapolis: University of Minnesota Press. 1957.

THOMAS, DOMINIC RICHARD. Oral Language, Sentence Structure and Vocabulary of Kindergarten Children Living in Low Socioeconomic Urban Areas. Doctoral Thesis. Detroit, Michigan: Wayne State University. 1962. 393 pp. Abstract: *Dissertation Abstracts,* Vol. 23, No. 3, 1962, p. 1014.

ZIGLER, EDWARD. Mental Retardation: Current Issues and Approaches. In: *Review of Child Development Research.* Edited by Lois Wladis Hoffman and Martin L. Hoffman. New York: Russell Sage Foundation, 1966. pp. 107-168.

14

EDUCATING INNER CITY CHILDREN: CHALLENGES AND OPPORTUNITIES

Wilson C. Riles

Associate Superintendent and Chief
Division of Compensatory Education
California State Department of Education

American education's most challenging problem in the latter half of the 20th century is indisputably in the large cities. Achievement test scores show that children in the central cities lag consistently behind the average in educational attainment. The concern over elimination and unification of small, rural, inefficient school districts has now been overshadowed by the controversy over the organization and administration of large metropolitan school districts such as New York, Washington, D.C., Chicago, and Los Angeles. Questions about quality of instructional programs and adequate educational expenditures are being raised as much in the cities with their large industrial tax base as in the poor communities of the South.

The so-called crisis in urban education appears to have materialized in the last few years, contemporaneously with our concern over civil rights and poverty. In effect, the crisis is in the center of our urban areas, in the ghettoes populated by the poor and the minority groups. But the fact that children of minority groups and/or low-income families do not do as well in school as middle-class Caucasian children is not a new problem nor a sudden discovery.

Educators have long known that there is a strong correlation between a student's educational achievement and his socio-economic background. Statistics in California show that the child from a disadvantaged background has traditionally achieved at the rate of .7 of a year for every year of instruction. This means that the disadvantaged child falls further and further behind, at the rate of three months for every school year. Thus, at the end of the third grade, he is already a full year behind

---

Presented to the President's Committee on Mental Retardation's Conference on Problems of Education of Children in the Inner City. Warrenton, Virginia, August 10-12, 1969.

the middle-class student and when he enters his teenage years, he is two years behind, and about to become a statistic—a dropout.

We have traditionally thought of a dropout in terms of the child's failure to succeed in school. But a more realistic appraisal is that dropouts reflect the school's failure to succeed with the child. In effect, the child has not dropped out; he has been pushed out by a school that has ignored his educational needs and by a school program that had no relevance to his aspirations or learning problems.

Although most of our children come from lower-class families, our schools have been geared to the middle-class child. Our teachers come from middle-class backgrounds and naturally are better able to understand and communicate with the middle-class child. Our curriculum, textbooks and recognized teaching methods are all aimed at the experiences and values of the middle-class child.

But the instructional program that is good for the middle-class child is not necessarily good for the child whose background is one of poverty. The child of poverty has not had many of the simple experiences which we assume are common with all youngsters. He has not been taught at home to place a high value on education, to think of education as the key to success. Instead of being prepared for school with a home full of books, magazines, and newspapers, his childhood is one of illness, hunger and threat of eviction. Because of the low status that society has accorded him and his family, he is likely to have a low image of himself and a lack of motivation to succeed, at least to attain what is considered success in middle-class terms. The most severe handicap is his lack of verbal communication skills that are foundations of reading and writing. He may not speak English at all, or if he does, it comes out in monosyllables and incomplete sentences.

This child is behind from the day he enters school. Failures pile upon failures until the child simply gives up.

The problem is not new. What is new is the attention that is finally being given to the problem. Most of the students who are dropping out today would never have attended high school at all 50 years ago. They would have quit school before reaching the secondary level and would have taken unskilled jobs which were then readily available. They would not have been considered dropouts, they would have simply joined the working class.

What is new is that a majority of Americans are now living in metropolitan areas, and among the "immigrants" are large proportions of persons from minority groups and low-income families. In effect, the educational problems which have always been with us are becoming more concentrated in certain parts of our large cities and are thus becoming more visible. Recent statistics published by the Bureau of the Census and the Bureau of Labor Statistics show that 69 percent of the Negroes and 64 percent of the whites now live in the cities or urban fringe areas. Negroes now constitute 25 percent of the residents of cities with more than one million population, and in some cities they are a majority.

And most significantly, what is new is that the poor and the alienated are no longer willing to accept the status quo. They are demanding what any middle-class parent would have demanded long ago if his child did not seem to be getting anything out of the educational system. They are demanding an accounting and a change in the system to make it more relevant to their needs.

COMPENSATORY EDUCATION

Compensatory education is based on the premise that the disadvantaged child *can* succeed if he is given the assistance and the adequate educational program that will enable him to maximize his potential. It is also based on a new concept of what is meant by the term equal educational opportunity.

Traditionally, educators and the public have spoken of equal educational opportunity in terms of sameness—the same textbooks, the same curriculum, the same class size, the same number of library volumes for all children. If every child received the same treatment, then every child was receiving an equal educational opportunity.

Compensatory education rejects this concept and recognizes that equal educational opportunity means an educational program geared to the needs of each individual child. This means that more money, more books, more individual attention through smaller class size, more curriculum experimentation and better teachers must be poured into the schools where economically and environmentally disadvantaged children are concentrated.

However, merely providing more money alone will not do the job, if that money is spent to provide more of the same program that has failed in the past. We cannot make a significant difference in the educational attainment of the urban disadvantaged by just patching up our normal school procedures with a few remedial band-aids. Too often, educators and the public tend to look for the easy solution, and in the case of the disadvantaged, the easy answer is to provide more money to reduce class size.

One of the most highly publicized programs for urban ghettos has been the "More Effective Schools" program in New York City. This effort consists of a substantial reduction in teacher load, along with an increase in supplementary personnel such as clerical help, counselors, and administrators. A recent evaluation by the Center for Urban Studies disclosed that while the program had definitely improved the morale and attitudes of the school staff, students, and community, it has not had a lasting effect in significantly increasing student achievement. One of the prime reasons, according to the evaluators, was that the teachers continued using the same curriculum and teaching techniques with 20 students that they used with 40. Our evaluation report of California compensatory education programs supports the finding that merely reducing class size alone will not do the job. An effective compensatory education program must change the *substance* as well as the *form* of the instructional program.

The California evaluation report, which was based on the first full year of operation of the Elementary and Secondary Education Act, Title I, projects in 1966-67, showed that the best gains in achievement occurred where a comprehensive program involving multiple activities was provided for the students. Piecemeal projects which attempted through a single activity to overcome the learning handicaps caused by poverty usually failed to result in demonstrable achievement gains.

Where a comprehensive program was provided, the average growth was more than one month per month of instruction, or more than one year per year of instruction, as compared to the participants' previous average for .7 year growth per year of instruction. This does not mean that the children in compensatory education caught up after one year. What it does mean is that they stopped falling further behind and the gap between them and the middle-class child decreased rather than increased as it normally would have.

The successful programs included a careful diagnosis of each individual student's learning difficulties. A comprehensive program that would attack that particular student's problems was then provided. The focus was on finding methods or techniques that would be successful with each student, rather than applying a blanket instructional program for all students.

What makes up a comprehensive compensatory education program depends on the needs of the students. Most of the programs in California center on changes in curriculum, especially in reading and language development. Supportive activities often include counseling and guidance, health and nutritional services, cultural enrichment, library expansion, after school study centers, preschool, inservice training of staff personnel and activities to improve school-home relationships.

Because of limited funds, a dilemma often arises as to whether to provide a concentrated program for a limited number of students or a limited program for all the students who may need compensatory education. When compensatory education funds became available in California, the large cities—and many smaller communities—faced the problem that the funds were insufficient to enable all the eligible students to participate. Without hesitation, we adopted the policy of doing an adequate job with a limited number of students rather than scattering bits and pieces among all the children, which would not have made a significant impact on any of the children.

Also essential is coordination and articulation between grades and grade levels to insure that achievement gains are lasting and not merely dramatic, short-term improvements. The story of what happened with Head Start and other preschool programs has been well-documented throughout the nation. Too many people were looking for a miracle and thought that if disadvantaged children were exposed to a few months of intensive classroom experience, all our educational problems in the ghettos would be solved. What resulted was that Head Start "graduates" proceeded to lose their gains when they were placed in regular kindergarten and primary grade classrooms that were not prepared to build upon the children's preschool experience.

Compensatory education activities, to be of maximum effectiveness, must start at an early age and continue until the student is able to maintain progress without extra help. The California findings show that greatest gains in compensatory education programs are achieved by students in the elementary grades, with least gains demonstrated at the high school level.

California guidelines for compensatory education provide that school districts place priority on elementary school students, so that the elementary schools are saturated before attempts are made to reach the secondary population. Within the elementary school level, school districts are to serve only the number of schools and children for which a comprehensive program—amounting to at least $300 over and above the regular school program—can be implemented.

This, of course, means that many eligible children are left out. But the solution to this is to provide an adequate funding level, rather than attempt to serve all the eligible children with less than half the funds.

DISADVANTAGED OR MENTALY RETARDED?

This paper will not attempt to go into depth in the complex issue of the relationship between environmental deprivation and mental retardation. However, I would like to offer a few comments on this topic.

Those who work in compensatory education as well as those who work in special education programs for the mentally retarded must give attention to the possible misclassification of children from poverty areas. California's annual survey of the racial and ethnic backgrounds of students in public school programs shows that the percentage of minority group children enrolled in special education classes is substantially higher than that of the majority group. The rate of placement of Spanish surname children in special education is about three times higher than for Anglo children; the Negro rate is close to four times higher than the Anglo rate. Children from all minority groups constitute about one-fourth of the public school enrollment in the state, but about half the special education enrollment.

To some extent, a higher rate of mental retardation in poverty areas may be due to the organic damage resulting from lack of adequate health care, dietary deficiencies, etc. But the question must be raised: to what extent are children classified as mentally retarded when the true nature of their learning disabilities stems from environmental factors? In California, educators are taking a second look at their classification criteria to see if language difficulties, deprivation of experiences, and deviation from the majority's culture and value system may be entering into the determination of who is mentally retarded.

Several school districts have developed programs whereby children identified as borderline mentally retarded are reclassified for compensatory education programs rather than classes for the mentally retarded. The children are provided intensive language development and enrichment activities to enable them to function in regular classroom activities.

There are also several such projects for children of preschool age. In one project, for example, half of the children who were thought to be mentally retarded were recommended for placement in regular kindergarten classes after participation in compensatory preschool programs.

INTEGRATION

Two recent national reports—one by the U.S. Civil Rights Commission and another by the U.S. Office of Education—show that most children in the United States, and especially in our urban centers, attend schools that are segregated, that is, where almost all of their fellow students are of the same racial background as they are.

The Civil Rights Commission's report, "Racial Isolation in the Public Schools," states that in a survey of 75 cities, 75 percent of the Negro students in the elementary grades attend schools that are at least 90 percent Negro, while 83 percent of the white students are in nearly all-white schools. Population trends indicate that the degree of segregation in the nation's schools is increasing and not decreasing. Eighty-four percent of the total Negro enrollment increase in a survey of Northern city school systems was absorbed in schools that are at least 90 percent Negro, and 97 percent of the students were enrolled in schools that were more than 50 percent Negro.

In the last few years, there has been much discussion in educational circles as to the best method of improving the education of disadvantaged minority group students. There are some who say, "Let's forget about integration. It's too hard to accomplish. We'll pour extra resources into our ghetto schools and do the job through compensatory education." And then there are those who say, "Let's forget about compensatory education. Just desegregate the schools and the problems of low achievement among minority groups will vanish."

This schism exists among leaders of minority groups as well as among school administrators. Among civil rights groups, there are leaders who feel that compensatory education is just an excuse for maintaining segregation. And lately, there are Negro leaders, including those who a few years ago were in the forefront of the integration battle, who now are urging that we accept the fact of segregation and concentrate on building the "golden ghetto" school.

The answer is not *either* compensatory education *or* integration. The two are not mutually exclusive. It is not an either/or situation, and neither can substitute for the other. Both compensatory education and integration are needed to reach the goal of maximizing educational opportunities for minority group youth.

The U.S. Office of Education's Study, "Equality of Educational Opportunity," commonly known as the Coleman report, points out that a student's achievement is strongly related to the educational backgrounds and aspirations of the other students in the school. Segregation of students from the same racial and economic background works to the disadvantage of those children whose family educational resources are meager. Such segregation deprives these children of the learning environment that is engendered by more advantaged students with their higher motivation, better verbal skills and vocabulary and higher achievement level.

For the minority child, the segregated school reinforces the attitudes and practices of the dominant society that have placed him in a subordinate position. Every day that the minority child enters his classroom and sees a sea of faces all of the same color, he is reminded that society considers him not equal enough to join it. The psychological effects of segregation on the student's learning cannot be erased by compensatory education alone.

But just as compensatory education is not a substitute for integration, neither can integration be a substitute for compensatory education. Just moving the bodies around will not insure that the deprivations resulting from poverty will somehow disappear into thin air. Many persons have interpreted the Coleman report to mean that integration alone will lead to increased student achievement. The author of the report, Professor James Coleman of Johns Hopkins University, has refuted this interpretation of his study.

In California, several city school districts have developed programs that involve both compensatory education and integration for disadvantaged minority group students. State guidelines for the Elementary and Secondary Education Act, Title I, programs provide that funds may be used to plan and implement integration, with compensatory education services following the children to their new schools. In this way, the enrichment and special services that children from poverty backgrounds need will be available in the integrated schools to facilitate their learning process. In Sacramento, for example, compensatory education funds are used to pay for transporting 1,000 Negro elementary school students to predominantly Caucasian schools. Remedial reading teachers, counselors, and a free lunch program have been added to the receiving schools.

The racially segregated school not only jeopardizes the minority child's potential for high academic achievement, but it fosters, among both minority and majority children, damaging attitudes and distorted behavior that have perpetuated isolation in all aspects of American life.

The U.S. Civil Rights Commission report cited statistics of a national survey of Caucasian and Negro adults on the relationship between the racial makeup of the schools they attended and their attitudes toward the other race. This survey indicated that Caucasians who attended desegregated schools expressed greater willingness to reside in an interracial neighborhood, to have their children attend integrated schools, to have Negro friends, and to support the elimination of discrimination in employment against Negroes. Similarly, Negroes who had attended schools where the majority of the students were Caucasians were more likely to have children in desegregated schools and were more willing to send their children out of the neighborhood, if necessary, to obtain the benefits of integrated education. And, regardless of their educational background or region of the country, Negroes with integrated school backgrounds were more likely to disagree with the statement, "If a Negro is wise he will think twice before he trusts the white man as much as he would another Negro."

Thus, aside from its effects on school achievement, integration of our schools is important if American society is to become truly multiracial. We must be just as concerned about the Caucasian student who is growing up in an isolated school environment as we are about the minority group child. An educational system which helps perpetuate the feelings of unrealistic superiority and racial prejudice of the majority group is not a quality educational system and is not preparing its students to live in a heterogenous society, regardless of the number of students it sends on to college.

To be realistic, it is not possible to integrate Watts of Los Angeles or the South Side of Chicago overnight or even in the near future. However, the massive size of the segregation problem or the difficulties, both financially and logistically, of implementing racial balance in the classroom should not be used as an excuse to stand still and fail to make any efforts toward providing our urban students with some form of integrated educational experiences. Such situations demand not less effort, but more creativity.

The area of extracurricular activities, for example, provides great opportunities for students from different parts of the cities and different racial and economic backgrounds to participate in integrated programs. Student government, debate, athletics, music, and drama lend themselves to interschool and interschool district participation and not merely as competitors. A city-wide or regional choir or orchestra would enable an integrated group of students to work together toward a common goal. Minority groups students could be exposed to life outside their neighborhood through field trips to cultural performances, city council meetings, and industrial firms.

If a city is unable to integrate its schools, it can at least prevent the problem from getting worse by stabilizing the transition areas. Special efforts must be made to insure that schools which are integrated now do not become predominantly minority group schools in the future. This requires that careful attention be given to the racial makeup of the integrated school and boundary changes adjusted when necessary to insure its heterogeneous composition. It also requires intensive efforts to maintain the quality of the educational program in that school and to make it a model institution where any parent would wish to send his son or daughter.

ADMINISTRATION OF THE URBAN SCHOOL SYSTEM

In the California evaluation report on compensatory education, we found that the greatest improvement in achievement was demonstrated by students in the medium-sized urban districts. These students did far better than did their counterparts in the state's largest cities. The U.S. Office of Education reports that similar findings are being reported from other states.

One reason is that the degree of educational deprivation and retardation is less severe in the medium-sized cities than in the largest cities. But another possible reason is that the administrative framework of large city school systems may be less flexible and less easily mobilized for change. The cumbersome bureaucracies that exist in many city educational structures often mean delay in implementing new programs.

However, the solution lies in making the large city administrative structure more flexible and more receptive to innovation, not in breaking it up completely. The proposals to create many small "community" school districts in a large city would eliminate the advantages as well as the disadvantages of size.

Real control comes with the purse strings—including the power to levy taxes and allocate resources. Most decentralization proposals retain this power in the central school board, which would determine how much each community district would receive although the community board can determine the spending of its own share.

In effect, what these proposals would do is to say to the community, "If you don't like the way we're running the schools, you try to do better." At the same time that the new system deprives the local community of the alibi that "they" are not educating "our children," it gives the central school board an alibi for its failures. There is a great danger that the ghettos will be locked in perpetual segregation and will find themselves at a disadvantage in competing with more attractively located community districts for the best personnel.

Large city school systems must become more responsive to the views of the community and involve parents in the decision-making processes, but this does not require turning over administration of the schools to a community which does not have the same expertise and resources that the central city administration can gather together. A large system can be sensitive to needs of its sub-parts without making each sub-part a separate organization. It is significant that the impetus for decentralizing city school systems has come largely from the demands of low-income communities for a larger voice in educational affairs rather than from the middle-income and high-income communities. This is because our school systems have always been able to be responsive to the concerns of the more affluent parents and it was not necessary to turn over the schools to these parents in the process.

Crucial to the success of a city school system in meeting the concerns of disadvantaged communities is a change in personnel policy and practice. It is common practice in many school districts for the inexperienced teachers and administrators to be placed in the ghetto area schools. Then, if they survive a few years, they are promoted "up the hill." Often this is not due to design, but to a seniority system where the experienced teachers are given their choice of assignment, leaving the younger teachers with no choice but to take what is left—what is usually the "difficult" schools. In the case of school principals, a common practice is to move them around the school district to different schools as training prior to promotion to the front office.

If we are to solve the educational problems of our ghettos, we cannot leave the selection of principals and teachers in those areas up to chance. We must recognize that not all principals and teachers, even good ones, have the temperament and skills to work effectively with children from disadvantaged socio-economic backgrounds. School personnel must be assigned on the basis of their ability to function in a specific situation.

Once the staff has been carefully placed in a school, it must be provided sufficient resources and flexibility to exert leadership and creativity. The principal must be able to make decisions and experiment with new ideas without going through a tortuous bureaucratic maze. It is possible to have decentralization within the large city school system. It is possible for the building principal to be as responsive to the needs of his immediate community and the wishes of parents as the suburban school principal is to his community if the principal is able to act without first checking upstairs.

Of course, there must be minimum standards and policies for conduct and procedures within the administrative structure. However, standardization—the old nemesis of the same program for every child—must not be allowed to take precedence over flexibility to meet the needs of diverse communities and student populations within a large city school system.

The future of the urban school system will be determined by its ability to make the necessary changes without breaking down—or being torn apart. What is at stake is not just the city school system—but public education itself. For education's most challenging problem in the latter half of the 20th Century is in the large cities. And, if public education cannot rise to its greatest challenge, it will be questionable whether public education is worth saving.

15

GENETICS AND EDUCABILITY
EDUCATIONAL IMPLICATIONS OF THE JENSEN DEBATE

Carl Bereiter, Ph.D.
The Ontario Institute for Studies in Education

In this paper I shall consider several educational issues growing out of A. R. Jensen's paper, "How Much Can We Boost IQ and Scholastic Achievement?" (Jensen, 1969). The first deals with the question of how education should adjust to the incontestable fact that approximately half the children in our schools are and always will be below average in IQ. Following this I take up some of the more moot points of the "Jensen controversy"—What does heritability tell us about teachability? What are the prospects for reducing the spread of individual differences in intelligence? And what are the educational implications of possible hereditary differences in intelligence associated with social class and race?—ending with some implications that these issues have for educational research.

INTELLIGENCE AS AN EXCUSE FOR POOR TEACHING

When children fail to learn, one may find fault either with the teaching or with the children. If the children who fail are in a minority, even if a fairly large minority, one has convenient grounds for a case that it is the children who are defective.

Every student of mental measurement knows the story of how the intelligence test was born, how French education authorities asked Alfred Binet to devise means of identifying children who were too dull to profit from regular schooling (c.f. Vernon, 1960). Thus from its outset intelligence testing has been rooted in the effort to locate the causes of school failure in the child rather than in the way he was taught. It is interesting to speculate that if a different type of instruction had been used in French schools in 1904, so that a different type of child failed, we might today have a different concept of intelligence. It is even more interesting to speculate that intelligence testing may have served to perpetuate the kind of instruction that happened to be in use in France at the turn of the century.

The rationale for this latter speculation is as follows. If children of adequate IQ are found not to learn, then it is supposed that something must be wrong with the teaching, and the teaching is accordingly changed. If, however, the failing children have low IQs, then there is no cause for altering the method of teaching, because such children are expected to fail. The result is not necessarily a perpetuation of the exact forms of traditional instruction. Style and content may change. What remains constant is the complex of mental abilities that the child must have in order to succeed in school—the complex that is variously called "scholastic aptitude," *g*, or IQ.

To challenge the IQ, as some of Jensen's critics have done, on grounds that it represents a limited or biased conception of intelligence, is easy but pointless. Jensen has taken the much more daring and constructive approach of challenging the instructional methods that make IQ significant in the first place. He has raised the question, is it really necessary to teach in such a way that only children of average or above-average IQ can learn?

There is a head-on and a dodge-to-the-left way of meeting this question. The dodge-to-the-left way is to say that schools should not expect the same things of all children, that children should be free to pursue their own goals in their own ways, rather than having to pursue the particular achievement goals set forth by the schools. Although the proposal may have merits, it dodges the question of whether the traditional goals could be achieved by children who are deficient in "scholastic aptitude" as it is conventionally measured, if they were taught by different methods. The original assumption that "some kids just can't get it" remains unchallenged by this digression to other goals.

Jensen has tried to meet the question head-on, but there has not been much evidence for him to bring to the encounter. He has expressed the faith that basic scholastic skills could be learned in a variety of ways that make use of different mental abilities (pp. 116-117).* Schools, however, have adhered to methods and criteria which allow only the child possessed of abstract, verbal cognitive abilities to succeed. He points out that functional mastery of skills such as arithmetic computation is not regarded as a sufficient criterion of success, that "understanding" in the abstract, verbal sense is required. Thus the same abilities that are involved in IQ predictors of success are used as criteria of success, producing self-fulfillfng prophecy.

I would suggest that a more basic factor in maintaining the self-fulfilling prophecy is the generally low quality of instruction. The more

---

* Unless otherwise designated, page numbers refer to pages in Jensen (1969).

confusing, inconsistent, and full of gaps that instruction is, the more the child has to figure out for himself. Thus the child must be able to form abstractions, to generalize from scattered and incomplete evidence, even when the material to be learned is itself not of a very abstract nature. To ensure that IQ predicts achievement, it is necessary merely to teach badly. But educators have managed to make a virtue out of poor teaching by asserting that they want to make children think. The implication is that if the child can't think, he has no business learning.

The term "thinking," as used above, ought perhaps to be severely qualified. It refers to the kinds of information processing that are called for on general intelligence tests. There are, of course, other sorts of mental activities that deserve to be called thinking—indeed, it would be difficult to justify assigning a very exalted place to the sort of thinking called for by intelligence tests. But for the present discussion, which deals exclusively with school learning, it will simplify the terminology a great deal if we understand the unqualified term "thinking" to refer to the kinds of thinking normally involved in mastering academic subjects.

The question Jensen has raised may then be given a more pointed form: Can we find ways for children to learn that require less thinking? It will immediately be seen that the main trend of curriculum reform in recent times has been in precisely the opposite direction—in the direction of requiring more thinking. Before considering whether this trend is a wise one, let us consider whether there are actually any viable alternatives.

An obvious alternative to thinking is rote memorization, and this is more-or-less the alternative that Jensen proposes. His own research has indicated that, among lower-class children at least, substantial numbers can be found who have adequate associative learning ability even though they have low IQs. Accordingly, he has proposed that educational methods might be developed that make greater use of this ability and less use of what I am referring to as thinking.

The prospect of an instructional program based entirely on rote learning is not an attractive one by any account. This is not the necessary alternative, however. In the first place, the problem is not that children of below-average IQ cannot think but that they may not be able to think well enough to cope with instruction as it is presently administered. In the second place, even the most rudimentary of scholastic skills, such as oral reading and arithmetic computation, require transformations of some complexity on the presented information, and hence some amount of thinking. Thus the implied alternative to existing methods of instruction would not be one that eliminated thinking but one that kept it within more attainable limits of difficulty.

On the face of it, programmed instruction would appear to be the embodiment of this alternative—particularly programmed instruction that follows the principle of small steps and the minimizing of error rate. From the evidence, the most that could be claimed is that on occasion programmed instruction has managed to produce learning that is less dependent on IQ than the learning that takes place through conventional instruction (Tuel, 1966). It is difficult to draw any far-reaching conclusions from these results, however, since programmed instruction is a medium that differs from ordinary instruction in a number of ways, and, moreover, does not necessarily entail any change in the basic strategy by which subject matter is organized for teaching.

The work that I have been associated with over the past six years, in the design of instructional programs for young disadvantaged children, has, on the other hand, been consciously aimed at reducing the conceptual and problem-solving difficulties of school learning. The approach we have taken does not have any magic key to it. It has been a matter of trying to locate the underlying sources of difficulty in grasping various concepts and operations and then trying to devise ways to overcome them. Expositions of the general approach and specific applications of it can be found in Engelmann (1969a), Engelmann (1969b), Bereiter and Engelmann (1966). Results reported by Engelmann in this volume indicate the striking achievements in subject-matter learning that have been obtained with this approach. How much can be accomplished through such an approach in raising achievement over the full span of school years and what overall value this might have to the individual learner remain to be seen. As they stand, however, the results lend strong support to Jensen's faith that basic scholastic skills can be put in the reach of children who lack the attributes needed to master them under conventional approaches.

While much remains unknown about the broader effects of reducing the thinking burden in learning, there are two consequences that are foreseeable enough to be worth considering at this time. One is that such instructional reforms cannot be expected to reduce the range of individual differences in achievement, nor in the long run to make achievement less dependent upon IQ. What such reforms can be expected to do, instead, is simply to raise the general level of achievement, while conceivably even increasing the spread of individual differences. Teach every child to read or to do multiplication, and you have raised the general level of attainment in these subjects; but the reasonable expectation, confirmed by results to date, is that "bright" children will still be able to read better and to solve more complex problems involving multiplication. By virtue of these superior skills, the "bright" children may be expected in consequence to show even greater attainment in more advanced mathematics and in what they learn through reading. Clearly, then, if our concern is purely with a child's attainment relative to his peers, we gain nothing much by improving instruction.

If, however, there is some value to be attached to absolute levels of attainment, then there is much to be hoped for from instructional reform. If under method A the lowest child in the class does not learn to read, while under method B he does, then he is better off under method B, even if he is still the lowest child in the class and just as far below the mean of his class as he would have been under method A. To the extent that scholastic skills have some value outside of school itself, one does children a service by increasing the general level of their attainment in them, regardless of individual differences; and if scholastic skills have no direct or indirect external value, they ought simply to be eliminated from the curriculum. Hence, what is worth teaching ought to be taught in ways that put it within the reach of the largest number of children, which means simply making it as easy as possible to learn. Any educational philosophy that insists on putting unnecessary thinking difficulties into the path of learning should be rejected as discriminatory.

Having made such a self-obvious pronouncement, however, it is necessary to look at its social implications. These implications can perhaps best be brought out by making them graphic. The kinds of children we have worked with have been ones who, by the usual sociological and psychometric predictors, would be expected to be at best plodding and unprepossessing students. In the course of our work with them, however, they consistently took on many of the characteristics of gifted or academically talented children—they were alert, confident often to the point of being cocksure, proud of their ability, and eager for new challenges. This is not what would have been expected from the view that learning is a degrading form of drudgery, but it makes sense in light of the fact that their whole school experience consisted of a series of challenges successfully met. However, the challenges were challenges to learning rather than to thinking, and by the same token what the children were good at and proud of was learning rather than thinking. Their confidence was easy to shatter, and their experiences after they left our program often managed to do this in short order. All that was needed to discourage them was to put them into a situation where they had to think at a higher level in order to succeed, and the ordinary school situation is well designed for that purpose.

One may speculate, however, as to what might happen if the entire school program were designed so as to permit continual progress in learning without excessive demands on thinking ability. One can imagine that under such a program children of below-average IQ could remain eager and self-confident learners throughout their school careers, emerging with a substantial fund of knowledge and skill and a readiness to go on learning in later life.

Presented in this way, the picture is a glowing one that almost anyone would endorse. But the other side of the picture is that such children would not necessarily have any deep understanding of what they were doing and might be severely limited in their ability to apply knowledge in new situations. We have to ask ourselves whether, in the prevailing climate of value, such children would indeed be accorded the respect without which their eagerness and self-confidence could never survive.

My view of the prevailing climate of value is largely based on the reactions of educators and child developmentalists to our program, and so it may be excessively jaundiced. But from this experience I conclude that the prevailing view is that high-achieving children who cannot think very well are impostors who ought to be exposed and their mentors denounced. Learning is viewed as a sub-human activity, more appropriate to rats or pigeons; among humans only what is acquired through thinking is deemed of any value. The response of one noted educator is typical. Viewing a kindergarten class engaged in solving algebraic equations, he was impressed and inquired as to how this phenomenon had been brought about. When he heard the story, he announced, like someone uncovering a fraud, "Why, you taught them how to do it!" The almost universal response of visiting educationists or child developmentalists has been to ask "Could they do such-and-such?" (or, if they are bolder, to quiz the children themselves) until they have managed to convince themselves that the children are, after all, still stupid.

Although these reactions may have been exaggerated by other situational factors, I have not been able to discover anything in current educational writing that suggests people are willing to view learning, apart from thinking, as a dignifiable human accomplishment. This elitist view seems to be so widespread that it is held by a number of people who can lay no claim to superior thinking abilities themselves. People who can't excel at thinking are allowed to dignify themselves through nonintellective accomplishments or personal virtue. And yet it seems clear that only a small minority of people are ever able to do much of the kind of thinking that is associated with intellectual disciplines. They may do a good deal of thinking in their daily lives, but it is thinking that owes practically nothing to school learning. So far as we know, schooling in modern societies does nothing to improve thinking abilities.

Schooling may do nothing to improve learning abilities either, but it can at least produce useful learning, including tool skills that permit further learning, and it could develop interest and confidence in learning. As technology assumes an increasingly prominent place in human activities, the need to figure things out becomes increasingly subordinated to the need to learn how to use equipment. Compare the old-

fashioned automobile mechanic, who had to possess a good deal of diagnostic, problem-solving and inventive skill, with the modern mechanic,
whose main problem is to keep up with the increasing number of
instruments, tools, procedures, and specifications that he must use.

It is all very well to speak, as Jensen does, of trying to discover ways
of utilizing "the great and relatively untapped reservoirs of mental
ability in the disadvantaged" (p. 117), but I see little prospect that any
good will come of this, either for disadvantaged children or for the
great mass of middle-class children of average or below-average IQ, so
long as non-thinking routes to scholastic achievement are held in such
low regard. A number of prejudices need to be eliminated. We need to
eliminate the prejudice that simple learning is tedious and boring;
it often is, just as what passes for thinking and problem-solving in our
schools is often tedious and boring, but it doesn't have to be. (Learning
to swim, for instance, is straight-forward learning that involves practically no thinking, yet only under the worst conditions of instruction is
it boring.) We need to eliminate the prejudice that managing simple
learning is a pedestrian task and that only the promotion of thinking
requires pedagogical art. (Those who think it is might try such a seemingly simple task as teaching an average class of second-graders how to
tell time.) Above all, however, we need to eliminate the prejudice that
thinking ability is the one true mark of scholastic achievement, all other
marks being in some wise inferior or spurious.

At the root of this prejudice seems to be the illusion that schools
teach children to think. There is no question that the kind of thinking
exemplified in the academic disciplines is one of man's highest achievements. Teachers will always be pleased to observe signs of such thinking
in their students, and they do right to encourage it. The trouble begins
when teachers claim credit for having produced such thinking, for it
is then but a small step to conclude that the less capable academic
thinkers have failed to learn what was taught. It seems to me that Jensen
has provided the most effective antidote available for this illusion, by
showing the strength of genetic influences on thinking ability and pointing out the lack of evidence that schooling has any effect on it.

WHAT DOES HERITABILITY TELL US ABOUT TEACHABILITY?

In the preceding section, individual differences in IQ were treated as
an unalterable fact, while attention was directed to the possibility of
improving the scholastic success of children despite it. That there will
always be IQ differences of some magnitude probably can be treated as
an unalterable fact. On the other hand, IQ scores themselves are known
to be in some measure influenced by experience. Hunt (1961) presented
evidence to show that they could be influenced a great deal. Jensen

(1969) has presented a documented case for the contrary conclusion. I do not propose to enter into weighing of the evidence, but to focus upon a question of interpretation that seems to be a pivotal one, namely the question of what can be inferred about modifiability of IQ from its heritability ratio. Since the issue is one of interpretation, I shall accept without discussion Jensen's estimate that the heritability of IQ is 80 per cent for the white population of the United States at the present time.

A heritability ratio, as Hirsch (1969) has emphasized, tells us about the population on which it is calculated, and tells us nothing of a fundamental nature about the determinants of the trait in question. It tells us what proportion of the variability of a trait in a particular population can be attributed to genetic differences. In principle, the same trait could show heritability ranging from zero in one population to 100 per cent in another, depending on gene frequencies and frequencies of relevant environmental conditions. Accordingly, Hirsch has declared that "High or low heritability tells us absolutely nothing about how a given individual might have developed under conditions different from those in which he actually did develop" (Hirsch, 1969, p. 19). He labels as fallacious Jensen's (p. 59) inference that the lower heritability of scholastic achievement indicates that it is potentially more susceptible to improvement through environmental means than is intelligence.

There seems to be no question that Hirsch is correct in saying that heritability tells us nothing about the *potential* susceptibility of a trait to environmental influence. Tomorrow somebody could stumble upon an environmental variation that would have much more influence on IQ than the normal run of genetic variations. Are we to conclude, therefore, that heritability estimates have no educational significance whatsoever?

I would say no for the simple reason that virtually all educational effort is concerned, not with the creation of new environmental conditions, but merely with the allocation of existing ones. We may take Head Start as an example. What it has consisted of is taking certain environmental conditions (nursery school experience, medical examinations, lunches, availability of playthings) which had been largely restricted to children of higher socio-economic status and applying them to children of lower socio-economic status. Thus it amounts to changing the distribution of existing environmental conditions.

If heritability ratios can tell us anything of practical importance, they can tell us something about the expected results of altering the distribution of existing variants. In order for them to tell us anything definite, however, it is necessary to introduce additional assumptions that go beyond what is given by a simple heritability ratio. To illustrate this I shall introduce a simplifying assumption that appears, from available evidence at least, not to fly in the face of fact.

Let us assume that the effects of heredity and environment on IQ are independent, that is, that the contribution of genetic and environmental sources of variation is the same for all levels of IQ. According to Jensen's calculations, as interpreted by Light and Smith (1969), interaction between source and level accounts for only about one per cent of the variation.

Ignoring this interaction, we may conceive of the observed distribution of IQ scores (approximately normal in shape with a standard deviation of 15 IQ points) as being due to the summation of two other normal distributions, one a distribution of genetic effects on IQ, and the other a distribution of environmental effects. With a heritability ratio of 80 per cent, the distribution of genetic effects will have a standard deviation of approximately 14 IQ points and the distribution of environmental effects will have a distribution of 7 IQ points.

One thing worth noting immediately is that the distribution of environmental effects does allow for substantial IQ differences due to environment. Each standard deviation of difference in environmental effectiveness should make a difference of 7 points in average IQ. Extreme environmental differences could have very large effects. Although the present representation is entirely abstract and says nothing about what the relevant environmental differences are or how they might be scaled, we might consider as one anchor point the extremely impoverished and restricted orphanage environment from which children were taken in the Skeels and Dye (1939) study. From what we know about conditions of learning and intellectual development, it seems reasonable to put such an environment at the bottom extreme of the distribution —at say four standard deviations below the mean.* The expected result of taking children out of such an environment and rearing them in an average one would be a gain of 4 times 7 or 28 IQ points. That is approximately what was found. Thus the Skeels and Dye findings, which have often been cited as evidence contrary to the hypothesis of high heritability of IQ (c.f. Hunt, 1964), are in fact adequately accounted for within a model based upon a heritability ratio of 80 per cent.

This model allows us to make some inferences about the effects to be expected from Utopian environmental conditions. Suppose, for instance, that the mean quality of environments, as they affect IQ, were

---

* It seems reasonable to assume that not only the distribution of observed IQ scores but also the distributions of hypothetical components of these scores are bounded. That is, just as IQ scores do not have an infinite range but vary from approximately zero to 200, it may be supposed that genetic environment factors are limited at the upper end by the fact that they consist of a finite number of pluses and at the lower end by the fact that if things are too bad the organism will perish. Setting the limits at $\pm$ 4 S. D., while arbitrary, produces results that are conformable to the observed range of IQs.

raised two standard deviations, while the standard deviation of environments was reduced by half. This would amount to compressing the whole distribution of environmental conditions into the top half of the existing distribution. Accordingly, the poorest conditions to be found would correspond to what is average for the population today, although the most favorable conditions would be no better than the most favorable conditions today. This is what could be expected from a major improvement in social welfare accomplished without the creation of any new environmental conditions. The expected result of such environmental improvement would be to increase the mean IQ of the population by 14 points. This would be a major change and undoubtedly one of far-reaching consequence. On the other hand, the effect of such environmental improvement on the spread of individual differences in intelligence would be negligible. The standard deviation of IQs would be reduced by only about one point.*

What a high heritability ratio implies, therefore, is that changes within the existing range of environmental conditions can have substantial effects on the mean level of IQ in the population but they are unlikely to have much effect on the spread of individual differences in IQ within that population. If one is concerned with relative standing of individuals within the population, the prospects for doing anything about this through existing educational means are thus not good. Even with a massive redistribution of environmental conditions, one would expect to find the lowest quarter of the IQ distribution to be about as far removed from the upper quarter as before. On the other hand, if one is willing to attach some absolute importance to IQ levels, the prospects are much brighter. A 14 point gain in mean IQ for the population would reduce the number of people having IQs below 70 by a factor of more than 10 and would increase the number of those with IQs above 130 by a factor of about 5. Thus there should be a substantial decrease in the number of people who are incapable of holding their own in the world and a substantial increase in the number capable of doing the more demanding kinds of intellectual work.

A high heritability ratio for IQ should not discourage people from pursuing environmental improvement in education or any other area. The potential effects on IQ are great, although it still remains to discover the environmental variables capable of producing these effects. It

---

* These observations are all implicit in Jensen's own account and have been noted explicitly by other writers (e.g., Stinchcombe, 1969). Jensen has emphasized the small potential effect of environmental change on variance; his critics have emphasized the large potential effect on mean IQ. What I have tried to make clear is that these two conclusions are not at odds, and furthermore that they presuppose only change in the allocation of existing environmental conditions. The possibilities opened up by the introduction of novel environmental conditions are much broader and unpredictable, as is indicated in the following section of this paper.

is clear from the Coleman report (Coleman et al, 1966) and subsequent analyses of it (Jencks, 1969) that the kinds of tangible environmental improvements usually sought by school administrators are not very relevant to intellectual differences.

WHAT ARE THE PROSPECTS FOR REDUCING THE SPREAD OF INDIVIDUAL DIFFERENCES IN INTELLIGENCE?

I shall leave aside for now the question of why anyone should be concerned about reducing the spread of individual differences in intelligence. The discussion of how such differences might be reduced will, I think, convert the question of why into the question of why not.

If a given environmental improvement affects everyone the same, regardless of their genetic endowment, then it may produce some general improvement in IQ but it will not reduce individual differences. On the other hand, if a given environmental improvement is more beneficial to those who would ordinarily manifest a low IQ than to those who would ordinarily manifest a high one, then it will have the effect of reducing the spread of individual differences in IQ. This is a heredity-environment interaction (Jensen, 1969, p. 39-41). Of course, the interaction can work the other way; the environmental improvement can be more beneficial to those more favored genetically, thus increasing individual differences. From the evidence cited by Jensen, it appears that what heredity-environment interaction has so far been demonstrated has been of this latter kind, leading to the expectation that general environmental improvement will increase individual differences in IQ.

There is, however, one dramatic instance of heredity-environment interaction that has had a compensatory or difference-rducing effect. This is the dietary treatment of phenylketonuria. Phenylketonuria, or PKU, is an inherited metabolic defect which under ordinary circumstances has a high probability of leading to severe mental retardation. Given a special diet, however, this probability is considerably reduced. The "environmental improvement" represented by this special diet, therefore, has the effect of raising the mean IQ of PKU children but is presumably not beneficial to other children. Thus it reduces individual differences.

We may suppose that in the days before this special diet was discovered, PKU children experienced the normal range of dietary variations found in the infant population at large. If these normal variations made any difference in IQ it was probably to the same small degree as for other children. What was required to make a real compensatory difference was an environmental variation that lay outside the normal range and that would probably never have been stumbled upon by chance.

This is a point worth keeping in mind when we consider Hirsch's statement, quoted previously, that "High and low heritability tells us absolutely nothing about how a given individual might have developed under conditions different from those in which he actually did develop." We do not know how changed environmental conditions will affect an individual's development, but on the other hand, it is wishful thinking to suppose that through conventional ameliorative efforts we will ever stumble upon environmental variations that will interact with genetic factors in such a way as to produce dramatic compensatory effects. If such effects could be produced in this way the means would probably already have been discovered centuries ago as a kind of folk psychological medicine.

A more reasonable supposition is that, although environmental conditions vary greatly within a society as heterogeneous as that of North America, the variations are not consistent enough to interact *strongly* with genotypes in determining IQ. Diets vary considerably, for instance, and some diets undoubtedly contain smaller amounts than others of phenylalinine (the critical substance in determining the effects of PKU). However, it is unlikely that any normally occurring variations in diet would be low enough in phenylalinine to produce a noticeable effect on PKU children. Similarly, we might suppose that if there are certain conditions of experience that could interact with genotypes to produce markedly higher intelligence among some kinds of children than are observed under other conditions, these special conditions would not occur in great enough concentration within the life history of individuals to reveal such effects.

This point may be made clearer by considering a conjectural example. Suppose that there are some children who could develop high intelligence except that they are lacking in the normal sort of sensitivity to cognitive conflict—they remain indifferent to contradictions and incongruities that influence other children and promote cognitive growth. Conceivably such a deficit could be offset by having people in the child's environment continually confronting him with the discrepancies which he is inclined to ignore. Now a certain amount of this confrontation goes on in any child's experience, and some children encounter more of it than others. But perhaps no adults normally instigate the amount of confrontation that would be necessary to produce noticeable results. Moreover, since adults themselves are sensitive to response from the child, it may be that the child who is most in need of such confrontations fails to respond in ways that would encourage adults to provide them.

If strong interactions between experience and heredity are to be obtained, it is likely that they must be created experimentally rather than discovered through observation of existing variations in experience. Blind probes are likely to have a very low probability of success. I am not in a position to offer specific suggestions of promising leads, but it may be worth noting some of the *least* promising sources of leads. Investigation of the differences in experience of high and low IQ children is not very promising. It might indicate experiential factors that would have a generally beneficial effect on IQ, but high and low IQ groups are so heterogeneous that the possibility of unearthing specific heredity-environment interactions is slight. Even the search for generally beneficial kinds of experience is likely to go astray in this kind of investigation because one will be comparing differences in home background of children whose parents probably differ significantly in geotype, so that differences in home experience may merely reflect the same genetic differences that are also reflected in IQ.

Another unpromising source of leads is the normal course of child development, as represented, for instance, in Piagetian stage theory. One cannot expect to discover the sources of individual differences by investigating those developmental changes that are universal. A final unpromising source is the developmental deficits of young children. These generally turn out to be time lags in development and in themselves tell nothing about why the children may turn out to be handicapped in the long run.

More promising sources of leads that might be mentioned are the following: (1) Intellectual deficits remaining at maturity. These may indicate specific intellectual skills or operations that some children never acquire, but which might be specifically taught to long-range effect. (2) Deficiencies in experience-producing behavior (Hayes, 1962). If certain children fail to engage in such activities as question-asking, exploration, verbal reconstruction of events (what Church, 1961, calls "thematization"), or solitary thought, these might have serious but preventable effects on learning to think. (3) Special abilities or interests of low IQ children. These might suggest assets that could be, but under normal educational conditions are not utilized in the development of general intelligence.

It is possible that no very strong interactive effects can be discovered. It is also possible that they might require such massive or radical deviations from normal child-rearing practices or might have such undesirable side-effects that no one would wish to bring them about. On the other hand, we cannot know this in advance and we ought not to be so wedded to the status quo in child-rearing and education that we refuse to investigate. The sorts of practices that have evolved over the centuries are undoubtedly ones that work fairly well on the average. But it may well be that there are other ways, equally reasonable and economical, that would work much better for some children and that these children are now being unnecessarily handicapped in intellectual development.

What I am proposing is not quite the same thing as adapting education to individual differences. The usual kind of adaptation assumes that individual differences cannot be altered and that children's life chances can be improved by allowing them to develop in accordance with their unique characteristics. Thus adaptation to individual differences is generally not compensatory in effect, but if anything augments differences. Seeking out specific heredity-environment interactions, on the other hand, is an effort to neutralize the effect of certain genetic characteristics which handicap children under standard environmental conditions. Thus it is a compensatory effort intended to make children less the victims of their heredity.

WHAT ARE THE EDUCATIONAL IMPLICATIONS OF POSSIBLE HEREDITARY DIFFERENCES IN INTELLIGENCE ASSOCIATED WITH RACE AND SOCIAL CLASS?

Lower-class children are known to score lower in IQ than middle-class children, and Negroes lower than whites. By far the most controversial part of Jensen's paper has been his suggestion that these observed group differences may be in part due to hereditary differences. Jensen does not claim to have proved that this is true, but only to have presented enough evidence to show that it is a reasonable possibility. So far as I know, the numerous rejoinders to Jensen have never directly attacked this claim; that is, no one has tried to show that it is *not* a reasonable possibility that social class and racial differences in IQ are partly due to heredity. Accordingly, I shall proceed on the grounds that it is a reasonable possibility and ask what the educational implications are if it should be true.

The issue of racial differences in intelligence has commanded much more attention among educators than the issue of socio-economic differences, largely, it would seem, because of its bearing on school desegregation. As I see it, however, the question of genetic differences in racial intelligence ought not to have any bearing on the issue of school desegregation, and the fact that it does indicates that the desegregation issue has been poorly drawn. Genetic considerations become pertinent only when one makes the claim that schools should be integrated because integration will be good for black children—i.e., it will eliminate their lag in IQ and scholastic achievement. This claim, however, has already been largely rejected, not on grounds that it is false, but on grounds that it is invidious. It is, when you get down to it, just as invidious as the counter-claim that schools should not be integrated because integration would be bad for white children. Both claims are at bottom similar in their environmentalist assumptions. The status of minority groups in relation to public institutions can pose exceedingly complex problems, as no one needs to be told, but one principle that seems clear to me is that policy decisions with respect to such problems should not be based on generalizations about the personal attributes of individuals composing those groups. Such generalizations, no matter how benignly intended, almost invariably turn out to be invidious and unfair to "minorities within the minority." If such generalizations are ruled out of policy consideration, issues will not be drawn in such a way that questions of genetic difference assume importance—and that it seems to me is the surest way to avoid the idealistic contrafactuality that can lead to paternalistic do-goodism on one hand or to apartheid on the other.

There has been a good deal of "all or nothing" thinking on both sides of the issue of genetic group differences. On the one side, environmentalists seem to be taking the position that so long as group differences in IQ *could* be explained by environmental factors, it follows that they are in fact solely due to such causes. Thus, Light and Smith (1969) have made use of hypothetical interaction effects to show that the Negro-white difference in IQ could be accounted for by environmental factors even within the limits of Jensen's estimate of heritability components. This is a significant point to have demonstrated,* but it should be recognized that Light and Smith have not demonstrated that genetic differences are not involved or even that an environmentalist explanation is the more likely one.

On the other side, one may discern a type of all-or-none thinking which holds that if there are genetically determined IQ differences between racial or social class groups, then efforts to raise the IQs of such groups through education are doomed to failure. Jensen himself has not made any such bald assertion, but is easy enough to infer it from the general structure of his argument, which begins by asserting that compensatory education has apparently failed to boost the IQs of disadvantaged groups, then goes on to discuss genetic influence on IQ and the possibility that group differences have a genetic basis, and ends by proposing that educational treatment of disadvantaged groups should concern itself with abilities other than general intelligence. The message would seem to be, "Forget about raising the IQ of lower-class and Negro children. It can't be done."

However, there is no question that lower-class and Negro children are disadvantaged environmentally. The possibility that they may also be

---

* The demonstration is, however, rather fanciful, for it seems to require that racial discrimination have the effect not merely of putting black people into generally unfavorable environmental conditions but of putting individuals into the particular environments that are worst for their particular genotypes. One result of such bizarre allocation would be greatly to increase the variance of IQ scores among blacks as compared to that among whites (a point brought to my attention by William Shockley, personal communication), whereas in fact the variance of IQs for blacks is less than that for whites.

"disadvantaged" genetically does not rule out the possibility that a large part of the IQ deficit shown by these groups is due to environmental factors and can thus be remedied by environmental means. Even if compensatory education has failed to produce demonstrable effects, it is going too far to excuse this failure on genetic grounds. We know that environmental changes can have an effect, as shown for instance in the studies of Negroes migrating to Philadelphia from the South (Lee, 1951). The last thing I think Jensen or any other genetically oriented behavioral scientist would want to see happen is for his ideas to be used as an excuse for not doing anything. There have been plenty of such excuses in the past. "Cultural deprivation" itself has been used as an excuse for giving up on disadvantaged children—misused, we should say; and there is danger that the notion of hereditary differences will be misused in the same way.

There are, however, two points in Jensen's discussion that have pessimistic indications for educational efforts to raise the IQs of disadvantaged children. One of these is the idea of environment as a threshold variable and the other is the indication that educational variables might be among the least potent of environmental variables for influencing IQ. The threshold idea implies that above a certain minimum level further improvements in environment make no difference in IQ. If the environments of so-called disadvantaged groups are already above this minimum level, then no effects can be expected from environmental improvement of any kind. Jensen does not provide strong evidence for his threshold hypothesis. It appears that he has constructed it mainly to account for the evidence of large IQ gains through environmental change in the Skeels and Dye (1939) study. However, as we have seen in the second section of this paper, these gains can be adequately accounted for by the hypothesis that environmental effects are additive across the whole range of environments. The other argument he employs is that he has found "no report of a group of children being given permanently superior IQs by means of environmental manipulations" (p. 60). There is, however, some evidence of this from work done in Israel, where Kibbutz-reared Oriental Jews show above-average IQs while those outside the kibbutzim show IQs substantially below average (cited in Bloom, 1969).

Although there is reason to be skeptical of these results because of unknown selection factors (only a small minority of Oriental Jews get into kibbutzim, and those who do may be exceptional in some way), it is nevertheless evidence that would have to be ruled out before one could be confident in resorting to the threshold hypothesis. To me a more reasonable and cautious hypothesis is that effectiveness of the environment in fostering IQ is not linearly related to gross indicators of socio-economic status. As one moves from a slum environment to an ordinary working-class environment, the difference in IQ-related effect may be much greater than it is when one moves from a working-class environment to that of a middle-income suburb. Accordingly, if one is dealing with slum children the more obvious sorts of environmental improvement, or those that would normally occur with increased prosperity, can be expected to have some effect on IQ, whereas if one is dealing with middle-class children the kinds of environmental improvements that would be effective in raising IQ may be much less obvious and more difficult to bring about. Another way of putting it is that such environmental variables as income, quality of housing, and supply of reading material in the home may indeed be threshold variables, which make no difference above a certain level, but other more primary variables (to which these are only indirectly related) may be significant at all levels.

The practical implication of this non-linearity notion is one with which I think few people would disagree, but it is also a fairly pessimistic one. It is that environmental improvement is likely to show diminishing returns in its effect upon IQ or any related variables. Alleviating the more obvious social ills that go with poverty may produce some notable gains in IQ among the formerly afflicted, but it cannot then be expected that further social improvements will automatically result in further IQ gains, and environmental improvements capable of producing such gains will take some deeper research to discover.

Jensen's other point, that education seems to be among the less potent environmental variables in affecting IQ, is of course only pessimistic in its implications for educators. In the larger social context, it would be a good thing if medical care and nutrition proved to be more potent variables, because the chances of doing something directly about them are much greater. We at least have a clearer idea of what constitutes good medical care and nutrition than we have of what constitutes effective education. However, it seems to me that there is much greater reason to suppose that physical factors in the environment function as threshold variables than that experiential factors do. Physical factors influence the condition of the neurological system, and by analogy with other biological systems we might assume that there are certain minimum requirements of nutriments and so forth that need to be met, and that beyond that further inputs are useless. Experience, on the other hand, determines what information is stored in the system, and there is no reason to suppose that this could not be improved upon indefinitely. So, again, it might be that for severely impoverished children physical improvements might make a decided difference, but for additional gains in intelligence or for gains among children whose physical conditions are already above the minimum level experiential factors might be the only ones that could make a difference.

All of this is highly conjectural, but it suggests a potentially fruitful direction for educational research. Perhaps what educational research should be doing is not concentrating upon improving the lot of severely impoverished children, whose main problems may be of a nonexperiential nature and ones that can only be alleviated by more general kinds of environmental change, but should rather be concentrating upon finding ways of improving the intellectual abilities of children whose physical conditions are already in good order. These would be children from the great mass of "Middle America" whose environments are physically adequate but not rich in intellectual stimulation. The justification for doing research on them would be that it could allow us to identify experiential factors that are separate from the physical factors that are also being dealt with in poverty programs and might thus make it possible for us to design educational programs for poorer children that would be beneficial over and above the general effects of eradicating poverty.

In raising the possibility that supposed cultural differences may in fact have genetic roots, Jensen has brought forth a point that casts profound doubt on a large range of research studies. I refer to studies that attempt to account for the behavior of children by examining the behavior of their parents toward them. Practically every psychological attribute of children, from creativity to bed-wetting, has been treated to a search for child-rearing antecedents, and the results of such studies have naturally been of considerable interest to educators, for they would seem to get at the causal experiential variables which educators in their turn might attempt to manipulate. Causal inferences from such studies must presume that the behaviors in question are environmentally determined. An alternate hypothesis is that the behaviors are genetically determined and that when correlations are found between parent behavior and subsequent child behavior, these correlations are due to genetic similarity of parents and children and reflect manifestations of the same inherited traits.

The genetic hypothesis has found considerable support in several areas where the hypothesis of experiential causation had previously held sway. Rimland (1964) has advanced such a hypothesis to account for the characteristics of parents of autistic children, rejecting experiential causation on grounds that the symptoms of infantile autism appear too early in life to have been influenced by parent behavior. Heston (1970), after substantiating the heritability of schizophrenia by evidence similar to that used by Jensen to demonstrate the heritability of IQ, went on to define a schizoid syndrome, shared by schizophrenics and their nonschizophrenic relatives alike, which accounts for parent-child relationships that had previously been interpreted as causal. In the case of intellectual abilities, it is easy to see how the same basic traits, which are manifested by children in their test performance, could be manifested by parents in how they talk to their children, teach them, discipline them, in their attitudes toward education, in what sorts of educational materials they have around the house, and so on. While one can always make a reasonable case for the causal influence of such parent characteristics, it is just as reasonable, even if less appealing to the educator, to treat them as evidence of genetic resemblance.

The practical upshot of this consideration is that findings on child-rearing antecedents of behavior must be regarded as ambiguous. At best they can suggest causal hypotheses that must be tested experimentally before they can be held with confidence.

The most profound and far-reaching implication of the hereditarian view of ethnic and other group differences is one that I don't believe has been touched on by Jensen, although it has been developed somewhat by Eckland (1967).

The implication is that culture may not only influence the phenotypic expression of inherited traits but may also, through selection pressures, influence the distribution of genes within cultural groups, and that cultural differences may represent not only adaptations to environmental conditions but also to distributional genetic differences between groups, with the result that culture and heredity are intimately interconnected.

If true, this would not be an argument for separatism, but it would add weight to arguments for pluralism, for allowing cultures to maintain their distinct identities and for not applying uniform standards of treatment and expectation, as has been done in public education. It could still be true that any given individual could adapt to any culture and might even be better suited to a culture different from the one into which he was born, while at the same time it was true that each culture was on the whole the best one for its members and should therefore not be willy-nilly absorbed into some other.

Although pluralism seems to be on its way to becoming a "good word" in education, the schools have not taken any but the most trivial steps toward achieving it (Green, 1969). The trend is toward individualization within heterogeneous pupil groups, an arrangement which among other things increases the opportunities and influences that might lead a child to deviate from the norms of his cultural group. Pluralism begins with a recognition of the right of groups to protect their members from such influences. The line between separatism or segregation and pluralism is a difficult one to establish in practice, as the current dilemmas in the education of black Americans reveals only too well, but it appears essential that the line be drawn in some rational and generalizable way. Thus far, education has had to deal largely with cultural groups defined on long-standing ethnic or religious lines. The future may well see the emergence of self-selected, experimental sub-cultures that cut across traditional lines and that have as a primary rather than a secondary distinction their rejection of the prevailing culture represented in the schools. These self-selected sub-cultures may well reflect, more strongly than sub-cultures of the past, complex differences in genetic disposition.

CONCLUSION

One apparently reasonable stance is that the educator need not concern himself with genetics because, in the first place, he is constrained to working with environmental variables and must therefore do the best he can with them, regardless of their relative potency compared to genetic variables; and because, in the second place, education deals with individual children of unknown genetic potential, so that normative data on genetic differences have no application. These are valid points with respect to the work of the teacher in the classroom, for whom genetic principles are most likely to function only as an after-the-fact excuse for educational failures.

At the level of policy, however, education deals with populations rather than with individuals, and it is at this level that genetics becomes potentially relevant. In this paper I have tried to indicate some ways in which genetic considerations can be relevant to educational policy. The mere fact of individual differences in intelligence should encourage us to look for alternative methods of achieving educational objectives that do not rely so heavily upon the abilities represented by IQ. The apparently high heritability of IQ should influence our expectations as to what may be accomplished through allocation of existing environmental variants: reallocation may produce substantial gains in mean IQ but should not be expected to produce much alteration in the spread of individual differences. The idea of specific heredity-environment interactions suggests the possibility of producing substantial environmental effects on individual differences in intelligence, but it appears that we are a long way from knowing how to produce such effects.

On the matter of social and racial differences, it is probably safe to say that the educational policy-maker need not concern himself with the question of whether these differences have a genetic basis. It is necessary to avoid both the oversimplification that says if there are genetic group differences nothing can be accomplished through educational improvement and the oversimplification that says if group differences in IQ are environmentally caused they can be eliminated by conventional social amelioration. The possibility that cultural differences are related to heredity, however, adds force to the need for schools to come to grips with the problem of providing for cultural pluralism without separatism or segregation. This may well be the major policy problem facing public education in our time.

REFERENCES

BEREITER, C., & ENGELMAN, S. *Teaching Disadvantaged Children in the Preschool.* Englewood Cliffs, New Jersey: Prentice-Hall, 1966.

BLOOM, B. S. Letter to the Editor. *Harvard Educational Review,* 1969, 39, 419-421.

CHURCH, J. *Language and the Discovery of Reality.* New York: Random House, 1961.

COLEMAN, J. S., *et al. Equality of Educational Opportunity.* U.S. Department of Health, Education, and Welfare, 1966.

ECKLAND, B. K. "Genetics and Sociology: A Reconsideration." *Amer. Sociol. Rev.,* 1967, 32, 173-194.

ENGELMANN, S. *Preventing Failure in the Primary Grades.* Chicago: Science Research Associates, 1969. (b)

ENGELMANN, S. *Conceptual Learning.* San Rafael, California: Dimensions Publishing Company, 1969. (a)

GREEN, T. F. "Schools and Communities: A Look Forward." *Harvard Educational Review,* 1969, 39, 221-252.

HAYES, K. J. "Genes, Drives, and Intelligence." *Psychol. Rep.,* 1962, 10 (2), 299-342. (Monogr. Suppl. No. 2-VIO).

HESTON, L. L. "The Genetics of Schizophrenic and Schizoid Disease." *Science,* 1970, 167, 249-256.

HIRSCH, J. "Behavior-Genetic Analysis and its Biosocial Consequences." Paper presented at University of Illinois, Conference on Contributions to Intelligence, November 14, 1969.

HUNT, J. McV. *Intelligence and Experience.* New York: Ronald Press, 1961.

HUNT, J. McV. "The Psychological Basis for Using Pre-School Enrichment as an Antidote for Cultural Deprivation." *Merrill-Palmer Quarterly,* 1964, 10, 209-248.

JENCKS, C. "A Reappraisal of the Most Controversial Educational Document of Our Time." *New York Times Magazine,* August 10, 1969, 12-13.

JENSEN, A. R. "How Much Can We Boost IQ and Scholastic Achievement." *Harvard Educational Review,* 1969, 39, 1-123.

LEE, E. S. Negro Intelligence and Selective Migration: A Philadelphia Test of the Klineberg Hypothesis." *Amer. Sociol. Rev.,* 1951, 16, 227-233.

LIGHT, R. J., & SMITH, P. V. "Social Allocation Models and Intelligence." *Harvard Educational Review.* 1969, 39, 484-510.

RIMLAND, B. *Infantile Autism.* New York: Appleton-Century-Crofts, 1964.

ROBINSON, H. B., & ROBINSON, N. M. *The Mentally Retarded Child: A Psychological Approach.* New York: McGraw-Hill, 1965.

SKEELS, H. M., & DYE, H. B. "A Study of the Effects of Differential Stimulation on Mentally Retarded Children. *Proc. Amer. Assoc, Ment. Def.,* 1939, 44, 114-136.

STINCHCOMBE, A. L. Environment: the Cumulation of Effects is Yet to Be Understood." *Harvard Educational Review.* 1969, 39, 511-522.

TUEL, J. K. "The Relationship of Intelligence and Achievement Variables in Programmed Instruction." *Calif. J. Educ. Res.,* 1966, 17, 68-72.

VERNON, P. E. *Intelligence and Attainment Tests.* New York: Philosophical Library, 1960.

16

MODIFICATION OF COGNITIVE SKILLS AMONG LOWER-CLASS BLACK CHILDREN

Irving E. Sigel, Ph.D. and Patricia Olmsted, M.A.

The Merrill-Palmer Institute, Detroit, Michigan

INTRODUCTION

Our 1967-1968 Head Start project was concerned with the modifiability of classification skills among lower-class black children by using training procedures that focused on decentration, the ability to shift point of view. It has been found that children increased in their ability to form classes, employed a greater variety of attributes and functions of objects in creating these classes, and increased in their capability for articulating

The research reported here was supported in part by OEO Head Start Subcontract #4118 with Michigan State University Head Start Evaluation and Research Center, 1967-68. Dr. Sigel is now at the State University of New York at Buffalo. Miss Olmsted is now at the University of Florida.

ACKNOWLEDGMENTS

The authors wish to acknowledge the help of many individuals in bringing this project to a successful conclusion. Our deepest thanks to Dr. Arthur Enzmann, Director, Early Childhood Education, Detroit Public Schools, for his assistance in the project and for enlisting the aid of the appropriate Board of Education personnel; to Mrs. Charlotte Gmeiner, Kindergarten Supervisor, Board of Education, our thanks for her wholehearted support and encouragement; to the following principals, who made the space and time available for us to test and train: Miss Elizabeth Sowell, Estabrook School; Mr. Roy Ossman, George School; Mr. Richard Blixberg, Marxhausen School; Mrs. Nola Wernette, Roosevelt School; and Mr. Sol Dunn, Assistant Principal, Bell School. To the principals of the other Detroit schools where many of our subjects were now students, our thanks for their cooperation in allowing us to continue working with these children. To the following research assistants, who carried out the testing program: Miss Elizabeth Ireland, Mr. Matthew Dodd, Miss Dessa Stone, Mr. Peter Vietze, Mr. Steven Terry, Mr. Michael Abramsky. To Mrs. Hazel McCutcheon, whose patience and skill made the completion of this project a reality. To Dr. Joseph Jackson for his critical reading of portions of this manuscript. To Miss Barbara Rybacki for putting the final manuscript in form.

the rationale for groupings after receiving classification training. (Sigel and Olmsted, 1967, 1970)

These results were based on post testing done shortly after the training period. Important as it was to demonstrate that classification skills can be modified by a particular educational experience, the more important issue is to examine what long-term effects may exist. Does the particular training employed in that study, in effect, create changes in classification skills that have some enduring quality?

It seems reasonable to expect that the result of short-term training would be short-lived, especially if the educational system does not create specific programs to enhance these skills. Consequently, it may be naive to expect that the one-month training program employed in 1966-67 would have long-term effects. On the other hand, one might reasonably assume that the training program might have had sufficient impact so that the basic learning is recoverable through review or further training a year later, thereby resulting in more rapid re-learning of classification skills. One can refer to this process, in effect, as "dosing." This is comparable to offering the child a booster shot. It is hypothesized that children who receive this booster treatment will do better on logical, analytic, and classification tasks than children who have not received such a booster. Thus, one purpose of this study was to examine the effects of such dosing.

In another study, cognitive skills were enhanced not only by training in classification but also by training children with experiences in discrimination and memory tasks (Shantz and Sigel, 1967). The fact that two apparently different training procedures yielded the same results on measures of children's ability to conserve mass and number led to the search for an overlap between the two training procedures which might account for the similar outcomes. Thus, the second purpose of this study is to compare these two approaches since one of the goals of our overall research program is to identify the most utilitarian and conceptually sound training procedures.

The rationale for this choice of a research problem rests on the seeming overlap between the two procedures. Before articulating the overlap, a word about each. In classification training, the children are asked to identify objects and their manifold attributes, focusing on the polydimensionality of objects, and the awareness that any one or more of these attributes may be used as a criterion for grouping. The child is encouraged to decenter and shift from one attribute to another. Children with such training employ a wider array of criteria for grouping as compared to children not having had experience (Sigel and Olmsted, 1967, 1970). The classification training program is, in a way, a guided discovery approach. The question remains, however, whether other training might not have had the same effect.

A second type of training that is proposed is attention training. This program is derived from a discrimination-memory training program used by Shantz & Sigel (1967). Discrimination-memory training is made up of discrimination and memory tasks. The children distinguish differences between objects, seriate items on the basis of details, retain knowledge from a story, reproduce body movements of another from memory, etc. (See Shantz & Sigel, 1967, for complete description). Discrimination-memory training was hypothesized as capable of being equally effective because it emphasizes manifest similarity and difference among items—a condition considered highly relevant for conservation. The results of that study, by the way, revealed no significant difference between groups of children trained by either method in ability to solve conservation problems.

Since the training programs employed influenced the acquisition of conservation equally then, it can be argued some overlap must exist between the two procedures; or at least, the solution to the conservation problem is multi-determined with some of determination residing in each of the training conditions.

Some commonality between classification and discrimination-memory training can be identified by analyzing each of the procedures, to wit, it is necessary to pay attention to details in order to distinguish some attributes from others; each training condition requires the child to discriminate, to scan arrays, and to see constancies and similarities among diverse objects. Since classification training and discrimination-memory training each involve these types of behaviors, and since each of these may be particularly relevant for performing on conservation tasks, no differences were obtained. Conservation skills were attributed in part as outcomes of the common-denominator, the *attention* variable (Shantz & Sigel, 1967). Hence, the idea of attention training.

Thus, the second purpose of this study—the comparison of classification training with attention training in terms of such cognitive outcomes as classification, logical, and analytic skills. Since attention training includes discrimination, scanning and generalization, and since classification training appears to involve these same processes, it is hypothesized that there will be no difference between classification training and attention training in terms of their influence on logical and analytic skills. The differences to be found between classification and attention training, however, would reside in types and range of criteria used in classification tasks, e.g., descriptions, relations, inferences. Attention training teaches the child to focus on observable attributes, discriminate among diverse observable attributes, scan for them and identify them in varying contexts—thereby generalizing on the basis of manifest cues. More likely, skills in differentiating items rather than grouping them result from such training (See Appendix B). In classification training, however, the goal is to make the children aware of the multi-dimensionality of objects including consideration of inferred attributes. Further, the children are taught that any criterion is possible for creating groupings. Thus a relativistic rather than absolutistic approach is encouraged in the building of groups or classes. Further, articulation of the rationale for such grouping encourages use of labels and verbalizations. Classification training should enhance verbal skills.

These are the effects anticipated for children who had no previous training; they were in fact children in the control group. It should be recalled, however, that about one-half the children in this study had received classification training a year earlier. Hypotheses have to be formulated integrating the fact that each of these children comes with some previous experience in classification to this study. For the sake of simplicity, let us first identify all the subgroups so that the reader can readily see the overall organization of the children into teaching groups.

(1) previous classification training (CT) (1966-67) followed by attention-training (AT) (1968-69), (Group designated CT-AT)

(2) previous classification training (CT) (1966-67) followed by booster of the same (1967-68), (CT-CT)

(3) previous classification training (1967-68) CT with no additional training (CT-NT)

(4) no previous classification training (NT) followed by attention-training (AT) (1967-68), (NT-AT)

(5) classification training (CT) (1966-67) followed by attention-training (AT) (1967-68), (CT-AT)

(6) a control group, no training (1966-67) and no training (1967-68) (NT-NT)

The effects of training with these groups are expected to be different than for the previous ones, since the degree to which a particular training procedure superimposed (about a year later) on a different trial must be considered. Where classification would encourage breadth, attention would narrow the focus. Children receiving additional classification training would be expected to be more varied in grouping criteria and hence be more able to provide a greater variety of responses. Children receiving attention training after classification training a year earlier would be able to create groupings by virtue of their previous training. Since, however, there is more emphasis on focusing on specifics, chances are they would show less variety than classification boosted children. Each of these procedures, however, should produce children more varied and more fluent than children who receive no further training.

The training procedures are expected to have differential effects on cognitive skills other than categorization. On the basis of previous research, classification training should induce conservation (Shantz &

Sigel, 1967; Sigel, Roeper, Hooper, 1966). Assuming the logic of our description of the attentional processes, we would expect enhancement of conservation skills as a result of this training. This expectancy is partly derived from results of Shantz & Sigel (1967) and from the report of Gelman (1969). In the latter study, Gelman reports indication of conservation in five year olds because of attention to relevant cues. Training children to focus on relevant details should thereby facilitate solution to conservation tasks.

It is also expected that children receiving attention training should do better on analytic tasks as compared to classification trained children because the former training condition provides greater emphasis on identifying and discriminating of relevant cues. Although the classification procedure does contain discrimination experience, the emphasis is on the grouping whereas in attention training the focus is on differentiation of elements of objects. Thus, superiority of the attention group over the classification trained is expected.

As for expectancies of training on logical tasks, e.g., multiple seriation, reversibility and multiple classification, we would base our expectation on the results of the Shantz & Sigel study where these operations were interpreted as independent of the training. That study was done with middle class children. The question is: Are these findings replicable with lower-class children?

In summary, the purposes of this study can be specified as follows:

(1) to test the long-range effects of classification training,
(2) to evaluate the effects of re-introducing classification training to those previously trained,
(3) to compare classification training at two age periods (5 and 6 year olds),
(4) to compare classification training with training in attentional processes.

DESIGN OF THE STUDY

Sample: To accomplish the above purposes, 69 of the 72 children who were involved in the 1966-67 study were located. Of the 69, 39 were in control groups and 30 received classification training .

The children in the 1966-67 study were identified as high scorers (at least 50% grouping responses on the Object-Picture categorization pretest) and low scorers (less than 50% grouping responses).* Of the 69 children located, 47 were low scorers and 22 were high scorers.

These 69 children were distributed into six groups in preparation for

---

* The Object-Picture categorization test requires children to classify three-dimensional objects and pictures of these objects. This test is reported in detail in Sigel & Olmsted, 1967, and Sigel & McBane, 1967.

TABLE 1

COMPOSITION OF AND TRAINING GIVEN IN EACH EXPERIMENTAL CONDITION

1967-68 Group	LCT	LNT	1966-67 Group HCT	HNT	Total
†CT-CT	6	—	3	—	9
NT-CT	—	6	—	4	10
CT-AT	7	—	4	—	11
NT-AT	—	6	—	4	10
CT-NT	9	—	1	—	10*
NT-NT	—	13	—	6	19**
Total	22	25	8	14	69

L = Low Responder
H = High Responder
CT = Classification Training
AT = Attention Training
NT = No Training

† Note: First abbreviation refers to 1966-67 training and the second abbreviation refers to 1967-68 training.
* One S (LCT) lost when family moved out of Detroit.
** Size of this group randomly reduced to be comparable to other groups. New composition = 6 LNT and 4 HNT.

the training programs in this study. Nine children were randomly eliminated from group 6 to equalize the size of all groups. The composition of the groups and the types of training given to each are presented in Table 1. As can be seen from Table 1, the six groups contain comparable proportions of high and low scores. These six groups were formed by making all possible combinations of the two conditions (CT and NT) included in 1966-67 and the three conditions (CT, AT, and NT) used in 1967-68.

Methods and Procedures: All 69 children were given a battery of pretests. The major criterion instruments in the 1966-67 study were the Object-Categorization Test (OCT) and Picture Categorization Test (PCT). Briefly, these two tests contain 12 items depicting familiar objects (see Figure 1). The OCT is made up of the three-dimensional items and the PCT 5"x8" colored photographs of these objects. Each test is administered separately. Within each test, two conditions are used—an Active and a Passive one. The Active condition is where the examiner selects an object from the array of 12 and asks the child to select as many or as few that belong or go with it. The child is free to select from the array any number to make a grouping. He is asked to explain the grouping. The examiner replaces the item, selects another and repeats the procedure. Twelve sub-groupings are made. In the Passive condition, the examiner selects a group of objects, presents it to the child, and asks

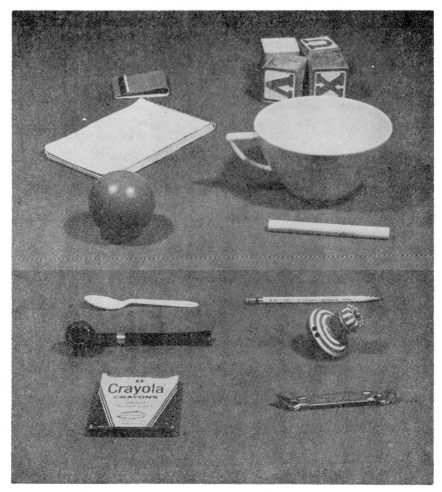

FIG. 1. Categorization Test Objects

for an explanation. The Passive condition is done at the end of the testing periods to avoid influencing Active groupings.

Two scores from this test were used, *grouping scores* and *style scores*. *Grouping* scores are those which contain a meaningful relationship between all the items selected. *Styles of categorization* are based on the content of the verbalization provided for each grouping. The following are the categories of styles: descriptive (form, color, structure); relational-contextual and categorical-inferential (See Appendix A for details).

A modification of the PCT was constructed for this study, the Multiple Categorization Test (MCT). In this task, the child is presented with twelve pre-arranged sets of pictures. For the first six presentations,

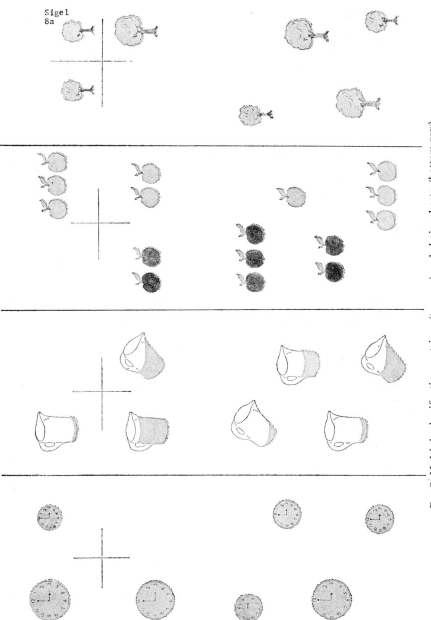

Sigel
8a

Fig. 2. Multiple classification matrices (top row) and choice sheets (bottom row).

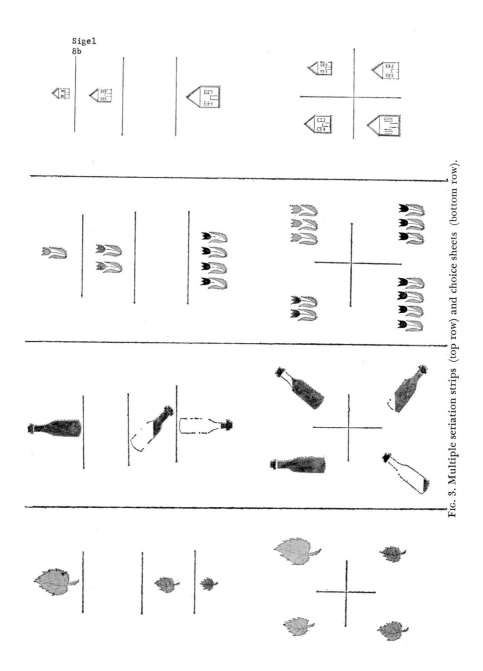

Sigel
8b

FIG. 3. Multiple seriation strips (top row) and choice sheets (bottom row).

the child is asked to give two reasons why the item may have been grouped. Three reasons are requested for the remaining six sets, yielding a total of 30 responses.

Other instruments in the pre-test battery were two classical Piagetian conservation tasks, number and quantity; and three measures of logical operations, multiple classification, multiple seriation, and reversibility. The multiple classification task requires that the child fill in one empty cell of a four cell matrix with a picture that includes *both* sub-class attributes relevant to the matrix (see Figure 2). The multiple seriation task requires that the child fill in one empty cell on a strip of four cells with a picture that includes both values of two continuous dimension from which the strip is constructed (see Figure 3). Finally, the reversibility task, requires the child to insert a missing picture in a series of pictures which are reversed horizontally from a standard series (see Figure 4). The Peabody Picture Vocabulary Test was included as a measure of general intellectual ability while the Block Design and Geometric Design sub-tests of the Wechsler Pre-school and Primary Scale of Intelligence were used as measures of analytic ability. Finally, the Draw-a-Line task was used as an impulse control measure to assess the degree to which the children would, as instructed, draw a line down a blank sheet of paper as slowly as possible.

The rationale for the test battery was as follows: First, we wanted to establish the degree to which children classified objects, and the kinds of cognitive styles they used in their classification; second, these measures allow for an assessment of the degree to which children classify *comparably* on three-dimensional *as compared to* two-dimensional objects; and third, it enables us to assess the relationship between cognitive measures which is in effect partly a replication of the Shantz & Sigel (1967) study.* The addition of the impulsivity measure is based on our interest in determining the degree to which attentional training, in particular, would slow down the child's performance.

Each child was seen twice, a week apart, in an individual testing session by a familiar and experienced examiner. All our examiners were white.

Training Procedures: For the classification training groups, ten sessions were held distributed over a two to three week period. Sample of the training program used this year is presented in Appendix B and also has been described previously (Sigel, Olmsted, 1970). For the new reader, let us briefly describe the task. The primary function of training is to provide the child with the opportunity to identify various attributes of objects and subsequently to use this information as bases for classifica-

---

* These three tasks were taken from Shantz-Sigel (1967).

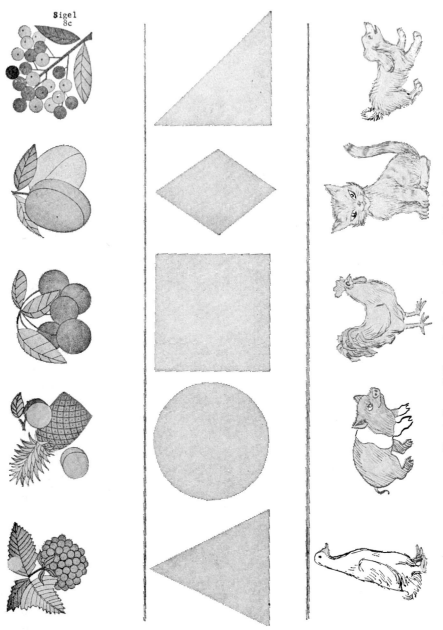

FIG. 4. Reversibility tasks (practice task not included).

tion. He is encouraged to build and rebuild classes and to combine and recombine classes of objects. The basic goal in the training is to acquaint the child with the multi-dimensionality of objects and to facilitate decentration. As can be seen from the curriculum samples, the teacher is encouraged to be non-evaluative, allowing the child to use whatever labels he desires in describing any attribute of an object. Pictures and objects were used in separate training sessions to facilitate learning that objects can be differentially represented by pictures, and thereby can be classified equivalently.

The attention training program was developed for this project and involved a series of tasks, samples of which are described in Appendix C. The focus was primarily on providing the children with opportunities for discrimination, for identifying sameness, difference, and degrees thereof, and for learning to analyze complex patterns.

Each of these training procedures was conducted in a group of four to seven children in a room away from the classroom by an experienced trainer, a member of our project team. The trainers had no knowledge of the children's scores on any tests. They did, however, meet with the children in the classroom to get to know them before the training began. Each trainer had a curriculum guide which she was instructed to follow as closely as possible. Tape recordings were taken of all the training sessions for two reasons: (1) to provide a monitoring effect by which the examiner could later on check his own behavior, and (2) as a check on the trainer—to be used by the project supervisors to be certain the curriculum guide was being followed.

RESULTS AND DISCUSSION

The results of this study will be presented in two sections. The first section will report pre-test data on the OCT, PCT, and MCT. In this way, the long-term effects of the initial training can be assessed. These pretest results are indicative of the long-term effects of the initial training in classification. The second section will deal with the effects of the subsequent training programs.

Pre-Test Results

Grouping Responses: The medians for each of the groups irrespective of training, mode of representation, and test condition are similar. Medians for the OCT active condition are 11 and 11.5 for the trained groups and 12 for each of the nontrained groups. For the PCT active condition, the median for the high non-trained group was 11.5 while a median of 10 was obtained for the other three groups. On the passive condition for the OCT, the medians ranged from four to six as follows: LCT, 5; LNT, 4; HCT, 6; HNT, 4.5. The PCT passive condition was equally difficult for each of the groups where the medians were three for the LNT group and four for each of the remaining three groups. Thus, we can conclude that performance level is equivalent among the four groups but the level of functioning varies with test material and test condition, not training experience.

Object-Picture Discrepancy: As indicated above, the mode of representation, i.e., objects or pictures, seems to influence the quantity and quality of grouping responses. We refer to the differential scores between the OCT and PCT as the *object-picture* discrepancy. We turn now to a discussion of this discrepancy.

TABLE 2

PERCENTAGE OF SUBJECTS PER GROUP SHOWING EACH TYPE OF
DISCREPANCY BETWEEN NUMBER OF GROUPING RESPONSES
GIVEN ON THE PRE-TEST OCT AND PCT

ACTIVE

Group	OCT>PCT	Direction of Discrepancy OCT=PCT	OCT<PCT	N
LCT	45	36	18	22
LNT	76	24	0	25
HCT	63	25	12	8
HNT	36	57	7	14

PASSIVE

Group	OCT>PCT	OCT=PCT	OCT<PCT	N
LCT	55	18	27	22
LNT	48	16	36	25
HCT	50	12	38	8
HNT	50	14	36	14

Table 2 contains the percentage of subjects in each group showing the various types of object-picture discrepancies. Inspection of the table reveals that discrepancies exist for both the active and passive conditions for each of the groups. Previous training does not appear to have reduced this discrepancy in any systematic way. Except for the HNT group in the active condition, a greater percentage of children give more grouping responses to objects than pictures. This result holds for each of the groups in the passive condition.

It is of interest to note that while most children produce grouping responses with objects, relatively large groups produce an equal number of grouping responses with objects and pictures in the active condition.

However, in the passive condition, while more grouping responses are still elicited by objects, grouping responses are frequently elicited by pictures, attesting to continued lack of equivalence between objects and pictures. Pictures elicit relatively more grouping responses in the passive condition than in the active one. In the active and in the passive condition, children produce more grouping responses with objects than with pictures. This finding reveals that equivalent performance does not occur at age six, a finding reported earlier with younger children (Sigel & Olmsted, 1970).

Explanation of these findings can be only speculative. The degree to which these discrepancies reflect difficulty in representational competence is still moot, since the results may be artifacts of the test materials and test conditions. For example, are equivalent responses to objects and pictures easier when the child is free to create his own grouping

TABLE 3

PERCENTAGE OF SUBJECTS IN EACH GROUP USING DIFFERENT NUMBERS OF STYLES OF CATEGORIZATION FOR EACH CONDITION OF EACH TEST

Object-Active

	n	0	1	2	3	4	5
LCT	(22)	—	50	27	9	14	—
LNT	(25)	—	48	36	16	—	—
HCT	(8)	—	50	38	12	—	—
HNT	(14)	—	71	14	14	—	—

Picture-Active

	n	0	1	2	3	4	5
LCT	(22)	4	50	23	23	—	—
LNT	(25)	4	44	40	12	—	—
HCT	(8)	—	50	38	—	12	—
HNT	(14)	—	64	14	21	—	—

Object-Passive

	n	0	1	2	3	4	5
LCT	(22)	9	32	32	18	9	—
LNT	(25)	8	38	36	16	4	—
HCT	(8)	—	25	50	25	—	—
HNT	(14)	—	64	29	7	—	—

Picture-Passive

	n	0	1	2	3	4	5
LCT	(22)	—	50	27	18	5	—
LNT	(25)	—	60	24	12	4	—
HCT	(8)	—	50	25	25	—	—
HNT	(14)	—	50	36	14	—	—

than when he has to respond to a pre-formed grouping? It may well be that such freedom of choice in the active condition elicits familiar criteria for grouping, while in the passive condition the child feels that he has to discover what the tester wants. This constraint might inhibit responsiveness. Does the difference in perceptual cues in the three-dimensional condition evoke more familiar associations than pictures? These are but some of the issues needing study.

Styles of Categorization: Comparability of grouping performance or variation as a function of mode of representation does not indicate the criteria employed in constructing groups. The bases for grouping are what we shall now discuss under the rubric of styles of categorization.

First, before we turn to analysis of the number of styles employed by each of the four groups, let us recall that one of the outcomes of the classification training reported in the 1966-67 study was the fact that children trained in classification increased significantly more in the number of styles used than the non-trained group. In Table 3 are presented the percentage of children using various numbers of styles for the active and passive condition with pictures and objects. The table reveals that some, but not dramatic, differences exist among the groups. Some children in each group are able to employ more than one basis of grouping. Thus, we can conclude that effects of training and original grouping capability are not necessary and sufficient conditions for influencing style variability performance eight months later. It might be recalled that initially larger proportions of children tended to persevere

TABLE 4

PERCENTAGE OF SUBJECTS PER GROUP USING EACH STYLE CATEGORY ON THE PRE-TEST OCT AND PCT FOR ACTIVE AND PASSIVE CONDITIONS

Style	OCT Active Group				PCT Active Group			
	LCT	LNT	HCT	HNT	LCT	LNT	HCT	HNT
Form	55	40	38	29	55	40	25	29
Color	27	40	75	64	27	44	62	64
Structure	23	24	12	7	27	20	25	21
Relational	32	36	25	21	23	32	25	21
Categorical	50	28	12	21	36	24	38	21

Style	OCT Passive Group				PCT Passive Group			
	LCT	LNT	HCT	HNT	LCT	LNT	HCT	HNT
Form	41	44	12	21	41	40	12	29
Color	59	40	100	64	59	44	62	64
Structure	23	8	12	14	14	8	—	14
Relational	27	36	38	14	32	36	38	29
Categorical	36	44	38	29	32	40	62	29

and use only one style. A year later many of the children are able to use more than one basis of similarity. There still is however, a relatively large percentage of one group (HNT) who use only one approach, e.g., 71% in the OCT active condition.

The percentage of children using each of the style categories is presented in Table 4 for the active and passive condition for each of the tests. Differences in style usage are evident between the active and passive condition for the OCT and the PCT. One most noticeable differences in the OCT active condition is that the high responders, irrespective of training, use more color responses than any other style. This is in contrast to the low responders who tend to use form equally or more so than color.

The results are similar for the active PCT task. The significance of this result is difficult to assess. It depends, in part, on the interpretation and significance attributed to color and form. From our previous studies, it is not clear whether color responses reflect increased experience in school where considerable emphasis is placed on teaching of colors and color labeling, or whether it is an artifact of our task. The latter interpretation seems doubtful in view of the variability among our groups in using color responses as a basis of classification. It may well be that children motivated to respond use the more blatant and dramatic criteria— namely, color. We are inclined to accept experiential and motivational interpretation for the present, at least in view of our previous results on color—form usage, where we found that children who had difficulty in verbalizing tended to use form responses (Sigel & Olmsted, 1967). Interesting is the fact that form responses are more evident among middle-class children than among lower-class children (Sigel & McBane, 1967). These results regarding use of form point up an intriguing problem. Can it be that the use of form has different meanings at different age levels? The non-verbal lower-class children use form because of the intact qualities of the figure, whereas middle class children may use form as an index of their vocabulary level.

Of relevance to this is the fact that in OCT passive condition, a usually more difficult test, color responses are more frequently used than form. It may be that color is easier in this condition because the words are more readily available. Form responses may be less obvious as a basis of grouping because the items are very diverse in form e.g., long, round, rectangular items. It is difficult to produce a form grouping response. Thus, the lack of form responses may be due to the difficulty level and variations within the task.

Other styles used in greater proportion than before are structural, relational, and categorical (Sigel & Olmsted, 1967). The increase in structural response is indeed of interest since this is interpreted as an analytic response, reflecting the ability to disengage items from an embedding context and hence reflect some independence from the environment. Further, such responses can be interpreted as indicating increased intellectual maturity (Witkin, 1962).

Employment of relational and categorical responses reflect increased capability to shift from physical attributes to a greater interest in relationships and class labeling.

It would seem that training effects wash out after an eight month period. Interestingly enough, *this is not a completely accurate statement for a significant and meaningful difference does persist,* and we turn now to this set of results—differences in multiple categorization.

Results of the Multiple Categorization Test: Since we discovered that all children were able to provide high frequencies of grouping responses to the original Object-Picture Categorization Test, it was concluded that the OCT and PCT were not sufficiently discriminating between the groups. It was, therefore, decided to introduce a more difficult task, the Multiple Categorization Test. This test, using pictures, requires the child to give two or three responses to a pre-formed set of pictures. Twelve sets are used.

A one-way analysis of variance was done using four groups: High Scorers, Classification Trained (HCT); Low Scorers, Classification Trained (LCT); High Scorers, Non-Classification Trained (HNT); and Low Scorers, Non-Classification Trained (LNT). (See Table 5). A significant F was found for the groups (F = 6.09, p < .005).

TABLE 5

MEANS AND STANDARD DEVIATIONS OF GROUPING RESPONSES FOR THE
PRE-TEST MULTIPLE CATEGORIZATION TEST FOR EACH GROUP

Group	N	X	SD
LCT	22	12.4	4.8
LNT	25	8.2	5.0
HCT	8	16.5	6.1
HNT	14	9.5	6.0

ANALYSIS OF VARIANCE OF GROUPING RESPONSES ON THE MULTIPLE
CATEGORIZATION TEST

Source	df	MS	F	p
Groups	3	168.1	6.09	<.005
Error	65	27.6		

Inspection of the means and standard deviations indicates little difference between classification-trained high and low scorers. Little difference was also found between the non-trained high and low scorers. Thus, the means of the two trained groups were combined and compared to the means of the two non-trained groups. A *t* test between these two combined groups indicates the difference is significant (t = 2.40, p < .01). Thus, it can be concluded that groups who were trained could, upon request, provide more alternative groupings than the untrained group. *Training did have a lasting effect at least as far as facilitating a more flexible approach to classification when requested to do so.*

Post-Test Results

Up to this point the results of the pre-test have been reported indicating the degree to which the earlier training persisted. Let us turn now to the results of the second training series. For this discussion the reader will have to think in terms of the *six* training groups described in Table 1.

In our discussion of pre-test results, it will be recalled that an analysis was made of the OCT and PCT in terms of grouping responses. Since the median for all groups was so high for the active condition and since the Multiple Categorization Test included the passive condition, the

TABLE 6

PERCENTAGE OF SUBJECTS PER GROUP SHOWING EACH TYPE OF DIS-
CREPANCY BETWEEN NUMBER OF GROUPING RESPONSES GIVEN ON EACH
CONDITION OF THE PRE- AND POST-TEST OCT AND PCT*

PRE-TEST

	Active Direction of Discrepancy			Passive Direction of Discrepancy		
Group	$OCT>PCT$	$OCT=PCT$	$OCT<PCT$	$OCT>PCT$	$OCT=PCT$	$OCT<PCT$
CT-CT	33	33	33	44	22	33
NT-CT	60	30	10	60	20	20
CT-AT	55	27	18	46	27	27
NT-AT	50	50	—	40	40	20
CT-NT	33	56	11	33	44	22
NT-NT	30	70	—	50	30	20

POST-TEST

	Active Direction of Discrepancy			Passive Direction of Discrepancy		
Group	$OCT>PCT$	$OCT=PCT$	$OCT<PCT$	$OCT>PCT$	$OCT=PCT$	$OCT<PCT$
CT-CT	11	67	22	44	33	22
NT-CT	30	50	20	30	50	20
CT-AT	9	46	46	18	46	36
NT-AT	40	50	10	60	40	—
CT-NT	22	78	—	22	56	22
NT-NT	20	40	40	40	20	40

* The pre-test data in this table include only those test items used in the short form of the OCT and PCT.

OCT and PCT were reduced to six sets each and it was this revision that was used for the post-test.*

In view of these changes in the post-test battery and in view of the high proportion of grouping responses in the active condition, analysis of grouping responses would not provide a meaningful test of the effects of training. Rather, the results from the Multiple Categorization Test, we believe, are more sensitive for assessing changes in classification skills and, therefore, will be used as a basis of examining effects of train-

---

* Correlation between this sub-set of six and the twelve OCT was .70 for the active and .81 for the passive; for the picture-condition, the active part was .82 and the passive was .76.

ing. However, the persistent problem of Object-Picture discrepancy will be reported.

Object-Picture Discrepancy: We have previously reported that children tended to categorize objects and pictures differently—as if treating each as a separate class of stimuli. After training there is a noticeable shift for the active and passive condition. Table 6 shows the changes—greater commonality in dealing with pictures and objects but also a tendency for the discrepancy to persist, now favoring pictures. This lack of equiv-

TABLE 7

MEANS AND STANDARD DEVIATIONS OF GROUPING RESPONSES FOR THE PRE-TEST, POST-TEST, AND PRE-POST-TEST CHANGE FOR THE SUBJECTS IN EACH GROUP ON THE MULTIPLE CATEGORIZATION TEST

Group	N	Pre-Test		Post-Test		Pre-Post-Test Change	
		X	SD	X	SD	X	SD
CT-CT	9	13.1	4.7	18.9	6.3	5.8	3.6
NT-CT	10	8.2	4.1	14.7	6.4	6.5	4.3
CT-AT	11	13.2	5.3	14.4	5.8	1.3	4.4
NT-AT	10	7.6	6.7	11.5	8.2	3.9	4.8
CT-NT	9	14.1	6.8	14.7	6.9	0.6	5.2
NT-NT	10	10.3	5.2	11.8	4.4	1.5	4.0

t VALUES OF PRE-POST-TEST CHANGE FOR EACH GROUP

Group	t	p
CT-CT	4.9	$<.001$
NT-CT	4.7	$<.001$
CT-AT	1.0	N.S.
NT-AT	2.6	$<.025$
CT-NT	0.4	N.S.
NT-NT	1.2	N.S.

alence raises the questions posed earlier, since no systematic changes are found as a function of training groups. Rather than venture speculation, there is need to examine this question further empirically. First, there is need to assess the groups. Sigel reported no discrepancy with older middle-class children (age 7) (Sigel, 1953). On this basis one might ask if using older children might not yield results different from those obtained here. Secondly, it may well be that lower-class black children have difficulty in the representational area and a more direct frontal research attack is still needed. All that can be concluded at this point is that more research is necessary.

Let us now move on to the Multiple Categorization Test (MCT).

Multiple Categorization Test: This task, it will be recalled, formed part of the pre-test battery. In that pre-test condition, the children who were trained a year earlier differed significantly in their ability to give multiple reasons for a grouping from those who were not trained.

Thus, in examining post-test results for each of the six experimental groups, it must be kept in mind that the 3 CT groups (as of 1966-67) did begin with an advantage. To cope with this bias, we compared pre and post gains for each of the groups separately—in effect using each group as its own control. With such analysis for each of the six groups we can focus on the gains for each group.

In Table 7, the pre and post-test scores and change scores are presented. From the table it can be seen that the NT-CT group made the greatest gains in absolute terms followed closely by the CT-CT group; the NT-AT group was far below the above two. The remaining groups made relatively little gain. The group that had classification training in 1966-67 and in 1967-68 received attention training showed very little change, no different from the control group. Another group that changed virtually not at all was the CT-NT group.

In effect, these results show that in the pre-test condition—eight months after the last contacts with the children, CT groups did better than non-CT groups. Dosing or introduction of classification training does facilitate the ability of children to produce several responses to a single set of objects. This is a confirmation of our hypothesis that reintroduction of classification training influences the ability of children to function more flexibly.

The imposition of attention training (AT) on classification training (CT) yielded no significant gain. This finding is interpreted as a function of the possible redundancy of AT in the context of previous CT experience, adding little to classificatory skill. Thus in that respect, AT training contributes no more than no training. It will be recalled that AT preceded by no training did lead to gains in multiple classification.

Thus, we might conclude that there is a "plus" factor in classification training that enhances the capability of the child to shift his focus— that he decenters more readily than children attention trained. Our data also demonstrates that for most effective change in classification training, one of the following two conditions is necessary for maximal gain: classification retraining or the most recent classification training; and second, attention training not preceded by classification training.

If review is not instituted, children do not show further gain. However, they do not lose what they have previously gained.

As was noted previously, the addition of attention training experience in the context of classification training experience contributes little to the child's comprehension of grouping. When AT is used *alone,* it does

TABLE 8

PERCENTAGE OF SUBJECTS IN EACH GROUP USING DIFFERENT NUMBERS OF
STYLES OF CATEGORIZATION ON THE PRE- AND POST-MULTIPLE
CATEGORIZATION TEST

	Pre-Test Number of Styles Used						Post-Test Number of Styles Used					
Group	0	1	2	3	4	5	0	1	2	3	4	5
CT-CT	—	11	22	56	11	—	—	—	—	56	22	22
NT-CT	—	20	30	50	—	—	—	10	10	40	30	10
CT-AT	—	18	9	27	27	18	—	—	46	18	36	—
NT-AT	20	10	40	10	10	10	10	—	30	30	10	20
CT-NT	—	—	33	11	44	11	—	—	22	33	22	22
NT-NT	—	50	40	10	—	—	—	40	10	40	—	10

	Number of Styles Used			
	Pre		Post	
Group	0-2	3-5	0-2	3-5
CT-CT	.. 33	67	—	100
NT-CT	50	50	20	80
CT-AT	27	73	45	55
NT-AT	70	30	40	60
CT-NT	33	67	22	78
NT-NT	90	10	50	50

PERCENTAGE OF SUBJECTS IN EACH GROUP INCREASING, DECREASING, OR
SHOWING NO CHANGE IN THE NUMBER OF STYLES USED FROM
PRE-TEST TO POST-TEST MCT

Group	Increase	No Change	Decrease
CT-CT	67	33	—
NT-CT	50	50	—
CT-AT	27	18	55
NT-AT	60	20	20
CT-NT	44	22	33
NT-NT	50	30	20

help focus the child on commonalities which is a necessity for classification. But the magnitude of the contribution is limited.

The MCT responses also allow for analysis of *number* of styles of categorization used as well as type of styles employed. Each of these sets of results will now be discussed.

Table 8 presents the results of the *change* in number of styles used. From Table 8 it is evident that the groups who received classification training once within the time confines of this study, 1966-67 or 1967-68, tended to produce more alternative ways of grouping than those who have *never* received any classification training. Sixty-nine percent of the children receiving classification training used more than three criteria for building classes as compared to 30% for the non-trained group.

This is the state of affairs prior to the second round of training but of significance of itself. It does show one type of long-term gain.

The groups that produce the highest percentage of 3 or more responses are those who received classification training during this year or last (CT-CT, NT-CT, CT-NT). The NT-AT and one CT-AT group ranked next with 60 and 55% of the children respectively using more than three grouping responses. The group receiving no training was equally divided 50% less than 3; 50% more than 3.

It is of interest to note that for most groups there was a tendency to increase in the number of styles used. No doubt experience in school and increased skill in verbalizations influence all groups, e.g. the group not trained in either year showed an increase of 40% of the children providing 3 or more styles. The significant index of change is the percentage of children who gave 2 or less styles. The fact that the groups who received only CT experience a year ago still maintained their capability of using varied styles attests to the potency of this type of training. This is particularly the case when one examines the effects of AT, either alone or subsequent to CT. In both cases AT negatively influences openness of classification.

Further support for the "narrowing" effect of attention training as well as the potency of classification training as a review or a new experience can be seen from inspection of individual changes depicted on Table 8. It is interesting to note that only for the CT-CT and NT-CT groups, not a single child decreased in the number of styles used, whereas some such decreases are found for each of the other groups. Note the particularly large number of children decreasing in the CT-AT group.

Thus, it can be concluded that the stable long-term result of classification training is the continued ability to utilize a variety of classification approaches.

Table 9 contains the percentages of children using the various style categories, i.e. form, color, structure, relational and categorical. As can be noted from that table, changes in styles appear for each group but these changes are not systematic. This may well be due to the fact that neither of our training programs emphasizes any particular style, rather a variety of criteria was accepted, thereby allowing the children to employ their own preferences. What these results may represent is, in fact, an increased opportunity and "know-how" for children to express their own preferences in grouping responses as well as increase their repertoire of responses. The fact that color responses, in particular, persist does raise a question of the maturity level of these children since it was found that privileged children tend to decrease in their use of color at age six (Bearison & Sigel, 1968). Aside from this, our results do indicate capability of the children to group and perhaps to have attained increased understanding of the methodology of classification and flexibility in choosing criteria.

Analytic Ability and Verbal IQ: Two tasks were included as measures of analytic ability—the Block Design and the Geometric Design, sub-

TABLE 9

PERCENTAGE OF SUBJECTS PER GROUP USING EACH STYLE CATEGORY ON
THE PRE-TEST AND POST-TEST MULTIPLE CATEGORIZATION TEST

Style	CT-CT	NT-CT	CT-AT	NT-AT	CT-NT	NT-NT
			Pre-Test Group			
Form	33	50	55	50	44	20
Color	67	40	82	40	67	60
Structure	44	40	64	20	33	20
Relational	33	40	55	40	100	30
Categorical	89	60	73	60	89	30
			Post-Test Group			
Style	CT-CT	NT-CT	CT-AT	NT-AT	CT-NT	NT-NT
Form	67	50	36	40	67	40
Color	89	70	91	70	78	80
Structure	56	60	73	50	56	40
Relational	67	90	36	60	56	40
Categorical	89	50	64	70	89	50
			Change			
Style	CT-CT	NT-CT	CT-AT	NT-AT	CT-NT	NT-NT
Form	+34	—	—19	—10	+23	+20
Color	+22	+30	+9	+30	+11	+20
Structure	+12	+20	+9	+30	+23	—
Relational	+34	+50	+18	+20	+44	+10
Categorical	—	—10	—9	+10	—	+20

tests of the Wechsler Preschool and Primary Scale of Intelligence (WPPSI). The IQ measure used was the Peabody Picture Vocabulary Test.

The results of the post-testing showed that all groups increased significantly irrespective of training status in Block Design Test performance. Apparently, just increasing age and consequent experience seems to make for the difference.

Turning now to the Geometric Design Task, we find that those groups receiving training of either type in 1967-68 regardless of previous training showed a significant change (See Table 10).

TABLE 10

MEANS AND STANDARD DEVIATIONS OF RAW SCORES FOR PRE-TEST, POST-TEST, AND PRE-POST-TEST CHANGE FOR THE SUBJECTS IN EACH GROUP ON GEOMETRIC DESIGN TEST*

Group	N	Pre-Test X	Pre-Test SD	Post-Test X	Post-Test SD	Pre-Post-Test Change X	Pre-Post-Test Change SD
CT-CT	9	9.4	5.5	15.9	4.9	6.5	3.8
NT-CT	10	11.9	4.0	16.8	4.1	4.9	5.4
CT-AT	11	10.5	2.8	15.1	3.3	4.6	3.6
NT-AT	10	13.7	6.1	17.8	4.1	4.1	4.3
CT-NT	9	14.8	4.8	14.3	4.6	—0.5	5.3
NT-NT	10	13.8	6.2	14.7	5.4	0.9	3.3

t VALUES OF PRE-POST-TEST CHANGE FOR EACH GROUP

Group	t	p
CT-CT	4.93	<.001
NT-CT	2.86	< .01
CT-AT	4.18	<.001
NT-AT	3.03	< .01
CT-NT	0.25	N.S.
NT-NT	0.87	N.S.

* Raw scores were used in the analysis as the ages of the subjects at the time of post-testing were not covered in the scaled score conversion charts given in the WPPSI manual.

TABLE 11

MEANS AND STANDARD DEVIATIONS OF INTELLIGENCE QUOTIENTS ON THE PEABODY PICTURE VOCABULARY TEST FOR EACH EXPERIMENTAL CONDITION

Group	N	X	SD
CT-CT	9	84.8	8.8
NT-CT	10	86.1	8.2
CT-AT	11	89.6	10.2
NT-AT	10	90.3	8.9
CT-NT	9	88.0	13.3
NT-NT	10	82.4	11.1

It was hypothesized that the AT groups should do significantly better than the CT groups since the former focused on detail and analysis more systematically than the latter. This hypothesis was not substantiated.

Peabody Picture Vocabulary Test reveals no difference among each of the six groups. Since this test was administered only as a post-test, we cannot assess whether gains were made. But it is of considerable interest

TABLE 12

MEANS AND STANDARD DEVIATIONS OF LOG TIME FOR EACH TRIAL OF
THE PRE-TEST AND POST-TEST IMPULSIVITY TEST FOR EACH GROUP

Group	Pre-Test Trial 1		Pre-Test Trial 2		Pre-Test Trial 1		Pre-Test Trial 2	
	X	SD	X	SD	X	SD	X	SD
CT-CT	1.32	0.29	1.26	0.30	1.44	0.24	1.40	0.26
NT-CT	1.16	0.32	1.16	0.25	1.38	0.29	1.36	0.22
CT-AT	1.14	0.29	1.24	0.28	1.08	0.34	1.19	0.52
NT-AT	1.12	0.22	1.09	0.25	1.08	0.34	1.19	0.28
CT-NT	1.08	0.24	1.01	0.28	1.33	0.19	1.35	0.28
NT-NT	1.14	0.20	1.19	0.35	1.19	0.31	1.02	0.30
					1.09	0.28	1.09	0.31

t VALUES OF CHANGE BETWEEN PRE-TEST AND POST-TEST FOR
TRIAL 1 AND TRIAL 2

Group	Trial 1		Trial 2	
CT-CT	1.68	N.S.	2.14	$< .05$
NT-CT	2.14	$< .05$	4.14	$< .005$
CT-AT	—1.00	N.S.	—0.38	N.S.
NT-AT	2.74	$< .025$	3.40	$< .005$
CT-NT	1.24	N.S.	0.10	N.S.
NT-NT	—0.76	N.S.	—0.62	N.S.

to note that differences among the groups in their other cognitive abilities cannot be attributed to differences in IQ. (See Table 11).

Impulsivity: It was hypothesized that AT would influence impulse control more than CT since AT contains training in scanning which is assumed to require delay in responding. CT also encourages scanning behavior but does not articulate such behaviors as a prerequisite to responding.

The results are presented in Table 12 separately for Trials 1 and 2. Two trials are used in order to assure reliability. However, it was found that there was only a moderate correlation for performance on the two trials. The correlation between trials for the groups trained in 1966-67 was .27 (N.S.) for the non-trained was .72 (p < .01). This lack of consistency was surprising since middle-class children tend to be highly consistent from Trial 1 to Trial 2 (r = .89, Sigel, unpublished data).

The lack of relationship between the two trials may be due to a variety of factors, e.g., the child's comprehension of the task, willingness, and ability to comply. Consequently, pre-post measures were done separately for each trial. Using separate analysis for each trial and comparing such results would allow for examination of consistency.

In Table 12, the pre-post results are presented for each trial showing where increase in impulse control was found. Significant changes are found for Trial 1, for NT-CT, NT-AT, the two groups trained only this year. This result tends to be a rejection of the hypothesis that AT would be superior. In Trial 2, significant changes are found for these two groups and, in addition, for the CT-CT group. Thus, particular training does not seem to have any effect.

We continue to be perplexed by the CT-AT results since at least for this measure there is every reason to expect significant changes which are not found. Whether this is a function of a sampling error or is a reflection of the redundancy rationale discussed earlier, is hard to say. Of course, there is the chance that in this case the results are a function of AT cancelling out CT experience by making a contradiction and hence conflict in the child. This conflict between the openness of CT experience followed by the closedness of AT training may well have immobilized him. Once again, further study of this issue is needed.

Logical Operations: Each child, it will be recalled received three Piagetian type tasks of logical operations, i.e., *multiple classification, multiple seriation,* and *reversibility.*

The question raised here is whether either of these training procedures would effect the children's performance on these cognitive tasks. This is a partial replication of the Shantz & Sigel study (1967). Inspection of Table 13 reveals that overall, the training is not effective in improving these skills. These results are consistent with those found by Shantz & Sigel (1967).

The performance of the children on each of these tasks is not consistent. Success on pre-test does not necessarily predict the success on post-testing. The instability may be due to the unreliability of the measure, or the tentativeness with which these children deal with these type problems.

Of all the tasks, reversibility was the easiest—with 61% of all children passing in both pre and post in contrast to 8.5% and 5.1% passing multiple seriation and multiple classification respectively. In fact, multiple classification and multiple seriation appear to be of equal difficulty (32.2% succeed in pre and post multiple classification and 39% succeed

TABLE 13

DISTRIBUTION OF THE SUBJECTS IN EACH EXPERIMENTAL CONDITION ON
THE LOGICAL OPERATIONS FOR PRE- AND POST-TESTING

MULTIPLE CLASSIFICATION

Tests Passed	Group CT-CT	NT-CT	CT-AT	NT-AT	CT-NT	NT-NT	Total N	%
Neither	7	6	9	6	4	8	40	67.8
Pre-Test only	1	2	2	—	—	1	6	10.2—Δ
Post-Test only	—	2	—	4	4	—	10	16.9+Δ
Both	1	—	—	—	1	1	3	5.1 No Δ
Total	9	10	11	10	9	10	59	100.0

Net Change
Pre-Test to
Post-Test

	CT-CT	NT-CT	CT-AT	NT-AT	CT-NT	NT-NT	Total
	—1	—	—2	+4	+4	—1	+4

MULTIPLE SERIATION

Tests Passed	Group CT-CT	NT-CT	CT-AT	NT-AT	CT-NT	NT-NT	Total N	%
Neither	8	5	9	3	5	6	36	61.0
Pre-Test only	—	2	2	2	2	—	8	13.6—Δ
Post-Test only	1	1	—	4	1	3	10	16.9+Δ
Both	—	2	—	1	1	1	5	8.5 No Δ
Total	9	10	11	10	9	10	59	100.0

Net Change
Pre-test to
Post-Test

	CT-CT	NT-CT	CT-AT	NT-AT	CT-NT	NT-NT	Total
	+1	—1	—2	+2	—1	+2	+1

REVERSIBILITY

Tests Passed	Group CT-CT	NT-CT	CT-AT	NT-AT	CT-NT	NT-NT	Total N	%
Neither	1	—	3	—	—	1	5	8.5
Pre-Test only	1	—	—	2	1	—	4	6.8—Δ
Post-Test only	1	5	1	2	2	3	14	23.7+Δ
Both	6	5	7	6	6	6	36	61.0 No Δ
Total	9	10	11	10	9	10	59	100.0

Net Change
Pre-Test to
Post-Test

	CT-CT	NT-CT	CT-AT	NT-AT	CT-NT	NT-NT	Total
	—	+5	+1	—	+1	+3	+10

in pre and post multiple seriation). Changes from pre to post are highest for reversibility, 23.7%, whereas for the other two operations 16.9% of the children change. Percentages increasing or decreasing in the success for each of these two operations are virtually equal. No systematic change is attributable to particular training conditions.

TABLE 14

DISTRIBUTION OF THE SUBJECTS IN EACH EXPERIMENTAL CONDITION ON
THE CONSERVATION TASKS FOR PRE- AND POST-TESTING*

NUMBER CONSERVATION

Tests Passed	Group						Total	
	CT-CT	NT-CT	CT-AT	NT-AT	CT-NT	NT-NT	N	%
Neither	8	9	9	6	9	7	48	81.3
Pre-Test only	1	—	1	—	—	2	4	6.8—Δ
Post-Test only	—	1	1	3	—	1	6	10.2+Δ
Both	—	—	—	1	—	—	1	1.7 No Δ
Total	9	10	11	10	9	10	59	100.0
Net Change Pre-Test to Post-Test	—1	+1	—	+3	—	—1	+2	

QUANTITY CONSERVATION

Tests Passed	Group						Total	
	CT-CT	NT-CT	CT-AT	NT-AT	CT-NT	NT-NT	N	%
Neither	9	10	11	6	9	10	55	93.2
Pre-Test only	—	—	—	1	—	—	1	1.7—Δ
Post-Test only	—	—	—	3	—	—	3	5.1+Δ
Both	—	—	—	—	—	—	—	—No Δ
Total	9	10	11	10	9	10	59	100.0
Net Change Pre-Test to Post-Test	—	—	—	+2	—	—	+2	

* The total number of children passing the number conservation pre-test is obtained by combining the number passing the pre-test only and the number passing both pre-test and post-test. (4 + 1 = 5 or 6.8% + 1.7% = 8.5%) This same procedure should be followed in comparable situations.

These results with lower-class black children are consistent with the Shantz and Sigel results as far as change in performance on multiple seriation and multiple classification are concerned. The difference between these two studies is in the percentage of children able to cope with these tasks.

In the Shantz & Sigel study of middle-class 5 year olds, many were able to solve each of these problems—while for this population the performance is considerably inferior. It can be concluded that the training in attention and in classification does not have any direct effect on reversibility, matrix-type classification problems, and multiple seriation.

Effects of Training in Conservation: It was hypothesized that classification and attention training would have equal effects in facilitating solution of conservation problems, similar to the results reported by Shantz & Sigel (1967).

Table 14 presents the results of performance on the conservation tasks. On the pre-test, only 8.5% of the children could conserve number and 1.7% could conserve quantity. These results are not very dramatic, when it is noted that 81.3% could *not* conserve number and 93.2% could *not* conserve quantity either before or after training. These results cannot be attributed to a lack of understanding of concept like more, same, or less since tests for this were administered. *All* children passed this test.

Where change, and this is not statistically significant, did occur was for groups receiving attention training. It may well be that aiding children in attending might facilitate acquisition of conservation, but perhaps longer training is needed.

It is important to point out that the difficulties these first-grade children have (both at the beginning and at the end of first grade) in not being able to conserve number and/or mass, reveals the seriousness of their cognitive deficit, especially if the criterion used is our data from middle-class whites. It is worth pointing out that among 5 year old white middle-class children, conservation of number and mass are soluble. Of the 75 children tested in the Shantz & Sigel study, approximately 50% could conserve in these areas without training and after a nine-session training program, 68% of the previous non-conservers could then conserve. For the lower-class population, however, the situation is dramatically different; very few conservers are found at age 6.

SUMMARY OF CONCLUSIONS

The purposes of this study were: (1) to examine the effects of classification skills a year after a one-month training program was completed; (2) to assess the effects of re-introducing classification training as compared to introducing training in discrimination, scanning, and generalization; (3) to test the efficiency of classification training at two age levels. The dependent variables are categorization skills, IQ, analytic skills, logical operations (multiple seriation, reversibility, multiple classification), and conservation. The rationale for expecting the training to have differential effects is based on previous studies (Shantz & Sigel, 1967; Sigel & Olmsted, 1967; Sigel, Roeper, Hooper, 1967).

Children involved in the 1966-67 program were identified and of the original group 69 were found and pre-tested; then 59 of these were placed in one of six groups, thereby providing for control and experimental groups. Assignments were made on the basis of previous roles in the 1966-67 study so that adequate representation for each of the necessary conditions was possible.

Training sessions in classification and in attention were developed—a total of ten sessions for each type of training.

As for pre-test results, (1) all children irrespective of training continued to show discrepancy in responses to objects and pictures; (2) children having had previous training in classification did not differ from their controls eight months later in giving single grouping responses; (3) children having been trained, however, were superior to the controls in being able to produce multiple responses when instructed to do so; (4) trained children were more able to use more varied criteria in classification.

Post-training results showed: (1) children receiving booster classification training showed a significant increase in grouping responses as did children receiving classification and attention training for the first time, while the remaining three groups showed no significant change in group responses; (2) all new training did affect analytic performance as measured by the Geometric Design Test (WPPSI); (3) new training regardless of type did seem to increase impulse control (motor inhibition); (4) training did not affect performance in logical operation and conservation.

CONCLUSIONS AND IMPLICATIONS

The results of this study demonstrate the value of classification training vis-a-vis subsequent classification behavior. However, contrary to expectation, such achievements did not have the transfer effects predicted.

The effectiveness of this training is, however, not just on the contemporary scene, but also has some long-term effect. It is interesting to have found some long-term gains in spite of the short-term training periods in 1966-67 and in spite of the fact that there is little likelihood of the first-grade experience reinforcing the training. One wonders what might have happened had the school curriculum incorporated our training program and built upon it.

From the theoretical point of view many unresolved issues remain, e.g., the Object-Picture discrepancy, the difficulty in conservation, etc. Why these phenomena exist will have to await further study. At least as far as is known now, these lower-class black children do show different patterns of cognitive functioning than their middle-class counterparts. There is still need to map out the cognitive functions of these children to ascertain the similarities and differences with their privileged peers. This is on the assumption, of course, that privileged status yields, in general terms, more efficient and effective cognitive behavior. For example, why did classification training have no effect on conservation for children in this study when it has been shown on three different occasions with middle-class children that this is the case. The children in this study have IQ's which are in the low "normal" end of the distribution and should, therefore, have made the necessary gains—assuming IQ is relevant of course.

The considerable variability of these children indicate that they are not of the same cloth in spite of commonality in economic and social position. There is much to be done in deepening our knowledge of them, and we have but scratched the surface.

In sum, we believe that the training programs do have educational heuristic value. At the same time, however, we must not feel smug, rather there is much research to be done identifying in more specific terms the causative basis for the kind of cognitive behavior we found. Armed with such data and given increased flexibility of public schools in incorporating the new knowledge, the cognitive competence necessary for maximizing educational opportunities can be brought about. The joint efforts of research and educational practice are, in our estimation, the necessary and sufficient conditions needed to create the long overdue change in educational level of impoverished children.

REFERENCES

BEARISON, DAVID J., & SIGEL, I. E. Study of hierarchial attributes for categorization. *Journal of Perceptual and Motor Skills,* 1968, 27, 147-153.

GELMAN, R. Conservation acquisition: A problem of learning to attend to relevant attributes. *Journal of Experimental Child Psychology,* 1969, 7, 167-187.

SHANTZ, CAROLYN U., & SIGEL, I. E. Logical operations and concepts of conservation in children: A training study. OE Report, Project No. 6-8463, June, 1967.

SIGEL, I. E. Developmental trends in the abstraction ability of children. *Child Development,* 1953, 24, (2), 131-144.

SIGEL, I. E., & McBANE, BONNIE. Cognitive competence and level of symbolization among five-year-old children. In J. Hellmuth (Ed.) *The Disadvantaged Child,* Vol. 1. New York, New York, Brunner/Mazel, Inc., 1967, 435-453.

SIGEL, I. E. & OLMSTED, PATRICIA. Styles of categorization among lower-class kindergarten children. Paper presented at the American Educational Research Association Annual Meeting, New York, New York, 1967.

SIGEL, I. E. & OLMSTED, PATRICIA. Modification of classificatory competence and level of representation among lower-class Negro children. In Passow, H. Reaching the Disadvantaged Learner. New York, Columbia University Teacher's College, 1970.

SIGEL, I. E., ROEPER, ANNEMARIE, & HOOPER, F. H. A training procedure for acquisition of Piaget's conservation of quantity: A pilot study and its replication. *British Journal of Educational Psychology,* 1966, 36, 301-311.

WITKIN, H. A., DYK, R. B., FATERSON, H. F., GOODENOUGH, D. R., & KARP, S. A. *Psychological Differentiation.* New York: Wiley, 1962.

ZEAMAN, D., & HOUSE, B. J. An attention theory of retardate discrimination learning. In N. R. Ellis (Ed.), *Handbook of Mental Deficiency.* New York: McGraw-Hill, 1963, 159-223.

APPENDIX A

STYLES OF CATEGORIZATION

All scorable (grouping and nongrouping) responses of the child are scored in one of the three following categories:

1) *Descriptive*

form —The use of measurement or shape properties, such as round, flat, long, small, fat, corners, is scored as a form response: e.g., "they are all long."

color —Use of a color label, as saying "same color" is scored as a color response.

structure —Designation of specific intrinsic or inherent parts or properties such as metal, wood, having writing on them; having similar parts like handles, knobs, points, etc., is a structure response.

2) *Relational Contextual*

functional —When the action of the functional-relation takes place directly between the items in a given sort, then the response is recorded as relational-functional: e.g., "light the cigarette with the matches."

Also, functions taking place between a person and single items in a given sort are scored as relational-functional: e.g., "write with the pencil and smoke the cigarette."

thematic —When the action between two or more items in a given sort takes place on an imported item, then the response is recorded as relational-thematic: e.g. "open the pop with the bottle opener and drink it out of the cup."

Also coded as thematic are those responses in which the objects are related in story sequence but their function is not otherwise interrelated: e.g., "smoke the cigarette while you drink a cup of coffee."

Thematic responses can also occur with single items: e.g., "you get up in the morning and drink juice in the cup," when the items are the cup, the crayons, and the pencil.

contextual —Responses in which objects are grouped because they are found in the same location, or belong to the same person are scored contextual: e.g., "my daddy has those," or "they are in the kitchen."

Contextual responses can also occur with single items: e.g., "this goes in the kitchen," when the items are the bottle opener and the top and child points to BO.

3) *Categorical*

low functional —*One* object or picture is related to the stimulus because both are used for the same purpose: e.g., "you write with them," or "you play with them," or inferred action properties such as rolling or spinning.

high	—*Two or more* objects or pictures are chosen to go with the stimu-
functional	lus because all are used for the same purpose or inferred action
	properties such as rolling or spinning.
class	—One term is used to define two or more items included in the
label	class: e.g., "toys," or "kitchen things," or "writing things."

This response can also be used with single items: e.g., "this ($\rightarrow$T) is a toy," when the objects are the top and the bottle opener.

All nonscorable responses are scored as having no classification ("None" on the score sheet.)

APPENDIX B

Sample of Categorization Training Procedures

SESSION 1

MATERIALS: Red and yellow large circles, squares and triangles
Red and yellow small circles and squares.

GENERAL PROCEDURE:

1. Sorting 4 pieces of cardboard two ways
   a. Introduce large red and large yellow circles and squares individually, discussing the attributes of each (i.e. color and form) with all the children.
   b. Ask Child #1 to put the pieces of cardboard (all four) into two piles. Each pile must be the *same* in *one* way.
   c. Ask Child #2 to give the reason for the first sort. (This may be in the form of a dialogue between the two children.)
   d. Ask Child #3 to put the pieces into two piles a *different* way, so that each pile is still the *same* in *one* way.
   e. Ask Child #4 to state why these piles are the same.
   f. Review the two sorts by the children to recall the ways in which the piles were the same.
2. Sorting 6 pieces of cardboard three ways
   a. Introduce large red and yellow triangles along with pieces from the first sort. Point out the straight edges and corners on the squares and triangles.
   b. Ask Child #2 to make a sort into 2 piles, have Child #1 explain. Repeat with all three sorts using different children to sort and explain.
   c. Possible sorts:
      1) color—2 piles
      2) form—3 piles
      3) form—2 piles—corners or straight edges vs. circles.
3. Sorting 8 pieces of cardboard three ways—1 dimension
   a. Introduce red and yellow, large and small circles and squares *without* discussing the new dimension of size.
   b. Ask a child to make a sort on one dimension using all of the pieces and making 2 piles. Have another child explain. Repeat for all possible sorts.
   c. Possible sorts
      1) color—2 piles
      2) form—2 piles
      3) size—2 piles

d. Have a short discussion with all of the children concerning size.

e. Review the sorts by having the children recall.

4. Sorting 8 pieces of cardboard 3 ways—2 dimensions

   a. Use the same pieces as in Sort 3.

   b. Ask a child to make a sort on a multidimensional basis using all of the pieces but putting them into 4 piles so that each pile is the *same* in *two* ways.

   c. Ask another child to explain the reason for the sort. Repeat with different children until all of the sorts have been made.

   d. Possible sorts

      1) color and size

      2) size and form

      3) color and form

   e. Short review.

5. Sorting 4 pieces of cardboard 3 ways

   a. Introduce large, red circle; large, yellow square; small, red square; and small, yellow circle.

   b., Ask a child to sort all of the pieces into 2 piles (one dimensional basis) so that each pile is the same.

   c. Have another child explain the sort. Repeat with different children until all the sorts have been made.

   d. Possible sorts

      1) color—L,R O and S,R □; L,Y. □ and S,Y O—2 piles

      2) form—L,Y □ and S,R □; L,R O and S,Y O—2 piles

      3) size—L,R O and L,Y □; S,R □ and S,Y O—2 piles

   e. If children only sort 2 ways, review the three attributes by recall and show them the two that they have used. Try to have the children figure out the missing sort by asking them to recall the ways they have sorted before.

SESSION 2

MATERIALS: Pair of shoes, shirt, tie, pair of gloves, watch, belt, socks

GENERAL PROCEDURE:

(avoid straight descriptive responses as much as possible)

1. Present *shirt*

   a. Identify—"Tell me about this."

      1) What can we do with it?   (Wear it)

      2) What is it made of?   (Cloth)

      3) Where does it come from?   (Store)

      4) Who uses this?   (Boy or girl)

   b. Compare it with shirts of the subjects noting similarities and differences.

   c. Class label of *Clothing*

      1) I have a new word for things like shirts that you wear. It's CLOTHING.

      2) Have children repeat the word.

      3) Clothing, now what does it mean?

2. Present *tie*

   a. Identify with open-ended question used above.

   b. Compare shirt and tie. (Note: do not use color.)

      1) Both cloth

      2) Wear both of them

      3) Both for boys

      4) Buy both of them in a store

      5) Wear on what part of the body

c. Establish that they are both pieces of clothing but at the same time, they are different kinds.
3. Present *watch*
   a. Identify with open-ended question.
   b. Compare same as above.
4. Present *belt*
   a. Identify
   b. Compare.

SESSION 3

MATERIALS: 5 trucks, 1 bus, 1 motorcycle, 1 big car, 3 small cars, 2 sailboats, 2 canoes, 4 big airplanes, 2 helicopters, 2 small planes, 1 stagecoach, 1 racing car

GENERAL PROCEDURE:

1. Place in center of table enough different kinds of vehicles so that there is one kind for each child. (Example: 1 truck, 1 plane, 1 car, 1 boat, 1 bus, etc.) For the groups of four children, have two vehicles for each child.
2. Have one child select one of the vehicles and identify it.
   a. (Name) pick up one of these things from this pile and tell us about it.
   b. Can you tell us what it does? Can you think of other kinds?
   c. Deal with the leftover objects in a group. . . . Who can tell me about this? . . . What does it do?
   d. Establish the use of the class label—vehicle.
      1) I'm going to tell you a new word for all of these things. That word is VEHICLES.
      2) Have the children repeat the word.
      3) Explain how this word is for all means of transportation and this includes things that carry people and loads of things.
3. Discuss the different attributes of the vehicles by making piles.
   a. Have one child put his vehicle in the center of the table.
   b. Question: Everyone who has a vehicle that does the same thing as this put it with the one on the table. What do they all do?
   c. For the leftover objects, have the children do it in a group.
   d. Piles:
      1) Function—things that fly, things that you drive, things that float—3 piles
      2) Location of use—ground, air, water—3 piles
      3) Material made from—plastic, metal, both—2 piles, then 1 pile
      4) One that carry people, ones that carry load of something, ones that do both —2 piles, then 1 pile
4. Discuss the differences of the vehicles in several groupings by asking how they are the same and how they are different.
   a. *E* makes the piles one at a time.
   b. Piles:
      1) Things that you drive.
      2) Things that you fly.
      3) Things that float.
   c. Emphasize that while they are different kinds of things they are all vehicles.
5. Class Inclusion
   a. Use 2 trucks, 1 plane, 3 cars.

b. Are there more trucks or vehicles?

c. Are there more cars, or things that go on the ground?

SESSION 4

MATERIALS: 4 large planes, 2 small planes, 2 helicopters; 1 large car, 3 small cars, 1 racing car; 5 trucks

GENERAL PROCEDURE:

1. Review Session #3—"Remember yesterday we talked about all kinds of things we called vehicles. What did we say about them?"
2. Today we are going to talk about some of the same vehicles, (Make sure they understand the word *vehicle*.)
3. Use the 8 planes
   a. Have one child give the common function for all 8 planes—They all fly.
   b. How are they different?
      1) Different kinds of planes—jets, helicopters, propellor (short discussion of propellors may be necessary)
      2) Different materials—rubber, hard plastic
      3) Different colors
   c. Establish that each can be a plane yet they are different kinds.
4. Use 5 cars
   a. Function—you drive them all.
   b. Differences
      1) Convertibles, station wagons, regular (sedans)
      2) Metal, plastic
      3) Colors
   c. Establish kinds with the class of cars.

APPENDIX C

SESSION 1: Safari

MATERIALS: *Original Jungle Contents*

Zebra	Motorcycle	Box 2
Pan	Jet	2 Moose: 1 green, 1 brown
House	Bus	2 Buffalo: 1 green, 1 grey
Baby	Car	2 Bears: 2 bronze
Fork	Soldier	3 Camels: 3 grey
		3 Hippos: 1 blue, 2 brown
Box 3		4 Elephants: 3 green, 1 black
4 Camels	6 Lions	4 Rhinos: 3 grey, 1 dark
7 Bears	9 Hippos	6 Gorillas: 6 dark
12 Moose	2 Rhinos	6 Lions: 2 grey, 4 dark
5 Gorillas	2 Giraffes	
5 Buffalo	8 Elephants	

PROCEDURE: 1. Explanation and Demonstration

a) "Do you know what a Safari is?" (If not, explain.) "A Safari is an animal hunt."

b) "Today we are going on a Safari. We are going into the jungle to hunt for animals to put into the zoo. (Place box on table.) Here is your jungle. After you catch the animals you have to put them in a cage or they will run away. Here is a cage." (Place cage in front of child

c) "I am going to put an animal in your cage. The animal will be all alone. You are the hunter. You go into the jungle to look for an animal like the one in your cage. When you catch him, put him in your cage too. Then you will have two animals that are just the same."

d) "Then we will put the animals in the zoo. (Place large cage on table.) Here is the zoo."

1. Continue with Trials 2 through 15.

3. (Add animals from Box 2 to the jungle.) "Now we are going to do something different. I'm going to put an animal into your cage and you go into the jungle and look for *all* the animals that are just like that one and put them in the big zoo. (Continue with Trials 16 through 19.)

4. (Add animals in Box 3 and animals in zoo to the jungle.) "Now I'm going to give you two animals in your cage and you have to find all the animals that are like both of them". (Trials 20 through 21.) (Note what strategy the child uses to find the animals, i.e., does he look for both at the same time or does he do one first and then the other.)

ERRORS: When the child makes an error in finding the correct animal, E should question him as to the similarity between the stimulus animal and the one he found. (Usually just the question "are these two the same?" is sufficient to elicit the correction of the error.)

PROCEDURE GUIDE:

1. | Trial | Put into Jungle | Take Out | Give Child |
|---|---|---|---|
| 1. | Blue Rhino | **** | Zebra |
| 2. | Olive Lion | Pan | Grey Rhino |
| 3. | Brown Bear | House | Grey Lion |
| | Blue Rhino | | |
| 4. | Black Camel | Baby | Grey Bear |
| | Olive Lion | | |
| 5. | Grey Moose | Fork | Grey Camel |
| | Brown Bear | | |
| 6. | Blue Elephant | Motorcycle | Grey Moose |
| | Black Camel | | |
| 7. | Olive Hippo | Jet | Grey Elephant |
| | Grey Moose | | |
| 8. | Grey Gorilla | Bus | Grey Hippo |
| | Blue Elephant | | |
| 9. | Brown Giraffe | Car | Grey Gorilla |
| | Olive Hippo | | |
| 10. | Black Buffalo | Soldier | Grey Giraffe |
| | Grey Gorilla | | |
| 11. | Brown Giraffe | **** | Grey Buffalo |
| 12. | Black Buffalo | **** | Grey Rhino |
| 13. | Blue Rhino | **** | Grey Lion |
| 14. | Green Lion | **** | Grey Bear |
| 15. | Brown Bear | **** | Grey Camel |

	2. *Trial*	*Put into Jungle*	*Take Out*	*Give Child*
	16.	Animals in Box 2	****	Grey Elephant
	17.	****	****	Grey Moose
	18.	****	****	Grey Gorilla
	19.	****	****	Green Hippo
3.	20.	Animals in Box 3	****	Grey Lion
				Dark Bear
	21.	****	****	Dark Camel
				Dark Buffalo

SESSION 3: Picture Card Game

MATERIALS: (1) Two brown elephants, one blue elephant, one blue hippo. One black, fifty gram weight
(2) Two Milton Bradley Memory Card Matching Games (arranged in special sequence)

PROCEDURE:

1. Introduction
   (To find out the child's understanding of 'same" ask:)
   "What do we mean if we say things are the same?"
   (If child seems to understand "same", continue to ask about "different", "identi-cal", and "similar"; if not, explain these as follows:)
   "If two things are the same, they can be *completely alike* or they can be *partly alike*. If they are *completely alike* we say they are *"identical."* If they are only *partly alike* we say they are *"Similar."* If things are *not alike* we say they are *"Different."*
   (Discuss these terms and let child repeat them a few times. Then, using the objects, do the following:)
   (Show two blue elephants.) "Are these two the same? These two elephants are the same because they are *completely alike*. They are both elephants and they are both the same color. If things are completely alike, what do we call them? (Wait for a response.) If things are *completely alike*, if they are alike in every way, we call them *IDENTICAL."*
   (Show the blue and the brown elephants.) "Are these two the same? These two elephants are the same because they are *partly alike*. They are both elephants but they are *not completely alike*. There is something that is not the same about them. What is it? (Wait for a response.) They are different colors. One is blue and one is. . . . If things are *partly alike,* they are not the same in *every* way. They are only the same in *some* ways. We call these things *SIMILAR*. They are not IDENTICAL."
   (Show blue elephant and blue hippo.) "Are these two the same? These two ani-mals are the same because they are *partly alike*. They are *SIMILAR*. Why are they similar? (Wait for response.) They are both the same color, they are blue. Are they identical? No, they are not identical, they are *SIMILAR*."
   (Show brown elephant and blue hippo.) "Are these two the same? These two animals are not the same. They are different colors and they are different animals. Is there any way that they are alike?" (Establish that they are both animals.)
   (Show brown elephant and black weight.) "Are these two the same? These two things are not the same. They are different colors and different things. We call them completely *DIFFERENT."*

2. Use of comparison terms with pairs of pictures

"Look at this card. It is a picture of a butterfly. Now look at this other card. What can you tell me about these two cards? . . . That's right, they are IDENTICAL. Now, look at this card. (Show Card #2—a tree, placing it on top of and covering one of the butterflies.) Is this one (Card #2) identical to this one (Card #1)? No, they are not identical. They are different."

"I am going to show you some cards, two at a time. Each time I show you some new ones, you tell me if they are IDENTICAL, SIMILAR, or DIFFERENT."

(Note: When you get to Trial 13, you will find two examples of the same class, i.e., flowers. If the child says they are different, ask him what is different about them. Bring out the idea that they are SIMILAR because they are flowers, but that they are not the same kind of flower. If he says that they are the same, find out why and show how they are different kinds of flowers. Point out that they are SIMILAR because they are both flowers.)

3. "Look at this card. It is a picture of a ball. I have two more pictures here. When I show them to you, I want you to pick the one that's IDENTICAL to this one." (Turn the other cards over.) "O.K., now find the one that's IDENTICAL to this one."

"Now, look at this card. It is a picture of a boat. I'm going to show you two more pictures and I want you to pick the one that is IDENTICAL to this one." (If they have trouble with IDENTICAL go over the meaning of IDENTICAL, SIMILAR, and DIFFERENT again.)

"Now we are going to look at some more pictures. Every time I am going to show you one card first and then two more. I want you to pick the card that is IDENTICAL to the one up here. (In many cases the other choice is similar but not identical to the sample and if the child picks this one, discuss his choice and how it is only partly like the sample card, i.e., similar and not identical.)

4. "This time I'm going to show you three cards to pick from and I want you to find the one that's IDENTICAL to the one I put up here. (Here again, in many cases, one alternative is similar but not identical to the sample card. Proceed as above.)

5. "Now we are going to do something different. I'm going to show you four cards and I want you to pick the two that are IDENTICAL. Pick the two that are the same in every way." (Sometimes a third card is similar to either the identical pair or to the fourth card. Proceed as above.)

17

THE EFFECTIVENESS OF DIRECT INSTRUCTION ON IQ PERFORMANCE AND ACHIEVEMENT IN READING AND ARITHMETIC

Siegfried Engelmann

Senior Educational Specialist,
University of Illinois College of Education (Urbana)

INTRODUCTION

The performance of a child on an IQ test is taken by some as an indication of the child's intelligence. It is suggested that the child's performance indicates something about the child's ability to learn and retain information and skills. On the surface, this interpretation has a certain face-value appeal; however, if it is analyzed more carefully, it becomes something of an absurd position. There is no learning in the abstract. The child who is learning is always taught. He is provided with models of behavior; he is corrected if his performance is incorrect; he is reinforced for appropriate behavior. In other words, the term "learning" is not a very accurate description of what happens in a "learning situation," since the child is always being taught. Even if he is working alone, with no "teacher" present, he is still being taught by the physical environment. The physical environment provides rather clear demonstrations of what can be done and what can't.

Since there can be no learning (except in trivial, autistic instances) without teaching, we can categorically assert that if a child performs appropriately on an IQ item, he has been taught the skills needed to handle that item. This does not mean that the item on which he is tested has been presented to the child. It means, however, that he has learned the words, the operations, and concepts that would allow him to handle that item or similar items dealing with the problem (assuming that the words used in the item are within the child's repertoire). The amount of teaching that has been required for two different children to achieve a particular criterion of performance on an IQ item may vary considerably. One child may have required only a minimum of "teaching" while another child may have required a considerable amount of instruction. The performance on the item provides for no inference about the amount of teaching that has been provided; therefore, the item cannot be seriously considered as an indicator of the child's innate capacity or genetic endowment. Two six-year-old children may score correctly on the same set of IQ items. One child may have received three times the amount of instruction that the other child received. Yet, the IQ score tells us nothing about the environment. Therefore, the IQ test can in no way be a very reliable indicator of the genetic composition of these children.

It may be argued that the children who respond to an IQ test appropriately are not actually taught the skills that would lead to correct performance. Such would be an ill-conceived argument. We could test the limits to see what the child had been taught. If we were to present the same item using a foreign language, such as Pali, the chances are that the child who responded appropriately when the task was presented in English would not respond appropriately. We could therefore conclude that successful performance on the item is contingent upon an understanding of the English language. How does a child acquire an understanding of this language? He is taught. To say that he learns it begs the question. The language is not a whole. It is the sum of various meanings and operations. He does not acquire the "language" as a whole. He acquires it as he is taught it, a meaning and operation at a time.

What if we were to change the IQ item so that it involved English, but a very anfractuous English. Would the child perform on the item? Probably not, simply because he has not been taught the meanings we refer to with the revised item. On the other hand, we could construct a number of items that are similar to the original that do not involve "difficult" language, but do involve different responses. (We may require the child to produce a verbal response, in which he answers a what question, a response to a yes-no question, a pointing response, etc.) We could also change the examples used in the original item. Through these procedures, we would be able to make some kind of strong statement about what the child has been taught about the operation being tested. Again, however, it would tell us precisely nothing about the child's genetic endowment, merely about the *effective* instruction that he has received.

It may be that some children are taught analogies, for example, through very oblique teaching demonstrations. It is quite probable that the teacher demonstrations of analogies that are effective for some children would not be effective for others. Unless, however, there are precise statements about the type of instruction that has been provided to teach the operations that underlie basic analogies, it is impossible to make precise statements about the nature of the child's genetic capacity. Two children may exhibit the same successful performance on Stanford-Binet analogies; yet, they may have received rather drastically different degrees of instruction. To attempt to derive conclusions about their genetic endowment, therefore, would be something verging on the absurd.

The work that has been conducted at the University of Illinois (formerly under the direction of Carl Bereiter, and currently under the direction of Wesley Becker) was based on the simple proposition that if disadvantaged or "normal" children are taught a wide variety of concepts at a faster-than-normal rate, they will become relatively "smart." Their smartness should be reflected in both performances on IQ tests and on achievement tests that deal with the specific skills taught in the program. These measures are admittedly poor, since they do not articulate precisely what has been taught. At best, they sample, and the sampling is sometimes obscured by items that test operations that the children have been taught but involve language that may not have been taught.

Note that the goal of the program is to teach specifics. The notion of non-specific operations is rejected. An operation is applicable only to certain concrete problems. The subject must somehow be able to see that certain aspects of the problem imply a particular operation. Without this assumption, the operation would be used either universally or randomly. If it is used in a discriminated manner, there must be a basis for discrimination, which means that the operation is specific to a certain set of cues. The operation can be applied to a wide variety of situations, but the operation still remains quite specific.

Also note that the idea of long-range effects of the program is rejected as a legitimate measure of the program's effectiveness. Granted, it is quite possible, even probable, that if children who receive an intensive preschool and kindergarten instruction are tested four years later, there should be a *tendency* for the children in the experimental program to perform better than the children who received no such intensive training. However, the argument is based on the idea that all things are equal. And when we deal with questions of intellectual growth, the question becomes a very troublesome one at best. It is one thing if we mean by "all things are equal" that the children are allowed to progress from the point at which they are and are taught according to the skills that they have at any given time. The "all things are equal" means something quite different if the children, regardless of the skills that they have at the time, are put through a lockstep program, which may in fact attempt to teach skills that have been taught or skills for which adequate preparation has not been provided. One would expect that the differences between the experimental children and the controls would be lessened—either because the experimental children are being relatively held back and are not receiving the opportunity to "develop" at an accelerated rate, or because both the controls and the experimental children would have an "equally" inadequate base for performing or "developing."

The measure of the "long range" effectiveness of an approach, unfortunately, is not a clean test of the program. It is a test of the program plus a host of intervening variables. Unless the nature of these variables is clearly specified, one would be at a loss to make strong inferential statements about the effectiveness of the experimental program. The results may lead the investigator to a number of spurious conclusions, such as: "The program shows a slight tendency to be better than the traditional program. . . ." "The gains that are realized through the program do not hold up over time. . . ." These conclusions may be spurious in the sense that different programs that intervene between the termination of the experimental program and the test of long-range effectiveness may change the outcomes astronomically, even if the same program is provided for both the control and experimental children.

In short, the position is this. Children get relatively smart if you teach more than they would be expected to be taught under "normal" conditions during a given period of time. Similarly children become relatively less smart if the rate of effective instruction is slowed. When children begin to regress, it means only one thing. They are not being taught at relatively the same rate that they had been taught before. It can mean nothing else. This is not to say that all of the instruction a child receives goes on in school. But it is axiomatic that if his performance begins to slow, he is not being taught at the rate that he had been taught. No statement of the child's genetic composition or capacity is implied. This statement is strictly one about what he is taught.

As an indication of what can be done with middle-class and disadvantaged children, I refer to the disadvantaged and middle-class children who graduated from the Bereiter-Engelmann kindergarten program in 1967. In one sense, this group received the most concerted instruction of any experimental classes from 1965-1969. Our best teachers were assigned to these children. We had no trainees working with the children (the instruction of whom tends to reduce by about one-third the rate at which the children are taught). Finally, there was a concerted attempt to make sure that the lowest performing children were taught. Program improvements were introduced. These were based on the performance of the low-performing children who had graduated the preceding year. Also during the school years of 1966-1967 a continuous program of program revision was adopted, based on the difficulties the lowest performing children were having.

The hypotheses investigated were:

1) effective instruction can dramatically increase the rate at which children are taught new behaviors that are relevant both to specific achievement tests (such as reading achievement) and more general achievement tests (such as the Stanford-Binet);

2) the children will achieve gains both in the first and second year of instruction if the instruction continues to teach skills at a faster-than-expected rate. The IQ drop noted during the second year of many pre-school programs (after a 4-8 point first-year gain) is a function of poor instruction, not of the genetic capacity of the children;

3) any child can be accelerated to at least "average" if the instruction is effective.

The goal of the program was not to achieve mere statistical differences between experimental and control groups, while demonstrating no obvious differences in performance between the groups. Rather it was to achieve changes of such magnitude that there could be little doubt (statistically or otherwise) that the changes were a function of instruction. The basic goal was to bring all of the children to "average" on some of the more common measures of achievement, such as IQ measures.

METHOD

Subjects

The disadvantaged subjects for the present experiment were four-year-old culturally disadvantaged children who would be eligible for Head Start. The selection criteria were:

1) according to Warner ratings of occupations (1949) and housing ratings obtained through the City Planning Commissioner's office, subjects were from low socioeconomic homes (mean weighted S.E.S. in the low 40's);

2) subjects were four years old by December 1, in keeping with public school's entrance policies;

3) subjects did not have previous preschool experience;

4) children with gross physical handicaps and severely retarded children were excluded.

Subjects received Stanford-Binet tests and were divided into three groups—high intelligence, middle intelligence, and low intelligence. Children were assigned to the experimental and comparison classes, each class receiving the same proportion of highs, middles, and lows. Adjustments were made so that each class had approximately the same proportion of Negro-whites, and a nearly equal number of male and female subjects. Fifteen children were assigned to the experimental group and twenty-eight to the comparison group. The composition of both groups is summarized in Table 1.

In addition to the disadvantaged subjects, eighteen middle-class four-year-old children were selected for a two-year program. These subjects were not given IQ tests upon entrance. They were introduced into the experiment to demonstrate the differential effects of the experimental program on children who might be considered developmentally impaired and those considered normal. The control for the middle-class children was a group of middle-class four-year-olds in a Montessori preschool. The middle-class subjects in the experimental program were referred by parents of the Montessori children as children whose parents would be interested in a Montessori type of education (or a relatively inten-

TABLE 1

CHARACTERISTICS OF DISADVANTAGED SUBJECTS

Subjects	Mean CA	Mean Binet IQ	White	Negro	Male	Female	Mean Weighted S.E.S.
Experimental							
N=15	4-3	95.33	6	9	8	7	41.93
Comparison							
N=15	4-3	94.50	11	17	15	13	42.50

sive preschool education). Some of the experimental children were on the Montessori waiting list. The selection criterion was adequate, it was felt, to identify children who should be roughly comparable to the Montessori children. The Montessori controls were the same age as the experimental children although the Montessori children had already had one year of schooling at the time the experimental children began their program.

Evaluation of Performance

The disadvantaged children were given Stanford-Binet IQ tests after the first and second year of instruction. The middle-class children received Stanford-Binets only after the second year of instruction. These tests were taken as a measure of "general achievement," primarily in language concepts. The disadvantaged and middle class subjects in the experimental program were also tested on reading, arithmetic, and spelling achievement with the Wide-Range Achievement Test (1965). This test was selected for evaluating the subjects because:

1) There are fewer potential sources of extraneous difficulty. The instructions are uncomplicated, and the tests are clearly tests of relevant

content. For a child to achieve a given score in reading, he has to read —not circle words or follow complicated instructions.

2) No multiple-choice items appear in the Wide Range, which means that the children cannot receive a spuriously high score because they happened to guess correctly.

3) The Wide Range is capable of measuring achievement below the first grade level.

The disadvantaged children in the comparison group were not given achievement tests, because they were not taught skills in reading, arithmetic, or spelling. The Montessori group was given the Wide Range Test once, after they had finished their pre-kindergarten year.

Procedure

The subjects in the disadvantaged comparison class received a traditional preschool education. During the first year, they attended a two-hour-a-day preschool based as closely as possible on the recommendations of child development authorities. The emphasis of the program was on play, self-expression, developing a positive self image through role playing, and typical nursery-school activities. The preschool was outfitted with a sand table, dress-up corner, and a variety of toys. The child to teacher ratio was about 5 to 1. During the second year, comparison subjects went to public-school kindergartens.

The middle-class comparison group attended a Montessori program which operated for three hours a day. The emphasis of the program was on non-verbal manipulative activity. The child to teacher ratio was about 10 to 1.

During the first year (1965-1966) 15 disadvantaged children and 19 middle-class children were enrolled in experimental programs for two hours a day. Three of the disadvantaged children were not continued in the program the second year, and 12 middle-class children were not continued. The 12 remaining disadvantaged children and 7 middle-class children were integrated in a single class and received a second year of two-hours-a-day instruction. Throughout the two-year treatment, the child to teacher ratio was about 5 to 1.

The Experimental Program

The emphasis of the experimental program was on rapid attainment of basic academic concepts. The children attended three twenty-minute classes daily—a language concept class, an arithmetic class, and a reading class. For these classes, the children were divided into small (4-7 children) relatively homogeneous groups (based on performance in the classroom). For the remaining hour the children engaged in a period of semi-structured activities (writing, drawing, working reading-readiness problems), a music period (in which the songs were geared to the concepts presented in the language-concepts program), and a juice-and-toilet period.

Both the content and the style of teacher presentation used in the language, arithmetic, and reading sessions derived from a relatively simple principle: teach in the fastest, most economical manner possible. In language, the children were taught how to use a "minimum" instructional language. The language derived from the requirements of future teaching situations. In future teaching situations, the teacher would present physical objects of some kind and call the children's attention to some aspect of the objects—perhaps the color, perhaps the relative size, perhaps the position in relation to another object. The teacher would also "test" the children, primarily by asking a child (or the group) questions. The basic language that is needed for all such instructional situations is one that adequately describes the objects presented, that adequately calls attention to the conceptual dimension to which the teacher is directing the children, and that allows for unambiguous "tests" or questions.

The language that satisfies the requirements of the teaching situation consists of the two statement forms,

This is a . . . .

This . . . . is . . . .

with plural and *not* variations (This is not a . . . .), with *yes-no* questions (Is this a ball?), and with the *what* question (What is this?).

The basic language of instruction was taught during the first year. The language teachers did not use a rich variety of expressions; rather, they confined themselves to the basic patterns noted above until the children had demonstrated through performance that they understood the statements and the relationships between statements and questions.

The content that was taught in connection with the basic language consisted of names of common objects, polars (hot-cold, wet-dry, big-little, long-short, etc.), colors, prepositions, and hierarchical classes (vehicles, buildings, tools, clothing, weapons, etc.). After the children mastered the basic language they were introduced to tense variations, action verbs, conditional statements, *and, or, if-then,* and *only.* Finally, during the second year, the children were taught methods for defining words (through genera and differentia), and for describing complex figures and events.

In arithmetic, the children were taught how to count both objects and events (Tell me how many times I clap). They were then shown how addition, subtraction, and multiplication reduce to counting operations. For example, the children were shown how to translate such a problem as

$$5 + 3 = b$$

into the counting operation: start out with five; get more; get three more; and you end up with ......; we have to count them to find out.

All addition problems were reduced to this operation. The children were taught some rote facts, such as the series

$$1 + 1 = 2$$
$$2 + 1 = 3$$
$$3 + 1 = 4$$

etc.,

which articulates the relationship between counting and adding. There was, however, no attempt to teach the children an exhaustive set of arithmetic facts. Rather, the emphasis was on the operations that would lead to a correct solution.

The children were introduced to algebra and story problems early. To work algebra problems, the children used a variation of the translation they were taught for handling regular problems. For example, the operation for handling the problem

$$5 + b = 8$$

was: start out with five; get more; we don't know how many more, but we know we end up with 8. By starting out with five and getting more until he ends up with eight, the child discovers how many more he has to get.

The initial story problems were quite similar to the statement operations taught in connection with each type of problem. For example: a man starts out with five balls; then he gets more; he gets three more; how many does he end up with? The problem translates directly into the arithmetic statement:

$$5 + 3 = b$$

Problems were then systematically de-structured. That is, synonymous expressions were systematically introduced. After the children had learned to handle the basic story problems, the children were introduced to problems in which a man *has* so many balls, in which he *finds* so many balls, in which he *makes* so many balls.

The children were taught to read according to a modified ITA approach (the first version of DISTAR reading, 1969). The innovations which were introduced into the experimental program (primarily with the low performing children) had to do with the formation of long-vowel sounds and the convention for blending words. The following symbols were introduced to designate long-vowel sounds: ā, ē, ī, ō. The rationale for these symbols was that they could be introduced to help the child "spell" or sound out a variety of long-vowel words; after the children learned these words (sō, gō, nō, hē, shē, mē, sāve, fīne, etc.), the diacritical mark could be dropped without grossly changing the total configuration of the word.

To help the children learn how to blend words, a skill disadvantaged children often fail to master after years of reading instruction, only continuous-sound words (*fan,* not *ban* or *tan*) were introduced initially. The children were taught how to proceed from letter to letter *without pausing.* In sounding out words in this manner, the children were actually saying the words slowly and could see the relationship between the slowly produced word and the word as it is normally produced. To assure adequate performance in blending, the children were given say-it-fast drills with spoken words. "Say it fast and I'll show you the picture: te-le-phone."

As early as possible, the children were introduced to controlled-vocabulary stories. After reading the stories, the children took them home. Taking stories home functioned as an incentive.

In each of the three study areas, the teachers proceeded as quickly as possible, but only after the children had demonstrated through performance that they had mastered the skills that they would be expected to use on higher-level tasks.

The above description of the curriculum is very rough. In each of the major subject areas, there are many sub-tasks. To teach each of the sub-tasks, the teacher had to take a number of steps. For example, to teach the children to blend words that are presented orally (a sub-task reading), the teacher first presented two-part words, each part of which is a word—ice-cream, motor-boat, snow-man. Next, the teacher introduced relatively long words the parts of which were not "words," sit-ting, shov-el, mon-ey, etc. Next, the teacher broke the words that had been presented into more than one part—mo-tor-boat, snow-ma-n, sh-ov-el. The teacher then introduced shorter words, broken into two parts: si-t, bea-t, c-ream, m-an. Finally, the teacher introduced short words that were divided into individual phonemes—m-a-n, s-i-t, sh-o-v-e-l. (A more detailed description of the arithmetic and language programs is contained in, *Teaching Disadvantaged Children in the Preschool* [1966].)

The Teacher's Behavior

The teacher had three primary roles in the experimental program:

1) she managed the group of children, keeping them on task;

2) she taught concepts;

3) she tested the children's knowledge of concepts before either providing a remedy or proceeding to the next task.

The general rules that guided her behavior in all three areas were:

1) don't assume that the children know anything unless they have demonstrated that they do;

2) get as many correct responses and as few incorrect responses out of the children during the alloted time as possible.

3) teach the behaviors necessary for successful classroom performance.

Since the goal of the program was to induce learning at an above average rate, procedures that induce learning at a normal rate were rejected. The teacher did not first "shape" behavior and then introduce academic content. She simultaneously introduced academic content and the rules of behavior associated with the content. The focus was always on the behavior related to the task, never on behavior in the abstract. The sanctions that were used were:

Negative:

Loss of food reinforcers (raisins, juice);

Additional work ("If you keep that up, you'll have to work when the other children are singing. You're here to work.");

Physical manipulation (tugging on an arm to secure attention, tapping leg, physically turning children around in seat, turning face toward presentation);

Scolding, usually in loud voice ("Cut that out! Sidney! Look here!");

Repetition of task ,"Do it again . . . Again . . . Again . . . Again. Now, after this when I tell you to do it, you do it.").

Positive:

The use of reinforcing objects in presentations ("Look at that silly number. That's 7. I can't stand a 7. I have to erase it. Oh, there's another 7. I can't stand a 7 . . .");

The use of personalization ("Here's a story about, guess who! Sidney!");

The use of mock shock ("Everybody knew the answer. And I just said nobody will know the answer. You guys really fooled me.");

The use of praise ("Now, did you hear Sidney? He's a smart boy. Let's clap for him. He is smart and he's working hard.");

Dramatic change of pace (After having the children repeat a series of statements in unison, the teacher stops. The room is dead silent. The children look at each other and smile. Then they laugh. The teacher interrupts in a loud voice, "Okay, let's hear it: four plus zero equals four.");

A dynamic presentation of objects (During a two-minute segment, the teacher may present as many as 30 objects—some repeated—and as many questions. "Tell me about this . . . What about this . . . And this . . . And this . . .");

Positive speculations ("Boy, will your mother ever be surprised when she finds out that you can read. She'll say, 'I never knew you were so smart.' That's what she'll say.");

Exercises with a reinforcing pay-off ("Everybody likes to erase numbers, right? So I'll point to it and you can erase it.");

Relating positive comments of others—both real and fictitious ("Do you know what the man who watched you read said to me? He said, 'These are the smartest kids I've ever seen in my life.' And you want to know something? He's right.") ;

Food rewards ("If you do a good job on this problem, I'll give you some raisins. So work hard.") ;

Fooler games (The children say that when they add 3 to 4, they end up with seven. The teacher says, "So I write a 7." She writes a 4. The children object, and the teacher pouts, "I guess I just can't fool you guys." The children laugh.) ;

Hand shakes ("Sidney did such a good job that I'm going to shake his hand. Good boy, Sidney.") ;

Special privileges ("Sidney is working so hard I'm going to let him be the teacher.") ;

Singling out a member of the group for praise ("Debby did it that time. I didn't hear the rest of you guys, but I sure heard Debby. Let's do it again; see if anybody else can say it like Debby does.") ;

Presenting take-homes ("Tell me this sound and you can take it home.").

The teacher had a full range of social and physical reinforcers at her disposal to use as the situation demanded. Some of the reinforcers listed as positive reinforcers are "acquired." Once taught, however, they proved to be quite effective in influencing behavior, increasing attention, and maintaining the kind of concerted participation that might be called "working hard."

Note that the primary reinforcing emphasis was on positive reinforcement. The teacher used herself as a model, "I'm smart. I can do this stuff." She used other children in the group as models. "Did you hear Sidney? He and I are the only ones who can do this. We're smart." She always tried to acknowledge the correct responses of every child in the group. "Hey, everybody did it that time. Boy you are smart kids. Good work, Tyrone. You too, Lisa."

Whenever the teacher taught, she utilized some of the reinforcing techniques noted above. She moved quickly so that the children were not confronted with a static presentation. She spoke loudly one moment, softly the next. She presented interesting examples of the concept, when the interesting aspects of the objects did not interfere with the concept being taught. She structured the presentation so that the children had a pay-off—perhaps playing a fooler game, perhaps a hand-out for correct responses.

In addition to the reinforcing aspects of the presentation, however, the teacher followed a basic rule in presenting any new concept: *The presentation must be consistent with one and only one concept.* When the teacher presented the concept big, for example, she used the same statement forms, "This .... is big," and "This .... is not big," to describe a variety of object pairs—cups, circles, figures, men. Each of the objects in the pair was identical except for size. Through this type of presentation, the teacher demonstrated what the invariant *big* means. She further demonstrated the type of statement that is used to describe the invariant. "This cup is big; this ball is big; this man is big . . ."

Because of the presentational requirements necessary to demonstrate a concept, the teacher presented a great many examples, usually 10-15 times more than are used by the average classroom teacher (a judgment based on the presentational suggestions of instructional programs designed for children in the early primary grades).

The teacher tested the children on various levels of performance. The first test of a concept was whether the children could find (or point to) the appropriate example. "Find the man that is big."

The next test was whether the children could answer *yes-no* questions about an object the teacher pointed to. "Is this ball big? . . . Is this ball big?"

The next test was whether the children could answer *what* questions. These are more difficult than *yes-no* questions because the children must supply the content word. "This ball is what? . . . Yes, this ball is *big*."

The teacher usually introduced the various tests rapid fire, in no particular order. However, if the children had difficulty with a *what* question, the teacher would re-structure the tasks, starting with the *finding* task and working up to the *what* task. "Sidney, find the ball that is big . . . Good. This ball is big. Is this ball big? . . . Yes, this ball is big. This ball is what? . . . Yes, this ball is big."

While the rate at which questions are presented to the group and to individuals in the group varied with the tasks, the teacher often introduced as many as 20 questions a minute. She used the children's responses to these questions as indications of whether or not they had learned the concepts she was presenting. She geared her presentation *to the lowest performer in the group,* because the goal of instruction was to teach every child each criterion skill. (If a child consistently lagged behind the others in the group, he was moved to a slower group in which his performance was more consistent with that of the other members.)

RESULTS

IQ Performance of Disadvantaged Subjects

The disadvantaged subjects in the experimental program achieved significantly greater Stanford-Binet IQ gains than the subjects in the

FIGURE 1

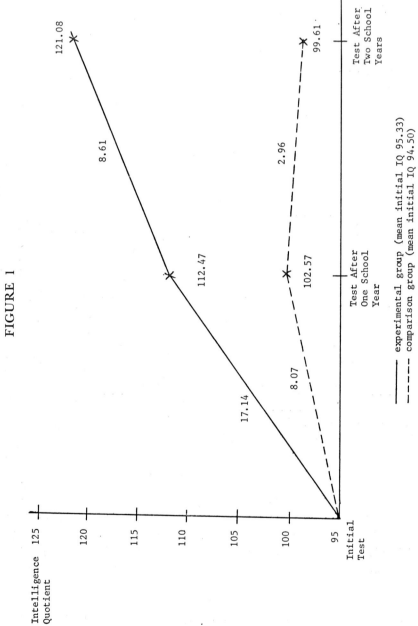

comparison program. More important, the mean IQ of the experimental subjects after two years of instruction was 121.08, well above the mean of normal, middle-class children. The mean of the comparison group was 99.61 after two years of instruction.

Figure 1 shows the IQ performance of the experimental and comparison groups after one and two years of instruction. The comparison

TABLE 2

STANFORD-BINET IQ PERFORMANCE OF DISADVANTAGED EXPERIMENTAL
SUBJECTS AFTER ONE AND TWO YEARS OF TRAINING

Subject*	Entering IQ	IQ After One Year	First Year Gain	IQ After Two Years	Second Year Gain	Total Gain
MA	92	113	+21	123	+10	+31
TA	93	94	+1	103	+9	+10
TB	105	112	+7	121	+9	+16
MB	89	101	+12	131	+30	+42
(DB)	(82)	(112)	(+30)	—	—	(+30)
RC	99	116	+17	119	+3	+20
MC	86	105	+19	112	+7	+26
(NC)	(70)	(89)	(+19)	—	—	(+19)
BG	119	130	+11	139	+9	+20
BP	90	107	+17	112	+5	+32
SV	85	101	+16	108	+7	+23
RV	109	127	+18	138	+11	+29
DD	99	118	+19	129	+11	+30
DW	101	123	+22	118	—5	+17
(BW)	(111)	(139)	(+28)	—	—	(+28)
X Total	95.33	112.47	17.14	—	—	24.20
X one-Year Subjects	87.66	113.33	25.67	—	—	25.67
X Two-Year Subjects	97.25	112.25	15.00	121.08	8.83.	23.83

* one-year subjects in parentheses

group achieved an 8.07 gain after the first year of instruction, but had a loss of 2.96 points after the second year (which is typical of early compensatory programs). The experimental group showed a 17.14 gain after the first year and an 8.61 gain after the second year.

Table 2 shows the performance of the individual disadvantaged subjects after one and two years of instruction. The mean first year gain of those children who were retained in the program for two years was 15.00 (IQ 112.25). The mean gain of those who were not continued a second year was 25.67 (IQ 113.33). The total mean gain for the two-year subjects after the second year of instruction was 23.83.

TABLE 3

IQ PERFORMANCE OF DISADVANTAGED COMPARISON SUBJECTS

Subject	Entering IQ	IQ After Two Years Training	Change
AB	94	115	+21
AC	118	115	−3
AD	83	94	+11
BA	90	92	+2
BB	88	74	−14
BC	76	93	+17
BD	92	90	−2
CR	101	87	−14
CS	82	95	+13
DB	85	100	+15
BC	79	83	+4
DF	107	97	−10
DJ	113	114	+1
DK	107	120	+13
EA	97	109	+12
EE	97	88	−9
EM	89	94	+5
EP	93	93	0
MA	92	107	+15
MB	88	87	−1
MC	79	87	+8
MR	93	89	−4
NB	94	104	+10
NS	91	106	+15
NT	101	109	+8
PA	109	127	+18
PB	111	117	+6
PR	97	103	+6
X	94.50	99.61	+5.11

There was only one instance of an IQ loss in either the first or second year of the experimental program. Subject DW had a second-year loss of 5 IQ points. None of the experimental subjects experienced an overall loss. The lowest gain was 10 points. The largest total gain was 42. The lowest IQ score after two years of instruction was 103 (subject TA). The highest IQ score after two years of instruction was 139 (subject BG).

Table 3 shows the IQ performance of the disadvantaged children in the comparison group after two years of instruction. Only 12 of the 28 control subjects scored higher than 103, the score of the lowest IQ performer in the experimental group. Eight control subjects had overall

IQ losses compared to no IQ losses for the experimental group. The highest IQ gain for the control group was 21 points, whereas the *mean* gain for the experimental group was 24 points.

Achievement Performance of Experimental Disadvantaged Subjects

Table 4 shows the achievement performance in reading, arithmetic, and spelling of the 12 subjects who finished two years of the experimental program. The mean reading achievement was grade level 2.60

TABLE 4

ACHIEVEMENT OF DISADVANTAGED EXPERIMENTAL
SUBJECTS AFTER TWO YEARS OF INSTRUCTION

| Subject | IQ | Grade Level on Wide Range Achievement Test | | |
		Reading	Arithmetic	Spelling
MA	123	2.7	2.2	1.8
TA	103	1.6	2.3	1.7
TB	121	3.1	3.3	2.2
MB	131	3.7	3.1	2.1
RC	119	2.7	2.9	2.0
MC	112	3.6	2.5	2.3
BG	139	3.1	3.3	2.1
BP	112	1.6	1.4	1.0
SV	108	2.0	2.2	1.7
RV	138	3.1	2.7	2.0
DD	129	1.7	2.2	1.9
DW	118	2.3	2.0	1.6
	121.08	2.60	2.51	1.57

with a range of 1.6-3.7. The mean arithmetic performance was 2.51 with a range of 1.4-3.3. The mean spelling performance was 1.87 with a range of 1.0-2.3. As Table 4 indicates, the correspondence between IQ scores and achievement scores is not perfect. Subject MC had the second highest reading achievement score and the highest spelling achievement score; yet, he had an IQ of only 112. Similarly, subject TB had achievement scores of 3.1, 3.3, and 2.2 in reading, arithmetic, and spelling; however, TB's IQ was only "average" for the group—121.

The Middle-Class Subjects

Table 5 summarizes the performance of the middle-class experimental subjects. After the end of the first year of instruction, the mean achievements of the middle-class subjects in reading and spelling had nearly

TABLE 5

Achievement and IQ Scores of Middle-Class Subjects After One and Two Years of Instruction

Subject	First-Year Achievement on Wide Range			Second-Year Achievement on Wide Range						IQ Stanford-Binet
	Read.	Ar.	Sp.	Read.	Gain	Ar.	Gain	Sp.	Gain	
MC	2.0	1.4	1.8							
M	3.5	2.0	2.0							
G	1.4	1.2	1.0	3.3	+1.9	2.2	+1.0	2.2	+1.2	113
H	2.0	1.2	1.9							
H	2.7	1.4	1.8							
H	2.7	1.2	1.9	3.9	+1.2	3.9	+2.7	2.3	+1.4	125
H	1.7	1.6	1.6	3.0	+1.3	2.9	+1.3	1.9	+.3	118
SK	2.7	1.2	1.9							
VK	3.4	2.0	2.1							
JL	1.8	1.4	1.5	3.4	+1.6	2.7	+1.3	1.8	+.3	121
KM	2.0	1.5	1.6							
BO	2.6	1.4	2.2							
CP	1.9	1.4	1.5	2.9	+1.0	3.1	+1.7	2.1	+.6	140
MP	2.2	1.4	1.8							
GS	1.7	1.4	1.2	3.5	+1.8	2.5	+1.1	2.0	+.8	110
KT	2.7	1.5	1.8							
T	3.0	1.4	2.1	3.9	+0.9	3.1	+1.7	2.1	—	137
SW	3.7	1.6	1.3							
M of two yr. sub.	2.03	1.37	1.54	3.41	+1.4	2.91	+1.5	2.06	+.66	123.43
M of one yr. sub.	2.68	1.51	1.84							
M of Total	2.43	1.46	1.72							

reached the level that was achieved by the disadvantaged subjects after two years of instruction. The middle-class children had achieved a mean grade level of 2.43 in reading and 1.72 in spelling (compared to 2.60 and 1.87 for the disadvantaged children after two years of instruction). At the end of the first year, the achievements of the seven children who continued in the program for two years was below the mean of those who did not continue for a second year in all achievement areas, but most noticeably in reading achievement. The mean reading achievement for the continuing children was 2.03 (compared to 2.68 for the one-year subjects); however, during the second year, continuing subjects progressed a full year and a half in reading achievement, terminating the program with a mean reading achievement score of 3.41 (eight tenths of a year above the mean of the disadvantaged children).

Interestingly enough, the IQ performance of the middle-class children was only about 2 points higher than that of the disadvantaged subjects, after two years of instruction. Both middle-class and disadvantaged subjects seem to be regressing toward a mean, but this mean is not IQ 100; it is considerably higher than that. This mean would be an operational indicator of the effective rate of "cognitive development" induced by the program in which these subjects were placed.

Table 6 shows the achievement scores of the middle-class comparison

TABLE 6

PERFORMANCE OF MIDDLE-CLASS COMPARISON FIVE-YEAR-OLDS ON WIDE RANGE ACHIEVEMENT TEST AFTER TWO YEARS OF INSTRUCTION

Test, May 1966

Subject	Reading	Arithmetic
DA	1.1	.7
SA	2.6	2.3
JD	.9	1.2
KD	.3	1.4
CE	1.3	1.0
CG	.5	1.0
MH	1.8	1.6
FJ	1.5	1.2
MK	1.3	1.4
EL	1.2	1.5
RM	1.2	1.5
JP	0	.3
LS	.9	1.2
AS	1.3	1.4
DV	.9	1.4
MV	.7	1.1
MW	.3	.6
X	1.04	1.21

children after they had two years of instruction (having finished pre-kindergarten). The mean grade levels of achievement for the Montessori-trained children in reading and arithmetic (1.04 and 1.21) were well below the means of the middle-class experimental children after one year of Bereiter-Engelmann training (2.43 and 1.46). Significantly the Montessori-trained children did not "burst into reading."

DISCUSSION

Performance of the Disadvantaged Children

The performance difference between the experimental and control disadvantaged children is most economically explained as a function of different training. The experimental children were taught new skills at a much higher rate than the children in the comparison program. The children in the comparison group were taught at a rate only slightly higher than the rate at which they would have been taught if they had not attended the preschool-kindergarten program. The experimental children, on the other hand, were taught at a rate substantially higher than they would have been taught if they had not been enrolled in the program.

There is a tendency in evaluating the effectiveness of instructional programs to look at the long-range effects of the program. While such effects are relevant, they are not of primary concern. The primary issue is: Can a program meet the educational objectives to which it addresses itself? In the case of the present experiment, can the program teach disadvantaged preschool and kindergarten children basic skills in reading, arithmetic, and the logical use of language? The IQ scores of the children reflects the effectiveness of the language program. The achievement scores in reading, arithmetic, and spelling indicate the effectiveness of the arithmetic and reading programs. Not one experimental child scored below 100 in IQ after two years of instruction (compared with 14 children in the comparison group who scored below 100). Not one experimental child scored below 1.6 grade level in reading or below 1.4 grade level in arithmetic. In other words, there were no instructional failures. All of the children were taught. The mean performance in arithmetic and reading indicates that the experimental subjects, after finishing their kindergarten year, performed as well as "average" disadvantaged children two or three years older. Mean achievement scores of 2.5 in reading and arithmetic are not unusual for fourth grade disadvantaged children. If children can be accelerated by 3 years (as the present experiment indicates), the general failure in the public schools is not necessarily a result of the children's innate inferiority or lack of aptitude. It is a function of inadequate instruction.

Middle-Class Children

At the end of the first year of reading instruction, the middle-class children performed on the 2.43 grade level, which means that they had progressed nearly a year and a half during the first year. Those children who continued for a second year in the program had progressed one year (achieving a mean reading score of 2.03 at the end of the first year). During the second year, however, the children who continued gained nearly a year and a half in reading. These children, in other words, were progressing at a faster rate than older children in the public schools.

By the end of the second year, two disadvantaged children scored above grade 3.4 in reading, the mean of the middle-class children, and interestingly, both of these children were Negroes who entered with IQ's in the 80's (MB and MC). Four disadvantaged children scored on or above the middle-class mean in arithmetic. By the end of the second year, there were disadvantaged children in the top-performing study group and there were middle-class children in the B and C groups.

The middle-class children did not have to be taught many of the sub-skills that had to be programmed for the disadvantaged children, especially in reading. For example, the middle-class children did not have to be taught how to blend the letters of a word. The disadvantaged children required a great deal of practice in this skill. By the end of the second year, the advantaged children were almost a full year ahead of the disadvantaged children in reading, although the disadvantaged children made more than one year's progress during the second year.

The reading performance of the middle-class and disadvantaged children was achieved with only about 96 hours of classroom instruction. The amount of time devoted to reading in the regular school program during the first two years of instruction is probably 3-6 times greater. It seems evident, in terms of the performance of children, that the public schools do not utilize their available time to good advantage.

The performance of the experimental children may be viewed as an example of the "hawthorn" effect. However, in the program there was very little interaction with the parents and correspondingly little attempt to change the patterns of behavior in the home. There was a total of three parent meetings over a two-year period. During these meetings, the staff members emphasized the good performance of the children and tried to persuade the parents that their children were smart. Beyond this, however, nothing was done to change the conditions which affected the outside-school learning of the children. The changes that took place in these children were changes that resulted primarily from the experimental treatment in the classroom.

The Effects of "Pressure" on Younger Children

One of the traditional encumbrances to early formal education is the belief that the pressure resulting from such instruction will developmentally malform the children. While it is difficult to evaluate the effects of the present program on the children's personality, interviews with parents and observations of the children disclosed no ill effect. In the program there were virtually no tantrums or behavior problems beyond the second week, although at least two of the disadvantaged children were considered emotionally disturbed. The children participated, and they seemed to enjoy participation. All children engaged in the music period. All complied with the rules—but not as automatons. If the program failed in any respect, it did not adequately prepare the children for the kind of behavior-for-behavior-sake rules which they would encounter in school. During free time or semi-structured activities, the children talked freely to each other. They made observations and asked questions. When given the slightest opportunity, they would relate personal experiences and engage in conversations that were sophisticated for four and five-year-old children. In short, they showed no engrams from the "pressure" of the program. They worked hard; but the parents noted no regressive behavior, bed wetting, thumb sucking, nightmares, etc. In fact, if the parents' reports are to be taken seriously, the children had fewer emotional problems than any sample of "unpressured" children.

Perhaps the most noticeable characteristic of the children after two years of instruction was their confidence. The easiest way for the teacher to capture their interest was to announce a difficult task. "This is so hard I shouldn't even be giving it to little kids like you. You'll never be able to do it." The children would respond to this type of challenge by insisting, "We can do it! You'll see." Their confidence had been programmed through fooler games in which the children proved to be "smarter" than the teacher. The children exhibited confidence because they had received many demonstrations that they were competent and could succeed in challenging situations. They had surprised—even crushed—the teacher with their smartness. This is not to say that the children would be confident in *all* situations or even all instructional situations. But they had firm and realistically based confidence about their capacity to perform in new-learning situations of the type presented in the B-E program.

SUMMARY

A group of disadvantaged four-year-olds and a group of middle-class four-year-old children were taught intensively in the Bereiter-Engelmann program for two years (the preschool and kindergarten years). The group of disadvantaged children was comparable in IQ and race-sex composition to a group of 28 children assigned to a traditional nursery-school and kindergarten program. The middle-class children were roughly comparable to a group of Montessori trained four-year-olds. The major hypothesis tested by the program was that children are taught at different rates; if the effective rate at which disadvantaged and middle-class children are taught is increased substantially, these children will perform at an above-normal level, which means that the disadvantaged subjects may become "superior" in specific areas of achievement.

The hypothesis was confirmed. The disadvantaged children in the comparison group showed no particular advantage over children in similar compensatory programs, such as Head Start programs. The program failed to bring half of the children up to an IQ of 100. The mean for the group was 99.6. The experimental program, however, brought the IQ's of every child to above 100. The mean IQ after two years of instruction was 121, with a range from 103 to 139. The mean achievements of the experimental group were: reading, 2.6; arithmetic, 2.5; and spelling, 1.9. The scores are what one would expect from 8-10-year-old disadvantaged children: the experimental subjects, however, were six years old at the end of the program.

After one year of instruction, the middle-class subjects had achievement scores of 2.4 in reading, 1.5 in arithmetic, and 1.7 in spelling. The comparison group did not score as well in any of these achievement areas, although the comparison children had been in a Montessori program for two years at the time of testing. By the end of the second year, those middle-class children who continued in the program scored 3.4 in reading, 2.9 in arithmetic, and 2.1 in spelling. The mean IQ of the group after the second year was 123, only several IQ points higher than the mean IQ of the disadvantaged experimental children.

The present experiments seem to indicate, rather strongly, that the reason disadvantaged children fail in public schools is not necessarily that they are genetically inferior or developmentally impaired but that they receive poor instruction. If younger children with initially lower mental ages can achieve at an above-normal rate, school-age disadvantaged children (who usually learn more rapidly) should have little trouble achieving at the rate of normal children in specific achievement areas if instruction is adequate.

The results of the experiment cast rather serious doubt on the validity of IQ measures as indicators of genetic endowment. The children in the experimental program were changed rather dramatically during the two years of instruction. Unless one knew what went on in the environment during these two years, one would be at something of a loss to describe these children. If we were to take their terminal IQ scores as indications of genetic endowment, then we would be faced with the difficult problem of explaining how the genetic composition of the children changed over the two year period. Was it something that they ate?

The fact that some of the children made relatively little progress compared to others may be taken as an indication of differential genetic influence. But again, this conclusion would be quite hasty. Before we can intelligently discuss what happened to individuals, we would have to know what went on in that individual's environment (his total waking environment and not merely the 2½ hours a day that he was in school) before we could presume to talk about the relative influence of the "environment" on intelligence. Probably everyone would agree that genetic endowment makes a difference, but the extent of that difference is far from obvious. At best, genetic influence seems to be a minor factor among the overwhelming majority of children.

18

YPSILANTI CARNEGIE INFANT EDUCATION PROJECT

Dolores Z. Lambie and David P. Weikart, Ph.D.

High/Scope Educational Research Foundation
Ypsilanti, Michigan

Part I
OVERVIEW OF THE PROJECT

The Ypsilanti-Carnegie Infant Education Project was established in January 1968 and funded by the Carnegie Corporation and the Ypsilanti Public Schools. This report presents the results of the first six months of the project, including quantitative data and a case study (Part 2). Of special importance is the discussion of the curriculum employed in the home, with illustrations of curriculum practices (Part 3). Research design changes from the original proposal are also reviewed (Part 4).

The infant education project is the outgrowth of the findings from the Ypsilanti Perry Preschool Project (Weikart, 1967) and the Ypsilanti Home Teaching Project (Weikart and Lambie, 1968). The project is based on two assumptions: 1) Preventative programming must start earlier than current preschool efforts since the essential framework for intellectual growth is completed by age three. 2) Preventative intervention has unusual potential for success when provided as a home teaching program for both the mother and her infant. Early infancy is a time of extremely rapid intellectual and physical growth, and it is the period when primary emotional relationships are established; most mothers from all cultural backgrounds hold high hopes for their infants and welcome assistance in attaining their goals.

This project is funded by the Carnegie Corporation; the Department of Health, Education, and Welfare, Public Health Service, Grant No. 1 R01 MH1761-01 JP; and the Ypsilanti Public Schools. This paper is a revised version of an illustrated progress report presented to the Carnegie Corporation in September 1969.

Specific recognition is made of the assistance given by (Mrs.) Nikki Miller and (Mrs.) Marilyn Jeffs with the case study, teaching plans, and techniques, by Robert Wozniak with the data analysis and instrumentation, and by Walter Hull with the language goals activities.

362

The purpose of the project is to assess the effectiveness of systematic intervention by public school teachers, starting at the period of infancy, in preventing the intellectual deficits commonly found in children from disadvantaged populations. In order to control some of the important variables, four groups have been established: an experimental group, a contrast group, and two control groups. The experimental group utilizes home teaching by public school teachers as the method of program operation. In this plan, a public school teacher goes into the home to work with the mother and her infant once each week for an hour. During the visit, the teacher expresses her genuine interest in the mother and what she is doing with the child, especially as it relates to language, motoric development and cognitive growth. The mother is helped to become aware of the infant's development in each of these key areas by learning to observe her child closely, and she is encouraged to respond to the child as each small step of growth evolves. By this process, the mother becomes deeply involved in the child's development. Specifically, the visits are organized around five points: individualized programming for each mother—child dyad; development of the mother's teaching style, language style, and control techniques; and direct tutoring of the child. Since the overall goal is to help each mother become an effective teacher of her child, the project staff strongly rejects the development of a standardized "script" of activities for the teacher, the mother, or the child. The home teaching process is carefully supervised and developed in a systematic fashion by the project staff.

The contrast group employs home visits by volunteer college students and young women from the community. The focus of these visits is adult attention for the child and service to the family. The "intuitive wisdom" of the volunteers is augmented by training from a professional social worker.

One control group is the traditional no-treatment group receiving only the same testing as the other groups. The other control group is a no-treatment, no-testing group created from those families who, for no reason under their control, had to drop out from one of the above three groups; in every case, the initial testing has been completed, and no further testing will be done with the family and child until the project is complete.

The groups are created by random assignment of mother-child dyads from the available disadvantaged families of the Ypsilanti school district. The groups are further subdivided by age of entry into the project. The youngsters are phased into the project at three, seven, and eleven months of age to provide information on the effect of entry age on program impact. The groups are also controlled for race and sex so far as this is possible.

The next section of this report presents the results of the pilot study completed in the spring of 1968. This section is followed by a presentation of the direction curriculum development is taking at this point and a review of the project design.

Part II

PILOT STUDY: RESULTS OF THE FIRST SIX MONTHS OF THE PROJECT

In order to develop explicit techniques, the first six-month period of the Infant Education Project was devoted to a pilot study. During this time the focus of the project was upon the organization of the home teaching program, the data collection procedures, and staff orientation. A pilot group of families was selected to serve as a trial group or "wave" throughout the period of the experiment. Some data collection was done with this group to obtain initial indication of programming impact.

Sample. The sample for this study was drawn from the available disadvantaged infants in the Ypsilanti Public School attendance district. These infants and their families were located through use of county birth records, school census data, and referrals from ongoing departmental projects. Both black and white families were included. The selection criterion was a low score on the cultural deprivation (CD) scale developed by the Perry Preschool Project, which is based on occupation, parent education, and number of persons in the living unit. In addition to clearly disadvantaged families, two families were selected to represent the lower middle class. Table 1 gives a brief description of the sample families selected for the pilot "wave." The actual period of visits was concentrated in three months (March, April and May 1968).

In addition to the families listed in the table, several others were initially involved. Two families who started with the project went South during spring vacation and failed to return to Ypsilanti at the end of the vacation period. One of these families has now returned and will be included in the pilot sample again. Two other families were served in the pilot group but are not included, since they were members of a pre-pilot study group and had had several months of home teaching before the testing. The curriculum developed during the pilot study for use with these families is presented in Part 3.

Two types of information from the project are presented in the following pages. The first is qualitative information concerning the impact of the program on a single family, and a case study approach is employed. The second type of information is quantitative data collected

TABLE 1

FAMILY INFORMATION

Name	Age of Mother	Edu- cation	No. of Children	No. of People	Birth Date	Sex	ADC	CD	No. of Visits
R.A.	24	8	2	5	11-20-67	M	x	7.6	9
T.C.[a]	30	11	5	3	4-12-67	F	x	10.8	6
O.J.[b]	30	11	5	7	3-1-67	F		8.93	5
M.G.	29	14	5	7	12-4-67	M		12.5	6
T.M.[c]	24	12	2	4	11-29-67	M	x	11.5	4
L.W.	33	12	4	6	11-7-67	F		15.9	7
I.K.	21	8	3	6	9-11-67	F		7.8	8

[a] T.C.—only two children currently in home, father absent.
[b] O.J. had complications in pregnancy with next child and was very ill. No visits were made after May 17, 1968.
[c] T.M.'s child was ill almost every other week, severely limiting visits.

through use of the Bayley Infant Scales of Development. While more extensive data were collected, they were primarily helpful in decisions involving instrument development and teaching strategies and are not presented at this time.

QUALITATIVE DATA

The project staff found that most mothers of the infants could be placed in one of four categories evolved as a result of past home teaching programs (Weikart and Lambie, 1968). These four types require somewhat different teaching patterns and definitely provide a range of home teaching conditions. 1) A few mothers have a good understanding, usually intuitive, of their children's needs and have already established a growth-encouraging relationship. These mothers receive extensive teacher support in what they are doing. 2) Most of the mothers want to do what is best for their infants but they do not know how to go about it. These mothers receive specific consultation from the teacher including ideas, demonstrations, and information. 3) Some mothers are not involved with their infants and see their children as "slow" or different in some way. A mother from this group demands to know what is wrong; then, if the problem can't be easily solved, she prefers to ignore the child. 4) Some mothers seem to provide detrimental assistance to their children, as everything they do with the baby seems to go wrong. These mothers react to these difficulties by becoming punitive, treating the infant with detachment, or showing overwhelming concern. These last two groups of mothers need considerable assistance in developing an equilibrium in child rearing. The teacher constructs, through carefully related educational activities, a responsive relationship between mother and child. She supports the vital interest the mother has in the child by helping her achieve success in some activity with the baby.

In order to illustrate the home teaching conditions and the methods the staff employed to work with parents and infants, a case study of one family is presented below in detail. While the family is somewhat atypical in that the mother represents category four (provides detrimental assistance), the teacher's report does indicate the range of problems a home teacher must face. It also outlines how a cognitive curriculum may operate within a framework of family dynamics with which it is very difficult to contend.

FAMILY CASE HISTORY: T. D.

I. *General Description*

A. Home Environment (Physical)

This family lives in four rooms plus a bathroom of a large run-down house which has been converted into several apartment units. The building is in very poor repair; the roof leaks, several windows are broken, and the whole house is infested with cockroaches. The landlord has been given a deadline by the city to complete repairs or the house will be condemned. A screenless front door opens onto a small hallway with a very strong musty odor. There are two apartments downstairs and one of the mothers living there takes care of five extra children on weekdays in addition to several of her own. An enclosed stairway leads to the second floor apartment where the project family lives. The main hallway of the apartment opens directly on this stairway. The door at the bottom of the stairs is usually kept bolted. The door to the stairway is not protected by a gate though T. D. is a toddler. The living room has an old and badly worn couch and chair, two T.V. sets only one of which works, two end tables with three children's banks, and a child's toy table with two chairs. There are pictures of the children on the walls and both end tables, a small radio, a large wooden toy chest, a walker, a jumper chair, and a baby swing. The wooden floor is usually clean but has no coverings. In one corner of the couch is a large memento pillow which designates the mother's side of the couch. No one else is allowed to sit on this end of the couch. The furniture in the room is rearranged at least once a week. The children's bedroom has a crib, a single bed, and dresser. One of the window panes in the dimly lighted room is broken. Clothes are scattered everywhere and the mother's room has more light but a large crack in the ceiling lets in huge quantities of water whenever it rains. A small child's wading pool catches the water on these occasions. The room has a large bed and dresser. The teacher has never seen the kitchen or the bathroom. Access to the attic for the whole house is off the apartment's upstairs hallway and there is often a ladder there with several people going up and down. The radio and the television are usually both going at the same time.

B. Family Members and Others

The family unit consists of the mother and two of her six daughters (half-sisters). The mother has recently divorced her husband although they still maintain a dating relationship. He gives her money for the children occasionally (on birthdays and holidays). This mother had three illegitimate children before she married, two by her husband and one illegitimate child since the divorce. The youngest legitimate child was taken away from her for child abuse and is presently in a foster home, as are the three older children. The children currently in the home are the five-year-old who just completed kindergarten and the illegitimate fourteen-month-old who is the mother's sixth child. The mother is 31 years old and has an eleventh grade education. She reports herself to have been a poor student. She is from a family of seven children and describes herself as the rejected child especially after having her first three children out of wedlock. She receives ADC. This mother has long blond hair and is very heavyset. She has an old boyfriend's name tatooed on her arm and writes her current boyfriend's name on her other wrist with a marking pen. She seems to have an active social life.

C. Teaching Conditions

The teaching sessions were always held in the living room. During the first two visits no teaching of the baby was attempted as the mother was extremely defensive and seemed to be "feeling the teacher out." The baby was sleeping and the teacher was invited to talk until she woke up, which did not happen during the first two sessions. At the first actual session with the baby, the mother's boyfriend was present and participated more than the mother, somehow relaxing the tension. The next session, the mother joined in and told the teacher that she had been on trial and that the mother had decided that the teacher could stay. The teaching sessions usually lasted at least an hour, thirty minutes of which were directed to the baby. These thirty minutes were spread out in short periods of concentration on the baby, sandwiched between a flow of mother-centered conversation. The teacher had to keep returning the mother to the teaching task or relating the mother's conversation to the task. Occasionally friends of the mother or the landlord sat in on the sessions. The lessons were conducted on the couch with the baby between teacher and mother.

II. *History of Teacher's Relationship with Family*

A. Mother

This mother comes across as a very dominating, independent woman completely uninhibited about revealing her problems and personal exploits. She is boastful and yet at the same time seems to have tremendous feelings of inadequacy. She constantly refers to herself as an "abusive" mother and yet has established a strong line of defenses to refute that accusation. On the surface, the first contacts with this mother were characterized by very casual, friendly, accepting exchanges. The teacher was given indirect messages, however, that any implied challenge to the mother's "mothering ability" would completely jeopardize any continuation of the program in this home. It was also apparent that any interaction with the baby would be mother-directed and controlled in equal if not "more-equal" partnership with the teacher. As a result the lessons took on the flavor of a mini-battlefield with each side trying to rattle a sabre and yet continue to maintain a relationship. The teacher became an information seeker and clarifier in an attempt to steer the conversation and return the focus to the baby. Eventually the teacher reinforced particular interactions between the mother and child and occasionally modified some of the mother's inappropriate teasing behaviors that were particularly detrimental to the child. Despite the difficulties of teaching interaction, both the teacher and mother seem to like each other and feel very confortable together. Mother says she feels the teacher is like a "girlfriend."

Some differences between the mother's and teacher's point of view have been bluntly particularized through statements by the teacher: "We have different ideas about that." The mother accepts this type of interaction if not yet the ideas transmitted. She is very interested in continuing home teaching, saying that she has a lot more fun than the baby. The teacher is not quite convinced but the mother is obviously gaining some satisfactions that mitigate the personal threat and meet her need to influence her baby's achievement.

B. Child

The mother encourages independence and competition between both children and herself. The baby was eleven and a half months old when this family was first contacted. Her test behavior was very spotty and she had a very short attention span. She did not carry many of the activities to completion; for example, she would grasp objects but couldn't imitate. Instead she would impose her own schemata—shaking, mouthing, and rocking—soon after each new activity was introduced. She seemed to spend nearly all of her waking time in the jumper chair. She was observed to do a great deal of rocking and had nearly worn out her second jumper chair. This rocking was accompanied by a lot of vocalizing but both behaviors could be interrupted when she was given a lot of direct attention. She was very responsive to social situations.

The child shows some stubbornness and independence. At the same time she is often very clinging when given an opportunity to hug mother or teacher. She often will come to the teacher for attention when the mother scorns her advances. She has abandoned all the rocking behavior and is very interested and persistent in object play.

III. *Mother's Teaching Interaction with Child*

A. Awareness of Development

This mother seems to have some appropriate expectations for motor development for her baby. However, her general expectation of independence is extended to many more areas than baby is ready to handle. For example, the child is expected to take a bath by herself, to win her own toys back from her older sister, and to stop crying on command, all at 11½ months of age. Mother feels that independence is important to prevent a child from becoming spoiled. This mother also watches "The Children's Doctor," a T.V. program that gives health and growth stages for children, and attempts to apply this knowledge to the baby.

B. Support of Child's Growth

The mother does not see herself in a supportive role to her child's growth. Her interactions are directive and thus, she believes, prevent undesirable behavior. Sometimes mother's own needs are put ahead of those of the baby. On one occasion one of teacher's often-made points became obvious: Baby worked longer and better when she received a reward and was not teased. Mother noticed this and said that she guessed teacher was right about reward but she liked to tease her baby anyway. Once when the project supervisor was visiting a teaching session, the mother tried forcing the child to walk, but the infant's legs kept buckling under. Then this mother half-teasingly started kicking the child, as if the child were purposely not trying to walk to displease her. The supervisor offered an alternative reason for the child's failure by commenting that babies who have been supported in a jumper chair for a while sometimes have difficulty in supporting themselves, in getting their feet under them immediately. The mother became very defensive and the subject was dropped. The next week, however, she reported that the baby was no longer using the jumper chair.

The mother has attempted to provide materials similar to those brought into the home by the teacher. She has bought standard materials and attempted to make a picture book for the baby. During the teaching sessions, the mother lets the child explore new materials freely and in teaching allows the child to move at her own pace. She also picks up and extends new approaches the baby may make to a specific activity. When the baby, who had been putting blocks through a hole in a can, suddenly began to pass blocks to her mother, the mother quickly started to play "Give it to . . ." This behavior by the mother may not be typical outside the teaching session as yet.

C. Description of Mother's Behavior

1. Language

This is a very talkative mother. She does a great deal of talking to the baby. Most of this is appropriate and specific to the situation: "Here is your teacher," or "Get that dog." The mother also usually responds to all vocalizations of the baby when the mother is focusing her attention on her and not engaging the teacher in conversation. She usually repeats what the child said or what she thinks she said. When in conversation with the teacher, she wants the baby to be quiet and not make any noise at all, however. Most of her language to the child consists of restrictive imperatives, such as "Put that in there," but during teaching she often is quite expansive.

The area of language has not been a focus of the teaching plan to date although the mother has been encouraged to participate and to direct many language oriented activities toward the baby.

2. Teaching Style

The mother has some very nice interactions with the baby as long as the baby is cooperative. When the baby begins to be less responsive, the mother becomes very negative and resorts to threats and physical punishment. Another problem area is that of rewards. At the beginning of the project, the mother was very interested in getting the baby to walk. She held out a toy and encouraged the baby to come and get it. The baby took three very halting steps and reached for the toy. The mother immediately changed the toy to the other hand and again invited the baby to get it. She reached again. This was repeated two or three more times until the baby gave up, sat down in the middle of the floor and started to cry. The mother then gave her a cookie to stop her crying. The teacher commented on the obvious distress of the baby, but at that point direct confrontation was not advisable. In several less tense situations the teacher pointed out how the child was continuing to pursue a task when she was getting a lot of positive reinforcement. The teasing behavior by the mother began to drop out completely during the teaching sessions. It appeared again during a video-taping toward the end of the sessions. In viewing the tape, teacher again commented that the baby gave up and didn't seem to like teasing. Mother agreed that the teacher was right about that, but said that *she,* the mother, still liked it. At least the impact was made, but one can't be sure how changed the mother was. She has begun to consistently reward in other situations, however.

Another difficult problem is to get the mother to help the baby make a transition from one activity to another. When the teacher gave any indication that it was time to change activities, the mother would snatch the toy away from the baby. The child would often come close to tears. It was necessary to find a way to help the mother make a transition from one activity to the next. The mother was told, "Let's try . . . . now. Why don't you see if T. D. will trade this toy for the one she has. Maybe that will be a way to get that toy away without upsetting her." This suggestion was only necessary once. No more snatching behavior has been observed in the teaching sessions.

This mother is sometimes irritated by some of the problem-solving behaviors that the child shows and responds very aggressively. The baby was putting wooden blocks in the can and was having a hard time getting one in. She finally tried to throw it in and by accident it missed and stung the mother; the mother yelled and threw the block at the baby, whereupon the baby got ready to throw another one at the mother. Teacher stepped in and got baby to throw her block in the can. This type of mollification is sometimes necessary to keep the child from punishment and to demonstrate a more neutral response to the mother although the original teaching goal may have been specifically for the child. Such interaction seems to be very helpful and the mother usually carries over these techniques to similar situations. It seems that often the mother welcomes more effective ways of maintaining the child's cooperation.

3. Control Techniques

This mother uses several control techniques. Threats and warnings are usually her first response to any misbehavior. Sometimes these are not followed up. Sometimes she uses both a threat and a promise of a reward: "If you stop it, I'll give you a cookie; if you don't, you'll get a slap." She sometimes does both no matter what the child does. Other times she slaps her playfully and says, "I was kidding about the cookie." This mother takes things away for discipline purposes but she also takes things away to teach the baby to stand up for herself. These controls usually disturb the baby and she cries and gets very upset. Then the mother gives her something to stop the crying or spanks her and puts her in her crib. The choice of which treatment she uses seems to depend on the mother's mood at the moment.

The mother seems to control only those things the baby does which interrupt or somehow personally affect her. She does not control, in particular, things necessary for the baby's safety, her play activity, or her fighting with the older sister, unless they become personally irritating to her. There is, therefore, a great deal of inconsistency in the general extent to which the mother exerts controls as well as in the type of controls used.

The teacher has begun work in this area by trying to clarify with the mother what her exact position is on controlling certain things in the hope that in crystallizing what it is she believes important, she may at least then handle that behavior consistently. The teacher reinforces the mother's position whenever she can agree with her in order to lend further support to the mother in establishing a consistent approach.

The teacher also tries to point out when the mother's expectations seem too high, with the hope that this will help to clarify whether things the child does are really misbehavior or whether they are simply too hard for her to do. For example, the mother was very anxious for the baby to take a bath by herself, but every time the mother left the room, the baby would start screaming and crying. The mother tried closing the door and letting her fuss and then she tried spanking her. When this problem was brought up in the teaching session, the teacher suggested that maybe the baby wasn't just misbehaving but was afraid to be by herself, and that most babies of 12 months really aren't quite ready to take a bath alone even if they can do many other things for themselves. The mother accepted this and later told the teacher that she guessed she would not try to force the baby to take a bath alone anymore since maybe she wasn't quite ready.

Although teacher and mother have begun to discuss this area of control more directly and the mother has exhibited some agreement with the teacher, only a small beginning has been made and much more needs to be done. Hopefully some successful control techniques can be demonstrated during teaching which the mother will be able to carry over to her later interactions with the child.

IV. *Developmental Steps in Child's Educational Growth*

A. Language

When this baby was first seen she was doing a lot of babbling accompanied by rocking. She was very socially responsive and would vocalize to people when they came to her. She did not seem very responsive to verbal commands or extraneous sounds.

All of the activities in the cognitive area were accompanied by specific language referents. Some attempt was made to include activities with familiar commands: "Put it in . . ." "Give it to . . ." "Show me . . ." Since the mother was very responsive to all of the expressive language of the baby, the baby seemed to be very imitative. More structured language-imitative activities were then included. Some pictures were found of familiar objects which the baby began to name in imitation of mother. She would also imitate various words yelled into a can or on a toy telephone. The baby seems to imitate very well at this point but her understanding of words seems poor. She does not discriminate her mother's name from that of her sister or teacher, although she says "mama" meaningfully when distressed. She continues to do a lot of babbling during play.

B. Cognitive

Early in the family contacts the baby seemed very friendly but was exhibiting an excessive amount of rocking. When given a task she would then show some goal-directed behavior but would not carry most tasks to completion; rather she would use the object in her own way, usually mouthing or banging it. She had an easy play style but short interest in any particular activity. Her performance on the Bayley Scales in the cognitive area was spotty and she would not release objects but tended to hoard the toys.

The program for the baby included the following types of cognitive activities with accompanying language:

a) Release Activities

1) Passing objects around
2) "Give it to"
3) Putting blocks in a can
4) Trading toys
5) Putting shapes through appropriate slots in can
6) Pulling pop-beads apart and putting in can

b) Activities for imitation

1) Block banging
2) Peek-a-boo
3) Picture naming
4) Mirror play

c) Object permanence

1) Finding toy behind a screen
2) String-operated jack-in-the-box
3) Finding toy given more than one screen

d) Stacking activities

1) Nesting small cups
2) Nesting measuring cup with handles
3) Stacking blocks
4) Nesting cans
5) Stacking cans
6) Stacking graduated rings

The release activities were especially difficult for the baby although she seemed to enjoy them most. She would hoard the objects or refuse to participate. She seemed to fear that she wouldn't get the toy back if she gave it up. This real fear had been reinforced by some of the mother's behavior. Concentrated effort by both mother and teacher to reward any release eventually helped her to successfully accomplish these tasks although she still is reluctant to give or trade a favorite or new toy.

The imitation activities were the most successful. She worked especially well with mother on these activities although the play was very aggressive by both. She seemed ready to extend her skills to more meaningful levels of imitative play.

Her object permanence skills have increased to the level of finding an object under one screen. When given more than one screen she returns to the position where the toy was found last, and then cries if it is not there.

Her skills in the stacking-nesting area were very poor. She was unable to nest anything and could only stack two blocks. She would not persist in these activities when met with the slightest frustration.

C. Motor

From the start, the baby seemed to have good muscle tone and adequate coordination of both fine and gross muscles. She could walk with help but would not walk alone. Her mother was very eager for her to walk and was spending about 45 minutes each night trying to get her to walk. The baby would take two steps to get something but mother would start the teasing and then the baby would stop and cry. Another problem was that the baby spent most waking hours in the jumper chair and seemed to have little time by herself to explore. After a visit from the project supervisor where the use of jumpers in general was mentioned, the mother began to let her out more. She is now walking very well but cannot get up without something to pull up on. Her general motor development is age appropriate.

V. *Evaluation*

In general the baby has made many improvements. Her attention span is much longer, and when encouraged, she will pursue a task to completion. She still needs a great deal of work in the cognitive area to bring her up to a level consistent with her motor and language skills. No rocking is observed.

The mother has also demonstrated that the teaching program has had some impact on her. A beginning has been made in changing her reward behavior as well as giving her some positive experiences with the baby. She shows potential for more change. Her teaching methods, which have received the major thrust of teacher's work with her, have improved significantly, at least during the teaching sessions. The mother has also experienced many successful interactions with her child, which did not seem to be a well-established pattern at the beginning of this program. Thus a small start has been made in mitigating some of her rejection of this child. This problem of rejection has been discussed quite openly. The mother brought it up herself in discussing her own mother's treatment of her and she admitted that sometimes she couldn't stand to be around her kids either. Teacher reassured her that most mothers have times when their children seem to be a burden, but went on to discuss some ways other mothers handle kids at these times. It was also pointed out that kids can pick up these feelings very easily and it can influence how they behave.

Only a beginning has been made. This mother has some deep-seated problems that are beyond the scope of this program but there is some evidence that some of the guilt she feels about her other children can be channeled into a more appropriate effort to do well with the baby. This mother is beginning to find some real satisfactions. Much work still needs to be done in the area of the mother's teaching methods to attempt to cut down the amount of negative reinforcement and to help the mother find new ways of expressing her pleasure with the child, which at this point comes across in a negative manner.

VI. *Overview*

One of the major difficulties faced by the teacher was the slow pace of the program for this family. Very limited, carefully planned goals had to be established. This seemed necessary for the stability of the teaching program, because there were so many problems that any large-scale approach would have discouraged the teacher and overwhelmed the mother. It would seem practical to continue with the present teaching program concentrating on one small aspect of behavior at a time in several different activities. It also would be helpful to continue to have the mother participate in preparing materials that she chooses. This seems to give her something positive to do during the week on her own. She is very open to such suggestions.

Another problem was how to work the baby into the mother's framework. The mother seemed to feel the teacher was someone for her and work with the baby was incidental. It seemed advisable not to challenge this mother but rather to try to fit the program into her framework. The idea of limited challenge seemed to be effective. It was very difficult for the teacher to reach a comfortable feeling of security in the home such that she could take a stand on some of the differences between herself and the mother. To say the least, this mother was very intimidating at first. It did seem necessary for the teacher to take the responsibility of maintaining the tentative relationship between herself and the mother. This idea of limited challenge seemed to establish a frankness on the part of both the teacher and the mother which was acceptable to both. The result was that a rather strong and comfortable relationship was established between the teacher and mother. This was necessary in order to begin to establish a common investment in the child, which is yet to come. Until this investment is made, hometeaching will not have fulfilled its potential.

QUANTITATIVE DATA

In addition to the general qualitative information on individual families, systematic data were collected employing the Bayley Infant Scales of Development. These scales were chosen to evaluate the general progrss of the infants in the pilot study. However, since the scales were in the pre-publication stage, a scoring manual was not available to the project and only individual basal and ceiling age-scores could be calculated directly. These are presented in Table 2.

This method of analyzing the data, however, is unsatisfactory as it neglects the patterns of passes in the pass-fail scatter which occur between the basal and ceiling scores. This neglect is a serious weakness since in the nine weeks of program intervention much of the relative effect might be manifested in the pass-fail pattern.

In the absence of a published scoring procedure, an arbitrary method of calculating a single age-placement score for each individual was developed. This method attempted to take into account both the basal level of the subject and his pass-fail scatter in a manner somewhat analogous to that utilized in the Stanford-Binet. The test was divided

TABLE 2

BASAL AND CEILING AGE-SCORES (in months) ON BAYLEY INFANT SCALES OF DEVELOPMENT

Name	PRE-TEST			POST-TEST		
	Chron. Age	Basal Age	Ceiling Age	Chron. Age	Basal Age	Ceiling Age
			MENTAL			
R.A.	4.30	3.40	4.60	6.67	7.00	9.30
T.C.	11.60	9.50	12.70	13.90	12.70	16.80
O.J.	12.90	10.90	13.50	15.33	13.20	19.00
M.G.	3.93	3.80	4.80	6.20	5.80	8.40
T.M.	4.00	3.90	5.20	6.27	5.80	7.60
L.W.	4.73	3.80	4.80	7.00	6.50	9.60
I.K.	6.57	6.90	7.00	9.00	7.60	9.60
			MOTOR			
R.A.	4.30	2.90	5.30	6.67	6.90	7.60
T.C.	11.60	11.30	11.80	13.90	14.20	16.80
O.J.	12.90	12.50	13.00	15.33	13.50	14.20
M.G.	3.93	3.90	4.00	6.20	5.90	7.20
T.M.	4.00	3.90	5.10	6.27	5.80	8.20
L.W.	4.73	2.90	5.20	7.00	6.00	6.90
I.K.	6.57	6.00	7.60	9.00	9.20	11.30

TABLE 3

WEIGHTS FOR POSSIBLE PASSES AT SIX-MONTH TIME INTERVALS

Time Interval in Months	MENTAL Number of Possible Passes	Weight	MOTOR Number of Possible Passes	Weight
0.0 to 5.9	70	.09	26	.23
6.0 to 17.9	29	.21	20	.30
12.0 to 17.9	24	.25	8	.75
18.0 to 23.9	19	.32	2	3.00

TABLE 4

PRE- AND POST-TEST MENTAL AGE-PLACEMENT SCORES

Name	Age at Pre-test	Pre-test Age Score	Diff.	Age at Post-test	Post-test Age Score	Diff.
R.A.	4.30	4.20	—.09	6.67	7.63	.96
T.C.	11.60	11.26	—.34	13.90	13.95	.05
O.J.	12.90	11.92	—.98	15.33	15.27	—.06
M.G.	3.93	4.16	.23	6.20	7.27	1.07
T.M.	4.00	3.98	—.02	6.27	7.27	1.00
L.W.	4.73	4.16	—.57	7.00	7.76	.76
I.K.	6.57	6.90	.33	9.00	8.02	—.98

into six-month intervals and the total number of possible passes in each of the intervals was calculated. This total was then divided into the six-month time span in order to arrive at the equal fractional month-weights assigned to each item in the interval. Table 3 presents the possible number of passes and the weights assigned to these passes for each of the respective intervals in both the mental and motor sub-tests.

TABLE 5

PRE- AND POST-TEST MOTOR AGE-PLACEMENT SCORES

Name	Age at Pre-test	Pre-test Age Score	Diff.	Age at Post-test	Post-test Age Score	Diff.
R.A.	4.30	3.59	—.71	6.67	7.50	.83
T.C.	11.60	11.30	—.30	13.90	14.20	.30
O.J.	12.90	12.50	—.40	15.33	13.50	—1.83
M.G.	3.93	3.90	—.03	6.20	6.20	.00
T.M.	4.00	4.59	.59	6.27	7.00	.73
L.W.	4.73	3.59	—1.14	7.00	6.42	—.58
I.K.	6.57	6.60	.03	9.00	9.50	.50

TABLE 6

T-TESTS OF THE MEAN DIFFERENCES BETWEEN CHRONOLOGICAL AND TEST AGE AGAINST AN EXPECTED MEAN DIFFERENCE OF ZERO FOR BOTH THE MENTAL AND MOTOR SUB-TESTS

M Chron. Age	M Test Age	Pre-test M Diff.	t-test	M Chron. Age	M Test Age	Post-test M Diff.	t-test
				Mental			
6.86	6.65	—.21	1.23 (n.s)	9.20	9.60	.40	1.951 (p<.05)
				Motor			
6.86	6.58	—.28	1.346 (n.s.)	9.20	9.19	—.01	.020 (n.s.)

The individual age-placement scores which resulted from this scoring method are presented separately for the mental and motor sub-tests in Tables 4 and 5.

A consistent trend is observable in the pre- to post-test progress shown by these infants. While in both the mental and motor sub-tests five of the seven infants performed at a level below that which might be expected from their chronological age at the pre-test, at the post-test five of the seven (not the same five) performed at a level *equal to or above* that which might be expected from their chronological age. In addition, for both sub-tests, six of the seven infants improved relative to their chronological ages during the period of intervention.

The mean differences between chronological age and test age and the results of t-tests of these sample means against expected means of zero are presented in Table 6.

After intervention, the infants' performance on the mental sub-test was significantly (p<.05) above the level which might be expected on

TABLE 7

T-TESTS OF THE DIFFERENCES BETWEEN CORRELATED MEANS
FOR BOTH THE MENTAL AND MOTOR SUB-TESTS

Name	Test Age/ Chron. Age	Expected Gain	Actual Gain	t
		Mental		
R.A.	.979	2.32	3.42	
T.C.	.971	2.23	2.69	
O.J.	9.24	2.25	3.35	
M.G.	1.058	2.40	3.11	
T.M.	.995	2.26	3.29	
L.W.	.879	1.99	3.60	
I.K	1.050	2.55	1.12	
MEAN	.979	2.29	2.94	2.03 (p<.05)
		Motor		
R.A.	.835	1.98	3.91	
T.C.	.974	2.24	2.90	
O.J.	.969	2.35	1.00	
M.G.	.992	2.25	2.30	
T.M.	1.147	2.60	2.41	
L.W.	.759	1.72	2.83	
I.K.	1.005	2.44	2.90	
MEAN	.954	2.23	2.61	1.15 (n.s.)

the basis of their chronological age, even though they performed, on the average, below (though not significantly below) their respective level before initiation of the project. On the motor sub-test, the results are not as clear. At the end of the project the sample was performing at a level essentially equal to that expected on the basis of their chronological age even though again they were below that level (though not significantly so) at the time of the pre-test.

These data from the pilot sample are suggestive of the potential impact of the Infant Education project. Certainly there is every reason to believe that home teaching as a method of altering the growth pattern of disadvantaged infants is worth an intensive trial.

Part III
CURRICULUM

While curriculum normally refers only to a course of study, in this project the term is used as an umbrella to include the entire process of home teaching interaction. Specifically, it includes both the development of the mother's ability to control and teach her child and the actual *teaching agenda* or activities carried out in the home with the mother-child dyad. What is done in the home is limited only by the relationship that can be established between the mother and teacher. As discussed in the case study, T.D.'s mother watched a T.V. series regarding child care and yet she was totally unable to apply the knowledge obtained. It is the carefully paced and carefully focused mother-teacher relationship that allows for the gradual improvement in the child's total environment. To be successful, the teacher must be aware of the dynamics in the home. This knowledge is part of the base the teacher draws upon to provide an individualized program of sequenced activities for support of the infant's growth and for encouraging the mother's interest as an effective participant in the child's learning process. After the dynamics of working in the home is discussed, this section will present information on the development of the teacher's role, individual programming, teaching style and control techniques, teaching agenda and teacher planning.

DYNAMICS OF WORKING IN THE HOME

Teachers working in the homes of disadvantaged families must accept a role different from that assumed when working in traditional classrooms or clinical settings. Professionally, teachers are trained to work with groups that are basically captive audiences making the sacrifice and effort to be present and assuming low "power" positions, i.e., sitting at desks, answering roll calls, performing to teacher expectations, etc. In addition, classroom teachers seldom have their performance judged in any immediate way other than being "liked" or "disliked" by their students. Only occasionally is long term achievement by students introduced as a possible consideration of teaching effectiveness. Home teaching, on the other hand, demands a very different performance on the part of the teacher; acceptance of a position of low power, immediate critical evaluation of teaching, and adjustment to economic and social differences are all required.

The teacher is a guest in the home of a mother. As a guest, the teacher must sit where told to sit and put up with many inconveniences, e.g., dirt, bugs, disease, poor heating, lack of work space, lack of access to teaching supplies, assorted visitors viewing the teaching, summary dismissal by the mother, cancellations of appointments by the mother, etc. In all of this the teacher basically assumes a position of low power.

In addition, the mother does an immediate evaluation of the teacher's performance during the working session. In the classroom the teacher is seldom judged in areas other than discipline and classroom management. In the home, trial and error teaching is not well received and negative reaction is immediate to teaching failure. The teacher must demonstrate that she can tap the child's ability, handle teaching situations correctly, and explain why something did or didn't work. If she fails in any of these categories, she seldom receives a second chance unless the mother is convinced of the teacher's expertise.

Even though the teacher focuses primarily on education of the child, knowledge of and feeling for the economic situation of the family is important. For instance, a mother with limited income cannot purchase many toys for the children. The teacher must show the mother ways to use everyday household objects for toys (such as coffee cans, clothespins, cartons, etc.) or use examples of good, serviceable, inexpensive toys available at the local discount stores. On the other hand, families who have money to spend must be helped to understand that many expensive toys that whirl and twirl neither maintain the child's interest nor aid his development as much as simpler toys, such as blocks, with which the child can perform innumerable manipulations.

It is essential that the teacher neither make moral judgements nor show surprise, disgust, or rejection of aspects of the social, cultural and moral make-up of the family which are poignantly apparent even though the teacher does not try to become aware of them. The teacher who focuses her interest on the child and on the mother as the child's teacher is more likely to reach the goals for improvement in the child and changes in the mother than the one who is overly absorbed in such things as cleanliness and presence or absence of fathers. Since culturally different situations do occur, however, the teacher needs ideas on how to handle them as well as a few well chosen rules, such as: "Do not enter the house if a child answers the door. Ask the child to get his mother, then wait outside until she knows you are present."

The project staff believes the *key element of concern* is that the mother stimulate and support the infant's growth. This single and narrow focus makes her role as teacher palatable to the mother over the long period of contact. Only those things which have a direct bearing on the infant's participation in the teaching session are brought up with the mother. For example, if the baby has diaper rash and is fussy and cannot sit for the activities, the teacher might mention using cornstarch and changing diapers frequently. If the rash is severe, the teacher would encourage the mother to keep her appointment at the well-baby clinic and to ask for suggestions from the doctor, or she would suggest the mother call the visiting nurse assigned to her for help in clearing up the rash. In any case, the teacher constantly reinforces for the mother that her narrow and only concern is the growth and intellectual development of the child with the mother acting as the child's teacher. (This position of only educational concern is possible in this Southeastern Michigan community because of the extensive agency service available to all families with need. Such a position is not feasible in centers operated by this Foundation in Mississippi, for example.)

DEVELOPMENT OF THE TEACHER'S ROLE

The role of educational consultant to disadvantaged families is not a natural one. The teacher is not a typical part of the home environment and must work very hard to be accepted. It is the mother's home and she definitely establishes the structure, which includes what is acceptable to her and to the infant and the general working conditions in the home, and which is influenced by whether or not she is actively seeking help in raising her child or sees the teacher's presence as reflecting "how nice it is that schools are so interested in infants." The responsive teacher must adapt to the various roles assigned by different mothers. For instance, in one home the teaching session starts at the door. When the teacher enters she is greeted, toys are carried to the table by a preschool youngster, and mother starts talking about the changes she has observed in the infant during the past week. The teacher may be direct she may demonstrate and suggest, and she may observe the family while the mother plays a favorite game with the child. In another home, the teacher and mother talk amiably for a few minutes about the baby while sitting in the living room. Then mother abruptly announces, "It is 1:30. Time to start." The trio then begin the business of the day at the kitchen table. The mother sees nothing before, after or between the activities with the child as related to the session.

As the teacher moves from "outsider" to "insider" with the family, the mother usually drops most pretenses (after about the third visit), such as assumed social mannerisms, carefully formulated language patterns, stiff rules (e.g., as to where each one sits in the room), and apologies for the condition of the room or the infant's appearance. She feels free to punish as she usually does, to speak naturally, and eventually in many instances to begin to bring up topics related to folklore, such as the "importance" of consuming clay during pregnancy or the "danger" to physical development by cutting a child's hair. With some mothers, this kind of acceptance and exchange facilitates discussions about growth and development and encourages activities. And it is rather unlikely that without these discussions permanent changes in attitudes toward child development will occur.

In essence, the creation of the teacher's role is determined by how the mother can accept the teacher and how the teacher can fulfill the objectives of the project after answering the question, "How do we work together?" We don't try to force mothers into the teacher's structure or concept of what is *the* most appropriate learning situation; rather the teacher determines how she can fit into the existing home structure and operate in a manner which gives support and impetus for change.

Teachers take a broad range of specific roles with individual mothers and may assume different roles at different times with the same mothers.

1. *Reinforcer*—Teacher supports everything good the mother does. This role is assumed with mothers who basically know what to do but are unsure of themselves.

2. *Activity director*—Teacher gives ideas to the mother who wants to do things with her baby but doesn't know what to do.

3. *Director*—The teacher is seen as an authority by the mother. In this role the teacher is very direct and specific in stating the kinds of activities to be employed, and their purposes.

4. *Casual friend*—Teacher imparts and shares information about the child's growth, development, toys, and activities with mother in an incidental way.

5. *Information seeker and giver*—Teacher assumes the role of observer with the mother who feels very insecure about her relationship with her child. The teacher gets and gives information unobtrusively during "games with the baby" time.

Regardless of role, most mothers respond well if the teacher maintains good communication, explains what the activities are, what the child is doing or learning, and keeps the focus on the child rather than on the mother's performance as a parent.

INDIVIDUAL PROGRAMMING

The process of being an effective teacher includes specific activities for teacher, mother, and child which intensify home teaching. The essential condition of effective home teaching by the teachers can be stated as the development of a perception of the mother's and infant's behavior or stage of development followed by a choice of course of action to produce growth based on that perception. Because a successful program must be carefully individualized for each mother-child dyad, this definition was adopted to insure accurate and sympathetic teacher observation of the mother's behavior and the child's development. Then, since the main goal of home teaching is to enable each mother to become an effective teacher to her child, we are interested in influencing the mother in terms both of her perception of the child and of the information available to her for choice of action.

The perception of the infant's behavior becomes more valid and the choice of action more effective for both the teacher and the mother by: 1) observing the child's responses (not pass-fail) to structured test items (e.g., observing the administration of the Bayley) ; 2) sharing knowledge and information about the many developmental steps established as descriptive of growth in language, motor skills and cognition; and 3) observing the infant's reaction to activities sequenced to fit his particular pattern of development.

TEACHING STYLE AND CONTROL TECHNIQUES

Before it is possible or even advisable to alter a mother's teaching style, language patterns and control techniques, it is necessary to observe and examine the interaction between the mother and the child. Teachers must become aware of such factors as the mother's attitude toward the child's intellectual development, her understanding of the growth process, the way she reacts to the child's experimentation, alternatives known and used by her in language training, infant stimulation and behavior controls, and the mother's expectations for the child's performance. The teacher must also determine the impact or implications of these factors as the mother employs them for the child's future responsiveness.

Because understanding these mother-child factors places a heavy burden on the teacher's observation at a time when she is struggling to develop rapport in the home and define activities that are developmentally appropriate to the child, the *Ypsilanti Picture Sorting Inventory* (YPSI) was developed to facilitate and systematize the process. This instrument is a collection of 122 drawings of infants engaged in a variety of motor, cognitive and verbal activities. The pictures were designed primarily to obtain diagnostic information for teachers on the mother's perception of child development in general and her observations of and expectations for her own child's development. This goal is achieved by presenting each picture individually to the mother and asking her to describe the pictured child's activity and to state whether or not she thinks her own child has ever engaged in that activity. When all of the pictures have been presented in this manner, those which the mother has stated do not show activities of her child are again presented individually and the mother is asked whether or not she thinks her child "will be doing this" in four months.

In addition to immediate diagnostic information, many YPSI items provide a direct measure of the accuracy of the mother's observations. The test also taps how realistic her expectations are for her child. This information is obtained by comparison of the mother's answers on certain of the YPSI items (designed to portray activities tested in the

Bayley) with the child's actual Bayley performance both immediately and four months after the administration of the YPSI.

In many ways, the definitions by O. K. Moore (1967) of "responsive environment" and "autotelic activities" have been useful to teachers in deciding how to help a mother achieve a responsive relationship with her child and facilitate her child's growth. *Responsive environment* permits the learner free exploration, self pacing, full use of his capacity for discovering relations, possibilities for interconnected discoveries and immediate information about the consequences of his actions. (p. 340) *Autotelic activity* is engaging in something for its own sake rather than for obtaining rewards or avoiding punishments that have no inherent connection with the activity itself. (p. 341) These criteria are not used by teachers in the same manner as in the highly organized curriculum established at the Hamden Hall Laboratory, but they can be of direct help in developing the control techniques and teaching style of the mother.

1. *Free exploration.* Many mothers have control problems very early because they do not see the necessity of allowing the child to explore or experiment. For example, on one visit it was noticed that while the mother and teacher were talking, the infant kept reaching for objects which the mother quickly withdrew from his reach. When all objects were removed or hidden, the child became interested in a shiny metal ashtray the mother was using. As the infant tried to reach the ashtray from the right side of the chair, the mother moved it to the left side. After the infant (12 months) slowly worked his way to the left side of the chair, the mother moved it to the right side. This was repeated several times until the baby sat down and cried. The mother was annoyed and ready to spank him rather than provide some suitable object for play.

2. *Self pacing.* The interests and whims of infants dictate what will maintain their attention. Since an infant has not yet learned to accept a learning situation which is not to his liking, he responds to such a situation by crying, fussing, refusing to participate or going to sleep. It is necessary to correctly read the concepts, schemas, and experiments in which the infant is involved in order to be able to choose activities that will match and stimulate his interests.

3. *Full use of capacity.* This element and self pacing are highly dependent on the mother's level of expectation being within a reasonable range of the child's possible performance. It is not self pacing if the child is expected to walk at six months, nor can it be a full use of capacity if the mother would prefer to retard the child's walking by keeping him confined in a play pen until 20 months of age.

4. *Autotelic activity.* If external rewards for performing activities in the teaching session are overused, a child begins to continually look

for approval of what he is doing, or to repeat a few rewarded behaviors rather than advance to new and more difficult activities. While external reinforcement is a useful technique for teachers and mothers to involve certain passive infants and curb overly active ones, careful programming will permit adequate matching of activities with the developmental level of the baby to encourage interest in the activity for its own sake.

In order to involve the mother in the primary relationship of education of her infant, the teacher employs a number of techniques. Some of these are illustrated next.

Techniques Employed by Teachers

A. To facilitate the mother's perception of her infant.
   1. Provide interpretations for behavior child is showing.
      a. Learning.
         "Oh, look, he's learned to dangle the beads."
         "He really seems to have learned to . . ."
      b. Controls.
         "Maybe he's tired of this game. Let's try . . ."
         "That noise seems to be much more interesting to him than this right now. We'll wait a minute and try again.'
   2. Point out effect of mother's action on baby by taking "talking" role for baby in indirect way.
      a. "She says, 'Oh, Mommy, that hurt.' "
      b. "He says, 'Oh, Mommy, that's very hard.' "
   3. Call attention to transference of new skills or use of basic skill in a new way: "He's trying to dangle the hammer just like he does the beads."
   4. Call attention to new skills or expectations by asking information from mother about:
      a. Behavior.
         "Has R. been dropping any of his toys on purpose yet?"
      b. Play.
         "What things did O. like to play with this week?"
      c. Comparisons with sibs.
         "What did his brother do when he was five months old?"
      d. Likes and dislikes.
         "Have you noticed if he is doing any . . . ?"
   5. Make schemata checklist and ask mother to help watch for several specified behaviors in child given a series of toys during lesson.
      a. Discuss doing it together—teacher check off list as mother observes.
      b. Have mother check off list as observer.
      c. Ask mother to do activities so teacher can be "free" to check off.

B. To encourage involvement of the mother.
   1. Reinforce any comments or participation of mother by picking up on suggestions and modifying lesson to include interest of mother.
   Mother: "He's trying to pull himself up in his crib now."
   Teacher: "Oh, really? Let's see if he can pull himself up by using someone's fingers. Maybe he will do that better with you."
   2. Elaborate idea of mother.
   Mother: "I don't know, maybe she's afraid of the water or she's just being stubborn."
   Teacher: "Well, most 12-month-old babies would probably put up a fuss if left in the water alone. She's probably still a little too young. Maybe you could play with her or leave some sponges in the water to make bath time fun and then she may get some confidence."
   3. Compliment mother on new insight.
      a. "That was a good idea. Do you mind if I pass it on to one of the other mothers?"
      b. *Mother*: "R. put his toys in a pail the other day."
      Teacher: "That really helps me in planning the lesson—to know what he does during the week."
   4. Ask the mother to do specific things during the lesson.
      a. "Maybe Mommy will play 'peek' with you."
      b. "Maybe he'll do this better for you."
      c. "Will you try this while I find something else in my bag?"
   5. Suggest that mother work on special things during the week.
      a. "He seems to be almost ready to sit. Maybe you could give him some more practice time a few minutes a day this week."
      b. "You might try dropping a toy with him this week. He is beginning to get the idea."
   6. Try to bring flow of general conversation back to child by relating some comment of mother to child's needs, etc.
      a. Mother discussing problems with welfare workers—teacher brings discussion focus to people in authority positions in general by recounting some school experience. Then—
      b. Mother talking about her own school problems—teacher talks about children's learning in general. Then—
      c. Mother talking about goals for own children—teacher discusses important concepts involved in attaining goals.
   7. Ask mother's opinion about a technique teacher has been using that is not very successful to see if mother can suggest an alteration that might improve activity.
      a. "She doesn't seem to like this very much. Maybe there's some other thing we can do with this."

b. "Would you like to try something else with this? She doesn't seem to be responding to me."

c. "Can you think of another way to get her interested in this? She just doesn't like this."

8. Include activities in lesson that need both teacher and mother involved.
   a. Rolling ball between baby and teacher—mother helping baby.
   b. Playing "pass it around," etc.

9. Share decision making about course of lesson plan for next time by asking mother if she has a choice about what area to work on next.
   a. "Well, she's doing very well on these things, isn't she? Do you think we should continue with this or should we concentrate on some language games?"
   b. "Is there anything that you would particularly like for us to work on next time?"

C. To support skill improvement of the mother.

1. Demonstrate more successful ways to control child when opportunity occurs in lesson.
   a. "Let's try . . ."
   b. "Maybe this would help."

2. Bring material or use some material present to distract "misbehaving" child and point out response to mother.
   a. "Maybe if we give him something more interesting, he'll cooperate again."
   b. "She (an older child) seems to mind better if we give her something specific to do while we play with the baby."

3. Explain or point out purpose of each activity to mother.
   a. "This will help him understand how to use things as tools."
   b. "This is important for good muscle development."

4. When mother is doing an activity with the baby, join in the activity briefly to introduce a new idea or expand mother's technique.
   a. *Language*: Mother telling baby to look in mirror saying, "Look, Jimmy!"
      Teacher joins in and says, "Touch the baby" or, "See the baby"; teacher withdraws when mother picks up expansion.
   b. *Teaching*: Mother trying to interest child in new toy. Teacher suggests, "Maybe she'll be more interested if you show her how it works first."

5. Join in activity to modify teaching style of mother that is unsuccessful or detrimental to child's learning.

6. Mother demanding that child give up toy to start a new game.

Teacher suggests mother try to "trade" toys with baby before mother starts to snatch toy away.

7. Reinforce those teaching styles of the mother that seem to be most successful with child or that seem to be most conducive to learning.

    a. "It was a good idea to get her interested first."

    b. "You're right! It's good that you answer her when she talks even if you're not sure just exactly what she said."

    c. "I'll try your way with this toy. She really seems to like that kind of game."

8. Explain what behavior or response you want from the child in order to get mother to discriminate the successful from the unsuccessful performances of the child and to see how her own or teacher's approach can affect the quality of the child's performance.

TEACHING AGENDA: PROGRAM OF SEQUENCED ACTIVITIES FOR
SUPPORTING THE INFANT'S GROWTH

In some ways the period of infancy is an easier time for teaching than the elementary school age, for the child is usually very curious and wants to investigate everything in as many ways as are known to him. Because of this, it is possible to provide a teaching environment as well as a responsive one. Five criteria are employed for choosing infant activities suitable for use in the home teaching session. 1) They must be play oriented as the child must enjoy his involvement or he will not attend. 2) They must be novel enough to maintain the child's attention. 3) They must be variable, alternating "old favorites" with new and challenging toys or games. 4) They must strengthen the nucleus of schemas and concepts that the child already understands or provide the basis for new understanding. 5) They must be something in which the child can actively participate rather than something done to him or for his entertainment.

Because of the individualized curriculum for each mother-child dyad, what is important is not which activities a teacher might choose, but rather their relation to three critical areas of development: language, motoric skills and cognition. A compilation of suggested activities helps the teachers create a teaching agenda which focuses on the dual goals of activities for mother and child and orientation to gross sequences in child development.

In the creation of a teaching agenda, the Piagetian developmental sequence, outlined by Uzgiris and Hunt (1967), provided a format for the gross organization of infant activities and became the "subject" areas in the traditional use of the word. As stated by Uzgiris (1967),

"The notion of an orderly sequence does not necessarily imply that development is predetermined. It can be equally assumed that the order is based upon a continuous interaction of the child and his environment, where earlier achievements make other higher level forms of interaction possible and in turn lead to new achievements." The scales may also be used to interpret child behavior to mothers and to determine levels of stimulation activity for each infant.

The teacher who is constantly assessing and analyzing an individual infant is able to choose, adjust or relate activities cross-sectionally from a sequence to fit the child if she knows the purpose of the activities and has a sense of total developmental organization. The present curriculum development includes two key areas. The first is the development of *cognitively related activities.* Teachers are governed in the presentation of activities in a unit by

(a) Always including the desired behavior in the activity so that the teacher can make alterations to assure the child success or create new but similar activities most appropriate to a particular child.
(b) Identifying concepts within the sequences as subtopics to clarify what is being taught (for example, putting an object inside of another object is essential to the concept of container).

Following is an outline of the Uzgiris-Hunt Scales and the sequences contained in each. A sample teaching agenda (range of potential activities) presently being developed for one of the areas is also presented.

OUTLINE OF INFANT ACTIVITY UNITS
FROM UZGIRIS-HUNT SCALES

Unit 1) Visual Pursuit and Permanence of Objects
Sequences: a. Visual Search
b. Partial Disappearance
c. Complete Disappearance
d. Superimposed Screens
e. Invisible Displacement
f. Series of Displacement

Unit 2) Development of Means for Achieving Desired Environmental Events
Sequences: a. Eye-hand Coordination
b. Secondary Circular Reactions
c. Differentiation of Means and Ends
d. Use of Other Objects as Intermediaries
e. Representation of Means

Unit 3) Development of Causality
        Sequences: a. Effort to Prolong Interesting Inputs
                  b. Use of Procedures to Maintain Interesting Inputs
                  c. Use of Direct Action to Maintain Interesting Inputs
                  d. Objectification of Causality
                  e. Representative Causality

Unit 4) The Construction of the Object in Space
        Sequences: a. Development of the Notion of Recognizable Object
                  b. Development of Understanding of Relationships Between Objects
                  c. Interest in the Phenomenon of Fall
                  d. Representation of Objects in Space

Unit 5) Development of Imitation
        Sequences: a. Beginning of Differentiation in Vocal Productions
                  b. Development of Imitation of Sound Patterns
                  c. Imitation of Words
                  d. Imitation of Familiar Gestures
                  e. Imitation of Unfamiliar Gestures

SAMPLE TEACHING AGENDA

ACTIVITY UNIT 4

THE CONSTRUCTION OF THE OBJECT IN SPACE

A. *Development of the Notion of Recognizable Object*

1. Present two different colored objects to baby lying in supine position to stimulate baby to look from one object to another.
2. Shake a noise maker on either side and above head to stimulate baby to locate object.
3. Present two stationary objects to baby in sitting position to stimulate baby to look from one to another.
4. Shake a container with objects in it to stimulate baby to look in container for noisemaker.
5. Attract baby's attention with a colorful object. Move the object slowly toward screen from the right, continue behind screen moving it to make it reappear on the opposite side of the screen. Repeat the sequence to stimulate baby to glance to the side of the screen where the object will reappear. Reverse directions—from left to right.

6. Drop a bright colored object from a height, to stimulate baby to follow object to floor and begin awareness of trajectory.
7. Drop object so that it hits another surface before it falls to the floor and rolls out of sight to stimulate baby to look in direction of fallen object.
8. Present object with definite reverse sides. Present object with wrong side to stimulate baby to turn object to the right side.

The second key area in the development of the curriculum is *language*. The general goal of the project in language development is to increase the mother's awareness of the child's developing language ability and to help her offer him appropriate aid and encouragement.

Specific goals may be stated in terms of developmental areas:

1. Vocabulary development.
   a. Word recognition, including the ability to recognize recurrence of words and to divide utterances into words.
   b. Word production, ranging from the replicable production of some collection of speech sounds, whether meaningful or not and without regard to occurrence in adult language, to progressively finer articulatory discrimination.
   c. Meaning, ranging from the discovery of some correspondence between a word and the real world to the development of a large vocabulary of definite and interrelated meanings.
2. Combination of words into longer utterances, with regard to both production and comprehension.
   a. Simple combination. Any words put together in any order to indicate that a situation talked about has to do with both, or comprehending that an adult utterance involving two words is about both of them in an interdependent way.
   b. Development of restrictions on word combinations.
      (1) Development of grammatical classes.
      (2) Development of a variety of grammatical structures.
3. Awareness and exploitation of language as communication.
   a. Awareness of speech as directed *to* child.
   b. Awareness of own vocalization as affecting environment.
   c. Progressively more discriminate awareness of relations between particular utterances and meanings.

Clearly most of these areas and sub-areas may be chronologically ordered, if at all, only with respect to their onsets, since there is overlap. Instead of taking each area in turn and completing it before going on to the next, the teachers try to help the mother to see that anything the child does which may be interpreted as linguistic activity is growth and an expression of his state of development. As with other areas of development, the mother's awareness and participation are encouraged largely through the use of activities which provide appropriate help for the infant and, at the same time, opportunities for the teacher to point out how the child's behavior reflects his growth.

Below are some samples of language activities used by teachers in this project, organized in terms of their structural similarity, with indications of the goals they may serve and the situations in which they may be used. It is usual for one activity or type of activity to serve several ends simultaneously or be appropriate to more than one stage of the child's development. All linguistic activities are used in conjunction with other teaching agenda activities, since there is no practical reason to regard them as separate.

Language Activities

A. Imitation

The specific aim of imitation activities is to introduce the child to new vocabulary, grammatical items, etc., and to improve auditory and articulatory discrimination. It is of less importance to vary the complexity of material imitated according to the child's developmental level than to vary the degree of accuracy with which he is expected to imitate.

1. Pure imitation by adult of child's prelinguistic vocalization during normal play is used as specific reinforcement of vocal play and to encourage repetition of particular sound patterns. It increases the child's awareness of language as a special form of interaction and as a means of affecting his environment. During the later prelinguistic stages, it is more useful to "answer" the child's babbling with English, however.

2. Games in which child is encouraged to imitate adult speech.
    a. Naming activities.
        (1) Preverbal children: objective is child's first word. In course of normal play, feeding, etc., name objects slowly, clearly, and repeatedly.
            (a) Objects such as bottle, familiar toys.
            (b) Address baby by name.
            (c) Mirror play ("There's a BABY; there's MOMMY . . .")
        (2) Older children: objectives are increased vocabulary, improvement of articulatory control, and increased accuracy in auditory discrimination.
            (a) Name variety of common objects, encouraging child to imitate.
            (b) Name pictures from magazines for child to imitate.
            (c) Gradually move to finer distinctions, both of sound (Doll: Ball) and meaning (Dog:Cat, Bowl:Cup).
        (3) Naming games are also used to introduce other linguistic areas, such as questions and simple predications ("What's that? That's a . . .").
    b. Imitation games involving both linguistic and nonlinguistic imitation. In general these activities stress the relation of words to

actions, as opposed to objects, and thus may lead to differentiation of grammatical classes.
  (1) Peek-a-boo.
  (2) Pat-a-cake.
  (3) Wave (and say) bye-bye.
  (4) Give it to . . .
c. Imitation with substitution. In general, these are activities holding some part of a situation and/or utterance constant while changing another part. The objective is to establish equivalences among substituted items.
  (1) Show me your nose/eyes/doll . . .
  (2) Give it to Mommy/Mrs. Miller/the doggie . . .
  (3) Find the block/ball/beads/clown . . .
  (4) Find/hide/give me the ball/block/doll . . .
  (5) Give me the red/blue/big . . . ball.

Note: In all the above, the child is encouraged to imitate the speech as well as the actions involved.

3. Imitations with expansion.
  a. Elaborations. Adult repeats nearest correct English equivalent of child's utterance, and encourages imitation. For example:
    (1) Child: Baw. Adult: That's right, ball.
    (2) Child: Dat baw. Adult: Yes, that's a ball.
    (3) Child: Mommy ball. Adult: Yes, Mommy has the ball.
  Clearly it is necessary to use situational clues for the best elaboration.
  b. Extensions. Child is encouraged to repeat a gradually extended utterance. Examples:
    (1) Ball
        It's a ball.
        It's a big ball, etc.
    (2) There's a ball.
        There's a ball and a duck, etc.

B. Comprehension

In general, this class of activities is very similar to that under A (imitation), except that the child is asked to show by some response, verbal or nonverbal. depending on his ability, that he understands what is said.

1. Vocabulary.
  a. Determine whether child responds differentially to own name.
  b. Ask child for familiar objects by name.
  c. Ask child to point to objects, persons in mirror, or in pictures.
  d. Use a simple imperative with a variety of verbs. For example: Show/give me the ball, hide/find it, etc.
  e. Ask child to pick out objects by size, shape.

2. Words in combination. Objective is to explore child's ability to respond to two or more parts of a single utterance as related.
  a. Show pictures of objects in pairs, ask child to point to pictures. (Show me the boy and the dog; the dog playing with the ball; etc.)

  b. Require child to respond to imperatives in which two parts are simultaneously varied.
   (1) Give *Mommy* the *ball;* give *me* the *block;* etc.
   (2) Where's *your nose?* Where's *Mommy's ear;* etc.
   (3) Show pictures of a variety of situations, ask child to point to the dog running, the boy sitting down, the girl playing ball, etc.

C. Production
  Production is distinguished from imitation in that the general goal is to encourage the child to use his own words and phrases to express his own thoughts and desires, rather than to parrot what adults have said.

 1. Vocabulary.
  a. Ask child to name familiar objects.
  b. Encourage child to ask for toys, bottle, etc. by name.
  c. Encourage child to name his reflection in mirror, to call people by name.
  d. Ask child for descriptions of situations (What's he doing? Where's your doll? etc.)

 2. Attempt to elicit longer utterances.
  a. Ask child for progressively more detailed descriptions of pictures, prompting (but not supplying too much) when he stops.
  b. Tell child familiar story, stop occasionally and ask him what he thinks will happen next.
  c. Encourage child to express desires verbally, rather than with gestures. When he asks for something with just its name, try to get him to expand before giving it to him.

  The sample activities listed above are not intended to constitute an exhaustive list; rather they are indications of what may be done, and our teachers vary their verbal interactions with the child considerably depending on the demands of the situation.

PLANNING, REPORTING AND IMPROVING TEACHER SKILLS

  The teachers use all information available to them (Bayley, YPSI, Teaching Agenda, etc.) to determine appropriate activities for mother and child. (See Part 4 for an annotated list of the testing instruments used.) It is not helpful for the teacher or mother to have a score on an infant test (and project research requirements do not permit it), but it is essential that both the mother and the teacher observe the test administration. This organized observation yields more usable information for initial planning than several observations of random behavior. In addition, it is planned to use the Uzgiris-Hunt scales as informal checklists of each child's progress to maintain the teacher's orientation to continual diagnosis.
  Another way of helping teachers improve their performance has been to use video tape. The initial intention of the video tapes was to show

various conditions the teachers must face in the home: active baby, responsive mother in loud environment, passive baby, passive mother in quiet environment, etc. The tapes were only fair representations of the situations. For example, in one filming session the passive baby-passive mother dyad turned into a responsive baby and frightened mother who could not even talk, leaving the impression on the tape of a teacher working with the baby alone, since the teacher's attempts with the mother were so subtle and "soft" most viewers missed them completely. However, the tapes have documented what does happen in the homes to some degree. The major strength of the tapes has been in teacher training through improvement of teaching skills and use with new teachers. As one staff member stated about the video tapes, "Just show them to the teacher, and a teacher with any sensitivity at all will respond to seeing her method of operation on tape." The gross magnification of errors and strengths and the opportunity to compare time samples are most effective in eliciting discussions about methods, techniques, and responsibilities.

A typical lesson plan and evaluation for one visit is given next. The format was devised to help the teacher concentrate on both mother and child during each activity. The first three categories (Goal, Conditions, Technique) are the lesson plan prepared before the home visit. The last three (Actual Performance, Teacher Intervention, Trends and Recommendations) are a record of what happened during the session.

Lesson Plan:

	Mother	Child (11 months of age)
GOAL Terminal Behavior for Acceptable Performance	To understand concept of activity	(construction of objects in space). Development of understanding relationships between objects.
CONDITIONS (activity)	1) Drop objects through hole in lid of container and remove objects by prying off lid. 2) Manipulating pegs in primary peg toy.	Drop objects through hole in lid of container and remove objects by prying off lid.
TECHNIQUE	Explain purpose of activity giving other examples of same concept and ask if he has done similar things before.	1) Give can with lid on the blocks separately. If unable to drop blocks in—demonstrate. If no attempt to remove lid—demonstrate prying. 2) Give primary pegs with pegs in place.
ACCEPTABLE PERFORMANCE (specifically)	Close observation and participation in activity, any comments made indicating understanding.	1) Will drop into can either spontaneously or with demonstration—will also make attempt to pry lid either spontaneously or with demonstration. 2) Will remove pegs—finger holes and make a brief attempt to replace one peg although unsuccessful in fitting peg accurately.
ACTUAL PERFORMANCE	Mother very involved in activity—discussed other activities baby did—only those with identical condition. During peg activity—mother suggested to T. that one peg at a time be used—mother did so—verbally encouraging baby to replace peg.	Immediately dropped blocks through hole in lid—at-tempted to get block by reaching through hole—with demonstration tried to pry lid up—also tried to put lid on himself to continue game. 2) Immediately pulled pegs out, inspecting each and mouthing them, banging and picking up toy itself, turning it over inspecting carefully—made no attempt to finger hole or to make contact with peg in hole—threw pegs on floor each time he finished mouthing and banging.
TEACHER INTERVENTION	Teacher explained similarity between activities.	Teacher noticed baby had some difficulty manipulating large can on highchair so held it next to side encouraging baby to put blocks in.
TRENDS & RECOMMENDATIONS	Mother needs experience in relating separate activities to a single concept.	Bring smaller can to make it easier to use on table top.

Lesson Plan:

	Mother	Child (11 months of age)
GOAL Terminal Behavior for Acceptable Performance	Mother's awareness of baby's interest in finding lost objects.	(visual pursuit and permanence of objects). Baby follows object through complete disappearance.
CONDITIONS (activity)		1) Hiding toy under one of two screens to stimulate following a hidden object. 2) Hiding toy under one of two screens alternately to stimulate following and finding a hidden object without returning to original position of screen.
TECHNIQUE	Verbalize purpose of activity providing mother with possible responses from baby.	1) Place 2 cans on table—hide favorite toy under one stimulating looking under to find it. 2) Hide toy first under 1 can then alternate with other can to stimulate finding toy without returning to original position.
ACCEPTABLE PERFORMANCE (specifically)	Observing activity, acknowledging Teacher's comments on baby's performance.	1 & 2) Will immediately follow and pick up appropriate can retrieving toy.
ACTUAL PERFORMANCE	Mother surprised when baby lifted each can until he found toy—asked Teacher how she thought up these activities.	1) Baby immediately began knocking down and grabbing can but not aware at first that toy was under it. After 2nd attempt, immediately grabbed for can to retrieve toy—repeated this several times. 2) Baby immediately grabbed for appropriate can, retrieving toy.
TEACHER INTERVENTION		
TRENDS & RECOMMENDATIONS	Mother interested and involved, will see if she relates any similar activities during next session.	Teacher actually watched baby increase skill in retrieving toy from appropriate can—will provide more experience in this area.

Lesson Plan:

	Mother	Child (11 months of age)
GOAL Terminal Behavior for Acceptable Performance	To realize need to stimulate baby in new developmental areas.	To develop imitation of sound patterns and to use direct action to maintain interesting inputs (development of imitation and causality).
CONDITIONS (activity)	1) Repeat infant's familiar sound patterns while he's looking in mirror. 2) Repeat infant's familiar sound patterns into a container.	
TECHNIQUE	1) Discuss purpose of new activity area. 2) Join in activity to modify language, if necessary.	1) Hold mirror in front of baby—repeat sounds baby makes—if silent, make familiar sounds to induce imitation of same from baby. 2) Holding can against mouth, Teacher vocalizes familiar sounds then hands can to baby for imitation.
ACCEPTABLE PERFORMANCE (specifically)	Mother performs language activity.	1 & 2) Baby imitates sounds and/or returns can or mirror to Teacher to repeat activity.
ACTUAL PERFORMANCE	1) Teacher had left mirror on kitchen table after going into living room —mother noticed mirror commenting, "We didn't show him this" and brought mirror in showing it to baby —she tried to encourage baby to look at self saying, "there's the baby see the baby"; also told how he became intrigued with a friend's full length mirror talking and playing with his image. 2) Mother observed activity quite excitedly as baby directed his responses to teacher.	1) Grabbed mirror excitedly, pushed face toward it smiling—non-verbal at first then began vocalizing for few seconds but more excited breathing rather than vocalizing—kept grabbing mirror pushing it away then close again. 2) Pushed can against face without producing sounds— handed can to teacher for continuation of activity—repeated this several times.
TEACHER INTERVENTION	Teacher joined in mirror activity producing familiar baby sounds rather than words mother was using—mother picked up teacher's style and continued activity.	

Lesson Plan:

	Mother	Child (11 months of age)
GOAL		Development of use of other objects as intermediaries (development of means for achieving ends).
Terminal Behavior for Acceptable Performance	Awareness of baby's ability to secure an out-of-reach object—induce mother to relate or give similar activity.	
CONDITIONS (activity)		1) Present baby with string attached to toy resting on floor to stimulate vertical pulling to obtain out of reach toy. 2) Present baby with string attached to toy out of reach to stimulate horizontal pulling. 3) Present baby with diaper and favorite toy at opposing end to stimulate pulling diaper to reach toy.
TECHNIQUE	Comments about baby's performance as he performs—wait for mother to take initiative.	1) Dangle toy by string—drop toy to floor—giving string to baby. 2) Place toy out of reach leaving string within baby's reach. 3) Place toy on far end of diaper leaving opposite end of diaper within reach.
ACCEPTABLE PERFORMANCE (specifically)	Mother assumes an active role by offering a similar toy and/or relating a similar experience she had with baby.	1) Will vertically pull on string until he reaches toy then immediately grabs toy. 2) Will manipulate and pull string toward him until toy is within reach, then grabs toy. 3) Will pull diaper toward him until toy is within reach, then grabs toy.
ACTUAL PERFORMANCE	Mother had related to teacher how older children had been playing with baby using pull toy and showing him how to manipulate it with the string. After baby finished playing with toys teacher brought, mother went to get toy children used with him and verbally tried to interest baby in pulling string—seemed pleased when baby began pulling string to reach toy.	2) On first attempt, baby succeeded in reaching toy by pulling string. On 2nd attempt, baby pulled with more force compelling toy to fall toward floor although baby held onto string. Baby began manipulating, watching toy dangle—repeated dangling several toys but unable to pull string vertically with enough force to reach toy. 3) Manipulated and pulled diaper toward him grabbing toy when it was within reach—repeated this several times.
TRENDS & RECOMMENDATIONS	Continue to encourage mother's active participation in lesson.	Since baby did not succeed in reaching toy by vertical pulling, will provide more activities in this area.

Part IV
REVIEW OF THE PROJECT DESIGN

The outcomes of the project are expected to be found in four major areas: (1) language style of the mother, (2) teaching style of the mother, (3) child management style of the mother, and (4) growth and intellectual development of the child. The work during the pilot phase of the project was directed mainly at the development of instruments and reporting procedures to meet the research demands of the project. It is recognized that most of the essential measures of concern to the project will not be made until the final testing sessions at the end of the project. The comparison among groups will produce the most important information about the impact of the intervention.

The basic design of the project has been altered in two ways to increase the amount of information that can be gained. First, two control groups have been added to the original experimental group and contrast group. Basically, the experimental group ($N = 33$) receives home teaching by qualified and supervised teachers who employ a theoretically based curriculum. The contrast group ($N = 33$) receives home visits by concerned community women and college-age girls who wish to help the family. The curriculum employed is "intuitive" to the volunteers. The first control group ($N = 33$) receives all testing but no other intervention, and the second control group (N undetermined) receives only initial and then final testing without further intervention of any sort.

The second change in the design was to include a study on "age-at-time-of-intervention." This is being accomplished by phasing in the children of all groups at three months, seven months, and eleven months of age. The addition of this factor was primarily an attempt to provide evidence on the question of possible differential effects of entering an education program at different times in infancy.

TESTING INSTRUMENTS USED

While most of the essential measures of project impact will be made at the end of the intervention period, a number of instruments have been employed throughout the project period. Most of these instruments pertain directly to the specific research goals of the project, while some are more directly concerned with description of either the sample being studied or the process of intervention. Special emphasis is given to the fact that a trained observer, i.e., the teacher, is in the home of experimental families once each week. The volunteers are also involved in the homes of the contrast group on a once-a-week basis and an attempt is made to solicit information from them as well.

Maternal Behavior Inventory. This 186 item inventory is completed by the teacher on each mother after the third visit to the home and at intervals throughout the project. The inventory, developed by Dr. Earl Schaefer of the National Institute of Mental Health, assesses a wide range of dimensions, such as the observer's rating of the mother's practice in discipline, amount of anxieties, irritabilities, sociabilities, etc.

Teacher's Report, Form B. This report form was developed by the project staff to provide assessment of each teaching session. The teacher records her observations of the infant and the mother and documents the instructional activities. The lesson plan included in Part 3 is from one of these report forms.

Infant Cognitive Home Environment Scale. This instrument represents an attempt to revise downward a Cognitive Home Environment Scale used with preschool children. It explores the stimulation provided by the home.

Infant Information Inventory. General information is obtained with this form on the physical surroundings of the home and the general family situation.

Infant and Maternal Medical History. This medical form is designed to obtain information on the prenatal and birth history of the mother and child. It was developed locally with consultants from the medical staff of the University of Michigan Hospital.

Ypsilanti Picture Sorting Inventory (YPSI). This instrument, developed by project staff, provides information on the mother's perception of her child and his stage of development. Especially important is the information gained from the test on the mother's ideas about the child's rate of growth and development. The instrument was discussed in more detail in the curriculum section of this report (Part 3).

Bayley Infant Scales of Development. These scales were accepted by the project as the major assessment device of the infant's growth and development, for several reasons. First, the BISD is the most recent major scale to be revised for publication and as such has had throughout its development the advantage of the availability of the previously published infant scales (Gesell, California, Cattell, etc.) and the more recent state of knowledge and theory in the field of child development. Second, the Bayley has greater age-specificity in its items, high saturation of the early age levels with items, and is at least as easily administered as any of the other scales. Third, the test does not suffer, as do several older scales, from the possible ambiguity of scoring introduced by either the use of substitutable items or the scoring of mother reports. Fourth, it is anticipated that the test will receive very wide use as an assessment device in infant educational research, and the use of the BISD by the Carnegie Project will then allow for a more ready comparison of the results of this program with those of similar programs. Fifth, and most importantly, the Bayley has gone through the most rigorous and sophisticated standardization process to be used with any infant scale (sponsored by the Psychological Corporation of New York). In addition, the standardization was accomplished in such a way as to allow for the calculation of a deviation IQ, a factor which greatly increases the value and reliability of the Bayley as a research instrument.

Attention to Transformations. While the Bayley Infant Scales of Development has been adopted as the basic assessment instrument of the program, a decision was made to adapt several techniques developed by Kagan (1968) in view of the impressive evidence he has found for what appear to be inherent differences in psychological organization and rate of cognitive growth. If such differences are relatively stable for an individual, there is a strong possibility that they may in some way interact with the overall effects of the intervention project. It would seem critical, therefore, that such differences be measured.

Traditional intelligence scales such as the Bayley do not seem to reflect inherent determiners to any great extent. One possible explanation for this lack is that, traditionally, intelligence tests have attempted to maintain a continuity over time by tapping essentially the same processes at all ages. Scott and Ball (1963) refer to this with respect to the earlier Bayley scale, the 1933 California First Year Mental Scale: "Effort was made also to provide continuity of content by using appropriate tests of the same functions at successive age levels, a condition so lacking in most intelligence scales." This is the type of continuity which Kagan refers to as "homotypic."

Kagan has distinguished another type of continuity between two behavioral variables that are manifestly different but *theoretically* related. "Crying to strangers at eight months, for instance, might index precocious schema development and, as such, not predict crying at five years but rather a large vocabulary." If there is in the child a stable underlying congenital process of the sort tacitly assumed in the development of the infant intelligence scales, perhaps it is not being measured as such because of different behavioral manifestations at different periods in the child's growth. Thus the approximately zero correlation which Bayley found in her test-retest of the California Scale from under a year to 18 months might well have been due to the attempt to enforce homotypic continuity.

In an attempt to trace one such underlying process with different behavioral manifestations at different ages and also to provide partial replication of Kagan's (1968) work, the project has adopted a portion of his assessment program. Included are three-dimensional faces and two-dimensional photographs of faces, an auditory stimulus situation and a free play situation. The variables to be employed are eye fixation, vocalization, smiling and fussing, head turning, length of attention, etc. Unlike the Bayley, the Attention to Transformations measure does not give a score but will be employed to provide basic growth and intellectual development data.

Part V
CONCLUSIONS

With the project now a year in operation, it is possible to see the potential of home teaching. Perhaps the most important observation is that the *process* of a teacher, a mother, and an infant *getting ready* to learn together is even more critical than what is actually done. To be sure, the teacher must have ideas and "expertise" to assist the mother and infant in learning, but that is a long way from simply providing a family with a series of exercises. The process of helping the family become prepared for teaching is still a fairly intuitive one on the part of the teacher. It includes great persistence by the teacher in focusing the mother's attention on the educational problems at hand. The process includes absolute flexibility in lesson plans to meet the mother half way in whatever direction is necessary to help her focus on her child. In short, the human relationship, in an almost romantic sense, is the essential condition for any educational growth. Without this relationship, nothing will occur.

Perhaps a second observation is the gradual realization that child development "theory," no matter how sophisticated, does not have as much to say as desired about specific children and their mothers. A teacher must be ready and willing to step slowly through the great distances that separate landmarks in the child's development. Using a baby's table-banging as the occasion to introduce "bang bang" vocalizations would be an example of "making do" within a real teaching situation. A teacher must blend the needs of the mother with the needs of the infant in such a way as to maximize the learning opportunity for both.

Whether or not the basic hypothesis of this research, that education in early infancy can prevent intellectual and educational handicaps, will be found to be true, the essential fact at this point is that disadvantaged families are willing to accept infant education. The job at hand is to do this effectively.

REFERENCES

KAGAN, J. Change and continuity in the first year: An inquiry into early cognitive development. Harvard University, duplicated, 1968.

MOORE, O. K. The preschool child learns to read and write. In Brackbill, Y. and Thompson, G. (Eds.) *Behavior in infancy and early childhood.* New York: The Free Press, 1967.

STOTT, L. & BALL, R. Infant and preschool mental tests: Review and evaluation. *Monographs of the Society for Research in Child Development,* No. 101, 1965.

UZGIRIS, I. Ordinality in the development of schemas for relating objects. In Hellmuth, J. (Ed.) *Exceptional infant,* Vol. 1: The Normal Infant. New York: Brunner/Mazel, Inc., 1967.

UZGIRIS, I. & HUNT, J. McV. Ordinal scales of infant development. Clark University, duplicated, 1967.

WACH, T., UZGIRIS, I. & HUNT, J. McV. Cognitive development in infants of different age levels and from different environmental back grounds. Paper presented at the biennial meeting of the Society for Research in Child Development, New York, 1967.

WEIKART, D. P. (Ed.) *Preschool intervention: preliminary results from the Perry Preschool project.* Ann Arbor, Mich.: Campus Publishers, 1967.

WEIKART, D. P. & LAMBIE, D. Z. Preschool intervention through a home teaching program. In Hellmuth, J. (Ed.) *The disadvantaged child,* Vol. 2: Head Start and Early Intervention. New York: Brunner/Mazel, Inc., 1968.

19

AN EDUCATION SYSTEM FOR HIGH-RISK INFANTS: A PREVENTIVE APPROACH TO DEVELOPMENTAL AND LEARNING DISABILITIES

John H. Meier, Ph.D.

Leslie L. Segner, Ph.D.

and

Barbara B. Grueter, M.D.

John F. Kennedy Child Development Center
University of Colorado Medical Center

INTRODUCTION

The effectiveness of several efforts to systematically intervene in the lives of children from the culture of poverty with compensatory educational programs has been obscured by the largely negative and extremely controversial reports about the efficacy of massive intervention programs. However, positive acknowledgment has been accorded several small, well-designed and carefully implemented compensatory preschool educational programs. This chapter makes no attempt to enter the impassioned polemics about why or in what way various large-scale compensatory programs have allegedly failed. This chapter is concerned with a consistently strong thread woven through the blanket statements about preschool educational intervention, namely that it should begin as early as infancy. This conviction certainly prompted Head Start officials to launch the first thirty-six pilot Parent-Child Centers, each serving about one hundred children three and younger, plus their families. Although preliminary findings are guarded and premature in terms of predicting

The writers gratefully acknowledge suggestions for and critiques of this paper by numerous colleagues representing several disciplines. Special thanks are given to Margaret Cranson and her staff at the La Junta Colorado Parent-Child Center where many ideas were germinated and are still being field-tested.

later performance of the infants, the results are very encouraging from programs which have been in operation for a year or more (Lazar, 1970). Therefore, this chapter presents a review of the relevant recent literature regarding infant education, marshals reasons for developing a systematic infant education program, and makes some suggestions as to how this might be accomplished, including recommendations for the empirical validation of an infant curriculum.

During the past decade, a significant portion of developmental research has been directed toward studying the effects of various high-risk situations on the developing organism. Attention has been focused primarily on two high-risk groups: the child with socio-economic deprivation, and the infant with high potential for neurologic damage. The premature or low birth weight baby makes up a large proportion of this latter group. In considering the outcome statistics of this research, it seems that experiential deprivation, whether extrinsically (environmentally) or intrinsically (neurologically) determined, is the predominant contributing factor to mental retardation and learning disability in the society today. If this factor can be eliminated or minimized by furnishing potentially handicapped children with more appropriate and therapeutic these developmental and/or learning disabilities, which affect about 15% of the nation's school children (Meier, 1970c), can be minimized or prevented.

In considering the extrinsic and intrinsic groups together, they represent a solid majority of the retarded population. According to the Mental Retardation Clinic statistics published by the U.S. Department of Health, Education and Welfare for the fiscal year 1968, 76% of the retarded population fell into these two categories. About one-third of this 76% was functioning as retarded, presumably due to environmental factors alone, with no neurological manifestations detected on routine examination. The remaining two-thirds of the group had neurological manifestations frequently associated with histories of pre- and peri-natal insults. Caution must be exercised in rigidly establishing a cause and effect relationship between the neurological manifestations and historical incidents which may, but may not, have caused the damage. Other causes of neurological damage such as infection, injury, etc. were classified separately. The reader is reminded that these statistics are misleading in terms of the incidence of retardation, since one of the characteristics of members of the culture of poverty is that they do not know how to avail themselves of such services as mental retardation clinics.

Further analysis of the HEW statistics, with regard to supplementary classification, revealed that 30% of the handicapped population has significant learning disability and an additional 25% falls into the category of minimal cerebral dysfunction. According to the government task force definition of minimal cerebral dysfunction, academic disability with normal or near normal intelligence is a major criterion of diagnosis. When one considers the etiologic studies of children with minimal cerebral dysfunction (studies admittedly retrospective), the majority of cases have histories of pre- or peri-natal insult and/or environmental deprivation. In essence, the intrinsically insulted baby and the extrinsically threatened baby are both at extreme statistical high risk to become significantly retarded or learning disabled.

The reader should not ignore the potential overlapping of groups: when statistics are reported from clinics, professionals must categorize children according to predominant factors. In truth, the two high-risk situations frequently co-exist. It is well known that poor prenatal care and prematurity are most prevalent in lower socio-economic groups; by the same token, Drillien's (1964) follow-up study of prematures has shown that the "outcome" (in terms of IQ, school problems, etc.) of prematures is significantly poorer in those babies reared in lower socio-economic homes than in those reared in middle-class homes. It becomes a frustrating intellectual exercise to see an eight-year-old ghetto child, born prematurely, whose young mother had no prenatal care, and to try to decide if his severe learning disability is predominantly the product of his environment or his damaged nervous system. We are most frequently forced into rigid classification systems which limit decisions in seeking and in applying appropriate intervention.

In analyzing existing intervention systems, several shortcomings are immediately evident, which also interfere with the adoption of sound treatment procedures. These may be summarized as follows:

1. A preventive approach is rarely taken; when it is, it is at an age too late to be most effective.

2. Treatment is initiated after the handicap has severely disabled the child, and complications have arisen.

3. Treatment focuses on only one aspect of the multiple problems presented, and the attempts to alleviate one symptom before others are attacked often result in incomplete or unsatisfactory results.

These shortcomings inhibit carrying out the interdisciplinary efforts expended in diagnosis. Such practices exist not only in the community, but also in clinical research facilities where the efficacy of one treatment approach is being compared to others. In order to facilitate the optimal development of any child's potential, a comprehensive program of multiphasic intervention, where the various phases of the program occur simultaneously, must be implemented. Optimal programming can only occur if it is initiated at as early an age as is possible, especially if it has as its goal the prevention of disability.

While the efficacy of early intervention has been established by research in this area (Bobath, 1967; Ellis, 1963; Westinghouse Report on

Head Start, 1969), the problems of getting to these populations at appropriately early ages are tremendous and need to be recognized in criticizing past and existing programs. Harkening back to the HEW statistics, it is found that *less than 3%* of the developmentally suspect population was referred under twelve months of age, and that less than 15% was referred under three years of age. Literally no report cases were discussed prenatally in terms of high risk or preventive intervention. This lack of referral of young infants and children, even to highly specialized facilities, is most striking when one considers that 97% of developmentally handicapped children are not even detected during their first year, the most critical period for efficacious intervention. It is clear that serious attention must be given to gaining access to this population. Even with the best of community screening and early detection devices, valuable time may be lost before diagnosis is confirmed and intervention is begun. Children with milder disabilities may be missed until they are of school age.

With the valuable information we have from various outcome and prospective studies (Drillien, 1964; Lubchenco, 1969; HEW Report, 1969) and with statistical risk figures for many situations available, populations significantly "at risk" can be identified with relative ease. Therefore, the primary detection effort should be toward "diagnosing" the high-risk situation, whenever possible in the prenatal period. Subsequent postnatal diagnosis and evaluation can then become an integral part of the intervention program. Such situational diagnosis will set the framework upon which a truly preventive intervention program can be built, one which is specifically designed to provide an optimal developmental environment for each child it serves.

RETARDATION BASED ON ENVIRONMENTAL DEPRIVATION

Research on the determinants of cultural retardation has revealed that more than two-thirds of "slow learners" and "school failures" are retarded on the basis of experiential deprivations which have left their scars before the child enters school (Bloom, 1964; Hunt, 1961; Masland, Sarason, & Gladwin, 1959; Riessman, 1962). The apparent irreversibility of the effects of early deprivation makes it evident that social planning in the area of mental retardation must include prevention as a first priority. Although the culturally determined retardation being considered here usually has no demonstrable organic correlates, it is as real and disabling to the individual as are the more grossly identifiable forms of brain damage and chromosomal defects. With the knowledge that preventive environmental measures are possible, it is necessary to discover the most effective ways to intervene in this problem which affects at least 5% of children entering school.

A primary thrust of the government's interventions in the poverty cycle has been the early childhood education efforts of Project Head Start. While it is recognized that the Head Start Program has promoted the socialization and emotional development of most of the children involved, recent evaluations have suggested that some basic research and reorganization are necessary before this program can be of maximum benefit in facilitating intellectual growth and development. One of the major recommendations growing out of the Westinghouse Learning Corporation's assessment of Head Start (1969) was that intervention must begin prior to the traditional preschool period of development in order to be maximally effective. The notion of education during the first three years of life is not a new one, and it receives support from knowledge of the critical significance of this developmental period for later learning and adjustment.

The literature on the effects of socio-economic class on development is uniform in its conclusion that there is strong, positive correlation between environmental deprivation and intellectual deficit (Deutsch & Brown, 1964; Masland *et al.,* 1959; Stevens & Heber, 1964). Although it has been demonstrated repeatedly that Negro children are at least equal, if not slightly superior, to white children in sensori-motor abilities very early in life, by eighteen months of age the adverse effects of environmental deprivation manifest themselves in the intellectual inferiority of the Negro child and from that point on the curves of normal intellectual growth for Negro and white children show a continuing divergence (Bayley, 1965; Deutsch, 1968; Knobloch & Pasamanick, 1953) since a significantly larger proportion of the Negro community is presently impoverished. In fact, Kagan (1968) has found that, as early as four months of age, lower-class babies vocalize significantly less than do upper-middle-class babies. Sears (1957) has hypothesized that the fundamental difference between lower- and middle-class child-rearing practices lies in the variable of "access to information." Bernstein (1961) has made a similar suggestion in his formulation of the linguistic difference between the classes. He suggests that communication in lower-class families is marked by an absence of verbal elaboration and language-mediated internal cues, as contrasted to the highly elaborated nuances of communication found in the verbal transactions of middle-class families. This reliance of lower-class families on nonverbal and implicit modes of communication results in a lack of stimulating verbal input which is so necessary to the development of language in young children. Since verbal facility has been shown to be the best predictor of later intelligence (Bayley, 1967), it is evident that ways must be found of providing children in the culture of poverty with models for language development in the earliest months of life. Developmental services, including day care programs for infants and toddlers, are becoming a central part of the anti-poverty effort, e.g., the Federally-sponsored Parent-Child Centers,

Community Coordinated Child Care (4-C), and Model Cities. These programs provide a convenient means of implementing language programs for disadvantaged children. Another method of stimulating language development is instructing parents to set aside some time each day for reading to their infants. Irwin (1960) did an experiment in which lower-class mothers read to their infants for ten minutes a day, beginning at thirteen months of age. When tested after seven months of this treatment at twenty months of age, the experimental infants were found to be superior to a control group in all language functions.

RETARDATION AND LEARNING DISABILITY BASED ON NEUROLOGICAL DYSFUNCTION

The neurologically high-risk infant has attracted a great deal of attention during the past decade. The thrust of this attention has been in two directions. Firstly, to improve methods of perinatal care by the establishment of intensive care units for these babies in larger teaching hospitals and medical centers. There is no question that infant mortality has decreased as a result of this improved care. Secondly, the question of "intactness" of infant survivors has been exhaustively reviewed in various follow-up studies. There is no doubt that the high-risk situation ultimately poses its greatest threat to the central nervous system of a developing infant, and that if permanent damage occurs, it is this system that bears the brunt of the insult on a long-term basis. Most of the babies considered to be of high risk are low birth weight, and hence most follow-up studies deal with outcome of these groups. Less information is available regarding follow-up of normal birth weight babies with perinatal complications which place them at significant risk. Although this latter group represents a relatively small percentage of the intensive care nursery population, they must be considered at significant high risk and are usually suffering from disorders similar to the complications of prematurity that do lasting damage. They are frequently babies with birth injury and hypoxia, respiratory distress, transient metabolic, hematologic, and/or infectious problems, all of which can permanently insult the nervous system.

Much more specific information is available concerning the outcome of the low birth weight baby. Virtually all follow-up studies have shown a striking excess in proportions of dull and retarded children in low birth weight follow-up groups (Drillien, 1961 & 1964, Collaborative Study Reports, and University of Chicago Controlled Follow-up Study). Even in the best environments, the proportion of children considered below average at two and four years of age ordinally increases as birth weight decreases. Because the general outcome for the larger low birth weight baby differs in characteristics from the smaller babies—i.e. less than 1580 grams (3 lbs. 8 oz.), they will be discussed separately in the following section.

When one considers the very small premature—less than 1580 grams—literally all statistics agree on a poor prognosis regarding future development (Drillien, 1964; Lubchenco, 1969). Lubchenco reports an incidence and severity of retardation, within this group, which is inversely related to birth weight. Her findings are collaborated by Drillien (1964), Knobloch (1956), and others, all of whom report an overall incidence of mild to moderate retardation in approximately 65% of the sample studies. In Lubchenco's population, 48% of the retarded children had associated findings of cerebral palsy. Of additional interest was the fact that, of the 35 children followed with normal intelligence in this very low birth weight group, 20 were experiencing difficulty in school characterized by significant underachievement, problems in speech, reading, mathematics, and behavior.

In low birth weight babies with birth weights greater than 1580 grams (3 lbs. 8 oz.), less severe but significant defects in intellectual development are also shown. This is particularly true of these babies in the lower social classes. The incidence of actual mental retardation in these larger preemies in good homes is only slightly increased over that of the full-term population, whereas the mental retardation incidence doubles when the matched low birth weight population is born into lower social classes. However, when one disregards social class, it has been demonstrated that most of these low birth weight babies performed significantly below their siblings from identical genetic and environmental milieus.

> From the findings reported so far, it seems likely that a combination of inferior genetic endowment, a poor environment, and restricted opportunity has a more marked effect on development in those who were small at birth than on maturely born children from a similar background. (Drillien, 1964, p. 188).

It must be pointed out that an IQ of 100 in a child of a middle- or upper-class home, where parents and siblings are of above average or superior intelligence, may represent mental retardation to that family. Again, the finding was prevalent that, of the small babies who did score within the average range of intelligence at ages 2 and 4, there is an increased incidence of learning disability and school maladjustment (Drillien, 1964).

All low birth weight babies are not premature, and further unpublished data from Lubchenco indicate that any baby that is small for gestational age is at statistical high risk when compared to babies of similar gestational age but appropriately sized for their gestational ages. This impression of Lubchenco's is collaborated by studies of Beargie *et al* (1970) and Van den Berg (1968). Many studies are in process to compare the outcome of the small-for-dates baby with that of the similarly sized, but appropriate for gestational age baby. It should be noted that the classification of size at birth with respect to gestational age is a relatively new endeavor in pediatrics and that, prior to 1967, almost all of these children were considered premature and in the same category. Follow-up studies then are rather short in duration, few in number, and many inconsistent data are emerging. It must also be mentioned that the small for gestational age infant may represent up to one-third of the total low birth weight population, and that these babies, prior to 1967 and 1968, were considered like any other premature, and may represent some contamination of data from follow-up studies which did not differentiate the two groups. At the present time, it does appear as if the small-for-dates baby of any gestational age is at some additional risk when compared to his age-mates.

Twinning may represent another example of small for gestational age babies, as most will fall into this category when compared with singleton birth weight babies. Statistics also indicate that twinning involves some additional high risk (Drillien, 1964; Mehrotra & Maxwell, 1949). Premature twins show a significantly poorer outcome than paired singletons of like birth weight. There are many theoretical explanations for this: the intrauterine environment is not as optimal in terms of nurturance and mechanical factors, there is a higher incidence of birth trauma; there is a higher incidence of psychological problems of early childhood. So, the poor outcome for premature twins as compared to matched singletons is probably due to a combination of the above factors.

While the incidence of mild brain damage and consequent learning disability is significantly high in all of the afore-mentioned follow-up studies, there are no prospective data to assist in determining the natural history of these disorders. The diagnosis is made when the child gets to school, and follow-up studies regarding this disorder are mostly retrospective. In addition to lack of prospective data, there is an associated lack of supportive pathological data, e.g., supportive of the fact that these children are indeed mildly damaged. Some animal experimentation is greatly illuminative, however. In the controlled asphyxia experiments recently reported by Windle (1969), all asphyxiated Rhesus monkeys had striking pathological findings. There was marked depletion of nerve cell populations, not only in the cortex, but also in the brain stem, thalamus, dorsal spinal columns, and basal ganglia.

> The main structural defects involve centers that process signals from the environment and others that control association and integration of information (Windle, p. 83).

When one associates these pathological findings with the clinical findings in the same monkeys of transient neurological symptoms and later defects in memory and learning (5 and 10 years later in some instances), it represents the experimental model of perceptual dysfunction with mild organic damage, albeit in the monkey. It is not surprising that workers like Lubchenco have found that 34% (or more) of high-risk babies with normal intelligence are school underachievers with multiple problems with learning.

Environmental manipulation and stimulation programs (other than intensive medical care nurseries) have not really been comprehensively tested on these neurologically high risk populations. Some practical nursery procedures, such as parent counseling programs and consistent mothering from nursing personnel, have been incorporated into intensive care as well as normal newborn nurseries. In the University of Colorado Medical Center Intensive Care Unit, foster grandmothers are frequently employed to give loving attention to sick newborn infants like any sick child. A recent sensory stimulation project on a premature nursery was reported by Solkoff (1969) to have a beneficial effect on both growth and development of the babies studied. Earlier studies by Hasselmeyer (1964) and Freedman *et al* (1966) demonstrated beneficial immediate effects of sensory stimulation and rocking on the nursery. The previous rigidly enforced "hands off" policies of premature nurseries are disappearing; however, when one considers that an infant might spend his first 3-6 months in an isolated environment with a dearth of stimulation, the possible effects of such intense sensory and affective deprivation are frightening.

Beyond innovations in nursery care, follow-up care for the high-risk infant has mainly focused on diagnosis. However, workers in the field of cerebral palsy have been able to demonstrate most success, and have shown the significance of early treatment (Bobath, 1963). While the effects of specific physical therapy on the neurologically handicapped population have been demonstrated to be efficacious, it remains to be shown that comprehensive, coordinated stimulation and therapeutic intervention will affect the outcome of these neurologically high-risk babies. A controlled clinical trial in this area is certainly warranted.

RATIONALE FOR AN INFANT EDUCATION CURRICULUM

There is an impressive body of evidence, from studies of both lower animals and human subjects, which points to the critical and pervasive influence of experience in infancy. Studies by Levine (1960), Dennenberg (1964), and Harlow (1963), with various kinds of laboratory animals, have all led to the conclusion that close physical contact and stimulation are essential for adequate physiological, emotional, and adaptive development. Another set of investigations relating to the importance of early experience has been concerned with critical periods of learning, particularly imprinting. The work of Scott (1962), Hess (1967) and others has suggested that, in certain lower animals, there exist functions capable of being learned only during circumscribed periods of development. A third group of animal studies bearing on early experience has compared the social development and learning of animals raised in "enriched" environments with those raised under isolated conditions. Thompson and Melzack (1956) found that dogs reared in cages providing minimal stimulation were emotionally disoriented and deficient in learning abilities when compared to dogs which had been reared in normal or enriched environments. Some recent investigations (Bennett, Diamond, Krech, and Rosenzweig, 1964; Krech, Rosenzweig & Bennett, 1962; Rosenzweig, Bennett & Diamond, 1962) have shown that rearing in enriched environments produces anatomical as well as biochemical differences in the brains of rats. Not only were the experimental animals more proficient on problem-solving tests, but they were also found, on autopsy, to have more of an enzyme (acetylcholinesterase) associated with transmission of neural messages in their brains.

The research relevant to infant education using human subjects has been mainly concerned with the consequences of maternal deprivation and institutionalization, and the developmental effects of handling and physical contact. The earliest studies on the effects of maternal deprivation (Bowlby, 1951; Spitz, 1946) were alarmingly grim in their description of the devastating and lasting consequences of early lack of mothering. Subsequent investigations (Dennis & Najarian, 1957; Goldfarb, 1955; Provence & Lipton, 1962) have led to similar, although perhaps less extreme, conclusions. In essence, they have shown that children deprived of a consistent mothering figure in early life are significantly behind normal children on almost all measures of growth and development. The most strikingly deficient areas are language behavior and social competence.

Since neither institutionalization nor mothering is a pure or unitary variable, subsequent investigations have endeavored to isolate the factors in the mothering process which are crucial for the infant's development. One such factor which is now known to be basic is the handling of the infant. Brody (1951) reports that visual attentiveness in infants is highly correlated with amount of handling by the caretaking person. Studies by Rheingold (1961), Casler (1965), and White, Castle & Held (1964) have shown that additional handling and attention of institutionalized infants facilitates their development and increases their alertness. The explanation for this phenomenon probably lies in the relationship between physical contact and visual curiosity. Spitz has suggested in his formulation of the "cradle of perception" that the infant can only begin to see and learn about his environment through his close physical relationship with his mother. Along these lines, Korner &

Grobstein (1967) recorded the visual scanning behavior of twelve neonates, and observed that their eyes were open 90% of the time when being held, and only 25% of the time when either left unhandled or moved to a sitting position. Clearly, this finding suggests that the development of early visual-motor schemata is facilitated by handling, since it is known that the child even at this young age can discriminate between visual cues (Fantz, 1967). Yarrow (1963) found a similar result in a study of children in foster care. He discovered a significant correlation between developmental test scores at six months, and ratings of amount and appropriateness of maternal handling. In the same vein, Rubenstein (1967) reported a significant positive relationship between ratings of maternal attentiveness and measures of exploratory behavior and preference for novel stimuli in five-month-old infants.

In a different tradition from the aforementioned studies of the effects of early experience, the work of Jean Piaget (1952) has equally important theoretical significance. The relevance of Piaget's work for the present discussion lies in its emphasis on the critical importance of the earliest learning experiences. His work clearly implies that the later expression of intelligent behavior has its roots in the schemata laid down during the earliest months and years of life. Piaget's observations on the continuity of development point to the cumulative nature of intelligent behavior, which he conceptualized as a sequential unfolding process. Although he did not discuss the effects of deviant environmental circumstances such as stimulus deprivation on cognitive development, one can infer that without intensive exchange between the infant and his environment during the sensori-motor period (the first eighteen months), there will be impairment of later adaptation and intellectual growth.

EXISTING INFANT EDUCATION PROGRAMS

The last set of studies to be reviewed deals with the effectiveness of programs of infant stimulation. Based on the assumption that environmental manipulations can alter the course of intellectual development, a number of infant education programs have been initiated during the past several years (Dittman, 1969). Although it is too soon to evaluate the results of most of these programs, the workers in this field are generally encouraged in regard to their effectiveness. Two approaches have generally been used, the first providing an enriched environment in a day care setting, and the second involving the training of disadvantaged mothers in home programs of infant stimulation.

A relatively large-scale study of stimulation for infants and toddlers has been underway for several years under the direction of Keister at the University of North Carolina at Greensboro. This project was designed to demonstrate that growth-facilitating and stimulating experiences could be implemented through group day care facilities for children from birth to age three. Unlike the typical nursery situation in which working mothers leave their infants for group day care, this program has a high ratio of care-givers to children, quality health care, and individualized learning programs geared to each child and his particular needs. A preliminary report on the evaluation of this project (Keister, 1969) compares fourteen infants treated in this enriched day care with fourteen "home reared" infants matched on age, sex, race, and education of parents. There were no significant differences between the two groups on either the Bayley Scales of Infant Development or the Vineland Social Maturity Scale, administered regularly between 18 and 36 months of age. Children from both middle- and lower-class homes were included in this analysis but, unfortunately, the social class of the subjects was not discussed as a variable. From these data, it is only possible to conclude that high quality group day care stimulates the infant's mental, motor, and social development equally as well as does rearing in a home environment.

The Children's Center in Syracuse, formerly under the direction of Caldwell, is another experimental program in group day care for children of lower-class working mothers. This project is seeking to instill in infants and young children the foundations of a positive self-concept, basic conceptual thinking, and enriched experiences with words and events. The primary goal of the program is to demonstrate that an enriched day care environment can offset the disadvantages of maternal separation and give additional cognitive and sensory input which the lower-class home is frequently unable to offer. Although a complete evaluation of the development of these children, in comparison to matched controls, has not yet been published, Caldwell's preliminary impressions of the effectiveness of the program are positive. Repeated intelligence assessments have revealed that participation in the enriched day care program seems to normalize the distribution of intelligence scores of disadvantaged infants. Those children who scored initially between 70 and 100, thus skewing the distribution negatively, were found, upon retest, to have moved into the middle or right half of the distribution. Caldwell reports that enrollment in the program for one year resulted in average IQ gains of 10 to 14 points. It is interesting to note that there was a negative correlation between the amount of educational experiences available in the home (as rated by the Syracuse Home Stimulation Scale) and magnitude of change in developmental quotient. That is, children from the most deprived environment showed the largest gains (Caldwell, 1967).

One concern which is inevitably raised in discussions of group day care for infants has to do with its effects on mother-child attachment. A recent report by Caldwell and her associates (1969) compared a group of home-reared 30-month-old children with a group of children of the same age who had been enrolled in an infant day care program in regard to patterns of child-mother and mother-child attachment. No differences were found. There was a positive relationship between strength of attachment and amount of stimulation and support for development available in the home. A related issue has to do with the effects of multiple mothering. On the basis of the results of Rheingold (1961) and Caldwell and Hersher (1964), it seems that the presence of more than one mothering person has no ill effects if all the "mothers" are good and are working together. What is known about the development of children raised in the Russian children's collectives (Meers and Madans, 1968) and the Israeli Kibbutzim (Spiro, 1958) gives no reason to believe that there is anything detrimental about multiple mothering (Wollin, 1969).

A longitudinal study of Negro males in New York City was recently reported by Palmer (1969), in which the experimental infants were given two one-hour education sessions a week in a one-to-one situation. There were two types of training: "concept training," which included systematic instruction; and "discovery," in which the same play materials were presented, but with no instructions. After eight months of such training, which was begun at age two, both experimental groups were superior to controls on such diverse tasks as the Stanford-Binet Intelligence Test, language comprehension and use, perceptual discrimination, motor behavior, delayed reaction, and persistence at a boring task. This superiority of the treated groups was still present on retesting one year later. Palmer proposed four factors to account for this effect: 1) the regularity of exposure to a structured learning condition; 2) the affective relationship between instructor and child; 3) the uninterrupted nature of the instructor-child interaction; and 4) the increasing realization by the child that he could respond to educational experiences and be rewarded for his response.

Probably the largest scale and most comprehensive infant education project undertaken to date by a single investigator is the one at the University of Florida under the direction of Gordon. This program utilizes disadvantaged women to train other disadvantaged mothers in techniques of infant stimulation used at home. A recent report (1969) of Gordon's findings indicates that, at the end of the first year of the project, the children whose mothers had been given instructions in infant education were superior to control children on the Griffiths Mental Development Scales. At the end of the second year, the same differences obtained for those children who had been in the program from 3 months to 24 months of age, as well as for those who had participated from 12 months to 24 months of age. However, those children who were enrolled only from 3 months to 12 months of age were not significantly different from their controls, which suggests that the "headstart" gained during the first year is lost unless the education program continues during the second year of life. It is interesting to note that there was a language lag on both the Griffiths and Bayley Scales for those children enrolled in the education program, as well as for the controls. This suggests that the language deficits in the environment of these children were not completely offset by the stimulation program. However, the fact that the developmental quotients of the "educated" children were elevated in comparison to controls gives encouragement for developing more effective programs.

Although these demonstration projects (Caldwell, 1967; Gordon, 1969; Keister, 1969, Palmer, 1969) have shown that education experiences in the first three years of life can enhance intellectual development, there has been no systematic evaluation of the effectiveness of various approaches to stimulating the infant. It is now known that infant education is efficacious, but little knowledge exists as to when and how to intervene with what experiences for maximal benefits. It is clear that projects are needed which have the primary goal of developing a detailed curriculum of materials which follows a hierarchical sequence and corresponds with existing knowledge about learning and development in the first three years of life. Based on the assumption that intellectual deficits can be prevented in children at risk for socio-cultural or neurological reasons through systematic programs of early education, there is a real need for the development of a series of learning episodes and curriculum materials which can be easily communicated to nonprofessionals and mothers.

INFANT EDUCATION CURRICULUM

As implied in the preceding rationale section, there are several assumptions underlying the notion that systematic education of infants facilitates their optimal development. A basic assumption is that the developmental process occurs as the result of a simultaneous mutual interaction between biological mechanisms and environmental factors (Bigge & Hunt, 1962). That is, the organism does not develop without use. Secondly, it is assumed that the infant actively seeks the experiences required for his growth and development. A third assumption is that information is processed for meaning, and the infant develops cognitively only when he performs certain learning acts within certain kinds of surroundings. A fourth assumption, suggested by Bloom (1964), is that the first three years is a critical period for intervention and "feeding" emerging abilities, because of the unparalleled growth of intelligence during this period. The fifth assumption is that the disproportionate amount of developmental disabilities in high-risk children is due to either inadequate or inappropriate educational experiences during the earliest years of life. Finally, the present thesis is that compensatory measures can be implemented with these high-risk infants to prevent later intellectual deficits.

Some first approximations to a curriculum for infant education have been developed and tested by Caldwell (1967), Gordon (1969), Gray (1968), Weikart & Lambie (1968), and others. The preliminary findings from their efforts to train indigenous paraprofessionals to assist parents in helping their infants to achieve the various prescribed developmental milestones have been encouraging. There are many opponents to such intervention, and many others who are either lukewarm to the idea, or feel ill-prepared to implement such programs, and thus remain adamantly uncommitted to any specific formulation of an individualized curriculum. Some of the reluctance on the part of the child development specialists is due to a genuine, albeit romantic, appreciation for the pristine innocence of the infant. Some already harassed parents prefer the greater convenience of having a more passive infant, and of not having to busy themselves about the additional task of tending to educational experiences for infants whose toileting, feeding, and sleeping needs are already too much for the harried mothering one to accomplish. The reticence frequently is also a function of the lack of familiarity with even the rudimentary requirements of curriculum building.

Several years ago, Barsch (1967) wrote a chapter in a book about exceptional infants which he entitled "The Infant Curriculum—A Concept for Tomorrow." The chapter was the last of a series of contributions from experts of many disciplines writing in regard to the exceptional, or more specifically, the developmentally disabled infant. It seemed quite fitting, after having presented the multiplicity of problems which occur in very early childhood from the viewpoint of numerous disciplines, that some prescription for the amelioration or, even better, the prevention of such disabilities be offered. Certainly, Barsch's interest and sophistication in the perceptual-motor development of the human organism qualified him to make informed recommendations about the optimal development of the human organism, particularly where efficient perceptual-motor functioning is concerned. However, as a reflection of the state of the art, Barsch admittedly had precious few concrete methods and materials to suggest in behalf of the education of infants.

The optimal content of this paper should be a carefully documented presentation of an Infant Curriculum which has already been tested and tried over a period of time and had a profitable outcome. The sequences of stimulation should be precisely described in handbook style as a ready reference for any parent or clinician who wish to pursue the same course with a given infant. It should be possible, perhaps, to have developed this curriculum to such a point of clarity that specific sequences might have been studied in each perceptual mode so that remedial sequences might be strategically employed to the benefit of those infants who have suffered specific losses or impairments. Unfortunately, the concept of infant curriculum is far from such an advanced stage of development. (1967, p. 553)

Some day in the future it might be possible to present a detailed listing of stimulation sequences which have been scientifically organized on the basis of a simplicity to complexity continuum much in the same manner as we can now prescribe a remedial course for the failing reader. For the present, however, we must content ourselves with providing an outline and a few suggestions in hope that those who find this an acceptable concept will fill in the details from their own creativity and dedication. (1967, p. 562)

In order to construct the infant curriculum which will produce an infant education system capable of simple, but highly specific, application, a basic structural framework must exist. This framework should contain five essential major parts. First, the entire system must be built from a solid conceptual rationale—one which supports the idea that the measurements, activities, and environmental manipulations in this system will validly indicate and foster optimum development. Secondly, there should be an inventory of infant development which will assess each infant's existing skills, his readiness to accomplish new tasks, and his environmental situation by using validated instruments of assessment and skilled observations. Third, there should be a systematic method of teaching those who will teach parents and babies, an educational system which will enable the most unsophisticated or most skilled learning facilitator to implement the curriculum and administer the inventory. Fourth, there must be a detailed curriculum of sequential and hierarchical experiences to carry out with the infants; this curriculum should carry the aforementioned conceptual framework as its core, and be continually guided by the inventory. Fifth, there must be an additional system of remediation which can be added to the core program when the inventory indicates a discrepancy in either performance or in the environment that necessitates special techniques of intervention. Lastly, it might be added that techniques must exist to evaluate the effectiveness of such programs so that objective evidence of their efficacy can be evaluated at a future date.

THE CONCEPTUAL RATIONALE

In developing a specific curriculum, the cognitive developments of the first three years have been conceptualized according to Piagetian theory. Piaget described six basic stages of development within the sensory-motor period. Using the theoretical framework of these stages, a hierarchy of behaviors and skills has been drawn up which utilizes not only Piagetian observations, but also infant developmental milestones as described or suggested by Gesell (1941), Havighurst (1953), Uzgiris & Hunt (1969), Stott & Ball (1965), and others. In other words, the hierarchy of skills and behaviors described by these workers has been translated into the Piagetian theoretical framework, and serves as a basis for the educational activities contained in the Infant Educational System.

The adoption of Piaget's theory of mental development as a rationale for a curriculum is desirable for two reasons. First, Piaget and his associates have formulated a theory in which the nature of the developmental process is the primary concern. Thus, curriculum sequences can be based on a dynamic rationale, the nature of which is explainable in terms of the unfolding intellect. Secondly, Piaget describes the process of mental development, not as a predetermined sequence of events or solely a biological maturation, but as a vital continuous interaction between an individual and his environment.

> Concerning the problem of intelligence, the lesson furnished by such an example seems to us to be the following. From its beginnings, due to the hereditary adaptations of the organism, intelligence finds itself entangled in a network of relations between the organism and the environment. Intelligence does not therefore appear as a power of reflection independent of the particular position which the organism occupies in the universe but is linked, from the very outset, by biological *a priori's*. It is not at all an independent absolute, but it is a relationship among others, between the organism and things. If intelligence thus extends an organic adaptation which is anterior to it, the progress of reason doubtless consists in an increasingly advanced acquisition of awareness of the organizing activity inherent in life itself, and the primitive stages of psychological development only constitute the most superficial acquisitions of awareness of this work of organization. One can therefore believe that intellectual activity, departing from a relation of interdependence between organism and environment, or lack of differentiation between subject and object, progresses simultaneously in the conquest of things and reflection of itself, these two processes of inverse direction being correlative. From this point of view, physiological and anatomical organization gradually appears to consciousness as being external to it and intelligent activity is revealed for that reason as being the very essence of the existence of our subjects. (Piaget, 1952, p. 19)

Using this theory as a point of departure for curriculum development, the appropriate manipulation of the environment in terms of both stimulation and interaction can be conceptualized as influencing the dynamic chain of events which is critical in intellectual development.

In other words, it is necessary to have a theoretical basis for a curriculum which is designed to facilitate intellectual development in the infant: such a theoretical base has been relatively clearly conceptualized by Piaget and his associates. Once a curriculum is developed, based on this rationale, it is possible to assign specific meanings to curriculum tasks, thus giving the tasks (activities) a defined representational role in the total schema of intellectual development.

Within the first three years of life, Piaget describes two periods of development: that of sensory-motor development, and the early phases of pre-operational thought, which encompass the child's preschool and early educational years, in addition to a period of time in the third year of life. Within the sensory-motor period, covering roughly the first 18 months, Piaget describes six stages of development:

Stages I and II. These stages generally deal with elementary sensory-motor adaptations and show early progression from automatic or reflexive behavior to a modification and differentiation of these responses. Stages I and II usually occur during the first four months of life. The final four stages of development deal generally with intentional sensory-motor adaptations and their refinement.

Stage III (4-8 months). The infant begins to make intentional adaptations toward various goals. "Intention" is primarily a generalized response directed toward maintaining or reproducing a pleasurable or stimulating experience.

Stage IV (8-12 months). The infant actively anticipates the goals, and consequent activity becomes less generalized and more specifically goal-directed, or intentional.

Stage V (12-18 months). Active exploration and experimentation become evident, and experimentation itself becomes goal-oriented.

Stage VI (18 months to beginning of subperiod of preoperational thought). The final stage of the sensory-motor period involves the use of inventiveness and creativity in goal-directed behavior, and the consequent transition into preoperational thought.

Final Stage (age 2 to 3). This stage encompasses the early phase of the subperiod of preoperational thought described by Piaget as existing in the child from age 2 until around age 7. During this period of time, the child learns to utilize his multiple sensory-motor adaptations from previous periods, and moves toward internalization of cognition and symbolic manipulation of reality. Using what is known about these 7 phases during an infant's first three years, activities can be planned, in a learning sequence fashion, which will not only provide appropriate stimulation, but will also facilitate the intellectual developments of that period.

THE DEVELOPMENTAL INVENTORY—A PROFILE AND
BASE FOR CURRICULUM PLANNING

The Bayley Infant Scales of Psychomotor and Mental Development (1969) the corresponding efforts by Uzgiris & Hunt (1969), the Yale Developmental Schedules (which incorporate much of the Gesell Institute findings), and more gross screening devices such as the Denver Developmental Screening Test (Frankenburg & Dodds, 1969) all indicate that there are specific behaviors and capabilities which are expected

FIGURE I

		Source
ENTRY BEHAVIOR	Stands up by furniture Pulls to stand	Bayley—Item 38 Yale—Gesell
	1. Supports full weight on legs (holding rail for stabilization, not using arms for support)	Yale—Gesell
LEARNING SEQUENCE	2. Lifts and replaces foot—standing at rail	Yale
	3. Stepping movements Reciprocal leg movements — two hands held	Bayley—Item 40 Yale
	4. Cruises at rail	Yale
TERMINAL BEHAVIOR	5. Walks forward Walks with help — one hand held	Yale Bayley—Item 42

of children at various chronological ages. Administration of these types of tests to an infant not only gives one an accurate picture of the infant's present development, but also serves as a guide to the systematic education of babies as specified by various students of early child development. As a matter of fact, the entry and terminal behaviors, particularly in the realm of sensory-motor-perceptual functioning, have already been rather thoroughly delineated by the observable behaviors enumerated in the aforementioned infant appraisal instruments.

In considering, for example, the evolution of standing and walking skills as delineated by a composite of these tests, a "learning sequence" can be designed by interjecting a hierarchy of precursor skills between an accomplished "entry behavior" and a projected goal—"terminal behavior" (See Fig. I). As illustrated by Figure I, Item 42 on the Bayley

Infant Scale for Psychomotor Development specifies that a child should be able to walk, with help, within the age range of 7 to 12 months (mean 9.6 months). A stimulation-learning sequence is suggested to enable an infant to develop the sensory-motor-perceptual skills requisite in walking without someone's holding one hand. The inventory is administered until the infant's highest point of mastery of a precursor task in this sequence is established. This accomplishment is considered an entry behavior if passed with a qualitative criterion performance. From this point of mastery, perhaps Item 40 (stepping movements) or Item 38 (stands up by furniture) to the normal achievement of terminal behavior, an orderly step-by-step sequence of training is instituted and practiced until mastery of the underlying skills and understandings is accomplished. Once the terminal behavior is accomplished at criterion levels, it may well become an entry behavior for a related and more advanced sequence.

The use of play objects to stimulate the motor behaviors listed will also stimulate the transition from simple motor schema development (e.g. standing) to that of more complex motor schemas (e.g. standing and cruising in order to obtain desired object).

The appropriateness of items on standardized test instruments is challenged by many defenders of the culture of poverty. If these items are being challenged as valid test items, they will equally well be challenged as accepted items in learning sequences in an infant education curriculum. Wechsler makes a cogent reply to this criticism.

> The I.Q. has had a long life and will probably withstand the latest assaults on it. The most discouraging thing about them is not that they are without merit, but that they are directed against the wrong target. It is true that the results of intelligence tests and of others, too, are unfair to the disadvantaged, deprived, and various minority groups, but it is not the I.Q. that has made them so. The culprits are poor housing, broken homes, a lack of basic opportunities, etc., etc. If the various pressure groups succeed in eliminating these problems, the I.Q.'s of the disadvantaged will take care of themselves. (1966, p. 66)

A history of the intelligence testing movement clearly demonstrates that standardized tests comprise a distillation of those skills and abilities which are most validly and reliably assessed, and most of which have been replicated by other investigators. Therefore, it is unnecessary to be apologetic or surreptitious about employing the current and rather well-conceptualized series of behaviors contained in various infant assessment instruments, at least as the skeletal framework for an infant curriculum. Although this procedure involves educating youngsters to successfully perform on test-like items, there is nothing inherently wrong in this, provided that the items, which become terminal behaviors, sample behaviors which are universally recognized as essential indices of normal infant growth and development, and constitute critical experiences in the building of intellect. Although addressing their concern to school children, Karp and Sigel (1965) make a strong case for a test's truly reflecting a desired constellation of terminal behaviors.

> . . . tests and trained observations should take on new meaning and different diagnostic significance. In addition to appraising learning difficulty, measurement and observation should lead to remedial and compensatory techniques which can be incorporated readily into the curriculum and translated easily into work in the classroom. Psychoeducational appraisal of the disadvantaged pupil confronts us anew with the need to develop assessment procedures that both clarify the mechanisms by which learning occurs and guide the teaching-learning process. (1965, p. 409-410)

It has been stated that the behavioral series contained in infant assessment instruments will comprise not only an initial profile of the child, but also a skeletal framework for the infant curriculum. In order to initiate curriculum planning, other factors must be taken into consideration. The fleshing out of such a curriculum is a function of the individual infant whose idiosyncratic style of dealing with his environment requires an equally individual match (Hunt, 1967) of education experiences suitable to his learning style, so that these individual idiosyncracies must be observed in a skilled way and taken into consideration in planning. Furthermore, the infant's existing environment must be assessed as it is his interaction with this environment which constitutes the first critical relationship in intellectual development. Much as a curriculum is based upon accepted sequences of performance, an environment may be assessed and manipulated in accordance with the infant's needs. In addition, each child's built-in physiological readiness must be taken into consideration in determining individual goals and underlying skills. This is true of mental development as well as physical development, e.g. the child's vocalizations and generalized language development are contingent not only on the linguistic environment, but also on the maturation of various oral and neurological structures for receiving, processing and expressing sounds and words.

Finally, as field test efforts proceed to empirically validate curricular content, new methods and materials inevitably are generated, much as necessity is the mother of invention. The extensive writings about observations of child growth and development in various natural settings by such authors as Church (1966), Gesell *et al.* (1943), Piaget (1952) Terman (1925), and others help to bridge gaps in the framework circumscribed by the aforementioned infant assessment instruments.

If an infant curriculum is to have maximum impact, either upon the culture of poverty or on other high-risk populations, it is essential that the mothering personnel who are ultimately responsible for providing it to the infants be appropriately trained. For the culture of poverty, it is particularly important that it be organized in a simple and highly specific fashion. Very little sophistication can be assumed on the part of parents of high-risk infants, who are the prime implementers of the infant curriculum in the last analysis. In this country today, educational programs are not available for persons who desire vocational training in infant care. In designing a useful Infant Education System, one must provide some vehicle to train a group of people who can become learning facilitators for the infants in the various programs utilizing the System. The provision of such programs can make training a prerequisite for vocational placement in either day care centers or community-sponsored home-based operations which will employ this Infant Education System.

In essence, this Infant Education System can best be implemented if facilities are provided where personnel can be appropriately trained to do so. In order to design an organizational structure which will permit the proper curriculum to reach the infant, an Organizational Flow Chart is herein proposed (See Figure II). Following such an organizational system, it should be noted that a professional staff which is responsible for the design of the inventory and curriculum (which comprises the Infant Education System) also provides center-based training programs for learning facilitators who can be placed in various situations. Some learning facilitators can be trained specifically to work in day care centers and provide direct education to the infants in the centers when it is not feasible for the babies to be treated at home.

Other personnel can be trained in the center to go into community agencies such as public health departments, maternal and child health facilities and Parent-Child Centers, and from there be responsible for the implementation of the educational system in the homes of the infants and for the parent education involved in such implementation. The training programs consist of some didactic presentation of a curriculum involving the inventory and the educational curriculum for the infants. Supervised practical experience can be offered in a center-based day care center for those going into day care center operations, and in the field for those going into agency-sponsored operations. Once adequately trained, these personnel are then placed in appropriate situations, but may return to the center for workshops or refresher courses, at which time they not only learn new techniques, but provide feedback based upon their field testing of various curriculum methods. In other words,

FIGURE II

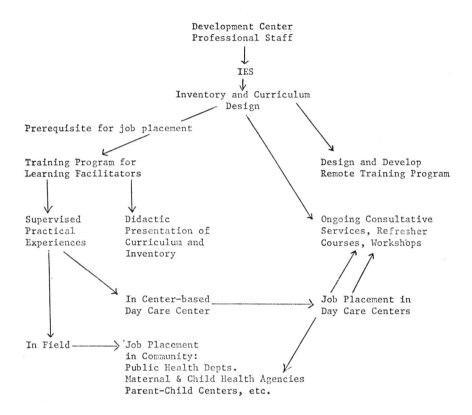

ongoing inservice training is offered to these learning facilitators once they are placed into the community, much as a teacher in public school takes summer courses in order to learn more current educational techniques, and to renew her certification.

THE INFANT EDUCATION SYSTEM

In spite of the many unknowns which exist in the knowledge of early cognitive development, there are some facts supported by research which can serve as guidelines in planning infant curriculum. It is known that vocalizing to the baby makes him more vocal (Luria, 1966; Meier, 1969a). Simple as this principle may sound, its application is the cornerstone of any infant education program. One practical suggestion to help accomplish this is to equip the mothering one or learning facilitator with an infant back pack which enables her to talk with the infant rider while doing routine household chores. Another simple, but equally important, principle is that smiling, playing with, and socially responding to the baby make him more alert and socially responsive (Rheingold, 1961). Giving him an opportunity to practice his emerging sensory-motor skills helps him to learn about himself in space, and also gives him variety in color, form, pattern, shadow, and movement. In fostering speech, it is known that associating words with as many actions and stimulus qualities as possible facilitates learning.

Another item of significance gained from recent research (Bower, 1966; Fantz, 1965) is that infants are capable of perceiving in all modalities from a very early age. This knowledge that the infant can register all sensory input, even if he can't process it in the same way that adults do, represents a tremendous advance. The research findings on stimulus parameters, such as novelty and complexity (Fantz, 1967; Friedlander, 1968; McCall & Kagan, 1967) also provide helpful guidance.

It is well to keep in mind the caution against overstimulating the infant, and trying unwisely to speed up those processes which must wait for nature's timeclock. While it has been shown that the normal infant has built-in protection against information-overload in the form of a stimulus barrier (Benjamin, 1965), caution must be used in introducing new experiences and tasks only when the child has demonstrated readiness. Little is known about the high-risk infant's abilities to either appropriately monitor stimuli or erect the stimulus barrier. In structuring the learning environment of the high-risk or environmentally deprived child, it is important to recognize that the problem is often not a lack of stimulation, but rather a lack of appropriate circumstances in which he can organize and assimilate educational experiences. Since the auditory (and visual) noise level around his crib is often execsive (Deutsch, 1968), it is important to provide a quiet background against which he can attend to and integrate new, carefully programmed educational experiences, rather than to indiscriminately bombard him with competing stimuli.

In the early months of an education program for the environmentally deprived infant, in addition to the manipulation of objects, it is desirable to get the baby to attend and respond to the human face as a distinct schema. Kagan (1968) has observed that, as early as four months of age, there are significant differences in the attentional responses of lower- and middle-class children. Although the lower-class babies attend visually to a drawing of a human face for as long as middle-class babies, they do not show a deceleration in heartbeat, which has been shown to be a physiologic correlate of attention (Lewis *et al,* 1966). Kagan suggests that this finding is due to the fact that the face is not a distinctive stimulus with the lower-class infants, because they have not experienced repeated presentations of the mother's face smiling down at them against a background of quiet. Because of crowded living conditions and other factors, the lower-class infant has experienced the mother's face under more confusing stimulus bombardment (the television's blaring, other siblings' voices and faces, etc.) and has not formulated it as a distinctive schema.

Since the foundation and necessary prerequisite for the baby's learning experiences is a trusting relationship with his learning facilitator, the importance of the early establishment of affectional relationships cannot be overstressed. There is much to be learned from observations of normal, nurturing mothers, and the ways in which they expose their babies to new experiences and communicate with them. One advantage of teaching mothers to set aside portions of the day for playful interaction with the babies is that the fulfillment which the mother experiences in such interactions will probably reinforce the frequency of their occurrence. It is believed that this will initiate a cycle of interactions in which the mother is pleased and rewarded by seeing her baby learn new things, and will seek more of these positive experiences by spontaneously talking to and playing with him more.

Since many of the experiences to which an infant might be exposed can be presented mechanically, Friedlander (1968), Grassi (1968), Kagan (1967), Lipsitt (1968), Meier (1967 and 1969c), and others have experimented with various infant education content and media for conveying it. The use of such media can be considered a valuable adjunct to the overall Infant Education System; when the use of such elegant and sophisticated equipment is impractical, the same programs can be presented by the learning facilitators. When such use of equipment is feasible, as in supervised day care centers, the essential motive for substituting various mechanically-mediated educational experiences for some of the quite desirable adult contact is not a mechanistic rejection of the importance of the human factor, but rather an attempt to use new media to complement and supplement the mothering one's affective and cognitive inputs which are typically attenuated by other children, employment out of the home, daily crises, etc.

The overriding principle guiding the introduction of media into the Infant Education System is that the infant must be able to control it himself. This is consistent with the notions of an autotelic (intrinsically attractive and rewarding) responsive environment (Moore & Anderson, 1968), which is suggested to comprise a cogent rationale for developing the positive feelings and the competent knowledge necessary for the satisfactory manipulation of one's environment (Meier, 1970a and 1968a; Nimnicht, McAfee & Meier, 1969). Thus, the infant learns to control a certain amount of the environment and actively selects and controls various educational experiences programmed for his optimal learning. As the infant masters simpler material, more complex hardware and software are introduced. (See illustrations on pages 436-439.)

The episodic or advertising format of the new educational program, "Sesame Street," is an example of one kind of approach which is appropriate for A-V presentation of cognitive content to the infant. Similar material, with considerable redundancy, is what comprises the programmed learning experiences which may be selected by the learner. Friedlander (1968 and 1969) has clearly documented that infants prefer a certain amount of redundancy. Counters may be used to determine the number of times each experience is selected, and as a child's rate of selection per unit of time peaks and begins to fall off, the content of that particular modality's stimulation is altered by replacing the now monotonous content with a novel and slightly more complex sensory-perceptual-cognitive experience. The learning facilitator is responsible for making the selections according to the Infant Education System, and his/her intuition regarding the child's response to previous stimuli. A lending "library" of infant education apparatus and materials makes the Infant Education System more economically feasible for those who wish to use expensive hardware and software for short periods of time and do not wish to purchase it or cannot afford it.

The learning facilitator is also instructed to reinforce any efforts the infant learner makes toward imitating sounds, identifying the visual items, etc. Like the framework of the learning sequences, the materials in the media become progressively more complex, and all of the mechanically-presented sequences have already been empirically validated or at least theoretically conceptualized to conform with the overall Infant Education System.

A general procedural flow chart depicting the total Infant Education System (IES) is provided by Figure III. As illustrated by this chart, the system is self-perpetuating if the infant responds according to expectations. If he does not, however, further diagnosis and remediation techniques are designed and incorporated into the core curriculum for a given time period. The remediation curriculum may include therapeutic techniques, additional parent counseling, environmental manipulation, etc.—responding to the individualized needs of the infant as delineated by the diagnostic profile. In these cases, the learning facilitator may need ongoing consultation and perhaps assistance from other professionals. For example, the infant with a motor developmental lag may need a physical therapy home program incorporated into the overall developmental program; thus, a PT consultant may work closely with the learning facilitator to plan appropriate curriculum and deliver it expertly to the baby.

Finally, Figure IV illustrates some details of the curriculum for infants between 4 and 8 months of age, corresponding to Piaget's sensory-motor Stage 3. This curriculum is an example of the type of basic procedures

FIGURE III

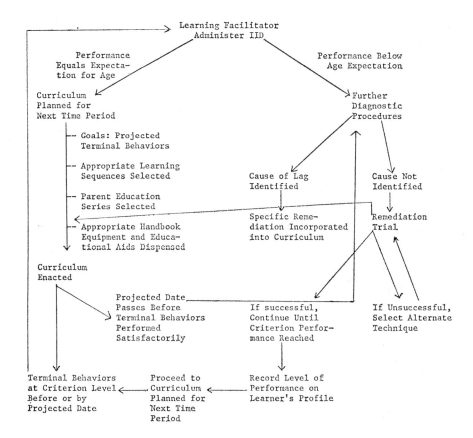

which would be implemented at other stages of development, and is offered as illustrative data. By study of the given sequences and sequence goals, it may be seen how validated landmarks of development are incorporated into the Piagetian framework, and how suggested activities would educate and stimulate an infant in such a way as to foster early and optimal learning, growth and development.

FIGURE IV

A. The following sequence involves the evolution of sensori-motor skills involved in maintaining sitting with good posture and stability. The learning situation is combined with several "game" situations: foot play, mirror play, and the removal of obstacles (diaper over face), and incorporate play, object and self-concept into activity.

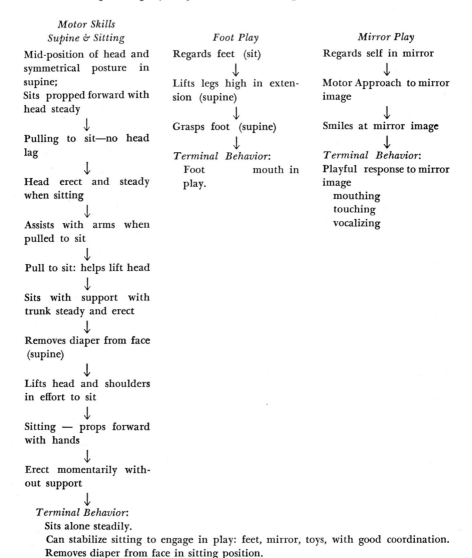

Motor Skills Supine & Sitting	*Foot Play*	*Mirror Play*
Mid-position of head and symmetrical posture in supine; Sits propped forward with head steady ↓	Regards feet (sit) ↓	Regards self in mirror ↓
Pulling to sit—no head lag ↓	Lifts legs high in extension (supine) ↓	Motor Approach to mirror image ↓
Head erect and steady when sitting ↓	Grasps foot (supine) ↓	Smiles at mirror image ↓
Assists with arms when pulled to sit ↓	*Terminal Behavior:* Foot mouth in play.	*Terminal Behavior:* Playful response to mirror image mouthing touching vocalizing
Pull to sit: helps lift head ↓		
Sits with support with trunk steady and erect ↓		
Removes diaper from face (supine) ↓		
Lifts head and shoulders in effort to sit ↓		
Sitting — props forward with hands ↓		
Erect momentarily without support ↓		
Terminal Behavior:		

Sits alone steadily.
Can stabilize sitting to engage in play: feet, mirror, toys, with good coordination.
Removes diaper from face in sitting position.

A. *Activities*: A general description.

All practice of motor skills will be associated with game or play situations so that they are more enjoyable for mother and/or facilitator and baby, and so that emerging skills in the areas of play object and self-concept, space concept, and time are both reinforced and reinforce the sensori-motor development. Motor activities stress reinforcement and stimulation of righting, propping, and equilibrium responses necessary in maintaining head and trunk stability. In beginning covering the face, a colored scarf is used which will eventually be used to hide objects, progressing from perceptual freeing of the face toward recovery of partially hidden objects.

B. The following sequences deal with stimulation of motor activities in prone and standing positions. Activities are reinforced with object and personal play. Conceptual development with respect to object, and space are both reinforced and reinforcing.

Entry Behaviors:

1. Head extended, weight on forearms, sustained in prone position; legs extended or semi-extended.
2. Attemps rolling to prone.
3. Brief supporting reaction—standing.

↓

1. Rolls to prone.
2. Scratches platform and uses hands in prone.
3. Can support weight on hands, arms fully extended.

↓

1. Removes diaper from face in prone.
2. Bears large fraction of weight—standing.
3. Bounces in standing.

↓

1. "Works" motorically (creeps, scoots, etc.) toward object out of reach in prone.
2. Early reciprocal stepping movements in standing position (with trunk support).

↓

Terminal Behaviors:

1. Prone—pivots toward object.
2. Standing—maintains full weight briefly, hands held.
3. Can be pulled to full stand by facilitator—traction on hands.

B. Activities to stimulate this series will be facilitated by use of a toy object, personal (affectionate) reinforcement, and nursery rhymes and songs. Use of the latter facilitates early development of rhythmic, sequenced motor activity. Generally, the infant will initiate the desired motor activities as he progresses from:

> Secondary circular reactions. The consolidation by repetition, of certain motor habits leading to effects in the milieu which are of interest to the infant (Effects—desirable toy play, social reinforcement, and auditory reinforcement)
>
> ↓
>
> Recognitory assimilation (recognition of the desired effect is acted out motorically)
>
> ↓
>
> Generalized assimilation—the act becomes represented in thought and is utilized toward a variety of objects (without recognition of novelty) in an effort to make interesting sights last. Motor schemas become progressively more complex.

C. The following sequences deal with the acquisition of language skills and imitation skills involved in language development. Early indication of auditory perceptual skills are included in the sequences.

Entry Behaviors:

1. Differentiation of vocalization from cry.
2. Excites, breathes heavily, strains.
3. Laughs.
4. Turns head to sound.

↓

1. Responds with mouth movements, smile, or vocalization to familiar sounds.
2. Squeals.
3. Vocalizes to toys, mirror image.
4. Vocalizes attitudes—pleasure, satisfaction, etc.

↓

1. Uses sound to localize in turning head after falling object.
2. Grunts and growls.
3. Bangs objects in play.
4. Reflects a facial mimic.

↓

1. Interest in sound production (obj.).
2. Vocalizes four syllables.
3. Lip closure voc. —m-m-m cry.
4. Polysyllabic sounds—vowels.

↓

Terminal Behaviors:

1. Vocalizes similar sounds in response to familiar sounds.
2. Attends (quietens, decreases activity) to unfamiliar sounds—may vocalize.
3. Says da-da or equivalent (ba-ba, ma-ma).
4. Listens selectively to familiar words (name, baby, bottle, etc.).

C. Activities center around auditory stimulation with visual and tactile reinforcement. Development of imitation begins with sounds already in the infant's repertoire with reinforcement of any attempt to imitate. Auditory skills of localizing, association, early discrimination are stimulated and reinforced. Investigatory mouth play and sensory stimulation around mouth are utilized.

D. The following sequences deal with the acquisition of fine motor and visual motor and conceptual skills regarding objects, space and causality.

Entry Behaviors:

1. Anticipates trajectory of moving objects.
2. Activates arms or hands with visual identification of stimulus object.
3. Retains object in hand and takes to mouth.
4. Hands together in midline.
5. Glances from hand to object and object to container.
6. Regards (visually) small objects.

↓

1. Precarious grasp of object, especially when near hand.
2. Visual pursuit of lost object.
3. Bilateral approach.
4. Sustained inspection with manipulation of object.

↓

1. Exploitation of objects (string, paper), using more complex motor schemas.
2. Palmar grasp.
3. Displeasure at loss of object; searching prehensory pursuit of lost object.
4. Playful responses to objects, people.

↓

1. Radial-palmar grasp of larger objects.
2. Unilateral approach to objects.
3. Visual rediscovery and anticipation of whole object after seeing part.

4. Transfers adeptly.
5. Imitates knocking with hand, banging toys on table top.

Terminal Behaviors:

1. Raking approach to small objects.
2. Retains two objects.
3. Holds object, regards container.
4. Exploitation more goal oriented:
   Retrieves partially hidden toy.
   Resists toy pull.
   Pulls string and secures tied toy.
   Motorically works to get toy out of reach.
   Manually rotates objects to get to desired portion of object
   (flashlight, bottle, etc.) .

A parent-educator on the staff of the La Junta, Colorado Parent and Child Center demonstrates, in the child's home, a learning episode (using large threaded pipe fittings) to improve eye-hand coordination and language labeling ability. Parents then continue and expand the learning episode.

Each learning episode is contained in a color-coded cloth sack which has instructions for its use printed on the outside of the sack itself. The sacks are conveniently stored and carried in the travel bag in background.

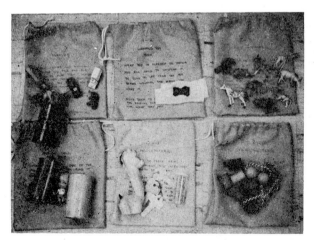

Six examples of experimental learning episodes from the Infant Education System are shown with the 3-dimensional contents placed on top of each brightly-colored sack.

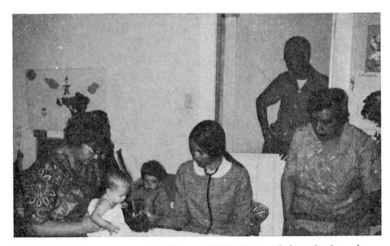

Developmental assessment of a Parent-Child Center infant is done by a pediatrician (center) while two staff nurses assist and the mother (partially hidden), father, and sibling observe and report how the infant functions at home.

The infant at lower left watches a TV-like audio-visual presentation (lower center) of a nursery rhyme. The control unit of the crib education hardware (lower right) enables the infant to control an 8mm single concept film projector, a crib vibrator or heartbeat simulator, the intensity of room illumination, a radio or audio-tape recorded program in one or more languages, an adult-summoning buzzer or bell, etc. Hanging objects (cartoon figures), when pulled, turn on or off motorized mobiles or illuminated face schema, abstract shapes, letters and words (upper left).

A young learner manipulates a control which turns on sequentially flashing lights placed around the ceiling of the nursery. While lying on his back the learner can visually follow the light patterns, the motorized mobile (s), or the moving pictures projected onto the ceiling. More advanced control units allow only one piece of the apparatus to operate at any one time and can be programmed to turn various educational experiences on and off for predetermined lengths of time once initiated by the infant learner.

REFERENCES

BARSCH, R. The infant curriculum, a concept for tomorrow. *Exceptional Infant,* Vol. I, J. Hellmuth (Ed.), New York: Brunner/Mazel, Inc., 1967, 543-568.

BATTAGLIA, F. C. & LUBCHENCO, L. O. A practical classification of newborn infants by weight and gestational age, *J. Pediat.,* 1967, 71, 159.

BAYLEY, N., CAMERON, J., & LIVSON, N. Infant vocalization and their relationship to mature intelligence, *Science,* 1967, 157, 331-333.

BAYLEY, N., & SCHAEFER, E. S. Relationships between socio-economic variables and the behavior of mothers toward young children, *J. Genet, Psychol.,* 1960, 96, 61-77.

BAYLEY, N. *Scales of Mental and Motor Development.* New York: The Psychological Corporation, 1969.

BEARGIE, R. A. Growth and development of small-for-date newborns, *Ped. Clinics of North America,* 1970, 17, 159.

BENJAMIN, J. D. Developmental biology and psychoanalysis. *Psychoanalysis and Current Biological Thought.* N. S. Greenfield and W. C. Lewis (Eds.), Madison: University of Wisconsin Press, 1965, 57-80.

BENNETT, E. L., DIAMOND, M. C., KRECH, D., & ROSENZWEIG, M. K. Chemical and anatomical plasticity of the brain, *Science,* 1964, 146, 610-617.

BERNSTEIN, B. Social class and linguistic development: A theory of social learning. *Education, Economy and Society,* A. Halsen, J. Floud & C. Anderson (Eds.), New York: The Free Press of Glencoe, Inc., 1961, 288-314.

BIGGE, M. & HUNT, M. *Psychological Foundations of Education.* New York: Harper, 1962.

BLOOM, B. S. *Stability and Change in Human Characteristics.* New York: Wiley, 1964.

BOBATH, B. Treatment principles and planning in cerebral palsy, *Physiotherapy,* 1963, 49, 122.

BOWER, R. G. R. The visual world of infants, *Scientific American,* 1966, 80-92.

BOWLBY, J. *Maternal Care and Mental Health.* World Health Organization, 1951.

BRENNAN, W. M., AMES, E. W., & MOORE, R. W. Age differences in infants' attention to patterns of different complexities, *Science,* 1966, 151, 355-356.

BRODY, S. *Patterns of Mothering.* New York: International Universities Press, 1951.

CALDWELL, B. M. & RICHMOND, J. B. Programmed day care for the very young child. A preliminary report, *J. of Marriage and the Family,* 1964, 26, 481-488.

CALDWELL, B. M. What is the optimal learning environment for the very young child? *Amer. J. Orthopsychiat.,* 1967, 37, 8-21.

CALDWELL, B. M. Descriptive evaluations of child development and of developmental settings, *Pediatrics,* 1967, 40, 46-54.

CALDWELL, B. M. & HERSHER, L. Mother-infant interaction during the first year of life, *Merrill-Palmer Quart.,* 1964, 10, 119-128.

CALDWELL, B. & RICHMOND, J. Social class level and stimulation potential of the home. *Exceptional Infant,* J. Hellmuth (Ed.), New York: Brunner/Mazel, Inc., 1967, 455-466.

CALDWELL, B. M., WRIGHT, C. M., HONIG, A. S. & TANNENBAUM, J. Infant day care and attachment. Unpublished manuscript, 1969.

CASLER, L. The effects of extra tactile stimulation on a group of institutionalized infants, *Genetic Psychology Monographs,* 1965, 135-175.

CHASE, P., & MARTIN, H. Undernutrition and child development, Abstract from Society for Pediatric Research, April, 1969.

CHURCH, J. (Ed.) *Three Babies: Biographies of Cognitive Development.* New York: Random House, 1966.

CRAVIOTO, J. Nutrition, growth, and neurointegrative development. An experimental and ecologic study, *Supplement to Pediatrics,* 1966, 38.

DANN, M., LEVINE, S. Z., & NEW, E. V. A long-term follow-up study of small premature infants, *Pediatrics,* 1964, 33, 945-960.

DAVIS, A., & HAVIGHURST, R. J. Social class and color differences in child rearing, *Amer. Sociol. Rev.,* 1946, 11, 689-710.

DeHirsch, K., Jansky, J., & Langford, W. S. Comparisons between prematurely and maturely born children of three age levels, *Amer. J. Orthopsychiat.*, 1966, 36, 616-628.

Denenberg, V. H. Critical periods, stimulus input and emotional reactivity: A theory of infantile stimulation, *Psychol. Rev.*, 1964, 71, 335-351.

Dennis, W., & Sayegh, Y. The effect of supplementary experiences upon the behavioral development of infants in institutions, *Child Develop.*, 1,65, 36, 81-90.

Deutsch, M. & Associates. *The Disadvantaged Child.* New York: Basic Books, 1968.

Deutsch, M., & Brown, B. Social influence in Negro-White intelligence differences, *J. Social Issues*, April, 1964, 24-35

Dittman, L. L. *Early Child Care The New Perspectives.* Atherton Press, 1968.

Drillien, C. *The Growth and Development of the Prematurely Born Infant.* Baltimore: Williams & Wilkins, 1964.

Ellis, E. The physical management of developmental disorders, *Clinics in Developmental Medicine*, 1967, No. 26.

Fantz, R. L. Pattern vision in newborn infants, *Science*, 1963, 140, 296-297.

Fantz, R. L. Visual perception from birth as shown by pattern selectivity. Whipple, H. F. (Ed.), New Issues in Infant Development, *Annals of the New York Academy of Sciences*, 118, 793-815, 1965.

Fantz, R. L., & Nevis, S. Pattern preferences in perceptual cognitive development in early infancy, *Merrill-Palmer Quart.*, 1967, 13, 77-108.

Frankenburg, W., & Dodds, J. *Denver Developmental Screening Test—Manual.* Denver: Univ. of Colo. Medical Center, 1969.

Foss, B. M. *Determinants of Infant Behavior.* New York: Wiley, 1966.

Fowler, W. Cognitive learning in infancy and early childhood, *Psychol. Bulletin*, 1962, 59, 116-152.

Freedman, D. G. *et al.* Effects of kinesthetic stimulation on weight gain and on smiling in premature infants. Paper presented at Meeting of American Orthopsychiatric Association, San Francisco, April, 1966.

Friedlander, B. Z. The effect of speaker identity, voice inflection, vocabulary and message redundancy on infants' selection of vocal reinforcement, *J. Exper. Child Psychol.*, 1968.

Gesell, A., & Amatruda, C. *Developmental Diagnosis.* New York: Hoeber, 1941.

Gesell, A., Ilg, F., Learned, J., & Ames, L. *Infant and Child in the Culture of Today.* New York, Harper & Row, 1943.

Goldfarb, W. Emotional and intellectual consequences of psychological deprivation in infancy: A re-evaluation. P. Hoch & J. Zubin (Eds.), *Psychopathology of Childhood.* New York: Grune & Stratton, 1955, 105-119.

Gorden, I. *Early Child Stimulation Through Parent Education: A Final Report to the Children's Bureau.* Gainesville: Univ. of Florida Press, 1969.

Gorden, I., & Lally, J. *Intellectual Stimulation of Infants and Toddlers.* Gainesville: Univ. of Florida Press, 1967.

Granger, R. *et al. The Impact of Head Start.* Preliminary draft, Westinghouse Learning Corporation, April, 1969.

Gray, S. *Project DARCEE Progress Report.* Nashville, Tenn.: Unpublished, 1967.

Harlow, H. F. The maternal affectional system. Foss, B. M. (Ed.), *The Determinants of Infant Behavior.* New York: John Wiley & Sons, 1963, 3-33.

Harmeling, J. D., & Jones, M. B. Birthweights of high school dropouts, *Amer. J. Orthopsychiat.*, 1968, 38, 63-66.

Hasselmeyer, E. G. The premature neonate's response to handling, *Amer. Nurses Association*, 1964, 11, 15-24.

Havighurst, R. J. *Human Development and Education.* New York: Longmans, 1953.

Hellmuth, J. (Ed.) *Exceptional Infant*, Vol. I. New York: Brunner/Mazel, 1967.

Hess, E. H. Ethology. A. M. Freeman & H. I. Kaplan (Eds.). *Comprehensive Textbook of Psychiatry.* Baltimore: Williams & Wilkins, 1967, 180-189.

Hoopes, J. *An Infant Rating Scales Its Validation and Usefulness.* New York: Child Welfare League of America, 1967.

HUNT, J. McV. The psychological basis for using preschool enrichment as an antidote for cultural deprivation. J. Hellmuth (Ed.), *Disadvantaged Child*, Vol. I., New York, Brunner/Mazel, 1967, 255-299.

HUNT, J. McV. *Intelligence and Experience*. New York: The Ronald Press, 1961.

Inventory of Home Stimulation for Ages 3 to 6. Children's Center, Syracuse University, Syracuse, N. Y., 1969.

IRWIN, O. C. Infant speech: Effect of systematic reading of stories, *The J. of Speech & Hearing Research*, 1960, 3, 187-190.

JONES, H. E. The environment and mental development. *Manual of Child Psychology*, L. Carmichael (Ed.). New York: John Wiley, 1954, 631-696.

KAGAN, J. On cultural deprivation. D. Glass (Ed.), *Proceedings of the Conference on Biology and Behavior*. New York: Rockefeller Univ. Press, 1968, 211-250.

KAGAN, J., & LEWIS, M. Studies of attention in the human infant, *Merrill-Palmer Quart.*, 1965, 11, 95-127.

KAGAN, J. Continuity in cognitive development during the first year, *Merrill-Palmer Quart.*, 1969, 15, 101-120.

KAGAN, J., HENKER, B., HEN-TOV, A., LEVINE, J., & LEWIS, M. Infants' differential re-actions to familiar and distorted faces, *Child Development*, 1966, 37, 519-532.

KARP, J. & SIGEL, I. The psychoeducational appraisal of disadvantaged children, *Rev. Educ. Res.*, 1965, 35:5, 401-412.

KEISTER, M. E. A demonstration project: the good life for infants and toddlers. A paper presented at a symposium sponsored by the Day Care Council of New York, Inc., 1969.

KNOBLOCH, H., & PASAMANICK, B. Further observations on the behavioral development of Negro children, *J. Genetic Psychology*, 1953, 83, 137-157.

KNOBLOCH, H., & PASAMANICK, B. Mental subnormality, *New England J. Med.*, 1962, 266, 1045, 1092-1155.

KNOBLOCH, H., & PASAMANICK, B. Neuropsychiatric sequelae of prematurity. *J.A.M.A.*, 1959, 161, 581.

KORNER, A., & GROBSTEIN, R. Visual alertness as related to soothing in neonates: Im-plications for maternal stimulation and early deprivation, *Child Development*, 1967, 37, 867-876.

KRECH, D., ROSENZWEIG, M. R., & BENNETT, E. L. Relations between brain chemistry and problem-solving among rats raised in enriched and impoverished environ-ments, *J. Comp. Physiol. Psychol.*, 1962, 55, 801-807.

KRECH, D., ROSENZWEIG, M. R., & BENNETT, E. L. Effects of environment complexity on brain chemistry, *J. Comp. Physiol. Psychol.*, 1960, 53, 509-519.

KRECH, D., ROSENZWEIG, M., & BENNETT, E. Environmental impoverishment, social isolation, and changes in brain chemistry and anatomy, *Physiology and Behavior*. London: Pergamon Press, 1966.

LAZAR, I. Private communication, February, 1970, regarding psychometric findings from a sample of six Parent and Child Centers. The contract with Kirschner Associ-ates prohibits publication of the data, and this restriction is herein honored.

LEVINE, S. Stimulation in infancy, *Scientific American*, 1960.

LEWIS, M., & GOLDBERG, S. Perceptual-cognitive development in infancy: A generalized expectancy model as a function of the mother-infant interaction, *Merrill-Palmer Quart.*, 1969, 15, 81-100.

LEWIS, M., KAGAN, J., CAMPBELL, H., & KALAFAT, J. The cardiac response as a correlate of attention in infants, *Child Develop.*, 1966, 37, 63-71.

LUBCHENCO, L. O. *et al.* Development of premature infants of low birth weight: Evaluation at ten years of age, *Amer. J. Dis. Child.*, 1962, 102, 752.

LUBCHENCO, L. *High Risk Infant Follow-up Study*. Unpublished Progress Report, 1969.

LUBCHENCO, L. O. Sequelae of premature birth. Evaluation of premature infants of low birth weights at ten years of age, *Amer. J. Dis. Child.*, 1963, 106, 101-115.

LUBCHENCO, L. O. Assessment of gestational age and development at birth, *Ped. Clinics of North America*, 1970, 17, 125.

LURIA, A. R. *Human Brain and Psychological Processes*. New York: Harper & Rowe, 1966.

MALLITSKAYA, M. K. A method for using pictures to develop speech comprehension in children at the end of the first and in the second year of life, *Voprosy Psikhol.*, 1960, No. 3, 122-126.

MASLAND, R. L., SARASON, S. B., & GLADWIN, T. *Mental Subnormality*, New York: Basic Books, 1958.

McCALL, R. B., & KAGAN, J. Attention in the infant: Effects of complexity, contour, perimeter, and familiarity, *Child Develop.*, 1967, 38, 938-952.

MEERS, D., and MARANS, A. Group care of infants in other countries. In L. Dittman (Ed.), *Early Child Care*. New York: Atherton Press, 1968.

MEHLER, J., & BEVER, T. G. Cognitive capacity of very young children, *Science*, 1967, 158, 141-142.

MEHROTRA, S. N., & MAXWELL, J. Intelligence of twins: A comparative study of eleven year old twins, *Population Studies*, 1949, 3, 295.

MEIER, J. An autotelic nursery school. In J. Masserman (Ed.), *Psychiatric Therapy Quart.*, Vol. 70 (in press-1970a).

MEIER, J. Causes and characteristics of communication disorders in elementary school children. In *Proceedings* for the Division for Children with Communication Disorders meeting at the 47th annual International Convention of the Council for Exceptional Children, 1969a.

MEIER, J. Developmental disabilities and problems of intellect. In Symposium on Spina Bifida, Univ. of Colo. Medical Center, 1969b, 39-56.

MEIER, J. Innovations in assessing the disadvantaged child's potential. In J. Hellmuth (Ed.), *Disadvantaged Child*, Vol. I. New York: Brunner/Mazel, Inc., 1967, 173-199.

MEIER, J. Some results of new nursery school language research, *Childhood Education*, 1968, 45:4, 228-236.

MEIER, J., & MARTIN, H. Diagnosis and management of developmental retardation. In H. Kempe, H. Silver, & D.O'Brien (Eds.), *Pediatric Current Diagnosis and Treatment. Los Altos*, Calif.: Lange, 1970d (in press).

MEIER, J. Prevalence and Characteristics of Learning Disabilities Found in Second Graders. *J. Learn. Disabilities*, 1970c (in press).

MOORE, O. K. Autotelic Responsive Environments and Exceptional Children. Mimeographed. Hamden, Conn.: Responsive Environments Foundation, 1963.

MOORE, O. K., & ANDERSON, A. R. Some principles for the design of clarifying educational environments. In *Handbook of Socialization Theory and Research*, D. Goslin (Ed.). Chicago: Rand McNally, 1968.

NEWTON, G., & LEVINE, S. *Early Experience and Behavior: The Psychobiology of Development*. Springfield: Charles C Thomas, 1968.

NIMNICHT, G., McAFEE, O., & MEIER, J. *The New Nursery School*. New York: General Learning Corp., 1969.

PALMER, F. Learning at two, *Children*, 1969, 16, 55-57.

PAVENSTEDT, E. A comparison of the child-rearing environment of upper-, lower- and very low-lower-class families, *Amer. J. Orthopsychiat.*, 1965, 35, 89-98.

PIAGET, J. *The Origins of Intelligence in Children*. New York: International Univ. Press, 1952.

PINES, M. *Revolution in Learning*. New York: Harper & Rowe, 1967.

Problems of neonatal intensive care units: Report of the Fifty-Ninth Ross Conference on Pediatric Research. Columbus, Ohio: Ross Laboratories, 1969.

PROVENCE, S., & LIPTON, R. C. *Infants in Institutions: A Comparison of Their Development with Family-reared Infants during the First Year of Life*. New York: International Univ. Press, 1962.

RAZRAN, G. The observable unconscious and the inferable conscious in current Soviet psychophysiology: Interoceptive conditioning, semantic conditioning and the orienting reflex, *Psychological Review*, 1961, 68, 81-147.

RHEINGOLD, H. L. The modification of social responsiveness in institutionalized babies. *Monographs of the S.R.C.D.*, Vol. 21, No. 2, Evanston, Ill.: Child Develop. Publications, 1956.

RHEINGOLD, H. L., GEWIRTZ, J. L., & ROSS, H. Social conditioning of vocalization in the infant, *J. Comp. Physiol. Psychol.*, 1958, 52, 68-73.

RHEINGOLD, H. L. The effect of environmental stimulation upon social and exploratory behavior in the human infant. B. Foss (Ed.), *Determinants of Infant Behavior.* New York: Wiley, 1961.

RIBBLE, M. *The Rights of Infants: Early Psychological Needs and Their Satisfactions.* New York: Columbia Univ. Press, 1943.

RIESSMAN, F. *The Culturally Deprived Child.* New York: Harper, 1962.

ROSENZWEIG, M. R., BENNETT, E. L., & DIAMOND, M. C. Transitory components of cerebral changes induced by experience. *Proceedings, 75th Annual Convention, APA,* 1967, 105-106.

SCHAEFFER, E., & BELLE, R. Development of a parental attitude research instrument, *Child Develop.,* 1958, 27, 337-361.

SCOTT, J. P. Critical periods in behavioral development, *Science,* 1962, 138, 949-956.

SCOTT, K. B., JENKINS, M. E., & CRAWFORD, R. P. Growth and development of Negro infants: I. Analysis of birth weights of 11,818 newly born infants, *Pediatrics,* 1950, 6, 425-431.

SEARS, R. R., MACCOBY, E., & LEVIN, H. *Patterns of Child Rearing.* Evanston, Ill.: Row-Peterson, 1957.

SKEELS, H., & DYE, H. A study of the effects of differential stimulation on mentally retarded children. *Proceedings of the American Association on Mental Deficiency,* 1939, 44, 114-136.

SOLKOFF, N., YAFFE, S., WEINTRAUB, D., & BLASE, B. Effects of handling on the subsequent developments of premature infants, *Developmental Psychology,* 1969, 1, 765-768.

SPIRO, M. *Children of the Kibbutz.* Cambridge, Mass.: Harvard Univ. Press, 1958.

SPITZ, RENE. *The First Year of Life: A Psychoanalytic Study of Normal and Deviant Development of Object Relations.* New York: International Univ. Press, 1965.

Statistical summary of patients served in mental retardation clinics of fiscal year, 1968. U.S. Dept. Health, Education & Welfare, National Center for Social Statistics.

STOTT, L., & BALL, R. Infant and preschool mental tests: Review and evaluation. *Monographs of the Society for Research in Child Development,* 1965, 30, No. 101.

TERMAN, L. M., *et al. Genetic Studies of Genius,* Vol. I. Palo Alto, Calif.: Stanford Univ. Press, 1925.

THOMPSON, W. R., & MELZACK, R. Early environment, *Scientific American,* 1956, 174, 38-42.

UZGIRIS, I. C., & HUNT, J. McV. A scale of infant psychological development. Unpublished manuscript. Urbana: Univ. of Ill.

UZGIRIS, I. Ordinality in the development of schemas for relating to objects. *Exceptional Infant,* Vol. I, J. Hellmuth (Ed.), New York: Brunner/Mazel, Inc., 1967, 315-334.

VALVERDE, F., & RUIZ-MARCOS, A. The effects of sensory deprivation on dendritic spines in the visual cortex of the mouse. In *Proceedings of Dyslexia Conference,* Wash., D.C.: National Research Council Committee on Brain Sciences, 1968.

VAN DEN BERG, B. J. Morbidity of low birth weight and/or pre-term children compared to that of the mature, *Pediatrics,* 1968, 42, 590.

WECHSLER, D. The IQ is an Intelligent Test. *The New York Times Magazine,* June 26, 1966.

WEIKART, D., & LAMBIE, D. Preschool intervention through a home teaching program. In J. Hellmuth (Ed.), *Disadvantaged Child,* Vol. II, New York: Brunner/Mazel, Inc., 1968, 435-501.

WHITE, B. L., CASTLE, P., & HELD, R. Observations on the development of visually directed teaching, *Child Develop.,* 1964, 35, 349, 364.

WHITE, B., & CASTLE, P. Visual exploratory behavior following postnatal handling of human infants, *Percept. Mot. Skills,* 1964, 18, 497-502.

WINDLE, W. Brain damage by asphyxia at birth, *Scientific American,* 1969, 221, 76-87.

WOLFF, P., & WHITE, B. Visual pursuit and attention in young infants, *J. Amer. Acad. Child Psychiatr.,* 1965, 4, 473-484.

WRIGHT, F. H. A controlled follow-up study of small prematures. *Final Report to Children's Bureau,* 1969.

YARROW, L. J. Research in dimensions of early maternal care, *Merrill-Palmer Quart.,* 1963, 101-114.

20

IS HEAD START A SUCCESS
OR FAILURE?

Robert Mendelsohn, M.D.

Department of Pediatrics, University of Illinois
Former Director of Medical Consultation Services for Head Start
American Academy of Pediatrics

Project Head Start is probably the most remarkable experiment in child development in this country's history. An understanding of some of its main characteristics is therefore of major importance. First, Head Start is not just an educational program and it is not a "junior kindergarten." This is important to recognize because it was so interpreted by many early observers. Nor is it just a medical or dental program. Nor is it just a social service program, or a psychological service program. It is none of these items by themselves, but rather Head Start is a combination of all of these components and others working in concert. It is vital to appreciate that no one of them works without the others. This has implications for the kind of direction that society is going to have to take in terms of solving the problems of the children and families that Head Start is designed to serve. Therefore, Head Start today can be defined as a multi-disciplinary program that is family-centered. Its purpose is to use the various components in order to assist people to help themselves out of poverty. Head Start is part of the War on Poverty and it would be difficult to imagine Head Start existing without being part of the total anti-poverty effort. This means that the goal of the program is not just to make children better educated, or just to make them healthier, or just to use the casework services to get the father a better job, or just to educate the mother. The purpose of the program is to use all of these "ends" and to convert them into means. In other words, it is a substitution of methods for what we are used to calling goals. A physician usually considers his job as finished when the patient gets well. However, Head Start has set a much higher goal than most of us are accustomed to seeking. This increases the responsibility on every professional who serves in Head Start. For example, the dentist's job is not finished just because the child has a set of perfect teeth. This is only the first step. He must simultaneously act in terms of his public role, his influence on existing institutions, in terms of community action and social action. In other words, the professional must emerge from the narrow role for which he has been trained and must collaborate with others. Health is too important to be left exclusively to the medical profession and education is too important to be left solely to the educators.

In Head Start the physician's job is not finished until the patient and his family are able to utilize good health to get out of poverty. The aim is to get people out of poverty and not merely to provide the kind of services for which we professionals have been trained. It has been accurately stated in the phrase "we are not in this work to make healthy poor people." The reason why an understanding of this concept is vital is because many proposed solutions to the poverty problem are presented in one dimensional terms. It is claimed that poverty could be eradicated if enough jobs were available. Others claim the solution lies in better health while still others stress education. Everyone seems to have his own pet ideas. But this approach has led universally to failure. As soon as a priority scale is established designating one facet as more important than the other, those in charge of funding choose the top item or the top two or three items for major effort. And when it doesn't work, the original planners and the plan are blamed for the failure. For example, if you place jobs in the highest priority, the Department of Labor or another agency of government may mount an extensive manpower development training program. Some people may actually secure jobs but if they don't stay in their jobs, the training program itself is faulted. The failing thus far of the anti-poverty effort in this country stems in part from the fact that many of us, and particularly professionals, talk in terms of priorities instead of in terms of a simultaneous all-out effort on all fronts. This is a major factor that explains why Head Start has succeeded to a greater extent than other programs. Head Start is a total effort. It really deserves the appellation of "War on Poverty" because in a war you put in everything. We don't give soldiers a choice between a tank or machine gun. Rather, we utilize all necessary weapons.

There is another reason for the success of Head Start other than its multidisciplinary approach. Originally, Head Start emphasized children. However, it soon became obvious that this was not adequate. It consequently evolved into and is generally now recognized to be a family-centered program. This is a significant development because those who serve children sometimes have some unfortunate tendencies. First, we tend to pay lip service to the American ideal of placing our greatest effort into children. We do this in many different ways. For example, we claim that if there is a certain amount of money available it should be spent on children instead of older folks. We talk about crucial ages with the implications that by the time a child reaches a certain designated age, be it age 3, or 5, or 8, or 18, virtually all hope is lost for meaningful change. The older a person gets the less hope we have. By the time adulthood is reached we tend to feel that there is very little chance left. And by the time you reach 75 there is really no opportunity at all for change, as far as most people are concerned. Yet those of us who have had experience in such activities as foster grandparent programs have seen that people between 65 and 98 can make far-reaching changes in their own lives and the lives of people around them if they are given the kind of inputs that enable them to properly function. Therefore, another achievement of Head Start has been to remove the undue emphasis from children and to place it in a more realistic framework—the family. We are aware that it is useless to try to give a child education unless something is done with the parents at the same time. As a matter of fact, there is a risk of potentially weakening family life by over-emphasizing the child. For example, in a program in 1965, for American Indian Head Start children, some 5- and 6-year-old Indian children who had no previous experience with utensils learned table manners in the Head Start school. There was little parent involvement effort in that first year. When the children went home, they tried to teach table manners to their fathers and created severe family tensions in some instances. Thus, in an attempt to focus on the child one can endanger and in some cases destroy family life. This kind of result occurs whenever we over-emphasize the children and whenever we imply that only children can be salvaged. Pediatricians may have to stop talking exclusively about children some day and start emphasizing families.

Has Project Head Start succeeded? The answer to this question depends, of course, on the definition of the goals. The ultimate goal of Head Start as stated earlier is to utilize its several components to help people to get themselves out of poverty. Let us consider the components. If one measures health and medical care, a difference will be found within the child upon entry to Head Start and upon leaving Head Start, since he has had a number of his health needs met. His principal defects have presumably been identified and evaluated. If he lives in a southern rural area he has been purged of intestinal parasites. He has received eye glasses and hearing aids and other medical and dental services. There are fewer dental caries in the children as a result of the dental component of the Head Start experience. The same applies to the educational experiences. By and large, almost every study demonstrates that, in terms of psychometric studies and educational achievements, the children show significant advances during their stay in the program. Similarly, as far as the nutrition program is concerned, the children who enter Head Start usually have poorer nutrition than the ones who are leaving

Head Start, since lunch and often breakfast are provided in the Head Start centers. Some centers serve three meals a day.

Good nutrition certainly leads to better physical and mental development. But it is not the only significant factor. For example, a study by the University of Pittsburgh demonstrated a good correlation between the Indian children's height and inside plumbing. Indian families living in homes with inside plumbing had a tendency to have taller children. Height was also associated with the square footage of living space inside the home. The families with bigger homes had taller children. Nutrition, therefore, cannot readily be separated from other socio-cultural and economic factors in determining effectiveness.

But let us return to the question of whether or not Head Start has really succeeded. There is some value in measuring results of the individual components, but the interpretation of these measurements is difficult. As previously indicated, each of the individual components can be shown to have had an effect. However, in terms of the real goal of Head Start, there can be only one ultimate measure of success. That criterion is whether families have been enabled to escape from the poverty cycle. That is the only valid way of judging the success of Head Start. Therefore, in addition to all the data-collecting in the fields of medical, dental, educational and casework services, we should study those families whose children were in Head Start in 1965, 1966, and succeeding years and compare their present incomes with their previous incomes. This must then be measured against a population similar in all respects but the Head Start experience. Has there been any change? Have these Head Start families been able to emerge from poverty or are they just as poor now as they were then? This will be the best indication of whether Head Start is a success. For example, one can measure educational performance, and there is general agreement that after leaving Head Start, the educational gains are soon lost. The question is to what extent does this deterioration occur? Also, to what extent do the gains in health deteriorate? This would apply to every component of the program. Some reports suggest that there may even be a "rebound phenomenon," that in the early Head Start graduates the incidence of those who drop out of school in later years may actually be higher. This may be due to the discrepancy realized by the child between his Head Start experience and the conditions actually existing in public schools. As Dr. William Glasser has written, sending a child to Head Start and then putting him into a public school is like preparing a soldier for combat by sending him on vacation to the French Riviera.

Head Start medical consultants have reported that the health components seem more satisfactory in programs that are run by community action agencies and churches than in programs that are run by public schools. There is a deadening depressing influence of the existing school system on children, and school bureaucracies are almost impossible to crack. New organizations, therefore, had a certain advantage. When health programs were freshly developed by the community action agencies or the church groups, they didn't have the dead weight of tradition to overcome. On the other hand, the schools had some sort of previous health program, usually inadequate, and they usually continued with the same kind of traditional program.

But why don't the schools respond? Part of the answer is because when it comes to poor people the traditional helping institutions in our country seem to work in reverse. The schools keep poor children from getting an education. The hospitals and medical system keep poor people from getting well and the welfare agencies and institutions keep poor people from getting money. More specifically, the public school systems have a most unAmerican quality. They have a monopoly on children. Poor children have no choice as to which school to attend nor do they even have the choice to attend school or to stay home. We need a basic change in the rules of the game. We should establish competing school systems, and perhaps Head Start might establish its own school so that Head Start graduates might never have to enter public school. Let us give the children choices between competing school systems or indeed even staying home. One might convincingly argue that poor children may be better off never entering school. It may be preferable for them to stay home, on the streets, because at least there they are not subject to the kind of brutal failure-oriented treatment that they get in public schools.

Head Start is a revolutionary activity in the full sense of the word revolutionary. One may begin by serving children, but will end up by fighting every establishment. Whether or not we are able to bring about the necessary changes in those establishments depends, first, on their store of information. One of the chief accomplishments of Head Start has been to inform the country, to make poverty visible. However, once informed, we will then have to depend on conscience, on will, and on motivation. If the majority in our country prove to have a strong conscience once they know the nature of the situation, then they will act responsibly. The alternative to responsible action by the majority is increased demands and aggressiveness by the oppressed minority.

One of our most serious problems is the division of thought from action. A most important group in this country responsible for this division are the professionals in the helping fields, and they carry a heavy burden. The general public often seems much more ready to act than the professionals, and certainly the poor people are ready to move. One wonders whether professional education, including medical education, prepares its graduates for contemplation rather than action. As a matter of fact, it may well be training us in the technique of avoiding action. Perhaps we enter our careers with a desire to perform and to accomplish and then this is systematically extinguished by the educational process.

However, this view may be too naive, since it is obvious that action per se is not enough. One can act and can still manage to do everything wrong because of unconscious motives. Operation Follow Through, which is supposed to take care of the "alumni" from Head Start who pass into the public school system, provides some good examples. For instance, this program provides funds to continue nutrition services to Head Start children. Thus, some Project Head Start children are enabled to have lunch in first, second and third grade.

Some of the public schools are reported to be segregating Follow-Through children in separate lunch rooms. Others give them special identification buttons; inevitably when they pass through the line their peers are aware of those receiving a free lunch. This kind of discrimination operates in other areas as well. A teacher recently fired from her position in a local school system for "unsatisfactory performance" said, "What good does all the Follow-Through and ESEA money do when the first week I was in the school the principal came into my room and demonstrated how to pinch a child's arm without causing black and blue marks." As everyone knows, if you want to do something wrong, you can take the best thing in the world and pervert it.

One of the reasons for Head Start's relative immunity to this kind of destructive process is due to the parent involvement aspect. The parents exercise a very considerable degree of control. They sit on the Boards, in significant numbers. They participate in the classrooms as teacher aides. They also participate in control of the budget and of the personnel policies and selection. One future measurement of the success of Head Start will be the degree of parent control and participation on Boards of Education and Boards of Health in a meaningful rather than a token fashion. There is a traditional tendency to exclude parents from this kind of involvement, much as universities have excluded students from the decision-making process. Yet, historically, universities came into being in central Europe around the 13th Century when groups of students organized themselves and hired teachers.

Therefore, when parents of poor children are properly represented at the policy-making levels of our major institutions designated to serve those children, we will know that Head Start has made its contribution towards achieving this kind of victory.

There has been a change in attitude and role of many professionals involved in local Head Start programs as a result of parent participation. For example, many of the teachers in Head Start summer programs are the very same teachers in public school the rest of the year. Yet they are usually able to accomplish far more in Head Start than in the traditional schools. The explanations are obvious, Head Start classes have 12 to 15 children and 3 to 4 adults; the public school system has 35 to 40 children and one adult. Head Start provides medical and dental services; the school system usually either gives none or inadequate service. Head Start serves lunch and often breakfast; the school systems usually give neither, or they may provide lunches in a degrading discriminatory manner. Head Start costs $1,400 per year per child and the school system spends about $550.

There are other reasons as well and the answers lie in the philosophy of the program. We must recognize that the answer does not lie in traditional teacher-education techniques. Head Start teachers and teacher aides receive little if any additional formal training, but much in-service experience. The presence of parents in a classroom inevitably influences the attitudes of the teacher and modifies her behavior. It is hoped that this influence may lead to greater identification on the part of the teachers with the parents of their students.

Furthermore, there is now considerable opinion that the single most important factor in determining the educational achievements of the child is the extent of involvement and concern of his parents. This in turn is influenced by many factors including the ability of the father to find and retain a meaningful job, the opportunity of the mother to keep a decent home, and the nutritional status of all family members. Therefore, the teacher must not behave as if she were operating in a vacuum. Rather, meaningful collaboration of parents and teachers is necessary to bring about the changes so vital to American education today. The same can be said of health personnel and all others involved in Head Start projects.

The non-professional teaching personnel are very valuable. Therefore, we must encourage participation by people who may have few formal credentials. When it is necessary to make cuts in the budget, logic would dictate that the aides without credentials should be retained, if necessary at the expense of some of the professionals who are not as close to the children. Yet experience teaches us that such is hardly ever the case in practice.

Consumer participation on Boards other than Head Start is still almost totally non-existent. Virtually all major hospitals serving many indigent patients have no poor people on their boards. Practically no private agency serving the poor has one-third of its Board consisting of poor people themselves.

Professionals will need a reeducation. They might begin by reading the important socio-cultural studies of our times, especially those works that concern themselves with the population in question. This list of recommended readings might include: Michael Harrington's "The Other America," Margaret Walker's "Jubilee," Jonathan Kozol's "Death at an Early Age," Grier & Cobbs' "Black Rage," and Andrew Billingsley's "The Black Family in White America." Also, it is important to familiarize oneself with the various community organizations of the poor, such as the Welfare Rights Organization, to support them and to encourage their activities. These organizations may become a significant source of power in the effort to bring about social change.

Professionals must understand that the goals of Head Start cannot be achieved merely by providing their own set of skills and abilities and applying them to poor children. They will have to begin to appreciate the importance of manpower development and training for new kinds of careers.

They must recognize that many of the poor with less formal education can be utilized not merely because they can carry out some of our tasks as well as we do, but because they can perform them better than the professional. The licensed physician, certified teacher and graduate caseworker are partially disabled precisely because of their education and their social class. This kind of outlook inevitably brings them into conflict with their own professional groups and many of their professional colleagues.

They will become aware of the arteriosclerosis of our professional guilds, of the conscious and unconscious exclusionary policies of our professional labor unions, of the irrationality and underlying discriminatory nature of our curriculum demands and our Board requirements.

One of the best measurements of the success of Head Start will be the extent to which the professional becomes reeducated. We will know success is near when doctors realize that they themselves are part of the problem. The health system they have helped to create and support is also part of the problem, rather than the solution. We will be near our goal when social workers free themselves of their air of professionalism and disregard the traditional teaching that discourages them from "overidentifying with the clients." It is high time that doctors, caseworkers and teachers begin to overidentify (whatever that means) and become involved with their patients, clients and students. We must begin to reverse the process and understand that in many instances the children and their families are the real faculty and we, the professionals, are the students.

These changes in the professionals will be at least as important as the changes in the children, because these newly educated professionals can help bring about the needed changes in our institutions. Institutional change is the third basic component of Head Start, the other two being service to the children and families and manpower development. Without institutional change in our hospitals, medical care system, schools, welfare system—in short, without basic changes in our social and economic structure, Head Start can never succeed.

It is vital to remember that we are changing children! For several generations they have been trained by their families and their culture to be passive, withdrawn, apathetic, controlled, unresponsive, and thick-skinned. They have been encouraged to exhibit a facade of mental retardation. This kind of training has come, not out of choice, but from the need to survive.

Now, in Head Start, we are training them to be outgoing, questioning, curious, sensitive, responsive, active, imaginative and ambitious. Yet this process of "coming alive" may be deadly! For, we are preparing these children for doors that may not be open, for doors that may be slammed in their faces. The new personalities that we have helped to foster can prove to be counter-adaptive if the opportunities to exploit their newly revealed powers and skills are denied. The resultant frustration may lead to internal reactions such as serious mental disease, or external reactions, such as revolutionary activity. Either path places their very lives in jeopardy. Thus, there is great danger that in the process of bringing about "improvements" in the children, we are endangering their very survival.

This is the reason why the simple measurement of "improvement" in the children is a naive and potentially misleading method of evaluation. Instead we must simultaneously measure the changes in ourselves and in the institutions and society we represent and support. As a matter of fact, a convincing argument could be constructed that if we worked harder and more successfully at opening doors for these children and their families, Project Head Start would not be necessary at all.

However, institutional change has been slow in coming and few dramatic breakthroughs can be cited. This is true even in well-motivated organizations of the "establishment" that have become involved in Head Start. I will cite one recent example. One of the major professional pediatric organizations in this country has been giving consultation service to Head Start and has not only provided important service, but has also undergone significant internal reorganization and change.

Yet, at the recent White House Conference on Nutrition, Food and Health, the representative of this pediatric organization failed to support the recommendations for a universal free school lunch program. He gave two reasons for his position. First, children should be encouraged to go home and eat lunch with their families, and, second, to give free lunches to rich children is socialism. These unrealistic expressions and attitudes emanate from a comparatively enlightened "member of the establishment," and indicate how far we still have to move in the direction of institutional change.

Head Start has been a noble experiment. It has not been a pilot project or a demonstration study. It has been an action program on a grand scale. Its future is uncertain and its effectiveness is problematic. But, in any event, it has had a remarkable effect on all those who have participated. It has served to open our eyes, to strengthen our better impulses, to change our lives. Many of Head Start's accomplishments will be measured, but these subtle factors cannot be quantitated. Yet, they may well prove to be the most enduring and powerful results.

Head Start has reached a crucial turning point. With the recedence of the large scale summer programs and the concentration on small full-year programs, the influence of the traditional educational establishment becomes markedly strengthened. The 1970's may well mark the transformation of Head Start into just another extension of this educational establishment. If so, regardless of how many IQ points the children temporarily gain, Head Start can be chalked up as a grand experiment that failed.

SUMMARY

In trying to decide whether Head Start is a success or a failure, we may be measuring the wrong items, and not measuring the right ones. We have concentrated on measuring the children. This is not adequate. Instead, we must measure ourselves. How have we changed? How have our social institutions changed? How are these changes reflected in the income of the parents of Head Start children?

Let no one regard Head Start as simply either beneficial or innocuous. It is true that Head Start may improve the condition of the children. It may also endanger their very lives! Those of us involved in providing service and in evaluating the results carry a heavy life and death responsibility.

21

THE IMPLICATIONS OF LEARNING THEORY FOR THE FADE-OUT OF GAINS FROM COMPENSATORY EDUCATION

Donald T. Campbell, Ph.D. and Peter W. Frey

Department of Psychology
Northwestern University

The gains from intensive compensatory interventions often "fade out" with time. Measures two or three years later show less effect than immediate posttests in terms of relative group performance. The gap between the disadvantaged and advantaged child reappears.

This fade out of effects is often mistakenly interpreted as casting doubt on the appropriateness of the intervention and on the assumption that abilities are learned which underlies compensatory educational efforts. So interpreted, the fade out may mistakenly seem to support efforts to interpret all group differences as innate. It is the purpose of this paper to point out that such interpretations are quite wrong. A fade out of effects is exactly what we would expect if group differences were totally or partially learned. Thus while such outcomes are regrettable, they should not be disappointing, in that they are perfectly consistent with the assumptions of learned abilities underlying compensatory efforts. The fade out effect does not mean that the measured gains were unreal or artifactual. The gains, albeit transient, are as real as the initial differences, and are to be explained on the basis of the same processes.

Performance on a learned task is dependent upon past opportunities to learn as well as upon differences in rate of learning and rate of forgetting. The theory of compensatory education assumes that major parts of observed group differences on achievement and ability tests are due to group differences in such opportunities. This paper assumes for sake of illustration the distribution of such opportunities shown in Figure 1.

Supported in part by National Science Foundation Grant GS 1309X and Public Health Service Research Grant MH17767.

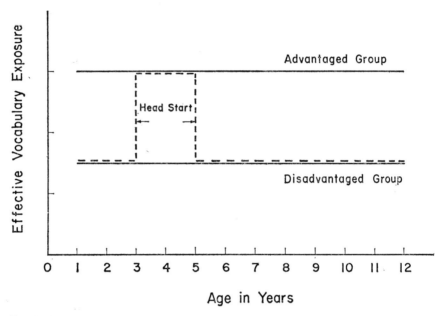

Fig. 1. A presumed distribution of learning opportunities or inputs for conventional and compensatory education programs.

For the advantaged child, a uniformly high opportunity structure is assumed. For the typical disadvantaged child a uniformly lower level of input is assumed. For an experimental group of disadvantaged children, it is assumed for this illustration that the input difference is completely removed during the two year Head Start period, during which the intellectual quality of the environment equals that of advantaged children. Following the compensatory effort, it is assumed that the input falls back to the level of other disadvantaged children. We are assuming for this illustration that the input during the 14 to 16 hour waking day is as different for advantaged and disadvantaged children after they start school as it is before. (This of course would not be because of poorer teachers, but rather because the schools of the disadvantaged for other reasons provide very poor learning opportunities. In addition they occupy only a minor part of the waking day.)

One could modify these assumptions and fade out would still be produced. Nonetheless, for future study of these problems, it seems imperative that we try to measure them as precisely as we do the child's performance. And for adequate communication about group differences to our fellow educators and the public, it would seem imperative that when we provide information on group differences on IQ, we accompany it by equally detailed data on an "EIPQ," an Environmental Intelligence

Producing Quotient. Looking at each aspect of our intelligence and achievement measures, one should score the environment in terms of the degree to which it has provided similar experiences. For example, if vocabulary is used as a dependent measure, information such as tape recordings of the vocabulary used in the home environment should be obtained. The EIPQ would be scored lower for children reared by illiterate grandmothers than for those getting constant hovering attention from otherwise unoccupied college graduates. The EIPQ for children regularly read to from picture books from an early age would be scored higher than that for those who have never had this experience. Important would be the frequency with which the child is allowed to provide the initiative in child-adult interactions, providing him with a truly responsive environment with high quality feedback. If Kohs' blocks are used as a performance measure, the child's familiarity with these blocks as playthings would contribute. The EIPQ would be low for children who have never had uniform colored blocks to play with, or who have lacked floor space they could dominate for play constructions.

Although the general form of the analysis suggested here can be applied to the acquisition of diverse problem solving skills other than verbal ones, for the sake of precision and clarity of exposition the present arguments will deal with the acquisition of vocabulary, an ubiquitous component of intelligence tests. Let us assume that the learning *input* situations diagramed in Figure 1 show the average level of *effective word exposure* for the advantaged and disadvantaged groups as a function of age. The example assumes that in terms of number of words present and in terms of effective verbal interaction between child and adult, the advantaged group receives double the test-relevant vocabulary exposure that the disadvantaged group receives. This estimate is probably reasonably consistent with the available data. The dashed line shows an exceptionally effective compensatory educational program which during a two year period, from age 3 to 5, completely compensates for the group differences as far as vocabulary input is concerned.

Given the input pattern of Figure 1, and assuming an equality among all three groups of children in rate of learning and in rate of forgetting, Figure 2 illustrates the outcome expected from learning theory. Let us consider first the two solid curves. Even with the equality in learning ability and even with the constancy over the years of the input difference, the gap between the advantaged and disadvantaged steadily increases. For the Head Start group, the temporary total closing of the input gap leads to a gradual lessening of the performance gap, but when the compensatory input ends, the gap gradually reappears, the immediate gains fade out.

In generating the simulated data of Figure 2, we have employed a mathematical learning theory. However the essential assumptions in-

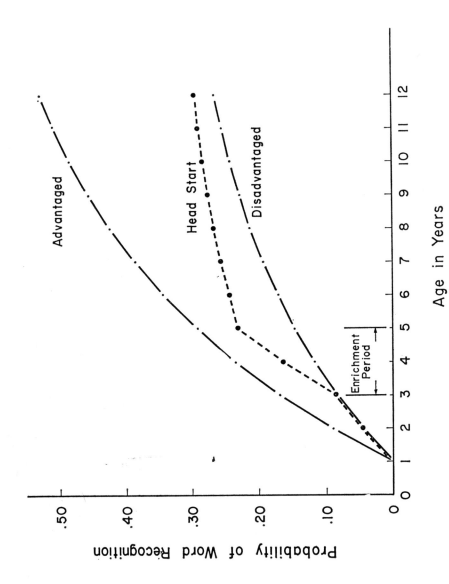

Fig. 2. Performance of normal, disadvantaged, and compensatory education groups, assuming the inputs of Fig. 1 and uniform rates of learning and forgetting for all groups.

volved are shared by all learning theories and have received empirical support in studies beginning with Ebbinghaus (1885). While our algebra is in the tradition of Estes (1959), our assumptions are explicit also in Hull (1943) and many others. The crucial assumptions are shown in Figure 3, namely that both learning and forgetting are negatively accelerated functions, changing rapidly at first, and more slowly later. These assumptions cut across the major disagreements within learning theory. Thus it does not matter whether one believes element learning to be all or none, or fractionally incremental. These assumptions hold whether one believes forgetting to be due to spontaneous recovery, or spontaneous recovery to be due to forgetting, etc.

For purpose of mathematically modeling the vocabulary learning situation, let us define a random variable, P_n, which indicates the probability that a child will recognize any given word randomly selected from a specified vocabulary population in his nth month after birth. Since it is a probability measure, it only takes on values between 0.0 and 1.0. The statement that $P_{47} = .12$ indicates that the child in his 47th month has a 12% chance of recognizing any given word randomly selected from the specific word population being sampled. The fundamental assumption is that the child learns a constant proportion each month of the unlearned material. The change in probability of word recognition each month can be expressed quantitatively as:

$$(1)$$
$$P_{n+1} = P_n + \theta(1 - P_n)$$

The learning rate parameter, θ, indicates the proportion of the unlearned items which are acquired each month. If one sets $P_1 = .01$ and $\theta = .04$, this function generates the growth curve depicted in Figure 3. The general form of this function would not be altered by the choice of different parameter values, only the rate at which the asymptote of the function is approached.

Since it seems reasonable to assume that the child may forget some items or not be able to retrieve them from memory due to interference, our model includes a forgetting function. This forgetting process can be assumed to have a detrimental effect on the number of words which a child can recognize at any given time. The model will make the common assumption that the amount which becomes unavailable each month is a constant proportion of the amount already learned and retained. If one assumes no new input, the change in word recognition due to the forgetting process each month can be expressed as:

$$(2)$$
$$P_{n+1} = P_n - \lambda \cdot P_n$$

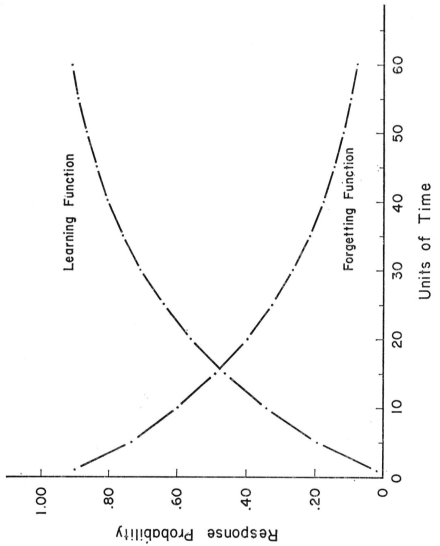

Fig. 3. Negatively accelerated learning and forgetting functions employed in the present model.

The rate parameter, λ, indicates the proportion of items which are lost each month. If one assumes an initial probability of .90 and sets $\lambda = .04$, this function generates the decay function depicted in Figure 2. If a different value were selected for λ, the general shape of the function would remain the same, only the rate of decay would change.

In order to analyze the vocabulary learning paradigm, the learning and forgetting functions are combined into a single model which merely assumes that the child learns and forgets some words each month. The change in the child's vocabulary each month can be depicted in terms of this general model as follows:

$$P_{n+1} = P_n + \theta \cdot (1 - P_n) - \lambda \cdot P_n \tag{3}$$

This model predicts an increase in the child's vocabulary each month as long as $\theta > \lambda$ and $P_n < \theta / (\theta + \lambda)$. Eventually, the proportion of the word population which the person recognizes will approach a steady state value of $\theta / (\theta + \lambda)$.

We are interested in applying this model to predict the effects of a short term enrichment program such as Head Start on the growth of disadvantaged children's vocabulary. As we have previously indicated, we will assume that the learning rate, θ, and the forgetting rate, λ, are the same for both advantaged and disadvantaged children. The only difference between these two groups in our model example will be in terms of the environmental input, the frequency of effective word exposure. The levels of this variable for the different groups is presented graphically in Figure 1. The advantaged group receives double the amount of word input stimulation that the disadvantaged group receives. The Head Start group receives the same inputs as the disadvantaged group except for the two year period of enrichment in which their level of input matches that of the advantaged group.

The predictions of performance based upon the model are presented in Figure 2. We have assumed that each child starts to learn vocabulary at 12 months and that $\theta = .008$ and $\lambda = .004$ for all groups. The advantaged and disadvantaged groups show very clear cut differences in the number of words acquired as a function of time. At the end of the second year, the advantaged group recognizes nearly twice as many words as the disadvantaged group. This difference is increased as the children grow older. The effects of the enrichment program are depicted by the dashed line. When the enrichment program is started after the third birthday, the program produces dramatic improvements in the disadvantaged child's vocabulary. At the 5th birthday, the enrichment program has narrowed the gap between the two groups such that the Head Start child's performance is almost equal to that of the advantaged child and is clearly superior to the performance of the non-enriched disadvantaged child.

However, when the enrichment program is discontinued and the Head Start children return to their normal word environment, the benefits of the enrichment program dissipate relative to the continued good performance of the advantaged group. At age 12, the vocabulary of the Head Start group is quite similar to that of the disadvantaged children who did not participate in the enrichment program and far smaller than that of the advantaged children.

The implications of the model do not depend on the particular details chosen for this illustration. Even if there were a marked overcompensation in input during the Head Start period or a longer enrichment period or less difference in environmental input between the groups, the fade out prediction would still be obtained. Choice of different rates of learning or forgetting would also have little effect on this basic outcome as long as the learning rate was greater than the forgetting rate. The only condition not entailing a fade out is a situation in which the compensatory input is maintained throughout the educational years.

For continuity with the existing literature, we have been willing to employ such terms as "disadvantaged" and "compensatory." Our argument however is not at all specific to this orientation, and can readily be translated into a culturally egalitarian, cultural-relativist position. Consider two equally complex, different, and partially overlapping languages, A and B. The performance test is in language A. Rehearsal on language B provides an input relevant to that performance only insofar as there is overlap in vocabulary. Children speaking language B are not disadvantaged in a general way but are so on the language A test. Instead of considering the intervention as "compensatory" education, it can be considered foreign language training. The results would take the same form.

This illustration, combined with the evidence of large subcultural differences in spoken language, raise another issue. We have assumed equality of all groups in rate of forgetting. Some modern learning theories interpret forgetting as a product of interference. In terms of such a theory, we have implicitly assumed equal interference rates. But if groups are using a partially overlapping vocabulary in different ways, pairing common words with different associates, the group with the usage most dissimilar from that employed in scoring the tests would have the higher interference rate, and hence the higher forgetting rate. This would contribute to further enlarging group differences, and to a faster fade out. Our simulation has dealt with the simpler situation, in which the inputs vary in volume (number of rehearsals, number of words) but not in "correctness" or the associates of words presented. Adding a consideration of differential interference, and hence a differential in effective forgetting rate, would no doubt improve its realism.

The simplistic model which we have assumed for the present demonstration also does not take into account the common finding that the items most recently learned are the ones which are most likely to be forgotten. Our model assumes that all items have an equal probability of being lost. If the model were altered by making assumptions which produced a recency phenomenon in the forgetting function, the fade out effects demonstrated by the present model would be further accentuated. In fact, when we have considered more realistic and necessarily more complex learning models, we have generally found that the fade out effects are predicted to be larger than those obtained with the more simplistic model.

We do not, of course, regard this demonstration as proving that differences in vocabulary or other tested abilities are totally learned. Rather, we wish to emphasize that the evidence of group differences and of fade out are completely compatible with that assumption, and cannot be used to argue any contrary conclusion.

REFERENCES

EBBINGHAUS, H. *Ueber das Gedächtnis*. Leipzig: Duncker & Humbolt, 1885. Translated as *Memory*. New York: Dover, 1964.

ESTES, W. K. The Statistical Approach to Learning Theory. In S. Koch, Ed. *Psychology: A Study of a Science*, Vol. 2, pp. 380-491. New York: McGraw-Hill, 1959.

HULL, C. L. *Principles of Behavior*, New York: Appleton-Century Company, 1943.

INDEX

465